FIRST-CLASS COUNTIES SECOND ELEVEN ANNUAL 2018

Edited by

Howard Clayton

Published by the Association of Cricket Statisticians and Historians, Bedford MK40 4FG.
2018
Typeset and printed by The City Press Leeds Ltd
ISBN: 978 1 908165 94 7

INTRODUCTION

Welcome to the First-Class Counties Second Eleven Annual for 2018. As usual, I hope the publication meets the needs of all Second Eleven Coaches and Scorers and that it provides hours of pleasant browsing for the numerous aficionados and followers of Second Eleven cricket around the country.

I next repeat a paragraph from last year's Review of the Season, which will be, I hope, self-explanatory.

Since the Counties were now restricted to nine three-day games, many of them arranged three or four day friendlies. Results of these games are included in the Annual, but all records are for Championship games only. However, player biographies reflect best batting and bowling performances in all three- and four-day games. Any player who played only in a friendly game is denoted by an asterisk, in the County Biographies and in the Index of Players, which has now been broken down and added to the end of each county section which also contains line scores and averages. Scotland A/Development Eleven played only friendly games. Again this season, 3- and 4-day friendly fixtures have seen teams comprised of players from two Clubs take the field. In such cases, the potted scores are given on the pages of the home team on the page of each of the two sides in the combined side.

Now a personal plea from the Editor. This year has again been particularly problematic in the compiling of the biographies of some Counties. In some cases, this was because forms given to players were not then returned to the Scorer. So for 2018, _**please be prepared to sit the new player down and complete the form with him. It will take but a few minutes, if that. If you are unsure whether a player has played before, a simple check in the 2018 Lists of Players will answer the question.**_

Some players play for as many five Counties in a single season and may only appear in Friendlies for one of those Counties. Such is indicated in the appropriate County Biography pages by an asterisk.

Some new records were set in 2017 and they are indicated, where necessary, in **_bold italic type_** for ease of recognition. Please also be aware that several loan transfers take place each season. Where a player's loan spell is known, it is indicated in his individual biography. Please note that, in the Second Eleven T20 Competition, teams played two T20 games on each date so, in the individual County pages and in the player biographies, these two games will be referred to as "Match 1" (pre-lunch) and "Match 2"

As usual, I am most grateful to the following for providing so speedily their counties' averages and biographical information and for sending all Second Eleven scorecards to Cricket Archive – John Wallis & Jane Hough (Derbyshire), Grahame Maddison (Durham), Paul Parkinson (Essex), Andrew Hignell, Byron Jones, Gareth Watkins & Robin Eyles (Glamorgan), Steve Cashmore & Keith Gerrish (Gloucestershire), Peter Danks & Alan Mills (Hampshire), Andy Bateup (Kent), Diana Lloyd and Mike Dixon (Lancashire), Peter Johnson (Leicestershire), Neil Smith (MCC Young Cricketers), Martyn Fryer (Middlesex), Mick Woolley

2

(Northamptonshire), Anne Cusworth (Nottinghamshire), David Johnson (Cricket Scotland), Polly Rhodes (Somerset), Jennifer Booth (Surrey), Graham Irwin (Sussex), Kevin O'Connell and Keith Coburn (Unicorns), Steve Smith (Warwickshire) and Phil Mellish & Sue Drinkwater (Worcestershire). The Editor provided all necessary information for Yorkshire and compiled the Biographies of the MCC Universities' players.

My thanks go also to John Anderson and all at City Press for the type-setting and printing.

The sharp-eyed amongst you will have noticed that there is no Second Eleven Player of the Year announced for 2017. This is due to circumstances utterly beyond the control of all connected to the publication. So the front cover shows a shot from the Gloucestershire v Glamorgan Second Eleven game at Bedminster CC and my grateful thanks go to Andrew Hignell of Glamorgan CCC for its provision. I must also thank Keith Gerrish (Gloucestershire) and Ian Smith (Cricket Archive) who have also helped with checking biographies and adding information from extensive work on Ancestry.co.uk. Finally, I would thank David Marshall, who has taken over from the late David Baggett as the chief proof-reader for the Annual. My heartfelt appreciation goes to Mr Marshall for the meticulous standard of his corrections to the manuscript.

Howard Clayton
22 Montagu Court
Oakwood Lane
LEEDS LS8 2TT
Tel – 0113-265-4401 or 07721-527727
(e-mail – howard.clayton@ntlworld.com)

REVIEW OF THE SEASON

Hello and welcome to the review of the 2017 season.

Once again, the three major honours were shared around and involved battles between North and South. The County Championship went to Lancashire. This was their fifth success and their first outright success since 1997, although they did share the title with Middlesex in 2013 when rain prevented a result in the play-off match.

Rain once again interfered with the final, for the first time played on the Isle of Wight as Hampshire played Lancashire. Lancashire had built a lead of 104 on first innings and had reduced Hampshire to 66/6 in their second innings when rain washed out the final day. Lancashire were awarded the title.

The One-Day Trophy also saw a north/south contest as Yorkshire took on Middlesex at Headingley. Yorkshire batted first and had reached 265/5 in 38.4 overs when the third rain interruption ended the innings. DLS dictated that Middlesex's target would be 279 runs to win from 38 overs and it looked likely that they may well have got there, as Nick Compton ensured that the chase maintained a rate of almost eight runs per over. But he and Rob White departed and a rebuild was required.

A recovery was underway , until, at 162/5, Yorkshire's off-spinner, Jack Shutt from Barnsley came on to bowl and finished the innings in 21 deliveries, returning 4/19, a performance which won him the Second XI Performance of the Year trophy at Yorkshire's end-of-season Gala Dinner. It was Yorkshire's fourth win of the Trophy and their first since 2009.

The T20 competition saw Sussex beat Hampshire in the final, after Lancashire and Yorkshire had lost in the Semi-Finals. Sussex batted first and ran up 171/6. They then dismissed Hampshire for 147, to win by 22 runs, their second success in this format, having won the inaugural tournament in 2011. It was Yorkshire's first appearance at Finals Day.

Two statistical oddities have occurred during the 2017 season. Firstly, several players have exactly equalled their personal bests with either bat or ball and these instances are all noted in the individual player biographies.

The second matter concerns the number of players who have been left either high and dry on 99* or who were dismissed agonizingly short of the magic three figures on 99. With due thanks to Philip Bailey, who compiled the information below, I list these unfortunates.

SCORE	PLAYER & CLUB	OPPONENTS	VENUE	COMPETITION
99*	J A Stamatis (Essex)	Hampshire	Ageas Bowl Nursery	Championship
99*	J J Bohannon (Lancashire)	Worcestershire	Great Crosby	Championship
99	C J Basey (Kent)	Surrey	Beckenham	Championship
99	A M Ali (Leicestershire)	Worcestershire	New Road	Championship
99	S M Imtiaz (MCC YC)	Lancashire	Urmston CC	Championship
99	J L Lawlor (Glamorgan)	MCC Universities	Mumbles	Championship
99	T C Lace (Middlesex)	Essex	Coggeshall	Championship

99	Z J Chappell (Leicestershire)	MCC YC	High Wycombe	Championship
99*	W A T Beer (Sussex)	Glamorgan	Blackstone	Trophy
99	A O Wiffen (Worcestershire)	Northamptonshire	Northampton	T20

As usual, all new records set in 2017 are indicated in bold italic script and there are several performance to which attention should be drawn.

Paul Horton's innings of 277* for Leicestershire against Warwickshire was the equal eighth-highest individual total ever made in the Championship. Tom Latham also went large with 241 for Durham against the MCC Young Cricketers.

A new fifth wicket record was established by George Scott and Rob White for Middlesex against the MCC Universities at Radlett as the pair added 389 in an unbroken stand. Such statistics may or may not have contributed to the Universities' decision to drop out of the Second XI Championship in 2018.

In the Trophy, Northamptonshire's score of 431/7 against Leicestershire at Northampton was the second highest team total in the competition, just seven runs away from beating Essex's record of 437/5, set in 2010 at the Oval. A new ninth wicket record was established by Tom Sole and Chad Barrett for Northamptonshire against Derbyshire at Denby.

In the T20 competition, Angus Robson of Sussex established a new season's best aggregate with his 471 runs. Ollie Robinson (Sussex) took 20 wickets and equalled the best return for a T20 season. New wicket partnerships were established for the second wicket when Zak Crawley and Jimmy Neesham of Kent added 195 (unbroken) against Middlesex at Polo Farm in Canterbury. It was also the highest partnership for any wicket in 2017.

At the other end of the scale, Yorkshire's Karl Carver and Jack Shutt added 48 (again unbroken) for the tenth wicket as Yorkshire completed the great escape against Worcestershire at Flagge Meadow, the home of Worcester RGS. Yorkshire had been 27/8 in their innings but the tail wagged (and how!) and a final total of 137/9 proved to be too many for Worcestershire as their efforts closed on 129/9.

Individual performances to note were as follows.

In the Championship, Robert Jones (Lancashire) scored three centuries in his 775 runs and ended with an average of 77.50. Stuart Whittingham (Sussex) had the season's best return with the ball as he claimed 30 wickets. Similar performances in the Trophy saw Brooke Guest (Lancashire) score 270 runs at an average of 103.50 and Dom Bess (Somerset) had 14 wickets, a total equalled by Matthew McKiernan for various teams.

As previously stated, Angus Robson led the way with the bat in then T20 competition and his team-mate at Hove, Ollie Robinson, took 20 wickets.

As some of you already be aware, it is all change at Surrey CCC as far as their scorers are concerned. Both Keith and Jennifer Booth have retired from their posts of first and second eleven Scorers respectively and we wish them well in their retirement. Debbie Beesley takes over the reins at the second eleven and we welcome her to the wonderful world of out-grounds and DLS and all that entails.

And that just about completes my Review of the Season. But I must finish with an enormous "Thank You" to all second eleven Scorers for submitting their scorecards to Cricket Archive so promptly, allowing the start of work on the Annual to begin as planned but please take note of my request, made in last year's annual in the Introduction, re the use of substitute scorers for second eleven matches and New Player forms.

I will not be seeing any of you in 2018 as Yorkshire CCC have decided to dispense with my services as second eleven scorer, retiring me on medical grounds. I was devastated to say the least as I felt it was the best job in the world so not sure how I am going to spend the summer months.

SECOND XI CHAMPIONSHIP 2017 - FINAL TABLES
NORTHERN GROUP

	P	W	L	D	A	Bt	Bl	Pts
1 Lancashire (2)	9	4	1	4	0	32	27	143
2 Warwickshire (6)	9	3	1	5	0	28	24	125
3 Worcestershire (3)	9	3	2	3	1	26	28	122
4 Yorkshire (5)	9	2	0	6	1	28	25	120
5 Derbyshire (8)	9	2	1	6	0	29	21	112
6 Nottinghamshire (7)	9	3	2	3	1	14	26	108
7 Leicestershire (9)	9	2	4	3	0	28	33	108
8 Durham (1)	9	2	2	4	1	19	27	103
9 MCC Young Cricketers (-)								
	9	0	4	5	0	26	21	71
10 Northamptonshire (10)	9	0	4	5	0	10	23	58

SOUTHERN GROUP

	P	W	L	D	A	Bt	Bl	Pts
1 Hampshire (8)	9	4	1	4	0	20	36	140
2 Middlesex (1)	9	3	0	5	1	22	26	126
3 Surrey (7)	9	3	2	4	0	24	33	125
4 Kent (4)	9	3	2	4	0	24	24	116
5 Somerset (9)	9	2	1	6	0	17	29	108
6 Sussex (2)	9	2	3	4	0	23	32	107
7 Gloucestershire (10)	9	3	2	3	1	14	17	99
8 Glamorgan (5)	9	0	3	6	0	24	29	83
9 MCC Universities (-)	9	0	2	7	0	21	26	82
10 Essex (6)	9	1	5	3	0	17	29	77

i) The MCC Young Cricketers & MCC Universities exchanged groups from the 2016 season
ii) Numbers in parentheses are the 2016 positions
iii) Ab = Abandoned
iv) BP = Bonus Points

Bonus Points are awarded as follows:
Batting – 150 = 1 point; 200 = 2 points;
250 = 3 points; 300 = 4 points
Bowling – 3 wkts = 1 point; 5 wkts = 2 points;
7 wkts = 3 points; 9 wkts = 4 points
(If a side is all out with 8 wkts or less, the fielding side can claim 4 bowling bonus points)

FIRST CLASS COUNTIES 2nd ANNUAL COUNTY CHAMPIONSHIP FINAL

The final was played at the Newclose CC ground, Newport, I of Wight on 5-8 September 2017. With no play on the final day, the match was officially drawn but Lancashire were awarded their fifth title, including one shared with Middlesex in 2013, on first innings lead.

Hampshire first innings		Runs
FS Hay	c Brown b Mahmood	59
JH Barrett	b Lester	0
OC Soames	lbw b Lester	11
FS Organ	b Mahmood	4
+CM Dickinson	c Turner b Sanders	34
*CP Wood	not out	76
AHJA Hart	c Jones b Hurt	16
HRC Came	c Guest b Bohannon	1
MET Salisbury	c Lilley b Bohannon	5
BTJ Wheal	c Jones b Mahmood	11
B Mugochi	c Lamb b Mahmood	0
C Searle	did not bat	
Extras	(6 b, 6 lb, 18 nb, 1 w)	31
Total	(all out, 67.5 overs)	248

Fall of wickets:
1-4 (Barrett, 5.2 ov), 2-50 (Soames, 15.3 ov), 3-57 (Organ, 18.4 ov), 4-109 (Dickinson, 32.6 ov), 5-121 (Hay, 37.3 ov), 6-175 (Hart, 51.1 ov), 7-176 (Came, 52.1 ov), 8-192 (Salisbury, 56.2 ov), 9-228 (Wheal, 63.1 ov), 10-248 (Mugochi, 67.5 ov)

Lancashire bowling	O	M	R	W
Mahmood	20.5	1	76	4
Lester	17	3	43	2
Hurt	14	3	40	1
Sanders	8	2	50	1
Lilley	2	1	2	0
Bohannon	6	1	25	21

Lancashire first innings		Runs
CK Turner	c Barrett b Wheal	0
KR Brown	c Wheal b Wood	23

*RP Jones	c Organ b Wheal	38
JJ Bohannon	c Dickinson b Hart	16
+BD Guest	b Wood	17
TJ Lester	lbw b Mugochi	47
DJ Lamb	c Organ b Hart	16
AM Lilley	c Salisbury b Mugochi	72
MH McKiernan	c Dickinson b Wood	34
LJ Hurt	not out	42
S Mahmood	st Dickinson b Mugochi	5
CWG Sanders	did not bat	
Extras	(14 b, 7 lb, 20 nb, 1 w)	42
Total	(all out, 104.4 overs)	352

Fall of wickets:
1-0 (Turner, 0.1 ov), 2-48 (Brown, 19.1 ov), 3-77 (Bohannon, 30.4 ov), 4-102 (Jones, 42.2 ov), 5-126 (Guest, 51.5 ov), 6-184 (Lamb, 73.5 ov), 7-200 (Lester, 78.6 ov), 8-241 (McKiernan, 85.3 ov), 9-344 (Lilley, 102.1 ov), 10-352 (Mahmood, 104.4 ov)

Hampshire bowling

	O	M	R	W
Wheal	24	9	64	2
Salisbury	19	2	86	0
Wood	27	10	61	3
Hart	14	6	37	2
Mugochi	12.4	2	46	3
Searle	7	1	31	0
Organ	1	0	6	0

Hampshire second innings

		Runs
FS Hay	c Brown b Mahmood	9
JH Barrett	lbw b Lester	16
OC Soames	c Guest b Bohannon	10
FS Organ	c Guest b Bohannon	14
+CM Dickinson	c Guest b Hurt	2
HRC Came	c Brown b Bohannon	10
*CP Wood	not out	0
AHJA Hart	not out	0
MET Salisbury	did not bat	
BTJ Wheal	did not bat	
B Mugochi	did not bat	
C Searle	did not bat	
Extras	(2 b, 1 lb, 2 nb)	5
Total	(6 wickets, 28 overs)	66

Fall of wickets:
1-26 (Barrett, 9.2 ov), 2-26 (Hay, 10.4 ov), 3-51 (Soames, 18.1 ov), 4-56 (Organ, 18.5 ov), 5-66 (Dickinson, 23.6 ov), 6-66 (Came, 24.3 ov)

Lancashire bowling

	O	M	R	W
Mahmood	7	2	21	1
Lester	8	2	25	1
Bohannon	7	5	8	3
Hurt	4	1	9	1
Lilley	2	2	0	0

Umpires - T Lungley & R J Warren
Scorers – Mike Dixon (Lancashire) & Alan C Mills (Hampshire)

i) SR = Strike-rate
ii) ER = Economy-Rate

SECOND ELEVEN CHAMPIONSHIP 2017 HIGHLIGHTS

BATTING 2017
Qual: 8 innings; Average of 40.00

	M	I	NO	Runs	HS	Avge	100s
R P Jones (Lancs)	9	13	3	775	138	77.50	3
G J Harte (Durham/MCC YC)							
	7	11	3	613	183	76.62	2
L A Procter (Lancs)	5	8	2	437	103	72.83	1
T C Fell (Worcs)	6	9	0	626	223	69.55	3
M J Lamb (Warwicks)	8	9	1	542	164	67.75	2
H R Hosein (Derbys)	9	14	4	615	115*	61.50	2
C J Basey (Kent)	5	8	2	350	99	58.33	-
L Banks (Warwicks)	7	11	1	570	181	57.00	1
W R Smith (Hants)	8	12	1	616	136	56.00	3
A J Robson (Sussex)	9	17	2	775	137	51.66	2
X G Owen (MCCU)	8	8	6	102	24	51.00	-
I G Holland (Hants)	6	10	0	506	192	50.60	2
A Hepburn (Worcs)	8	13	2	556	98	50.54	-
W M H Rhodes (Yorks)	7	11	0	551	147	50.09	1
A K Dal (Notts)	8	11	2	449	125	49.88	2
A Harinath (Surrey)	7	9	1	399	127	49.87	1
R Patel (Surrey)	8	12	0	598	226	49.83	1
H E Dearden (Leics)	5	9	0	446	141	49.55	1
A J Hickey (Durham)	5	8	1	346	144	49.42	1
A N Kervezee (Worcs)	5	8	0	395	140	49.37	1
J J Weatherley (Kent)	6	9	1	394	104*	49.25	1
A R I Umeed (Warwicks)	7	11	0	535	203	48.63	1
J J Bohannon (Lancs)	8	11	1	471	99*	47.10	-
J M Kettleborough (Derbys / Northants)							
	6	10	1	417	150*	46.33	2
M A Jones (Derbys / Durham/ Leics)							
	9	13	0	595	172	45.76	2
A O Morgan (Glam)	7	11	1	436	151*	43.60	1
W N Fazackerley (Leics)	7	10	1	387	83	43.00	-
S T Evans (Leics)	5	9	2	298	107	42.57	1
T P Alsop (Hants)	5	8	2	253	106*	42.16	1
J A Tattersall (Yorks)	8	14	2	501	117	41.75	2
A M Ali (Leics)	5	9	0	373	99	41.44	-
J Coughlin (Durham)	7	8	1	287	87	41.00	-
F O E van den Bergh (Surrey)	9	13	3	404	135	40.40	
T C Lace (Middx)	7	9	0	363	106	40.33	1

BOWLING 2017
Qual: 15 wickets; Average of 32.00

	O	M	R	W	Avge	BB
N Brand (Glam)	62.5	19	152	15	10.13	6/14
R N Sidebottom (Northants / Notts / Warwicks)						
	110.3	25	356	27	13.18	8/33
R H Patel (Middx)	110.4	26	285	17	16.76	3/23
T E Barber (Middx)	89.1	15	348	19	18.31	5/27
E O Hooper (Sussex)	74	8	300	16	18.75	6/110
H R Bernard (Kent)	97.5	16	341	17	20.05	5/20
G S Virdi (Surrey)	202.3	60	533	26	20.50	6/77
L A Procter (Lancs)	125.1	18	381	18	21.16	3/49
B J Taylor (Hants)	136.4	25	466	22	21.18	3/6
A Hepburn (Worcs)	170.4	30	595	28	21.25	5/43
M E Milnes (Notts)	140	34	425	20	21.25	4/41
G Stewart (Kent)	137	33	406	19	21.36	4/54
S G Whittingham (Sussex)	177.3	34	668	30	22.26	6/66
F O E van den Bergh (Surrey)						
	171.2	18	525	23	22.82	5/57
A S S Nijjar (Essex)	166.3	36	553	24	23.04	6/113
P A van Meekeren (Somerset)						
	130.1	33	404	17	23.76	5/44
A T Thomson (MCCU/Warwicks)						
	119.2	13	468	19	24.63	7/148
M E T Salisbury (Essex/Hants)						
	178.5	40	592	24	24.66	5/82
A P Beard (Essex)	147.4	28	520	21	24.76	4/58
S C Kerrigan (Lancs / Northants)						
	153.2	33	446	18	24.77	6/26
Imran Qayyum (Kent)	104.3	16	373	15	24.86	5/50
O E Robinson (Sussex)	147.5	27	430	17	25.29	5/37
I G Holland (Hants)	148.2	32	481	19	25.31	5/46
B A Hutton (Notts)	126.5	18	436	17	25.64	7/44
L J Hurt (Durham / Lancs / MCC YC)						
	183.4	34	576	22	26.18	3/21
A Sakande (Sussex)	148.1	21	577	22	26.22	6/96
K Carver (Yorks)	150	43	432	16	27.00	6/53
D Manthorpe (Leics)	167	31	626	22	28.45	3/36

7

W N Fazackerley (Leics)	101.5	12	484	17	28.47	6/55
M Carter (Notts)	211.5	59	524	18	29.11	4/47
T J Lester (Lancs)	172	28	644	22	29.27	5/79
K A Bull (Glam)	198	28	603	20	30.15	5/30
M W Parkinson (Lancs)	134	22	521	17	30.64	6/49
B J Twohig (Worcs)	196.3	18	698	22	31.72	5/87
Sukhjit Singh (Warwicks)	148.1	34	510	16	31.87	4/93

WICKET-KEEPERS (15 victims or better)

	CT	ST	Total
H J Swindells (Leics)	28	1	29
C M Dickinson (Hants)	21	2	23
H R Hosein (Derbys)	22	-	22
B D Guest (Lancs)	21	-	21
A A Shafique (Surrey)	15	1	16
O G Robinson (Kent)	13	2	15
A G Milton (Worcs)	14	1	15
A J Hodd (Yorks)	12	3	15

FIELDERS (7 catches or better)

	Total
W R Smith (Hants)	12
M Carter (Notts)	12
K A Bull (Glam)	9
K R Brown (Lancs)	9
R P Jones (Lancs)	9
J W Jenner (Sussex)	9
N J Selman (Glam)	8
A E N Riley (Kent)	8
J H Barrett (MCC YC)	8
B J Twohig (Worcs)	8
J H K Adams (Hants)	7
S D Robson (Middx)	7
J M Kettleborough (Northants)	7
E J Byrom (Somerset)	7
T D Rouse (Somerset)	7
E D Woods (Surrey)	7
D M W Rawlins (Sussex)	7
Sukhjit Singh (Warwicks)	7

HIGHEST TEAM TOTALS (400 or better)

612/4d	Middx v MCCU (Radlett)
585/8d	Yorks v Lancs (Scarborough)
573/5d	Warwicks v Derbys (EFCSG)
553/8d	Hants v Kent (Polo Farm SG, Canterbury)
526/8d	Yorks v MCC YC (High Wycombe)
521/9d	Worcs v MCC YC (Barnt Green)
508	Yorks v Durham (Riverside)
501	Leics v Northants (Desborough)
495/9d	Leics v Warwicks (EFCSG)
492/9d	Middx v Kent (Radlett)
469	Leics v MCC YC (HighWycombe)
459/3d	Middx v Essex (Coggeshall)
455/9d	Warwicks v Leics (EFCSG)
447/9d	Warwicks v Durham (S Northumberland CC)
446/5d	Surrey v Glos (Purley)
434/3d	Durham v Northants (Milton Keynes)
426/3d	Yorks v Derbys (York)
418/8d	Glos v MCCU (Bath)
417/4d	Durham v MCC YC (High Wycombe)
408	Glos v Essex (Billericay)
406/6d	Sussex v MCCU (Hastings)
403	Somerset v MCCU (Taunton Vale)
402/5d	Yorks v Northants (York)
400/9d	Sussex v Surrey (Hove)

LOWEST TEAM TOTALS (up to 129)

663	Essex v Surrey (Billericay)
82	Middx v Hants (Ageas Bowl Nursery)
92	Hants v Somerset (Taunton Vale)
93	Sussex v Hants (Newclose CC)
99	Essex v Glos (Billericay)
104	MCCU v Glam (Marespool)

118	Durham v Notts (Riverside)
120	Glos v Kent (Longwood, Bristol)
124	Northants v Durham (Milton Keynes)
125	Surrey v Kent (Beckenham)

HIGHEST INDIVIDUAL INNINGS (150 or better)

277*	P J Horton (Leics) v Warwicks (EFCSG)
241	T W M Latham (Durham) v MCC YC (High Wycombe)
230	T Kohler-Cadmore (Yorks) v Derbys (York)
226	R Patel (Surrey) v Glos (Purley)
223	T C Fell (Worcs) v MCC YC (Barnt Green)
212*	G F B Scott (Middx) v MCCU (Radlett)
208	L W P Wells (Sussex) v Surrey (Hove)
203	A R I Umeed (Warwicks) v Leics (EFCSG)
202	A Z Lees (Yorks) v Durham (Riverside)
192	B J Curran (MCC YC) v Yorks (High Wycombe)
192	I G Holland (Hants) v Kent (Polo Farm SG, Canterbury)
192	M K Andersson (Middx) v Essex (Coggeshall)
183	G J Harte (Durham) v Northants (Milton Keynes)
181	L Banks (Warwicks) v Derbys (EFCSG)
172	M A Jones (Durham) v Northants (Milton Keynes)
170*	J D Libby (Notts) v Worcs (Notts SG)
169	N J Dexter (Leics) v Northants (Desborough)
164	M J Lamb (Warwicks) v Durham (S Northumberland CC)
162	M E Trescothick (Somerset) v Sussex (Horsham)
161	H C Brook (Yorks) v Lancs (Scarborough)
160*	R G White (Middx) v MCC Uns (Radlett)
160*	G J Harte (Durham) v Yorks (Riverside)
151*	A O Morgan (Glam) v Glos (Newport)
151	T B Abell (Somerset) v MCCU (Taunton Vale)
150*	J M Kettleborough (Northants) v Durham
	(Milton Keynes)

A total of 107 centuries was scored in the Championship.

TWO DOUBLE CENTURIES IN THE SAME MATCH
277* by P J Horton (Leics) & 203 by A R I Umeed (Warwicks) (EFCSG)

THREE CENTURIES IN ONE INNINGS
212* by G F B Scott; 160* by R G White & 106 by T C Lace (all Middx) v MCCU (Radlett)

TWO CENTURIES IN ONE MATCH
There were no instances in 2017.

CARRYING BAT THROUGH A COMPLETED INNINGS
150* J M Kettleborough (Northants) v Durham
(Milton Keynes)

BEST BOWLING IN AN INNINGS (6 wkts or better)

8/33	R N Sidebottom (Warwicks) v Northants (EFCSG)
7/22	K Noema-Barnett (Glos) v Essex (Billericay)
7/44	B A Hutton (Notts) v Durham (Riverside)
7/148	A T Thomson (MCCU) v Sussex (Hastings)
6/14	N Brand (Glam) v Essex (Pontarddulais)
6/26	S C Kerrigan (Lancs) v Leics (Desborough)
6/47	W J Weighell (Durham) v Lancs (Todmorden)
6/49	M W Parkinson (Lancs) v Leics (Desborough)
6/52	A G Salter (Glam) v Hants (Basingstoke)
6/53	K Carver (Yorks) v Leics (Kibworth)
6/55	W N Fazackerley (Leics) v Yorks (Kibworth)
6/57	M D Sonczak (Derbys) v Leics (Kibworth)
6/66	S G Whittingham (Sussex) v Somerset (Horsham)
6/74	A J Hickey (Durham) v Leics (Riverside)
6/77	G S Virdi (Surrey) v Glam (Neath)
6/79	S Reeves (Durham) v Northants (Milton Keynes)
6/96	A Sakande (Sussex) v Kent (Polo Farm SG, Canterbury)
6/110	E O Hooper (Sussex) v MCCU (Hastings)
6/113	A S S Nijjar (Essex) v Sussex (Halstead)
6/162	A D Tillcock (MCC YC) v Somerset (Taunton Vale)

BEST BOWLING IN A MATCH (9 wkts or better)

11/131	G S Virdi (Surrey) v Glam (Neath)
10/59	R N Sidebottom (Warwicks) v Northants (EFCSG)
10/95	M W Parkinson (Lancs) v Leics (Desborough)
10/120	A Hepburn (Worcs) v MCC YC (Barnt Green)
10/160	A J Hickey (Durham) v Leics (Riverside)
9/100	S Reeves (Durham) v Northants (Milton Keynes)
9/131	M E T Salisbury (Hants) v Kent
	(Polo Farm SG, Canterbury)
9/136	I G Holland (Hants) v Essex (Ageas Bowl Nursery)
9/137	B A Hutton (Notts) v Durham (Riverside)
9/166	A S S Nijjar (Essex) v Sussex (Halstead)
9/170	A T Thomson (MCCU) Glos (Bath)
9/278	A T Thomson (MCCU) v Sussex (Hastings)

HAT-TRICKS
There were no instances in 2017

MATCHES ABANDONED WITHOUT A BALL BOWLED
Glos v Middx (Longwood, Bristol)
Durham v Worcs (Burnopfield)
Yorks v Notts (Stamford Bridge)

Only three games suffered this fate.

MOST WICKET-KEEPER DISMISSALS IN AN INNINGS

6	T J Moores (Notts) v Durham (Riverside)
6	A J Hodd (Yorks) v Warwicks (Harrogate)
5	A A Shafique (Surrey) v Glos (Purley)
5	G H Roderick (Glos) v Essex (Billericay)
5	J W Jenner (Sussex) v Hants
	(Newclose CC Gd, I of Wight)
5	T R Ambrose (Warwicks) v Northants (EFCSG)
5	H J Swindells (Leics) v MCC YC (High Wycombe)

MOST WICKET-KEEPER DISMISSALS IN A MATCH

8	A A Shafique (Surrey) v Glos (Purley)
8	A J Hodd (Yorks) v Warwicks (Harrogate)
8	B D Birkhead (Yorks) v Worcs (Worcester RGS)
7	H J Swindells (Leics)v Warwicks (EFCSG)
7	T J Moores (Notts) v Durham (Riverside)
7	J C Martin (Sussex) v Glam (Fulking)
7	T R Ambrose (Warwicks) v Northants (EFCSG)
7	H J Swindells (Leics) v MCC YC (High Wycombe)

MOST CATCHES BY A FIELDER IN AN INNINGS

4	R P Jones (Lancs) v Derbys (Stoke-on-Trent)
4	T J Moores (Notts) v Northants (Milton Keynes)
4	M Carter (Notts) v MCC YC (High Wycombe)
4	B D Guest (Lancs) v Yorks (Scarborough)
4	S D Robson (Middx) v Glam (Merchant Taylors' S)
4	W A Tavare (Glos) v MCCU (Bath CC)
3	K R Brown (Lancs) v Derbys (Stoke-on-Trent)
3	W R Smith (Hants) v Essex (Ageas Bowl Nursery)
3	J M Kettleborough (Northants) v Lancs (Liverpool)
3	M A Leask (Somerset) v Kent (Taunton Vale)
3	K S Carlson (Glam) v Kent (Neath)
3	E D Woods (Surrey) v Somerset (New Malden)
3	N R Welch (Essex) v Glam (Pontarddulais)
3	N J Selman (Glam) v Middx (Merchant Taylors' S)
3	D M W Rawlins (Sussex) v Essex (Halstead)
3	M E Trescothick (Somerset) v Essex (Taunton Vale)

MOST CATCHES BY A FIELDER IN A MATCH

6	S D Robson (Middx) v Glam (Merchant Taylors' S)
5	W A Tavare (Glos) v MCCU (Bath)

BEST PARTNERSHIPS 2017

First Wicket

326	G J Harte & M A Jones (Durham) v Northants
	(Milton Keynes)
257	R P Jones & S Chanderpaul (Lancs) v MCC YC (Urmston)
218	H C Brook & J A Tattersall (Yorks) v Leics (Kibworth)
189	B S Gilmour & M A H Hammond (Glos) v Glam (Newport)
176	A Z Lees & J A Tattersall (Yorks) v Northants (York)
168	A Harinath, R Patel & N R Welch (Surrey) v Middx
	(New Malden) *
166	Z Crawley & C J Basey (Kent) v Surrey (Beckenham)
162	A Harinath & R Patel (Surrey) v Glos (Purley)
151	A R I Umeed & I J Westwood (Warwicks) v Leics (EFCSG)
151	T C Lace & S Perera (Middx) v Essex (Coggeshall)
144	N J Selman & C R Brown (Glam) v Hants (Basingstoke)
139	A R I Umeed & L Banks (Warwicks) v Worcs
	(Worcester RGS)
137	P D Salt & A J Robson (Sussex) v Kent
	(Polo Farm SG, Canterbury)
131	G H Rhodes & O E Westbury (Worcs) v Warwicks
	(Worcester RGS)
122	C K Turner & R P Jones (Lancs) v Northants (Liverpool)
121	M A H Hammond & P J Grieshaber (Glos) v Sussex
	(Blackstone)
118	P J Horton & H J Swindells (Leics) v Warwicks (EFCSG)
117	A Harinath & R Patel (Surrey) v Glam (Neath)
116	B J Curran & L Banks (Warwicks) v Derbys (EFCSG)
115	J M Kettleborough & H R D Adair (Northants) v Lancs
	(Liverpool)
104	A J Robson & T J Haines (Sussex) v Glos (Blackstone)
103	B J Curran & D S Manuwelege (MCC YC) v Yorks
	(High Wycombe)
102	A R I Umeed & L Banks (Warwicks) v Lancs (EFCSG)

* A Harinath retired hurt, having scored 64, with the team score at 118/0.

Second Wicket

261	G P Smith & A K Dal (Notts) v Northants (Milton Keynes)
210	A Z Lees & W M H Rhodes (Yorks) v Durham (Riverside)
182	A R I Umeed & L Banks (Warwicks) v Leics (EFCSG)
171	W R Smith & I G Holland (Hants) v Essex
	(Ageas Bowl Nursery)
165	L W P Wells & H Z Finch (Sussex) v Surrey (Hove)
159	B S Gilmour & A W R Barrow (Glos) v Glam (Newport)
156	J R Bracey & W A Tavare (Glos) v MCCU (Bath CC)
153	R Patel & O J D Pope (Surrey) v Somerset (New Malden)
151	I J Westwood & L Banks (Warwicks) v Yorks (Harrogate)
148	T C Fell & A O Wiffen (Worcs) v Leics (Worcester RGS)
144	A O Morgan & W D Bragg (Glam) v Glos (Newport)
127	H E Dearden & N J Dexter (Leics) v MCC YC
	(High Wycombe)
121	A Harinath & O J D Pope (Surrey) v Middx (New Malden)
120	G A Bartlett & G D Rouse (Somerset) v Glam (Taunton S)
106	T P Alsop & W R Smith (Hants) v MCCU (Horsham)
101	B A Raine & L J Hill (Leics) v Durham (Riverside)
100	Z Crawley & J J Weatherley (Kent) v Glos (Longwood)

Third Wicket

276	M K Andersson & R G White (Middx) v Essex
	(Coggeshall)
269	P J Horton & N J Dexter (Leics) v Northants (Desborough)
249	T Kohler-Cadmore & J A Leaning (Yorks) v Derbys (York)
234	T C Fell & A N Kervezee (Worcs) v MCC YC (Barnt Green)
219	M E Trescothick & T B Abell (Somerset) v Sussex
	(Horsham)
197	G T Hankins & G L van Buuren (Glos) v Essex (Billericay)
194	L Banks & M J Lamb (Warwicks) v Derbys (EFCSG)
183	R M Yates & M J Lamb (Warwicks) v Notts (Notts SG)
175	T C Lace & S S Eskinazi (Middx) v MCCU (Radlett)
174	D S Manuwelege & F H Allen (MCC YC) v Yorks
	(High Wycombe)
169	A Z Lees & W M H Rhodes (Yorks) v Warwicks
	(Harrogate)
162	H Hameed & L A Procter (Lancs) v Warwicks (EFCSG)
158	K C Appleby & A J Ball (Kent) v Middx (Radlett)
154	R Patel & R Ratnasabapathy (Surrey) v Glos (Purley)

147 J J Weatherley C J Basey (Kent) v MCCU (Beckenham)
141 B J Curran & G J Harte (MCC YC) v Yorks
(High Wycombe)
138* G H Rhodes & A Hepburn (Worcs) v Warwicks
(Worcester RGS)
136 A K Dal & J E P Hebron (Notts) v MCC YC
(High Wycombe)
136 A Z Lees & G S Ballance (Yorks) v Durham (Riverside)
131 M A Jones & A J Hickey (Durham) v Leics (Riverside)
130* S T Evans & W N Fazackerley (Leics) v Derbys (Kibworth)
130 G H Rhodes & A Hepburn (Worcs) v Lancs
(Northern CC, Crosby)
128 R P Jones & L A Procter (Lancs) v Yorks (Scarborough)
121 A M Ali & M A Jones (Leics) v Worcs (Worcester RGS)
121 T C Fell & A Hepburn (Worcs) v Leics (Worcester RGS)
120 D M W Rawlins & P D Salt (Sussex) v Surrey (Hove)
118 C M Macdonell & A Patel (Derbys) v Leics (Kibworth)
117 A Javid & M J Lamb v MCC YC (High Wycombe)
114 R P Jones & J J Bohannon (Lancs) v Derbys
(Stoke-on-Trent)
109 A Javid, M J Lamb & S R Hain (Warwicks) v Worcs
(Worcester RGS) *
107 P J Horton & C F Parkinson (Leics) v Warwicks (EFCSG)
104 K C Appleby & G Fatouros (Kent) v Surrey (Beckenham)
103 M D Lezar & S M Imtiaz (MCC YC) v Leics
(High Wycombe)

* M J Lamb retired at 146/2, when 13*, and after 29 runs had been
added in the stand.

Fourth Wicket
316 T W M Latham & B A Carse (Durham) v MCC YC
(High Wycombe)
259 E J Byrom & R C Davies (Somerset) v Glos
(Longwood, Bristol)
220 W R Smith & I G Holland (Hants) v Kent
(Polo Farm SG, Canterbury)
196 W M H Rhodes & R Gibson (Yorks) v MCC YC
(High Wycombe)
189 C M Macdonell & M J J Critchley (Derbys) v Lancs
(Stoke-on-Trent)
169 N R D Compton & T C Lace (Middx) v Kent (Radlett)
166* R P Jones & J J Bohannon (Lancs) v Worcs
(Northern CC, Crosby)
155 M J Lamb & A J Mellor (Warwicks) v Durham
(S Northumberland)
152 J R Murphy & D L Lloyd (Glam) v Somerset (Taunton S)
145 A J Robson & O E Robinson (Sussex) v MCCU (Hastings)
139 A N Kervezee & A Hepburn (Worcs) v Northants (Holcot)
128 F O E van den Bergh & C J Whittock (Surrey) v MCCU
(New Malden)
127 A J Robson & P D Salt (Sussex) v MCCU (Hastings)
125 L A Procter & J J Bohannon (Lancs) v Worcs
(Northern CC, Crosby)
122 M S Pepper & R H Sheemar (Essex) v Middx (Coggeshall)
120 L W P Wells & D M W Rawlins (Sussex) v Surrey (Hove)
118* T J Moores & A K Dal (Notts) v Durham (Riverside)
112 H Hameed & S Chanderpaul (Lancs) v MCC YC (Urmston)
108* A Hepburn & A G Milton (Worcs) v Leics (Worcester RGS)
108 A O Morgan & H A J Allen (Glam) v Glos (Newport)
108 G H Roderick & J R Bracey (Glos) v Surrey (Purley)
105 J M Kettleborough & E A J Cox (Northants) v Notts
(Milton Keynes)
105 A N Kervezee & A Hepburn (Worcs) v Derbys (Amblecote)
104 A J Hickey & T M Hewison (Durham) v Notts (Riverside)
104 M K Andersson & S Perera (Middx) v Surrey
(New Malden)
100 J J Weatherley & A J Ball (Kent) v Essex
(Polo Farm SG, Canterbury)

Fifth Wicket
389* G F B Scott & R G White (Middx) v MCCU (Radlett)
170 H R Hosein & T P Milnes (Derbys) v Durham
(Belper Meadows)
163 A J Mellor & A D Thomason (Warwicks) v Derbys
(EFCSG)
161* M G K Burgess & O E Robinson (Sussex) v Somerset
(Horsham)
159 G J Harte & J Coughlin (Durham) v Yorks (Riverside)
155* M J J Critchley & A Patel (Derbys) v MCC YC (Glossop)
152 I G Holland & C M Dickinson (Hants) v Kent
(Polo Farm SG, Canterbury)
144 J D Marshall & J D Cooke (MCCU) v Somerset
(Taunton Vale)
128 H C Brook & J A Thompson (Yorks) v Lancs (Scarborough)
124 J D Libby & C F Gibson (Notts) v Worcs (Notts SG)
120 O C Soames & R T Sehmi (MCCU) v Kent (Beckenham)
117 A J Blake & C J Haggett (Kent) v Glam (Neath)
113 R A Whiteley & J J Dell (Worcs) v Lancs
(Northern CC, Crosby)
112 W M H Rhodes & A J Hodd (Yorks) v MCC YC
(High Wycombe)
110 M L Pettini & A M Ali (Leics) v Notts (Notts SG)
104 J L Lawlor & A O Morgan (Glam) v MCCU (Mumbles)
102 L A Procter & D J Lamb (Lancs) v Yorks (Scarborough)
101 A Javid & M R Adair v MCC YC (High Wycombe)

Sixth Wicket
163* T R Ambrose & A T Thomson (Warwicks) v Northants
(EFCSG)
140 Z Crawley & O G Robinson (Kent) v Sussex
(Polo Farm SG, Canterbury)
137 Z J Chappell & R J Sayer (Leics) v MCC YC
(High Wycombe)
132 O C Soames & J C Tetley (MCCU) v Middx (Radlett)
125* G J Harte & H W Podmore (Durham) v Yorks (Riverside)
116 J A Thompson & J Shaw (Yorks) v Lancs (Scarborough)
115 T B Abell & M A Leask (Somerset) v MCCU
(Taunton Vale)
111* B R M Taylor & C R Marshall (Notts) v Lancs (Notts SG)
109 S M Imtiaz & L A Jones (MCC YC) v Notts
(High Wycombe)
108 J W Tetley J M Cooke (MCCU) v Sussex (Hastings)
107 C M Macdonell & C A J Brodrick (Derbys) v Lancs
(Stoke-on-Trent)

Seventh Wicket
157 H R Hosein & C A J Brodrick (Derbys) v Worcs
(Amblecote)
152 H R Hosein & T A I Taylor (Derbys) v Leics (Kibworth)
122 J Dass & J Coughlin (Durham) v Leics (Riverside)
118* L P Smith & E O Hooper (Sussex) v MCCU (Hastings)
110 J M Cooke & A D Tillcock (MCCU) v Hants (Horsham)
102 M H Cross & B L Brookes (MCC YC) v Warwicks
(High Wycombe)

Eighth Wicket
148 L A Jones & B L Brookes (MCC YC) v Derbys (Glossop)
122 B J Twohig & J D Shantry (Worcs) v Northants (Holcot)
100 J A Stamatis & M W Dixon (Essex) v Hants
(Ageas Bowl Nursery)

Ninth Wicket
157 T N Cullen & C A J Meschede (Glam) v Sussex (Fulking)
119 J E Poysden & S E Grant (Warwicks) v MCC YC
(High Wycombe)
103 A M Lilley & M J Hurt (Lancs) v Hants
(Newclose, I of Wight)

Tenth Wicket
123 N A Sowter & R H Patel (Middx) v Sussex (Richmond)

SECOND ELEVEN TROPHY 2017 - FINAL TABLES
NORTHERN GROUP

		P	W	L	NR	Ab	Pts	NRR
1	Lancashire (1)	6	5	0	1	0	11	1.883
2	Yorkshire (7)	6	3	0	1	2	9	1.770
3	Worcestershire (10)	6	4	2	0	0	8	0.303
4	Warwickshire (5)	6	3	2	0	1	7	-0.064
5	Nottinghamshire (3)	6	3	3	0	0	6	0.309
6	Northamptonshire (9)	6	3	3	0	0	6	-0.183
7	Derbyshire (4)	6	2	4	0	0	4	-0.290
8	MCC Young Cricketers (-)	6	1	4	1	0	3	-0.622
9	Durham (6)	6	1	4	0	1	3	-1.517
10	Leicestershire (2)	6	0	3	1	2	3	-1.587

SOUTHERN GROUP

		P	W	L	NR	Ab	Pts	NRR
1	Somerset (1)	6	5	1	0	0	10	1.292
2	Middlesex (7)	6	4	1	1	0	9	1.185
3	Essex (6)	6	4	2	0	0	8	0.655
4	Sussex (4)	6	4	2	0	0	8	-0.007
5	Glamorgan (10)	6	2	2	1	1	6	0.451
6	Hampshire (3)	6	2	2	1	1	6	0.195
7	Surrey (5)	6	2	3	0	1	5	-0.059
8	Kent (2)	6	2	3	0	1	5	-1.227
9	Gloucestershire (8)	6	1	4	1	0	3	-0.599
10	Unicorns (-)	6	0	6	0	0	0	-1.370

i) MCC Young Cricketers & the Unicorns exchanged groups from the 2016 season
ii) Numbers in parentheses are the 2016 positions
iii) NR = No Result
iv) Ab = Abandoned
v) NRR = Net Run Rate

FIRST CLASS COUNTIES 2nd ANNUAL SECOND ELEVEN TROPHY FINAL

The Final was played at Headingley on 8 June 2017 under floodlights.

Yorkshire won by 99 runs (DLS). The game started as 50 overs per side but rain then intervened. Yorkshire's innings was finally declared closed at 38.4 overs after three interruptions. Middlesex's innings was thus reduced to 38 overs and their target was 279 to win.

Yorkshire innings | | Runs
HC Brook	b Barber	112
JA Tattersall	c Compton b Godsal	13
R Gibson	c Compton b Barber	58
*WMH Rhodes	not out	50
E Callis	c Godsal b Sowter	17
JA Thompson	b Higgins	0
J Shaw	not out	2
+J Read	did not bat	
JW Shutt	did not bat	
JC Wainman	did not bat	
JD Warner	did not bat	
Extras	(2 lb, 4 nb, 7 w)	13
Total	(5 wickets, innings closed, 198 minutes, 38.4 overs)	265

Fall of wickets:
1-65 (Tattersall, 12.3 ov), 2-173 (Gibson, 27.6 ov), 3-206 (Brook, 31.5 ov), 4-251 (Callis, 36.4 ov), 5-257 (Thompson, 37.3 ov)

Middlesex bowling

	O	M	R	W
Podmore	7	1	50	0
Barber	9	1	58	2
Godsal	6	0	43	1
Higgins	8	1	38	1
Sowter	5.4	0	46	1
Scott	3	0	28	0

Middlesex innings | | Runs
RF Higgins	c Callis b Wainman	4
TC Lace	retired not out	0
GFB Scott	c Read b Shaw	19
*NRD Compton	lbw b Thompson	57
+RG White	c Callis b Thompson	15
J Davies	st Read b Shutt	29
DS Manuwelege	b Shaw	40
HW Podmore	b Shutt	0
NA Sowter	not out	2
A Godsal	st Read b Shutt	2
TE Barber	b Shutt	0
Extras	(3 lb, 2 nb, 6 w)	11
Total	(all out, 131 minutes, 27.3 overs)	179

Fall of wickets:
1-4 (Higgins, 0.5 ov), 2-32 (Scott, 5.4 ov), 3-93 (White, 12.3 ov), 4-102 (Compton, 14.6 ov), 5-162 (Davies, 25.2 ov), 6-162 (Podmore, 25.4 ov), 7-174 (Manuwelege, 26.5 ov), 8-178 (Godsal, 27.1 ov), 9-179 (Barber, 27.3 ov)

Yorkshire bowling

	O	M	R	W
Wainman	5	0	25	1
Shaw	5	0	49	2
Rhodes	5	0	42	0
Warner	4	0	12	0
Thompson	5	0	29	2
Shutt	3.3	0	19	4

Umpires – I D Blackwell & M Newell
Scorers – Howard Clayton (Yorkshire) & Neil Smith (Middlesex)

COMPETITION SEMI-FINALS

Lancashire v Middlesex (Stanley Park, Blackpool) – 2 June. The match was reduced to 25 overs per side before the start. Lancashire made 128/9 and Middlesex won by five wkts on 131/5 (R G White 54*; M W Parkinson 3/14)

Somerset v Yorkshire (County Ground, Taunton) – 2 June. The match was reduced to 47 overs per side before the start. Somerset 328 (J Allenby 101, T D Rouse 64, E J Byrom 51; M D Fisher 4/67). Yorkshire's innings was ended by rain after just 12 overs on 76/1. Yorkshire were awarded the tie on a better Net Run Rate in the qualifying groups.

SECOND ELEVEN TROPHY 2017 HIGHLIGHTS

BATTING 2017
Qual: 4 innings; average of 40.00

	M	I	NO	Runs	HS	Avge	100s
B D Guest (Lancs)	7	5	1	270	110*	103.05	1
G F B Scott (Middx)	8	7	1	504	153*	92.98	3
R Gibson (Yorks)	5	5	2	237	76*	79.00	-
G P Smith (Notts)	4	4	1	209	103*	69.66	1
R C Davies (Somerset)	7	7	1	396	135	66.00	1
O E Westbury (Worcs)	6	6	0	383	143	63.83	2
W R Smith (Hants)	5	4	0	252	130	63.00	1
G A Bartlett (Somerset)	7	7	1	375	142*	62.50	1
P I Walter (Essex)	5	5	1	249	145*	62.25	1
C M Jones (Essex)	5	4	2	124	52	62.00	-
F O E van den Bergh (Surrey)	5	4	1	180	96*	60.00	-
M A Richardson (Northants)	4	4	3	58	46*	58.00	-

	M	I	NO	Runs	HS	Avge	100
C J Taylor (Essex)	4	4	1	170	73*	56.66	-
E J Byrom (Somerset)	6	5	1	224	75	56.00	-
A R I Umeed (Warwicks)	4	4	0	214	87	53.50	-
G H Rhodes (Worcs)	6	6	1	262	134*	52.40	1
K C Appleby (Kent)	4	4	1	152	59	50.66	-
D S Manuwelege (MCC YC/ Middx)	6	5	2	145	82	48.33	-
A Harinath (Surrey)	6	5	0	237	115	47.70	1
M S Pepper (Unc)	6	5	0	235	103	47.00	1
P D Salt (Sussex)	6	6	0	280	123	46.66	2
J H Barrett (Hants/MCC YC)	4	4	0	184	109	46.00	1
A M Ali (Leics)	4	4	0	183	96	45.75	-
A J Woodland (Sussex / MCCU)	5	5	2	134	55*	44.66	-
C J Haggett (Kent)	4	4	0	178	88	44.50	-
J G Myburgh (Somerset)	5	5	1	177	101	44.25	1
H R Hosein (Derbys)	6	6	1	218	87	43.60	-
M H Cross (Kent/MCC YC)	5	4	0	174	75	43.50	-
A H J A Hart (Hants)	5	4	1	127	72	42.33	-
T A Wood (Derbys)	6	6	0	248	126	41.33	1
G J Harte (Durham/Kent/MCC YC)	6	6	1	205	124*	41.00	1

BOWLING 2016

Qual: 10 wickets; average of 27.00

	O	M	Runs	Wkt	Avge	BB
M W Parkinson (Lancs)	29	2	107	12	8.91	5/14
M H McKiernan (Durham / Lancs / Unc)	47.5	1	232	14	16.57	5/45
D M Bess (Somerset)	56	2	269	14	19.21	5/63
A Hepburn (Worcs)	47	3	233	11	21.18	4/56
J E Poysden (Warwicks)	48.3	0	262	10	26.20	5/47

WICKET-KEEPERS (8 victims or better)

	CT	ST	Total
E C Davies (Somerset)	4	6	10
M S Pepper (Unc)	5	3	8

FIELDERS (4 catches or better)

	Total
M J J Critchley (Derbys)	6
F H Allen (MCC YC)	6
C A J Brodrick (Derbys)	5
K S Velani (Essex)	5
J J Bohannon (Lancs)	5
T A Wood (Derbys)	4
A O Morgan (Glam)	4
N J Selman (Glam)	4
M A H Hammond (Glos)	4
A J Ball (Kent)	4
R P Jones (Lancs)	4
G F B Scott (Middx)	4
R G White (Middx)	4
B M Kitt (Notts)	4
L A Patterson-White (Notts)	4
M R Adair (Warwicks)	4
J E Poysden (Warwicks)	4
A Hepburn (Worcs)	4
J A Thompson (Yorks)	4

HIGHEST TEAM TOTALS (280 or better)

431/7	Northants v Leics (Northampton)
383/6	Worcs v Derbys (Kidderminster)
364/7	Middx v Kent (Radlett)
362/7	Yorks v Warwicks (York)
355/9	Derbys v Worcs (Kidderminster)
349/7	Somerset v Surrey (Purley)
338/4	Middx v Unc (Newbury)
338/9	Hants v Glam (Ageas Bowl Nursery)
337/8	Somerset v Glos (Bristol Un SG)
336/5	Lancs v Northants (Northop Hall)
332/3	Kent v Glos (Beckenham)
332/7	Middx v Surrey (Purley)
332	Leics v Northants (Northampton)
328/7	Notts v Durham (Riverside)
328	Somerset v Yorks (Taunton)
327/6	Worcs v MCC YC (Kidderminster)
325	Unc v Middx (Newbury)
323/8	Somerset v Kent (Taunton Vale)
315/7	Glam v Glos (Newport)
315/8	Derbys v Northants (Denby)
309/2	Derbys v Notts (Denby)
307	Worcs v Warwicks (Shirley)
301	Hants v Essex (Ageas Bowl Nursery)
300/6	Sussex v Glam (Blackstone)
298/7	Glam v Sussex (Blackstone)
295	Yorks v Derbys (York)
294/6	Notts v Derbys (Denby)
289/3	Sussex v Hants (Fulking)
288/7	Hants v Sussex (Fulking)
288/7	Surrey v Glos (Purley)
287/9	Surrey v Essex (Billericay)
285	Kent v Somerset (Taunton Vale)
284/9	MCC YC v Worcs (Kidderminster)
283/7	Glos v Somerset (Bristol Un)
283/8	Kent v Hants (Polo Farm SG, Canterbury)

LOWEST TEAM TOTALS (129 or less)

91	Sussex v Surrey (Horsham)
93	Durham v Northants (Milton Keynes)
109	Leics v Lancs (Hinckley)

HIGHEST INDIVIDUAL INNINGS (120 or better)

157	C S Delport (Leics) v Northants (Northampton)
153*	G F B Scott (Middx) v Kent (Radlett)
152*	A J Ball (Kent) v Glos (Beckenham)
149	S S Eskinazi (Middx) v Unc (Newbury)
145*	P I Walter (Essex) v Somerset (Taunton Vale)
143*	J M Kettleborough (Unc) v Somerset (Taunton Vale)
143	O W Westbury (Worcs) v Derbys (Kidderminster)
142*	G A Bartlett (Somerset) v Somerset (Taunton Vale)
140	B J Taylor (Hants) v Essex (Ageas Bowl Nursery)
139*	B T Slater (Derbys) v Notts (Denby)
139	K S Carlson (Glam) v Glos (Newport)
135	R C Davies (Somerset) v Glos (Bristol U)
134*	G H Rhodes (Worcs) v Notts (Oakham S)
134	L A Procter (Lancs) v Northants (Northop Hall)
130	W R Smith (Hants) v Unc (Ageas Bowl Nursery)
126	T A Wood (Derbys) v Northants (Denby)
124*	G J Harte (Durham) v Worcs (Worcester)
123	W T Root (Notts) v Leics (Notts SG)
123	A Rath (Middx) v Kent (Radlett)
123	P D Salt (Sussex) v Hants (Fulking)
121	T Kohler-Cadmore (Worcs) v Derbys (Kidderminster)
121	L Wood (Notts) v Durham (Riverside)

In all, a total of 41 centuries was scored in the competition in 2017

TWO CENTURIES IN ONE INNINGS

153* by G F B Scott & 123 by A Rath (both Middx) v Kent (Radlett)

124 by L A Procter & 110* by B D Guest (both Lancs) v Northants (Northop Hall)

143 by O W Westbury & 121 by T Kohler-Cadmore (both Worcs) v Derbys (Kidderminster)

149 by S S Eskinazi & 106 by G F B Scott (both Middx) v Unc (Newbury)

TWO CENTURIES IN ONE MATCH

153* by G F B Scott & 142* by G A Bartlett (Somerset) (Taunton Vale)

115* by S P Crook (Northants) & 157 by C S Delport (Leics) (Northampton)

139* by B T Slater (Derbys) & 119 by B A Hutton (Notts) (Denby)

100 by G F B Scott (Middx) & 109* by V Chopra
(Essex) (Radlett)
143* by J M Kettleborough (Unc) & 142* by G A Bartlett
(Somerset) (Taunton Vale)
109 by J H Barrett (Hants) & 123 by P D Salt (Sussex) (Fulking)
135 by R C Davies (Somerset) & 113 by G T Hankins (Glos)
(Bristol U)

CARRYING BAT THROUGH COMPLETED INNINGS
There were no instances in 2017.

BEST BOWLING (5 wkts or better)
7/33	G S Virdi (Surrey) v Sussex (Horsham)
7/36	G Burrows (Lancs) v Leics (Hinckley)
6/53	T J Wells (Leics) v Lancs (Hinckley)
5/14	M W Parkinson (Lancs) v Durham (Bowdon)
5/45	M H McKiernan (Durham) v Worcs (Worcester)
5/47	J E Poysden (Warwicks) v Derbys
	(Bull's Head Gd, Coventry)
5/62	M E T Salisbury (Essex) v Hants (Ageas Bowl Nursery)
5/63	D M Bess (Somerset) v Kent (Taunton Vale)

MOST WICKET-KEEPER DISMISSALS IN AN INNINGS
5	W E L Buttleman (Essex) v Somerset (Taunton Vale)
5	S J W Sall (Surrey) v Glos (Purley)
4	J Davies (Middx) v Surrey (Purley)

MOST CATCHES BY A FIELDER IN AN INNINGS
3	C A Barrett (Northants) v Derbys (Denby)
3	M R Adair (Warwicks) v Worcs (Scorers, Shirley)
3	T A Wood (Derbys) v Yorks (York)
3	B M Kitt (Notts) v Durham (Riverside)
3	L A Patterson-White (Notts) v Worcs (Oakham S)
3	J C Wainman (Yorks) v Warwicks (York)
3	J L Lawlor (Glam) v Hants (Ageas Bowl Nursery)
3	D Davies (Northants) v Notts (Bedford S)
3	J A Thompson (Yorks) v Somerset (Taunton)

MATCHES ABANDONED WITHOUT A BALL BEING BOWLED
A total of 5 matches never began and were as follows. The period
between 15 & 19 May was the cause of the majority of these
matches to be lost.

Surrey v Hampshire (Whitgift S)
Leicestershire v Yorkshire (Lutterworth CC)
Durham v Yorkshire (Brandon CC)
Glamorgan v Kent (Newport CC)
Leicestershire v Warwickshire (Hinckley)

TIED MATCHES
There were no tied matches in 2017

HAT-TRICKS
R J Gleeson (Northants) achieved the feat against Derbys at
Denby, dismissing M J J Critchley, H R Hosein & T P Milnes.

BEST PARTNERSHIPS
First Wicket
199	T Kohler-Cadmore & O E Westbury (Worcs) v Derbys
	(Kidderminster)
184	J M Kettleborough & S S Arthurton (Unc) v Somerset
	(Taunton Vale)
147	A R I Umeed & S R Hain (Warwicks) v Worcs (Shirley)
132	P D Salt & A J Robson (Sussex) v Middx (Southgate)
122	A Harinath & R Patel (Surrey) v Glos (Purley)
118	J G Myburgh & G A Bartlett (Somerset) v Glam (Newport)
114	M L Pettini & C S Delport (Leics) v Northants
	(Northampton)
110	J J Cobb & B M Duckett (Northants) v Leics
	(Northampton)
107	N R D Compton & P R Stirling (Middx) v Surrey (Purley)

105	B S Gilmour & M A H Hammond (Glos) v Kent
	(Beckenham)
104	A R I Umeed & L Banks (Warwicks) v Yorks (York)
102	J Allenby & G A Bartlett (Somerset) v Surrey (Purley)
101	T P Alsop & W R Smith (Hants) v

Second Wicket
250	S S Eskinazi & G F B Scott (Middx) v Unc (Newbury)
192	J L Lawlor & K S Carlson (Glam) v Glos (Newport)
186	A Rath & G F B Scott (Middx) v Kent (Radlett)
185	C J Haggett & A J Ball (Kent) v Glos (Beckenham)
177	G A Bartlett & R C Davies (Somerset) v Unc
	(Taunton Vale)
163	T C Lace & G F B Scott (Middx) v Sussex (Southgate)
156	J L Lawlor & N Brand (Glam) v Sussex (Blackstone)
147	L Wood & G P Smith (Notts) v Durham (Riverside)
136	O E Westbury & T C Fell (Worcs) v MCC YC
	(Kidderminster)
108	V Chopra & C J Taylor (Essex) v Middx (Radlett)
108	H C Brook & R Gibson (Yorks) v Middx (Headingley)
108	J A Tattersall & E Callis (Yorks) v Warwicks (York)

Third Wicket
183	A M Ali & W N Fazackerley (Leics) v MCC YC
	(Merchant Taylors' S, Northwood)
177	G A Bartlett & R C Davies (Somerset) v Glos (Bristol U)
165*	B T Slater & H R Hosein (Derbys) v Notts (Denby)
120*	V Chopra & J S Foster (Essex) v Middx (Radlett)
116	J H Barrett & F S Hay (Hants) v Sussex (Fulking)

Fourth Wicket
204	L A Procter & B D Guest (Lancs) v Northants
	(Northop Hall)
189*	M J Lamb & A Javid (Warwicks) v Derbys
	(Bull's Head SG, Coventry)
172	T A Wood & A L Hughes (Derbys) v Northants (Denby)
140*	J A Leaning & R Gibson (Yorks) v MCC YC
	(Merchant Taylors' S)
138	G H Rhodes & A Hepburn (Worcs) v Notts (Oakham S)
121	O E Westbury & R A Whiteley (Worcs) v Warwicks
	(Shirley)
113	A Harinath & M W Pillans (Surrey) v Essex (Billericay)

Fifth Wicket
102	W A T Beer & L P Smith (Sussex) v Glam (Blackstone CC)

Sixth Wicket
168	S P Crook & G G White (Northants) v Leics (Northampton)
148	U Arshad & S Steel (Durham) v MCC YC (Riverside)
129	B A Hutton & T G Keast (Notts) v Derbys (Denby)
114	J R Murphy & C L Herring (Glam) v Somerset (Newport)
112	B J Taylor & A H J A Hart (Hants) v Essex
	(Ageas Bowl Nursery)
101	K C Appleby & O G Robinson (Kent) v Hants
	(Polo Farm SG, Canterbury)

Seventh Wicket
114	H R Hosein & T A I Taylor (Derbys) v Worcs
	(Kidderminster)
101	A K Dal & M Carter (Notts) v Worcs (Oakham S)
100*	P I Walter & C M Jones (Essex) v Somerset (Taunton Vale)

Eighth Wicket
90*	N R Welch & L G Cammish (Sussex) v Kent (Canterbury)
87	D J Willey & Azeem Rafiq (Yorks) v Derbys (York)

Ninth Wicket
106	T B Sole & C A Barrett (Northants) v Derbys (Denby)

Tenth Wicket
65	R Rampaul & T M Homes (Surrey) v Somerset (Purley)
61*	S Reeves & G T Main (Durham) v Notts (Riverside)

SECOND ELEVEN T20 COMPETITION 2017
FINAL GROUP TABLES

NORTHERN GROUP

		P	W	L	T	Ab	Pts	NRR
1	Yorkshire (7)	12	7	2	0	3	17	1.351
2	Lancashire (3)	12	7	3	0	2	16	0.829
3	MCC Young Cricketers (-)							
		12	7	3	0	2	16	0.748
4	Warwickshire (2)	12	7	5	0	0	14	0.069
5	Durham (1)	12	5	5	1	1	12	-0.127
6	Northamptonshire (8)	12	5	7	0	0	10	0.250
7	Nottinghamshire (6)	12	5	7	0	0	10	-0.639
8	Leicestershire (5)	12	4	6	0	2	10	-0.927
9	Worcestershire (10)	12	4	8	0	0	8	-0.390
10	Derbyshire (4)	12	1	6	1	4	7	-1.024

SOUTHERN GROUP

		P	W	L	T	NR	Ab	Pts	NRR
1	Sussex (9)	12	8	3	1	0	0	17	0.875
2	Hampshire (5)	12	7	3	0	0	2	16	0.320
3	Middlesex (2)	12	7	5	0	0	0	14	0.045
4	Kent (3)	12	6	5	0	0	1	13	0.627
5	Glamorgan (4)	12	5	5	0	0	2	12	-0.483
6	Surrey (6)	12	4	5	0	1	2	11	0.289
7	Essex (10)	12	5	6	0	0	1	11	-0.857
8	Gloucestershire (7)	12	5	7	0	0	0	10	0.272
9	Somerset (1)	12	4	8	0	0	0	8	-0.554
10	Unicorns (-)	12	2	6	1	1	2	8	-0.838

i) Tied = Tied matches
ii) NRR = Net Run Rate
iii) NR = No result
iv) MCC Young Cricketers & the Unicorns
exchanged groups from the 2016 season
v) Numbers in parentheses are the 2016 positions

FIRST CLASS COUNTIES 2nd ANNUAL
T20 FINALS DAY

The Semi-Finals and the Final were all played at Arundel Castle
on 10 August 2017.

First Semi-Final – Hampshire beat Yorkshire by nine wkts.

Yorkshire innings		Runs
JA Tattersall	run out (Lintott)	12
+BD Birkhead	c Wheal b Salisbury	12
B Anjum	lbw b Lintott	3
*WMH Rhodes	c Hay b Sole	11
MJ Waite	c Holland b Wheal	29
JA Thompson	c Adams b Salisbury	10
E Barnes	st Hay b Lintott	0
JC Wainman	run out (Adams)	4
JD Warner	run out (Adams)	6
K Carver	not out	1
JW Shutt	b Wheal	1
Extras	(2 b, 2 lb, 2 nb, 5 w)	11
Total	(all out, 73 minutes, 18.2 overs)	100

Fall of wickets:
1-21 (Tattersall, 3.4 ov), 2-26 (Birkhead, 4.5 ov), 3-32 (Anjum,
6.3 ov), 4-50 (Rhodes, 9.6 ov), 5-76 (Thompson, 12.6 ov), 6-77
(Barnes, 13.3 ov), 7-86 (Wainman, 15.3 ov), 8-97 (Waite, 16.3 ov),
9-99 (Warner, 17.1 ov), 10-100 (Shutt, 18.2 ov)

Hampshire bowling	O	M	R	W
Wheal	3.2	0	12	2
Salisbury	4	0	22	2
Holland	3	0	12	0
Lintott	4	0	26	2
Sole	4	0	24	1

Hampshire innings		Runs
*JHK Adams	not out	57
+FS Hay	c Wainman b Carver	26
IG Holland	not out	9
FS Organ	did not bat	
WR Smith	did not bat	
TAR Scriven	did not bat	
CB Sole	did not bat	
AHJA Hart	did not bat	
JB Lintott	did not bat	
MET Salisbury	did not bat	
BTJ Wheal	did not bat	
Extras	(2 lb, 2 nb, 5 w)	9
Total	(1 wicket, 44 minutes, 11.4 overs)	101

Fall of wickets:
1-62 (Hay, 6.3 ov)

Yorkshire bowling	O	M	R	W
Wainman	4	0	33	0
Waite	1	0	15	0
Shutt	1	0	13	0
Barnes	1	0	11	0
Warner	1	0	9	0
Carver	3	0	15	1
Thompson	0.4	0	3	0

Umpires – T Lungley & J D Middlebrook
Scorers – Peter J W Danks (Hampshire) & John R Virr (Yorkshire)

Second Semi-Final – Sussex beat Lancashire by four wkts.

Lancashire innings		Runs
CK Turner	run out (Jenner)	29
*+AL Davies	c Wells b Sakande	11
RP Jones	lbw b Hooper	27
H Hameed	c Robson b Barton	26
LA Procter	lbw b Hooper	18
JJ Bohannon	not out	15
DJ Lamb	not out	8
TE Bailey	did not bat	
LJ Hurt	did not bat	
TJ Lester	did not bat	
MH McKiernan	did not bat	
Extras	(4 lb, 3 nb, 8 w)	15
Total	(5 wickets, innings closed,	
	74 minutes, 20 overs)	149

Fall of wickets:
1-24 (Davies, 2.4 ov), 2-67 (Jones, 8.6 ov), 3-83 (Turner, 11.1 ov),
4-121 (Hameed, 16.5 ov), 5-125 (Procter, 17.3 ov)

Sussex bowling	O	M	R	W
Rawlins	2	0	21	0
Whittingham	3	0	17	0
Sakande	3	0	26	1
Hooper	4	0	28	2
Oxley	4	0	30	0
Barton	4	0	23	1

Sussex innings		Runs
AJ Robson	not out	90
LWP Wells	c Bohannon b Hurt	25
*HZ Finch	c and b Bohannon	3
DMW Rawlins	c Hameed b Bohannon	3
+MGK Burgess	b Procter	4
JW Jenner	run out (Bailey)	2
NS Oxley	b Procter	15
EO Hooper	not out	5
SG Whittingham	did not bat	
A Sakande	did not bat	
AP Barton	did not bat	
TJ Haines	did not bat	

Extras (2 lb, 1 w)
Total (6 wickets, 76 minutes, 19.2 overs) 150

Fall of wickets:
1-54 (Wells, 7.1 ov), 2-77 (Finch, 9.1 ov), 3-81 (Rawlins, 9.6 ov), 4-97 (Burgess, 12.6 ov), 5-107 (Jenner, 14.3 ov), 6-135 (Oxley, 17.4 ov)

Lancashire bowling	O	M	R	W
Procter	4	0	24	2
Bailey	3.2	0	31	0
Lester	2	0	13	0
Lamb	3	0	30	0
McKiernan	4	0	19	0
Hurt	1	0	18	1
Bohannon	2	0	13	2

Umpires – J D Middlebrook & C M Watts
Scorers – Mike Dixon (Lancashire) & Graham J Irwin (Sussex)

The Final – Sussex beat Hampshire by 24 runs.

Sussex innings		Runs
AJ Robson	b Wheal	3
LWP Wells	b Sole	28
*HZ Finch	c Sole b Wheal	54
DMW Rawlins	c Hay b Holland	40
+MGK Burgess	c Lintott b Salisbury	20
JW Jenner	run out (Lintott->Salisbury)	13
NS Oxley	not out	0
EO Hooper	did not bat	
SG Whittingham	did not bat	
A Sakande	did not bat	
AP Barton	did not bat	
TJ Haines	did not bat	
Extras	(1 b, 4 lb, 7 nb, 1 w)	13
Total	(6 wickets, innings closed, 80 minutes, 20 overs)	171

Fall of wickets:
1-13 (Robson, 2.4 ov), 2-51 (Wells, 5.5 ov), 3-112 (Rawlins, 12.4 ov), 4-157 (Finch, 18.3 ov), 5-162 (Burgess, 19.1 ov), 6-171 (Jenner, 20 ov)

Hampshire bowling	O	M	R	W
Wheal	4	0	23	2
Salisbury	4	0	33	1
Holland	3	0	28	1
Sole	4	0	34	1
Lintott	4	0	39	0
Smith	1	0	9	0

Hampshire innings		Runs
*JHK Adams	c Finch b Sakande	20
+FS Hay	b Hooper	4
IG Holland	c Rawlins b Sakande	14
FS Organ	c Wells b Whittingham	1
WR Smith	b Rawlins	31
TAR Scriven	c Burgess b Sakande	3
CB Sole	c Whittingham b Barton	22
AHJA Hart	st Burgess b Rawlins	12
JB Lintott	c Rawlins b Barton	29
MET Salisbury	c Burgess b Barton	1
BTJ Wheal	not out	3
Extras	(2 lb, 5 w)	7
Total	(all out, 71 minutes, 19.3 overs)	147

Fall of wickets:
1-6 (Hay, 0.4 ov), 2-39 (Adams, 4.1 ov), 3-39 (Holland, 4.2 ov), 4-45 (Organ, 5.5 ov), 5-60 (Scriven, 8.3 ov), 6-93 (Sole, 11.6 ov), 7-105 (Smith, 14.3 ov), 8-114 (Hart, 16.2 ov), 9-126 (Salisbury, 17.2 ov), 10-147 (Lintott, 19.3 ov)

Sussex bowling	O	M	R	W
Hooper	4	0	44	1
Whittingham	3	0	23	1
Sakande	4	0	26	3
Oxley	3	0	25	0
Barton	3.3	0	9	3
Rawlins	2	0	18	2

i) SR = Strike –Rate
ii) ER = Economy Rate

Umpires – T Lungley & C M Watts
Scorers – Peter J W Danks (Hampshire) & Graham J Irwin (Sussex)

SECOND ELEVEN T20 COMPETITION
2017 HIGHLIGHTS

BATTING 2017
Qual: 6 innings; average of 40.00

	M	I	NO	Runs	HS	Avge	100s
A J Robson (Sussex)	12	12	5	471	90*	67.28	-
N J Selman (Glam)	6	6	2	250	63*	62.50	-
T P Alsop (Hants)	8	8	3	277	68*	55.40	-
T A R Scriven (Hants)	8	7	4	144	42*	48.00	-
M H Cross (Kent / MCC YC)	9	8	1	324	69	46.28	-
Z Crawley (Kent)	11	11	2	404	109*	44.88	1
G F B Scott (Middx)	10	9	3	268	75*	44.66	-
N R Welch (Essex/Surrey)	6	6	1	218	75*	43.60	-
T Banton (Somerset)	12	12	3	376	94	41.77	-
W G Jacks (Surrey)	8	8	1	290	65*	41.42	-
S A Zaib (Northants)	10	10	0	411	76	41.10	-

BOWLING 2017
Qual: 10 wickets

	O	M	Runs	Wkt	Avge	BB
G L S Scrimshaw (Worcs)	14	1	68	10	6.80	5/12
S J Cook (Essex)	19	1	123	12	10.25	4/15
A Shahzad (Sussex)	18.1	1	110	10	11.00	3/29
C F Parkinson (Leics)	22	0	121	11	11.00	4/13
O J Hannon-Dalby (Warwicks)	20.2	0	138	11	12.54	4/14
O W Smithson (MCC YC)	27	0	152	12	12.66	3/15
B G F Green (Somerset)	20.1	0	169	13	13.00	4/22
M W Parkinson (Lancs)	27	1	146	11	13.27	4/18
B J Taylor (Hants)	34	0	217	16	13.56	4/23
C N Miles (Glos)	29	0	178	13	13.69	3/16
A P Barton (Sussex)	22.3	0	137	10	13.70	3/9
O E Robinson (Sussex)	46.5	1	299	20	14.95	5/33
B T J Wheal (Hants)	24.2	1	153	10	15.30	3/23
A S S Nijjar (Essex)	32.5	0	226	14	16.14	2/8
C J Haggett (Kent)	27.4	0	211	13	16.23	4/22
K A Bull (Glam)	32	1	197	12	16.41	2/10
J B Lintott (Essex/Hants)	29	0	214	13	16.46	4/18
U Arshad (Durham)	26.5	0	211	12	17.58	3/18
O R T Sale (Somerset)	20	0	176	10	17.60	3/23
R J Sayer (Leics)	27	0	198	11	18.00	3/31
M D Fisher (Yorks)	24	0	199	11	18.09	3/46
T M Homes (Surrey)	30.3	1	199	11	18.09	3/14
A Kapil (Northants/Unc)	32.2	0	221	12	18.41	3/26
M Carter (Notts)	32	1	204	11	18.54	4/11
J C Wainman (Yorks)	22.3	0	208	11	18.90	4/21
L J Hurt (Lancs/MCC YC)	32	0	216	11	19.63	2/20
P I Burgoyne (Unc)	32	0	238	11	21.63	4/43
J E Poysden (Warwicks)	46	0	303	14	21.64	2/15
D M W Rawlins (Sussex)	35	0	242	11	22.00	4/15
P A Sivirajah (MCC YC)	35.2	1	225	10	22.50	2/15
S G Whittingham (Sussex)	42.3	0	283	12	23.58	3/19
J Shaw (Glos)	29.4	1	260	11	23.63	3/31
R A J Smith (Glam)	27	0	268	11	24.36	3/32
B J Twohig (Worcs)	37.1	0	277	10	27.70	3/20

WICKET-KEEPERS Minimum of 6 victims

	CT	ST	Total
A J Mellor (Warwicks)	9	4	13
G H Roderick (Glos)	10	1	11
T Banton (Somerset)	9	2	11
C M Dickinson (Hants)	7	3	10
A J A Wheater (Essex)	9	-	9
T N Cullen (Glam)	6	2	8
T G Keast (Notts)	4	4	8
A A Shafique (Surrey)	5	3	8
C L Herring (Glam)	4	2	6
J H Barrett (MCC YC)	5	1	6
M G K Burgess (Sussex)	4	2	6
O B Cox (Worcs)	4	2	6
M H Cross (Kent / MCC YC)	6	-	6

FIELDERS Minimum of 5 catches

	Total
L A Jones (MCC YC)	9
S A Zaib (Northants)	9
J J Weatherley (Kent)	8
C J Taylor (Essex)	7
F H Allen (MCC YC)	7
T B Abell (Somerset)	7
C P Wood (Hants)	6
L J Hurt (MCC YC)	6
J W Jenner (Sussex)	6
C B Sole (Hants)	5
Z Crawley (Kent)	5
C J Haggett (Kent)	5
R P Jones (Lancs)	5
R J Sayer (Leics)	5
B L Brookes (MCC YC)	5
L Wood (Notts)	5
E J Pollock (Warwicks)	5
J G Myburgh (Somerset)	5
B J Twohig (Worcs)	5

BEST PARTNERSHIPS

First Wicket

137 V Chopra & A J A Wheater (Essex) v Unc (Great Tew)
135 A P Rouse & S W Billings (Kent) v Unc (Saffron Walden) (2nd match)
132 S Kelsall & E R Kilbee (Unc) v Essex (Great Tew)
130 S R Dickson & Z Crawley (Kent) v Unc (Saffron Walden) (1st match)
110 Waqas Husain & E R Kilbee (Unc) v Surrey (New Malden)
103 L Trevaskis & A J Hickey (Durham) v Worcs (Burnopfield CC)
102* A Hepburn & Z A Malik (Worcs) v MCC YC (Merchant Taylors' S, Northwood)

Second Wicket

195* Z Crawley & J D S Neesham (Kent) v Middx (Polo Farm SG, Canterbury)
150 R Gibson & J A Leaning (Yorks) v Durham (Marske CC)
146 J Allenby & P D Trego (Someret) v Middx (Uxbridge CC)
144* T C Lace & R G White (Middx) v Hants (Ageas Bowl Nursery)
130 Z Crawley & J D S Neesham (Kent) v Surrey (Polo Farm SG, Canterbury)
129 O J D Pope & F O E van den Bergh (Surrey) v Sussex (New Malden)
128 M H Cross & J H Barrett (MCC YC) v Durham (Merchant Taylors' S, Northwood)
122 C T Steel & G J Harte (Durham) v Warwicks (S Northumberland CC)
107 P D Salt & S van Zyl (Sussex) v Somerset (Horsham)

Third Wicket

113* C J Whittock & L J Thomason (Unc) v Sussex (Long Marston)

Fourth Wicket

125 F I N Khushi & A P Beard (Essex) v Somerset (Chelmsford)

Fifth Wicket

115 M J Lumb & S J Mullaney (Notts) v Northants (Grantham)

Sixth Wicket

93* T Banton & R C Davies (Somerset) v Glos (Taunton Vale)

Seventh Wicket

51 C R Brown & T R Bevan (Glam) v Glos (Bristol U)

Eighth Wicket

49 P I Burgoyne & B S Phagura (Unc) v Essex (Great Tew)

Ninth Wicket

62 J C Wainman & K Carver (Yorks) v Worcs (Worcester RGS)

Tenth Wicket

48* K Carver & J W Shutt (Yorks) v Worcs (Worcester RGS)

HIGHEST TEAM TOTALS (170 or better in a completed innings in an uninterrupted match)

219/1 Kent v Middx (Polo Farm SG, Canterbury)
212/7 Kent v Unc (Saffron Walden)
210/3 Yorkshire v Durham (Marske CC)
209/6 Middx v Glam (Richmond)
207/7 Yorks v Notts (Barnsley)
207/7 Sussex v Somerset (Horsham)
204/5 Durham v Warwicks (S Northumberland)
201/4 Yorks v Northants (Pudsey Congs CC)
200/6 Northants v Yorks (Pudsey Congs CC)
199/5 Durham v Leics (Riverside)
195/4 Somerset v Middx (Uxbridge CC)
195/4 Notts v Derbys (Worksop Coll)
195/5 Northants v Worcs (Northampton)
194/3 Sussex v Somerset (Horsham)
194/7 Derbys v Notts (Worksop Coll)
193/7 Somerset v Sussex (Horsham)
191/5 Middx v Essex (Coggeshall)
190/6 Unc v Kent (Saffron Walden)
188/3 Kent v Surrey (Polo Farm SG, Canterbury)
184/4 MCC YC v Durham (Merchant Taylors' S, Northwood)
184/5 Somerset v Glos (Taunton Vale)
180/6 Worcs v Northants (Northampton)
180/6 Leics v Durham (Riverside)
180/9 Essex v Middx (Coggeshall)
179/4 Middx v Essex (Coggeshall)
179/5 Essex v Glam (St Fagans)
179/7 Northants v Leics (Lutterworth CC)
178/5 Glam v Middx (Richmond)
174/2 Yorks v Northants (Pudsey Congs)
174 Northants v Leics (Lutterworth CC)
173/1 Leics v Unc (Great Tew)
173/4 Notts v Derbys (Worksop C)
173/7 Northants v Yorks (Pudsey Congs)
173/8 Middx v Kent (Polo Farm SG, Canterbury)
172/2 Glam v Somerset (Taunton Vale) (2nd match)
172/5 Glam v Somerset (Taunton Vale) (1st match)
171/3 Unc v Essex (Great Tew)
171/6 Sussex v Hants (Arundel)
171/9 Somerset v Glam (Taunton Vale) (2nd match)
170/5 Notts v Northants (Grantham)
170/7 Glos v Essex (Chelmsford)
170/8 Somerset v Glam (Taunton Vale) (1st match)

LOWEST TEAM TOTALS (99 or less in a completed innings in an uninterrupted match)

73 Leics v Northants v Leics (Lutterworth CC)

85	Kent v Sussex (East Grinstead)
94	Worcs v MCC YC (Merchant Taylors' S, Northwood)
94	Derbys v Lancs (Westhoughton)
96	MCC YC v Lancs (Westhoughton)
98	Notts v Yorks (Barnsley)

HIGHEST INDIVIDUAL INNINGS (Centuries)

116*	A Z Lees (Yorks) v Northants (Pudsey Congs)
109*	Z Crawley (Kent) v Middx (Polo Farm SG, Canterbury)
109*	C T Steel (Durham) v Warwicks (S Northumberland)
103	R Gibson (Yorks) v Durham (Marske CC)
101	K R Brown (Lancs) v Northants (Northampton)

CARRYING BAT THROUGH COMPLETED INNINGS

No instances were recorded in 2017.

BEST BOWLING (4 wkts or better)

5/11	R N Sidebottom (Warwicks) v Durham (S Northumberland)
5/12	G L S Scrimshaw (Worcs) v Yorks (Worcester RGS)
5/12	K van Vollenhoven (MCC YC) v Durham (Merchant Taylors' S, Northwood)
5/15	T E Bailey (Lancs) v MCC YC (Westhoughton)
5/22	A M Ali (Leics) v Northants (Lutterworth)
5/26	L B K Hollman (Middx) v Essex (Coggeshall)
5/33	O E Robinson (Sussex) v Unc (Long Marston)
4/5	Azeem Rafiq (Yorks) v Notts (Barnsley)
4/11	M Carter (Notts) v MCC YC (Merchant Taylors' S, Northwood)
4/12	J W Shutt (Yorks) v Derbys (Alvaston & Boulton)
4/13	C F Parkinson (Leics) v Warwicks (Scorers, Shirley)
4/13	T Bulcock (Unc) v Sussex (Long Marston)
4/14	O J Hannon-Dalby (Warwicks) v Northants (Scorers, Shirley)
4/15	F O E van den Bergh (Surrey) v Sussex (New Malden)
4/15	D M W Rawlins (Sussex) v Hants (Newclose, I of Wight)
4/15	S J Cook (Essex) v Somerset (Chelmsford)
4/17	T B Sole (Northants) v Leics (Lutterworth CC)
4/18	M W Parkinson (Lancs) v Northants (Northampton)
4/18	J B Lintott (Hants) v Middx (Ageas Bowl Nursery)
4/21	B D Cotton (Derbys) v Durham (Belper)
4/21	J C Wainman (Yorks) v Derbys (Alvaston & Boulton)
4/22	L Trevaskis (Durham) v Worcs (Burnopfield)
4/22	C J Haggett (Kent) v Middx (Polo Farm SG, Canterbury) (1st match)
4/22	B G F Green (Somerset) v Hants (Taunton Vale)
4/23	B J Taylor (Hants) v Unc (Great Tew)
4/26	S J Cook (Essex) v Glam (St Fagans)
4/29	C A J Meschede (Glam) v Essex (St Fagans)
4/31	B W Sanderson (Northants) v Worcs (Northampton)
4/31	L J Fletcher (Notts) v Northants (Grantham)
4/36	C J Haggett (Kent) v Middx (Polo Farm SG, Canterbury) (2nd match)
4/38	O E Robinson (Sussex) v Somerset (Horsham)
4/43	P I Burgoyne (Unc) v Kent (Saffron Walden)

HAT-TRICKS

J C Wainman (Yorks) v Northants (Pudsey Congs)
T Bulcock (Unc) v Sussex (Long Marston)

TIED MATCHES

Unc v Sussex (Long Marston)
Derbys v Durham (Belper Meadows)

MATCHES ABANDONED WITHOUT A BALL BOWLED.

There were twelve abandoned matches in 2017 as follows

Derbys v MCC YC (Glossop) (both matches)
Glam v Unc (Port Talbot) (both matches)
Yorks v Durham (Marske CC)
Kent v Essex (Polo Farm SG, Canterbury)
Leics v Derbys (Leicester GS) (both matches)
Lancs v Yorks (Stanley Park, Blackpool) (both matches)
Hants v Surrey (Ageas Bowl Nursery) (both matches)

MOST VICTIMS BY A WICKET-KEEPER IN AN INNINGS

5	G H Roderick (Glos) v Essex (Chelmsford)
5	A J A Wheater (Essex) v Glam (St Fagans)
4	C L Herring (Glam) v Surrey (Neath)
4	J M Cox (Kent) v Glos (Longwood, Bristol)

MOST CATCHES BY A FIELDER IN AN INNINGS

4	N O Priestley (Derbys) v Yorks (Alvaston & Boulton)
3	R H Patel (Middx) v Surrey (Sunbury)
3	A J Hickey (Durham) v Worcs (Burnopfield)
3	G H I Harding (Durham) v Worcs (Burnopfield)
3	A J Robson (Sussex) v Glos (Fulking)
3	T Banton (Somerset) v Middx (Uxbridge)
3	A L Hughes (Derbys) v Durham (Belper)
3	G T Thornton (Warwicks) v Lancs (Bull's Head Gd, Coventry)
3	C M Dudley (Lancs) v Warwicks (Bull's Head Gd, Coventry)
3	O J Hannon-Dalby (Warwicks) v Lancs (Bull's Head Gd, Coventry)
3	S A Zaib (Northants) v Leics (Lutterworth CC)
3	T B Abell (Somerset) v Sussex (Horsham)
3	A Z Lees (Yorks) v Worcs (Worcester RGS)
3	E J H Eckersley (Leics) v Durham (Riverside)
3	S Reingold (Midx) v Essex (Coggeshall)

SECOND ELEVEN CRICKETERS OF THE YEAR

1989	J.C.Pooley (Middlesex)	2003	S.A.Newman (Surrey)
1990	R.J.Bartlett (Somerset)	2004	Z.K.Sharif (Essex)
1991	A.R.Caddick (Somerset)	2005	T.J.Phillips (Essex)
1992	R.C.Williams (Gloucestershire)	2006	G.T.Park (Durham)
1993	K.P.Dutch (Middlesex)	2007	W.R.S.Gidman (Durham)
1994	D.L.Maddy (Leicestershire)	2008	G.J.Muchall (Durham)
1995	A.R.Roberts (Northamptonshire)	2009	A.Carter (Nottinghamshire)
1996	K.P.Dutch (Middlesex)	2010	M J Richardson (Durham)
1997	M.J.Powell (Glamorgan)	2011	M.T.C.Waller (Somerset)
1998	K.J.Innes (Northamptonshire)	2012	W A T Beer (Sussex)
1999	K.P.Dutch (Middlesex)	2013	N L J Browne (Essex)
2000	R.M.S.Weston (Middlesex)	2014	C D Piesley (MCC Young Cricketers)
2001	G.J.Batty (Surrey)	2015	S R Dickson (Kent)
2002	B.M.Shafayat (Nottinghamshire)	2016	A J Hose (Somerset)

DERBYSHIRE

PLAYING RECORDS 2017
Championship – P9 W2 L1 D6 - fifth in the northern group
2nd XI Trophy – P6 W2 L4 - seventh in the northern group
2nd XI T20 Competition – P12 W1 T1 L6 Ab4 - tenth in the northern
group

2nd XI SUCCESSES
2nd XI Champions – Best finish – Runners-up in 1999 and 2002
2nd XI Trophy – Winners – 1987, 2015
2nd XI T20 – Best finish – second in the group in 2011 & 2014

SECOND ELEVEN CHAMPIONSHIP AVERAGES

BATTING	M	I	NO	Runs	HS	Avge	100s	C/S	BOWLING	O	M	Runs	Wkt	Avge	BB
M J J Critchley	5	7	1	398	135	66.33	1	1	M D Sonczak	40.3	4	118	8	14.75	6/57
H R Hosein	9	14	4	615	115*	61.50	2	22	G S Sandhu	106.1	20	314	14	22.42	5/65
C A J Brodrick	6	8	0	308	76	38.50	-	3	W S Davis	16	2	78	3	26.00	3/55
M A Jones	5	6	0	227	100	37.83	1	-	T P Milnes	116	28	391	14	27.92	5/37
T A I Taylor	2	3	0	112	107	37.33	1	-	B D Cotton	94	29	255	8	31.87	3/41
T A Wood	4	6	1	185	68	37.00	-	2	S Connors	38	6	141	4	35.25	3/59
C M Macdonell	9	14	1	447	149	34.38	1	5	R P Hemmings	103	26	293	8	36.62	2/24
A Patel	4	7	1	206	84	34.33	-	3	G T G Cork	63	15	202	5	40.40	2/17
B T Slater	5	8	1	232	109*	33.14	1	-	A C F Wyatt	61.2	12	202	4	50.50	3/84
G T G Cork	6	8	3	165	75	33.00	-	6	T A I Taylor	54	7	220	4	55.00	2/83
R P Hemmings	5	4	0	104	48	26.00	-	5	C M Macdonell	117.1	26	533	9	59.22	2/5
T P Milnes	7	11	1	219	89	21.90	-	4	H Qadri	69	17	282	4	70.50	2/62
Rahib Ali	3	5	1	83	42	20.75	-	-	A F Gleadall	49.5	7	227	3	75.66	2/120
Ramanpreet Singh	2	4	0	57	23	14.25	-	-	M J J Critchley	74	8	303	4	75.75	3/48
H Qadri	3	2	1	14	11*	14.00	-	-							
B D Cotton	4	4	2	13	7*	6.50	-	2							
A F Gleadall	5	3	1	13	10	6.50	-	1							

Also bowled – H R Bernard 4-0-14-0; D J Gibbs 18-0-101-0; M A
Jones 4-1-57-0; D O`Sullivan 17-5-40-1; A Patel 9-1-41-2; Rahib
Ali 2.4-0-46-0; B T Slater 4.2-0-17-0; J P A Taylor 15-2-48-1.

Also batted – 4 matches - G S Sandhu 1*. 3 matches – S Conners
DNB. 2 matches – J L Morgan 6; M D Sonczak 29 (1 ct); A C F
Wyatt – DNB. 1 match – H R Bernard DNB; W S Davis DNB; M A
Gapes DNB; D J Gibbs 6, 1*; J P Hancock 0, 19; J M Kettleborough
32, 9; J T Lacey 8; D O`Sullivan DNB; N O Priestley 5, 0; J R
Redman 24; J P A Taylor DNB (2 ct).

SECOND ELEVEN TROPHY AVERAGES

BATTING	M	I	NO	Runs	HS	Avge	100s	C/S	BOWLING	O	M	Runs	Wkt	Avge	BB
B T Slater	3	3	1	199	139*	99.50	1	1	R P Hemmings	15	2	31	4	7.75	3/18
L M Reece	2	2	0	96	51	48.00	-	2	A L Hughes	5	0	44	3	14.66	3/44
H R Hosein	6	6	1	218	87	43.60	-	6/1	D J Gibbs	15	0	69	3	23.00	2/43
T A Wood	6	6	0	248	126	41.33	1	4	H Qadri	9	0	73	3	24.33	3/73
M J J Critchley	6	5	1	146	77*	36.50	-	6	L M Reece	12	0	80	3	26.66	2/33
G T G Cork	4	3	1	70	37	35.00	-	-	B D Cotton	30	3	148	4	37.00	2/41
C M Macdonell	5	5	0	152	48	30.40	-	1	C M Macdonell	22	1	114	3	38.00	2/16
T A I Taylor	5	3	0	79	66	26.33	-	-	T A I Taylor	42.3	2	310	8	38.75	3/75
B D Cotton	3	2	1	25	18*	25.00	-	-		50.4	1	291	6	48.50	4/26
T P Milnes	3	3	0	61	38	20.33	-	2							
C A J Brodrick	6	5	1	33	21	8.25	-	5							
A F Gleadall	4	3	0	24	23	8.00	-	-							

Also bowled – C J Ball 1-0-18-0; C A J Brodrick 4-0-30-0; G T G
Cork 18-0-146-0; A F Gleadall 23-0-112-2; T P Milnes 13-0-53-1;
G C Viljoen 6-0-44-0; A C F Wyatt 10-0-43-2.

Also batted – 2 matches – D J Gibbs 10*, 0; R P Hemmings 4; H
Qadri 10*. 1 match - J Ball 0 (1ct); J P Hancock 2; A L Hughes
66 (1ct); M A Jones 4; Rahib Ali 3; L J Thomason 0; G C Viljoen
32*; B D Wright DNB; A C F Wyatt 3.

SECOND ELEVEN T20 AVERAGES

BATTING	M	I	NO	Runs	HS	Avge	100s	C/S
R P Hemmings	4	4	2	60	43*	30.00	-	1
B T Slater	6	6	0	170	75	28.33	-	1
T A Wood	6	6	1	141	60	28.20	-	4
H R Hosein	8	7	1	144	36	24.00	-	1/2
C A J Brodrick	7	6	1	113	60	22.60	-	3
T P Milnes	5	5	2	60	22*	20.00	-	1
M J Henry	3	3	0	54	47	18.00	-	4
T A I Taylor	8	7	3	51	17	12.75	-	-
B D Cotton	6	5	1	28	15	7.00	-	-
G T G Cork	5	4	0	10	6	2.50	-	3

BOWLING	O	M	Runs	Wkt	Avge	BB
G C Viljoen	4	0	30	3	10.00	3/30
H Qadri	16	0	78	6	13.00	2/14
B D Cotton	21.5	0	182	7	26.00	4/21
T P Milnes	16	0	156	6	26.00	2/26
T A I Taylor	26.2	0	233	8	29.12	3/19

Also bowled – C A J Brodrick 1-0-21-1; G T G Cork 11-0-86-1; M J Critchley 4-0-34-1; W S Davis 9-0-79-0; A F Gleadall 4-0-18-0; R P Hermmings 4-0-36-1; M J Henry 4-0-18-0; A L Hughes 3-0-29-0; C M Macdonell 4.4-0-43-1; L M Reece 1-0-6-1; M D Sonczak 3-0-44-2; J S Sykes 7.5-0-48-1; J P A Taylor 3-0-26-1.

Also batted – 5 matches – H Qadri 0. 4 matches – W S Davis DNB. 2 matches – M J J Critchley 37, 9; A L Hughes 16, 45 (3ct); C M Macdonell 6, 10; T Maxfield 0, 1; A Patel 4, 11*; N O Priestley 0 (5ct); M D Sonczak 0* (1ct); J S Sykes 0, 6. 1 match - A F Gleadall 0; L M Reece 26 (2ct); J P A Taylor 0; G C Viljoen 1; G C Wilson 31.

HOME MATCHES: SECOND ELEVEN CHAMPIONSHIP

v Lancashire (Dennis Viollet Av, Stoke-on-Trent) – 18-20 April – Derbys 386 (C M Macdonell 149, M J J Critchley 89; T J Lester 5/79, D J Lamb 3/83) & 174/4 d (B T Slater 109*) drew with Lancs 268/4 d (R P Jones 130*, J J Bohannon 53) & 241/7 (D J Lamb 89; B D Cotton 3/41)

v Northamptonshire (Belper Meadows) – 5-7 June - Derbys 201/8 d (H R Hosein 53*; R J Gleeeson 3/56) drew with Northants DNB.

v MCC Young Cricketers (Glossop) – 26-28 June - MCC YC 335 (L A Jones 79, B L Brookes 71, M H Cross 51; G S Sandhu 4/81, A C F Wyatt 3/84) drew with Derbys 266/4 (M J J Critchley 87*, A Patel 63*; L J Hurt 3/61)

v Durham (Belper Meadows) – 11-13 July – Derbys 305/5 d (H R Hosein 115*, T P Milnes 89, C A J Brodrick 73) & 122/5 d beat Durham 84/1 d & 226 (B J Yates 57; T P Milnes 5/37) by 117 runs.

v Nottinghamshire (Swarkestone) – 14-16 July - Notts 217 (L Wood 57, L W James 54*; G S Sandhu 5/56, W S Davis 3/55) & 215 (M Carter 52; T P Milnes 3/29) lost to Derbys 275 (H R Hosein 69; M Carter 4/68, L Wood 3/60) & 158/6 (B T Slater 51; M Carter 4/47) by four wkts.

HOME MATCHES: FRIENDLIES

v Unicorns (Ticknall CC) – 10 Apr – Unc 278/7 (S Kessall 88, M S Pepper 53) lost to Derbys 280/6 (B T Slater 69; M H McKiernan 3/62)

v Nottinghamshire (Chesterfield) – 11-14 Sept – Notts 303/5d (W T Root 145*, L W James 93) & inns forfeited drew with Derbys inns forfeited & 119/4 (T A Wood 50*)

v Hampshire (Denby) – 18-20 Sept – Match abandoned without a ball bowled.

HOME MATCHES: SECOND ELEVEN TROPHY

v Lancashire (Dennis Viollet Av, Stoke-on-Trent) – 17 Apr – Lancs 204/9 (B D Guest 73; R P Hemmings 3/18) beat Derbys 173 (M J J Critchley 77*; A M Lilley 3/18, D J Lamb 3/38) by 31 runs.

v Nottinghamshire (Denby) – 24 Apr – Derbys 309/2 (B T Slater 139*H R Hosein 64*) beat Notts 294/6 (B A Hutton 119, T G Keast 66*) by 15 runs.

v Northamptonshire (Denby) – 25 Apr – Derbys 315/8 (T A Wood 126, L M Reece 51; R J Gleeson 3/19, A Kapil 3/68) beat Northants 222 (T B Sole 53*; A L Hughes 3/44) by 93 runs.

HOME MATCHES : SECOND ELEVEN T20 COMPETITION

v MCC Young Cricketers (Glossop) – 29 June – Match 1 – Match abandoned without a ball bowled.

v MCC Young Cricketers (Glossop) – 29 June – Match 2 – Match abandoned without a ball bowled.

v Durham (Belper) – 10 July – Match 1 – Durham 154/8 (M J Richardson 58;B D Cotton 4/21) tied with Derbys 154/7 .

v Durham (Belper) – 10 July – Match 2 – Derbys 154/4 (B T Slater 75) beat Durham 147/7 by seven runs.

v Yorkshire (Alvaston & Boulton) – 31 July – Match 1 – Yorkshire 158 (T A I Taylor 3/19) beat Derbys 136 (J W Shutt 4/12, J C Wainman 4/21) by 22 runs.

v Yorkshire (Alvaston & Boulton) – 31 July - Match 2 – Derbys 75/5 lost to Yorks 67/1 by nine wkts (DLS)

PLAYERS WHO HAVE REPRESENTED DERBYSHIRE 2ND XI IN 2017 (48)

*D Andrew	A F Gleadall	*B M A J Mendis	B T Slater
C J Ball	J P Hancock	T P Milnes	M D Sonczak
H R Bernard	R P Hemmings	J L Morgan	J S Sykes
*T Brett	M J Henry	D O'Sullivan	J P A Taylor
C A J Brodrick	H R Hosein	A Patel	T A I Taylor
S Connors	A L Hughes	N O Priestley	L J Thomason
G T G Cork	*D Jacobs	H Qadri	G C Viljoen
B D Cotton	M A Jones	Rahib Ali	*H Wansford
M J J Critchley	J M Kettleborough	Ramanpreet Singh	G C Wilson
W S Davis	J T Lacey	J R Redman	T A Wood
M A Gapes	C M Macdonell	L M Reece	B D Wright
D J Gibbs	T Maxfield	G S Sandhu	A C F Wyatt

DERBYSHIRE CRICKETERS

*Daniel ANDREW (Trent Coll; Loughborough Coll; AECC, Bournemouth) b Nottingham, 9.9.98. RHB WK. Debut 2017. Played v Notts, Chesterfield, 2017. Did not bat or bowl.

Cameron James BALL (Longdendale HS, Hyde, Cheshire; Loretto S, Manchester) b Hadfield, 22.11.98. RHB RM. Debut 2016. HS 28 v Durham, Darlington, 2016. BB 0/14 in the same match. HSSET 0 v Yorks, York, 2017. BBSET 0/18 in the same match.

Hugh Robert BERNARD (Archbishop's S, Canterbury) b Canterbury, 14.9.96. RHB RMF. Debut Kent 2014. F/C debut (Kent) v Glam, Canterbury, 2016. Debut Derbys 2017. Eng U19 to Aus, 2014/15; v Aus 2015. HS 14* (Kent) v Glos, Polo Farm SG, Canterbury, 2016. BB 5/20 (Kent) v Surrey, Beckenham, 2017. HSSET 7*(Kent) v Hants, Canterbury, 2014. BBSET 4/41 (Kent) v Glos, Canterbury, 2015. HS T20 5* (Kent) v Essex, Billericay, 2016 (1st). BBT20 4/22 (Kent) v Durham, Arundel, 2015 (SF).

Thomas BRETT (Latimer Community Arts Coll, Kettering) b Kettering, Northants, 13.11.89. RHB SLA, Debut Northants 2007. F/C debut (Northants) v Oxford MCCU, the Parks, 2010. Debut Derbys 2017. HS 43 (Northants) v Sussex, Finedon Dolben, 2010. BB 5/44 (Northants) v Notts, Rugby S, 2010. HSSET 3 (Northants) v Sussex, Wellingborough S, 2010. BBSET 2/35 in the same match. HSKO 1 (Northants) v Leics, Dunstable, 2010. BBKO 0/13 in the same match.

Callum Ashley James BRODRICK (John Taylor HS, Barton-under-Needwood, Staffs) b Burton-upon-Trent, Staffs, 24.1.98. LHB. Debut 2016. F/C debut v W Indians, Derby, 2017. HS 76 v Worcs, Amblecote, 2017. HSSET 21 v Worcs, Kidderminster, 2017. BBSET 0/30 v Warwicks, Bull's Head Gd, Coventry, 2017. HST20 60 v Notts, Worksop C, 2017 (2nd). BBT20 1/21 v Yorks, Alvaston & Boulton, 2017 (1st)

Samuel CONNERS (George Spencer Acad, Nottingham) b Nottingham, 13.2.99. RHB RM. Debut 2016. HS 20 v Yorks, Belper Meadows, 2016. BB 3/59 v Yorks, Belper Meadows, 2016. HSSET 2 v Yorks, Alvaston & Boulton, 2016. BBSET 0/24 in the same match.

Gregory Teodor Gerald CORK (Denstone Coll) b Derby, 29.9.94. Son of D.G (England, 37 Tests & 32 ODIs 1995/2002. Derbys, Lancs, Hants, 1995/2012). RHB LMF. Debut 2012. F/C debut v Worcs, New Road, 2016. HS 102 v Warwicks, Derby, 2014. BB 5/56 v Notts, Denby, 2016. HSSET 44* v Yorks, Marske-by-the-Sea, 2015. BBSET 2/34 v Northants, Belper, 2015. HST20 40* v Lancs, Ormskirk, 2013 (2nd) & v Notts, Derby, 2016 (2nd). BBT20 3/18 v Lancs, Ormskirk, 2013 (2nd). Released at the end of the 2017 season.

Benjamin David COTTON (Clayton Hall Business & Lang Coll, Newcastle-under-Lyme; Stoke SFC) b Stoke-on-Trent, Staffs 13.9.93. RHB RMF. Debut 2011. F/C debut v Surrey, the Oval, 2014. HS 30 v Leics, Desborough, 2016. BB 5/31 v Notts, Notts SG, 2016. HSSET 30* v Lancs, Parkgate, Neston, 2016. BBSET 4/47 v Leics, Grace Road, 2013. HST20 15 v Notts, Worksop C, 2017 (2nd). BBT20 4/21 v Durham, Belper, 2017 (1st). Derbys Staff.

Matthew James John CRITCHLEY (St Michael's, Chorley, Lancs; Cardinal Newman Coll, Preston) b Preston, Lancs, 13.8.96. RHB LB. Debut 2014. F/C debut v Glam, SWALEC, 2015. HS 135

v Warwicks, EFCSG, 2017. BB 5/50 v Notts, Denby, 2014. HSSET 77* v Lancs, Stoke-on-Trent, 2017. BBSET 4/26 v Yorks, York, 2017. HST20 37 v Durham, Belper, 2017 (1st). BBT20 1/11 Notts, Derby, v 2016(1st). Derbys Staff.

William Samuel DAVIS (Stafford GS) b Stafford, 6/3/96. RHB RMF. Debut (Derbys) 2013. F/C debut v the Australians, Derby, 2015. Eng U19 (T20s only) 2013; to Australia 2014/15. HS 12 v Lancs, Derby, 2016. BB 5/62 v Notts, Denby, 2014. HSSET 1 v Warwicks, Derby, 2014. BBSET 3/25 v Lancs, Glossop, 2015. HST20 23* v Notts, Loughborough,, (1st). BBT20 2/26 v Notts, Derby, 2016 (2nd). Derbys Staff.

Matthew Alan GAPES (Padua Coll, Brisbane, Queensland) b Frankston, Melbourne, Aus, 28.3.89. RHB RM. Debut 2017 v Durham (Belper) but did not bat or bowl.

Daniel John GIBBS (St John Fisher RC HS, Newcastle-u-Lyme; Newcastle-u-Lyme Coll) b Newcastle-u-Lyme, Staffs, 14.9.98. RHB RMF. Debut 2016. HS 18 v Leics, Desborough, 2016. BB 2/49 v Yorks, Belper Meadows, 2016. HSSET 10* v Yorks, York, 2017. BBSET 2/43 in the same match.

Alfie Frank GLEADALL (Westfield Sp Coll, Sheffield) b Chesterfield, 28.5.00. LHB RFM. Debut 2017. List A debut v S Africa A, Derby, HS 10 v Warwicks, ECFSG, 2017. BB 2/120 in the same match. HSSET 23 v Yorks, York, 2017. BBSET 1/21 v Lancs, Stoke-on-Trent, 2017. HST20 0 v Notts, Worksop C, 2017 (1st).

John Patrick HANCOCK (St Joseph's Coll, Stoke-on-Trent) b Newcastle-under-Lyme, Staffs, 16.1.92. RHB RM. Debut 2017. HS 19 v Lancs, Stoke-on-Trent, 2017. HSSET 2 v Lancs, Stoke-on-Trent, 2017.

Robert Phillip HEMMINGS (Sir Thomas Boughey S, Stoke-on-Trent; Denstone Coll) b Newcastle-under-Lyme, Staffs, 28.2.96. RHB RA. Debut 2015. F/C debut v Worcs, Derby, 2016. HS 87 v MCCU, Denby, 2015. BB 5/65 v Durham, Darlington, 2016. HSSET 36 v Yorks, Alvaston & Boulton, 2016. BBSET 3/18 v Lancs, Stoke-on-Trent, 2017. HST20 43* v Notts, Worksop C, 2017 (1st). BBT20 2/30 v Yorks, Harrogate, 2016 (2nd). Released at the end of the 2017 season.

Matthew James HENRY (St Bedes Coll, Christchurch, NZ) b Christchurch, NZ, 14.12.91. RHB RF. Debut 2017.Tests (NZ) 8 (2015 to date) & 32 ODIs. HST20 47 v Lancs, Westhoughton, 2017 (1st).

Harvey Richard HOSEIN (Denstone Coll) b Chesterfield, 12.8.96. RHB WK. Debut 2010, aged 13 yrs & 287 days. F/C debut v Surrey, the Oval, 2014. Eng U19 (T20s only) 2013. HS 115* v Durham, Belper, 2017. HSSET 87 v Worcs, Kidderminster, 2017. HST20 36 v Notts, Worksop C, 2017 (2nd). Derbys Staff.

Alex Lloyd HUGHES (Ounsdale HS, Wombourne) b Wordsley, Staffs 29.9.91. RHB RM. Debut 2009. F/C debut v Sussex, Hove, 2013. Derbys Cap 2017. HS 216* v Durham, Belper, 2015. BB 3/30 v Glos, Bristol, 2011. HSSET 67 v Warwicks, Repton S, 2016. BBSET 3/44 v Northants, Denby, 2017. HST20 56* v Yorks, Harrogate, 2016 (1st). BBT20 3/30 v Durham, Glossop, 2014 (1st). Derbys Staff.

*David JACOBS (Moranatha Christian S, Gauteng, S Africa; Juegland HS; Un of SA) b Johannesburg, S Africa, 3.5.89. RHB RF. Debut 2017. BB 1/76 v Notts, Chesterfield, 2017.

20

Michael Alexander JONES (Ormskirk GS; Myerscough Coll) b Ormskirk, Lancs, 5.1.98. RHB OB. Debut Derbys, Durham, Leics & Scotland A 2017. HS 173* (Scotland A) v Durham, Riverside, 2017. HSSET 34 (Durham) v Lancs, Bowden, 2017. HST20 35 (Leics) v Durham, Riverside, 2017 (1st).

James Michael KETTLEBOROUGH (Bedford S) b Huntingdon, Cambs, 22.10.92. RHB OB Debut Middx 2011; Northants 2012. F/C debut (Northants) v Sri Lankans, 2014. Debut Glam 2015; Derbys, Unc & ret to Northants 2017. HS 209* (Glam) v Essex, Bishop's Stortford, 2016. BB 2/24 (Northants) v Notts, Milton Keynes, 2017. HSSET 143* (Unc) v Somerset, Taunton Vale, 2017. BBSET 1/28 (Middx) v MCCYC, Radlett, 2011. HST20 52* (Glam) v Essex, Chelmsford, 2016 (1st). BBT20 2/13 (Unc) v Kent, Saffron Walden, 2017 (2nd).

Joshua Thomas LACEY (Heanor Gate Science Coll) b Derby, 25.11.00. RHB OB. Debut 2017. HS 8 v Yorks, York, 2017.

Charles Michael MACDONELL (Wellingborough S, Northants; Durham U) b Basingstoke, Hants, 23.2.94. RHB OB. Debut Northants 2013; Durham 2015; Derbys 2016. F/C debut (Durham MCCU) v Somerset, Taunton Vale, 2015. HS 149 v Lancs, Stoke-on-Trent, 2017. BB 2/5 v Yorks, York, 2017. HSSET 67* v Notts, Worksop Coll, 2016. BBSET 2/16 v Northants, Denby, 2017. HST20 10 v Yorks, Alvaston & Boulton, 2017 (2nd). BBT20 1/35 v Lancs, Westhoughton, 2017 (1st).

Timothy MAXFIELD (Wood Green HS, Wednesbury, W Midlands) b Walsall, Staffs, 28.12.90. LHB RM. Debut Leics 2013; Unc 2014, Derbys 2017. HS 50 (Leics) v Derbys, Ashby-de-la-Zouch, 2013. BB 0/6 in the same match. HSSET (Unc) 23 v Middx, Saffron Walden, 2014. BBSET 3/49 (Unc) v Warwicks, Bull's Head Ground, 2016. HST20 54* (Unc) v Lancs, Liverpool, 2015 (1st). BBT20 2/13 (Unc) v Leics, Loughborough Town CC, 2015 (1st).

***Balapuwaduge Mankulasuriya Amith Jeevan MENDIS** (St Thomas Coll, Colombo, Sri Lanka) b Colombo, 15.1.83. Debut 2017. ODIs (Sri Lanka) 54 (2010 to 2014/15) Brother of Balapuwaduge Mankulasuriya Thiwantha Tharindu (Colombo CC, Sri Lanka Ports Authority & Moors Sp Club, 2000/01 to 2016/17. HS40 v Unc, Ticknall, 2017. BB2/58 in the same match.

Thomas Patrick MILNES (Heart of England S, Coventry) b Stourbridge, Worcs 6.10.92. RHB RFM. Debut Warwicks 2009 aged 16 years and 233 days. F/C debut (Warwicks) v Durham MCCU, the Racecourse, 2011. Debut Derbys 2015 (on loan). Eng U19 to Sri Lanka 2010/11. HS 102 (Warwicks) v Notts, Edgbaston, 2014. BB 6/25 v Northants, Swarkestone, 2015. HSSET 51 (Warwicks) v Leics, Grace Road, 2014. BBSET 5/25 (Warwicks) v Derbys, Dunstall, 2010. HST20 54* v Leics, Derby, 2016 (2nd). BBT20 2/14 v Leics, Derby, 2016 (2nd). BBKO 1/20 (Warwicks) v Worcs, Worcester, 2010.

Joss Lloyd MORGAN (Repton S) b Durban, S Africa, 3.6.98. RHB. Debut 2017. Brother-in-law Wayne Madsen (Derbys 2009 to present day) Debut 2017. HS 31 v Yorks, Harrogate, 2017.

David O'SULLIVAN (Merchant Taylors' S, Northwood; Cardiff Met) b Sydney, Australia, 11.6.97. RHB RFM. Debut Derbys & Glam 2017. F/C debut (Cardiff MCCU) v Hants, Ageas Bowl Nursery, 2017. BB 1/40 v MCC YC, Glossop, 2017.

Akhil PATEL (Kimberley CS) b Nottingham 18.6.90. LHB SLA Chinamen. Brother of S.R. (6 Tests & 36 ODIs, Eng, 2008 to 2015/16). Debut Derbys 2007 aged 16 years and 304 days; F/C debut (Derbys) v Cambridge MCCU, Fenner's, 2007; debut Notts 2009. Ret to Derbys 2012. Debuts Kent & Northants 2012; Surrey 2013; ret to Northants 2014; debut Essex & Sussex 2017. HS 174 (Notts) v Northants, Finedon Dolben 2011. BB 4/53 (Notts) v Yorks, Barnsley, 2011. HSSET 105 (Notts) v Leics, Leicester, 2010. BBSET 4/25 (Northants) v Sussex, Desborough, 2014. HST20 35 (Northants) v Leics, Grace Road, 2015 (2nd). BBT20 2/16 (Notts) v Derbys, Long Eaton, 2011 (1st.) HSKO 63(Notts) v Derbys, Alvaston & Boulton, 2010. BBKO 0/21 in the same match.

Nils Oscar PRIESTLEY (Blessed Robert Sutton S, Burton-on-Trent; Abbotsholme SFC) b Sutton Coldfield, Warwicks, 18.9.00. LHB RM. Debut 2017. HS 23 v Yorks, Harrogate, 2017. BB 0/30 v Notts, Chesterfield, 2017. HST20 0 v Yorks, Alvaston & Boulton, 2017 (1st).

Hamidullah QADRI (Derby Moor S; Chellaston Acad) b Kandahar, Afghanistan, 5.12.00. RHB OB. Debut 2017. F/C debut v Glam, SWALEC, 2017. Eng U19 v India, 2017; to SA 2017/18. HS 11* v Yorks, York, 2017. BB 2/62 in the same match. HSSET 10* v Worcs, Kidderminster, 2017. BBSET 3/73 in the same match. HST20 0 v Yorks, Alvaston & Boulton, 2017 (1st). BBT20 2/14 in the same match.

RAHIB ALI (Littleover Common S; Derby Coll; Derby U) b Derby 15.10.95. RHB RM. Debut 2014. HS 42 v Yorks, York, 2017. HSSET 12 v Yorks, Marske-by-the-Sea, 2015. HST20 1 v Yorks, Derby, 2014 (1st).

RAMANPREET SINGH (Gosforth HS) b Newcastle upon Tyne, Northumberland 19.2.93. RHB OB. Debut Durham 2009 aged 16 years and 181 days. F/C debut (Durham) v Australia A, 2012. Debut Derbys & Leics 2015. Eng U19 to Sri Lanka 2010/11; v S.Africa 2011. to Bangladesh & to Australia 2011/12, HS 139 (Durham) v Ireland, A Darlington, 2012. BB 0/4 (Durham) v Lancs, Old Trafford, 2013. HSSET 106 (Durham) v Lancs, the Tyldesleys, Westhoughton, 2013. BBSET 0/9 (Durham) v Lancs, Middlesbrough, 2013. HST20 75 (Durham) v Derbys, Brandon, 2014 (2nd). HSKO 2 (Durham) v Yorks, Weetwood, 2010.

Jack Richard REDMAN (Sir Thomas Boughey S, Stoke-on-Trent; Denstone Coll) b Stoke-on-Trent, 30.11.00. LHB OB. Debut 2017. HS 24 v Notts, Swarkestone, 2017.

Luis Michael REECE (St Michael's S, Chorley; Myerscough Coll, Bilsborrow; Leeds Met U) b Taunton, Somerset 4.8.90. LHB LM. Debut Lancs 2008; Worcs 2010; MCCU & Unicorns A 2011. Ret to Lancs 2011. F/C debut (Leeds/Bradford MCCU) v Surrey, The Oval, 2012. Debut Derbys 2016. HS 201* (Lancs) v Durham, Old Trafford, 2013. BB 4/29 v Notts, Denby, 2016. HSSET 139* (Lancs) v Worcs, Ombersley, 2014. BBSET 2/22 (Lancs) v Sussex, Horsham, 2014. HST20 49 (Lancs) v Derbys, Ormskirk, 2013 (2nd). BB T20 3/13 (Unc A) v Northants, Wellingborough S, 2011 (2nd).

Gurjit Singh SANDHU (Isleworth & Syon S) b Isleworth, Middx, 24.3.92. RHB LMF. Debut (Middx) 2008 aged 16 years and 85 days. F/C debut (Middx) v the Sri Lankians, Uxbridge, 2011. Debut Durham & Derbys 2016. HS 49* (Middx) v Surrey, Radlett, 2010. BB 7/31 (Middx) v Surrey, Wimbledon, 2015 (and match figs of 10/76). HSSET 31 (Middx) v MCCYC, Radlett, 2011. BBSET 3/13 (Middx) v Northants, Dunstable, 2014. HST20 0 (Middx) v Leics, Uxbridge, 2013 (1st) & (Middx) v Northants, Bedford S, 2013 (2nd). BBT20 3/25 (Middx) v Northants, Uxbridge, 2014 (1st).

Benjamin Thomas SLATER (Netherthorpe S, Staveley; Leeds Met U) b Chesterfield 26.8.91. LHB OB. Debut 2009. F/C debut (Leeds/Bradford MCCU) v Surrey, The Oval, 2012. HS 156* v Warwicks, Deer Park, Dunstall, 2011. BB 0/4 v Notts, Notts Sp Gr, 2014. HSSET 139* v Notts, Denby, 2017. HST20 75 v Durham, Belper, 2017 (2nd). BBT20 2/34 v Unc, Long Marston, 2016 (2nd). HSKO 20 v Notts, Alvaston & Boulton, 2010. Derbys Staff.

Matthew David SONCZAK (Audenshaw S, Manchester) b Hadfield, Derbys, 5.9.98. RHB SLA. Debut 2017. F/C debut v West Indies, Derby, 2017. HS 29 v Notts, Swarkestone, 2017. BB 6/57 v Leics, Kibworth, 2017. HST20 0* v Notts, Worksop C, 2017 (1st). BBT20 2/44 in the same match.

James Stuart SYKES (St Ivo S, St Ives, Cambs) b Huntingdon 26.4.92. LHB SLA. Debut Leics 2009. F/C debut (Leics) v Essex, Chelmsford, 2013; Debut Derbys 2017. HS 66 (Leics) v Worcs, Kidderminster, 2015. BB 8/55 (Leics) v Durham, Chester-le-Street, 2011. HSSET 28* (Leics) v MCCYC, High Wycombe, 2014. BBSET 4/16 (Leics) v Worcs, Grace Road, 2014. HST20 33 (Leics) v Unc, Loughborough CC, 2015 (1st). BBT20 3/13 (Leics) v Derbys, Grace Road, 2015 (2nd)

James Philip Arthur TAYLOR (Trentham HS, Stoke-on-Trent) b Stoke-on-Trent, 19.1.01. RHB RFM. Debut 2017. F/C debut v W Indians, Derby, 2017. Brother of T A I Taylor (below). BB 1/48 v MCC YC, Glossop, 2017. HST20 3 v Yorks, Alvaston & Boulton, 2017 (1st). BBT20 1/26 in the same match.

Thomas Alexander Ian TAYLOR (Trentham HS, Stoke-on-Trent; Newcastle-under-Lyme Coll) b Stoke-on-Trent, Staffs, 21.12.94. RHB RFM. Debut 2011. (Brother of J P A above) F/C debut v Leics, Grace Road, 2014. HS 107 v Leics, Kibworth, 017. BB 5/24 v Worcs, Derby, 2014. HSSET 66 v Worcs, Kidderminster, 2017. BBSET 4/33 v Yorks, Swarkestone, 2014. HST20 17 v Yorks, Alvaston & Boulton, 2017 (1st). BBT20 3/19 in the same match. Joins Leicestershire for 2018.

Lee James THOMASON (Barr Beacon S, Walsall; U of Wolverhampton) b Sutton Coldfield, 22.1.95. RHB WK.. Brother of A D (Warwicks 2013 to date). Debut Warwicks & Unc 2014; Derbys 2017. HS 31 (Unc) v MCC YC, Saffron Walden, 2017. HSSET (Unc) 58 v Durham, Burnopfield, 2015. BBSET 2/32 (Unc) v Glos, Bristol U, 2017. HST20 47* (Unc) v Sussex, Long Marston, 2017 (1st). BBT20 2/11 (Unc) v Hants, Great Tew, 2017 (1st)

G C VILJOEN (G C is his name, not his initials. Known as Hardus) b Witbank, S Africa, 6.3.89. RHB RFM. Debut Easterns 2008/09; Titans 2009/10; Lions 2012/13; Kent 2016; Derbys 2017. F/C debut (Easterns) v E Prov, Benoni, 2008/09.Tests (SA) 1 (2015/16). HSSET 32* v Worcs, Kidderminster, BBSET 0/44 in the same match. HST20 1 v Lancs, Westhoughton, 2017 (1st). BBT20 3/30 in the same match.

*Henry WANSFORD (Anthony Gell S, Wirksworth) b Derby, 18.4.00. RHB RF. Debut 2017. BB 1/70 v Notts, Chesterfield, 2017.
Thomas Anthony WOOD (Heanor Gate Science Coll) b Derby, 11.5.94. RHB RM. Debut 2012. F/C debut v Leics, Derby, 2016. Debut Unc 2016. HS 200* v Worcs, Derby, 2016. BB 1/20 v Notts, Notts SG, 2014. HSSET 126 v Northants, Denby, 2017. HST20 67 (Unc) v Notts, Notts SG, 2016 (1st). Released at the end of the 2017 season.
Benjamin David WRIGHT (St Benedict`s S, Derby) b Southend-on-Sea, Essex, 7.1.00. RHB RM. Debut 2017. HS 4 v Notts, Chesterfield, 2017.
Alexander Charles Frederick WYATT (Oakham S) b Roehampton, Surrey, 23.7.90. RHB RMF. Debut Leics 2007, F/C debut (Leics) v Loughborough MCCU, Grace Road, 2009; debut Northants 2016; Derbys 2017. HS 31* (Leics) v Derbys, Denby, 2014. BB 5/40 (Leics) v Notts, Kibworth, 2012. HSSET 32* (Leics) v Yorks, Grace Road, 2011. BBSET 3/23 (Leics) v Worcs, Leicester, 2010. HST20 13 (Leics) v Unicorns A, Bishop`s Stortford, 2013 (1st). BBT20 4/18 (Leics) v Northants, Northampton, 2014 (2nd).

DURHAM

PLAYING RECORDS 2017
Championship – P9 W2 L2 D4 Ab1 – eighth in the northern group
2nd XI Trophy – P6 W1 L4 Ab1 – ninth in the northern group
2nd XI T20 Competition – P12 W5 T1 L5 Ab 1 – fifth in the northern group

2nd XI SUCCESSES
2nd XI Champions – 2008, 2016
2nd XI Trophy – Losing Finalists – 1996, 2015
2nd XI T20 – Losing Finalists - 2011

SECOND ELEVEN CHAMPIONSHIP AVERAGES

BATTING	M	I	NO	Runs	HS	Avge	100s	C/S
G J Harte	6	10	3	535	183	76.42	2	2
M A Jones	3	5	0	308	172	61.60	1	3
H W Podmore	2	3	2	58	51*	58.00	-	-
A J Hickey	5	8	1	346	144	49.42	1	4
B A Carse	4	5	1	192	113*	48.00	1	1
J Coughlin	7	8	1	287	87	41.00	-	4
S Bell	2	3	0	84	38	28.00	-	-
J T A Burnham	2	3	1	49	40*	24.50	-	2
S Steel	8	11	1	243	42	24.30	-	4
U Arshad	4	4	0	83	38	20.75	-	1
T M Hewison	3	4	0	76	53	19.00	-	1
G H I Harding	4	4	1	44	23	14.66	-	2
R L Greenwell	3	4	0	52	21	13.00	-	-

BOWLING	O	M	Runs	Wkt	Avge	BB
W J Weighell	26	5	84	7	12.00	6/47
U Arshad	36	10	100	7	14.28	2/23
S Reeves	54.5	13	169	11	15.36	6/79
B G Whitehead	16.3	1	82	5	16.40	4/71
Faizan Hussain	22.4	3	74	3	24.66	2/26
A J Hickey	101.3	11	376	13	28.92	6/74
O W Smithson	26	3	98	3	32.66	3/53
G T Main	42.3	4	214	6	35.66	2/51
B J McCarthy	28	3	148	4	37.00	3/73
S Steel	20	2	111	3	37.00	2/47
G Onions	97.5	22	349	9	38.77	4/65
J Coughlin	81.5	12	347	4	86.75	3/15

Also batted – 5 matches – G Onions 17*, 6*, 21*, 20*. 3 matches – B G Whitehead DNB (1ct). 2 matches – J Dass 55, 0 (2ct); E J Hurst 2 (1ct); I A Karim 60, 27 (4ct/1st); B J McCarthy 12; G T Main DNB (1ct); W J Weighell 7, 8 (1ct). 1 match – C Appleby DNB; N Borkhatria DNB (1ct); A D F Brewster DNB; C J Carter 0, 0; G Clark 0; B G Compton 36* (1ct); Faizan Hussain DNB; M J Fisher 6 (1ct); L J Hurt DNB; S M Imtiaz 0, 42 (5ct); T W M Latham 241; C M McBride 17, 13; R McKendray 0*; M Oswell DNB; J R Philippe 37, 2 (4ct); M J Potts 0, 6 (2ct); S W Poynter 1 (3ct); S Reeves 0, 4 (1ct); C J Shoebridge 0*, 9*; O W Smithson 7, 0; S J Tindale 4, 1 (1ct); L Trevaskis 10; B J Yates 57 (4ct).

Also bowled – C Appleby 13-2-53-1; A D F Brewster 12-1-59-1; B A Carse 8-2-33-1; B G Compton 5.1-0-15-1; J Dass 1-0-1-0; M J Fisher 13-2-56-1; G H I Harding 51-5-257-2; L J Hurt 22-7-40-1; C M McBride 2.4-0-13-1; R McKendray 17-3-37-1; M Oswell 6-0-28-2; H W Podmore 34-8-125-1; M J Potts 14.4-24-2; C J Shoebridge 10.5-2-53-0; S J Tindale 11-0-49-0; L Trevaskis 13.5-0-76-1.

SECOND ELEVEN TROPHY AVERAGES

BATTING	M	I	NO	Runs	HS	Avge	100s	C/S
G J Harte	4	4	1	151	124*	75.00	1	-
S Steel	4	3	1	57	53*	28.50	-	3
A J Hickey	5	5	0	103	44	20.60	-	1
M A Jones	5	5	0	94	34	18.80	-	1
I A Karim	4	4	0	49	23	12.25	-	6/1
J Coughlin	5	4	0	41	20	10.25	-	1
T M Hewison	3	3	0	19	11	6.33	-	-

BOWLING	O	M	Runs	Wkt	Avge	BB
M H McKiernan	16.1	0	75	7	10.71	5/45
G T Main	28.2	0	184	6	30.66	3/21
A J Hickey	32	0	151	3	50.33	2/43

Also batted – 4 matches – G T Main 3*, 18*, 5* (1ct). 3 matches – M H McKiernan 26; G Onions 0, 25 (1ct). 2 matches – M J Potts 30*, 0. 1 match – C Appleby DNB (1ct); U Arshad 92; G R Breese 21; J Dass 1*; G H I Harding 9; L J Hurt 13; J McCann 28; R D Pringle 4; S Reeves 54*; A C Simpson DNB; C T Steel 26; S J Tindale 3; R Wallace 0.

Also bowled – C Appleby 10-0-46-2; J Coughlin 22.5-0-139-1; G H I Harding 5-1-14-0; T M Hewison 8-0-49-0; L J Hurt 5-0-25-1; G Onions 23-1-110-2; M J Potts 11-1-50-2; R D Pringle 10-0-76-0; S Reeves 10-0-47-1; S Steel 11-1-67-1.

SECOND ELEVEN T20 AVERAGES

BATTING	M	I	NO	Runs	HS	Avge	100s	C/S
A J Hickey	6	6	1	177	77*	35.40	-	3
M J Richardson	5	5	2	106	58	35.33	-	-
U Arshad	8	6	0	193	70	32.16	-	-
S Steel	9	6	2	127	41	31.75	-	4
G J Harte	11	10	1	212	61	23.55	-	3
B A Carse	10	9	2	164	42	23.42	-	4
L Trevaskis	10	10	0	193	52	19.30	-	1
J T A Burnham	3	3	0	54	33	18.00	-	2
B J McCarthy	5	4	1	54	28	18.00	-	5
R L Greenwell	3	3	0	41	39	13.66	-	1

BOWLING	O	M	Runs	Wkt	Avge	BB
P Coughlin	2.3	0	31	3	10.33	3/31
R D Pringle	8	0	67	0	15.00	3/35
B J McCarthy	11	0	77	5	15.40	2/19
U Arshad	26.5	0	211	12	17.58	3/18
L Trevaskis	20	0	159	9	17.66	4/22
A J Hickey	21.3	0	139	6	23.16	2/22
B G Whitehead	13	0	103	4	25.75	2/24
J Coughlin	20	1	187	6	31.16	2/16
G H I Harding	30	0	240	7	34.28	2/31
G Onions	31	0	206	3	68.66	1/14

Also batted – 9 matches – J Coughlin 0, 1*, 3, 0, 3 (3ct). 8 matches – G H I Harding 1*, 13 (4ct). 7 matches – G Onions 0, 11 (2ct). 5 matches - B J Yates 14, 0* (2ct). 4 matches – B G Whitehead 1, 1. 2 matches – C Appleby 1* (1ct); J Dass 3, 1*; E J Hurst 2*, 4* (1ct/1st); S W Poynter 14, 12* (1ct); R D Pringle 6, 0 (3ct); C T Steel 2, 109*; W J Weighell DNB. 1 match – A D F Brewster DNB; G Clark 14; P Coughlin 1; C Rushworth 9*.

Also bowled – C Appleby 3-0-28-0; A D F Brewster 2-0-6-1; B A Carse 9-0-83-2; J Dass 2-0-19-0; R L Greenwell 0.5-0-14-0; C Rushworth 3-0-39-0; C T Steel 1-0-3-0; S Steel 2-0-18-0; W J Weighell 7-0-68-0.

HOME MATCHES: SECOND ELEVEN CHAMPIONSHIP

v Nottinghamshire (Emirates Riverside) – 9-11 May - Durham 118 (I A Karim 60; B A Hutton 7/44) & 304 (A J Hickey 144, T M Hewison 53; T P Milnes 4/41) lost to Notts 201 (J D Libby 114; A J Hickey 3/41) & 222/3 (T J Moores 101*) by seven wkts.

v Leicestershire (Emirates Riverside) – 23-25 May - Durham 219 (J Coughlin 87, J Dass 55; C E Shreck 4/30, W N Fazackerley 3/34) & 352/9 d (M A Jones 88, A J Hickey 81) beat Leics 270 (B A Raine 66; A J Hickey 4/86, B J McCarthy 3/73) & 284 (W N Fazackerley 83, A M Ali 77; A J Hickey 6/74, O W Smithson 3/53) by 17 runs.

v Worcestershire (Burnopfield CC) – 27-29 June - Match abandoned without a ball bowled

v Warwickshire (South Northumberland CC) – 18-20 July - Warwicks 447/9d (M J Lamb 164, A T Thomson 95, A J Mellor 64; G Onions 4/65) drew with Durham 271 (A J Hickey 64, J Coughlin 64; R N Sidebottom 5/64) & 63/4 (A D Thomason 3/31)

v Yorkshire (Emirates Riverside) – 15-17 Aug - Durham 393/5d (G J Harte 160*, H W Podmore 51*) & 256/5d (G J Harte 96, J Coughlin 72*) drew with Yorks 508 (A Z Lees 202, W M H Rhodes 77, G S Balance 69, M J Waite 59*; B G Whitehead 4/71)

HOME MATCHES: FRIENDLIES

v Scotland A (Riverside) – 19-21 April – Durham 285 (G Clark 106, M J Richardson 51; M R J Watt 3/32, T B Sole 3/45) & 153 (A J Hickey 69; A C Evans 4/65) lost to Scotland A 370/8d (M A Jones 173*, D E Budge 67; J Coughlin 3/75) & 69/2 by eight wkts.

v Essex (Richmond CC) – 19 June – Essex 277 (J A Wheater 83, A S S Nijjar 51; A D F Brewster 4/33, U Arshad 3/38) lost to Durham 278/6 (A J Hickey 108) by four wkts.

v Essex (Richmond CC) – 20-22 June – Essex 111 (J Coughlin 5/26) & 333 (C J Taylor 136, J S E Ellis-Grewal 77; G H I Harding 6/48) lost to Durham 421/9d (S Steel 86, M J Richardson 84, G H I Harding 74, J Coughlin 65; M W Dixon 3/107) & 25/2 by eight wkts.

v Yorkshire (Emirates Riverside) – 14 Aug – Durham 179 (J T A Burnham 80; M D Fisher 3/24) lost to Yorks 181/3 (J A Tattersall 69*) by seven wkts.

v Scotland A – 30 Aug – Scotland A 258/4 (M A Jones 120*, S M O Shah 61) beat Durham 130 (T B Sole 5/51, M R J Watt 3/6) by 128 runs.

v Scotland A (Burnopfield CC) – 31 Aug – Scotland A 185 (M M English 76; G H I Harding 3/46) lost to Durham 186/6 (U Arshad 66*, M A Wood 55*; I Malik 3/20) by four wkts.

HOME MATCHES: SECOND ELEVEN TROPHY

v Nottinghamshire (Emirates Riverside) – 8 May – Notts 328/7 (L Wood 121, G P Smith 93; G T Main 3/69) beat Durham 224/9 (S Reeves 54*; M Carter 3/28) by 104 runs.
v Yorkshire (Brandon CC) – 19 May – Match abandoned without a ball bowled.

v MCC Young Cricketers (Emirates Riverside) – 22 May – Durham 257/6 (U Arshad 92, S Steel 53*) lost to MCC YC 259/6 (D S Manuwelege 82) by four wkts.

HOME MATCHES: SECOND ELEVEN T20 COMPETITION

v Worcestershire (Burnopfield) – 26 June - Match 1 – Worcs 150/6 (A Hepburn 53; U Arshad 3/18) lost to Durham 152/1 (A J Hickey 77*, L Trevaskis 52) by nine wkts.
v Worcestershire (Burnopfield) – 26 June - Match 2 – Worcs 114 (L Trevaskis 4/22) lost to Durham 115/3 by seven wkts.
v Warwickshire (S Northumberland) – 17 July - Match 1 – Durham 127 (R N Sidebottom 5/11) lost to Warwicks 131/5 (M J Lamb 54) by five wkts.

v Warwickshire (S Northumberland) – 17 July - Match 2 – Durham 204/5 (C T Steel 109*, G J Harte 61) beat Warwicks 168 E J Pollock 50; P Coughlin 3/31, R D Pringle 3/35) by 36 runs.
v Leicestershire (Riverside) – 27 July - Match 1– Leics 180/6 (H E Dearden 53) beat Durham 138 (H E Dearden 3/7, R J Sayer 3/31) by 42 runs.
v Leicestershire (Riverside) – 27 July - Match 2 – Durham 199/5 (U Arshad 69) beat Leics 167/8 (E J H Eckersley 53, A M Ali 50); L Trevaskis 3/17) by 32 runs.

PLAYERS WHO HAVE REPRESENTED DURHAM 2ND XI IN 2017 (62)

C Appleby	M J Fisher	J McCann	C Rushworth
U Arshad *B M Baig	R L Greenwell	B J McCarthy	*B M A Seabrook
S Bell	G H I Harding	*J McCarthy	C J Shoebridge
N Borkhatria	G J Harte	R McKendray	A C Simpson
G R Breese	T M Hewison	M H McKiernan	O W Smithson
A D F Brewster	A J Hickey	* L Mulley	C T Steel
J T A Burnham	* S S Hunt	G Onions	S Steel
B A Carse	E J Hurst	* J Ormandy	S J Tindale
C J Carter	L J Hurt	M Oswell	L Trevaskis
G Clark	S M Imtiaz	J R Phillipe	R Wallace
B G Compton	M A Jones	H W Podmore M J Potts	W J Weighell
J Coughlin	I A Karim	S W Poynter	*T M Wing
P Coughlin	T W M Latham	R D Pringle	B G Whitehead
J Dass	*E Litvin	S Reeves	*M A Wood
Faizan Hussain	C M McBride	M J Richardson	B J Yates

DURHAM CRICKETERS

Callum APPLEBY (Fynedourne Community Coll, Sacriston, Co Durham) b Durham, 31.8.95. RHB RM. Debut 2016. BB 1/10 v Northants, Riverside, 2016. BBSET 2/46 v MCC YC, Riverside, 2017. HST20 1* v Leics, Riverside, 2017 (1st). BBT20 0/28 v Leics, Riverside, 2017 (2nd).
Usman ARSHAD (Beckfoot GS, Bingley,Yorks) b Bradford, Yorks, 9.1.93. RHB RFM. Debut 2010. F/C debut v Surrey, the Riverside, 2013. HS 105 v MCCU, Gosforth, 2016. BB 6/35 in the same match. HSSET 92 v MCC YC, Riverside, 2017. BBSET 3/29 v Yorks, S Northumberland, 2013. HST20 79* v Derbys, Brandon, 2013 (2nd). BBT20 5/10 v Lancs, Parkgate, Neston, 2013 (1st). Durham staff.
* Bilal Mirza BAIG (Nunthorpe C; Teesside U) b Lahore, Pakistan, 12.3.99. RHB RM. Debut 2017. BB 1/21 v Yorks, Scarborough, 2017.
Soloman BELL (Durham S) b Newcastle, 27.2.01. RHB LB. Debut 2017. HS 38 v Yorks, Riverside, 2017.
Nikhil BORKHATRIA (The John Lyon S, Harrow, Middx; Loughborough U) b London 18.4.95. RHB LB. Debut 2017 v MCC Young Cricketers, High Wycombe, but did not bat or bowl.
Gareth Rohan BREESE (Wolmer's BHS, Kingston; Kingston U of Technology, Jamaica) b Montego Bay, Jamaica 9.1.76. RHB OB. F/C Debut (Jamaica) v Barbados, Bridgetown, 1995/96, Tests (WI) 1 (2002). Debut Durham 2003, cap 2005. HS 109 v Yorks, Headingley, 2010. BB 7/48 v Durham, Hove, (11/99 in the match) 2010. HSSET 90 v Derbys, Alvaston & Boulton, 2010. BBSET 5/29 v Warwicks, Longhirst Hall, Morpeth, 2011. HST20 30 v Notts, Notts SG, 2014 (2nd). BBT20 2/36 in the same match.
Andrew David Francis BREWSTER (Tadcaster GS & SFC) b York, 1.2.97. RHB RFM. Debut Glam 2016; Durham, Northants & MCCU 2017. F/C debut (Cardiff MCCU) v Glam, SWALEC, 2017.

BB 4/33 v Essex, Richmond, N Yorks, 2017. HST20 5* (Northants) v Notts, Grantham, 2017 (2nd). BBT20 1/6 v Worcs, Burnopfield CC, 2017 (2nd).
Jack Tony Arthur BURNHAM (Deerness Valley CS, Durham) b Durham 18.1.97. RHB RM. Debut 2013. F/C debut v Yorks, Scarborough, 2015. Eng U19 v Australia, 2015. HS 116 v Worcs, Darlington, 2015. BB 2/21 v MCCYC, Shenley, 2014. HSSET 78* v Lancs, Middlewich, 2015. BBSET 1/8 v MCCYC, Shenley, 2014. HST20 46 v Kent, Arundel, 2015 (SF). BBT20 2/11 v Yorks, York, 2014 (2nd). Durham Staff.
Brydon Alexander CARSE (Pearson HS, Port Elizabeth, Eastern Cape, S Africa) b Port Elizabeth, 31.7.95. RHB RMF. Debut 2014. F/C debut v Durham MCCU., Riverside, 2016. HS 113* v MCC YC, High Wycombe, 2017. BB 6/42 v Worcs, Darlington, 2015. HSSET 43 v Yorks, York, 2016. HST20 42 v MCC YC, Merchant Taylors' S, Northwood, 2017 (2nd). BBT20 4/30 v Yorks, York, 2015 (2nd).
Christopher James CARTER (Hale S, Perth, W Australia) b Hong Kong, 9.9.97. RHB WK. Debut 2017. HS 0 v Notts, Riverside, 2017.
Graham CLARK (St Benedict's Catholic HS, Whitehaven) b Whitehaven, Cumberland, 16.3.93. RHB LB. Brother to J (Lancs 2010 to date). Debut Durham 2011, Durham, MCCYC 2013F/C debut (Durham) v Hants, Ageas Bowl, 2015. 151 v Northants, Northampton, 2015.2/16 (MCCYC) v Glos, Downend, 2013. 122 v MCCYC, Shenley, 2014.BBSET 2/3 v Glam, Newport, Isle of Wight, 2013. 85* v Warwicks, Benwell Hill, 2015 (1st). Durham Staff.
Benjamin Garnet COMPTON (Clifton Coll, Durban, S Africa) b Durban, Natal, S Africa, 29.3.94. LHB OB. Debut Hants & MCC YC 2015; Durham 2017. HS 120 (Hants) v Somerset, Taunton Vale,

2015. BB 1/15 v Northants, M Keynes, 2017.

Josh COUGHLIN (St Robert of Newminster Catholic CS, Washington) b Sunderland 29.9.97. Brother of P below (Durham 2012 to date). LHB RM. Debut 2015. F/C debut v Sri Lanka A, Riverside, 2016. Eng U19 v Sri Lanka, 2016. HS 87 v Leics, Riverside, 2017. BB 5/26 v Essex, Richmond, N Yorks, 2017. HSSET 20 v Lancs, Bowden, 2017. BBSET 1/9 v Yorks, Chester-le-Street, 2015, HST20 13* v Yorks, Brandon, 2016 (1st). BBT20 2/28 v Yorks, Brandon, 2016 (1st).

Paul COUGHLIN (St Robert of Newminster S, Washington, Co Durham) b Sunderland, 23.10.92. Debut Durham 2011. F/C debut v Australians A, Riverside, 2012. Brother of J (above).RHB RM. HS 231 v Middx, Riverside, 2016. BB 5/36 v Essex/Kent, Billericay, 2015. HSSET 50 v Unc, Burnopfield, 2016. BBSET 3/22 v Northants, Brandon, 2012. HST20 91* v Warwics, Edgbaston, 2016 (2nd). BBT20 3/18 v Derbys, Alvaston & Boulton, 2011 (2nd). Joins Notts for the 2018 season.

Jamie DASS (Bishop Barrington S, Bishop Auckland) b Middlesbrough, N Yorks, 2.5.99. RHB RM. Debut 2017. HS 55 v Leics, Riverside, 2017. BB 0/1 v MCC YC, High Wycombe, 2017. HSSET 1* v MCC YC, Riverside, 2017. HST20 3 v MCC YC, Merchant Taylors' S, Northwood, 2017 (1st). BBT20 0/19 v MCC YC, Merchant Taylors' S, Northwood, 2017 (2nd).

FEZAIN HUSSAIN (MacMillan C, Middlesbrough) b Middlesbrough, North Yorks, 3.9.98. RHB SLA. Debut 2017. BB 2/26 v Leics, Riverside, 2017.

Mark James FISHER (Easingwold S) b York, 6.8.92. RHB RM. Debut 2017. Brother of M D (Yorks). HS 6 v Warwics, S Northumberland, 2017. BB 1/56 in the same match.

Ross Liam GREENWELL (Emmanuel Coll, Gateshead) b Newcastle-upon-Tyne, 19.9.98. RHB RFM. Debut 2016. HS 24 v Sussex, Blackstone CC, 2016. HST30 39 v Leics, Riverside, 2017 (1st). BBT20 0/14 v MCC YC, Merchant Taylors' S, Northwood, 2017 (2nd).

George Harvey Idris HARDING (Brine Lees HS, Nantwich, Cheshire; Myerscough Coll, Preston, Lancs) b Poole, Dorset 12.10.96. RHB SLA. Debut 2015. F/C debut v Glam, M Keynes, 2017. HS 74 v Essex, Richmond, N Yorks, 2017. BB 6/48 in the same match. HSSET 9 v Northants, M Keynes, 2017. BBSET 3/61 v Northants, Riverside, 2016. HST20 13 v Leics, Riverside, 2017 (1st). BBT20 2/18 v Worcs, Amblecote, 2016 (2nd).

Gareth Jason HARTE (King Edward VII HS, Johannesburg) b Johannesburg, Transvaal, S Africa, 15.3.93. RHB RM. Debut Somerset & Middx 2012; Kent 2014; MCCYC & Sussex 2016; Durham 2017. List A (T20) debut v Lancs, Old Trafford, 2017. HS 199 (Sussex) v Surrey, New Malden, 2016. BB 4/47 (MCCYC) v Glam, Panteg, 2016. HSSET 124* v Worcs, New Road, 2016. BBSET 2/29 (Sussex) v Glam, St Fagans, 2016. HST20 61 v Warwics, S Northumberland, 2017 (2nd). BBT20 0/21 (Kent) v Hants, Ageas Bowl, 2014 (2nd).

Thomas Max HEWISON (Grangefield S; Stockton SFC) b Stockton-on-Tees, Co Durham, 24.8.99. RHB RM. Debut 2016. HS 100 v Sussex, Blackstone, 2016. HSSET 11 v Northants, M Keynes, 2017. BBSET 0/49 v MCC YC, Riverside, 2017.

Adam James HICKEY (Biddick Sp Coll, Washington) b Darlington, 1.3.97. LHB OB. Debut 2013. F/C debut v Sri Lanka A, Riverside, 2016. Eng U19 v Australia, 2015. HS 144 v Notts, Riverside, 2017. BB 6/74 v Leics, Riverside, 2017. HSSET 95* v Notts, Richmond, N Yorks, 2015. BBSET 3/30 v Lancs, Middlewich, 2015. HST20 77 v Worcs, Burnopfield, 2017 (1st). BBT20 4/12 v Leics, Brandon, 2015 (1st).

Edward James HURST (St Joseph's Catholic Acad, Hebburn, Co Durham) b South Shields, 13.10.98. RHB WK. Debut 2016. HS 51* v Essex/Kent, Billericay, 2017. HST20 8* v MCC YC, Merchant Taylors' S, Northwood, 2017 (1st).

Liam Jack HURT (Balshaws C of E HS, Leyland; Training 2000, Blackburn) b Preston 15.3.94. RHB RFMF. Debut Lancs 2013; Derbys & Leics 2015. List A debut (Leics) v Durham, Grace Road, 2015. Glos, Northants & Warwicks 2016. Debut Durham 2017. HS 42* (Lancs) v Hants, Newclose CC, I of Wight, 2017. BB 4/43 v Essex/Kent, Billericay, 2017. HSSET 24 v Lancs, Kidderminster, 2017. BBSET 3/58 (Lancs) v Leics, Middlewich, 2014. HST20 19*

(Leics) v Unc, Long Marston, 2016 (2nd). BBT20 3/41 (Lancs) v Yorks, Marske-by-the-Sea, 2013 (2nd).

Safwaan M "Saf" IMTIAZ (Chigwell S) b London 16.3.96. RHB WK. Debut Essex 2013; Durham , MCCYC & Northants 2016; Kent & Surrey 2017. HS 175 (MCC YC) v Essex, High Wycombe, 2016. BB 0/129 (MCC YC) v Lancs, Urmston, 2017. HSSET 100 (MCC YC) v Somerset, Taunton Vale, 2015. HST20 67 (MCC YC) v Surrey, High Wycombe, 2016 (1st).

Michael Alexander JONES (Ormskirk GS; Myerscough Coll) b Ormskirk, Lancs, 5.1.98. RHB OB. Debut Derbys, Durham, Leics & Scotland A 2017. HS 173* (Scotland A) v Durham, Riverside, 2017. HSSET 34 v Lancs, Bowden, 2017. HST20 35 (Leics) v Durham, Riverside, 2017 (1st).

Irfan Ali KARIM (Braeburn HS, Nairobi, Kenya; Braeburn SFC; Loughborough U) b Hendon, Middx, 25.9.92. LHB OB. ODIs (Kenya) 9 (2011 to 2013/14) & 7 T20s. Debut MCCU 2014; Leics 2016; Durham 2017. F/C debut (Kenya) v Ireland, Mombassa SC, 2011/12. HS 68 (Leics) v Notts, Hinckley, 2016. HSSET 50* (Leics) v Notts, Loughborough CC, 2016.

Thomas William Maxwell LATHAM b Christchurch, Canterbury, New Zealand 2.4.92. Tests 32 (NZ) (2013/14 to date) & 61 ODIs. Son of R T (Tests 4 NZ 1990/91 to 1993/94 & 33 ODIs) LHB RM. Debut 2010. F/C debut (Canterbury v C Districts, Napier, NZ, 2010/11). HS 241 v MCC YC, High Wycombe, 2017. HSSET 27* v Lancs, Riverside, 2010. HSKO 15 v Yorks, Weetwood, 2010.

***Eitan LITVIN** (Leeds GS) b I of Wight, 3.9.99. RHB WK. Debut 2017. HS 16 v Yorks, Scarborough, 2017.

Christopher M McBRIDE b Dumfries, Scotland, 26.9.99. RHB RM LB. Debut 2016. HS 17 v Warwics, S Northumberland, 2017. BB 1/13 in the same match.

Jacob McCANN (Westfield Sports S, Sheffield) b Liverpool, NSW, Australia, 21.5.91. LHB WK. Debut 2017. HSSET 28 v MCC YC, Riverside, 2017.

Barry John McCARTHY (St Michael's Cath Boys Coll, Dublin; University Coll, Dublin) b Dublin, Ireland, 13.9.92. RHB RM. Debut Durham 2014. F/C debut v Notts, Trent Bridge, 2015. HS 41* v Yorks, York, 2016. BB 5/18 v Essex/Kent at Billericay, 2016. HSSET 39 v Notts, S.Northumberland, Gosforth, 2014. BBSET 4/50 v Unc, Burnopfield, 2015. HST20 28 v Derbys, Belper, 2017 (2nd). BBSET 3a v Leics, Brandon, 2015 (1st). Durham Staff.

Ryan McKENDRAY b November 1992. Debut Unc 2016; Durham 2017. HS 0* v Northants, M Keynes, 2017. BB 1/3 in the same match. BBT20 2/11 (Unc) v Notts, Notts SG, 2016 (2nd).

Matthew Harry "Mattie" McKIERNAN (Lowton HS, Leigh; St John Rigby Coll, Wigan) b Billinge, Merseyside, 14.6.94. RHB LB. Debut Lancs 2011; Northants 2012 (on loan). Ret to Lancs 2013; Leics & Unc 2016; Durham 2017. HS 49 (Lancs) v Leics, Liverpool, 2014. BB 4/64 (Leics) v Northants, Desborough, 2017. HSSET 42 (Lancs) v Leics, Grace Road, 2014. BBSET 5/45 v Worcs, New Road, 2017. HST20 18* (Unc) v Hants, Great Tew, 2017 (2nd). BBT20 3/11 (Unc) v Leics, Long Marston, 2016 (2nd).

Gavin Thomas MAIN b Lanark, Scotland, 28.2.95. RHB RMF. Debut Durham 2013; F/C Debut v Notts, Trent Bridge, 2014. Debut MCC YC 2017. HS 17 v Yorks, York, 2016. BB 4/56 v Essex/Kent. Billericay, 2014. HSSET 18* v Notts, Riverside, 2017. BBSET 3/21 v Northants, M Keynes, 2017. BBT20 2/19 v Yorks, Brandon, 2014. Durham Staff.

Graham ONIONS (St Thomas More RC HS, Blaydon) b Gateshead, 9.9.82. RHB RMF. Tests (Eng) 9 (2009/12) & 4 ODIs (2009/2009/10). Debut 2001. F/C debut v Durham MCCU, Chester-le-Street, 2004. HS 40 v Yorks, Stamford Bridge, 2003. BB 6/62 in the same match. HSSET 25 v Notts, Riverside, 2017. BBSET 3/39 v Yorks, Stamford Bridge, 2005. HST20 15* v Worcs, Chester-le-Street CC, 2015 (2nd). BBT20 2/24 Worcs, Chester-le-Street CC, 2015 (1st). Joins Lancs for the 2018 season.

Matthew OSWELL b Newcastle, 7.11.00. RHB RM. Debut 2017. BB 2/28 v Yorks, Riverside, 2017.

Joshua Ryan PHILLIPE (Carine HS, W Australia; U of WA) b Australia, 1.6.97. RHB WK. Debut 2017. HS 37 v Yorks, Riverside, 2017.

Harry William PODMORE (Twyford HS, Acton) b Hammersmith,, 23.7.94. RHB RM. Debut Middx 2011; Glam (on loan) 2016. F/C debut (Glam) v Kent, Canterbury, 2016. Debut Durham (on loan) 2017. HS 116* (Middx) v Essex, Billericay, 2015. BB 6/52 (Middx) v Somerset, Merchant Taylors' S, 2015. HSSET 36* (Middx) v Surrey, Purley, 2017. BBSET 4/41 (Middx) v Kent, Radlett, 2015. HST20 31* (Middx) v Hants, Ageas Bowl Nursery, 2017 (2nd). BBT20 3/4 (Middx) v Somerset, Merchant Taylors` S, 2015 (2nd).

Matthew James POTTS (St Robert's of Newminster S, Washington) b Sunderland, 29.10.98. RHB RM. Debut 2016. F/C debut v Kent, Canterbury, 2017. Eng U19 v India, 2017. HS 32 v Lancs, Brandon, 2016. BB 3/14 v Northants, Riverside, 2016. HSSET 30* v Worcs, New Road, 2017. BBSET 2/30 in the same match.

Stuart William POYNTER (Teddington S) b Hammersmith, Middx 18.10.90. RHB WK. Brother of A.D. (Middx 2004/06). Debut Middx 2007. Ireland U19 2007/08. F/C debut (Oxford MCCU) v Middx, the Parks, 2010. Debut Middx 2007; MCCYC 2011; Durham 2013. HS 172 (MCCYC) v Durham, Brandon, 2013. HSSET 67 v Northants, Finedon Dolben, 2015. HST20 65 v Worcs, Amblecote, 2016 (1st). HSKO 4 (Middx) v Surrey, Wimbledon, 2010. Durham staff.

Ryan David PRINGLE (Hetton Comp S; Durham SFC; Sunderland U) b Sunderland 17.4.92. RHB OB. Debut 2009. F/C debut v Somerset, Taunton, 2014. HS 125 v Derbys, Marton, 2011 & v Leics, Hinckley, 2014 & v Northants, Northampton, 2014. BB 4/15 v Essex/Kent, Billericay, 2013. HSSET 72 v Lancs, Stockton-on-Tees, 2014. BBSET 3/45 v Derbys, Middlesbrough, 2013. HST20 35 v Yorks, York, 2015 (2nd). BBT20 3/35 v Warwicks, S Northumberland (2nd). Durham staff.

Stephen Dean Puttenham REEVES (Hilton Coll, KZN; U of Teesside) b Kwa-Zulu Natal, S Africa, 1.10.95. RHB SLA. Debut Durham 2016; Kent 2017. HS 24* v Northants, Riverside, 2016. BB 6/79 v Northants, M Keynes, 2017. HSSET 54* v Notts, Riverside, 2017. BBSET 1/47 in the same match.

Michael John RICHARDSON (Rondebosch HS, Cape Town; Stonyhurst C, Clitheroe, Lancs; Nottingham U) b Port Elizabeth, S.Africa 4.10.86. Son of D.J. (Eastern Province, Northern Transvaal, S.Africa 1977/78-1997/98). RHB WK. Debut MCCYC 2008; Durham 2009; F/C Debut v Durham MCCU, the Racecourse, 2011. HS 165* v Worcs, New Road, 2011. HSSET 109 v Yorks, Marske-by-the-Sea, 2012. HST20 58 v Derbys, Belper, 2017 (1st). HSKO 2* v Yorks, Weetwood, 2010. Durham staff.

Christopher RUSHWORTH (Castle View Comprehensive S, Sunderland) b Sunderland, 11.7.86. RHB RFM. Debut 2004. F/C debut v Yorks, Headingley, 2010. HS 57* v Kent / Essex, Billericay, 2011, BB 6/20 in the same match. HSSET 33 v Yorks, Bingley, 2006. BBSET 5/22 v Notts, Sunderland, 2004. HST20 17* v Derbys (2nd), Repton S, 2012, BBT20 3/38 v Lancs, Blackpool, 2011. Durham Staff.

Cameron J SHOEBRIDGE (U of St Andrews, Scotland) b Greenwich, London, 7.10.97. RHB RM. Debut 2017. HS 9* v Leics, Riverside, 2017. BB 0/12 in the same match.

Alexander Charles SIMPSON (Sedbergh S) b Darlington, 6.2.98. RHB RM. Debut Durham 2014; Worcs 2017. HS 39 v Sussex, Fulking, 2014. BB 0/ 13 v Northants, Riverside, 2016.

Oliver William SMITHSON (Bradfield C) b Lisbon, Portugal 6.1.96. RHB LMF. Debut Glos 2014; MCC YC 2015; Durham & Northants 2017. HS 12* (Glos) v Hants, WE Nursery 2014. BB 3/24 (MCC YC) v Glos, Shenley, 2016. HSSET 27 (Glos) v Northants, Thornbury CC 2014. BBSET 3/41 (MCC YC) v Leics, Merchant Taylors' S, Northwood, 2017. HST20 15 (MCC YC) v Worcs, Merchant Taylors' S, Northwood, 2017 (2nd). BBT20 3/15 (MCC YC) v Notts, Merchant Taylors' S, Northwood, 2017 (1st).

Cameron Tate STEEL (The Scotch Coll, Perth, W Australia; Durham U) b Greenbrae, California, USA, 13.9.95. RHB LB. Debut Middx & Somerset 2013; Durham 2016. F/C debut (Durham MCCU) v Derbys, Derby, 2014. HS 104 (Middx) v Sussex, Richmond, Surrey, 2015. BB 3/5 (Middx) v Essex, Coggeshall, 2013. HSSET 68* (Middx) v MCC YC, Radlett, 2015. BBSET 2/37 (Somerset) v Sussex, Taunton Vale, 2013. HST20 109* v Warwicks, S Northumberland, 2017 (2nd). BBT20 2/17 (Middx) v Durham, Arundel, 2013.

Scott STEEL (Belmont Community S, Durham) b Durham, 20.4.99. RHB OB. Debut 2016. HS 86 v Essex, Richmond. N Yorks, 2017. BB 2/47 v Yorks, Riverside, 2017. HSSET 53* v MCC YC, Riverside, 2017. BBSET 1/51 in the same match. HST20 41 v MCC YC, Merchant Taylors' S, Northwood, 2017 (2nd). BBT20 0/18 v MCC YC, Merchant Taylors' S, Northwood, 2017 (1st).

Sean Jamie TINDALE b Durham 28.4.96. RHB RM. Debut 2017. HS 4 v Notts, Riverside, 2017. BB 0/9 v Lancs, Stockton-on-Tees, 2014. HSSET 3 v Notts, Riverside, 2017.

Liam TREVASKIS (Queen Elizabeth GS, Penrith, Cumberland) b Carlisle, Cumberland, 18.4.99. LHB SLA. Debut 2015 aged 16 yrs & 128 days. F/C debut v Worcs, New Road, 2017. Eng U19 v India, 2017. HS 22 v Middx, Riverside, 2016. BB 6/31 v Middx, Riverside, 2016. HST20 52 v Worcs, Burnopfield, 2017 (1st). BBT20 4/22 v Worcs, Burnopfield, 2017 (2nd).

Ryan WALLACE (Kearsney C, Durban, S Africa) b Pietermaritzburg, Kwa-Zulu, Natal, S Africa, 18.10.95. RHB RM. Debut 2017. BB 1/8 v Essex, Richmond, N Yorks, 2017. HSSET 0 v Lancs, Bowden, 2017.

William James WEIGHELL (Stokesley S) b Middlesbrough, Yorks, 28.1.94. LHB RM. Debut 2012. F/C debut v Middx, Chester-le-Street, 2015. HS 84 v Lancs, Great Crosby, 2015 & v Derbys, Darlington, 2016. BB 6/47 v Lancs, Todmorden, 2017. HSSET 37 v Derbys, Chester-le-Street, 2015. BBSET 4/26 v Lancs, Middlewich, 2015. HST20 54 v Kent, Arundel, 2015 (SF). BBT20 1/39 in the same match.

Benjamin Guy WHITEHEAD (Hetton S, Houghton-le-Spring, Tyne & Wear) b Sunderland, 28.4.97. RHB LB. Debut 2014. HS 3* v Derbys, Belper, 2015. BB 4/71 v Yorks, Riverside, 2017. HST20 11* v Lancs, Chester-le-Street, 2014 (1st). BBT20 2/24 v Leics, Riverside, 2017 (2nd).

* Thomas Matthew WING (Billingham Coll; U of Teesside) b Middlesbrough, 17.8.96. RHB RM. Debut 2017. BB 0/50 v Yorks, Scarborough, 2017.

Bradley John YATES (Thornley Sec S, Bolton; Canon Slade School, Bolton) b Bolton, 10.7.97. RHB WK. Debut Lancs 2015; Durham 2017. HS 57 v Derbys, Belper, 2017. HSSET 10 (Lancs) v Derbys, Parkgate, Neston, 2016. HST20 22 (Lancs) v Unc, Knypersley, 2016 (1st).

26

ESSEX

PLAYING RECORDS 2017
Championship – P9 W1 L5 D3 – ninth in the southern group
2nd XI Trophy – P6 W4 L2 – third in the southern group
2nd XI T20 Competition – P12 W5 L6 Ab1 – seventh in the southern group

2nd XI SUCCESSES
2nd XI Champions – 1973
2nd XI Trophy – Winners - 2010
2nd XI T20 – Beaten Semi-Finalists in 2012

SECOND ELEVEN CHAMPIONSHIP AVERAGES

BATTING	M	I	NO	Runs	HS	Avge	100s	C/S
R K Patel	4	6	2	242	116*	60.50	1	3
F I N Khushi	3	5	1	180	101*	45.00	1	3
J A Stamatis	5	7	1	234	99*	39.00	-	2
O S Bocking	3	4	2	76	40	38.00	-	-
M S Pepper	5	9	1	257	136	32.12	1	4/1
N L J Browne	5	9	1	250	92	31.25	-	4
A S S Nijjar	6	9	0	269	58	29.88	-	5
K S Velani	8	15	1	373	95	26.64	-	-
W E L Buttleman	3	5	1	100	62	25.00	-	3
R H Sheemar	2	3	0	75	39	25.00	-	-
C J Taylor	7	13	1	289	64	24.08	-	1
A J A Wheater	2	4	1	71	32	23.66	-	2/1
Kashif Ali	5	8	0	176	76	22.00	-	-
D W Lawrence	2	3	0	59	28	19.66	-	3
S J Cook	4	5	3	39	19*	19.50	-	-
C M Jones	3	5	1	53	26	13.25	-	1
G Fatouros	2	4	0	48	30	12.00	-	1
A P Beard	8	13	1	143	45*	11.91	-	4
M W Dixon	5	7	2	32	31	6.40	-	-
J S E Ellis-Grewel	3	5	1	23	15	5.75	-	-

Also batted – 6 matches – B J Hyam 3* (2ct). 3 matches – B M J Allison 5, 2, 0 (1ct). 2 matches – D R Melton 7, 6 (1ct); J H Plom 2, 0* (1ct); 1 match – E Kalley 16*; A D L Russell 0 (5ct); J S Rymell 14*; M E T Salisbury DNB (1ct); T A Shah 37; S Singh DNB; S Snater 3, 0; I S Sohi 4, 49; S C Sullivan 6, 1 (1ct); R L Vickery 0, 11 (2ct); P I Walter 10, 19; B A Waring 0, 14 (1ct); N R Welch 25, 0 (3ct).

BOWLING	O	M	Runs	Wkt	Avge	BB
S Snater	21.3	6	61	6	10.16	4/26
A S S Nijjar	166.3	36	553	24	23.04	6/113
A P Beard	147.4	28	520	21	24.76	4/58
J A Stamatis	15	1	80	3	26.66	2/25
D R Melton	34.3	4	167	6	27.83	3/40
M E T Salisbury	21	4	84	3	28.00	2/54
S J Cook	103.5	29	269	8	33.62	3/34
B A Waring	27.3	3	107	3	35.66	1/14
M W Dixon	78	14	340	9	37.77	5/84
O S Bocking	55	10	202	4	50.50	2/25
C J Taylor	74	10	267	5	53.40	3/71
K S Velani	46.4	6	170	3	56.66	2/52

Also bowled – B M J Allison 36-6-154-1; J S E Ellis-Grewel 25-3-121-2; C M Jones 24.5-2-96-2; E Kalley 11-1-65-0; Kashif Ali 4-0-36-0; F I N Khushi 1-0-10-0; D W Lawrence 2-0-10-0; R K Patel 13-0-55-0; J H Plom 15-0-84-1; S Singh 18-2-79-1; I S Sohi 9-1-51-1; P I Walter 16.2-2-71-2.

SECOND ELEVEN TROPHY AVERAGES

BATTING	M	I	NO	Runs	HS	Avge	100s	C/S
J S Foster	3	3	2	104	67*	104.00	-	4/1
P I Walter	5	5	1	249	145*	62.25	1	2
C M Jones	5	4	2	124	52	62.00	-	1
C J Taylor	4	4	1	170	73*	56.66	-	-
K S Velani	6	5	1	147	56*	36.75	-	5
Kashif Ali	5	4	0	38	24	9.50	-	1
W E L Buttleman	4	3	0	22	11	7.33	-	7

Also batted – 6 matches - J S E Ellis-Grewel 28*, 5 (3ct). 5 matches – M W Dixon 15 (3ct). 3 matches – A P Beard 13 (1ct); J A Stamatis 3, 54 (2ct). 2 matches – V Chopra 11, 109* (2ct); J H Plom 10* (2ct); M R Quinn 2; R L Vickery 10, 15 (2ct); B A Waring 0. 1 match – F I N Khushi DNB; D W Lawrence 23 (1ct); J A Porter DNB; S S Prabhakar 0; A D L Russell DNB (1ct); M E T Salisbury 7; T A Shah 77 (2ct).

BOWLING	O	M	Runs	Wkt	Avge	BB
M R Quinn	18	4	71	6	11.83	4/36
M E T Salisbury	9.2	1	62	5	12.40	5/62
A P Beard	27	1	148	9	16.44	4/58
C J Taylor	31	3	138	6	23.00	3/41
P I Walter	44.4	1	207	9	23.00	4/58
M W Dixon	44	1	256	9	28.44	3/51
J S E Ellis-Grewel	36	1	221	3	73.66	2/55

Also bowled – C M Jones 15-0-80-0; D W Lawrence 5-0-31-0; J H Plom 12-0-83-1; J A Porter 10-1-42-2; J A Stamatis 16-1-78-2; B A Waring 10-0-31-2.

SECOND ELEVEN T20 AVERAGES

BATTING	M	I	NO	Runs	HS	Avge	100s	C/S
V Chopra	3	3	1	103	73*	51.50	-	1
A J A Wheater	5	5	0	192	88	38.40	-	9
F I N Khushi	4	4	0	138	69	34.50	-	3
K S Velani	11	10	0	267	88	26.70	-	2
A S S Nijjar	11	9	3	100	21	16.66	-	1
G Fatouros	3	3	1	33	27	16.50	-	1
C J Taylor	9	9	1	123	47	15.37	-	7
W E L Buttleman	4	4	2	29	20	14.50	-	-
A P Beard	11	10	1	114	50	12.66	-	-
N L J Browne	3	3	0	31	20	10.33	-	-
P I Walter	4	3	0	5	4	1.66	-	3

BOWLING	O	M	Runs	Wkt	Avge	BB
J A Porter	3	0	17	3	5.66	3/17
S J Cook	19	1	123	12	10.25	4/15
J H Plom	6	0	59	4	14.75	3/41
A S S Nijjar	32.5	0	226	14	16.14	2/8
C J Taylor	25	0	176	9	19.55	2/5
P I Walter	13	0	113	4	28.25	2/26
M W Dixon	17	0	143	5	28.60	2/17
A P Beard	31	0	357	3	119.00	1/22

Also bowled – A Zaidi 5-0-43-1; O S Bocking 5-0-50-1; J S E Ellis-Grewel 2-0-15-1; Kashif Ali 2-0-19-0; D R Melton 8-0-75-1; S Snater 5-0-55-1; S C Sullivan 7-0-60-2; K S Velani 6-0-54-0.

Also batted – 7 matches – S J Cook 0, 1* (1ct). 6 matches – M W Dixon 7, 14. 4 matches – O S Bocking 1, 1 (1ct); Kashif Ali 21, 27* (2ct). 3 matches – Asher Zaidi 4, 39* (1ct); J S E Ellis-Grewel 1, 2*(1ct); A D L Russell 26*, 32. 2 matches – B J Hyam – 1*; D R Melton 5*; R K Patel 25, 21; J H Plom 14 (2ct); R H Sheemar 1*, 1; S Snater 20 (2ct); J A Stamatis 11 (2ct); S C Sullivan 0, 8*; N R Welch 5, 0. 1 match – B M J Allison 16*; R S Bopara 17; J S Foster 9 (2ct); C M Jones 9; J A Porter DNB.

HOME MATCHES: SECOND ELEVEN CHAMPIONSHIP

v Surrey (Billericay) – 15-17 May – Essex 63 (R Patel 3/15) & 225 (N L J Browne 92; G S Virdi 4/24) lost to Surrey 311 (R Ratnasabapathy 90, E D Woods 61; C J Taylor 3/71) by an inns & 23 runs.
v Gloucestershire (Billericay) – 6-8 June – Glos 408 (G T Hankins 114, I A Cockbain 77, G L van Buuren 73; A P Beard 3/40) & 42/2d beat Essex 72/3d & 99 (K Noema-Barnett 7/22) by 279 runs.
v MCC Universities (Billericay) – 25-27 June – MCCU 160 (A P Beard 4/58, S J Cook 3/34) & 119/1(J D Marshall 52*) drew with Essex 191 (X G Owen 4/56)

v Middlesex (Coggeshall) – 1-3 Aug – Middx 459/3d (M K Andersson 192, R G White 101*, T C Lace 99) & 84/4d (D R Melton 3/40) drew with Essex 185/4d (F I N Khushi 101*) & 305/7 (M S Pepper 136, W E L Buttleman 62)
v Sussex (Halstead) – 16-18 Aug – Essex 297 (R K Patel 116*, M S Pepper 50; S G Whittingham 4/57, van Vollenhoven 3/95) & 160 (R K Patel 54*; O E Robinson 5/37) lost to Sussex 306 (M G K Burgess 75, H Z Finch 68; A S S Nijar 6/113) & 153/3 (N S Oxley 50; A S S Nijjar 3/53) by seven wkts.

HOME MATCHES: FRIENDLIES

v Sussex (Halstead) – 15 Aug – Essex 273/8 (F I N Khushi 120, M S Pepper 60) beat Sussex 217 (O E Robinson 72; D R Melton 3/53) by 56 runs.

COMBINED FRIENDLY MATCHES INVOLVING ESSEX

Essex & Kent v Durham (Billericay) – 10 Apr – Essex & Kent 239 (C J Haggett 55, A J Ball 53; A J Hickey 3/36, B J McCarthy 3/48) beat Durham 158/9 (G J Harte 52) by 68 runs (DLS)
Essex & Kent v Durham (Billericay) – 11-12 Apr – Durham 385/9d (G Clark 125, A J Hickey 97, J Coughlin 58, E J Hurst 51*; Imran Qayyum 5/70) & 250/7d (G Clark 110; Imran Qayyum 3/86) beat Essex & Kent 347 (C J Taylor 68, A J Blake 52, W E L Buttleman 50*; G H I Harding 4/87, W J Weighell 3/31) & 232 (A J Ball 97, C J Taylor 87; G H I Harding 5/49, L J Hurt 4/43) by 56 runs.

HOME MATCHES: SECOND ELEVEN TROPHY

v Sussex (Billericay) – 24 Apr – Essex 211 (C M Jones 52; S G Whittingham 3/44, A Sakande 3/53) lost to Sussex 207/8 (D R Briggs 70, M G K Burgess 62; M R Quinn 4/36, C J Taylor 3/41) by 21 runs (DLS)
v Surrey (Billericay) – 3 May – Surrey 287/9 (A Harinath 115; A P Beard 4/58, M W Dixon 3/57) lost to Essex 130/5 (K S Velani 56*) by 5 wkts (DLS)
v Unicorns (Billericay) – 23 May – Unc 208 (M S Pepper 77; P I Walter 4/26, A P Beard 3/36) lost to Essex 212/2 (P I Walter 74, C J Taylor 73*) by eight wkts.

HOME MATCHES: SECOND ELEVEN T20 COMPETITION

v Gloucestershire (Chelmsford) – 5 June – Match 1 – Glos 170/7 beat Essex 100 by 70 runs.
v Gloucestershire (Chelmsford) – 5 June – Match 2 – Essex 128/8 lost to Glos 132/2 (I A Cockbain 61*) by eight wkts.
v Somerset (Chelmsford) – 24 July - Match 1 – Somerset 122/7 beat Essex 102/5 by 20 runs.
v Somerset (Chelmsford) – 24 July - Match 2 – Essex 169/5 (F I N Khushi 50, A P Beard 50; J H Davey 3/37) beat Somerset 116/9 (S J Cook 4/15, J A Porter 3/17) by 39 runs (DLS).
v Middlesex (Coggeshall) – 4 Aug – Match 1 – Middx 179/4 (R G White 65*) lost to Essex 180/9 (K S Velani 88; L B K Hollman 5/26) by one wkt.
v Middlesex (Coggeshall) – 4 Aug - Match 2 – Middx 191/5 (G F B Scott 68*, T C Lace 54) beat Essex 165/7 by 26 runs.

PLAYERS WHO HAVE REPRESENTED ESSEX 2ND XI IN 2017 (46)

B M J Allison	J S Foster	M S Pepper	I S Sohi
Asher Zaidi	*J W N Gray	J H Plom	J A Stamatis
A P Beard	B J Hyam	J A Porter	S C Sullivan
O S Bocking	C M Jones	S S Prabhakar	C J Taylor
R S Bopara	E Kalley	M R Quinn	K S Velani
N L J Browne	Kashif Ali	A D L Russell	R LVickery
W E L Buttleman	F I N Khushi	J S Rymell	P I Walter
V Chopra	D W Lawrence	M E T Salisbury	B A Waring
S J Cook	D R Melton	T A Shah	N R Welch
M W Dixon	A S S Nijjar	R H Sheemar	A J A Wheater
J S E Ellis-Grewel	*A Patel	S Singh	
G Fatouros	R K Patel	S Snater	

ESSEX CRICKETERS

Benjamin Michael John ALLISON (New Hall S, Boreham, Chelmsford College) b Colchester, 18.12.99. RHB RFM. Debut 2017. Eng U19 v India, 2017. HS 51 v Kent, Beckenham, 2017. BB 1/46 in the same match. HST20 16* v Glos, Chelmsford, 2017.

Syed ASHAR Ahmed ZAIDI b Karachi, Sind, Pakistan, 13.7.81. LHB SLA. Debut & F/C debut (Islamabad) v Faisalabad, Islamabad, 1999/00; Pak Tel Comm Ltd & Rawalpindi 2003/04; Khan Research Labs 2006/07; Federal Areas 2007/08; Sussex 2013; Essex 2016. HS 192* (Sussex) v Durham, Fulking, 2013. BB 5/35 (Sussex) v Somerset, Blackstone, 2014. HSSET 146* (Sussex) v Middx, Richmond, Surrey, 2015. BBSET 3/19 (Sussex) v Glos. Hove, 2014. HST20 70* v Glam, Chelmsford, 2016 (1st). BBT20 4/11 (Sussex) v Surrey, Horsham, 2015 (1st).

Aaron Paul BEARD (The Boswells S, Chelmsford) b Chelmsford, 15.10.97. LHB RFM. Debut 2015. F/C debut v Sri Lankans, Chelmsford, 2016. Eng U19 v Sri Lanka, 2016; to Ind 2016/17. HS 80* v Middx, Radlett, 2016. BB 4/58 v Kent, Polo Farm, Canterbury, 2017 & v MCCU, Billericay, 2017. HSSET 33 v Middx, Billericay, 2016. BBSET 4/58 v Surrey, Billericay, 2017. HST20 50 v Somerset, Chelmsford, 2017 (2nd). BBT20 2/46 v Kent, Billericay, 2016 (1st). Essex Staff.

Oliver Stuart BOCKING (Ipswich S) b Colchester, 25.4.96. RHB RFM. Debut Essex 2012; MCCU 2017. F/C debut (Leeds/Bradford MCCU) v Kent, Canterbury, 2017. HS 40 v MCCU, Billericay, 2017. BB 4/32 v Kent, Beckenham, 2017. HSSET 8* v Somerset, Halstead, 2016. BBSET 2/28 v Hants, Coggeshall, 2016. HST20 1 v Kent, Polo Farm SG, Canterbury, 2017 (2nd) & v Middx, Coggeshall, 2017 (1st). BBT20 1/17 v Somerset, Chelmsford, 2015 (2nd).

Ravinder Singh BOPARA (Brampton Manor S; Barking Abbey Sports Coll) b Forest Gate. 4.5.85. RHB RM. Tests (Eng) 13 & 120 ODIs (2006/07 to 2015). Debut 2001; F/C debut v Northants, Northampton, 2002. Essex Cap 2005. HS 164 v Middx, Chelmsford, 2002. BB 2/15 v Leics, Halstead, 2003. HSSET 82 v Surrey, Coggeshall, 2004. BBSET 4/30 v Sussex, Eastbourne, 2004. HST20 70 v Unicorns A, Chelmsford (2nd), 2012. BBT20 1/14 v Leics, Chelmsford, 2014 (1st). Essex staff.

Nicholas Laurence Joseph BROWNE (Trinity Catholic HS, Woodford Green) b Leytonstone 24.3.91. LHB LB. Debut 2007 aged 16 years and 171 days; debut MCCYC 2008. F/C debut v Worcs, New Road, 2013. HS 219* v Somerset, Taunton Vale, 2013. BB 2/0 in the same match. HSSET 103* v Somerset, Taunton Vale, 2013. BBSET 4/30 v Somerset, Taunton Vale, 2011.HST20 51* v Leics, Hinckley, 2013 (2nd), BBT20 3/18 v Northants, Chelmsford, 2013 (2nd). Essex staff.

William Edward Lewis BUTTLEMAN (Felstead S) b Chelmsford, 20.4.00. RHB OB WK. Debut 2017. HS 72 v Kent, Beckenham, 2017. HSSET 11 v Somerset, Taunton Vale, 2017. HST20 20 v Kent, Coggeshall, 2017 (2nd).

Varun CHOPRA (Ilford County HS) b Barking, Essex, 21.6.87. RHB LB. Debut Essex 2003; F/C debut v Loughborough MCCU, Chelmsford, 2006. Debut Warwicks 2010 & Cap 2012. Eng U19 v SL 2005; v India 2006. HS 227 v Kent, Beckenham, 2009. BB 2/8 v Kent, Beckenham, 2007. HSSET 136* v Northants, Northampton,

2008. HST20 86 (Warwicks) v Leics, Edgbaston, 2015 (2nd). Essex Staff.

Samuel James COOK (Great Baddow HS, Great Baddow SFC) b 4.8.97, Chelmsford. RHB RFM. Debut 2014. F/C debut (Loughborough MCCU) v Surrey, the Oval, 2016. HS 19* v Kent, Polo Farm SG, Canterbury, 2017. BB 5/50 v Durham, Richmond, N Yorks, 2017. HSSET 1 v Somerset, Halstead, 2016. BBSET 3/38 v Sussex, Blackstone, 2016. HST20 6 v Middx, Billericay, 2015 (2nd). BBT20 4/15 v Somerset, Chelmsford, 2017 (2nd). Essex Staff.

Matthew William DIXON (Servite Coll, Tuart Hill, Perth, W Australia) b Subiaco, W Australia, 12.6.92. RHB RF. Debut 2016. F/C debut (W Australia) v New South Wales, Sydney, 2010/11. HS 31 v Hants, Ageas Bowl Nursery, 2017. BB 5/29 v Middx, Radlett, 2017. HSSET 15 v Hants, Ageas Bowl Nursery, 2017. BBSET 3/51 v Middx Radlett, 2017. HST20 14, v Kent, Polo Farm SG, Canterbury, 2017 (2nd). BBT20 2/17 v Unc, Great & Little Tew, 2017 (2nd). Essex Staff.

Joseph Sukhdev Edwin ELLIS-GREWAL (Beal HS, Leeds U) b. Walthamstow 18.2.92. LHB, SLA. Debut Glam & MCCU 2014; Essex 2016. F/C debut (Leeds/Brad MCCU) v Sussex, Hove, 2015. HS 77 v Durham, Richmond, N Yorks, 2017. BB 5/51 (MCCU) v Surrey, Cheam, 2014. HSSET 28* (Glam) v Sussex, Fulking, 2015 & v Sussex, Billericay, 2017. BBSET 2/43 (Glam) v Derbys, Cardiff, 2014. HST20 18 v Kent, Billericay, 2016 (2nd). BBT20 3/32 v Glam, Chelmsford, 2016 (2nd).

Gerasimos FATOUROS (Christchurch GS, Perth, W Australia) b Johannesburg, Gauteng, S Africa, 21.7.97. RHB OB. Debut Kent 2016; Essex 2017. HS 121 (Kent) v Hants, Polo Farm SG, Canterbury, 2017. HSSET 98 (Kent) v Glam, Canterbury, 2016. HST20 56 (Kent) v Glos, Polo Farm SG, Canterbury, 2016 (2nd). BBT20 0/7 (Kent) v Surrey, Purley, 2016 (2nd).

James Savin FOSTER (Forest S, Walthamstow; Durham U) b Leytonstone. 15.4.80. RHB WK. Tests (Eng) 7 & 11 ODIs (2001/02 to 2002/03). Debut Essex 1997. F/C debut (British Un) v Zimbabweans, Fenner's, 2000. Essex Cap 2001. HS 116 v Yorks, Harrogate, 2000. HSSET 77 v Kent, Canterbury, 1999. HST20 9 v Glos, Chelmsford, 2017 (1st). Essex staff.

Barry James HYAM (Havering SFC; Westminster C) b Romford 9.9.75. RHB WK. Debut 1992. F/C debut v Glam, Sophia Gardens, 1993. Debut MCC YC 1995. Essex Cap 1999. HS 182 v Kent, Coggeshall, 2003. HSSET 69* v Sussex, B Stortford, 2002. HST20 1* v Glam, St Fagans, 2017 (2nd).

Christopher Michael JONES (Ash Manor S, Aldershot, Hants; Farnborough SFC) b Frimley Park, 10.8.97. RHB OB. Debut Surrey 2014; Essex 2017. HS 79 (Surrey) v Somerset, Bath, 2016. BB 3/52 in the same match. HSSET 52 v Sussex, Billericay, 2017. BBSET 3/29 (Surrey) v Glos, Bristol, 2014. HST20 9 v Glos, Chelmsford, 2017 (2nd). BBT20 4/25 (Surrey) v Glam, Purley, 2016 (1st).

Eshun Singh KALEY (Barking Abbey S) b Ilford, 23.11.01. RHB RM. Debut 2017, aged 15 yrs & 251 days. HS 16* v Middx, Coggeshall, 2017. BB 0/65 in the same match.

KASHIF ALI (Dunstable Coll) b Kashmir, Pakistan, 7.2.98. RHB LB. Debut Essex 2016; Leics 2017. HS 76 v Kent, Polo Farm G,

Canterbury, 2017. BB 0/14 v Middx, Coggeshall, 2017. HSSET 24 v Sussex, Billericay, 2017. HST20 27* v Middx, Coggeshall, 2017. BBT20 0/19 in the same match.

Feroze Isa Nazir KHUSHI (Kelmscott S, Walthamstow) b Whipps Cross, 23.6.99. RHB OB. Debut 2015. HS 138 v Hants, Coggeshall, 2016. BB 0/10 v Middx, Coggeshall, 2017. HSSET 106* v MCC YC, Halstead, 2015. BBSET 0/4 v Somerset, Halstead, 2016. HST20 69 v Somerset, Chelmsford, 2017 (2nd). Essex Staff.

Daniel William LAWRENCE (Trinity Cath HS, Woodford Green) b Whipps Cross, 12.7.97. RHB LB. Debut 2013. F/C debut v Kent, Chelmsford, 2015. Eng U19 v Australia, 2015. HS 185 v Sussex, Southend-on-Sea, 2015. BB 2/11 v Surrey, Cheam, 2016. HSSET 77 v Middx, Coggeshall, 2013. BBSET 3/39 v Hants, the Ageas Bowl, 2014. HST20 39 v Kent, Maidstone, 2015 (1st). BBT20 1/15 v Kent, Maidstone, 2015 (1st). Essex staff.

Dustin Renton MELTON (Pretoria Boys HS, S Africa; U of Pretoria) b Zimbabwe, 11.4.95. RHB RFM. Debut Leics 2016; Essex 2017. HS 29 (Leics) v Derbys, Swarkestone, 2016. BB 3/40 v Middx, Coggeshall, 2017. BBSET 0/65 (Leics) v Unc, Loughborough CC, 2016. HST20 5* v Middx, Coggeshall, 2017 (1st). BBT20 1/39 (Leics) v Derbys, Derby, 2016 (1st).

Aron Stuart Singh NIJJAR (Ilford County HS) b Goodmayes, 24.9.94. LHB SLA. Debut 2013. F/C debut v Leics, Chelmsford, 2015. HS 170 v Somerset, Halstead, 2016. BB 6/113 v Sussex, Halstead, 2017. HSSET 82* v Sussex, Blackstone, 2016. BBSET 3/32 v Kent, Halstead, 2014. HS T20 30 v Glam, SWALEC, 2015 (2nd). HST20 3/19 v Glam, SWALEC, 2015 (2nd). Essex Saff.

*Akhil PATEL (Kimberley CS) b Nottingham 18.6.90. LHB SLA Chinaman. Brother of S.R. (6 Tests & 36 ODIs, Eng, 2008 to 2015/16). Debut Derbys 2007 aged 16 years and 304 days; F/C debut (Derbys) v Cambridge MCCU, Fenner's, 2007; debut Notts 2009. Ret to Derbys 2012. Debuts Kent & Northants 2012; Surrey 2013; ret to Northants 2014; debut Essex & Sussex 2017. HS 174 (Notts) v Northants, Finedon Dolben 2011. BB 4/53 (Notts) v Yorks, Barnsley, 2011. HSSET 105 (Notts) v Leics, Leicester, 2010. BBSET 4/25 (Northants) v Sussex, Desborough, 2014. HST20 35 (Northants) v Leics, Grace Road, 2015 (2nd). BBT20 2/16 (Notts) v Derbys, Long Eaton, 2011 (1st.) HSKO 63(Notts) v Derbys, Alvaston & Boulton, 2010. BBKO 0/21 in the same match.

Rishi Ketan PATEL (Brentwood S) b Chigwell, 26.7.98. RHB LB. Debut 2015 aged 16 yrs & 360 days. HS 116* v Sussex, Halstead, 2017. BB 0/55 v Middx, Coggeshall, 2017. HST20 25 v Middx, Coggeshall, 2017 (1st).

Michael-Kyle Steven PEPPER (The Perse S) b Harlow, 25.6.98. Brother of C A (Essex 2013 to 2016). RHB WK. Debut Unc 2016; Essex & Northants 2017. HS 136 v Middx, Coggeshall, 2017. HSSET 103 (Unc) v Middx, Radlett, 2017. HST20 38 (Northants) v Lancs, Northampton, 2017 (2nd).

Jack Henry PLOM (Gable Hall S, Essex; S Essex Coll, Southend) b Basildon, 27.8.99. LHB RFM. Debut 2016. Eng U19 v India, 2017; to SA 2017/18. HS. 2 v Glam, Pontarddulais, 2017. BB 1/39 in the same match. HSSET 10* v Hants, Ageas Bowl Nursery, 2017. BBSET 1/58 in the same match. HST20 14 v Glam, St Fagans, 2017 (2nd). BBT20 3/41 v Glam, St Fagans, 2017 (1st).

James Alexander PORTER (Oaks Park HS, Ilford; Epping Forest Coll, Loughton) b Leytonstone, Essex, 25.5.93. RHB RFM. Debut MCCYC 2011, Essex 2014. F/C debut v Kent, Chelmsford, 2014. HS 23* (MCCYC) v Yorks, Weetwood, 2011. BB 8/48 v Sussex, Southend-on-Sea, 2014. HSSET 9* (MCCYC) v Kent, Shenley, 2012. BBSET 3/26 v Surrey, Sunbury, 2014. HST20 15* (MCCYC) v Kent, Radlett, 2013 (1st). BBT20 3/5 (MCCYC) v Surrey, Purley, 2013 (2nd). Essex Staff.

Saurav Sanjay PRABHAKAR (Brentwood S) b Ilford, 15.11.96. LHB SLA. Debut Essex & Kent 2016. HS 60* v MCC YC, Halstead, 2015.

Matthew Richard QUINN (Sacred Heart Coll, Auckland, NZ; Massay U, Auckland) b Auckland, NZ, 28.2.93. RHB RF. Debut 2016. F/C debut (Auckland, NZ) v Central Districts, Eden Park, 2012/13. HS 4 v Middx, Radlett, 2016. BB 5/42 in the same match. HSSET 2 v Sussex, Billericay, 2017. BBSET 4/36 in the same match. HST20 1 v Somerset, Taunton Vale, 2016 (1st). BBT10 1/31 in the same match.

Alistair David Lewis RUSSELL (Eton Coll) b Cambridge, 29.8.97. RHB WK. Debut 2015. HS 5 v Sussex, Blackstone, 2016. HSSET 13 v Middx, Uxbridge, 2015. HST20 32 v Glos, Chelmsford, 2107 (2nd).

Joshua Sean RYMELL (Ipswich S; Colchester SFC) b Ipswich, 4.4.01. RHB. Debut 2017, aged 16 yrs & 139 days. HS 14* v Somerset (Taunton Vale), 2017.

Matthew Edward Thomas SALISBURY (Shenfield HS; Anglia RU) b Chelmsford 18.4.93. RHB RMF. Debut Essex 2011; MCC Un 2012. F/C debut (Cambridge MCCU) v Essex, Fenner's, 2012. Debuts Somerset 2016; Hants 2017. HS 52 v Glos, Bishop's Stortford, 2015. BB 6/37 v Middx, Billericay, 2014. HSSET 41 v Hants, Ageas Bowl Nursery, 2015. BBSET 5/62 v Hants, Ageas Bowl Nursery, 2017. HST20 17* v Northants, Northampton, 2014 (1st). BBSET 3/37 in the same match.

Tanveer Abbas SHAH (National Foundation S, Jhelum, Pakistan) b Jhelum, Pakistan, 12.10.94. RHB LB. Debut 2017. HS 37 v Hants, Ageas Bowl Nursery, 2017. HSSET 77 v Hants, Ageas Bowl Nursery, 2017.

Rahul Hari SHEEMAR (Bedford S) b Bedford, 22.4.01. LHB OB. Debut 2017, aged 16 yrs & 99 days. HS 39 v Middx, Coggeshall, 2017. HST20 1* v Middx, Coggeshall, 2017 (1st).

Sandeep SINGH (Little Ilford S, Manor Park, London; New Vic SFC, Newham) b Punjab, India, 16.7.96. RHB OB. Debut Durham 2014; Essex 2017. BB 1/79 v Middx, Coggeshall, 2017.

Shane SNATER (St John`s Co, Harare, Zim) b Harare, Zim, 24.3.96. RHB RFM. Debut 2017. F/C debut (Netherlands) v Afghanistan, Voorburg, Netherlands, 2016. HS 3 v Glam, Pontarddulais, 2017. BB 4/26 in the same match. HST20 20 v Glam, St Fagans, 2017 (2nd). BBT20 1/13 v Glam, St Fagans, 2017 (1st)

Ishwarjot Singh SOHI (Isleworth & Syon S; Brunel U) b Punjab, India, 7.8.94. RHB RFM. Debut Northants & Surrey 2014; MCCYC 2016. HS 49 v Sussex, Halstead, 2017. BB 3/83 (Northants) v Glos, Thornbury, 2014. HSSET 1* (Northants) v Somerset, Milton Keynes, 2014. BBSET 1/25 (Northants) v Sussex, Desborough, 2014. HST20 21* (Surrey) v Glam, 2017 (1st). BBT20 2/29 (Surrey) v Kent, Polo Farm SG, Canterbury, 2017 (1st).

James Arthur STAMATIS (Kearsney C, Durban, SA; IMM Graduate S, Durban) b Richards Bay, Durban, 24.5.98. RHB RM. Debut 2017. HS 99* v Hants, Ageas Bowl Nursery, 2017. BB 2/25 v Glos, Billericay, 2017. HSSET 54 v Hants, Ageas Bowl, Nursery, 2017. BBSET 1/28 in the same match. HST20 11 v Kent, Polo Farm SG, Canterbury, 2017 (2nd).

Sean Christopher SULLIVAN (New Hall S) b Chelmsford, 12.9.00. RHB RM. Debut 2017, aged 16 yrs & 338 days. HS 6 v Sussex, Halstead, 2017. HST20 8* v Middx, Coggeshall, 2017 (2nd). BBT20 1/28 in the same match.

Callum John TAYLOR (Cromer HS, Norfolk; Eastern Coll, Norwich) b Norwich, Norfolk, 26.6.97. RHB RM. Debut 2013. F/C debut v Glam, SWALEC, 2015. Eng U19 to Australia, 2014/15; v Australia 2015. HS 136 v Durham, Richmond, N Yorks, 2017. BB 4/21 v Glam, Mumbles, 2015. HSSET 129 v Hants, Coggeshall, 2016. BBSET 13/41 v Sussex, Billericay, 2017. HST20 47 v Unc, Great & Little Tew, 2017 (2nd). BBT20 3/21 v Somerset, Chelmsford, 2015 (2nd). Essex Staff.

Kishen Shailesh VELANI (Brentwood S) b Newham, Essex, 2.9.94. RHB RM/OB. Debut 2012. Eng U19 to Bangladesh 2011/12; to Australia (World Cup) 2011/12; to S Africa, 2012/13. F/C debut v Hants, the Ageas Bowl, 2013. HS 127 v MCC Un, Bishop's Stortford, 2013. BB 4/28 v Surrey, Bishop's Stortford, 2013. HSSET 106 v MCCYC, High Wycombe, 2016. BBSET 1/17 v Surrey, Bishop's Stortford , 2013. HST20 88 v Middx, Coggeshall, 2017 (1st). BBT20 1/ 16 v Glam, SWALEC, 2015 (1st). Released at the end of the 2017 season.

Ryan Lee VICKERY (Alec Hunter Acad; Colne Comm Coll; U of Beds) b Braintree, 17.11.95. RHB WK. Debut 2017. HS 11 v Hants, Ageas Bowl Nursery, 2017. HSSET 15 v Hants, Ageas Bowl Nursery, 2017.

Paul Ian WALTER (Billericay S) b Basildon, 28.5.94. LHB LM. Debut 2015. F/C debut v Derbys, Derby, 2016. HS 50* v Glam, Bishop's Stortford, 2016. BB 4/65 v Hants, Coggeshall, 2016. HSSET 145* v Somerset, Taunton Vale, 2017. BBSET 4/26 v

Unc, Billericay, 2017. HST20 30* v Glam, Chelmsford, 2016 (1st). BBT20 4/30 v Middx, Radlett, 2016 (1st). Essex Staff.
Ben Alexander WARING b Harlow, 12.4.98. RHB SLA. Debut Essex 2015; Unc 2017. HS 14 v Hants, Ageas Bowl Nursery, 2017. BB 2/36 v Somerset, Halstead, 2016. HSSET 0 v Hants, Ageas Bowl Nursery, 2017. BBSET 3/55 v Somerset, Taunton Vale, 2015. BBT20 3/15 (Unc) v Sussex, Long Marston, 2017 (2nd).
Nicholas Roy WELCH (St John's Coll, Harare, Zim) b Harare, Zim, 5.2.98. RHB LB. F/C debut (Mashonaland Eagles, Zim) v Mountaineers, Harare, 2013/14. Debuts Surrey 2015, Sussex 2016, Essex & Northants 2017. HS 88 (Surrey) v Middx, New Malden,

2017. HSSET 72* (Sussex) v Kent, Canterbury, 2017. HST20 75* (Surrey) v Unc, New Malden, 2017 (2nd).
Adam Jack Aubrey WHEATER (Millfield S; Anglia Ruskin U) b Leytonstone, Essex, 13.2.90. RHB WK. Debut Essex 2006 aged 16 years and 190 days. Debut Matabeleland Tuskers 2010/11; Badureliya Sports Club, Colombo 2011/12; Northern Districts, NZ, 2012/13; Hants 2013. F/C debut (Cambridge MCCU) v Essex, Fenner's, 2008. Eng U19 to S.Africa 2008/09 and v Bangladesh 2009. HS 147 (Hants) v Glam, Neath, 2016. HSSET 74 v Minor Counties, Milton Keynes 2007. HST20 88 v Glam, St Fagans, 2017 (1st). HSKO 22* v Kent, Billericay, 2010. Essex Staff.

GLAMORGAN

PLAYING RECORDS 2017
Championship – P9 W0 L3 D6 – tenth in the southern group
2nd XI Trophy – P6 W2 L2 Ab1 NR1 - fifth in the southern group
2nd XI T20 Competition – P12 W5 L5 Ab2 - fifth in the southern group

2nd XI SUCCESSES
Championship – Winners – 1965, 1980
2nd XI Trophy – Beaten Semi-Finalists in 2008 and 2011
2nd XI T20 Competition – Best finish – 2nd in the group in 2011

SECOND ELEVEN CHAMPIONSHIP AVERAGES

BATTING	M	I	NO	Runs	HS	Avge	100s	C/S
A O Morgan	7	11	1	436	151*	43.60	1	2
G G Wagg	2	4	0	156	112	39.00	1	1
N Brand	5	10	0	375	106	37.50	1	4
J L Lawlor	7	14	4	321	99	32.10	-	3
H A J Allen	2	4	0	127	59	31.75	-	2
A G Salter	2	3	0	94	44	31.33	-	1
J R Murphy	8	14	1	406	86*	31.23	-	3
R A J Smith	8	13	2	325	122	29.54	1	3
T N Cullen	5	8	0	223	85	27.87	-	9/1
C Z Taylor	2	3	2	25	24*	25.00	-	1
C A J Meschede	5	10	0	237	91	23.70	-	1
C R Brown	5	10	1	193	61	21.44	-	4
N J Selman	4	8	1	141	78	20.14	-	8
L Machado	3	6	0	119	46	19.83	-	3
K A Bull	8	11	8	45	26*	15.00	-	9
K S Carlson	5	10	0	143	29	14.30	-	6
L J Carey	3	4	0	52	39	13.00	-	-
S W Griffiths	3	6	1	57	23*	11.40	-	3
C L Herring	4	7	0	47	27	6.71	-	6

BOWLING	O	M	Runs	Wkt	Avge	BB
C R Brown	10	1	45	5	9.00	3/45
K Szymanski	16	6	39	4	9.75	3/25
N Brand	62.5	19	152	15	10.13	6/14
T van der Gugten	13	4	41	3	13.66	3/41
L J Carey	56.4	8	208	13	16.00	3/12
A G Salter	40.2	6	170	10	17.00	6/52
H A J Allen	35	2	133	5	26.60	2/42
C A J Meschede	103	33	288	10	28.80	3/21
K A Bull	198	28	603	20	30.15	5/30
R A J Smith	105	21	331	8	41.37	3/61
A O Morgan	82	17	296	7	42.28	2/32

Also bowled – K S Carlson 11.5-0-88-1; S W Griffiths 10-0-48-0; J L Lawlor 45-5-132-2; D L Lloyd 16-4-55-1; J P McIlroy 18-7-45-1; J R Murphy 18-1-69-0; T D Murphy 21-3-71-1; D O'Sullivan 13-1-59-0; S J Pearce 36-2-165-2; O M R Pringle 13-0-82-1; N J Selman 1-0-11-0; C Z Taylor 24-2-96-1; R J Tonkin 5-2-13-0; G G Wagg 23-10-35-1; R I Walker 14-5-38-1.

Also batted – 2 matches – S J Pearce 6*, 1, 0 (1ct); K Szymanski 1*, 0*, 0; R I Walker 0*, 0. 1 match – W D Bragg 93, 12; A H T Donald 13 (2ct); D L Lloyd 100 (2ct); J P McIlroy DNB; T D Murphy DNB; D O'Sullivan DNB (1ct); O M R Pringle 2*; S H Roberts 3, 6; R J Tonkin DNB; T van der Gugten 0; J H Voke 24 (1ct).

SECOND ELEVEN TROPHY AVERAGES

BATTING	M	I	NO	Runs	HS	Avge	100s	C/S
J R Murphy	5	4	1	100	60	33.33	-	1
R A J Smith	4	3	2	29	20*	29.00	-	-
A O Morgan	5	4	0	97	56	24.25	-	4
S W Griffiths	3	3	0	38	38	12.66	-	2
N J Selman	3	3	0	29	25	9.66	-	4

BOWLING	O	M	Runs	Wkt	Avge	BB
O M R Pringle	18	0	104	6	17.33	3/30
S J Pearce	37	2	204	8	25.50	3/35
A O Morgan	32.3	1	171	6	28.50	2/16
J R Murphy	18	0	118	4	29.50	2/45
T van der Gugten	15	0	100	3	33.33	3/34
R A J Smith	22	1	148	4	37.00	2/57
J L Lawlor	22	1	120	3	40.00	2/27

Also batted – 5 matches – S J Pearce 7, 1 (3ct). 4 matches – K A Bull 9* (1ct). 3 matches – N Brand 29, 102 (1ct); C R Brown 10, 0 (1ct); T N Cullen 23*, 10* (1ct); C L Herring 63, 36 (3ct); J L Lawlor 70, 90 (4ct). 2 matches – K S Carlson 139, 14 (2ct); C A J Meschede 4, 25*; O M R Pringle DNB (2ct); T van der Gugten 26*. 1 match - H A J Allen 11; A H T Donald 4; K Szymanski DNB.

Also bowled – N Brand 11-1-56-1; K A Bull 18.3-0-95-2; S W Griffiths 10-0-51-0; C A J Meschede 8-0-34-0; K Szymanski 9.3-1-42-2.

SECOND ELEVEN T20 AVERAGES

BATTING	M	I	NO	Runs	HS	Avge	100s	C/S
N J Selman	6	6	2	250	63*	62.50	-	4
N Brand	10	10	2	296	56	37.00	-	3
R A J Smith	8	5	1	134	53	33.50	-	2
T N Cullen	7	3	1	59	32*	29.50	-	6/2
J L Lawlor	10	10	1	225	58	25.00	-	2
A O Morgan	6	5	4	24	9*	24.00	-	1
C A J Meschede	4	4	1	62	26	20.66	-	1
K S Carlson	4	4	0	71	44	17.75	-	2
C R Brown	10	8	0	132	39	16.50	-	3
T R Bevan	4	3	0	29	18	9.66	-	1
C L Herring	4	3	1	11	8	5.50	-	4/2
J R Murphy	7	7	1	33	11	5.50	-	-

BOWLING	O	M	Runs	Wkt	Avge	BB
K A Bull	32	1	197	12	16.41	2/10
C A J Meschede	14.4	0	87	5	17.40	4/29
L J Carey	18	0	160	7	22.85	3/34
H A J Allen	7.2	0	73	3	24.33	3/32
R A J Smith	27	0	268	11	24.36	3/32
J L Lawlor	18.4	0	156	6	26.00	2/16
A O Morgan	20	0	161	4	40.25	3/17
N Brand	20	0	163	4	40.75	1/13

Also batted – 8 matches – K A Bull 1*, 1, 1* (1ct). 6 matches – K Szymanski DNB (1ct). 5 matches – L J Carey DNB. 3 matches – L Machado 3*, 2 (1ct). 2 matches – H A J Allen 2; D L Lloyd 1, 26; S J Pearce DNB; S H Roberts 24, 17.

Also bowled – T R Bevan 1-0-6-0; C R Brown 10-0-71-2; K S Carlson 2-0-20-0; J R Murphy 3-0-29-1; S J Pearce 3-0-29-1; K Szymanski 10-0-78-2.

HOME MATCHES: SECOND ELEVEN CHAMPIONSHIP

v Gloucestershire (Newport) – 26-28 Apr – Glam 377/4d (A O Morgan 151*, W D Bragg 93, H A J Allen 59) & 273/9d (R A J Smith 122; C J W Gregory 4/71, O C Currill 3/59) drew with Glos 108, B S Gilmour 55) & 250/4 (M A H Hammond 126*, B S Gilmour 84)

v Kent (Neath) – 30 May to 1 June – Glam 213 (J R Murphy 79, J L Lawlor 55; H R Bernard 5/72) & 290/9d (G G Wagg 112; Imran Qayyum 4/92, M D Hunn 3/60) lost to Kent 257 (A J Blake 61; L J Carey 3/65) & 247/6 (A J Blake 86) by four wkts.

v Surrey (Neath) – 19-21 June – Surrey 344 (R Patel 61, A Harinath 53; N Branjd 4/52) & 203/4d (R Patel 52) drew with Glam 242 (N Brand 106; G S Virdi 6/77) & 166/8 (N Brand 60; G S Virdi 5/54 [and match figs of 11/131])

v Essex (Pontarddulais Park) – 4-6 July – Essex 244 (L J Carey 3/40) & 150 (A S S Nijjar 58, C J Taylor 53; N Brand 6/14, C A J Meschede 3/21) beat Glam 223 (N Brand 58; A S S Nijjar 4/61, A P Beard 3/51) & 157 (S Snater 4/26) by 14 runs.

HOME MATCHES: FRIENDLIES

v Worcestershire (Abergavenney) – 18-20 July – Worcs 268 (J J Dell 70, A G Milton 60; L J Carey 6/71) & 196 (J J Dell 95*, A Hepburn 55; K A Bull 5/61) lost to Glam 432 (J R Murphy 155, N Brand 111, N J Selman 60, C R Brown 55; Z A Malik 4/55, G L S Scrimshaw 3/69) & 33/3 by seven wkts.

v Somerset (Newport) – 29-31 Aug – Glam 301/8d (C R Brown 68; M T C Waller 3/28) & 193/7d (C R Brown 83; R D Edwards 4/54) beat Somerset 178/4d (P D Trego 68, G A Bartlett 54*) & 315 (T Banton 117, G A Bartlett 65, F R Trenouth 52; K A Bull 4/129, S J Pearce 3/45) by one run.

HOME MATCHES: SECOND ELEVEN TROPHY

v Gloucestershire (Newport) – 25 Apr – Glam 315/7 (K S Carlson 139, J L Lawlor 70; M A H Hammond 4/50) beat Glos 218 (M A H Hammond 84; T van der Guigten 3/34) by 97 runs.

v Somerset (Newport) – 3 May – Glam 229/8 (C L Herring 63, J R Murphy 60; P A van Meekeren 4/42) lost to Somerset 230/6 (J G Myburgh 101, R C Davies 52*; S J Pearce 3/35) by four wkts.

v Kent (Newport) – 19 May – Match abandoned without a ball bowled.

HOME MATCHES : SECOND ELEVEN T20 COMPETITION

v Surrey (Neath) – 18 June – Match 1 – Surrey 127/8 (W G Jacks 61; H A J Allen 3/32) lost to Glam 128/3 by seven wkts.
v Surrey (Neath) – 18 June – Match 2 – Glam 111/8 (T M Homes 3/14) lost to Surrey 113/2 (W G Jacks 65*) by eight wkts.
v Essex (St Fagans) – 3 July – Match 1 – Essex 179/5 (A J A Wheater 88; R A J Smith 3/34) beat Glam 127 (J H Plom 3/41) by 52 runs.

v Essex (St Fagans) – 3 July – Match 2 – Glam 167/8 (S J Cook 4/26) beat Essex 128 (C A J Meschede 4/29) by 39 runs.
v Unicorns (Port Talbot) – 4 Aug – Match 1 – Match abandoned without a ball bowled.
v Unicorns (Port Talbot) – 4 Aug – Match 2 – Match abandoned without a ball bowled.

PLAYERS WHO HAVE REPRESENTED GLAMORGAN 2ND XI IN 2017 (40)

H A J Allen	T N Cullen	J P McIlroy	A G Salter
T R Bevan	*L Dixon	C A J Meschede	N J Selman
W D Bragg	A H T Donald	A O Morgan	R A J Smith
N Brand	S W Griffiths	J R Murphy	K Szymanski
*A D F Brewster	C L Herring	T D Murphy	C Z Taylor
C R Brown	* S J Jardine	D O'Sullivan	R J Tonkin
K A Bull	J L Lawlor	S J Pearce	T van der Gugten
L J Carey	D L Lloyd	O M R Pringle	J H Voke
K S Carlson	L Machado	*E A Rees	G G Wagg
*L M Cheshire	*C D Matthews	S H Roberts	R I Walker

GLAMORGAN CRICKETERS

Harry Andrew John ALLEN (Epsom Coll; Cardiff U) b. Carshalton, Surrey, 25.3.96. RHB, SLA. Debuts Surrey 2012; Cardiff MCCU 2016; Glam & MCCU 2017. HS 59 v Glos, Newport, 2017. BB 2/42 in the same match. HSSET 11 v Unc, Newbury, 2017. BBSET 3/24 (Surrey) v Essex, Sunbury-on-Thames, 2014. HST20 5 (Surrey) v MCCYC, Purley, 2013 (2nd). BBT20 3/32 v Surrey, Neath, 2017 (1st).

Thomas Rhys BEVAN (Millfield S) b Cardiff, 9.9.99. RHB OB. Debut 2017. HST20 18 v Glos, Bristol U, 2017 (2nd). BBT20 0/6 v Essex, St Fagans, 2017 (1st).

William David BRAGG (Rougemont S, Newport, Gwent; UWIC) b Newport, 24.10.86. LHB WK. Debut 2003. F/C debut v Somerset, Taunton, 2007. Glam Cap 2015. HS 182* v Somerset, SWALEC, 2008. HSSET 108 v Notts, Notts SG, 2010. BBSET 1/20 v Kent, Newport, 2015. HST20 53 v Somerset, Diamond Ground, Cardiff, 2012. BBT20 1/25 v Glos, Bristol U, 2015 (2nd). Retired at the end of the 2017 season.

Neil BRAND (King's Coll, Taunton; Cardiff Met U) b Johannesburg, South Africa 12.4.96. LHB SLA. Debut Glam & Somerset 2014. F/C debut (Cardiff MCCU) v Glam, SWALEC, 2015. HS 162 v Sussex, Abergavenny, 2016. BB 6/14 v Essex, Pontarddulais, 2017. HSSET 102 v Sussex, Blackstone, 2017. BBSET 2/34 v Glos, Diamond Ground, 2015. HST20 56 v Middx, Richmond, 2017 (2nd). BBT20 1/12 v Somerset, Taunton Vale, 2015 (2nd).

***Andrew David Francis BREWSTER** (Tadcaster GS & SFC) b York, 1.2.97. RHB RFM. Debut 2016; Debuts Durham, Northants & MCCU 2017. F/C debut (Cardiff MCCU) v Glam, SWALEC, 2017. HS 0 v Glos, Bower Ashton, 2017. BB 4/33 (Durham) v Essex, Richmond, N Yorks, 2017. HST20 5* (Northants) v Notts, Grantham, 2017 (2nd). BBT20 1/6 (Durham) v Worcs, Burnopfield CC, 2017 (2nd).

Connor Rhys BROWN (Y Pant CS) b Caerphilly 28.4.97. RHB OB Debut 2014. F/C debut (Cardiff MCCU) v Glam, SSE SWALEC, 2017. HS 170 v Hants, Newport, 2016. BB 3/45 v Middx, Merchant Taylors`S, Northwood, 2017. HSSET 21 v Kent, Newport, 2015. BBSET 3/43 v Kent, Newport, 2015. HST20 39 v Middx, Richmond, 2017 (2nd). BBT20 3/22 v Glos, SWALEC, 2016 (2nd).

Kieran Andrew BULL (Queen Elizabeth HS, Haverfordwest; Cardiff Met U) b Haverfordwest 5.4.95 RHB OB Debut 2012. F/C debut v Kent, Canterbury, 2014. HS 40* v Glos, Thornbury, 2013. BB 8/73 v Durham, Middlesbrough, 2014. HSSET 14 v Durham, Middlesbrough, 2014. BBSET 5/36 v Durham, Middlesbrough 2014. HST20 15* v Glos, SWALEC Stadium, 2014. BBT20 3/21 in the same match. Glam staff.

Lukas John CAREY (Pontarddulais CS, Gower SFC) b Carmarthen 17.7.1997 RHB, RFM. Debut 2014. F/C debut v Northants, Swansea, 2016. HS 39 v Middx, Merchant Taylors' S, Northwood, 2017. BB 6/71 v Worcs, Abergavenny, 2017. HSSET 22 v Durham, Middlesbrough, 2014. BBSET 4/37 v MCCYC, Cardiff, 2014. HST20 6* v Surrey, Diamond Ground, Cardiff, 2015 (1st). BBT20 3/25 v Surrey, Purley, 2016 (2nd).

Kiran Shah CARLSON (Whitchurch HS, Cardiff) b Cardiff 16.5.98. RHB OB Debut 2014. F/C debut v Northants, Northampton, 2016. HS 150 v Leics, SWALEC, 2015. HS 144 v Surrey, Neath, 2017. HSSET 139 v Glos, Newport, 2017. BBSET 2/28 v Hants, Newport, 2016. HST20 44 v Essex, St Fagans, 2017 (2nd). BBT20 1/19 v Surrey, Diamond Ground, Cardiff, 2015 (1st).

***Luke Mark CHESHIRE** b Wantage, Oxon, 8.9.99. RHB LFM. Debut 2017. HS 0 v Glos, Bristol U, 2017. BB 0/16 in the same match.

Thomas Nicholas CULLEN (Aquinas Coll, Stockport, Cardiff Met U) b. Perth W Australia, 4.1.92. RHB. Debut Leics 2015; F/C debut (Cardiff MCCU) v Glos, Bristol, 2015. Debut Glam 2016. HS 85 v Sussex, Fulking, 2017. HSSET 23 v Glos, Newport, 2017. HST20 32* v Middx, Richmond, 2017 (2nd).

***Liam DIXON** (Stanley Coll of Tech, Co Durham; Hild-Bede Coll, Durham) b Durham 26.4.93. RHB, RM. F/C debut (Durham MCCU) v Derbys, Derby, 2014. Debut Glam 2017. HS 16 v Northants, Northampton. 2017. BB 3/67 in the same match.

Aneurin Henry Thomas DONALD (Pontarddulais CS, Gower SFC) b Swansea 20.12.96. RHB, OB, occ WK. Debut 2012. F/C debut v Hants, SWALEC, 2014. Eng U19 v S Africa, 2014; to Australia 2014/15; v Australia 2015. HS 240 v Glos, Panteg, 2015. HSSET 53 v Durham, Middlesbrough, 2014. HST20 44 v Glos, Bristol, 2013. Glam staff.

Sean William GRIFFITHS (Dyffryn Comp S; Llandarcy SFC; Cardiff Met U) b 16.5.95. RHB RM. Debut 2012; Cardiff MCCU 2014. F/C debut (Cardiff MCCU) v Glam, SWALEC, 2014. HS 72* v Essex, Southend, 2012. BB 4/50 v Glos, Bristol, 2012. HSSET 38 v Unc, Newbury, 2017. BBSET 0/24 v Somerset, Newport, 2017. HST20 18* v Glos, Cardiff 2012. BBT20 4/28 v Warwicks, Cardiff, 2013.

Cameron Lee HERRING (Tredegar CS) b Abergavenny, Monmouthshire 15.7.94. RHB WK. Debut Glos 2011 aged 16 years and 315 days. F/C debut (Glos) v Essex, Chelmsford 2013. Debut Glam 2016. HS 203* (Glos) v MCC Univs, Cheltenham Victoria 2013. HSSET 82* (Glos) v Middx, Downend CC, 2015. HST20 39 (Glos) v Glam, Bristol U, 2015 (2nd).

***Samuel John JARDINE** (St Joseph`s S, Neath) b Neath, Glam, 17.10.01. RHB RM. Debut 2017. BB 2/42 v Somerset, Newport, 2017.

33

Jeremy Lloyd LAWLOR (Llandaff Cathedral S; Monmouth S; Cardiff Met. U) b Cardiff 4.11.95 RHB, OB Son of PJ Lawlor (Glam 1981) Debut 2012. F/C debut (Cardiff MCCU) v Glam, SWALEC, 2015. HS 99* v MCCU, Mumbles, 2017. BB 2/32 v Hants, Ageas Bowl Nursery, 2015. HSSET 90 v Sussex, Blackstone, 2017. BBSET 2/27 v Glos, Newport, 2017. HST20 58 v Glos, Bristol U, 2017 (1st) BBT20 2/16 v Glos, Bristol U, 2017 (2nd). Glam staff.

David Liam LLOYD (Darland HS, Wrexham; Shrewsbury S) b St Asaph, Dengighshire, 15.5.92. Debut 2008. F/C debut v Yorks, Headingley, 2012. HS 243 v Warwicks, Coventry and North Warwick, 2014. BB 2/62 v Lancs, SWALEC Stadium, 2014. HSSET 57 v Glos, Bristol, 2012. HST20 109* v Surrey, Diamond Ground, Cardiff, 2015 (2nd). BBT20 2/26 v Surrey, Diamond Ground, Cardiff, 2015 (2nd). Glam staff.

Jamie Peter MURPHY (Builth Wells HS; Coleg Powys, Newtown) b Hereford, 19.6.94. RHB LFM. Debut 2017. BB 1/11 v Somerset, Taunton Vale, 2017.

Lorenzo MACHADO (St Benedict's, Johannesburg; Kings S, Taunton) b Johannesburg, Gauteng, 1.2.98. RHB WK. Debut 2016. HS 57* v Glos, Bower Ashton, 2017. HSSET 40* v Sussex, St Fagans, 2016. HST20 3* v Middx, Richmond, 2017 (1st).

***Christopher Daniel MATTHEWS** (St Clare's S, Bridgend) b Bridgend, Glam, 18.11.99. RHB WK. Debut 2015, aged 15 years & 294 days. HS 29* v Somerset, Newport, 2017.

Craig Anthony Joseph MESCHEDE (King's Coll, Taunton) b Johannesburg, Gauteng, South Africa 21.11.91. RHB RMF. Debut 2008. F/C debut (Somerset) v Sussex, Hove, 2011. Debut Glam 2015. HS 109 (Somerset) v Surrey, The Oval, 2010. BB 5/61 (Somerset) v Kent, Maidstone, 2011. HSSET 101*(Somerset) v Glam, Diamond Ground, Cardiff, 2012. BBSET 5/18 (Somerset) v Middx, Richmond, 2011. HST20 43 (Somerset) v Glos, Bristol, 2011 (1st). BBT20 4/29 v Essex, St Fagans, 2017 (2nd). HSKO 32 (Somerset) v Glam, Croft-y-Genau, St Fagans, 2010. BBKO 2/34 in the same match.

Alun Owen MORGAN (Ysgol Gyfun yr Strade Cardiff Met U) b Swansea 11.4.94 RHB, SLA. Debut Glam & Cardiff MCCU 2014. F/C debut (Cardiff MCC) v Glos, Bristol, 2014. Debut (Kent) on loan 2015. HS 151* v Glos, Newport, 2017. BB 5/15 v Glos, Bath, 2016. HSSET 66* v Somerset, Taunton Vale, 2016. BBSET 3/18 v MCCYC, Cardiff, 2014. HST20 18 v Essex, Chelmsford 2016 (1st). BBT20 3/15 v Glos, SWALEC, 2016 (1st).

Jack Roger MURPHY (Greenhill School, Tenby. Cardiff Met U) b Haverfordwest 15.7.95 LHB, LFM. Brother of T D (below). Debut Glam 2011. F/C debut (Cardiff MCCU) v Glam, SWALEC, 2015. HS 155 v Worcs, Abergavenny, 2017. BB 6/68 v Kent, Canterbury, 2016. HSSET 60 v Somerset, Newport, 2017. BBSET 3/35 v Somerset, Taunton Vale, 2016. HST20 18 v Essex, Chelmsford, 2016 (1st). BBT20 2/14 v Somerset, Newport, 2016 (1st). Glam staff.

Thomas David MURPHY (Greenhill S, Tenby, Pembrokeshire) b Haverfordwest, Pembrokeshire, 22.4.99. RHB RFM. Debut 2015, aged 16 years & 111 days. Brother of J R (above). Debut 2015. BB 3/32 v Somerset, Taunton Vale, 2016.

David O'SULLIVAN (Merchant Taylors' S, Northwood; Cardiff Met U) b Sydney, NSW, Aus, 11.6.97. RHB RFM. Debut Derbys & Glam 2017. F/C debut (Cardiff MCCU) v Hants, Ageas Bowl Nursery, 2017. BB 1/40 (Derbys) v MCC YC, Glossop, 2017.

Samuel James PEARCE (Archbishop McGrath CS, Bridgend) b Bridgend 2.9.97 RHB, LB Debut 2013. HS 58 v Northants, Northampton, 2017. BB 5/69 v Hants, Ageas Bowl Nursery, 2017. HSSET 28 v Sussex, St Fagans, 2016. BBSET 3/35 v Somerset, Newport, 2017. HST20 45 v Surrey, Purley, 2016 (1st). BBT20 3/28v Somerset, Taunton, 2013.

Oliver Morgan Reynolds PRINGLE b Auckland, NZ 27.5.92. LHB RMF. Son of M.R. (Auckland 1984/85-1991/92). Debut

Surrey, Glos 2010, Notts, Somerset 2012, Glam 2017. HS 34* (Notts) v Surrey, (Notts SG) 2012. BB 4/21 v Leics, Lutterworth, 2017. HSSET 17* (Glos) v Kent, Beckenham 2010. BBSET 3/30 v Unicorns, Newbury 2017.

***Elliot Adam REES** b Pontypridd, Glam, 5.10.99. RHB RM. Debut 2017. HS 0* v Glos, Bristol U, 2017. BB 0/15 in the same match.

Steffan Howard ROBERTS (Maesteg CS) b Bridgend 8.10.97 RHB OB Debut 2014. HS 35 v Middx, Radlett, 2016. HST20 24 v Surrey, Neath, 2017 (1st).

Andrew Graham SALTER (Milford Haven SFC, Cardiff Met U) b Haverfordwest 1.6.93 RHB OB Debut Glam 2010. Eng U19 to S Lanka, 2011/12. F/C (Cardiff MCCU) v Somerset, Taunton Vale, 2012. HS 77 v Kent, Canterbury, 2016. BB 6/52 v Hants, Basingstoke, 2017. HSSET 31 v Kent, Canterbury, 2016. BBSET 4/28 v Surrey, Charterhouse S, 2012. HST20 16 v Essex, SWALEC, 2015 (1st). BBT20 2/11 v Essex, SWALEC, 2015 (2nd). Glam staff.

Prem SISODIYA (Clifton Coll) b Cardiff, 21.9.98. RHB SLA. Eng U19 to SA, 2017/18. Yet to make his 2nd XI debut.

Nicholas James SELMAN (Matthew Flinders Anglican C, Buderim, Queensland, Aus) b Brisbane, Queensland, 18.10.95. RHB RM. Debut Kent 2014; Glam & Glos 2015. F/C debut v Worcs, SWALEC, 2016. HS 151* (Kent) v MCCYC, High Wycombe 2015. BB 1/9 v Hants, Neath, 2016. HSSET 78 v Leics, SWALEC, 2015. HST20 91* v Surrey, Purley, 2016 (2nd). BBT20 1/5 v Somerset, Newport, 2016 (1st).

Ruaidhri Alexander James SMITH (Llandaff Cathedral School, Shrewsbury S; Bristol U) b Glasgow 5.8.94. RHB, RM Debut Glam 2010. F/C debut v Kent,SWALEC, 2013. HS 122 v Glos, Newport, 2017. BB 5/60 v Sujssex, Fulking, 2015. HSSET 43* v Leics, Leicester 2013. BBSET 4/25 v Glos, Panteg, 2015. HST20 53 v Somerset, Taunton Vale, 2017 (2nd). BBT20 3/32 v Somerset, Taunton Vale, 2017 (1st). Glam staff.

Kazimir SZYMANSKI (King's Coll, Taunton) b Torquay, Devon, 5.9.99. RHB RM. Debut 2017. HS 6* v Northants, Northampton, 2017. BB 3/25 v Middx, Merchnt Taylors' S, Northwood, 2017. BBSET 2/42 v Somerset, Newport, 2017. BBT20 1/17 v Middx, Richmond, 2017 (1st).

Callum Zinzan TAYLOR (The Southport S) b Newport, Monmouthshire, 19.6.98. RHB OB. Debut 2017. HS 36 v Somerset, Newport, 2017. BB 1/22 v Glos, Newport, 2017.

Ryan John TONKIN (Mullion S, Helston, Cornwall; Truro Coll) b Truro, 4.12.98. RHB RM. 2017.

Timm van der GUGTEN b Hornsby, NSW, Aus, 25.2.91. RHB RFM. ODIs (Netherlands) 4 & 25 T20s (2011/12 to 2016/17). Debuts & F/C debut (NSW) v W Aus, Sydney, 2011/12; Tasmania 2012/13; Glam 2016. HS 0 v Hants, Basingstoke, 2017. BB 3/41 in the same match. HSSET 26* v Somerset, Newport, 2017. BBSET 3/34 v Glos, Newport, 2017.

Joseph Harry VOKE (Caldicott S, Slough; Cardiff Met U) b Newport, Gwent, 31.7.98. RHB RM. Debut 2017. HS 45 v Somerset, Newport, 2017.

Graham Grant WAGG (Aslawn CS, Rugby) b Rugby, Warwicks, 28.4.83. RHB, LM, occ SLA. Debut Warwicks 2002. F/C debut (Warwicks) v Somerset, Edgbaston, 2002 Debut Derbys 2006; Cap 2007; Debut Glam 2011; Cap 2013. HS 112 v Kent, Neath, 2017. BB 5/14 (Warwicks) v Northants, Stockton 2002. HSSET 100* v Warwicks, Walmley 2014. BBSET 2/17 (Warwicks) v Northants, West Bromwich Dartmouth, 2003. HS T20 5 v Glos, Bristol U, 2015 (1st). BBT20 1/25 in the same match. Glam staff

Roman Isaac WALKER (Ysgol Bryn Alyn, Wrexham, N Wales) b Wrexham, 6.8.00. RHB RFM. Debut 2016. Eng U19 to S Africa, 2017/18. HS 30 v Northants, Northampton, 2017. BB 2/50 in the same match.

GLOUCESTERSHIRE

PLAYING RECORDS 2017
Championship – P9 W3 L2 D3 Ab1 – sixth in the southern group
2nd XI Trophy – P6 W1 L4 NR1 - ninth in the southern group
2nd XI T20 Competition – P12 W5 L7 – eighth in the southern group

2nd XI SUCCESSES
2nd XI Champions – 1959
2nd XI Trophy – Losing Finalists – 1995, 1997
2nd XI T20 – Losing Semi-Finalists – 2011, 2013

SECOND ELEVEN CHAMPIONSHIP AVERAGES

BATTING	M	I	NO	Runs	HS	Avge	100s	C/S
C N Miles	3	3	2	110	76*	110.00	-	1
G T Hankins	2	3	0	231	114	77.00	2	-
G H Roderick	3	5	0	180	105	36.00	1	13
M A H Hammond	8	12	2	352	126*	35.20	1	3
J R Bracey	6	8	0	279	119	34.87	1	2/1
W A Tavare	5	8	1	243	73	34.71	-	6
J L N Garrett	3	5	2	92	46*	30.66	-	3
C D J Dent	3	4	1	86	45	28.66	-	2
B A C Howell	2	3	0	82	66	27.33	-	3
G L van Buuren	2	3	0	81	73	27.00	-	-
L C Norwell	3	3	1	53	26	26.50	-	1
B S Gilmour	7	11	0	274	84	24.90	-	1
P J Grieshaber	5	6	1	112	57	22.40	-	4
G S Drissell	8	5	2	62	41*	20.66	-	1
A W R Barrow	2	3	1	38	27	19.00	-	-
O C Currill	3	3	1	14	8	7.00	-	2

BOWLING	O	M	Runs	Wkt	Avge	BB
K Noema-Barnett	12	4	22	7	3.14	7/22
L C Norwell	69	11	193	11	17.54	3/37
C J W Gregory	94.3	10	505	14	36.07	4/71
M A H Hammond	153.5	17	549	14	39.21	4/59
C N Miles	59	11	202	5	40.40	4/56
G S Drissell	83.4	7	362	7	51.71	3/56
O C Currill	59.4	4	262	5	52.40	3/59
J Shaw	97.1	24	302	5	60.40	2/39

Also bowled – C T Bancroft 1-0-1-0; C D J Dent 3-0-10-0; J H Gibbs 12-1-46-0; B S Gilmour 47-7-216-2; B A C Howell 2-0-7-1; H A Jordan 8-1-41-0; B Knyman 14-1-49-1; C J Liddle 8-1-34-0; J B Lintott -7-2-28-1; T J Price 5-1-15-0; O M R Pringle 8-3-17-0; T M J Smith 2-2-0-1; M D Taylor 20-6-61-2; G L van Buuren 32-4-111-1.

Also batted – 6 matches – C J W Gregory 17, 17 (1ct). 5 matches – J Shaw 28, 4. 2 matches – C T Bancroft 1, 5 (1ct); M D Taylor 25, 0 (1ct). 1 match – C L M Burnstone DNB (2ct); B G Charlesworth 59, 1(2ct); I A Cockbain 77, 53: O A Dawkins DNB; J S E Dunford 32, 8 (1ct); B A T S Ellis-Dabrowski 38, 7 (1ct); J H Gibbs DNB (1ct); H A Jordan 0*, 14; B Knyman 0, 0; C J Liddle DNB; J B Lintott 26*; K Noema-Barnett 31; T J Price 37, 13; O M R Pringle 21*; T M J Smith DNB.

SECOND ELEVEN TROPHY AVERAGES

BATTING	M	I	NO	Runs	HS	Avge	100s	C/S
G T Hankins	3	3	0	222	113	74.00	1	-
M A H Hammond	6	5	0	190	84	38.00	-	4
B S Gilmour	6	6	0	181	63	30.16	-	2
J L N Garrett	5	4	0	88	39	22.00	-	1
W A Tavare	3	3	1	38	19	19.00	-	1
C J W Gregory	6	4	2	22	11	11.00	-	-
O C Currill	5	3	1	58	42*	29.00	-	-

BOWLING	O	M	Runs	Wkt	Avge	BB
J H Gibbs	12.5	0	81	7	11.57	4/29
G S Drissell	10	0	44	3	14.66	3/44
D A Payne	10	2	49	3	16.33	3/49
M A H Hammond	42	2	214	6	35.66	4/50
O C Currill	29	1	168	4	42.00	2/51
C J W Gregory	40	3	255	6	42.50	3/36

Also bowled – B S Gilmour 26-1-141-1; G T Hankins 5-0-45-0; H J Hankins 7-0-58-1; B A C Howell 9-0-58-2; H A Jordan 7-0-42-0; C J Liddle 7-0-60-1;K Noema-Barnett 13-0-60-0; O M R Pringle 6-2-13-0; T M J Smith 10-052-0; M D Taylor 7-0-41-1.

Also batted – 4 matches – C L M Burnstone 0*, 0 (ct). 3 matches – G S Drissell14, 6 (1ct); K Noema-Barnett 24, 18. 2 matches – C T Bancroft 11*, 29; I A Cockbain 5, 80 (2ct); B A T S Ellis-Dabrowski 0, 5; J H Gibbs DNB; D J Lincoln 15*, 78; G H Roderick 11, 10 (1ct). 1 match – J R Bracey DNB; H J Hankins DNB; D J Hooper DNB; B A C Howell 30; H A Jordan 1*; C J Liddle 1* (1ct); D A Payne 2; O M R Pringle 8; T M J Smith 0; M D Taylor 9.

SECOND ELEVEN T20 AVERAGES

BATTING	M	I	NO	Runs	HS	Avge	100s	C/S
G L van Buuren	6	5	1	136	57*	34.00	-	3
T M J Smith	3	3	1	65	27	32.50	-	2
C N Miles	8	5	3	51	18	25.50	-	4
K Noema-Barnett	6	5	2	75	41*	25.00	-	2
C D J Dent	8	7	0	172	44	24.57	-	2
I A Cockbain	6	6	1	117	61*	23.40	-	-
M D Taylor	7	6	2	88	51*	22.00	-	1
J R Bracey	6	5	0	105	46	21.00	-	3
G H Roderick	8	7	1	119	38	19.83	-	10/1
W A Tavare	5	5	1	78	34	19.50	-	-
J M R Taylor	3	3	1	36	17	18.00	-	-
J L N Garrett	4	3	0	52	44	17.33	-	1
G T Hankins	8	8	0	127	35	15.87	-	4
B S Gilmour	4	4	0	60	30	15.00	-	2
C T Bancroft	4	4	0	47	31	11.75	-	2
B A C Howell	6	6	0	53	20	8.83	-	1
J Shaw	9	6	3	25	14	8.33	-	2
M A H Hammond	11	9	0	50	15	5.55	-	2

BOWLING	O	M	Runs	Wkt	Avge	BB
C N Miles	29	0	178	13	13.69	3/16
D A Payne	7	0	44	3	14.66	2/23
L C Norwell	12.4	0	64	4	16.00	2/19
G J van Buuren	18	0	110	5	22.00	2/12
J Shaw	29.4	1	260	11	23.63	3/31
M A H Hammond	21	0	154	6	25.66	3/22
K Noema-Barnett	15	0	108	4	27.00	2/23
C J Liddle	18.3	0	155	5	31.00	2/9
M D Taylor	24.5	0	164	5	32.80	2/20
B A C Howell	18.3	0	151	4	37.75	2/13

Also bowled – C D J Dent 0.4-0-3-1; G S Drissell 1-0-10-0; C J W Gregory 3-0-23-0; G T Hankins 1-0-12-0; J B Lintott 3-0-21-0; T M J Smith 11-0-70-2; W A Tavare 1.2-0-10-0; J M R Taylor 6-0-36-2.

Also batted – 6 matches – C J Liddle 2, 0 (1ct). 4 matches – L C Norwell 0*, 0. 3 matches – C J W Gregory 1* (1ct). 2 matches – G S Drissell 35, 12; J B Lintott 2, 20* (1ct); D A Payne DNB. 1 match – P J Grieshaber 10 (1st).

HOME MATCHES: SECOND ELEVEN CHAMPIONSHIP

v Middlesex (Longwood CC) – 16-18 May – Match abandoned without a ball bowled.

v Hampshire (Bristol Un SG) – 17-19 July – Glos 289 (C N Miles 76*; I G Holland 4/58) & 245/7d (W A Tavare 65, B G Sole 3/58) lost to Hants 287 (C N Milers 4/56, C J W Gregory 3/38) & 248/5 (T P Alsop 106*; G S Drissell 3/56) by five wkts.

v Kent (Longwood CC) – 25-27 July – Glos 120 (A J Ball 4/15, C F Hartley 4/48) drew with Kent 211/2 (J J Weatherley 104*, Z Crawley 56)

v Somerset (Longwood CC) – 1-3 Aug – Somerset 390/7d (E J Byrom 141, R C Davies 124; L C Norwell 3/50) drew with Glos 31/1.

v MCC Universities (Bath CC) – 15-17 Aug – Glos 418/8d (J R Bracey 119, W A Tavare 73, B G Charlesworth 59*, M A H Hammond 57; A T Thomson 4/102) & 181/7d (G H Roderick 51; A T Thomson 5/68) beat MCCU 197 (L C Norwell 3/37, M A H Hammond 3/62) & 261 (J D Marshall 102; M A H Hammond 4/59, L C Nowell 3/53) by 141 runs.

HOME MATCHES: FRIENDLIES

v Glamorgan (Bristol U SG) – 2 May – Glam 175/9 lost to Glos 176/1 (B S Gilmour 84*, G T Hankins 52*) by nine wkts.

v Worcestershire (Cheltenham Coll) – 30 May to 1 June – Glos 455/7d (G H Roderick 170, G T Hankins 74, K Noema-Barnett 56) & 239/5d (B S Gilmour 88, C T Bancroft 86; G H Rhodes 4/55) beat Worcs 291/3d (O E Westbury 118, A Hepburn 70*, G H Rhodes 61) & 282 (G H Rhodes 125; G S Drissell 5/54) by 121 runs.

v Scotland A (Bath CC) – 8-10 August – Scotland A 170 (H G Munsey 68; M D Taylor 4/37, G L van Buuren 3/5) & 135 (O C Currill 6/21) lost to Glos 64/7d (A C Evans 5/33) & 243/2 (C T Bancroft 119*, J R Bracey 63*) by eight wkts.

v Glamorgan (The Clanage, Bower Ashton) – 22-24 Aug – Glos 450/3d (G T Hankins 181, W A Tavare 158) & 180/6d (C D J Dent 104; A D F Brewster 4/61) drew with Glam 266 (L Machado 57*, T N Cullen 50; C J Liddle 3/13, M D Taylor 3/70) & 257/6 (T N Cullen 78*, R A J Smith 62)

v MCC Young Cricketers (Rockhampton) – 29-31 Aug – Glos 400/9d (B A C Howell 133, J Shaw 57*, J R Bracey 53; A Karvelas 4/57) & 168 drew with MCC YC 268/5d (S M Imtiaz 104*, J H Barrett 73; M A H Hammond 3/85) & 173/8.

HOME MATCHES: SECOND ELEVEN TROPHY

v Somerset (Bristol U SG) – 5 May – Somerset 337/8 (R C Davies 135, G A Bartlett 97; D A Payne 3/49, J H Gibbs 3/52) beat Glos 283/7 (G T Hankins 113; M J Leach 4/41) by 54 runs.

v Middlesex (The Clanage, Bower Ashton) – 15 May - Glos 26/1 v Middx DNB. No Result.

v Unicorns (Bristol U SG) – 22 May – Glos 257/9 (I A Cockbain 80) beat Unc 140 (J H Gibbs 4/29, C J W Gregory 3/36) by 117 runs.

HOME MATCHES : SECOND ELEVEN T20 COMPETITION

v Glamorgan (Bristol U SG) – 14 July – Match 1 – Glam 166/5 (J L Lawlor 58; J Shaw 3/31) beat Glos 146/9 (A O Morgan 3/17, L J Carey 3/34) by 20 runs.

v Glamorgan (Bristol U SG) – 14 July – Match 2 – Glam 128/8 (J Shaw 3/33) lost Glos 129/4 (G L van Buuren 57*) by six wkts.

v Hampshire (Clifton Coll) – 20 July – Match 1 – Hants 157/8 (M A H Hammond 3/22) beat Glos 142/8 (B T J Wheal 3/23) by 15 runs.

v Hampshire (Clifton Coll) – 20 July – Match 2 – Glos 146/8 (J B Lintott 3/30) lost to Hants 149/6 (C N Miles 3/16) by four wkts.

v Kent (Longwood) – 24 July – Match 1 – Kent 72/6 lost to Glos 76/6 by four wkts.

v Kent (Longwood) – 24 July – Match 2 – Glos 114 (C F Hartley 3/20) beat Kent 109/9 by five runs.

PLAYERS WHO HAVE REPRESENTED GLOUCESTERSHIRE 2ND XI IN 2017 (44)

*M C Ayres	G S Drissell	H J Hankins	L C Norwell
C T Bancroft	*J A Dryell	D J Hooper	D A Payne
A W R Barrow	J S E Dunford	B A C Howell	T J Price
J R Bracey	B A T S Ellis-Dabrowski	H A Jordan	O M R Pringle
C L M Burnstone	J L N Garrett	B Knyman	G H Roderick
B G Charlesworth	J H Gibbs	C J Liddle	J Shaw
*R B A Coates	B S Gilmour	D J Lincoln	T M J Smith
I A Cockbain	C J W Gregory	J B Lintott	W A Tavare
O C Currill	P J Grieshaber	C N Miles	J M R Taylor
O A Dawkins	M A H Hammond	*A Neill	M D Taylor
C D J Dent	G T Hankins	K Noema-Barnett	G L van Buuren

GLOUCESTERSHIRE CRICKETERS

*Milo Calvin AYRES (Ashton Park S & 6th Form C) b Bristol 19.9.99. LHB. Debut 2017. HS 41 v MCCYC, Rockhampton 2017.

Cameron Timothy BANCROFT (Aquinas C, Perth, WA) b Attadale, Perth, WA 19.11.92. RHB RM WK. F/C debut W.Australia v Victoria, Melbourne 2013/14. Tests (Aus) 2 (2017/18). Debut 2016. HS 119* v Scotland A, Bath C.C. 2017. HSSET 29 v Unicorns, Bristol University 2017. HST20 31 v Hants, Clifton College 2017 (2nd). Glos staff.

Alexander William Rodgerson BARROW (Selwood S, Frome; King's C, Taunton) b Bath 6.5.92. RHB OB WK. Debut Somerset 2009, Eng U19 v SL 2010, F/C debut (Somerset) v Hants, Rose Bowl, 2011; debut Glos & Northants 2017. HS 150* (Somerset) v Kent, Maidstone 2011. HSSET 93 (Somerset) v MCCYC, North Perrott 2011. HST20 56* (Somerset) v Glos, Taunton Vale 2015 (2nd).

James Robert BRACEY (Filton C; Loughborough U) b Bristol 3.5.97. LHB WK. Brother of S.N. (Glos 2011/14). Debut Glos 2014, MCCYC 2015. F/C debut v Sussex, Bristol 2016. HS 119 v MCC Univs, Bath C.C. 2017. BB 1/2 v Ireland Wolves, Rockhampton 2017. HSSET 72 v Middx, Radlett 2016. HST20 46* v Glam, Cardiff 2016 (1st). Glos staff.

Calum Leo M. BURNSTONE (Beechen Cliff S, Bath; Sth Glos & Stroud C). b Bath 17.4.98. RHB WK. Debut 2017. HSSET 0* v Glam, Newport 2017.

Ben Geoffrey CHARLESWORTH (St Edward's S, Oxford) b Oxford 19.11.00. LHB RM. Son of GM (Warwicks 2nd XI 1982/91, Griqualand West, Cambridge U 1989/90-1993). Debut 2016 aged 15 years and 144 days. HS 59* v MCC Univs, Bath C.C. 2017.

*Ross Bradman Amos COATES (Blythe Bridge HS, Stoke–on-Trent) b Stoke-on-Trent 2.2.99. RHB WK. Nephew of A.J.Brassington (Glos 1974/88). Debut 2017. HS 3 v Warwicks, Bull's Gd, Coventry 2017.

Ian Andrew COCKBAIN (Maghull HS; Liverpool John Moores U) b Liverpool, Lancs 17.2.87. Son of I. (Lancs 1979/83). RHB RM. Debut Lancs 2006, MCCYC 2008, Glos 2010, F/C debut v Derbys, Bristol 2011. HS 224 v MCCU, Cheltenham CC 2013. BB 2/39 v Essex, Southend-on-Sea 2013. HSSET 113 v Surrey, Bristol 2014. HST20 73 v Glam, Bristol 2011 (2nd). BBT20 1/4 v Glam, Bristol U 2015(2nd). Glos staff.

Oliver Charles CURRILL (Chipping Campden Acad.) b Banbury, Oxon 27.2.97. RHB RMF. Debut 2015. F/C debut v Durham MCCU, Bristol 2017. HS 13 v Glam, Bath CC, 2016. BB 6/21 v Scotland A, Bath C.C,. 2017. HSSET 42* v Somerset, Bristol U, 2017. BBSET 2/18 v Glam, Bristol U, 2017. BBT20 1/15 v Glam, Bristol U 2015 (1st).

Owen Alun DAWKINS (Crickhowell HS) b Cheltenham 23.11.78. RHB LB. Debut MCCYC, Somerset and Worcs 1997, Glam 1998, Middx and Northants 2000, Glos and Notts 2001, Essex and Minor Counties 2002, Sussex 2003. HS 83 (Worcs) v Hants, Southampton, 1997. BB 3/94 (Somerset) v Middx, Taunton, 1997. HSSET 25 (MCC YC) v Sussex, Shenley, 1997. BBSET 3/42 (Minor Counties) v Leics, Milton Keynes,, 2002. HST20 3* v Somerset, Bristol U, 2016 (2nd). Glos 2nd XI Coach.

Christopher David James DENT (Backwell CS; Alton C). LHB SLA. Debut 2007 aged 16 years and 199 days. F/C debut v Northants, Bristol 2010. Eng U19 to NZ 2010 (U19 World Cup)

and v SL 2010. HS 110* v Middx, Bristol 2009. BB 6/54 v Kent, Maidstone 2014. HSSET 81 v Hants, Cheltenham Coll 2011. HST20 92 v Kent, Cheltenham Coll 2015 (1st). BBT20 2/12 v Glam, Bristol 2013 (1st). Glos staff.

George Samuel DRISSELL (Bedminster Down S, Bristol; Filton C) b Bristol 20.1.99. RHB OB. Debut 2016. F/C debut v Northants, Northampton 2017. HS 41* v Glam, Newport 2017. BB 5/54 v Worcs, Cheltenham College 2017. HSSET 14 v Glam, Newport 2017. BBSET 3/44 v Surrey, Purley 2017. HST20 35 v Sussex, Fulking 2017 (1st).

*Joe Aiden DRYELL (Colston's S, Bristol) b Bristol 12.3.01. RHB RM. Debut 2016 aged 15 years and 39 days. HS 6 v MCCYC, Rockhampton 2017.

Jake Samuel Edward DUNFORD (Victoria C, Jersey; Durham U). b Jersey 24.6.94. RHB WK. Debut 2017. F/C debut Durham MCCU v Glos, Bristol 2016. HS 32 v Surrey, Purley 2017.

Benedict Alexander Theodore Sidney ELLIS-DABROWSKI (known as B.Ellis) (Bournside S, Cheltenham; Filton C). b Cheltenham, 21.7.98. RHB OB. Debut 2017. HS 38 v Glam, Newport 2017. HSSET 5 v Somerset, Bristol U 2017.

Jordan Laurence Norman GARRETT (Henry Box S) b Oxford 14.5.99. RHB OB. Debut Glos 2014 aged 14 years and 336 days; debut Hants 2017. HS 96* v Warwicks, Bristol 2016. HSSET 77 v Somerset, Bristol CC 2015. HST20 44 v Somerset, Taunton Vale 2017 (2nd). Debut Hants 2017as a mutually agreed guest for Hants in the 2nd XI T20 competition at Bristol, due to injuries and first eleven call-ups.

Jack Henry GIBBS (King's C, Taunton) b Birmingham, Warwicks 3.6.00. RHB RMF. Debut 2016 aged 16 years and 63 days. BB 0/20 v Glam, Newport, 2017. HSSET 1* v Kent, Cheltenham Vic, 2016. BBSET 4/29 v Unicorns, Bristol U 2017.

Brandon Stuart GILMOUR (Park House S) b Bulawayo, Zimbabwe 11.4.98. LHB RM. Debut 2013. HS 103 v MCCYC, Bath CC 2015. BB 4/26 v Middx, Richmond 2014. HSSET 84* v Glam, Bristol U 2017. BBSET 2/48 v Middx, Richmond 2014. HST20 49 v Somerset, Taunton Vale 2015 (2nd). BBT20 1/25 in the same match. Released at the end of the 2107 season. .

Callum James William GREGORY (Maiden Erlegh S) b Reading, Berks 14.2.97 RHB RMF. Debut Glos 2015, MCCYC 2016. HS 20 v Somerset, Taunton Vale 2015. BB 4/71 v Glam, Newport 2017. HSSET 11 v Surrey, Purley 2017. BBSET 3/36 v Unicorns, Bristol U 2017. HST20 1* v Sussex, Fulking 2017 (1st).

Patrick James GRIESHABER (Sheldon S, Chippenham) b Bath, Somerset 24.11.96. RHB WK. Debut 2012 aged 15 years and 180 days. F/C debut v Glamorgan, Bristol 2014. HS 66 v Ireland Wolves, Rockhampton 2017. HSSET 56 v Middx, Richmond 2014. HST20 17* v Somerset, Bristol U 2016(2nd). Released at the end of the 2107 season.

Miles Arthur Halhead HAMMOND (St Edward's S, Oxford) b Cheltenham 11.1.96. LHB OB. Debut 2010 aged 14 years and 120 days. F/C debut v Glam, Bristol 2013. Eng U19 in S.Africa 2012/13. HS 128 v Glam, Bristol CC 2015. BB 5/105 v Surrey, Bath CC 2016. HSSET 190* v MCCYC, Bath CC 2015. BBSET 4/50 v Glam, Newport 2017. HST20 34 v Glam, Bristol U 2015 (1st). BBT20 3/22 v Hants, Clifton College 2017 (1st). Glos staff.

George Thomas HANKINS (Millfield S) b Bath, Somerset 4.1.97. RHB OB. Brother of H.J. (below). Debut 2014. F/C debut v Durham MCCU, Bristol 2016. Eng U19 v S.Lanka 2016. HS 181 v Glam, Bedminster C.C. 2017. BB 1/2 v Glam, Bristol CC 2015 and v Middx, Radlett 2016. HSSET 113 v Somerset, Bristol U 2017. BBSET 1/60 v Surrey, Guildford 2015. HST20 35 v Somerset, Taunton Vale 2017 (2nd). Glos staff.

Harry John HANKINS (Beechen Cliff S) b Bath, Somerset 24.4.99. RHB RMF. Brother of G.T. (above). Debut 2017. BBSET 1/58 v Kent, Beckenham 2017.

Dominic Jonty HOOPER (Backwell S; S Glos & Stroud Coll, Filton) b Bristol 25.9.98. RHB RMF. Debut 2015 aged 16 years and 218 days. HS 6 v Surrey, Bath CC 2016. BB 1/25 in the same match. HST20 1* v Glam, Bristol U 2015 (2nd). BBT20 2/15 in the same match.

Benjamin Alexander Cameron HOWELL (Oratory S, Reading) b Bordeaux, France 5.10.88. RHB RM. Debut Hants 2005, F/C debut (Hants) v Lancs, Rose Bowl 2011. Debut Gloucs 2012. HS 207* v Surrey, Bristol 2012. BB 4/49 (Hants) v Sussex, Hove 2011. HSSET 103 (Hants) v Glam, Cardiff 2008. BBSET 3/27 (Hants) v Glam, West End Nursery 2011. HST20 53* (Hants) v Sussex, West End Nursery 2011. BBT20 2/13 v Essex, Chelmsford 2017 (1st). Glos staff.

Harry Alexander JORDAN (The Windsor Boys' S) b Windsor 15.10.98. LHB RF. Debut 2017. HS 14 v Surrey, Purley 2017. HSSET 1* v Surrey, Purley 2017.

Ben KYNMAN b Torquay, Devon 18.4.95. RHB RFM. Debut Kent 2016, Glos 2017. HS 0 v Surrey, Purley 2017. BB 1/49 in the same match. HSSET 2* (Kent) v Glam, Canterbury 2016. BBSET 1/28 in the same match.

Christopher John LIDDLE (Nunthorpe S; Teesside Tertiary C) b Middlesbrough, Yorks 1.2.84. RHB LFM. Debut Leics 2003, F/C debut (Leics) v Durham UCCE, Leicester 2005, debut Sussex 2007, Glos 2016. HS 63* (Sussex) v Ireland A, Blackstone 2012. BB 5/31 (Sussex) v Kent, Canterbury 2007. HSSET 27 (Leics) v Yorks, Leicester 2006. BBSET 4/43 (Sussex) v Surrey, Winbledon 2012. HST20 23* (Sussex) v Surrey, Fulking 2013 (2nd). BBT20 4/26 (Sussex) v Surrey Horsham 2015 (2nd). Glos staff.

Daniel John LINCOLN (Edgbarrow S, Crowthorne, Berks) b Frimley Park, Surrey 26.5.95. RHB RM. Debut 2017. HSSET 78 v Surrey, Purley 2017.

Jacob Benedict LINTOTT (Queen's C, Taunton) b Taunton 22.4.93. RHB SLA Debut Somerset 2010, Warwicks 2013, Hants 2016, Glos 2017. List A (T20) debut (Hants) v Somerset, Ageas Bowl 2017. HS 78 (Somerset) v Surrey, Taunton 2011. BB 4/111 (Warwicks) v Middx, Merchant Taylors' S, Northwood 2013. HSSET 26 (Warwicks) v Glam, Cardiff CC 2013. BBSET 3/39 (Somerset) v Surrey, Taunton 2014. HST20 29 (Hants) v Sussex, Arundel Castle 2017 (F). BBT20 4/18 (Hants) v Middx, Ageas Bowl Nursery 2017 (2nd).

*Dominic Oliver W. MAY (Skinners' S; Bristol U) b Tunbridge Wells, Kent 31.10.95. RHB SLA. Debut 2017. BBSET 2/24 v Glam, Bristol U, 2017.

Craig Neil MILES (Bradon Forest S, Swindon; Filton C) b Swindon, Wilts 20.7.94. Brother of A.J. (Glos 2007, MCCYC 2009). RHB RMF. Debut 2009 aged 14 years and 317 days, F/C debut v Northants, Bristol 2011. HS 76* v Hants, Bristol U, 2017. BB 4/22 v Kent, Bristol 2016. HSSET 30 v Middx, Radlett 2016. BBSET 3/47 v Glam, Bath CC 2016. HST20 18 v Kent, Bristol C.C. 2017 (2nd). BBT20 4/25 v Somerset, Bristol 2011 (2nd). Glos staff.

*Adrian NEILL (Nairn Academy, Inverness) b Riversdale, Western Cape, S.Africa 22.3.94. RHB RMF. Debut Scotland A 2016, Glos 2017. HS 8 (Scotland A) v Lancs, Blackpool 2016 and (Scotland A) v Ireland A (Alloway) 2016. BB 3/30 (Scotland A) v Durham, Chester-le-Street 2016.

Kieran NOEMA-BARNETT (Kavanagh College) b Dunedin, Otago, NZ 4.6.87. LHB RM. F/C debut (Central Districts) v Auckland 2008/09. NZ U19 in World Cup 2005/06. Debut Glos 2014. HS 118 v Surrey, Bath CC 2016. BB 7/22 v Essex, Billericay 2017. HSSET 91 v Glam, Bath CC 2016. BBSET 1/26 v Glam, Bristol U 2017. HST20 53* v Somerset, Taunton Vale 2015 (1st). BBT20 3/15 in the same match. Glos staff.

Liam Connor NORWELL (Redruth S) b Bournemouth, Dorset 27.12.91. RHB RMF. Debut 2009. F/C debut v Derbys, Bristol 2011. HS 46 v Kent, Canterbury CC 2016. BB 4/37 v MCCU, Bristol CC 2014. HSSET 9* v Unicorns A, Bradfield Coll, 2013. BBSET 3/22 v Glam, Cardiff CC 2015. HST20 27 v Kent, Canterbury CC 2016 (2nd). BBT20 5/14 in the same match. Glos staff.

David Alan PAYNE (Lytchett Minster S, Poole) b Poole, Dorset 15.2.91. RHB LFM. Debut 2008, F/C debut v Derbys, Bristol 2011. Eng U19 v Bangladesh 2009, to NZ 2010 (U19 World Cup) and v SL 2010. HS 65* v Northants, Bristol 2010. BB 6/33 v Yorks, Bristol 2015. HSSET 25* v Northants, Dunstable Town CC 2013. BBSET 6/9 v Glam, Cardiff CC 2015. HST20 13* v Worcs, Ombersley 2013 (2nd). BBT20 2/23 v Essex, Chelmsford 2017 (2nd). Glos staff.

Thomas James PRICE (Magdalen College S) b Oxford 2.1.00. RHB RM. Debut 2015 aged 15 years and 199 days. HS 37 v MCCU, Bath C.C. 2017. HSSET 4 v Kent, Cheltenham Victoria 2016.

Oliver Morgan Reynolds PRINGLE b Auckland, NZ 27.5.92. LHB RMF. Son of M.R. (Auckland 1984/85-1991/92). Debut Surrey, Glos 2010, Notts, Somerset 2012, Glam 2017. HS 34* (Notts) v Surrey, (Notts SG) 2012. BB 4/21 (Glam) v Leics, Lutterworth, 2017. HSSET 17* v Kent, Beckenham 2010. BBSET 3/30 (Glam) v Unicorns, Newbury 2017.

Gareth Hugh RODERICK (Maritzburg C, Durban) b Durban, S.Africa 29.8.91. RHB WK. F/C debut (KwaZulu-Natal) v Free State, Bloemfontein 2010/11. Debut Northants 2011, Glos 2012. HS 175 v Glam, Newport 2013. HSSET 144* v Somerset, Taunton Vale 2012. HST20 58* v Glam, Cardiff 2014 (1st). Glos staff.

Joshua SHAW (Crofton HS, Wakefield; Skills Exchange C, Wakefield) b Wakefield, Yorks 3.1.96. RHB RMF. Debut Yorks 2012, Glos (on loan) 2016.. F/C debut v Durham MCCU, Bristol 2016. Eng U19 to S.Africa 2012/13, v Pak & Bang 2013, to UAE 2013/14 (Tri-Series),v S.Africa 2014. HS 100* (Yorks) v MCCYC, High Wycombe 2017. BB 5/28 (Yorks) v Durham, Harrogate 2014 (match figures of 10/71). HSSET 19 (Yorks) v Glam, Cardiff 2014. BBSET 2/24 (Yorks) v Warwicks, York 2017. HST20 25 (Eng U19) v Yorks, Loughborough 2013 (1st). BBT20 3/25 (Yorks) v Derbys, Derby 2014 (1st). Yorks staff but on loan to Glos.

Thomas Michael John SMITH (Seaford Head Community C) b Eastbourne, Sussex 22.8.87. RHB SLA. Debut Sussex 2004, F/C debut Sussex v S.Lanka A, Hove 2007, debut Surrey 2009, Middx 2010, Gloucs 2013. HS 280 v Durham, Bristol 2015. BB 7/62 (Middx) v Sussex, Horsham 2012. HSSET 67* (Middx) v Somerset, Richmond 2011. BBSET 5/36 (Sussex) v MCCYC, RAF Vine Lane 2008. HST20 31 v Kent, Canterbury CC 2016 (1st). BBT20 4/29 v Glam, Bristol 2013 (2nd). Glos staff.

William Andrew TAVARE (Bristol GS; Loughborough U) b Bristol 1.1.90. RHB RM. Nephew of C.J. (England, Kent, Somerset, MCC, Oxford U). Debut Glos 2006, Somerset 2009, MCCU 2010, F/C debut (Loughborough MCCU) v Kent, Canterbury 2010, debut Northants & Warwicks 2011. HS 179* v Sussex, Frocester CC 2013. HSSET 75 v Kent, Canterbury 2015. BBSET 4/36 v MCCYC, Shenley 2016. HST20 34 v Hants, Clifton College 2017. (1st) Glos staff.

Jack Martin Robert TAYLOR (Chipping Norton S) b Banbury, Oxon 12.11.91. Brother of M.D. (see below). RHB OB. Debut 2007 aged 15 years and 297 days, F/C debut v Derbys, Bristol 2010. HS 179 v Essex, Bishop's Stortford 2015. BB 6/75 v Sussex, Horsham 2010. HSSET 114 v Glam, Bristol 2012. BBSET 4/26 v Hants, Cheltenham College 2011. HST20 97* v Glam, Cardiff C.C. 2012 (1st). BBT20 2/8 v Warwicks, Bristol 2012 (1st). Glos staff.

Matthew David TAYLOR (Chipping Norton S) b Banbury, Oxon 8.7.94. Brother of J.M.R. (see above). RHB LM. Debut 2010 aged 16 years and 60 days. F/C debut v Leics, Bristol 2013. HS 44* v MCC YC, Downend CC 2013. BB 5/50 (and 10/130 in the match) v MCCYC, Lansdown CC 2014. HSSET 37 v Surrey, Cheltenham Vic 2016. BBSET 4/21 v Somerset, Taunton Vale 2012. HST20 51* v Somerset, Taunton Vale 2017 (1st). BBT20 3/15 v Somerset, Bristol 2013 (1st). Glos staff.

Graeme Lourens VAN BUUREN b Pretoria, Transvaal, S.A. 22.8.90. RHB SLA. F/C debut (Northerns) v Griqualand West, Kimberley 2009/10. SA U19s v Eng 2008/09. Debut Glos, Sussex

2015. HS 170* v Glam, Bristol CC 2015. BB 5/70 in the same match. HSSET 0 (Sussex) v Middx, Richmond 2015. BBSET 2/50 in the same match. HST20 57* v Glam, Bristol U 2017 (2nd). BBT20 2/12 v Kent(Bristol CC 2017 (1st). Glos staff.

HAMPSHIRE

HAMPSHIRE
CRICKET

PLAYING RECORDS 2017
Championship – P10 W4 L2 D4 – Winners of the southern group & beaten finalists
2nd XI Trophy – P6 W2 L2 Ab1 NR1 – sixth in the southern group
2nd XI T20 Competition – P14 W8 L4 Ab2 – second in the southern group & beaten finalists

2nd XI SUCCESSES
2nd XI Champions – 1967, 1971, 1981, 1995, 2001
2nd XI Trophy Winners – 2003, 2008
2nd XI T20 –Beaten Finalists 2017

SECOND ELEVEN CHAMPIONSHIP AVERAGES

BATTING	M	I	NO	Runs	HS	Avge	100s	C/S
W R Smith	8	12	1	616	136	56.00	3	12
J H K Adams	3	5	1	219	105	54.75	1	7
I G Holland	6	10	0	506	192	50.60	2	2
C P Wood	4	6	2	176	76*	44.00	-	-
T P Alsop	5	8	2	253	106*	42.16	1	7
A H J A Hart	8	10	5	154	51*	30.80	-	1
C M Dickinson	10	13	0	391	86	30.07	2	21/2
C B Sole	6	8	1	187	75	26.71	-	3
F S Hay	10	16	3	310	59	23.84	-	6
F S Organ	4	7	0	142	38	20.28	-	3
J Goodwin	4	6	2	75	19	18.75	-	4
B J Taylor	8	9	0	168	48	18.66	-	5
T A R Scriven	4	7	0	101	37	14.42	-	2
B J Duggan	5	7	0	98	30	14.00	-	4
M E T Salisbury	7	7	4	38	11*	12.66	-	1
B T J Wheal	4	5	1	20	11	5.00	-	2

BOWLING	O	M	Runs	Wkt	Avge	BB
R J W Topley	40	17	61	7	8.71	4/20
B Mugochi	12.4	2	46	3	15.33	3/46
M S Crane	18	2	85	5	17.00	5/77
C P Wood	80	28	219	11	19.90	4/34
B J Taylor	136.4	25	466	22	21.18	3/6
R A Stevenson	24	6	87	4	21.75	3/33
M E T Salisbury	157.5	36	508	21	24.19	5/82
F H Edwards	42.2	8	147	6	24.50	4/42
I G Holland	148.2	32	481	19	25.31	5/46
B T J Wheal	56.4	10	209	8	26.12	3/35
C B Sole	90.4	15	354	11	32.18	4/69
A H J A Hart	139.5	28	509	15	33.93	3/19

Also bowled – T P Alsop 5-1-33-0; F A Hay 12-2-17-0; R Jerry 9-0-27-2; J B Lintott 6-0-21-0; J I McCoy 36-7-149-2; F S Organ 1-0-6-0; Z Organ 2-0-13-1; T A R Scriven 9-0-56-2; C Searle 7-1-3-10; W R Smith 15-0-77-2.

Also batted – 4 matches – J I McCoy 2, 3*. 2 matches – F H Edwards 0*; J B Lintott 2, 1, 6 (2ct); R A Stevenson 29 (1ct); R J W Topley 18 (1ct). 1 match – J H Barrett 0, 16 (1ct); H R C Came 1, 10; C Campbell 0, 19 (1ct); J Campbell DNB; M A Carberry 19 (1ct); M S Crane 1; C R M Freeston DNB; R Jerry DNB; S W Mead 0, 4; B Mugochi 0; Z Organ DNB; C Searle DNB; O C Soames 11, 10.

SECOND ELEVEN TROPHY AVERAGES

BATTING	M	I	NO	Runs	HS	Avge	100s	C/S
J B J Taylor	4	3	0	263	140	87.66	1	2
W R Smith	5	4	0	252	130	63.00	1	2
A H J A Hart	5	4	1	127	72	42.33	-	-
F S Hay	6	5	0	173	75	34.60	-	-
B J Duggan	5	5	1	93	45	23.25	-	-
J Goodwin	5	4	0	47	23	11.75	-	2
C M Dickinson	6	5	0	54	26	10.80	-	3
J I McCoy	6	4	1	18	14	6.00	-	3

BOWLING	O	M	Runs	Wkt	Avge	BB
I G Holland	10	1	29	4	7.25	4/29
W R Smith	21	0	99	4	24.75	2/38
F S Hay	18	1	114	4	28.50	3/35
B J Taylor	19	0	104	3	34.66	2/48
J I McCoy	24	3	151	4	37.75	3/49
A H J A Hart	26.2	2	167	4	41.75	2/60

Also batted – 3 matches – I G Holland 5, 55; F S Organ 0, 12. 2 matches – T P Alsop 36, 6; S J S Assani 0*, 20*; M E T Salisbury 3*, 1*. 1 match – J H K Adams DNB; J H Barrett 109 (1ct); J Campbell DNB; M S Crane 17*; D A Griffiths DNB; A T E Hazeldine DNB; R A Lock 1; Z MaCaskie 26; S W Mead 3; C B Sole 12; P Wood 15.

Also bowled – S J S Assani 10-1-45-1; J Campbell 6-0-35-0; M S Crane 8-0-33-0; J Goodwin 4-0-57-0; D A Griffiths 8.1-2-23-0; R A Lock 10-0-51-1; M E T Salisbury 10-3-46-2; C B Sole 8-0-37-0; C P Wood 9-1-38-1.

SECOND ELEVEN T20 AVERAGES

BATTING	M	I	NO	Runs	HS	Avge	100s	C/S
T P Alsop	8	8	3	277	68*	55.40	-	4
T A R Scriven	8	7	4	144	42*	48.00	-	2
R A Stevenson	3	3	2	24	19*	24.00	-	-
W R Smith	5	3	0	67	31	22.33	-	1
I G Holland	9	9	2	138	28*	19.71	-	3
C M Dickinson	10	10	0	185	57	18.50	-	7/3
J H K Adams	7	7	1	106	57*	17.66	-	3
F S Organ	10	9	1	130	39	16.25	-	-
F S Hay	10	6	0	92	26	15.33	-	4/1
B J Taylor	10	8	1	102	30	14.57	-	4
C B Sole	9	6	1	70	25	14.00	-	5
B T J Wheal	8	3	2	11	7*	11.00	-	2
C P Wood	7	4	0	23	14	5.75	-	6

BOWLING	O	M	Runs	Wkt	Avge	BB
R J W Topley	15.3	0	76	7	10.85	3/15
B J Taylor	34	0	217	16	13.56	4/23
J B Lintott	26	0	193	13	14.84	4/18
B T J Wheal	24.2	1	153	10	15.30	3/23
M E T Salisbury	28.4	0	198	8	24.75	2/22
I G Holland	26.5	0	175	7	25.00	3/14
C P Wood	19	0	109	4	27.25	2/19
C B Sole	33	0	252	7	36.00	3/10

Also bowled – L A Dawson 8-0-47-1; A H J A Hart 6-0-69-0; Shhad Afridi 4-0-20-0; W R Smith 6-0-45-2; R A Stevenson 1-0-5-0.

Also batted – 8 matches – M E T Salisbury 0*, 0*, 0*, 1. 7 matches – J B Lintott 7, 29 (1ct). 5 matches – A H J A Hart 18*, 12 (1ct). 4 matches – R J W Topley 3, 1 (1ct). 2 matches – M A Carberry 13, 6 (3 ct); L A Dawson 10, 35 (1ct). 1 match – J Garrett 12*; Shahid Afridi 11.

HOME MATCHES: SECOND ELEVEN CHAMPIONSHIP

v Surrey (Ageas Bowl Nursery) – 18-20 April – Surrey 231 (O J D Pope 92; B J Taylor 3/26, R A Stevenson 3/33) & 186 (M S Crane 5/77, C P Wood 4/34) lost to Hants 218 (C P Wood 75; F O E van den Bergh 3/27, G S Virdi 3/55) & 203/3 (W R Smith 108*) by seven wkts.

v Essex (Ageas Bowl Nursery) – 8-10 May – Essex 349 (J A Stamatis 99*, K S Velani 50; I G Holland 5/46, B J Taylor 3/60) & 243 (K S Velani 66; I G Holland 4/90, B J Taylor 3/66) lost to Hants 294/9d (I G Holland 109*; M W Dixon 5/84) & 299/4 (W R Smith 136, I G Holland 89) by six wkts.

v Glamorgan (Basingstoke) – 15-17 May – Glam 287 (N J Selman 78, C J Brown 61; M E T Salisbury 4/50) & 28/0 drew with Hants 185 (C B Sole 59; A G Salter 6/52, T van der Gugten 3/41)

v Sussex (Newclose County Ground, Newport, I of Wight) – 10-12 July – Sussex 93 (B J Taylor 3/6, A H J A Hart 3/19, B T J Wheal 3/35) & 175/6 (B J Taylor 3/17) drew with Hants 202 (A Sakande 5/57)

v Middlesex (Ageas Bowl Nursery) – 24-26 July – Hants 177 (C M Dickinson 60) & 302/8 (J H K Adams 105; J A R Harris 3/50) drew with Middx 82 (M E T Salisbury 4/12, B T J Wheal 3/35)

v Lancashire (Newclose County Ground, Newport, I of Wight) – 5-8 Sept – Hants 248 (C P Wood 76*, F S Hay 59; S Mahmood 4/76) & 66/6 (J J Bohannon 3/8) drew with Lancs 352 (A M Lilley 72; B Mugochi 3/46, C P Wood 3/61)

This was the Final Play-Off for the 2nd XI Championship of 2017. As no play was possible on the final day, Lancashire were awarded the title by virtue of their first innings lead.

HOME MATCHES: FRIENDLIES

v Lancashire (Ageas Bowl Nursery) – 6-7 Apr – Lancs 297 (K R Brown 137; J I McCoy 3/48, R A Stevenson 3/52) & 109/2d (R P Jones 58) drew with Hants 205 (T P Alsop 61; S C Kerrigan 5/37, A M Lilley 3/55) & 89/1.

v Worcestershire (Ageas Bowl Nursery) – 14-17 Aug – Hants 376 (I G Holland 159, A H J A Hart 76, T P Alsop 72; J D Shantry 4/49, C A J Morris 4/80) & 349/6d (T A R Scriven 124*, I G Holland

95, F S Hay 64*; Z Ul-Hassan 3/78) beat Worcs 223 (G H Rhodes 54, A G Milton 54; C P Wood 3/30) & 191 (A G Milton 55; J J Weatherley 5/15)

v Glamorgan (Ageas Bowl Nursery) – 11-14 Sept – Hants 404/9d (F S Organ 104, M H McKiernan 100; S J Pearce 5/69) & inns forfeited drew with Glam inns forfeited & 177/5 (C R Brown 58*)

HOME MATCHES: SECOND ELEVEN TROPHY

v **Unicorns** (Ageas Bowl Nursery) – 25 Apr – Hants 242/8 (W R Smith 130; B S Phagura 3/36, M B Wareing 3/55) beat Unicorns 225/8 (A J Woodland 55*: I G Holland 4/29) by 17 runs.
v **Essex** (Ageas Bowl Nursery) – 11 May – Hants 301 (B J Taylor 140; M E T Salisbury 5/62) beat Essex 250 (T A Shah 77, J A Stamatis 54; J I McCoy 3/49) by 51 runs.
v **Glamorgan** (Ageas Bowl Nursery) – 18 May – Hants 338/9 (W R Smith 86, I G Holland 55, F S Hay 50; O M R Pringle 3/74) v Glam DNB. No result.

HOME MATCHES: SECOND ELEVEN T20 COMPETITION

v **Sussex** (Newclose County Ground, Newport, I of Wight) – 13 July – Match 1 – Sussex 119/9 (B J Taylor 3/31) lost to Hants 123/4 by six wkts.
v **Sussex** (Newclose County Ground, Newport, I of Wight) – 13 July – Match 2 – Sussex 169/6 (D M W Rawlins 59) beat Hants 135/8 (D M W Rawlins 4/15) by 34 runs.
v **Middlesex** (Ageas Bowl Nursery) – 27 July – Match 1 – Hants 145/8 (T P Alsop 56*) lost to Middx 146/1 (T C Lace 80*, R G White 55*) by nine wkts.
v **Middlesex** (Ageas Bowl Nursery) – 27 July – Match 2 – Hants 128/7 lost to Middx 129/6 (M K Andersson 54; J B Lintott 4/18) by four wkts.
v **Surrey** (Ageas Bowl Nursery) – 2 Aug – Match 1 – Match abandoned without a ball bowled.
v **Surrey** (Ageas Bowl Nursery) – 2 Aug – Match 2 – Match abandoned without a ball bowled.
v **Yorkshire** (Arundel) – 10 Aug – Yorks 100 lost to Hants 101/1 (J H K Adams 57*) by nine wkts. *This was the first Semi-Final of the 2017 competition*
v **Sussex** (Arundel) – 10 Aug – Sussex 171/6 (H Z Finch 54) beat Hants 147 (A P Barton 3/9, A Sakande 3/26) by 24 runs. *This was the Final of the 2017 competition*

PLAYERS WHO HAVE REPRESNTED HAMPSHIRE IN THE 2ND XI IN 2017 (47)

J H K Adams	B J Duggan	M E Kantolinna	Shahid Afridi
T P Alsop	F H Edwards	J B Lintott	W R Smith
S J S Assani	*J Emanuel	R A Lock	O C Soames
J H Barrett	C R M Freeston	Z McCaskie	C D Sole
H R C Came	*R Gibson	J I McCoy	R A Stevenson
C Campbell	J Goodwin	S W Mead	B J Taylor
J Campbell	D A Griffiths	B Mugochi	R J W Topley
M A Carberry	A H J A Hart	F S Organ	*J J Weatherley
M S Crane	F S Hay	Z Organ	B T J Wheal
L A Dawson	A T E Hazeldine	M E T Salisbury	C P Wood
C M Dickinson	I G Holland	T A R Scriven	*B Worcester
*B L Draper	R Jerry	C Searle	

HAMPSHIRE CRICKETERS

James Henry Kenneth ADAMS (Sherborne S, Dorset; U Coll, London; Loughborough U) b Winchester, 23.9.80. LHB LM. Debut 1999. F/C debut (British Us) v Sri Lankans, Northampton, 2002. Hants Cap 2006. HS 200* v Derbys, Denby, 2002. BB 2/23 v Warwicks, Walmley, 2005. HSSET 170 v Glam, Cardiff, 2008. BBSET 3/12 v Glam, Pontarddulais, 2001. HST20 107* v Surrey, Purley, 2011 (1st).
Thomas Philip ALSOP b High Wycombe, Bucks, 26.11.95. LHB WK Brother of O J (Hants 2010-12). Debut 2013. F/C debut v Kent, the Ageas Bowl, 2014. Eng U19 to S Africa 2012/13; v S Africa, 2014; v Aus 2015. HS 195 v Sussex, Ageas Bowl Nursery, 2015. BB 1/17 v Lancs, Ageas Bowl Nursery, 2017. HSSET 151 v MCCYC, Ageas Bowl Nursery, 2016. BBSET 0/6 v Sussex, Eastbourne, 2014. HST20 68* v Sussex, Newclose CC, I of Wight, 2017(1st). BBT20 1/38 v Somerset, Ageas Bowl Nursery, 2016 (1st).
Shailen J S ASSANI (Harrow S; Cardiff U) b Brent, Middx, 13.12.96. RHB Debut 2016. HS 15 v Worcs, Ageas Bowl Nursery, 2016. BB 1/30 in the same match. HSSET 20* v Essex, Ageas Bowl Nursery, 2017. BBSET 1/28 v Sussex, Fulking, 2017.
Joseph Hedley BARRETT (Burford S, Oxon) b Chipping Norton, Oxon, 13.12.95. LHB RM. Debut Glos 2010; MCCYC & Notts 2016; Hants & Leics 2017. HS 108 (MCC YC) v Lancs, Urmston, 2017. BB 0/10 (MCCYC) v Sussex, Eastbourne, 2016. HSSET 109 v Sussex, Fulking, 2017. BBSET 0/22 (MCCYC) v Hants, Ageas Bowl Nursery, 2016. HST20 63* (MCC YC) v Durham, Merchant Taylors' S, Northwood, 2017 (2nd). BBT20 2/28 (MCCYC) v Hants, 2016 (1st). HSKO 4 (Glos) v Somerset, Taunton Vale, 2010
Harry Robert Charles CAME (Bradfield Coll) b Hants, 27.8.98. RHB OB. Debut 2016; Kent 2017. Great grandson of R W V Robins, 19 Tests (Eng) 1929/37; Great nephew of RVC Robins (Middx 1953/60). HS 14 v Glam , Ageas Bowl Nursery, 2017.

HSSET 6 v Glam, Newport, 2016.
Cole Rusty CAMPBELL (Hampton Boys S, London) b Hammersmith, London, 11.6.00. RHB OB. Debut 2017. HS 19 v Somerset, Taunton Vale, 2017.
Jack CAMPBELL (Churcher`s Coll, Petersfield) b Portsmouth, 11.11.99. RHB LMF. Debut 2017. BBSET 0/35 v Sussex, Fulking, 2017.
Michael Alexander CARBERRY (St John Rigby RCC) b Croydon, Surrey, 29.9.80. LHB OB. Debut Surrey 1998. F/C debut (Surrey) v Leics, Grace Road, 2001. Debut Kent 2003; debut & Cap Hants 2006. Tests (Eng) 6; 2009/10 to 2013/14 & 6 ODIs. HS 198 (Kent) v Essex, Coggeshall, 2003.HSSET 127 (Surrey) v Sussex, Hove, 2001. HST20 13 v Somerset, Taunton Vale, 2017 (1st). Joins Leicestershire for the 2018 season.
Mason Sydney CRANE (Lancing Coll, Sussex) b Shoreham-by-Sea, Sussex, 18.2.97. RHB LB. Debut 2013. F/C debut v Durham, Ageas Bowl, 2015. Eng U19 to Aus 2014/15; v Aus 2015. HS 45 v Glos, Cheltenham, 2015. BB 5/41 v Sussex, Ageas Bowl Nursery, 2015. HSSET 35 v Surrey, Ageas Bowl Nursery, 2016. BBSET 4/31 v Middx, Radlett, 2014. HST20 9 v Middx, Ageas Bowl Nursery, 2015 (2nd). BBT20 1/5 v Surrey, Purley, 2015 (1st).
Liam Andrew DAWSON (John Bentley S, Calne) b Swindon, Wilts 1.3.90. RHB SLA. Debut 2005 aged 15 years and 112 days, F/C debut v Yorks, Headingley, 2007. Debut MCCYC 2011. Tests 3 (Eng) 2016/17-2017 & 1 ODI. Eng U19 v Pakistan 2007, v N.Zealand 2008 and to S.Africa 2008/09. Hants Cap 2013. HS 200* v MCCYC, West End Nursery, 2010. BB 4/111 v Sussex, Stirlands CC, 2010. HSSET 120 v Sussex, Horsham, 2010. BBSET 6/35 v MCCYC, Vine Lane 2008. HST20 48 v Sussex, Ageas Bowl Nursery, 2011 (2nd). BBT20 2/25v Sussex, Hove, 2015 (2nd). HSKO 18 v Sussex, Stirlands CC, 2010. BBKO 3/43 in the same match. Hants staff.

Calvin Miles DICKINSON (St Edward's S, Oxford) b Durban. KwaZulu-Natal, S Africa, 3.11.96. RHB WK. Debut Worcs 2015; Essex & MCCU 2016. F/C debut (Oxford MCCU) v Worcs. The Parks, 2016. Debut Hants 2017. HS 185 (MCCU) v Warwicks, EFCSG, 2016. HSSET 28 (Essex) v Sussex, Blackstone, 2016. HST20 57 v Somerset, Taunton Vale, 2017 (2nd).

*Ben Liam DRAPER (Burgate S, Fordingbridge) b Salisbury, Wilts, 5.4.98. RHB WK. HS 17 v Glam, Ageas Bowl Nursery, 2017.

Benjamin Jason DUGGAN (Cowes Enterprise Coll) b Newport, Isle of Wight, 28.3.98. LHB SLA. Debut 2015. HS 178 v Worcs, Ageas Bowl Nursery, 2016. HSSET 45 v Essex, Ageas Bowl Nursery, 2017.

Fidel Henderson EDWARDS b St Peter, Barbados, 6.2.82. RHB RF. Tests 55 (WI) 2003 to 2012/13 & 50 ODIs. Debut Hants 2015. F/C debut (Barbados) v Windward Islands, Bridgetown, Barbados, 2001/02. HS 0* v MCCU, Horsham, 2017. BB 4/42 in the same match. BBT20 0/38 v Sussex, Hove, 2015 (1st).

*Joseph (Joe) EMMANUEL Debut 2017. HS 9 v Somerset, Bath, 2017. BB 0/32 in the same match.

Charlie Richard Maxwell FREESTON (Sandown HS, I of Wight; St Mary's Coll) b Liverpool, 4.9.79. RHB RM. Debut 2006. HS 46 v Yorks, West End Nursery, 2006. BB 2/30 in the same match. HSSET 44 v Surrey, Normandy, 2006. BBSET 3/45 v Kent, Bournemouth SC, 2006.

Jordan Laurence Norman GARRETT (Henry Box S) b Oxford 14.5.99. RHB OB. Debut Glos 2014 aged 14 years and 336 days; debut Hants 2017. HS 96* (Glos) v Warwicks, Bristol 2016. HSSET 77 (Glos) v Somerset, Bristol CC 2015. HST20 44 (Glos) v Somerset, Taunton Vale 2017 (2nd). Debut Hants 2017 as a mutually agreed guest for Hants in the 2nd XI T20 competition at Bristol, due to injuries and first eleven call-ups.

* Ryan GIBSON (Fylinghall S & SFC) b Middlesbrough, 22.1.96. RHB RM. Debut Yorks 2012. F/C debut (Yorks) v Pak A, Headingley, 2016. Debut Hants 2017. HS 162* (Yorks) v Leics, York, 2016. BB 3/1 (Yorks) v Northants, York, 2015. HSSET 87 (Yorks) v Durham, York, 2016. BBSET 3/35 (Yorks) v MCC YC, Merchant Taylors' S, Northwood, 2017. HST20 103 (Yorks) v Durham, Marske CC, 2017 (2nd). BBT20 2/37 (Yorks) v Derbys, Harrogate, 2016 (2nd).

Jake GOODWIN (Kingsdown S, Swindon) b Swindon, Wilts, 19.1.98. RHB RM. Debut 2015. List A (T20) debut v Somerset, Ageas Bowl, 2016. Debut MCC YC 2017. HS 131 v Surrey, Ageas Bowl Nursery, 2016. BB 1/47 v Kent, Newclose, I of Wight, 2016. HSSET 44 v Essex, Coggeshall, 2016. BBSET 2/20 v MCCYC, Ageas Bowl Nursery, 2016. HST20 29 v Somerset, Ageas Bowl Nursery, 2016 (1st). BBT20 1/7 v MCCYC, Shenley, 2016 (1st).

David Andrew GRIFFITHS (Sandown HS, IOW) b Newport, IOW 10.9.85. LHB RFM. Debut Hants 2003, F/C debut v Loughborough UCCE, the Rose Bowl, 2006. Debut Kent 2014. HS 70 v Essex, Southend 2009. BB 6/41 v Glam, Bournemouth SC 2007. HSSET 36 v Northants, West End Nursery 2009. BBSET 5/40 v Warwicks, West End Nursery 2006. HST20 14 (Kent) v MCCYC, Canterbury, 2014 (1st). BBT20 4/26 v Kent, Rose Bowl, 2012 (1st).

Asher Hale-bopp Joseph Arthur HART (Ullswater Community Coll, Penrith, Cumberland) b Carlisle, Cumberland 30.3.97. RHB RM. Debut Durham 2015;Hants 2017; F/C debut v Cardiff MCCU, Ageas Bowl, 2017. HS 76 v Worcs, Ageas Bowl Nursery, 2017. BB 3/19 v Sussex, Newclose CC, I of Wight, 2017. HSSET 72 v Kent, Polo Farm SG, Canterbury, 2017. BBSET 2/17 v Notts, Notts SG, 2016. HST20 18* v Sussex, Newclose CC, I of Wight, 2017 (2nd). BBT20 0/16 v Sussex, 2017 (2nd)

Fraser Steven HAY (Trinity Coll, Perth, WA; U of W Australia) b Perth, WA, 9.7.96. RHB RA, Debut 2016. HS 90 v Surrey, Ageas Bowl Nursery, 2016. BB 3/39 v Worcs, Ageas Bowl Nursery, 2016. HSSET 75 v Sussex, Fulking, 2017. BBSET 2/39 v MCCYC, Ageas Bowl Nursery, 2016. HST20 26 v Unc, Great Tew, 2017 (1st). BBT20 2/25 v Surrey, Purley, 2016 (1st).

Andrew Thomas Edward HAZELDINE (St Andrew's Coll, Christchurch, NZ) b Portsmouth, Hants, 13.7.94. LHB LF. Debut Essex, Hants, Somerset & MCCYC 2016. List A (T20) debut (Canterbury, NZ) v C Districts, Nelson, 2017/18. HS 8*

(MCCYC) v Essex, High Wycombe, 2016. BB 5/37 (MCCYC) v Sussex, Eastbourne, 2016. HSSET 7 (MCCYC) v Hants, Ageas Bowl Nursery, 2016. BBSET 2/86 (MCCYC) v Somerset, High Wycombe, 2016. BBT20 2/31 (MCCYC) v Hants, Shenley, 2016 (2nd).

Ian Gabriel HOLLAND (Ringwood Sec Coll, Melbourne, Australia) b Stevens Point, Wisconsin, USA, 3.10.90. RHB RM. Debut Leics 2013; Hants 2015. F/C Debut (Victoria, Aus) v Tasmania, 2015/16. HS 192 v Kent, Polo Farm SG, Canterbury, 2017. BB 6/26 v Kent, Polo Farm SC, Canterbury, 2015. HSSET 101 v Sussex, Ageas Bowl Nursery, 2015. BBSET 4/29 v Unc, Ageas Bowl Nursery, 2017. HST20 28* v Unc, Great Tew, 2017 (2nd). BBT20 3/14 in the same match.

Richard JERRY (St Thomas Senior Sec S, Kerala, India; Kent Adsult Ed; Southampton City Coll) b Ludhiana, Punjab, India, 2.5.92. RHB RA. HS 0 v Somerset, Bath, 2017. BB 2/16 in the same match.

Miles E KANTOLINNA (Bishop Wordsworth GS) b Salisbury, Wiltshire, 5.9.00. RHB WK. Debut 2017. HSSET 2 v Ageas Bowl Nursery, 2017.

Jacob Benedict LINTOTT (Queens Coll, Taunton) b Taunton, Somerset, 22.4.93. RHB SLA. Debut Somerset 2010; Warwicks 2013; Hants 2016. Glos 2017. List A (T20) debut v Somerset, Ageas Bowl, 2017. HS 78 (Somerset) v Surrey, Taunton, 2011. BB 4/111 (Warwicks) v Middx, Merchant Taylors S, Northwood, 2013. HSSET 26 (Warwicks) v Glam, Cardiff CC, 2013. BBSET 3/39 (Somerset) v Surrey, Taunton Vale, 2011. HST20 29 v Sussex, Arundel, 2017 (F). BBT20 4/18 v Middx, Ageas Bowl Nursery, 2017 (2nd).

Richard Anthony LOCK (Whitgift S; Southampton Solent U) b Zim, 2.1.97. LHB OB. Debut Unc 2015; Hants 2017. HSSET 1 v Sussex, Fulking, 2017. BBSET 1/51 in the same match.

Joshua Ian McCOY (Millfield S) b 2.3.98. RHB RFM. Debut 2016. Eng U19 v Sri Lanka, 2016. HS 28* v Middx, Uxbridge CC, 2016. BB 4/52 v Glam, Newport, 2016. HSSET 14 v Essex, Ageas Bowl Nursery, 2017. BBSET 3/49 in the same match. HST20 7* v Somerset, Ageas Bowl Nursery, 2016 (2nd). BBT20 3/24 v Surrey, Purley, 2016 (1st).

Zachary McCASKIE (Christ Church Foundation; Barbados Community Coll) b Barbados 18.11.96. RHB OB. Debut 2016. HS 69 v Glam, Newport, 2016. HSSET 26 v Sussex, Fulking, 2017.

*Matthew Harry "Mattie" McKIERNAN (Lowton HS, Leigh; St John Rigby Coll, Wigan) b Billinge, Merseyside, 14.6.94. RHB LB. Debut Lancs 2011; Northants 2012 (on loan). Ret to Lancs 2013. Debut Leics 2016; Hants 2017. HS 100 v Glam, Ageas Bowl Nursery, 2017. BB 4/64 (Leics) v Northants, Desborough, 2017. HSSET 42 (Lancs) v Leics, Grace Road, 2014. BBSET 3/36 (Lancs) v Yorks, Todmorden, 2013. HST20 2 (Lancs) v Durham, Parkgate, Neston, 2013 (1st). BBT20 2/12 (Lancs) v Derbys, Ormskirk, 2013 (2nd).

S W "Billy" MEAD (Marlborough Coll) b Winchester, 3.2.99. RHB OB. Debut 2015. Great grandson of Stewart Caithie "Billy" Griffith CBE, DFC, TD (Surrey, MCC, Sussex & England [3 Tests 1948-49]) and great nephew of Mike Grenville Griffith (Sussex 1962 to 1972). HS 13 v Surrey, the Ageas Bowl Nursery, 2016. HSSET 3 v Essex, the Ageas Bowl Nursery, 2017.

Brighton Ian MUGOCHI (Prince Edward HS, Zim; Solent U) b Harare, Zim, 23.7.88. LHB SLA.Debut 2017. F/C debut (Centrals, Zim) v Westerns, Bulawayo, 2006/07. HS 0 v Lancs, Newclose CC, I of Wight, 2017. BB 3/46 in the same match.

Felix S ORGAN (Canford S, Dorset) b Sydney, NSW, Australia, 2.6.99. Brother of Z H (below). RHB OB. Debut 2015. F/C debut v Middx, Uxbridge, 2017. Eng U19 v Ind 2017; to S Africa 2017/18. HS 107* v Middx, Uxbridge CC, 2016. BB 2/31 v Glam, Newport, 2016. HSSET 22 v Surrey, Ageas Bowl Nursery, 2016. BBSET 0/12 v Essex, Coggeshall, 2016. HST20 39 v Somerset, Taunton Vale, 2017 (1st). BBT20 1/34 v Somerset, Taunton Vale, 2015 (2nd).

Zachary Huxley ORGAN (Canford S, Wimborne, Dorset) b Sydney, Aus, 11.2.01. Brother of F S (above). RHB OB. Debut 2017. BB 1/13 v Somerset, Taunton Vale, 2017.

Matthew Edward Thomas SALISBURY (Shenfield HS; Anglia RU) b Chelmsford 18.4.93. RHB RMF. Debut Essex 2011; MCC

Un 2012. F/C debut (Cambridge MCCU) v Essex, Fenner's, 2012. Debuts Somerset 2016; Hants 2017. HS 52 (Essex) v Glos, Bishop's Stortford, 2015. BB 6/37 (Essex) v Middx, Billericay, 2014. HSSET 41 (Essex) v Hants, Ageas Bowl Nursery, 2015. BBSET 5/62 (Essex) v Hants, Ageas Bowl Nursery, 2017. HST20 17* (Essex) v Northants, Northampton, 2014 (1st). BBT20 3/37 in the same match.

Thomas Antony R SCRIVEN (Magdalen College S, Oxford) b Oxford, 18.11.98. RHB RMF. Debut 2016. Eng U19 to SA 2017/18. HS 124* v Worcs, Ageas Bowl, 2017. BB 2/37 v Sussex, Newclose CC, I of Wight, 2017. HSSET 26 v Sussex, Horsham, 2016. BBSET 0/20 v Glam, Newport, 2016. HST20 42* v Glos, Clifton Coll, 2017 (1st),

Christopher SEARLE (Hampton S) b Frimley, Surrey, 23.12.98. RHB RMF. Debut 2016. HS 13 v Essex, Coggeshall, 2016. BB 1/21 v Glam, Newport, 2016.

Sahibzada Mohammed SHAHID Khan ARFIDI b Khyber Agency, 1.3.80. Debut & F/C debut (Combined XI) v Eng A, Karachi, 1995/96. Debut Karachi Whites 1995/96; Habib Bank & Karachi 1997/98; MCC 2001; Leics & Cap 2001; Derbys 2003; Griqualand West 2003/04; Kent 2004; Ireland 2006; Sind 2007/08; S Australia 2009/10; Hants 2011; Northants 2015. Tests (Pak) 27 (1998/99 to 2010) & 393 ODIs. HST20 38* v Surrey, Purley, 2011 (1st). BBT20 3/21 v Sussex, Ageas Bowl, 2016 (1st).

William Rew SMITH (Bedford S; Collingwood Coll, Durham U; Staffordshire U) b Luton, Beds, 28.9.82. RHB OB. Debut Notts 1999; F/C Debut (Notts) v West Indies A, Trent Bridge, 2002. Debut Durham 2007; Cap 2009; debut Hants 2014. HS 293 (Notts) v Durham, Gosforth, 2005. BB 4/62 (Durham) v Northants, Milton Keynes, 2011. HSSET 130 v Unc, Ageas Bowl Nursery, 2017. BBSET (Notts) 4/16 v Middx, Worksop Coll, 2005. HST20 57* (Durham) v Yorks, Chester-le-Street, 2011 (1st). BBT20 2/15 v Yorks, Chester-le-Street, 2011 (2nd). HSKO 32 (Durham) v Lancs, Parkgate, Neston, 2010. Re-joins Durham for the 2018 season.

Oliver Courtenay SOAMES (Cheltenham Coll, Loughborough U) b Kingston-upon-Thames, Surrey, 27.10.95. RHB RM OB. Debut Hants & MCCU 2017. HS 106* (MCCU) v Kent, Beckenham, 2017. BB 0/8 (MCCU) v Sussex, Hastings, 2017.

Christopher Barclay SOLE (Merchiston Castle S) b Edinburgh 27.2.94. RHB RM. Brother of T.B. (Northants 2015) son of D. (Scotland and British Lions rugby). Nephew of C.R.Trembath (Glos 1982/84). Debut 2016. F/C debut (Scotland) v UAR (Ayr) 2016. HS 75 v MCCU, Horsham, 2017. BB 4/69 v Somerset, Taunton Vale, 2017. HSSET 12 v Kent, Polo Farm SG, Canterbury, 2017. BBSET 0/37 in the same match. HST20 25 v Glos, Clifton Coll, 2017 (2nd). BBT20 3/10 v Somerset, Taunton Vale, 2017 (2nd).

Ryan Antony STEVENSON (King Edward VI Comm Coll, Totnes, Devon) b Torquay, Devon, 2.4.92. RHB RMF. Debut 2015.

F/C debut v Durham, Chester-le-Street, 2015. HS 97* v Surrey, Ageas Bowl Nursery, 2016. BB 4/20 v Kent, Polo Farm SC, Canterbury, 2015. HSSET 5 v Sussex, Horsham, 2016. HST20 37* v Somerset, Ageas Bowl Nursery, 2016 (1st). BBT20 0/5 v Unc, Great Tew, 2017 (1st).

Bradley Jacob TAYLOR (Eggar's S, Alton) b Winchester, 14.3.97. RHB OB. Debut 2013. F/C debut v Lancs, Southport, 2013. Eng U19 v S Africa, 2014; to Aus 2014/15; v Aus 2015. HS 87 v Notts, Notts SG, 2016. BB 5/86 v MCCU, the Ageas Bowl, 2014. HSSET 140 v Essex, Ageas Bowl Nursery, 2014. BBSET 4/28 v Glam, Newport, 2016. HST20 30 v Somerset, Taunton Vale, 2017 (1st). BBT20 4/23 v Unc, Great Tew, 2017 (1st). Hants staff.

Reece James William TOPLEY (Royal Hospital S, Holbrook) b Ipswich, Suffolk 12.2.94. ODI 10 (Eng) 2015 to 2015/16 & 6 T20s. RHB LFM (Son of TD Essex, Surrey.1985 to 1994) Debut Essex 2010. F/C debut (Essex) v Cambridge MCCU, Fenner's, 2011. Essex Cap 2013. HS 26 (Essex) v Middx, Billericay, 2015. BB 4/20 (Essex) v Derbys, Derby, 2013 & v MCCU, Horsham, 2017. HSSET 17 (Essex) v Glos, Bristol, 2014. BBSET 3/41 (Essex) v Hants, Rose Bowl Nursery, 2012. HST20 6 (Essex) v Leics, Chelmsford, 2014 (2nd). BBT20 3/15 v Somerset, Taunton Vale, 2017 (1st).

***Joe James WEATHERLEY** (King Edward VI S, Southampton) b Winchester, 19.1.97. RHB OB. Debut 2014. Eng U19 to Aus 2014/15. F/C debut v Cardiff MCCU, Ageas Bowl, 2016. HS 180* v Notts, Notts SG, 2016. BB 5/15 v Worcs, Ageas Bowl Nursery, 2017. HSSET 111 v Glam, Ageas Bowl Nursery, 2015. BBSET 1/31 v Kent, Polo Farm Nursery, 2015. HST20 92 v Sussex, Ageas Bowl Nursery, 2016 (2nd). BBT20 1/23 v MCCYC, Shenley, 2016 (2nd).

Bradley Thomas James WHEAL b Durban, KwaZulu-Natal, S Africa, 28.8.96. RHB RFM. Debut & F/C debut v Middx, the Ageas Bowl, 2015. HS 23 v Surrey, Ageas Bowl Nursery, 2015. BB 7/42 v Middx, Radlett, 2015. HSSET 23* v Essex, Ageas Bowl Nursery,2015. BBSET 3/33 v Glam, Ageas Bowl Nursery, 2015. HST20 7* v Somerset, Taunton Vale, 2017 (1st). BBT20 3/17 v MCCYC, Shenley, 2016 (1st).

Christopher Philip WOOD (Alton Coll) b Basingstoke 27.6.90. RHB LFM. Debut 2007. F/C debut v Oxford MCCU, the Parks, 2010. Eng U19 to S.Africa 2008/09; v Bangladesh 2009. HS 143 v Middx, Ageas Bowl, 2014. BB 9/48 v Kent, Canterbury, 2010. HSSET 58 v Essex, Southend-on-Sea, 2011. BBSET 5/23 v Northants, Milton Keynes, 2010. HST20 44 v Sussex, the Ageas Bowl Nursery, 2011 (1st). BBT20 2/5 v Surrey, Purley, 2015 (1st). Hants Staff.

***Bailey WORCESTER** (Woodhouse Grove S, Bradford) b Leeds, 2.8.97. RHB WK. Debut 2017 v Sussex, Horsham, but did not bat.

KENT

PLAYING RECORDS 2017
Championship – P9 W3 L2 D4 – fourth in the southern section
2nd XI Trophy – P6 W2 L3 Ab1 – eighth in the southern section
2nd XI T20 Competition – P12 W6 L5 Ab1 - fourth in the southern section

2nd XI SUCCESSES
Championship – Champions – 1961, 1969, 1970, 1976, 2002, 2005, 2006, 2012
(Joint Champions with Yorkshire in 1987)
2nd XI Trophy – Winners – 1999, 2002
2nd XI T20 Competition – Winners of the southern group and beaten finalists 2015

SECOND ELEVEN CHAMPIONSHIP AVERAGES

BATTING	M	I	NO	Runs	HS	Avge	100s	C/S
A J Ball	3	5	2	239	86	79.66	-	1
C J Basey	5	8	2	350	99	58.33	-	3
J J Weatherley	6	9	1	394	104*	49.25	1	4
A J Blake	3	5	1	174	86	43.50	-	1
Z Crawley	7	12	0	467	134	38.91	1	6
G Fatouros	5	8	1	264	121	37.71	1	3
O G Robinson	5	9	1	272	117	34.00	1	13/2
C J Haggett	4	7	2	169	72*	33.80	-	1
K C Appleby	9	14	0	424	68	30.28	-	5
A E N Riley	7	6	2	120	37*	30.00	-	8
G Stewart	7	7	2	136	50*	27.20	-	2
Imran Qayyum	5	7	2	88	31	17.60	-	-
J M Cox	3	3	0	47	39	15.66	-	8
S R Dickson	2	3	0	42	26	14.00	-	2
C F Hartley	5	6	2	56	21*	14.00	-	3
M D Hunn	4	4	2	18	12*	9.00	-	1
H R C Ellison	3	5	0	37	17	7.40	-	2

BOWLING	O	M	Runs	Wkt	Avge	BB
H R Bernard	97.5	16	341	17	20.05	5/20
G Stewart	137	33	406	19	21.36	4/54
Imran Qayyum	104.3	16	373	15	24.86	5/50
A E N Riley	89	18	228	9	25.33	3/33
A J Ball	62	12	199	7	28.42	4/15
C J Haggett	61	10	232	7	33.14	3/27
M D Hunn	87	17	293	8	36.62	3/60
I A A Thomas	35	5	157	4	39.25	3/100
C F Hartley	83	15	332	8	41.50	4/48
J W N Gray	38	4	144	3	48.00	2/31

Also Bowled – J S Bassan 7-1-18-0; Z Crawley 19-0-96-1; W R S Gidman 9-2-31-0; O A M Hills 30-4-112-2; D Paul 1-0-4-0; S Reeves 15-0-48-1; T Richards 5-1-15-1; M Richardson 12-2-53-2; J J Weatherley 9-1-41-1.

Also Batted – 5 matches – H R Bernard DNB (2ct). 3 matches – J W N Gray DNB (1ct); O A M Hills 0 (1ct). 2 matches – I A A Thomas DNB (1ct). 1 match – J S Bassan DNB; H R C Came 5, 9; W Garvey DNB; W R S Gidman 47, 44 (1ct); Harsh Kumar 22, 38*; S M Imtiaz 3, 0; B A D Manenti DNB (1ct); D Paul 21; S Reeves 9, 11; T Richards DNB; M Richardson 7*; R A Smith 10.

SECOND ELEVEN TROPHY AVERAGES

BATTING	M	I	NO	Runs	HS	Avge	100s	C/S
A J Ball	3	3	1	226	152*	113.00	1	4
K C Appleby	4	4	1	152	59	50.66	-	1
C J Haggett	4	4	0	178	88	44.50	-	3
O G Robinson	5	4	0	90	46	22.50	-	5/1
J J Weatherley	3	3	0	65	50	21.66	-	-
Z Crawley	5	5	0	103	40	20.60	-	1
Imran Qayyum	3	3	1	27	16*	13.50	-	-
C F Hartley	4	3	0	22	10	7.33	-	-

BOWLING	O	M	Runs	Wkt	Avge	BB
M D Hunn	22	4	121	6	20.16	4/48
C J Haggett	38.5	2	222	9	24.66	4/54
H R Bernard	18	0	109	3	36.33	2/56
Imran Qayyum	28	0	146	4	36.50	2/49
C F Hartley	36	2	219	6	36.50	3/63

Also Bowled – A J Ball 18-0-116-1; J S Basan 10-0-56-1; Z Crawley 10-0-62-1; W R S Gidman 4-1-5-0; J W N Gray 4-0-27-0; S Reeves 2-0-26-0; A E N Riley 10-0-59-1; G Stewart 12-0-80-1; I A A Thomas 25-1-144-2; A D Tillcock 2-0-15-0; J J Weatherley 2-0-21-0

Also Batted – 3 matches – G Fatouros 37, 50; M D Hunn 0*, 6 (1ct); I A A Thomas 1 (1ct). 2 matches – H R Bernard 1*; A J Blake 4, 13; G Stewart 26, 20*. 1 match – J S Bassan 1*; M H Cross 28 (2ct); W R S Gidman 22 (2ct); J W N Gray DNB (1ct); G J Harte 33; S Reeves 4; A E N Riley 13; A P Rouse 1; A D Tillcock 1..

SECOND ELEVEN T20 AVERAGES

BATTING	M	I	NO	Runs	HS	Avge	100s	C/S
Z Crawley	11	11	2	404	109*	44.88	1	5
S R Dickson	4	4	1	126	68	42.00	-	2
C F Hartley	5	4	2	37	18*	18.50	-	2
A J Ball	4	3	0	51	27	17.00	-	1
A J Blake	6	6	1	69	31	13.80	-	-
J J Weatherley	9	6	0	79	27	13.16	-	8
A E N Riley	11	4	3	13	5	13.00	-	3
O G Robinson	5	3	0	39	24	13.00	-	1
Imran Qayyum	8	4	1	37	118	12.33	-	3
K C Appleby	10	9	2	77	17	11.00	-	4
C J Haggett	8	5	0	34	16	6.80	-	5
G Stewart	9	6	3	20	17*	6.66	-	2
B A D Manenti	3	3	0	14	11	4.66	-	2

BOWLING	O	M	Runs	Wkt	Avge	BB
C F Hartley	15.1	0	78	8	9.75	3/20
A J Ball	13.4	0	76	6	12.66	3/14
O A M Hills	9	0	77	5	15.40	2/12
B A D Manenti	8.2	0	63	4	15.75	2/21
C J Haggett	27.4	0	211	13	16.23	4/22
G Stewart	28.5	0	217	9	24.11	3/23
A E N Riley	27	0	206	8	25.75	2/16
Imran Qayyum	29	1	207	6	34.50	2/21

Also Bowled – H R Bernard 13.5-0-108-1; A J Blake 0.1-0-4-0; Z Crawley 1-0-5-0; J W N Gray 1-0-16-1; A F Milne 7-0-51-2; J D S Neesham 8-0-66-2; J J Weatherley 2-0-18-0.

Also Batted – 4 matches – H R Bernard 3*. 3 matches – J M Cox 12 (4ct & 1st); M H Cross 25, 14 (1ct); O A M Hills 4* (2ct); A F Milne 33*, 1; J D S Neesham 78*, 81 (1ct). 2 matches – C J Basey 22, 7 (1ct); S W Billings1*, 84; G Fatouros 0, 4 (1ct); A P Rouse 53 (2ct). 1 match – M Grant 12; J W N Gray DNB; R A Smith DNB.

HOME MATCHES: SECOND ELEVEN CHAMPIONSHIP

v Sussex (Polo Farm SC, Canterbury) – 9-11 May – Kent 392 (Z Crawley 134, O G Robinson 117; A Sakande 6/96) & 245/9d (S G Whittingham 5/58) beat Sussex 246 (H R Bernard 4/75) & 227 (A J Robson 70; Imran Qayyum 5/50) by 164 runs.

v Hampshire (Polo Farm SC, Canterbury) – 22-24 May – Hants 553/8d (I G Holland 192, W R Smith 130, C M Dickinson 86; G Stewart 4/100) & 7/0 beat Kent 164 (M E T Salisbury 4/49, A H J A Hart 3/30) & 394 (G Fatouros 121, J J Weatherley 53, Z Crawley 51; M E T Salisbury 5/82) by 10 wkts.

v Surrey (Beckenham) – 5-7 June – Kent 337/4d (C J Basey 99, K C Appleby 68, Z Crawlwy 66, G Fatouros52; M W Pillans 3/73) & inns forfeited beat Surrey inns forfeited 125 (H R Bernard 5/20, C J Haggett 3/27) by 212 runs.

v Essex (Polo Farm SC, Canterbury) – 17-19 July – Essex 257 (K S Velani 76, K S Velani 59; G Stewart 4/54) drew with Kent 276 (A J Ball 58, J J Weatherley 56; A P Beard 4/58, S J Cook 3/58) & 196/6 (A J Ball 57*)

HOME MATCHES: FRIENDLIES

v Leicestershire (Beckenham) – 31 July to 3 Aug – Leics 457 (A Raine 66, E J H Eckersley 66, N J Dexter 62, B M W Mike 59, P J Horton 58; O A M Hills 3/37) & 152/5d lost to Kent 293/3d (J J Weatherley 135*, Z Crawley 103) & 320/9 (J J Weatherley 111, A J Ball 85; D Manthorpe 4/86) by one wkt.

v Essex (Beckenham) – 28-30 Aug – Essex 269 (B M J Allison 51, J S Rymell 50; M D Hunn 5/61) & 254/4d (R K Patel 96, W E L Buttleman 72) drew with Kent 123 (O S Bocking 4/32, M W Dixon 3/27) & 203/2 (K Ali 81, W R S Gidman 73*)

COMBINED FRIENDLY MATCHES INVOLVING KENT

Essex & Kent v Durham (Billericay) – 10 Apr – Essex & Kent 239 (C J Haggett 55, A J Ball 53; A J Hickey 3/36, B J McCarthy 3/48) beat Durham 158/9 (G J Harte 52) by 68 runs (DLS).

Essex & Kent v Durham (Billericay) – 11-12 Apr – Durham 385/9d (G Clark 125, A J Hickey 97, J Coughlin 58, E J Hurst 51*; Imran Qayyum 5/70) & 250/7d (G Clark 110; Imran Qayyum 3/86) beat Essex & Kent 347 (C J Taylor 68, A J Blake 52, W E L Buttleman 50*; G H I Harding 4/87, W J Weighell 3/31) & 232 (A J Ball 97, C J Taylor 87; G H I Harding 5/49, L J Hurt 4/43) by 56 runs.

Kent & Northamptonshire v Warwickshire (Canterbury) – 13-16 June – Kent & Northants 241 (C J Basey 57; O J Hannon-Dalby

3/41, M R Adair 3/55) & 425 (S A Zaib 114, J M Kettleborough 84, H R D Adair 69; Sukhjit Singh 5/87, G D Panayi 3/74) lost to Warwicks 255 (S R Hain 115, A J Mellor 60; R J Gleeson 6/78, M D Hunn 3/61) & 415/3 (A R I Umeed 174, S R Hain 149*) by seven wkts.

Kent & Northamptonshire v Scotland A (Northampton) – 12-14 Sept – Kent & Northants 329 (A P Rouse 108, S A Zaib 61; A C Evans 4/84, S M Sharif 3/67) & 151/9d (A C Evans 5/66, S M Sharif 3/29) lost to Scotland A 99 (N L Buck 4/35, G Wade 3/22) & 382/7 (C S MacLeod 145, S M Sharif 75*, M H Cross 63) by three wkts.

HOME MATCHES: SECOND ELEVEN TROPHY

v Gloucestershire (Beckenham) – 3 May – Kent 332/3 (A J Ball 152*, C J Haggett 88) beat Glos 263/5 (G T Hankins 97, B S Gilmour 63, M A H Hammond 60) by five runs (DLS).

v Sussex (Canterbury) – 8 May – Sussex 222/7 (N R Welch 72*) beat Kent 133 by 89 runs.

v Hampshire (Polo Farm SC, Canterbury) – 25 May – Hants 279 (B J Taylor 81, A H J A Hart 72; C J Haggett 4/54) lost to Kent 283/8 (K C Appleby 59, G Fatouros 50; F S Hay 3/35) by two wkts.

HOME MATCHES: SECOND ELEVEN T20 COMPETITION

v Middlesex (Polo Farm SC, Canterbury) – 3 July – Match 1 – Kent 149/8 (G F B Scott 3/10, T N Walallawita 3/26) beat Middx 118 (C J Haggett 4/22) by 31 runs.

v Middlesex (Polo Farm SC, Canterbury) – 3 July – Match 2 – Kent 219/1 (Z Crawley 109*, J D S Neesham 78*) beat Middx 173/8 (C J Haggett 4/36) by 46 runs.

v Surrey (Polo Farm SC, Canterbury) – 5 July – Match 1 – Kent 144/8 (A A P Atkinson 3/24) lost to Surrey 150/1 (O J D Pope 81*, W G Jacks 50) by nine wkts.

v Surrey (Polo Farm SC, Canterbury) – 5 July – Match 2 – Kent 188/3 (J D S Neesham 81, Z Crawlwy 59) beat Surrey 167/7 (G Stewart 3/23) by 21 runs.

v Essex (Polo Farm SC, Canterbury) – 20 July – Match 1- Match abandoned without a ball bowled.

v Essex (Polo Farm SC, Canterbury) – 20 July – Match 2- Essex 112 lost to Kent 118/3 (Z Crawley 50) by seven wkts.

PLAYERS WHO HAVE REPRESENTED KENT 2nd XI IN 2017 (43)

*K Ali	M H Cross	O A M Hills	T Richards
K C Appleby	H R C Ellison	M D Hunn	M Richardson
A J Ball	G Fatouros	Imran Qayyum	A E N Riley
C J Basey	W Garvey	S M Imtiaz	O G Robinson
J S Bassan	W R S Gidman	*H Kingston	A P Rouse
H R Bernard	M Grant	B A D Manenti	R A Smith
S W Billings	J W N Gray	A F Milne	G Stewart
A J Blake	C J Haggett	J D S Neesham	A D Tillcock
H R C Came	G J Harte	*W T O'Donnell	I A A Thomas
J M Cox	Harsh Kumar	D Paul	J J Weatherley
Z Crawley	C F Hartley	S Reeves	

KENT CRICKETERS

Kai Charles APPLEBY (Kent Coll, Canterbury; Canterbury Acad) b Canterbury, 5.2.98. RHB LB WK. Debut 2016. HS 68 v Surrey, Beckenham, 2017. HSSET 64 v Glam, Canterbury, 2016. HST20 17 v Sussex, E Grinstead, 2017 (2nd).

Adam James BALL (Beths GS, Bexley) b Greenwich 1.3.93. RHB LMF. Debut 2009 aged 16 years and 136 days. F/C debut v Glos, Canterbury, 2011. Eng U19 to New Zealand 2009/10; v Sri Lanka 2010; to Sri Lanka, 2010/11; v South Africa, 2011; to Bangladesh & to Australia 2011/12; to Australia, World Cup, 2011/12. HS 125 v Surrey, Whitgift S, 2013. BB 7/26 v Sussex, Canterbury, 2015. HSSET 152* v Glos, Beckenham, 2017. BBSET 3/29 v Hants, Maidstone, 2012. HST20 74* v MCCYC, Beckenham, 2016 (1st). BBT20 3/14 v Unc, Saffron Walden, 2017 (1st). Released at the end of the 2017 season.

Calum J BASEY (Langley Park Boys S, Bromley) b Croydon, Surrey, 28.1.96. RHB WK. Debut 2017. HS 99 v Surrey, Beckenham, 2017. HST20 22 v v Sussex, E Grinstead, 2017 (1st).

Jasdev Singh BASSAN (Harris Acad, Falconwood, Bexley; Leeds Met U) b Sidcup, 11.4.96. RHB SLA. Debut 2015. HS 0 v Middx, Radlett, 2015. BB 2/31 v Somerset, Taunton Vale, 2015. HSSET 0 v Glos, Canterbury, 2015. BBSET 0/27 in the same match. BBT20 2/20 v Surrey, Maidstone, 2015 (1st).

Hugh Robert BERNARD (Archbishop's S, Canterbury) b Canterbury, 14.9.96. RHB RMF. Debut Kent 2014. F/C debut (Kent) v Glam, Canterbury, 2016. Debut Derbys 2017. Eng U19 to Aus, 2014/15; v Aus 2015. HS 14* v Glos, Polo Farm SG, Canterbury, 2016. BB 5/20 v Surrey, Beckenham, 2017. HSSET 7*v Hants, Canterbury, 2014. BBSET 4/41 v Glos, Canterbury, 2015. HS T20 5* v Essex, Billericay, 2016 (1st). BBT20 4/22 v Durham, Arundel, 2015 (SF). Released at the end of the 2017 season.

Samuel William BILLINGS (Haileybury & Imperial Coll) b Pembury 15.6.91. RHB WK. Debut 2007 aged 16 years and 46 days. F/C debut (Loughborough MCCU) v Northants, Loughborough, 2011. Kent Cap 2015. 13 ODIs (Eng) 2015-2017. HS 152 v Glos, Bristol, 2012. BB 1/14 v Glos, Beckenham, 2012. HSSET 180* v Glos, Beckenham, 2012. HST20 84* v Unc, Saffron Walden, 2017 (2nd). Kent Staff.

Alexander (Alex) James BLAKE (Hayes S; Leeds Met U) b Farnborough, Kent 25.1.89. LHB RM. Debut 2005, F/C debut v the New Zealanders, Canterbury, 2008. Kent Cap 2017. Eng U19 to Malaysia, 2006/07. HS 206 v Somerset, Beckenham 2009. BB 5/17 v Middx, Richmond 2006. HSSET 151 v Hants, Polo Farm, Canterbury, 2015. BBSET 5/31 (inc hat-trick) v Hants,

Bournemouth SC 2008. HST20 69 v Hants, Ageas Bowl, 2014 (1st). BBT20 0/4 v Middx, Arundel, 2015 (F). & v Sussex, E Grinstead, 2017 (2nd). Kent staff.

Harry Robert Charles CAME (Bradfield Coll) b Hants, 27.8.98. RHB OB. Debut 2016; Kent 2017. Great grandson of R W V Robins, 19 Tests (Eng) 1929/37; Great nephew of RVC Robins (Middx 1953/60). HS 14 (Hants) v Glam , Ageas Bowl Nursery, 2017. HSSET 6 (Hants) v Glam, Newport, 2016.

Jordan Matthew COX (Felsted S) b Margate, 21.10.00. RHB WK. Debut 2017. HS 39 v MCCU, Beckenham, 2017. HST20 12 v Glos, Longwood, 2017 (2nd).

Zak CRAWLEY (Tonbridge S; Tonbridge SFC) b Orpington, 3.2.98. RHB RM. Debut 2013 aged 15 years & 199 days. F/C debut v West Indians, Canterbury, 2017. HS 134 v Sussex, Polo Farm SG, 2017. BB 1/50 v Hants, Polo Farm SG, 2017. HSSET 114* v Hants, Ageas Bowl Nursery, 2016. BBSET 1/20 v Somerset, Taunton Vale, 2017. HST20 109* v Middx, Polo Farm SG, Canterbury, 2017 (2nd). BBT20 0/5 v Glos, Longwood, Bristol, 2017 (2nd). Kent Staff.

Matthew Henry CROSS (Robert Gordon Coll; Loughborough U) b Aberdeen, Scotland, 15.10.92. RHB WK. Debut Scotland A 2009; 32 ODIs & 23 T20s (Scotland), 2013 to date. Debut Notts 2011. F/C debut (Loughborough MCCU) v Sussex, Hove, 2013. Debut Leics 2015; Essex 2016; Kent, MCC YC & Northants 2017. HS 105* (Notts) v MCCU, Notts Sports Ground, 2012. HSSET 80 (Notts) v Derbys, Notts SG, 2014. HST20 69 (MCC YC) v Merchant Taylors' S, Northwood, 2017 (1st).

Sean Robert DICKSON b Johannesburg, Transvaal, S Africa, 2.9.91. RHB RM. Debut Somerset 2010; F/C debut (Northerns) v Border, United CC, E London, E Cape, S Africa, 2013/14; debut Kent 2015. HS 177 v Essex, Maidstone, 2015. BB 1/28 v MCC YC, High Wycombe, 2015. HSSET 124 v Middx, Radlett, 2015. HST20 108 v MCC YC (High Wycombe, 2015 (2nd). BBT20 0/19 v MCC YC (High Wycombe, 2015 (1st). Kent Staff.

Harry Richard Clive ELLISON (Millfield S; Anglia Ruskin U) b Canterbury, Kent, 22.2.93. RHB OB. F/C debut (Cambridge MCCU) v Essex, Fenner's, 2014. Debut MCCU 2015; Kent & Northants 2017. HS 68 (Northants) v Yorks, Weetwood, 2015.

Gerasimos FATOUROS (Christchurch GS, Perth, W Australia) b Johannesburg, Gauteng, S Africa, 21.7.97. RHB OB. Debut Kent 2016; Essex 2016. HS 121 v Hants, Polo Farm SG, Canterbury, 2017. HSSET 98 v Glam, Canterbury, 2016. HST20 56 v Glos, Polo Farm SG, Canterbury, 2016 (2nd). BBT20 0/7 v Surrey, Purley, 2016 (2nd).

46

William Michael GARVEY (Chatham GS for Boys; Sir Joseph Williamson`s Mathematical School for Boys; Brighton U) b Chatham, 25.9.89. Debut 2017.

William (Will) Robert Simon GIDMAN (Wycliffe Coll, Glos; Berks Coll of Agriculture) b High Wycombe, Bucks, 14.2.85. Younger brother of A P R (Glos, Otago & Worcs, 2001 to date). LHB RM. Debut Glos 2003; MCC YC 2004; Worcs 2005; Durham 2006; F/C debut (Durham) v Sri Lanka A, Chester-le-Street, 2007; debut Glos & Cap 2011; Notts 2015; Kent 2017. HS 137* (Notts) v Kent, Birley's Field, Canterbury, 2016. BB 6/28 (Durham) v Scotland, Norton-on-Tees, 2008. HSSET 78* (MCC YC) v Hants, Bournemouth SC, 2005. BBSET 4/18 (MCC YC) v Hants, High Wycombe, 2005. HST20 60* (Notts) v Yorks, Harrogate (2nd). BBT20 2/43 (Notts) v Yorks, Harrogate, 2015 (1st). HSKO 46 (Durham) v Lancs, Parkgate Neston, 2010. BBKO 2/31 in the same match.

M GRANT Debut 2017. HST20 12 v Surrey, Polo Farm SG, 2017 (1st).

Jan Willem Nall GRAY (Simon Langton GS for Boys) b Ashford, 1.1.99. RHB LB. Debut 2016. BB 2/29 v Sussex, Blackstone, 2016. BBSET 0/27 v Glos, Beckenham, 2017. BBT20 1/16 v Glos, Longwood, Bristol, 2017 (1st).

Calum John HAGGETT (Crispin S & Millfield S, Street) b Taunton, Somerset, 30.10.90. LHB RFM. Debut Somerset 2005 aged 14 years and 241 days. Debut Hants & Kent 2012. F/C debut v MCCU, Canterbury, 2013. England U19 to Bangladesh 2009/10. HS 148 v Hants, Newclose, I of Wight, 2016. BB 4/50 v Leics, Grace Road, 2012. HSSET 88 v Glos, Beckenham, 2017. BBSET 6/27 v Glos, Maidstone, 2014. HST20 47 (Somerset) v Glam, Taunton Vale, 2011 (2nd). BBT20 4/22 v Middx, Polo Farm SG, Canterbury, 2017 (1st). Kent Staff.

HARSH KUMAR (Chadwell Heath S, London; Shenfield HS) b Gaya, Bihar, India, 24.2.00. RHB RFM. Debut 2017. HS 38* v MCCU, Beckenham, 2017.

Gareth Jason HARTE (King Edward VII HS, Johannesburg) b Johannesburg, Transvaal, S Africa, 15.3.93. RHB RM. Debut Somerset & Middx 2014; Kent 2014; MCCYC & Sussex 2016; Durham 2017. List A (T20) debut (Durham) v Lancs, Old Trafford, 2017. HS 199 (Sussex) v Surrey, New Malden, 2016. BB 4/47 (MCCYC) v Glam, Panteg, 2016. HSSET 124* (Durham) v Worcs, New Road, 2017. BBSET 2/29 (Sussex) v Glam, St Fagans, 2016 . HST20 61 (Durham) v Warwicks, S Northumberland, 2017 (2nd). BBT20 0/21 v Hants, Ageas Bowl, 2014 (2nd).

Charles Frederick HARTLEY (Millfield S) b Redditch, Worcs, 4.1.94. RHB RMF. Debut 2013. F/C debut v Leics, Grace Road, 2014. HS 71* v Essex, Maidstone, 2013. BB 5/19 v Surrey, Polo Farm Sports Complex, Canterbury, 2014. HSSET 60* v Glos, Maidstone, 2014. BBSET 4/59 v Essex, Maidstone, 2013. HST20 39* v Surrey, Purley, 2016 (2nd). BBT20 3/29 v Surrey, Purley, 2016 (1st). Released at the end of the 2017 season.

Oliver Alexander M HILLS b Maidstone, 14.8.99. RHB LMF. Debut 2017. HS 0 v Essex, Polo Farm SG, 2017. BB 2/46 in the same match. HST20 4* v Glos, Longwood, Bristol, 2017 (2nd). BBT20 2/12 in the same match.

Matthew David HUNN (St Joseph's Coll, Ipswich) b Colchester, Essex, 22.3.94. RHB RFM. Debuts Essex 2012, Kent 2013. F/C debut v Lancs, Canterbury, 2013. HS 46* v Essex, Billericay, 2016. BB 6/93 v Middx, Canterbury, 2016. HSSET 15* v Essex, Halstead, 2014. BBSET 4/48 v Somerset, Taunton Vale, 2017. HST20 1 v Essex, Billericay, 2016 (1st). BBT20 4/20 v MCC YC, High Wycombe, 2015 (1st). Kent staff.

IMRAN QAYYUM (Villiers HS, Southall; Greenford SFC, Southwark; City U, London) b Ealing, London, 23.5.93. RHB SLA. Debut Kent, Northants, Sussex, Unc A, 2013. F/C debut v Northants, Northampton, 2016. HS 68* v MCC YC, High Wycombe, 2015. BB 6/58 v Middx, Radlett, 2013. HSSET 20 v Unc, Long Marston, Herts, 2014. BBSET 4/43 v Hants, Ageas Bowl Nursery, 2016. HST2011* v Middx, Polo Farm SG, Canterbury, 2017 (1st). BBT20 3/14 v Sussex, Horsham, 2015 (1st). Kent Staff.

Safwaan M "Saf" IMTIAZ (Chigwell S) b London 16.3.96. RHB WK. Debut Essex 2013; Durham , MCCYC & Northants 2016; Kent & Surrey 2017. HS 175 (MCC YC) v Essex, High Wycombe,

2016. BB 0/129 (MCC YC) v Lancs, Urmston, 2017. HSSET 100 (MCC YC) v Somerset, Taunton Vale, 2015. HST20 67 (MCC YC) v Surrey, High Wycombe, 2016 (1st).

***KASHIF ALI** (Dunstable Coll) b Kashmir, Pakistan, 7.2.98. RHB LB. Debut Essex 2016; Somerset 2017. HS 76 (Essex) v Kent, Polo Farm G, Canterbury, 2017. BB 0/14 (Essex) v Middx, Coggeshall, 2017. HSSET 24 (Essex) v Sussex, Billericay, 2017. HST20 27* (Essex) v Middx, Coggeshall, 2017. BBT20 0/19 in the same match.

***Hamish Philip KINGSTON** (St Virgil's College, Hobart, Tasmania) b Hobart, Tasmania, 17.12.90. RHB RM. Debut 2017.

Benjamin Andrew Davey MANENTI (St Patrick's Coll, Queensland, Aus) b Sydney, NSW, Aus, 23.3.97. RHB OB. Debut 2017. HST20 11 v Glos, Longwood, Bristol, 2017 (2nd). BBT20 2/21 in the same match.

Adam Fraser MILNE b Palmerston North, Manawatu, NZ, 13.4.92. RHB RFM. 40 ODIs (NZ) 2012/13 to 2017/18. Debut 2017. BBT20 2/10 v Middx, Polo Farm SG,, Canterbury, 2017 (1st).

James Douglas Sheehan NEESHAM b Auckland, NZ, 17.9.90. LHB RM. F/C debut (Auckland) 2009/10; debut Otago 2011/12; Derbys 2016; Kent 2017. Tests (NZ) 12 (2013/14 to 2016/17) & 41 ODIs. BBSET 0/25 (Derbys) v Notts, Worksop Coll, 2016. HST20 81 v Surrey, Polo Farm SG, Canterbury, 2017 (2nd). BBT20 4/21 (Derbys) v Yorks, Harrogate, 2016 (1st).

***William Taylor O'DONNELL** (Westlake Boys HS, Auckland, NZ) b Randburg, S Africa, 29.9.97. RHB OB. Brother RR O'Donnell FC Auckland. Debut 2017.

Dipayan PAUL (Sir John Cass S, Stepney) b Sylhet, Bangladesh 3.11.92. RHB OB. Debut 2017. HS 21 v MCCU, Beckenham, 2017. BB 0/4 in the same match.

Stephen Dean Puttenham REEVES (Hilton Coll, KZN; U of Teesside) b Kwa-Zulu Natal, S Africa, 1.10.95. RHB SLA. Debut Durham 2016; Kent 2017. HS 24* (Durham) v Northants, Riverside, 2016. BB 6/79 (Durham) v Northants, M Keynes, 2017. HSSET 54* (Durham) v Notts, Riverside, 2017. BBSET 1/47 in the same match.

Thomas Steven RICHARDS (Homewood S & SFC) b Ashford, 22.4.96. RHB RMF. Debut 2017. BB 1/15 v Somerset, Taunton Vale, 2017.

Miles Andrew RICHARDSON (Sackville S, E Grinstead, Sussex) b Maidstone, 26.8.91. RHB RMF. Debut Surrey & Kent 2014; Northants 2016. F/C debut (Northants) v Loughborough MCCU, Northampton, 2017. HS 84* (Northants) v Worcs, Kidderminster, 2016. BB 3/74 (Northants) v Derbys, Northampton, 2016. HSSET 46* (Northants) v Lancs, Northop Hall, 2017. BBSET 3/41 (Northants) v MCC YC, Totternhoe, 2017. HST20 10 (Northants) v Lancs, Westhoughton, 2016 (1st). BBT20 4/25 (Northants) v Lancs, Westhoughton , 2016 (2nd).

Adam Edward Nicholas RILEY (Beths GS, Bexley; Loughborough U) b Sidcup 23.3.92. RHB OB. Debut 2009.F/C debut v Northants, Canterbury, 2011. HS 53* v Hants, Newclose, I of Wight, 2016. BB 5/60 v Middx, The King's S, 2010. HSSET 23* v Minor Counties, Horsford, 2010. BBSET 4/44 v Surrey, Canterbury, 2010. HST20 12* v MCCYC, Radlett, 2011 (2ⁿᵈ). BBT20 4/19 v MCCYC, Radlett, 2011 (1st). HSKO 4* v Essex, Billericay, 2010. BBKO 0/34 in the same match. Kent Staff.

Oliver Graham ROBINSON (Hurtsmere S, Greenwich) b Sidcup, 1.12.98. RHB RM WK. Debut 2015. List A debut v West Indies U19, North Sound, Antigua, W Indies, 2016/17. Eng U19 v India 2017. HS 117 v .Sussex, Polo Farm SG, Canterbury, 2017. HSSET 46 v Hants, Polo Farm SG, Canterbury, 2017. HST20 24 v Unc, Saffron Walden, 2017 (2nd).

Adam Paul ROUSE (Perrins Comm Sp Coll; Alresford; Peter Symonds Coll, Winchester) b Harare, Zim, 30.6.92. RHB WK. Debut Hants 2008 aged 16 yrs & 331 days; F/C debut (Hants) v Kent, Canterbury, 2013; debut Glam, Glos, Kent & Surrey 2014. Eng U19 v SL, 2010. HS 117* (Hants) v Sussex, Horsham , 2013. BB 1/8 (Hants) v Northants, Ageas Bowl Nursery, 2013. BBKO 0/34 in the same match. HSSET 104 (Hants) v Kent, the Ageas Bowl, 2013. HST20 71 (Surrey) v Hants, Ageas Bowl Nursery, 2014. Kent Staff.

Rory Andrew SMITH (Sir Roger Manwood's School, Sandwich) b Canterbury, 4.8.98. RHB RM. Debut 2017. HS 10 v MCCU, Beckenham, 2017. BB 1/55 in the same match.

Grant STEWART (All Saints Coll, St Mary's Campus, Maitland, NSW, Aus; U of Newcastle, NSW) b Klagoorlie, W Aus, 19.2.94. RHB RMF. Debut 2017. F/C debut v Glam, Canterbury, 2017. HS 50 v MCCU, Beckenham, 2017. BB 4/54 v Essex, Polo Farm SG, Canterbury, 2017. HSSET 26 v Somerset, Taunton Vale, 2017. BBSET 1/64 in the same match. HST20 17* v Unc, Saffron Walden, 2017 (2nd). BBT20 3/23 v Surrey, Polo Farm SG, Canterbury, 2017 (2nd).

Ivan Alfred Astley THOMAS (John Roan S, Greenwich; Leeds U) b Greenwich, 25.9.91. RHB RMF. Debut 2011. F/C debut (Leeds/ Bradford MCCU) v Surrey, The Oval, 2012. HS 21* v Essex, Halstead, 2014 & v Leics, Market Harborough, 2014. BB 5/47 v Glos, Beckenham, 2012. HSSET 9* v Middx, Canterbury, 2012. BBSET 4/14 v Surrey, Cheam, 2011. HST20 1* v Glos, Polo Farm SG, Canterbury, 2016 (2nd) & v Essex, Billericay, 2016 (1st). BB T20 4/26 v Essex, Billericay, 2016 (2nd). Kent staff.

Adam David TILLCOCK (Trent Coll, Long Eaton; South Notts Coll) b Nottingham 13.10.93. RHB SLA. Debut Notts 2011; Kent 2016. List A debut (Notts) v Bang A, Trent Bridge, 2013. HS 115 (Notts) v Yorks, Notts SG, 2014. BB 4/22 (Notts) v Warwicks, Notts SG, 2015. HSSET 50* (Notts) v Derbys, Trent Coll, 2013. BBSET 5/39 (Notts) v Durham, Gosforth, 2014. HST20 50* (Notts) v Lancs, Ormskirk, (1st). BBT20 4/18 (Notts) v Durham, Trent Coll, 2013 (2nd).

Joe James WEATHERLEY (King Edward VI S, Southampton) b Winchester, 19.1.97. RHB OB. Debut Hants 2014; Kent 2017 (on loan). Eng U19 to Aus 2014/15. F/C debut (Hants) v Cardiff MCCU, Ageas Bowl, 2016. HS 180* (Hants) v Notts, Notts SG, 2016. BB 3/20 (Hants) v Glam, Ageas Bowl Nursery, 2015. HSSET 111 (Hants) v Glam, Ageas Bowl Nursery, 2015. BBSET 1/31 (Hants) v Kent, Polo Farm Nursery, 2015. HST20 92 (Hants) v Sussex, Ageas Bowl Nursery, 2016 (2nd). BBT20 1/23 (Hants) v MCCYC, Shenley, 2016 (2nd)

LANCASHIRE

2nd XI COUNTY CHAMPIONS 2017

PLAYING RECORDS 2017
Championship – P10 W4 L1 D5 – winners of the northern group & County Champions
2nd XI Trophy – P7 W5 L2 – winners of the northern group & beaten semi-finalists
2nd XI T20 Competition – P13 W7 L4 Ab2 – second in the northern group & beaten semi-finalists

2nd XI SUCCESSES
Championship – Winners – 1964, 1986, 1997, 2013 (joint with Middlesex), 2017
2nd XI Trophy – Winners – 1990, 2012, 2013, 2016
2nd XI T20 Competition – Beaten Semi-Finalists 2014, 2015, 2017

SECOND ELEVEN CHAMPIONSHIP AVERAGES

BATTING	M	I	NO	Runs	HS	Avge	100s	C/S	BOWLING	O	M	Runs	Wkt	Avge	BB
R P Jones	9	13	3	775	138	77.50	3	9	T E Bailey	45	12	147	12	12.25	4/46
L A Procter	5	8	2	437	103	72.83	1	2	B Woolley	29	7	80	6	13.33	3/30
H Hameed	3	3	0	200	110	66.66	1	-	S Mahmood	54.5	10	180	9	20.00	4/76
J J Bohannon	8	11	1	471	99*	47.10	-	6	L J Hurt	88.4	17	293	14	20.92	3/21
B D Guest	9	12	2	395	96*	39.50	-	21	L A Procter	125.1	18	381	18	21.16	3/49
D J Lamb	8	9	2	271	89	38.71	-	2	S C Kerrigan	112.5	28	318	13	24.46	6/26
T J Lester	9	8	4	147	47	36.75	-	1	J J Bohannon	38	9	132	5	26.40	3/8
A M Lilley	6	7	1	170	72	28.33	-	5	T J Lester	172	28	644	22	29.27	5/79
L J Hurt	6	5	1	82	42*	20.50	-	2	M W Parkinson	134	22	521	17	30.64	6/49
C F K Turner	9	14	1	262	54	20.15	-	4	A M Lilley	92	18	261	7	37.28	3/105
G Lavelle	3	4	0	77	33	19.25	-	5/3	D J Lamb	98	15	402	7	57.42	3/83
K R Brown	6	10	1	136	30	15.11	-	9							
M W Parkinson	8	5	2	40	14	13.33	-	-							
S C Kerrigan	5	4	0	28	18	7.00	-	1							

Also Batted – 3 matches – C M Dudley 28, 15 (1cvt); E Moulton 4 (1ct). 2 matches – T E Bailey 1, 11 (1ct); G Burrows 2*; S Chanderpaul 50, 111*, 103; D Houghton DNB; M H McKiernan 16*, 34; S Mahmood 5; C W G Sanders DNB. 1 match – M P Breetzke 50; A L Davies 51 (3ct); K M Jarvis 6; C Laker 2 (1ct); F Shafiq 7 (2ct); B Woolley DNB (1ct).

Also Bowled – K R Brown 5-0-52-1; G Burrows 26-4-77-1; B D Guest 4-0-19-1; H Hameed 3-0-8-0; D Houghton 17-2-53-0; K M Jarvis 10-2-29-1; R P Jones 2-0-8-1; M H McKiernan 11-6-24-1; E Moulton 28-6-106-0; C W G Sanders 18-3-89-1; F Shafiq 2-0-10-0; C K Turner 9.4-0-95-2.

SECOND ELEVEN TROPHY AVERAGES

BATTING	M	I	NO	Runs	HS	Avge	100s	C/S
L A Procter	3	3	1	227	134	113.50	1	1
B D Guest	7	5	1	270	110*	103.05	1	3/2
K R Brown	4	4	1	80	44	26.66	-	2
A M Lilley	5	4	2	53	25*	26.50	-	2
R P Jones	6	5	0	127	66	25.40	-	4
T J Lester	6	3	1	32	16	16.00	-	-
J J Bohannon	7	5	0	56	37	11.20	-	5
D J Lamb	5	4	0	35	24	8.75	-	1
C K Turner	7	7	1	165	74	-		2

BOWLING	O	M	Runs	Wkt	Avge	BB
G Burrows	6	0	36	7	5.14	7/36
M W Parkinson	29	2	107	12	8.91	5/14
S C Kerrigan	15	2	40	4	10.00	3/22
M H McKiernan	11.4	0	52	5	10.40	3/24
A M Lilley	36	3	152	6	25.33	3/18
L A Procter	16	2	77	3	25.66	2/37
D J Lamb	38.3	1	213	8	26.62	3/38
T J Lester	35.1	0	209	6	34.83	3/42
J J Bohannon	28	1	155	4	38.75	2/32

Also Batted – 4 matches – M W Parkinson 0*. 3 matches – T E Bailey DNB (1ct); S C Kerrigan 42, 0 (1ct); G Lavelle 3, 1 (4ct & 1st); M H McKiernan 17, 8 (1ct). 1 match – M P Breetzke 4; G Burrows DNB; S Chanderpaul 27* (1ct); D Houghton 0* (1ct); L J Hurt 9*; E Moulton DNB. C Oldham 4; F Shafiq 20; B Woolley DNB.

Also Bowled – T E Bailey 20-1-82-2; B D Guest 1-0-13-0; D Houghton 6-1-20-1; L J Hurt 1-0-19-0; E Moulton 5.4-0-41-1; C K Turner 1.2-0-14-0; B Wooley 2-0-16-0.

SECOND ELEVEN T20 AVERAGES

BATTING	M	I	NO	Runs	HS	Avge	100s	C/S
L S Livingstone	3	3	0	111	64	37.00	-	2
C K Turner	5	5	0	179	55	35.80	-	1
K R Brown	5	5	0	147	101	29.40	1	3
L A Procter	5	5	1	115	35*	28.75	-	1
A L Davies	7	7	1	159	44	26.50	-	3
B D Guest	4	4	1	73	32*	24.33	-	3
R P Jones	7	6	0	135	66	22.50	-	5
A M Lilley	6	5	0	112	39	22.40	-	4
J J Bohannon	5	4	1	60	24	20.00	-	4
D J Lamb	9	7	2	89	35*	17.80	-	1
D J Vilas	4	3	1	33	20	16.50	-	1st
H Hameed	3	3	0	48	26	16.00	-	1
S C Kerrigan	7	4	2	32	12	16.00	-	1
C M Dudley	5	5	1	45	18	11.25	-	3
T E Bailey	5	3	3	8	7*	8.00	-	2
J Clark	4	3	1	12	8	6.00	-	2

BOWLING	O	M	Runs	Wkt	Avge	BB
A M Lilley	15	0	86	7	12.28	2/10
M W Parkinson	27	1	146	11	13.27	4/18
S D Parry	9	0	55	4	13.75	3/30
J Clark	6	0	42	3	14.00	1/12
L A Procter	16.5	0	117	8	14.62	2/14
T E Bailey	16.2	0	107	7	15.28	5/15
S C Kerrigan	25	0	145	7	20.71	2/14
K M Jarvis	13.5	0	115	5	23.00	2/22
S Mahmood	13	1	102	4	25.50	1/9
D J Lamb	25	0	236	9	26.22	3/48
T J Lester	19	0	137	5	27.40	3/8

Also Bowled – J J Bohannon 3-0-24-21; S J Croft 5-0-34-1; L J Hurt 6-0-62-2; R P Jones 1-0-9-0; L S Livingstone 2-0-6-0; M H McKiernan 4-0-19-0; R McLaren 6-0-35-1.

Also Batted – 7 matches – T J Lester 2*, 0*; M W Parkinson DNB (1ct). 5 matches – S Mahmood DNB. 4 matches – L J Hurt 5*, 13*; K M Jarvis DNB. 3 matches – S J Croft 24, 36 (2ct); S D Parry DNB (2ct). 2 matches - R McLaren 43*. 1 match – M P Breetzke 32; M H McKiernan DNB.

HOME MATCHES: SECOND ELEVEN CHAMPIONSHIP

v Northamptonshire (Liverpool) – 9-11 May – Lancs 321 (R P Jones 138; A Kapil 3/33, D Davies 3/57) & 262/4d (R P Jones 67, J J Bohannon 65, C K Turner 64) beat Northants 265 (F A J Cox 62, D Davies 51; T E Bailey 4/53, B Woolley 3/30) & 269 (H R D Adair 98, J M Kettleborough 61; T E Bailey 4/48, Woolley 3/50) by 49 runs.

v Worcestershire (Great Crosby) – 23-25 May – Worcs 239 (Z A Malik 63*; L J Hurt 3/21) & 327 (A Hepburn 68, R A Whiteley 65, G H Rhodes 58) lost to Lancs 303 (L A Procter 103, J J Bohannon 63; M B Wareing 3/48) & 265/3 (J J Bohannon 99*, R P Jones 80*) by seven wkts.

v MCC Young Cricketers (Urmston) – 18-20 Jul - Lancs 317/9d (H Hameed 110, S Chanderpaul 50; F J Hudson-Prentice 3/53)

& 257/0d (R P Jones 137*, S Chanderpaul 111*) beat MCC YC 300/7d (J H Barrett 108, M H Cross 53; L A Procter 3/49) & 207 (S M Imtiaz 99; M W Parkinson 4/46, T J Lester 3/38) by 67 runs.

v Durham (Todmorden) – 21-23 Aug – Durham 201 (T E Bailey 4/46, L J Hurt 3/30) drew with Lancs 256 (S Chanderpaul 103*, A L Davies 51; W J Weighell 6/47)

v Hampshire (Newclose County Ground, Newport, I of Wight) – 5-8 Sept – Hants 248 (C P Wood 76*, F S Hay 59; S Mahmood 4/76) & 66/6 (J J Bohannon 3/8) drew with Lancs 352 (A M Lilley 72; B Mugochi 3/46, C P Wood 3/61)

This was the Final Play-Off for the 2nd XI Championship of 2017, As no play was possible on the final day, Lancashire were awarded the title by virtue of their first innings lead.

HOME MATCHES: FRIENDLIES

v Yorkshire (Old Trafford) – 10-13 Apr – Lancs 257 (S C Kerrigan 56; J C Wainman 5/42, D J Willey 3/47) & 185/5 (J J Bohannon 74*; M J Waite 4/33) drew with Yorks 428 (W M H Rhodes 176, M J Waite 64; S C Kerrigan 5/54)

v Scotland A (Stanley Park) – 17/18 Aug – Match abandoned without a ball bowled

v Middlesex (Liverpool) – 28-31 Aug – Middx 305 (R G White

102, G F B Scott 84; T E Bailey 5/42) & 249 (R G White 91, M K Anderson 58; C W G Sanders 3/27, T E Bailey 3/31) lost to Lancs 289 (J J Bohannon 64; R H Patel 3/35) & 264/4 (C K Turner 78, B D Guest 77*) by six wkts.

v Leicestershire (Southport) – 12-14 Sept – Lancs 315 (D J Lamb 100*, C K Turner 56; G T Griffiths 4/73, T J Wells 3/52) drew with Leics 140 (C W G Sanders 3/25, A M Lilley 3/37) & 71/3.

HOME MATCHES: SECOND ELEVEN TROPHY

v Northamptonshire (Northop Halll) – 8 May – Lancs 336/5 (L A Procter 134, B D Guest 110*) beat Northants (M H McKiernan 3/24, M W Parkinson 3/31) by 167 runs.

v Durham (Bowden CC) – 16 May – Durham 149 (M W Parkinson 5/14) lost to Lancs 151/2 (C K Turner 74) by eight wkts.

v Worcestershire (Parkgate, Neston) – 22 May - Worcs 275 (G H Rhodes 62, R A Whiteley 55; T J Lester 3/42) lost to Lancs 276/9 (L A Procter 67, B D Guest 62; A Hepburn 4/56) by one wkt.

v Middlesex (Blackpool) – 2 June - Lancs 128/9 lost to Middx 131/5 (R G White 54*; M W Parkinson 3/14) by five wkts. *This was the Semi-Final of the One-Day Trophy.*

HOME MATCHES : SECOND ELEVEN T20 COMPETITION

v Derbyshire (Westhoughton) – 5 July – Match 1 – Derbys 141 (S D Parry 3/30) lost to Lancs 142/6 by four wkts.

v Derbyshire (Westhoughton) – 5 July – Match 2 – Lancs 159/7 (L S Livingstone 64; G C Viljoen 3/30) beat Derbys 94 by 65 runs.

v MCC Young Cricketers (Westhoughton) – 17 July – Match 1 – Lancs 138/5 (C K Turner 52) lost to MCC YC 139/7 by three wkts.

v MCC Young Cricketers (Westhoughton) – 17 July – Match 2 – Lancs 132/7 (R P Jones 66) beat MCC YC 96 (T E Bailey 5/15) by 36 runs.

v Yorkshire (Blackpool) – 2 Aug – Match 1 – Match abandoned without a ball bowled.

v Yorkshire (Blackpool) – 2 Aug – Match 2 – Match abandoned without a ball bowled.

v Sussex (Arundel) – 10 Aug – Lancs 149/5 lost to Sussex 150/6 (A J Robson 90*) by four wkts.

This was the second Semi-Final of the 2017 competition

PLAYERS WHO HAVE REPRESENTED LANCASHIRE 2nd XI IN 2017 (39)

T E Bailey	C M Dudley	D J Lamb	S Oldham
J J Bohannon	*E Fluck	G Lavelle	M W Parkinson
M P Breetzke	B D Guest	T J Lester	S D Parry
K R Brown	H Hameed	A M Lilley	L A Procter
G Burrows	D Houghton	L S Livingstone	C W G Sanders
S Chanderpaul	L J Hurt	M H McKiernan	F Shafiq
J Clark	K M Jarvis	R McLaren	C K Turner
*T Cornell	R P Jones	S Mahmood	D J Vilas
S J Croft	S C Kerrigan	E Moulton	B Woolley
A L Davies	C Laker	C Oldham	

LANCASHIRE CRICKETERS

Thomas Ernest BAILEY (Myerscough Coll, Bilsborrow) b Preston, 21.4.91. RHB RFM. Debut Lancs 2010. F/C debut v Surrey, Liverpool, 2012. HS 69 v Yorks, Liverpool, 2016. BB 5/42 v Middx, Liverpool, 2017. HSSET 32 v Warwicks, Coventry & N Warwicks, 2013. BBSET 4/34 in the same match. HST20 20* v Durham, Blackpool, 2011 (1st). BBT20 5/15 v MCC YC, Westhoughton, 2017 (2nd). Lancs Staff.

Joshua James BOHANNON (Harper Green HS, Bolton) b Bolton, 9.4.97. RHB. Debut 2014. HS 99* v Worcs, Great Crosby, 2017. BB 3/8 v Hants, Newclose, I of Wight, 2017. HSSET 47* v Northants, Westhoughton, 2015. BBSET 2/32 v Worcs, Parkgate, Neston, 2107. HST20 39* v Notts, Worksop Coll, 2015 (1st). BBT20 2/13 v Sussex, Arundel, 2017 (SF).

Matthew Paul BREETZKE (Grey HS, P Elizabeth, SA) b P Elizabeth, S Africa, 3.11.98. RHB RM. Debut 2017. F/C debut v E Province, SA) v Free State, Bloemfontein, 2017. HS 50 v Leics, Desborough, 2017. HSSET 4 v Middx, Blackpool, 2017. HST20 32 v Notts, Trent Coll, 2017 (1st).

Karl Robert BROWN (Hesketh Fletcher HS, Atherton) b Bolton 17.5.88. RHB RMF. Debut 2003 aged 15 years and 94 days, F/C debut v Durham UCCE, the Racecourse, Durham, 2006. HS 171 v Glam, Crosby 2006. BB 2/41 v Warwicks, Moseley 2006. HSSET 118 v Leics, Todmorden, 2010 BBSET 2/48 v Leics, Unsworth 2006. HST20 101* v Yorks, Marske-by-the-Sea, 2013 (1st). HSKO 26 v Durham, Parkgate, Neston, 2010. Lancs Staff.

George BURROWS b 22.6.98. RHB RM WK. Debut 2016. HS 2* v Derbys, Stoke-on-Trent, 2017. BB 1/24 v Derbys, Derby, 2016. BBSET 7/36 v Leics, Hinckley, 2017.

Shivnarine CHANDERPAUL (Gibson S, Unity Village; Cove & John HS, U Village) b Unity Village, Demerara, Guyana, 16.8.74. LHB LB. Debut & F/C debut Guyana v Leeward Is, Georgetown, 1991/92; debuts Durham 2007, Lancs 2010, Warwicks 2011. Tests 164 (WI) 1993/94 to 2014/15 & 268 ODIs. HS 111* v MCCYC, Urmston CC, 2017. HSSET 27* v Durham, Bowdon, 2017.

Jordan CLARK (Sedbergh S) b Whitehaven, Cumberland, 14.10.90. RHB RM. Debut 2008. Brother to G (Durham & MCCYC 2011 to date). F/C debut v Kent, Old Trafford, 2015. HS 139* v Sussex, Blackstone, 2014. BB 5/36 v Derbys, Middlewich, 2012. HSSET 109 v Worcs, Northop Hall, 2011. BBSET 3/20 v Middx, Radlett, 2012. HST20 96* v Northants, Westhoughton, 2016 (2nd) BBT20 2/21 v Derbys, Glossop, 2016 (1st). HSKO 15 v Durham, Parkgate, Neston, 2010. Lancs Staff.

*T CORNELL Debut 2017. HS 44 v Middx, Liverpool, 2017. BB 0/2 v Leics, Southport, 2017.

Steven John CROFT (Highfield HS, Blackpool; M|yerscough Coll, Bilsborough, Preston) b Blackpool 11.10.84. RHB RMF/ OB. Debut 2001. F/C debut v Oxford UCCE, The Parks, 2005. Debut Auckland, NZ, 2008/09. Lancs Cap 2010. HS 149* v Glam, Crosby, 2006. BB 5/51 v Hants, Old Trafford, 2006. HSSET 142 v Derbys, Chester, 2005. BBSET 4/53 v Yorks, Pudsey Congs, 2005. HST20 77 v Notts, Worksop, 2013 (2nd). BBT20 1/10 v Northants, Northampton, 2017 (2nd). Lancs Staff.

Alexander Luke DAVIES (Queen Elizabeth GS, Blackburn) b Darwen, 23.8.94. RHB WK. Debut 2011. F/C debut v Surrey, Liverpool, 2012. Eng U19 to Australia, World Cup, 2012. HS 119 v Yorks, Scarborough, 2013. HSSET 116* v Derbys, Glossop, 2013. HST20 65 v Notts, Ormskirk, 2014 (1st). Lancs Staff.

Connor M DUDLEY (Pulteney GS, Adelaide, S Australia) b Sydney NSW, Aus, 1.12.98. RHB RM. Debuts Worcs 2016; Lancs 2017. HS 35 (Worcs) v Lancs, Great Crosby, 2017. HSSET 2 (Worcs) v Lancs, Parkgate, Neston, 2017. HST20 18 v Warwicks, Bull's Head Gd, 2017 (1st).

*Edward FLUCK (Cheadle Hulme GS) b 14.1.99. RHB. Debut 2017. HS 0 v Leics, Southport, 2017.

Brooke David GUEST (Kent Street Sen HS, Perth, W Australia; Murdoch U, Perth) b Perth, WA, 14.5.97. RHB WK Debut 2016. HS 130 v Glos, Bristol, 2016. BB 1/19 v Derbys, Stoke-on-Trent, 2017. HSSET 110* v Northants, Northop Hall, 2017. BBSET 0/13 v Yorks, Headingley, 2017. HST20 32* v Notts, Trent Coll, 2017 (2nd).

Haseeb HAMEED (Bolton GS) b Bolton, 17.1.97. RHB LB. Debut 2013. F/C debut v Glam, Old Trafford, 2015. Cap 2016. Eng U19 v Pak & Bang, 2013; to Aus 2014/15; v Aus 2015. Tests 2 (Eng) 2016/17. HS 110 v MCC YC, Urmston, 2017. BB 0/3 v Worcs, Worcester RGS, 2016. HSSET 112 v Glam, SWALEC, 2014. HST20 35 v Northants, Oundle S, 2015 (1st).

Daniel HOUGHTON (Burscough Priory Science Coll, W Lancs) b Ormskirk, 5.7.98. RHB RM. Debut 2016. BB 1/28 v Derbys, Derby, 2016. Eng U19 in Ind, 2016/17. HSSET 0* v Derbys, Stoke-Trent, 2017. BBSET 1/20 in the same match.

Liam Jack HURT (Balshaw's C of E HS, Leyland; Training 2000, Blackburn) b Preston 15.3.94. RHB RMF. Debut Lancs 2013; Derbys & Leics 2015. List A debut (Leics) v Durham, Grace Road, 2015. Glos, Northants & Warwicks 2016. Debut Durham 2017. HS 42* v Hants, Newclose CC, I of Wight, 2017. BB 4/43 (Durham) v Essex/Kent, Billericay, 2017. HSSET 24 (Durham) v Worcs, Kidderminster, 2017. BBSET 3/58 v Leics, Middlewich, 2014. HST20 19* (Leics) v Unc, Long Marston, 2016 (2nd). BBT20 3/41 v Yorks, Marske-by-the-Sea, 2013 (2nd).

Kyle Malcolm JARVIS (St John's Coll, Harare, Zim) b Harare, 16.2.89. Son of M P Jarvis; 5 Tests (Zim) & 12 ODIs, 1987/88 to 1994/95. RHB RFM. Debut Mashonaland Eagles 2009/10; F/C debut Zim XI v Kenya, Kwe-Kwe, 2009/10. 8 Tests & 33 ODIs (Zim) 2009 to 2013. Debut Essex 2011; debut Lancs 2013; Cap 2015. HS 13 v Scotland A, Alderley Edge, 2013. BB 6/47 v Yorks. Northop Hall, 2014. HSSET 6 v Warwicks, Westhoughton, 2014. BBSET 2/33 v Derbys, Parkgate, Neston. BBT20 2/22 v Derbys, Westhoughton, 2017 (1st). Released at the end of the 2107 season.

Robert Peter JONES (Bridgewater HS, Warrington, Cheshire) b Warrington, 3.11.95. RHB LB. Debut Lancs 2013; F/C debut v Surrey, the Oval, 2016. Eng U19 (T20 only) 2013; to UAE 2013/14 (Tri/Series) v S Africa 2014. HS 138 v Northants, Liverpool, 2017. BB 3/43 v Yorks, Headingley. 2014. HSSET 66 v Leics, Hinckley, 2017. BBSET 2/32 v Leics, Middlewich, 2014. HST20 66 v MCC YC, Westhoughton, 2017 (2nd). BBT20 2/28 (Eng U19) v Yorks, Loughborough, 2013 (1st).

Simon Christopher KERRIGAN (Preston Coll) b Preston 10.5.89. RHB SLA. Debut 2007. F/C debut v Warwicks, Old Trafford, 2010. Lancs Cap 2013. Tests (Eng) 1 2013. Debut Northants (on loan) 2017. HS 52 v Notts, Liverpool 2009. BB 6/26 v Leics, Desborough, 2017. HSSET 42 v Leics, Hinckley, 2017. BBSET 4/8 v Yorks, Pudsey Congs, 2015. HST20 14 v Durham, Gosforth, 2012 (2nd). BBT20 2/14 v MCC YC, Westhoughton, 2017 (2nd). BBKO 0/5 v Derbys, Glossop, 2010. Lancs staff.

Christopher Michael LAKER (Wellacre Academy, Flixton, Greater Manchester) b Trafford, 5.9.96. LHB RM. Debut Lancs 2016; Leics 2017. HS 46 (Leics) v Durham, 2017.

Daniel " Danny" John LAMB (St Michael's HS, Chorley; Cardinal Newman Coll, Preston) b Preston 7.9.95. RHB RMF. Debut 2013. List A debut v Notts, Trent Bridge, 2017. HS 100* v Leics, Southport, 2014. BB 5/54 Scotland A, Blackpool, 2014. HSSET 36 v Durham, Brandon, 2016. BBSET 3/38 v Derbys, Stoke-on-Trent, 2017. HST20 35* v Warwicks, Bull's Head GD, 2017 (2nd). BBT20 5/25 v Notts, Worksop Coll, 2015 (1st).

George Isaac D LAVELLE (Merchant Taylors' S, Crosby, Lancs) b Lancs, 24.3.00. LHB WK. Debut 2017. HS 33 v Leics, Desborough, 2017. HSSET 3 v Derbys, Stoke-on-Trent, 2017.

Toby James LESTER (Baines HS, Blackpool; Rossall S; Loughborough U) b Blackpool, 5.4.93. LHB LFM. Debut MCC Un 2012. F/C debut (Loughborough MCCU) v Notts, Trent Bridge, 2012. Debut Lancs 2013. HS 47 v Hants, Newclose CC, 2017. BB 6/27 v Derbys, Derby, 2016. HSSET 20* v MCCYC, Radlett, 2013. BBSET 3/42 v Worcs, Parkgate, Neston, 2017. HST20 11 v Notts, Worksop Coll, 2015 (2nd). BBT20 4/33 v Northants, Westhoughton, 2016 (2nd).

Arron Mark LILLEY (Mossley Hollins HS, Ashton-under-Lyne) b Tameside, Lancs, 1.4.91. RHB OB. Debut Lancs 2010. F/C debut v Glam Old Trafford, 2013. HS 93 v Yorks, Crosby, 2014. BB 7/67 v Glos, Bristol, 2016. HSSET 25* v Worcs, Parkgate, Neston, 2013. BBSET 6/26 v Unicorns A, Old Trafford, 2013. HST20 41 v Unc,

Knypersley, 2016 (2nd). BBT20 3/26 Derbys, Ormskirk, 2013 (1st). Lancs Staff.

Liam Stephen LIVINGSTONE (Chetwynde S, Barrow) b Barrow-in-Furness, Cumberland, 4.8.93. RHB LB. Debut 2011. F/C debut v Notts, OldTrafford, 2016. HS 204 v Yorks, Headingley, 2014. BB 2/8 v Yorks, Todmorden, 2013. HSSET 162 v Worcs, Old Trafford, 2015. BBSET 3/46 v Derbys, Glossop, 2015. HST20 103 v Unc, Liverpool, 2015 (2nd). BBT20 3/7 v Notts, Worksop Coll, 2015 (1st). Lancs staff.

Matthew Harry "Mattie" McKIERNAN (Lowton HS, Leigh; St John Rigby Coll, Wigan) b Billinge, Merseyside, 14.6.94. RHB LB. Debut Lancs 2011; Northants 2012 (on loan). Ret to Lancs 2013; Leics & Unc 2016; Durham 2017. HS 49 v Leics, Liverpool, 2014. BB 4/64 (Leics) v Northants, Desborough, 2017. HSSET 42 v Leics, Grace Road, 2014. BBSET 5/45 (Durham) v Worcs, New Road, 2017. HST20 18* (Unc) v Hants, Great Tew, 2017 (2nd). BBT20 3/11 (Unc) v Leics, Long Marston, 2016 (2nd).

Ryan McLAREN (Grey Coll, P Elizabeth, SA; Free State U) b Kimberley, SA, 9.2.83. LHB RM. Debut & F/C debut (Free State, SA) v Easterns, Benoni; Eagles 2004/05; Warwicks 2005; Kent 2007 & Cap; Knights 2010/11; Middx 2011; Hants 2015; Lancs 2017.Tests 1 (SA) & 10 ODIs, 2009/10 to 2010). HS 220* (Warwicks v Hants, Rose Bowl Nursery, 2002. BB 3/24 (Warwicks) v Derbys, Dunstall, 2005. HST20 43* v Derbys, Westhoughton, 2017 (1st). BBT20 1/18 (Middx) v Leics, Uxbridge CC, 2011 & v Northants, Northampton, 2017 (1st).

Saqib MAHMOOD (Matthew Moss HS, Rochdale) b Birmingham, 25.2.97. RHB RFM. Debut 2013. F/C debut v Hants, the Ageas Bowl, 2016. Eng U19 to Aus 2014/15; v Aus 2015. HS 21 v Middx, Liverpool, 2017. BB 4/23 v Derbys, Denby, 2015. HSSET 2 v Leics, Grace Road, 2014 & v Durham, Middlewich, 2015. BBSET 2/57 v Leics, Grace Road, 2014. HST20 2* v Unc, Liverpool, 2015 (1st). BBT20 4/20 v Derbys, Parkgate, Neston, 2015 (1st). Lancs Staff.

Edwin MOULTON Debut 2017. HS 4 v Northants, Liverpool, 2017. BB 0/24 in the same match. BBSET 1/41 v Durham, Bowdon, 2017.

C OLDHAM Debut 2017.HSSET 4 v Middx, Blackpool, 2017.

Sam OLDHAM (Balshaws HS, Leyland) b 23.10.98. RHB RFM. Debut 2017. HS 42 v Middx, Liverpool, 2017. BB 2/32 in the same match. HSSET 76* v Leics, Hinckley, 2017.

Matthew William PARKINSON (Bolton S) b Bolton, 24.10.96. RHB LB. Twin brother of C F (Leics 2017). Debut 2013. F/C debut v Warwicks, Old Trafford, 2016. Eng U19 to Aus 2014/15; v Aus 2015. HS 23 v Yorks, Scarborough, 2015. BB 6/49 v Leics, Desborough, 2017. HSSET 16 v Northants, Northampton, 2016. BBSET 6/28 v Glam, SWALEC, 2014. BBT20 5/17 v Unc, Knypersley, 2016 (1st).

Stephen David PARRY (Audenshaw HS) b Manchester 12.1.86. RHB SLA. Debut 2003, F/C debut v Durham UCCE, the Racecourse, Durham, 2007. Cap 2015. ODIs 2 (Eng) 2013/14. HS 109 v Durham, Southport, 2011. BB 6/38 v Notts, Aigburth, 2016. HSSET 68* v Leics, Hinckley 2007. BBSET 5/35 v Derbys, Parkgate, Neston, 2014. HST20 29 v Unc, Liverpool, 2015 (1st). BBT20 3/5 v Notts, Aigburth, 2016 (1st). HSKO 8 v Durham, Parkgate, Neston, 2010. BBKO 1/35 in the same match. Lancs staff.

Luke Anthony PROCTER (Counthill S, Oldham) b Oldham 24.6.88. LHB RM. Debut Lancs 2006, MCCYC 2007. F/C debut v Warwicks, Edgbaston, 2010. HS 150 v Leics, Todmorden, 2010. BB 7/37 v Warwicks, Southport, 2014 (and match-figures of 12/81). HSSET 134 v Northants, Northop Hall, 2017. BBSET 4/44 v Worcs, Ombersley, 2010. HST20 70* v Derbys, Parkgate Neston, 2015 (2nd). BBT20 4/14 v Derbys, Ormskirk, 2013 (2nd).HSKO 1 v Derbys, Glossop, 2010. BBKO 1/36 v Durham, Parkgate, Neston, 2010. Joins Northamptonshire for the 2018 season.

Christopher W G SANDERS (Loughborough U) Debut 2017. HS 3* v Hants, Ageas Bowl Nursery, 2017. BB 3/25 v Leics, Southport, 2017.

Furqan SHAFIQ (Parrs Wood Sixth Form Centre, Manchester) b 29.11.96. RHB OB. Debut 2015. HS 7 v Northants, Liverpool, 2017. BB 0/10 in the same match. HSSET 20 v Worcs, Parkgate, Neston, 2017.

Calum Kirby TURNER (Urmston GS) b Manchester, 14.9.96. LHB LB. Debut 2015. HS 103 v Yorks, Todmorden, 2016. BB 2/95 v Derbys, Stoke-on-Trent, 2017. HSSET 74 v Durham, Bowdon, 2017. BBSET 0/14 v Middx, Blackpool, 2017. HST20 55 v Notts, Trent Coll, 2017 (1st)
Dane James VILAS b Johannesburg, SA, 10.6.85. RHB WK. Debut & F/C debut Gauteng (SA) v Free State, Bloemfontein, 2006/07; debuts Lions 2008/09; Western Province 2010/11; Cape Cobras 2011/12; Lancs 2017; Dolphins 2017/18. Tests 6 (SA) 2015 to 2015/16 & 1 T20. HST20 20 v Derbys, Westhoughton, 2017 (2nd).
Bradley WOOLLEY Debut 2017. BBSET 0/16 v Durham, Bowdon, 2017. BB 3/30 v Northants, Liverpool, 2017. BBSET 0/16 v Durham, Bowdon, 2017.

LEICESTERSHIRE

PLAYING RECORDS 2017
Championship – P9 W2 L4 D3 – seventh in the northern group
2nd XI Trophy – P6 W0 L3 NR1 Ab2 – tenth in the northern group
2nd XI T20 Competition – P12 W4 L6 Ab2 – eighth in the northern group

2nd XI SUCCESSES
Championship – Winners – 1983, 2014
2nd XI Trophy – Winners – 1993, 1995, 1996, 2000, 2014
2nd XI T20 Competition – Winners 2014

SECOND ELEVEN CHAMPIONSHIP AVERAGES

BATTING	M	I	NO	Runs	HS	Avge	100s	C/S
P J Horton	4	6	1	521	277*	104.20	2	3
N J Dexter	3	4	0	287	169	71.50	1	2
H E Dearden	5	9	0	446	141	49.55	1	2
L J Hill	2	3	0	134	87	44.66	-	3
W N Fazackerley	7	10	1	387	83	43.00	-	4
S T Evans	5	9	2	298	107	42.57	1	-
A M Ali	5	9	0	373	99	41.44	-	3
M Hussain	2	3	0	88	39	29.33	-	-
R J Sayer	4	7	0	194	80	27.71	-	2
H J Swindells	7	11	1	265	60	26.50	-	28/1
B W M Mike	7	8	0	211	49	26.37	-	2
B A Raine	4	7	1	148	66	24.66	-	-
T J Wells	2	4	1	64	24	21.33	-	3
J S Sykes	2	4	0	83	46	20.75	-	1
M L Pettini	2	3	0	61	50	20.33	-	1
J H Barrett	2	4	0	79	38	19.75	-	-
C F Parkinson	5	9	1	149	46	18.62	-	1
R A Jones	4	4	1	54	30	18.00	-	1
C E Shreck	3	3	0	46	24	15.00	-	-
J W Dickinson	3	3	1	28	22*	14.00	-	1
J E Bailey	4	6	2	20	12	5.00	-	4
M H McKiernan	2	3	1	10	8	5.00	-	1
D Manthorpe	7	7	4	11	5*	3.66	-	3

BOWLING	O	M	Runs	Wkt	Avge	BB
C E Shreck	67.5	21	179	10	17.90	4/30
T J Wells	33	7	100	5	20.00	2/27
J E Bailey	31	3	170	8	21.25	4/57
B A Raine	81.5	29	179	8	22.37	3/18
Z J Chappell	21	2	94	4	23.50	3/46
R J Sayer	101.5	24	263	10	26.30	4/29
R A Jones	72	13	224	8	28.00	4/64
D Manthorpe	167	31	626	22	28.45	3/36
W N Fazackerley	101.5	12	484	17	28.47	6/55
C F Parkinson	104.1	29	302	10	30.20	4/8
N J Dexter	33	7	100	3	33.33	2/11
M H McKiernan	80	17	261	7	37.28	4/64
D Klein	20.5	1	117	3	39.00	2/68
B W M Mike	96.3	13	488	12	40.66	3/63
J S Sykes	47	9	157	3	52.33	2/51
A Shahzad	59.2	10	237	4	59.25	3/68
A M Ali	46	1	202	3	67.33	2/83

Also Bowled – M Ahmed 8-1-36-0; D N Butchart 13-0-92-0; H E Dearden 15-0-74-1; J W Dickinson 18-0-82-0; J Graham 7-0-45-0; M Rafique 13.2-2-56-1.

Also Batted – 2 matches – Z J Chappell 99, 22; A Shahzad 12*, 0* (2ct). 1 match – M Ahmed DNB; I Amjad 9, 27; R N Bell 5 (4ct); J C Blunt 0; D N Butchart 9 (4ct); M H Cross 12; B J Curran 37, 33; J Graham DNB; M A Jones 45, 15 (2ct); Kashif Ali 8, 0; D Klein DNB; C M Laker 11 (1ct); M Rafique 12.

SECOND ELEVEN TROPHY AVERAGES

BATTING	M	I	NO	Runs	HS	Avge	100s	C/S
A M Ali	4	4	0	183	96	45.75	-	2
T J Wells	3	3	0	80	78	26.66	-	1
L J Hill	3	3	0	49	35	16.33	-	4
J S Sykes	3	3	0	19	19	6.33	-	2

BOWLING	O	M	Runs	Wkt	Avge	BB
T J Wells	29.5	0	180	8	22.50	6/53
D Klein	20	0	139	5	27.80	3/48

Also Bowled – A M Ali 4-0-20-0; Z J Chappell 15-1-102-0; C S Delport 7.4-0-62-2; N J Dexter 10-2-41-1; W N Fazackerley 6-1-23-1; G T Griffiths 11-2-72-0; R A Jones 2.2-0-18-0; B W M Mike 4-0-21-0; C F Parkinson 7-0-47-1; R J Sayer 18-0-123-2; J S Sykes 15-0-64-2.

Also Batted – 2 matches – Z J Chappell 7, 11; C S Delport 157, 61 (1ct); N J Dexter 10, 0 (2ct); W N Fazackerley 33, 102 (1ct); G T Griffiths 0 (1ct); D Klein 2*, 5 (1ct); B W M Mike 4*; R J Sayer 11*, 1; H J Swindells 4, 4*. 1 match –J E Bailey DNB; J C Blunt DNB; M J Cosgrove 1; E J H Eckersley 14; J Graham DNB; M Hussain 7; M A Jones 6; R A Jones DNB; Kashif Ali 13*; D Manthorpe DNB; C F Parkinson 40; M L Pettini 44; B A Raine 27.

SECOND ELEVEN T20 AVERAGES

BATTING	M	I	NO	Runs	HS	Avge	100s	C/S
E J H Eckersley (WK)	4	4	0	176	61	44.00	-	8 (5 as WK)
M L Pettini	4	4	1	117	81*	39.00	-	3
C S Delport	4	4	0	103	60	25.75	-	1
A M Ali	9	9	0	189	50	21.00	-	2
L J Hill	3	3	0	53	23	17.66	-	1
H E Dearden	7	7	0	119	53	17.00	-	3
W N Fazackerley	10	9	2	98	40	14.00	-	3
T J Wells	5	5	0	69	21	13.80	-	2
D N Butchart	3	3	1	25	11	12.50	-	4
C F Parkinson	6	5	1	49	17*	12.25	-	1
R N Bell	4	3	1	18	11*	9.00	-	2/3
H J Swindells	4	3	1	18	10	9.00	-	1/2
R A Jones	4	2	0	13	11	6.50	-	-
N J Dexter	3	3	0	15	9	5.00	-	1
R J Sayer	7	6	1	18	10	3.60	-	5
B W M Mike	6	4	2	5	5	2.50	-	-

BOWLING	O	M	Runs	Wkt	Avge	BB
H E Dearden	3.5	0	24	3	8.00	3/7
C F Parkinson	22	0	121	11	11.00	4/13
G T Griffiths	6.1	0	48	3	16.00	2/9
M W Pillans	7	0	54	3	18.00	2/26
R J Sayer	27	0	198	11	18.00	3/31
D Klein	7	0	65	3	21.66	2/36
A M Ali	23.4	0	180	8	22.50	5/22
D Manthorpe	15	1	116	5	23.20	2/19
C S Delport	8.4	0	78	3	26.00	2/26
T J Wells	13	0	104	4	26.00	3/33
W N Fazackerley	16	0	137	4	34.25	2/25

Also Bowled – C N Ackermann 2-0-20-1; J E Bailey 4-0-39-2; D N Butchart 4-0-39-1; N J Dexter 3-0-24-2; H Funnell 2-0-14-1; J Graham 2-0-16-0; R A Jones 11-0-97-1; B W M Mike 10-0-99-0; J S Sykes 7-0-51-0.

Also Batted – 5 matches – D Manthorpe 0*, 2*. 4 matches – J E Bailey 1*, 0 (3ct). 2 matches – S T Evans 29, 3 (2ct); G T Griffiths 0* (1ct); M A Jones 35, 16; D Klein 12, 0; M W Pillans 20*, 4; J S Sykes 11*, 9. 1 match – C N Ackerman 6 (1ct); H Funnell 1*; J Graham DNB; P J Horton 56* (1ct); J Nightingale 0; A Trusz 7.

HOME MATCHES: SECOND ELEVEN CHAMPIONSHIP

v Yorkshire (Kibworth CC) – 30 May to 1 June – Yorks 270 (M J Waite 85, W M H Rhodes 50; W N Fazackerley 6/55) & 293/4d (H C Brook 127, J H Tattersall 117) beat Leics 158 (W N Fazackerley 50; W M H Rhodes 4/23) & 223 (H J Swindells 58*; K Carver 6/53) by 182 runs.

v Lancashire (Desborough) – 19-21 June – Leics 164 (M W Parkinson 6/49) & 142 (S C Kerrigan 6/42, M W Parkinson 4/46 [and match figs of 10/95]) lost to Lancs 271 (B D Guest 60, M P Breetzke 50; R J Sayer 3/59, B W M Mike 3/63) & 36/0 by 10 wkts.

v Derbyshire (Kibworth CC) – 19-21 July - Leics 296 (S T Evans 107; M D Sonczak 6/57) & 276/2d (P J Horton 83, S T Evans 82*, W N Fazackerley 72*) drew with Derbys 292/8d (T A I Taylor 107, H R Hosein 85*; W N Fazackerley 4/72, D Manthorpe 3/54) & 269/7 (J M Clarke 91, A Patel 84; R A Jones 4/64)

v Northamptonshire (Desborough CC) – 22-24 Aug – Northants 323/7d (D Murphy 92*, E A J Cox 57; M H McKiernan 4/64) & 154/5 drew with Leics 501 (N J Dexter 169, P J Horton 130; S C Kerrigan 5/128)

HOME MATCHES: FRIENDLIES

v Glamorgan (Lutterworth) – 9 May – Leics 254 (S T Evans 69, A M Ali 68; O M R Pringle 4/21) lost to Glam 260/1 (N J Selman 112*, A O Morgan 99) by nine wkts.

v Worcestershire (Desborough) – 19-21 Sept – Match abandoned without a ball bowled.

HOME MATCHES: SECOND ELEVEN TROPHY

v Lancashire (Hinckley) – 26 Apr – Lancs 246/8 (S Oldham 76*, R P Jones 66; T J Wells 6/53) beat Leics 109 (C S Delport 61; G Burrows 7/36) by 137 runs.

v Yorkshire (Lutterworth CC) – 15 May – Match abandoned without a ball bowled.

v Warwickshire (Hinckley) – 19 May - Match abandoned without a ball bowled.

HOME MATCHES : SECOND ELEVEN T20 COMPETITION

v MCC Young Cricketers (Kibworth) – 20 Apr – Match 1 – Leics 143/8 (P J Horton 56*) beat MCC YC 141/6 (M H Cross 64; T J Wells 3/33) by two runs.

v MCC Young Cricketers (Kibworth) – 20 Apr – Match 2 – MCC YC 164/3 (M H Cross 67*, B J Curran 51) beat Leics 113/8 by 51 runs.

v Northamptonshire (Lutterworth) – 18 July – Match 1 – Northants 174 (A M Ali 5/22) beat Leics 136/9 (T B Sole 3/21) by 38 runs.

v Northamptonshire (Lutterworth) – 18 July – Match 2 – Northants 179/7 (S A Zaib 76) beat Leics 73 (T B Sole 4/17) by 106 runs.

v Derbyshire (Leicester GS) – 24 July – Match 1 – Match abandoned without a ball bowled.

v Derbyshire (Leicester GS) – 24 July – Match 2 – Match abandoned without a ball bowled.

PLAYERS WHO HAVE REPRESENTED LEICESTERSHIRE 2nd XI IN 2017 (52)

C N Ackerman	M H Cross	P J Horton	C F Parkinson
M Ahmed	B J Curran	M Hussain	M L Pettini
A M Ali	H E Dearden	* C M Jones	M W Pillans
I Amjad	C S Delport	M A Jones	M Raffique
J E Bailey	N J Dexter	R A Jones	B A Raine
J H Barrett	J W Dickinson	Kashif Ali	* J A J Rishton
*A J Ball	E J H Eckersley	D Klein	R J Sayer
*C J Ball	S T Evans	* B I W Ladd-Gibbon	A Shahzad
R N Bell	W N Fazackerley	C M Laker	C E Shreck
J C Blunt	H Funnell	D Manthorpe	H J Swindells
D N Butchart	J Graham	M H McKiernan	J S Sykes
Z J Chappell	G T Griffiths	B W M Mike	A Trusz
M J Cosgrove	L J Hill	J Nightingale	T J Wells

LEICESTERSHIRE CRICKETERS

Colin Niel ACKERMAN (Grey HS, P Eliz,; U of S Africa) b George, Cape Province, S Africa, 4.4.91. RHB OB. F/C debut E Prov v Gauteng, Johannesburg, 2010/11; debuts Warriors 2013/14; Leics 2017. HS 13 v Glam, Lutterworth, 2017. HST20 6 v Worcs, Worcester RGS, 2017 (1st). BB T20 1/20 in the same match.

AADIL MASUD ALI (Lancaster Boys; Wyggeston & Queen Elizabeth I Coll, Leicester) b Leicester, 29.12.94. RHB OB. Debut 2013. F/C debut v Kent, Grace Road, 2015. HS 126 v Worcs, Kidderminster, 2015. BB 2/20 v Warwicks, Shirley, 2015. HSSET 96 v MCC YC, Merchant Taylors' S, Northwood, 2017. BBSET 2/34 v Durham, Grace Road, 2014. HST20 61 v Worcs, Kidderminster, 2015 (2nd). BBT20 5/22 v Northants, Lutterworth, 2017 (1st). Leics Staff.

Mohammed AHMED (Small Heath S; Solihull Coll) b Birmingham, 18.3.99. LHB LA Chinaman. Debut 2017. BB 0/36 v Warwicks, EFCSG, 2017.

Irfan AMJAD (Batley Bus & Ent Coll; Park Lane SFC; Huddersfield U) b Dewsbury, W Yorks, 14.10.93. RHB OB. Debut Derbys 2015; Leics 2017. HS 27 v Worcs, Worcester RGS, 2017.

Jacob Edward BAILEY (The Market Bosworth S; Bosworth Acad) b Leicester, 27.5.99. RHB RM. Debut 2017. HS 12 v Durham, Riverside, 2017. BB 4/57 v Warwicks, EFCSG, 2017. HST20 1* v Northants, Lutterworth, 2017 (1st). BBT20 2/16 v Warwicks, Scorers, 2017 (2nd).

Adam James BALL (Beths GS, Bexley) b Greenwich 1.3.93. RHB LMF. Debut Kent 2009 aged 16 years and 16 days. F/C debut (Kent) v Glos, Canterbury, 2011. Debut Leics 2017. Eng U19 to New Zealand 2009/10; v Sri Lanka 2010; to Sri Lanka, 2010/11; v South Africa, 2011; to Bangladesh & to Australia 2011/12; to Australia, World Cup, 2011/12. HS 125 (Kent) v Surrey, Whitgift S, 2013. BB 7/26 (Kent) v Sussex, Canterbury, 2015. HSSET 103 (Kent) v Hants, Polo Farm, Canterbury, 2015 & v Middx, Beckenham, 2016. BBSET 3/29 (Kent) v Hants, Maidstone, 2012. HST20 74 (Kent) v MCCYC, Beckenham, 2016 (1st). BBT20 2/21 (Kent) v Sussex, Horsham, 2015 (1st).

*Cameron James BALL (Longdendale HS, Hyde, Cheshire; Loretto S, Manchester) b Hadfield, 22.11.98. RHB RM. Debut Derbys 2016; Leics 2017. HS 28 (Derbys) v Durham, Darlington, 2016. BB 0/14 in the same match. HSSET 0 (Derbys) v Yorks, York, 2017. BBSET 0/18 in the same match.

Joseph Hedley BARRETT (Burford S, Oxon) b Chipping Norton, Oxon, 13.12.95. LHB RM. Debut Glos 2010; MCCYC & Notts

2016; Hants & Leics 2017. HS 108 (MCC YC) v Lancs, Urmston, 2017. BB 0/10 (MCCYC) v Sussex, Eastbourne, 2016. HSSET 109 (Hants) v Sussex, Fulking, 2017. BBSET 0/22 (MCCYC) v Hants, Ageas Bowl Nursery, 2016. HST20 63* (MCC YC) v Durham, Merchant Taylors' S, Northwood, 2017 (2nd). BBT20 2/28 (MCCYC) v Hants, 2016 (1st). HSKO 4 (Glos) v Somerset, Taunton Vale, 2010

Richard Nicholas BELL (King Edward VI GS, Louth, Lincs) b Lincoln, 25.12.00. RHB WK. Debut 2017. HS 5 v Derbys, Kibworth, 2017. HS 0 v Lancs, Desborough, 2017. HST20 11* v Northants, Lutterworth, 2017 (1st).

Joshua Carl BLUNT (Longfield Acad, Melton Mowbray; Loughborough GS) b Leicester, 17.9.98. RHB LB. Debut 2017. HS 0 v Lancs, Desborough, 2017.

Donald Norton BUTCHART (Oakham S) b Harare, Zim, 18.12.98. RHB RM. Son of I P. Tests (Zim) 1 & 20 ODIs, 1993 to 1994/95. Debut 2017. HS 9 v Derbys, Kibworth, 2017. BB 0/34 in the same match. HST20 11 v Northants, Lutterworth, 2017 (1st). BBT20 1/18 v MCC YC, Kibworth, 2017 (2nd).

Zachariah John CHAPPELL (Stamford S, Lincs) b Grantham, Lincs, 21.8.96. RHB RFM. Debut 2015. F/C debut v Derbys, Derby, 2015. HS 99 v MCC YC, High Wycombe, 2017. BB 3/23 v Notts, Notts SG, 2017. HSSET 24 v Warwicks, Bull's Head Ground, Coventry, 2016. BBSET 2/36 v Northants, Lancot Park, Totternhoe, 2015. HST20 22* v Northants, Grace Road, 2015 (1st). Leics Staff.

Mark James COSGROVE b Elizabeth, Adelaide, S Aus, 14.6.84. LHB RM. ODIs (Aus) 3 (2005/06 to 2006/07). Debut (S Aus) & F/C debut v Queensland, the Gabba, 2002/03. Debut Glam 2006; Leics 2015. HSSET 22 (Glam) v Yorks, Barnsley, 2009. HST20 76 (Glam) v Glos, Bristol, 2011,

Matthew Henry CROSS (Robert Gordon Coll; Loughborough U) b Aberdeen, Scotland, 15.10.92. RHB WK. Debut Scotland A 2009; 32 ODIs & 23 T20s (Scotland), 2013 to date. Debut Notts 2011. F/C debut (Loughborough MCCU) v Sussex, Hove, 2013. Debut Leics 2015; Essex 2016; MCC YC, Kent & Northants 2017. HS 105* (Notts) v MCCU, Notts Sports Ground, 2012. HSSET 80 (Notts) v Derbys, Notts SG, 2014. HST20 69 (MCC YC) v Merchant Taylors' S, Northwood, 2017 (1st).

Benjamin Jack CURRAN (Wellington Coll) b Northampton, 7.6.96. LHB OB. Brother of T K Tests 1 (Eng) 2017/18 & 1 ODI (2017) & S M (both Surrey) and son of K M (Northants, Glos,

Boland, SA & Natal, SA, 1980/81 to 1999. ODIs 11 (Zim) 1983 to 1987/88). Debut MCC YC 2015; Notts & Surrey 2016; Warwicks & Leics 2017. HS 192 (MCC YC) v Yorks, High Wycombe, 2017. HSSET 141* (MCC YC) v Middx, Radlett, 2016. HST20 87* (MCC YC) v Notts, Merchant Taylors' S, Northwood, 2017 (2nd).

Harry Edward DEARDEN (Tottington HS, Bury) b Bury, Lancs, 7.5.97. LHB OB. Debut Lancs 2013 aged 16 years & 14 days. Debut Hants & Leics 2016. F/C debut (Leics) v Derbys, Derby, 2016. HS 141 v MCC YC, High Wycombe, 2017. BB 1/26 in the same match. HSSET 81 (Hants) v Surrey, Ageas Bowl Nursery, 2016. BBSET 0/16 (Hants) v Glam, Newport, 2016. HST20 53 v Durham, Riverside, 2017 (1st). BBT20 3/7 in the same match.

Cameron Scott DELPORT (Kloof Sen S; Westville Boys HS, KZN) b Durban, Natal, S Africa, 12.5.89. LHB RM. Debut Kent 2007; F/C debut (Kwa-Zulu Natal) v E Province, Port Elizabeth, 2009/10. Debut Dolphins 2009/10; Leics 2016. HS 99* v Middx, Uxbridge, 2017. BB 1/26 in the same match. HSSET 157 v Northants, Northampton, 2017. BBSET 2/57 in the same match. HST20 60 v Warwicks, Scorers, 2017 (1st). BBT20 2/32 v Warwicks, Scorers, 2017 (2nd).

Neil John DEXTER (Northwood HS, Hillingdon; Varsity Coll, U of S Africa) b Johannesburg, Transvaal, S Africa, 21.8.84. RHB RM. Debut Kent 2004; F/C debut (Kent) v Bangladesh A, Canterbury, 2005; debut Essex 2008; Middx 2009; Cap 2010; debut Leics 2016. HS 169 v Northants, Desborough, 2017. BB 3/24 (Kent) v MCC YC, RAF Vine Lane, Uxbridge, 2006. HSSET 147 (Middx) v Glos, Bristol, 2015. BBSET 5/35 (Kent) v Surrey, Tonbridge S, 2007. HST20 43 (Middx) v Leics, Uxbridge CC, 2011. BBT20 3/21 (Middx) v Northants, Uxbridge CC, 2012 (2nd).

James William DICKINSON (Loretto S, Musselburgh, Scotland) b Edinburgh, 14.9.98. RHB BLB. Debut 2016. HS 22* v Durham, Riverside, 2017. BB 1/19 v Notts, Coalville CC, 2017.

Edmund John Holden "Ned" ECKERSLEY (St Benedict's GS, Ealing) b Oxford, 9.8.89. RHB OB WK. Debut MCCYC 2007; Middx 2008, Northants 2010, Leics 2011. F/C debut v Surrey, Grace Road, 2011. Debut Mountaineers, Zim, 2011/12. Leics Cap 2013. HS 133* v Yorks, Hinckley, 2011. BB 2/10 (MCCYC) v Glos, Cheltenham, 2010. HSSET 112 v Derbys, Grace Road, 2013. HST20 61 v Worcs, New Road, 2017 (2nd). Leics Staff.

Samuel Thomas EVANS (Lancaster Boys S, Leicester; Wyggeston & Queen Elizabeth I Coll, U of Leicester) b Leicester, 20.12.97. RHB. Debut 2015. F/C debut (Loughborough MCCU) v Leics, Grace Road, 2017. HS 107 v Derbys, Derby, 2017. BB 1/5 v Lancs, Ashby-de-la-Zouch, 2015. HSSET 57 v Warwicks, Bull's Head Ground, Coventry, 2016. HST20 29 v Durham, Riverside, 2017 (1st).

William "Will" N FAZACKERLEY (Lancing Coll, Sussex) b Guernsey, 19.6.98. RHB RFM. Debut 2016. F/C debut v Sussex, Arundel, 2017. HS 83 v Durham, Riverside, 2017. BB 6/55 v Yorks, Kibworth, 2017. HSSET 102 v MCC YC, Merchant Taylors' S, Northwood, 2017. BBSET 1/23 v Notts, Notts SG, 2017. HST20 40 v MCC YC, Kibworth, 2017 (2nd). BBT20 2/25 v Durham, Riverside, 2017 (2nd). Retired from cricket at the end of the 2017 season.

Harry FUNNELL (Uppingham S) b Leicester. 31.5.99. LHB RM. Debut 2017. HST20 1* v MCC YC, Kibworth, 2017 (2nd). BB T20 1/14 in the same match.

James GRAHAM (Brockington Coll, Enderby; Sir Frank Whittle Studio S, Lutterworth) b Leicester, 2.9.99. RHB LM. Debut 2017. BB 0/12 v Worcs, Worcester RGS, 2017.

Gavin Timothy GRIFFITHS (St Michael's C of E HS, Chorley; St Mary's Coll, Crosby) b Ormskirk, 19.11.93. RHB RMF. Eng U19 v S.Africa, 2011 & to S Africa 2012/13. Debut Lancs 2011. List A debut (Lancs) v Northants, Old Trafford, 2014. Debut Hants & Leics 2016. HS 36 (Lancs) v Derbys, Denby, 2015. BB 5/58 (Lancs) v Sussex, Hove, 2011. HSSET 6* (Lancs) vDurham, Middlewich, 2015 & v Kent, Ageas Bowl Nursery, 2016. BBSET 6/27 (Hants) v Kent, Ageas Bowl Nursery, 2016. HST20 14 (Lancs) v Durham, Parkgate, Neston, 2013 (1st) BBT20 3/8 (Lancs) v Yorks, Parkgate, Neston, 2017 (2nd).

Lewis John HILL (Hastings HS, Hinckley; John Cleveland Coll, Hinckley) b Leicester 5.10.90. RHB RM. Debut Leics 2009;

Unicorns 2012. F/C debut v Kent, Canterbury, 2015. HS 143 v Notts, Notts Sports Ground, 2011. BB 1/2 v Durham, Darlington, 2013. HSSET 125 v Northants, Kibworth, 2016. HST20 65* v Derbys, Derby, 2016 (2nd), BBT20 1/20 v Essex, Chelmsford, 2012 (1st). HSKO 12* v Northants, Dunstable, 2010.

Paul James HORTON (St Margaret's HS, Liverpool) b Sydney, NSW, Australia, 20.9.82. RHB RM.Debut Lancs 2001; F/C debut v Durham UCCE, racecourse, 2003; Lancs Cap 2007; debut Matabeleland Tuskers, Zim, 2010/11; Leics 2016. HS 277* v Warwicks, EFCSG, 2017. BB 3/11 (Lancs) v Middx, Liverpool, 2015. HSSET 61 (Lancs) v Durham, Liverpool, 2006. HST20 56* v MCC YC, Kibworth, 2017 (2nd). HSKO 43 (Lancs) v Derbys, Glossop, 2010 .

Mosun HUSSAIN (City of Leeds S) b Leeds, 27.3.97. RHB RM. Debut Yorks 2012; Leics 2017. Eng U19 to Aus 2014/15. HS 104 (Yorks) v Northants, York, 2015. BB 0/11 (Yorks) v Glos, Bristol, 2014. HSSET 48 (Yorks) v Warwicks, Knowle & Dorridge, 2016. HST20 48 (Yorks) v Durham, York, 2013 (2nd).

***Christopher Michael JONES** (Ash Manor S, Aldershot, Hants; Farnborough SFC) b Frimley Park, Surrey, 10.8.97. RHB OB. Debut Surrey 2014; Leics 2017. HS 79 (Surrey) v Somerset, Bath, 2016. BB 3/52 in the same match. HSSET 14* (Surrey) v Sussex, Horsham, 2014. BBSET 3/29 (Surrey) v Glos, Bristol, 2014. HST20 6 (Surrey) v Hants, Purley, 2015 (1st). BBT20 4/25 (Surrey) v Glam, Purley, 2016 (1st).

Michael Alexander JONES (Ormskirk GS; Myerscough Coll) b Ormskirk, Lancs, 5.1.98. RHB OB. Debut Derbys, Durham, Leics & Scotland A 2017. HS 173* (Scotland A) v Durham, Riverside, 2017. HSSET 34 (Durham) v Lancs, Bowden, 2017. HST20 35 v Durham, Riverside, 2017 (1st).

Richard Alan JONES (Grange S, Stourbridge; King Edward VI S, Stourbridge; Loughborough U). b Wordsley, Stourbridge, 6.11.86. RHB RMF. Debut Worcs 2004, F/C debut (Worcs) v Loughborough MCCU, New Road, 2007. Worcs Cap 2007. Debut Warwicks 2014; Leics 2017. HS 72* (Worcs) v Lancs, Nantwich, 2014. BB 6/29 (Worcs) v Warwicks, Worcester RGS, 2011 HSSET 34 (Worcs) v Durham, New Road, 2011. BBSET 4/61 (Warwicks) v Notts, Notts SG, 2016. HST20 11 v Northants, Lutterworth, 2017 (2nd). BBT20 3/5 (Warwicks) v Worcs, Shirley, 2016 (1st).

KASHIF ALI (Dunstable Coll) b Kashmir, Pakistan, 7.2.98. RHB LB. Debut Essex 2016; Leics 2017. HS 76 (Essex) v Kent, Polo Farm SG, Canterbury, 2017. BB 0/14 (Essex) v Middx, Coggeshall, 2017. HSSET 24 (Essex) v Sussex, Billericay, 2017. HST20 27* (Essex) v Middx, Coggeshall, 2017. BBT20 0/19 in the same match.

Dieter KLEIN (Hoerskool, Lichtenburg) b Lichtenburg, NW Province, S Africa, 31.10.88. RHB LMF. Debut & F/C debut (N West) v Free State, Bloemfontein, 2007/08; debut Kent & Hants 2012; Lions (SA) 2012/13; Somerset 2015; Leics 2016. HS 22* v Notts, Notts SG, 2017. BB 5/35 (Hants) v Sussex, Fulking, 2012. HSSET 10 (Kent) v Glam, SWALEC, 2012. BBSET 3/48 v Notts, Notts SG, 2017. HST20 12 v Northants, Lutterworth, 2017 (1st). BBT20 2/36 v Northants, Lutterworth, 2017 (2nd).

***Benjamin Ian William LADD-GIBBON** (Clayesmore S, Blandford Forum, Dorset; Bryanston S, B Forum, Dorset; Loughborough U) b Dorchester, Dorset, 20.5.94. RHB RMF. Debut Somerset 2015;Leics 2017. HS 9* (Somerset) v Middx, Merchant Taylors' S, 2015 & v Glam, Lutterworth, 2017. BB 3/47 (Somerset) v Glam, SWALEC, 2015. BBT20 1/32 (Somerset) v Glos, Taunton Vale, 2015 (1st).

Christopher Michael LAKER (Wellacre Acad, Manchester; Pendleton SFC; Edge Hill U, Ormskirk) b Trafford, Manchester, 5.9.96. LHB RM. Debut Lancs 2016; Leics 2017. HS 66 (Lancs) v Derbys, Derby, 2016.

Matthew Harry "Mattie" McKIERNAN (Lowton HS, Leigh; St John Rigby Coll, Wigan) b Billinge, Merseyside, 14.6.94. RHB LB. Debut Lancs 2011; Northants 2012 (on loan). Ret to Lancs 2013; Leics & Unc 2016; Durham 2017. HS 49 (Lancs) v Leics, Liverpool, 2014. BB 4/64 v Northants, Desborough, 2017. HSSET 42 (Lancs) v Leics, Grace Road, 2014. BBSET 5/45 (Durham) v Worcs, New Road, 2017. HST20 18* (Unc) v Hants, Great Tew, 2017 (2nd). BBT20 3/11 (Unc) v Leics, Long Marston, 2016 (2nd).

Dominic MANTHORPE (Hadleigh HS, Suffolk; St Joseph's Coll, Ipswich) b Bury St Edmunds, Suffolk, 18.7.97. LHB LFM. Debut Essex 2015; Leics 2017. HS 5* v Yorks, Kibworth, 2017. BB 4/86 v Kent, Beckenham, 2017. HST20 2* v Durham, Riverside, 2017 (2nd). BBT20 2/19 v Northants, Lutterworth, 2017 (2nd).

Benjamin Wentworth Munro MIKE (Loughborough GS) b Nottingham, 24.8.98. RHB RM. Son of G M (Notts 1989 to 1996). Debut 2017. HS 59 v Kent, Beckenham, 2017. BB 3/63 v Lancs, Desborough, 2017. HSSET 4* v Notts, Notts SG, 2017. BBSET 0/21 in the same match. HST20 5 v MCC YC, Kibworth, 2017 (2nd). BBT29 0/7 v Warwicks, Scorers, 2017 (2nd).

Jack NIGHTINGALE (Ratcliffe Coll) b Leicester, 13.11.99. RHB RMF. Debut 2017. HST20 0 v MCC YC, Kibworth, 2017 (2nd).

Callum Francis PARKINSON (Bolton S; Canon Slade S, Bolton) b Bolton, Lancs, 24.10.96. RHB SLA. Debut Derbys 2016; Leics 2017. Twin brother of M W (Lancs 2013 to date). F/C debut (Derbys) v Leics, Grace Road, 2016. HS 46 v Warwicks, EFCSG, 2017. BB 5/64 (Derbys) v Glam, Belper Meadows, 2016. HSSET 40 v Notts, Notts SG, 2017. BBSET 2/17 (Derbys) v Yorks, Harrogate, 2016 (2nd). HST20 17* v Warwicks, Scorers, 2017 (1st). BBT20 4/13 v Warwicks, Scorers, 2017 (2nd).

Mark Lewis PETTINI (Comberton Village Coll, Hills Road SFC, Cambridge, Cardiff U) b Brighton, Sussex 7.8.83. RHB RM. Eng U19 v India 2002. Debut Essex 1999. F/C debut (Essex) v Yorks, Scarborough, 2001. Essex Cap 2006. Debut Leics 2016. HS 217 (Essex) v Warwicks, Chelmsford, 2003. HSSET 88 (Essex) v Unc, Billericay, 2014. HST20 84 (Essex) v Northants, Chelmsford, 2013 (2nd).

Mathew William PILLANS (Pretoria Boys HS, Gauteng, S Africa; U of Pretoria) b Westville, KwaZulu-Natal, S Africa, 4.7.91. RHB RFM. Debut (Northerns) v N West, Pretoria, 2012/13; debut KZN & Dolphins 2013/14; Somerset 2014; Glam 2015; Surrey 2016; Leics 2017. HS 73 (Surrey) v Hants, Ageas Bowl Nursery, 2016. BB 5/42 (Surrey) v Glos, Purley, 2017. HSSET 49 (Surrey) v Essex, Billericay, 2017. BBSET 3/37 (Surrey) v Glos, Purley, 2017. HST20 23 (Surrey) v Middx, Sunbury, 2017 (1st). BBT20 3/23 (Surrey) v MCCYC, High Wycombe, 2016 (1st).

Mustafa RAFIQUE (Roundhay HS; U of E London) b Leeds 2.3.98. RHB RMF. Debut 2017. HS 12 v Worcs, Worcester RGS, 2017. BB 1/31 in the same match.

Benjamin Alexander RAINE (St Aidan's RC Sec S, Sunderland) b Sunderland 14.9.91. RHB RMF. Debut Durham 2009. F/C debut (Durham) v Sri Lanka A, Chester-le-Street, 2011. Debut Leics & Sussex 2013. HS 208 (Leics) v Essex, Chelmsford, 2014. BB 5/31 (Leics) v Yorks, York, 2014. HSSET 69 (Durham) v Notts, Acklam Park, Mbro, 2010. BBSET 2/3 (Leics) v Notts, Notts SG, 2013. HST20 29 (Durham) v Glos, Fenner's, 2011. BBT20 3/8 (Durham) v Lancs, Blackpool, 2011 (2nd). Leics staff.

*James Andrew John "Andy" RISHTON (Bradfield Coll; Loughborough U) b Boston, Mass, USA, 14.2.95. RHB RM. Debut 2017. HS 6 v Lancs, Southport, 2017. BB 0/14 in the same match.

Robert John SAYER (Abbey Coll, Ramsey, Cambridgeshire) b Huntingdon, 25.10.95. RHB OB. Debut Leics & Unicorns A 2013. F/C debut v Derbys, Grace Road, 2015. Eng U19s (T20 only) 2013; to UAE 2013/14 (Tri/Series). HS 94* v Yorks, York, 2016. BB 5/57 v Somerset, Taunton Vale, 2016. HSSET 23 v MCCYC, High Wycombe, 2014. BBSET 2/24 v Worcs, Grace Road, 2014. HST20 30 v Unc, Long Marston, 2016 (2nd). BBT20 3/19 v Worcs, Kidderminster, 2015 (2nd).

Ajmal SHAHZAD (Woodhouse Grove S, Bradford) b Huddersfield, Yorks, 27.7.85. RHB RMF. Debut Yorks 2003;F/C debut (Yorks) v Middx, Scarborough, 2006. Cap 2010. Debut Lancs 2012 (on loan); Debut Notts 2013; Sussex 2015; Leics & Northants 2017. Tests (Eng) 1 & 11 ODIs (2010-2010/11). HS 57 (Yorks) v Derbys, Barnsley, 2008. BB 6/42 in the same match. HSSET 91 (Yorks) v Leics, Bingley, 2008. BBSET 3/55 (Yorks) v Durham, Seaton Carew, 2006. HST20 27 (Sussex) v Surrey, Purley, 2016 (1st). BB 3/29 (Sussex) v Surrey, New Malden, 2017 (1st).

Charles Edward SHRECK (Truro S, Cornwall) b Truro, 6.1.78. RHB RFM. Debut Worcs 1996; Middx & Northants 1999; Notts 2002; F/C debut v Durham UCCE Trent Bridge,2003, Notts Cap 2006; debut Wellington (NZ) 2005/06; debut Kent 2012; Leics 2014. Notts cap 2006. HS 34 (Notts) v Surrey, Notts SG, 2005. BB 6/17 (Notts) v MCC Un, Weetwood, 2011. HSSET 22* (Notts) v Leics, Nottingham HS, 2009. BBSET 5/31(Notts) v Northants, Papplewick & Linby 2005.

Harry John SWINDELLS (Brockington Coll, Leics; Lutterworth Coll) b Leicester, 21.2.99. RHB WK. Eng U19 v India, 2017. Debut 2015. HS 60 v Worcs, Worcester RGS, 2017. HSSET 19 v Warwicks, Bull's Head Ground, Coventry, 2016. HST20 29 v Warwicks, Edgbaston, 2015 (1st).

James Stuart SYKES (St Ivo S, St Ives, Cambs) b Huntingdon 26.4.92. LHB SLA. Debut Leics 2009. F/C debut (Leics) v Essex, Chelmsford, 2013; Debut Derbys 2017. HS 66 v Worcs, Kidderminster, 2015. BB 8/55 v Durham, Chester-le-Street, 2011. HSSET 28* v MCCYC, High Wycombe, 2014. BBSET 4/16 v Worcs, Grace Road, 2014. HST20 33 v Unc, Loughborough CC, 2015 (1st). BBT20 3/13 v Derbys, Grace Road, 2015 (2nd). Left Leics at the end of the 2017 season.

Ashish "Ash" TRUSZ (Loughborough GS) b Leicester, 9.7.99. RHB RMF. Debut 2017. HS 34* v Lancs, Southport, 2017. HST20 7 v MCC YC, Kibworth, 2017 (2nd).

Thomas Joshua WELLS (Gartree & Beauchamp C, Oadby) b Grantham, Lincs 15.3.93. (Son of John Wells, Leicester Tigers RUFC, 1982-2006. Coach to England's forwards 2006-12; Newcastle Falcons 2013 to date) RHB RMF. Debut 2009 aged 16 years and 163 days. F/C debut v Lancs, Grace Road, 2013. HS 148 v Durham, Darlington, 2013. BB 5/51 v Durham, Desborough, 2016. HSSET 111 v Lancs, Lutterworth, 2013. BBSET 6/53 v Lancs, Hinckley, 2017. HST20 55 v Worcs, Kibworth, 2016 (2nd). BBT20 3/33 v MCC YC, Kibworth, 2017 (1st). HSKO 3 v Sussex, Lutterworth, 2010. BBKO 1/18 in the same match. Leics Staff.

MCC UNIVERSITIES

PLAYING RECORD 2017
Championship – P9 W0 L2 D7 - eighth in the southern group

2nd XI SUCCESSES
Championship – Best finish – third in the northern group in 2016

SECOND ELEVEN CHAMPIONSHIP AVERAGES

BATTING	M	I	NO	Runs	HS	Avge	100s	C/S
X G Owen	8	8	6	102	24	51.00	-	2
N R Kumar	4	7	1	299	76*	49.83	-	3
K S Leverock	3	5	3	96	46*	48.00	-	1
J W Tetley	8	12	1	413	94	37.54	-	4
J M Cooke	8	9	1	291	105	36.37	1	2
J D Marshall	7	12	2	359	102	35.90	-	4
O C Soames	9	15	2	462	106*	35.53	1	4
A D Tillcock	4	4	0	135	79	33.75	-	2
W A R Fraine	6	10	0	325	65	32.50	-	3
B M Broughton	4	5	1	110	48	27.50	-	3
R T Sehmi	6	9	1	196	58	24.50	-	5/3
A T Thomson	3	4	1	63	39*	21.00	-	2
H J Palmer	4	7	0	92	31	13.14	-	-
H A J Allen	3	3	0	36	22	12.00	-	2
J A L Scriven	4	5	0	42	35	8.40	-	5
A H McGrath	5	6	0	45	15	7.50	-	1
O S Bocking	5	5	1	23	7	5.75	-	1
J A Clifford	4	4	0	16	14	4.00	-	2

BOWLING	O	M	Runs	Wkt	Avge	BB
A T Thomson	118	12	467	19	24.57	7/148
J A Clifford	58	7	213	7	30.42	3/68
X G Owen	173	39	582	18	32.33	4/56
A D F Brewster	64	16	249	7	35.57	3/38
A D Tillcock	128.2	14	445	11	40.45	6/162
J M Cooke	39	6	176	4	44.00	2/45
H A J Allen	41	3	163	3	54.33	2/72
A H McGrath	88	16	289	5	57.80	2/30
O S Bocking	112	22	406	7	58.00	2/44
S R Green	58.2	6	261	4	65.25	4/47
S E Rippington	73.3	6	358	4	89.50	3/96

Also bowled – M H Azad 5-0-39-1; B M Broughton 2.2-0-18-1; L A Jones 13-1-78-2; N R Kumar 4-0-33-0; M Lake 17-2-60-1; K S Leverock 38-3-159-1; D Scott 2-1-7-2; J A L Scriven 40.4-9-119-2; O C Soames 1-0-8-0; J W Tetley 2-1-1-0.

Also batted – 4 matches – S E Rippington 0 (1 ct). 3 matches – A D F Brewster DNB. 2 matches – S R Green 17*, 6. 1 match – M H Azad 25, 2 (1ct); L A Jones 8, 4 (1ct); M Lake 58, 0 (1ct); D Scott 0, 11.

HOME MATCHES: SECOND ELEVEN CHAMPIONSHIP

v Hampshire (Horsham) – 27-29 June – MCCU 213 (A D Tillcock 79; R J W Topley 4/20, F H Edwards 4/42) & 174/4 (N R Kumar 76*) drew with Hants 377 (W R Smith 81, C B Sole 75, T P Alsop 50; S E Rippington 3/96).
v Sussex (Hastings) – 5-7 July – Sussex 406/6d (A J Robson 137, L P Smith 82*, O E Robinson 71, E O Hooper 67*) & 321/9d (A J Robson 97, P D Salt 64; A T Thomson 7/148) drew with MCCU 396 (J M Cooke 105, J W Tetley 65, M R Kumar 65, W A R Fraine 57; E O Hooper 6/110)

v Middlesex (Radlett) – 17-19 July – MCCU 370/9d (O C Soames 94, J W Tetley 80; H W Podmore 3/73, R H Patel 3/88) & 226/6 drew with Middx 612/4d (G F B Scott 212*, R G White 160*, T C Lace 106, S S Eskinazi 97; X G Owen 3/106)
v Glamorgan (The Mumbles) – 1-3 Aug – Glam 189 (J L Lawlor 99*; S R Green 4/47, A D F Brewster 3/38) & 154/3 (J R Murphy 86*) drew with MCCU 104 (K A Bull 5/30)
v Kent (Beckenham) – 7-9 Aug – Kent 347/7d (J J Weatherley 76, C J Basey 73, G Stewart 50*) & 117/1(K C Appleby 63) drew with MCCU 349/5d (O C Soames 106*, W A R Fraine 65, R T Sehmi 58)

MCC UNIVERSITIES CRICKETERS

Harry Andrew John ALLEN (Epsom Coll; Cardiff U) b. Carshalton, Surrey, 25.3.96. RHB, SLA. Debuts Surrey 2012; Cardiff MCCU 2016; Glam & MCCU 2017. HS 59 (Glam) v Glos, Newport, 2017. BB 2/42 in the same match. HSSET 11 (Glam) v Unc, Newbury, 2017. BBSET 3/24 (Surrey) v Essex, Sunbury-on-Thames, 2017. HST20 5 (Surrey) v MCCYC, Purley, 2013 (2nd). BBT20 3/32 (Glam) v Surrey, Neath, 2017 (1st).
M H AZAD (Fernwood Comp S, Nottingham; Bilborough Coll, Nottingham; Loughborough U) b Quetta, Balochistan, Pakistan, 7.1.94. LHB LB. Debut Notts 2012; MCCU 2015. F/C debut (Loughborough MCCU) v Hants, Ageas Bowl Nursery, 2015. HS 123 v Northants, Desborough, 2016. BB 1/2 (Notts) v Yorks, Notts

SG, 2014. HSSET 57 (Notts) v Yorks, Notts SG, 2014. HST20 42 (Notts) v Lancs, Worksop Coll, 2013 (2nd)
Oliver Stuart BOCKING (Ipswich S) b Colchester, 25.4.96. RHB RFM. Debut Essex 2012; MCCU 2017. F/C debut (Leeds/Bradford MCCU) v Kent, Canterbury, 2017. HS 40 (Essex) v MCCU, Billericay, 2017. BB 4/32 (Essex) v Kent, Beckenham, 2017. HSSET 8* (Essex) v Somerset, Halstead, 2016. BBSET 2/28 (Essex) v Hants, Coggeshall, 2016. HST20 1 (Essex) v Kent, Polo Farm SG, Canterbury, 2017 (2nd) & (Essex) v Middx, Coggeshall, 2017 (1st). BBT20 1/17 (Essex) v Somerset, Chelmsford, 2015 (2nd).

Andrew David Francis BREWSTER (Tadcaster GS & SFC) b York, 1.2.97. RHB RFM. Debut Glam 2016; Durham, Northants & MCCU 2017. F/C debut (Cardiff MCCU) v Glam, SWALEC, 2017. BB 4/33 (Durham) v Essex, Richmond, N Yorks, 2017. HST20 5* (Northants) v Notts, Grantham, 2017 (2nd). BBT20 1/6 (Durham) v Worcs, Burnopfield CC, 2017 (2nd).

Bruno Miles BROUGHTON (Cranleigh S) b Lambeth, Surrey, 10.10.94. RHB SLA. Debut 2015. F/C debut (Oxford MCCU) v Northants, The Parks, 2017. HS 48 v Essex, Billericay, 2017. BB 1/15 v Glos, Bath, 2017.

James Andrew CLIFFORD (Great Baddow HS) b Chelmsford, 2.9.96. RHB OB. Debut Essex, 2014; MCCU 2017. HS 42* (Essex) v MCCYC, High Wycombe, 2016. BB 3/68 v Somerset, Taunton Vale, 2017.

Joseph M COOKE b Hemel Hempstead, Herts, 30.5.97. LHB RFM. Debut 2017. F/C debut (Durham MCCU) v Glos, Bristol, 2017. HS 105 v Sussex, Hastings, 2017. BB 2/45 v Hants, Horsham, 2017.

William Alan Richard FRAINE (Silcoates S, Wakefield; Bromsgrove SFC; Durham U) b Huddersfield, Yorks, 13.6.96. RHB RM. Debut Worcs 2015; MCCU & Notts 2017. F/C debut (Durham MCCU) v Glos, Bristol, 2017. HS 87* (Worcs) v Yorks, Scarborough, 2016. HSSET 75 (Worcs) v Lancs, Worcester RGS, 2016. HST20 27* (Worcs) v Leics, Kidderminster, 2015 (1st).

Steven R GREEN (St Edward's S, Oxford) b 9.11.96. RHB LM. Debut MCCU 2016. HS 17* v Middx, Radlett, 2017. BB 4/47 v Glam, Mumbles, 2017.

Luke Adam JONES (Nicholas Chamberlaine S; Bedworth, Warwicks; King Edward VI, Nuneaton) b Nuneaton, Warwicks, 31.7.97. LHB OB. Debut Unc & Warwicks 2016; MCCU 2017. HS 8 v Surrey, New Malden, 2017. BB 2/78 in the same match. HST20 2* (Unc) v Durham, Burnopfield, 2016 (2nd). BBT20 0/29 in the same match.

Nitesh Roenik KUMAR (Repton S; Loughborough U) b Scarborough, Ontario, Canada, 21.5.94. RHB OB. F/C debut (Canada) v Kenya, ICC Inter-Continental Cup, King City, Ontario, Canada, 2009/10. Debut MCCU 2016. ODIs (Canada) 16 (2009/10 to 2013/14). HS 79 v Yorks, Stamford Bridge, 2016. BB 2/61 v Durham, Gosforth, 2016.

Malcolm Blair LAKE (Oxford Brookes University) b Harare, Zim, 3.8.94. LHB RM. Debut 2017. F/C debut (Oxford MCCU) v Worcs, The Parks, 2017. HS 58 v Surrey, New Malden, 2017. BB 1/22 in the same match.

Kamau Sadiki LEVEROCK (Bermuda Institute of Higher Education; Priory SFC, Dorking, Surrey; Cardiff Met U) b Hamilton, Bermuda, 19.10.94. LHB RFM. Nephew of D, 32 ODIs (Bermuda) 2006-09. Debut Surrey & Sussex 2011; MCC YC 2014; Glam & MCCU 2015. F/C debut (Cardiff MCCU) v Glos, Bristol, 2015. Debut Somerset 2016. HS 48 v Warwicks, EFCSG, 2016. BB 3/31 v Worcs, Kidderminster, 2016. HSSET 13 (Glam) v Glos, Diamond Ground, Cardiff, 2015. BBSET 3/54 in the same match.

Alexander Halliday McGRATH (Durham U) b Bishop Auckland, Co Durham, June 1997. RHB LM. Debut 2017. F/C debut (Durham MCCU) v Glos, Bristol, 2017. HS 15 v Glos, Bath, 2017. BB 2/30 v Surrey, New Malden, 2017.

Jason David MARSHALL (Michael S, Kwa-Zulu Natal, S Africa; Durham U) b London, 20.6.96. RHB Debut 2017. F/C debut (Durham) v Glos, Bristol, 2017. HS 102 v Glos, Bath, 2017.

Xavier George OWEN (Durham U) b High Wycombe, Bucks, Aug 1997. RHB RM. F/C debut v Glos, S, Bristol, 2017. HS 24 v Glos, Bath, 2017. BB 5/66 v Durham, Gosforth,016.

Harrison John PALMER b Enfield, Middx, 13.10.96. RHB WK. Debut Unc 2016; MCCU 2017. F/C debut (Cambridge MCCU) v Essex, Fenner's, 2016. HS 31 v Hants, Horsham, 2017. HSSET 22 (Unc) v Essex, Billericay, 2017.

Samuel Edward RIPPINGTON (Abbey Coll, Ramsey) b Waltham Forest, Essex, 8.1.94. LHB LFM.. Debut Northants & MCCU 2017. F/C debut (Cambridge MCCU) v Notts, Fenner's, 2017. HS 10* (Northants) v Warwicks, EFCSG, 2017. BB 3/96 v Hants, Horsham, 2017.

David Neil Cullinan SCOTT b 27.7.98. RHB RM. Debut Glos 2016; MCCU 2017. F/C debut (Oxford MCCU) v Surrey, The Parks, 2017. HS 11 v Surrey, New Malden, 2017. BB 2/7 in the same match. HSSET 5 (Glos) v Somerset, Taunton Vale, 2016. BBSET 2/73 in the same match.

Jack Ashley Luke SCRIVEN (Cranleigh S; U of S Wales) b Oxford, 4.6.95. RHB OB. Son of T J A (Somerset 1998/94). Debut Somerset 2016; MCCU 2017. F/C debut (Cardiff MCCU) v Glam, SWALEC, 2017. HS 35 v Surrey, New Malden, 2017.BB 2/22 in the same match.

Robert Thomas SEHMI (Sutton Valence S, Maidstone) b Macclesfield, Cheshire, 1.8.96. RHB WK. Debut Kent 2013; MCCU 2016. HS 58 v Kent, Beckenham, 2017. BB 0/4 v Derbys, Weetwood, 2016. HSSET 18 (Kent) v Hants, Polo Farm SC, Canterbury, 2015.

Oliver Courtenay SOAMES (Cheltenham Coll; Loughborough U) b Kingston-upon-Thames, Surrey, 27.10.95. RHB RM OB. Debut Hants & MCCU 2017. HS 106* v Kent, Beckenham, 2017. BB 0/8 v Sussex, Hastings, 2017.

Joseph William TETLEY (Mount St Mary's S, Sheffield; Anglia Ruskin U) b Sheffield, Yorks, 14.4.95. LHB WK. Debut 2015. F/C debut (Cambridge MCCU) v Northants, Fenner's, 2015. HS 94 v Surrey, New Malden, 2017. BB 0/1 v Sussex, Hastings, 2017.

Alexander Thomas THOMSON (The King's S, Macclesfield, Cheshire; Denstone Coll, Uttoxeter; Cardiff Met) b Macclesfield, Cheshire, 30.10.93. RHB OB. Debut Leics 2013; Unc 2015. F/C debut (Cardiff MCCU) v Glam SWALEC, 2015. Debut MCCU 2016; Warwicks 2017. HS 101* (Warwicks) v Worcs, Bull's Head Gd, 2017. BB 7/148 v Sussex, Hastings, 2017. HST20 39* (Warwicks) v Notts, Worksop Coll, 2017 (2nd). BBT20 2/20 in the same match.

Adam David TILLCOCK (Trent Coll, Long Eaton; South Notts Coll; Loughborough U) b Nottingham 13.10.93. RHB SLA. Debut Notts 2011. List A debut (Notts) v Bang A, Trent Bridge, 2013. Debut Kent & Leics 2016. MCCU 2017. HS 115 (Notts) v Yorks, Notts SG, 2014. BB 6/162 v Somerset, Taunton Vale, 2017. HSSET 50* (Notts) v Derbys, Trent Coll, 2013. BBSET 5/39 (Notts) v Durham, Gosforth, 2014. HST20 50* (Notts) v Lancs, Ormskirk, (1st). BBT20 4/18 (Notts) v Durham, Trent Coll, 2013 (2nd).

MCC YOUNG CRICKETERS

PLAYING RECORDS 2017
Championship – P9 L4 D5 – ninth in the northern group
2nd XI Trophy – P6 W1 L4 NR1 – eighth in the northern group
2nd XI T20 Competition – P12 W7 L3 Ab2 – third in the northern group

2nd XI SUCCESSES
Championship – Best finish – fifth in the group in 2010
2nd XI Trophy – Best finish – second in the group in 2006 and 2007
2nd XI T20 Competition – Best finish – second in the group in 2014

SECOND ELEVEN CHAMPIONSHIP AVERAGES

BATTING	M	I	NO	Runs	HS	Avge	100s	C/S
F H Allen	7	11	1	386	95	38.60	-	4
F J Hudson-Prentice	2	4	1	100	68	33.33	-	1
S M Imtiaz	9	15	0	497	118	33.13	1	9/1
J H Barrett	6	9	0	286	108	31.77	1	8
B J Curran	9	15	0	465	192	31.00	1	2
L A Jones	8	11	1	297	79	29.70	-	3
M H Cross	6	9	2	199	53	28.42	-	10
D S Manuwelege	3	6	0	163	82	27.16	-	1
T F Smith	5	9	0	230	79	25.55	-	1
B L Brookes	8	13	1	298	84	24.33	-	2
A T E Hazeldine	5	5	1	96	44	24.00	-	2
M D Lezar	8	13	0	293	58	22.53	-	3
P A Sivirajah	6	7	4	52	16*	17.33	-	4
M Renwick	3	4	1	38	14	12.66	-	1
O W Smithson	8	8	1	878	25	12.42	-	2
L J Hurt	4	6	2	44	35*	11.00	-	-

BOWLING	O	M	Runs	Wkt	Avge	BB
S E Grant	17	3	64	3	21.33	3/64
G T Main	31	2	172	6	28.66	4/101
T E Barber	35	6	149	5	29.80	3/59
L J Hurt	73	10	243	7	34.71	3/61
F J Hudson-Prentice	35	6	108	3	36.00	3/53
B L Brookes	121.5	13	506	13	38.92	4/67
O W Smithson	144.3	20	616	13	47.38	3/54
L A Jones	82	5	435	7	62.14	3/95
P A Sivirajah	106	16	374	5	74.80	5/78

Also bowled – F H Allen 35.1-4-154-2; J H Barrett 9-0-127-0; A T E Hazeldine 66.4-4-302-2; S M Imtiaz 9.2-0-129-0; A Karvelas 18-4-73-2; D S Manuwelege 9-0-65-2; B V Sears 11-1-75-0; T F Smith 30-3-175-2; I S Sohi 1.2-0-2-0; K van Vollenhoven 24-3-106-2; M B Wareing 17-4-48-1.

Also batted – 3 matches – K van Vollenhoven 3* (1ct). 1 match – B L Allen 16, 1; T E Barber DNB (1ct); J Goodwin 7; S E Grant 8*; G J Harte 78; A Karvelas DNB; G T Main 1*; B V Sears 0, 5; I S Sohi 4*; M B Wareing DNB.

SECOND ELEVEN TROPHY AVERAGES

BATTING	M	I	NO	Runs	HS	Avge	100s	C/S
L A Jones	4	3	2	83	53*	83.00	-	3
M H Cross	4	3	0	146	75	48.66	-	2/1
M D Lezar	5	4	0	136	53	34.00	-	-
B J Curran	5	4	0	115	83	28.75	-	-
P A Sivirajah	4	4	3	28	20*	28.00	-	2
J H Barrett	3	3	0	75	44	25.00	-	2
S M Imtiaz	5	4	1	72	33*	24.00	-	2/1
F H Allen	6	5	0	117	64	23.40	-	6
T F Smith	6	5	0	105	41	21.00	-	1
O W Smithson	6	4	1	42	16*	14.00	-	2
B L Brookes	5	4	2	15	6*	7.50	-	2

BOWLING	O	M	Runs	Wkt	Avge	BB
G T Main	19	0	120	4	30.00	2/50
O W Smithson	52	0	302	10	30.20	3/41
B L Brookes	41	2	200	6	33.33	3/45
P A Sivirajah	32	0	142	3	47.33	2/40
L J Hurt	31.3	1	203	4	50.75	2/66
T F Smith	47	0	233	3	77.66	2/45

Also bowled – T E Barber 18-0-95-1; F L Hudson-Prentice 10-0-49-1; L A Jones 24.1-0-141-2; B V Sears 10-0-57-1; M B Wareing 5-0-22-0.

Also batted – 4 matches - L J Hurt 11, 24. 2 matches – T E Barber 17(1ct); G T Main 1, 3. 1 match – G J Harte 21 (2ct); F J Hudson-Prentice 7; D S Manuwelege 82; B V Sears 39; M B Wareing DNB.

SECOND ELEVEN T20 AVERAGES

BATTING	M	I	NO	Runs	HS	Avge	100s	C/S
M H Cross	6	6	1	285	69	57.00	-	5
B J Curran	10	10	2	310	87*	38.75	-	1
S M Imtiaz	8	6	3	90	34	30.00	-	1/2
M Renwick	4	4	2	56	25	28.00	-	-
J H Barrett	10	10	1	231	63*	25.66	-	5/1
T F Smith	6	6	2	43	15*	10.75	-	1
F H Allen	8	7	1	59	21	9.83	-	7
L J Hurt	8	5	2	18	14*	6.00	-	6
P A Sivirajah	10	3	1	10	5	5.00	-	3
B L Brookes	8	4	0	17	14	4.25	-	5
M D Lezar	6	5	0	21	9	4.20	-	1
L A Jones	10	5	1	15	9*	3.75	-	9

BOWLING	O	M	Runs	Wkt	Avge	BB
K van Vollenhoven	7	1	22	8	2.75	5/12
O W Smithson	27	0	152	12	12.66	3/15
T F Smith	19	0	102	7	14.57	2/19
L J Hurt	26	0	154	9	17.11	2/20
B L Brookes	24	1	193	9	21.44	2/16
P A Sivirajah	35.2	1	225	10	22.50	2/15
L A Jones	25	0	168	7	24.00	2/12

Also bowled – F H Allen 7-0-44-1; A T E Hazeldine 5-0-29-0; F J Hudson-Prentice 8-0-47-1; G T Main 5-1-38-1.

Also batted – 8 matches – O W Smithson 15, 11*. 3 matches – A T E Hazeldine 9. 2 matches – F J Hudson-Prentice 5, 9 (1ct); G T Main DNB (1ct); K van Vollenhoven DNB.

HOME MATCHES: SECOND ELEVEN CHAMPIONSHIP

v **Warwickshire** (High Wycombe) – 10-12 April – Warwicks 270 (S E Grant 76; T E Barber 3/59) & 350/7d (A Javid 105, G T Thornton 71*, M R Adair 66, M J Lamb 62; G T Main 4/101) drew with MCC YC 349 (B L Brookes 84, F H Allen 53; M J Lamb 4/30) & 150/6 (Sukhjit Singh 3/25).

v **Yorkshire** (High Wycombe) – 3-5 May - MCC YC 362 (F H Allen 95, D S Manuwelege 82; J A Brooks 3/46) & 390 (B J Curran 192, G J Harte 78; J E G Logan 4/107, A Drury 3/74) drew with Yorks 526/8d (W M H Rhodes 147, J Shaw 100*, R Gibson 71; B L Brookes 4/71) & 121/5 (O W Smithson 3/54).

v **Nottinghamshire** (High Wycombe) – 12-14 June – Notts 376 (A K Dal 122, O M D Kolk 59, J E P Hebron 54; B L Brookes 3/50, L A Jones 3/95) & 40/0 beat MCC YC 158 (R N Sidebottom 4/53, M E Milnes 3/37) & 255 (S M Imtiaz 59, L A Jones 53; R N Sidebottom 4/55) by 10 wkts.

v **Durham** (High Wycombe) – 1-3 Aug – Durham 417/4d (T W M Latham 241, B A Carse 113*) drew with MCC YC 179/4 (J H Barrett 52).

v **Leicestershire** (High Wycombe) – 15-17 Aug – MCC YC 227 (F H Allen 81; R J Sayer 4/29, Z J Chappell 3/46) & 328 (S M Imtiaz 118, M D Lezar 58; B A Raine 3/18, A Shahzad 3/68) lost to Leics 469 (H E Dearden 141, Z J Chappell 99, R J Sayer 80; P A Sivirajah 5/78) & 87/1 by nine wkts.

HOME MATCHES: SECOND ELEVEN TROPHY

v **Warwickshire** (Merchant Taylors' S) – 13 Apr – Warwicks 274/7 (L Banks 78) beat MCC YC 213 (M H Cross 75, M D Lezar 53; A D Thomason 3/36) by 61 runs.

v **Yorkshire** (Merchant Taylors' S) – 2 May – MCC YC 219/9 (M D Lezar 52; R Gibson 3/35, J E G Logan 3/53) lost to Yorks 220/3 (J A Leaning 77*, R Gibson 76*) by seven wkts.

v **Leicestershire** (Merchant Taylors' S) – 18 May – Leics 279/5 (W N Fazackerley 102, A M Ali 96; O W Smithson 3/41) v MCC YC DNB. No result.

HOME MATCHES: SECOND ELEVEN T20 COMPETITION

v **Worcestershire** (Merchant Taylors' S) – 7 June – Match 1 – Worcs 94 lost to MCC YC 98/1 by nine wkts.

v **Worcestershire** (Merchant Taylors' S) – 7 June – Match 2 – MCC YC 101 (B J Twohig 3/20) lost to Worcs 102/0 (Z A Malik 52*) by 10 wkts.

v **Nottinghamshire** (Merchant Taylors' S) – 15 June – Match 1 – Notts 108/8 (O W Smithson 3/15) lost to MCC YC 111/9 (M Carter 3/23) by one wkt.

v **Nottinghamshire** (Merchant Taylors' S) – 15 June – Match 2 – Notts 134/8 (G P Smith 70) lost to MCC YC 136/6 (B J Curran 87*; A Carter 4/11) by four wkts.

v **Durham** (Merchant Taylors' S) – 31 July – Match 1 – MCC YC 184/4 (M H Cross 69, J H Barrett 58) beat Durham 113 (K van Vollenhoven 5/12) by 71 runs.

v **Durham** (Merchant Taylors' S) – 31 July – Match 2 – Durham 118/8 (K van Vollenhoven 3/10) lost to MCC YC 119/3 (J H Barrett 63*) by seven wkts.

PLAYERS WHO HAVE REPRESENTED THE MCC YOUNG CRICKETERS IN 2nd XI COMPETITIONS IN 2017 (30)

B L Allen	J Goodwin	A Karvelas	T F Smith
F H Allen	S E Grant	M D Lezar	O W Smithson
T E Barber	G J Harte	G T Main	I S Sohi
J H Barrett	A T E Hazeldine	D S Manuwelege	*B S Twine
B L Brookes	F J Hudson-Prentice	M Renwick	K van Vollenhoven
*S Cameron	L J Hurt	B V Sears	M B Wareing
M H Cross	S M Imtiaz	*W Sheffield	
B J Curran	L A Jones	P A Sivirajah	

Brandon Louis ALLEN (Aylesbury GS; St Edwards, Oxford SFC) b Aylesbury, Bucks 6.9.98. RHB WK. Debut Glos 2015 aged 16 years and 345 days. Debut MCC YC 2017. HS 68 (Glos) v Scotland A, Alveston, 2016. HSSET 16 v MCCYC, Shenley, 2016.

Finnley Hugh ALLEN (St Kentigern Coll, Auckland, NZ) b Auckland, NZ, 22.4.99. RHB WK. Debut MCC YC & Surrey 2017. List A debut (T20) (Auckland) v Central Districts, Auckland, 2016/17. HS 95 v Yorks, High Wycombe, 2017. BB 1/28 v Leics, High Wycombe, 2017. HSSET 64 v Northants, Totternhoe, 2017. HST20 21 v Leics, Kibworth, 2017 (2nd). BBT20 1/23 v Durham, Merchant Taylors' S, Northwood, 2017 (1st).

Thomas "Tom" Edward BARBER (Bournemouth GS) b Poole, Dorset, 31.8.95. RHB LFM. Debut Hants 2012. List A Debut (Hants) v Sri Lanka A, the Ageas Bowl, 2014. Debut Somerset 2016; Middx & MCC YC 2017. Eng U19 to S Africa, 2012/13; v Pak & Bang 2013. HS 27* (Hants) v Somerset, Taunton Vale, 2015. BB 5/27 (Middx) v Sussex, Richmond, 2017. HSSET 17 v Warwicks, Merchant Taylors' S, Northwood, 2017. BBSET 2/29 (Middx) v Lancs, Blackpool, 2017. HST20 5* (Middx) v Somerset, Uxbridge, 2017 (2nd). 3/12 (Hants) v Surrey, Purley, 2015 (1st).

Joseph Hedley BARRETT (Burford S, Oxon) b Chipping Norton, Oxon, 13.12.95. LHB RM. Debut Glos 2010; MCCYC & Notts 2016; Hants & Leics 2017. HS 108 v Lancs, Urmston, 2017. BB 0/10 v Sussex, Eastbourne, 2016. HSSET 109 (Hants) v Sussex, Fulking, 2017. BBSET 0/22 v Hants, Ageas Bowl Nursery, 2016. HST20 63* v Durham, Merchant Taylors' S, Northwood, 2017 (2nd). BBT20 2/28 v Hants, 2016 (1st). HSKO 4 (Glos) v Somerset, Taunton Vale, 2010

Benjamin Louis BROOKES (Tudor Grange S, Solihull; Alden SFC) b Solihull, 29.6.97. RHB LM. Brother of J H H (Warwicks). Debut Warwicks 2015; MCC YC 2017. HS 84 v Warwicks, High Wycombe, 2017. BB 4/44 (Warwicks) v Kent/Northants, Beckenham, 2015. HSSET 25 (Warwicks) v Yorks, Knowle & Dorridge, 2016. BBSET 3/45 v Northants, Totternhoe, 2017. HST20 14 v Notts, Merchant Taylors' S, Northwood, 2017 (1st). BBT20 2/12 (Warwicks) v Leics, Edgbaston, 2015 (2nd).

* Scott James CAMERON (Craigie High School, Dundee) b Dundee, Scotland 24.9.96. RHB RMF. Debut 2017.HS 10* v Glos, Rockhampton, 2017. BB 2/68 in the same match.

Matthew Henry CROSS (Robert Gordon Coll; Loughborough U) b Aberdeen, Scotland, 15.10.92. RHB WK. Debut Scotland A 2009; 32 ODIs & 23 T20s (Scotland), 2013 to date. Debut Notts 2011. F/C debut (Loughborough MCCU) v Sussex, Hove, 2013. Debut Leics 2015; Essex 2016; MCC YC, Kent & Northants 2017. HS 105* (Notts) v MCCU, Notts Sports Ground, 2012. HSSET 80 (Notts) v Derbys, Notts SG, 2014. HST20 69 v Merchant Taylors' S, Northwood, 2017 (1st).

Benjamin Jack CURRAN (Wellington Coll) b Northampton, 7.6.96. LHB OB. Brother of T K Tests 1 (Eng) 2017/18 & 1 ODI (2017) & S M (both Surrey) and son of K M (Northants, Glos, Boland, SA & Natal, SA, 1980/81 to 1999. ODIs 11 (Zim) 1983 to 1987/88). Debut MCC YC 2015; Notts & Surrey 2016; Warwicks & Leics 2017. HS 192 v Yorks, High Wycombe, 2017. HSSET 141* v Middx, Radlett, 2016. HST20 87* v Notts, Merchant Taylors' S, Northwood, 2017 (2nd).

Jake GOODWIN (Kingsdown S, Swindon) b Swindon, Wilts, 19.1.98. RHB RM. Debut Hants 2015. List A (T20) debut (Hants) v Somerset, Ageas Bowl, 2016. Debut MCC YC 2017. HS 131 (Hants) v Surrey, Ageas Bowl Nursery, 2016. BB 1/47 (Hants) v Kent, Newclose, I of Wight, 2016. HSSET 44 (Hants) v Essex, Coggeshall, 2016. BBSET 2/20 (Hants) v MCCYC, Ageas Bowl Nursery, 2016 (2nd). HST20 29 (Hants) v Somerset, Ageas Bowl Nursery, 2016 (1st). BBT20 1/7 (Hants) v MCCYC, Shenley, 2016 (1st).

Samuel Edward GRANT (Brighton Coll; Loughborough U) b Shoreham-by-Sea, Sussex, 30.8.95. LHB LMF. Debut Sussex 2013; F/C debut (Loughborough MCCU) v Kent, Canterbury, 2014. Debuts Durham & Somerset 2016; Warwicks & Worcs 2017. HS 76 (Warwicks) v MCC YC, High Wycombe, 2017. BB 4/19 (Sussex) v Surrey, Blackstone, 2013. HSSET 15* (Sussex) v Unc, East Challow, Oxon. 2014. BBSET 2/18 (Sussex) v Somerset, Arundel, 2014. HST20 29* (Somerset) v Hants, Ageas Bowl Nursery, 2016

(1st). BBT20 3/4 (Somerset) v Warwicks, Arundel, 2016 (SF).

Gareth Jason HARTE (King Edward VII HS, Johannesburg) b Johannesburg, Transvaal, S Africa, 15.3.93. RHB RM. Debut Somerset & Middx 2012; Kent 2014; MCCYC & Sussex 2016; Durham 2017. List A (T20) debut (Durham) v Lancs, Old Trafford, 2017. HS 199 (Sussex) v Surrey, New Malden, 2016. BB 4/47 v Glam, Panteg, 2016. HSSET 124* (Durham) v Worcs, New Road, 2017. BBSET 2/29 (Sussex) v Glam, St Fagans, 2016. HST20 61 (Durham) v Warwicks, S Northumberland, 2017 (2nd). BBT20 0/21 (Kent) v Hants, Ageas Bowl, 2014 (2nd).

Andrew Thomas Edward HAZELDINE (St Andrew's Coll, Christchurch, NZ) b Portsmouth, Hants, 13.7.94. LHB LF. Debut Essex, Hants, Somerset & MCCYC 2016. HS 44 v Notts, High Wycombe, 2017. BB 5/37 v Sussex, Eastbourne, 2016. HSSET 7 v Hants, Ageas Bowl Nursery, 2016. BBSET 2/86 v Somerset, High Wycombe, 2016. HST20 9 v Worcs, Merchant Taylors' S, Northwood, 2017 (2nd). BBT20 2/31 v Hants, Shenley, 2016 (2nd).

Fynn Jake HUDSON-PRENTICE (Warden Park S, Cuckfield; St Bede`s S, Upper Dicker, Hailsham) b. Haywards Heath, Sussex, 12.1.96. RHB RMF. Debut Sussex 2012. Debut Eng U19 (T20s only) 2013. F/C debut (Sussex) v Hants, Hove, 2015. HS 125 (Sussex) v Somerset, Taunton Vale, 2016. BB 4/34 (Sussex) v Glos, Hove, 2014. HSSET 147* (Sussex) v Middx, Fulking, 2016. BBSET 3/25 (Sussex) v Kent, Beckenham, 2015. HST20 44 (Sussex) v Hants, the Ageas Bowl, 2013 (1st). BBT20 3/19 (Eng U19) v Derbys, Alvaston & Boulton, 2013 (2nd).

Liam Jack HURT (Balshaw's C of E HS, Leyland; Training 2000, Blackburn) b Preston 15.3.94. RHB RMF. Debut Lancs 2013; Derbys & Leics 2015. List A debut (Leics) v Durham, Grace Road, 2015. Glos, Northants & Warwicks 2016. Debut Durham 2017. HS 42* (Lancs) v Hants, Newclose CC, I of Wight, 2017. BB 4/43 (Durham0 v Essex/Kent, Billericay, 2017. HSSET 24 (Durham) v Worcs, Kidderminster, 2017. BBSET 3/58 (Lancs) v Leics, Middlewich, 2014. HST20 19* (Leics) v Unc, Long Marston, 2016 (2nd). BBT20 3/41 (Lancs) v Yorks, Marske-by-the-Sea, 2013 (2nd).

Safwaan M "Saf" IMTIAZ (Chigwell S) b London 16.3.96. RHB WK. Debut Essex 2013; Durham, MCCYC & Northants 2016; Kent & Surrey 2017. HS 175 v Essex, High Wycombe, 2016. BB 0/129 v Lancs, Urmston, 2017. HSSET 100 v Somerset, Taunton Vale, 2015. HST20 67 v Surrey, High Wycombe, 2016 (1st).

Luke Adam JONES (Nicholas Chamberlaine S; Bedworth, Warwicks; King Edward VI, Nuneaton) b Nuneaton, Warwicks, 31.7.97. LHB OB. Debut Unc & Warwicks 2016; MCC YC 2017. HS 79 v Derbys, Glossop, 2017. BB 3/95 v Notts, High Wycombe, 2017. HSSET 53* v Worcs, Kidderminster, 2017. HST20 9* Lancs, Westhoughton, 2017 (1st). BBT20 2/12 v Worcs, Merchant Taylors' S, Northwood, 2017 (1st).

Aristides "Ari" KARVELAS b Johannesburg, Gauteng, S Africa, 20.3.94. RHB RMF. Debut 2017. HS 32 v Sussex, Eastbourne, 2017. BB 4/57 v Glos, Rockhampton, 2017.

Marc Daniel LEZAR (Filton C, Bristol) b Johannesburg, S.Africa 14.11.95. RHB RM. Brother of D.R. (Glos 2013). Debut Glos 2013; MCC YC 2015; Notts 2017. HS 87 v Hants, Ageas Bowl Nursery, 2016. BB 3/17 v Glos, Shenley, 2016. HSSET 54 (Glos) v Sussex, Hove 2014. BBSET 0/12 v Somerset, High Wycombe, 2016. HST20 59 (Glos) v Somerset, Taunton Vale 2014 (1st). BBT20 0/10 (Glos) v Kent, Cheltenham Coll, 2015 (1st) & v Hants, Shenley, 2016 (2nd).

Gavin Thomas MAIN b Lanark, Scotland, 28.2.95. RHB RMF. Debut Durham 2013. F/C Debut (Durham) v Notts, Trent Bridge, 2014. Debut MCC YC 2017. HS 17 (Durham) v Yorks, York, 2016. BB 4/56 (Durham) v Essex/Kent. Billericay, 2014. HSSET 6* (Durham) v Derbys, Ticknall, 2014. BBSET 3/21 (Durham) v Northants, M Keynes, 2017. BBT20 2/19 (Durham) v Yorks, Brandon, 2014.

Don Sithira MANUWELGE (Heathlands S) b Colombo, Sri Lanka, 25.9.96. RHB. Debut Middx 2014; MCC YC 2017. HS 92 (Middx) v Essex, Billericay, 2016. BB 2/65 v Yorks, High Wycombe, 2017. HSSET 89 (Middx) v Sussex, Fulking, 2016. BBSET 2/6 (Middx) v MCC YC, Radlett, 2015. HST20 35 (Middx) v Glam, Port Talbot, 2016 (2nd). BBT20 2/8 (Middx) v Surrey, Purley, 2016 (1st).

Mitchell "Mitch" RENWICK (Palmerston North Boys HS, NZ) b Palmerston North, Manawatu, NZ, 23.2.93. RHB LB WK. Debut Hants 2015; MCC YC 2017. F/C debut (C Districts) v Wellington, Napier, NZ, 2015/16. HS 28 (Hants) v Glos, Cheltenham, 2015. HST20 25 v Lancs, Westhoughton, 2017 (1st).

Benjamin Vincent SEARS (Hutt International Boys S, Upper Hutt, Wellington, NZ) b Lower Hutt, Wellington, NZ, 11.2.98. Son of M J (Wellington 1990/91 to 1993/94) RHB RMF. Debut 2017. HS 5 v Yorks, High Wycombe. 2017. BB 0/75 in the same match. HSSET 39 v Yorks, Merchant Taylors' S, Northwood, 2017. BBSET 1/57 in the same match.

*William SHEFFIELD Debut 2017. BB 0/10 v Sussex, Eastbourne, 2017.

Praven Ashley SIVIRAJAH (Haberdashers'Aske's S, Elstree, Herts; U of Southampton Solent) b Islington, 3.4.94. RHB SLA. Debut MCC YC 2016; Northants 2017. HS 21* v Sussex, Eastbourne, 2016. BB 5/78 v Leics, High Wycombe, 2017. HSSET 20* v Worcs, Kidderminster, 2017. BBSET 2/40 v Warwicks, Merchant Taylors' S, Northwood, 2017. HST20 5 v Worcs, Merchant Taylors`s S, Northwood, 2017 (2nd). BBT20 2/1 v Essex, Southend-on-Sea, 2016 (1st).

Thomas Frederick SMITH (Clifton C) b Bristol 21.5.96. RHB OB. Debut Glos 2012 aged 16 years and 99 days; debut MCC YC 2015. Debuts Glam & Sussex 2016. List A debut (Glam) v Pakistan A, Newport, 2016. HS 106 v Kent, Beckenham, 2016. BB 2/13 v Unc, Saffron Walden 2017. HSSET 73 (Glos) v Surrey, Guildford, 2015. BBSET 2/38 v Essex, High Wycombe, 2016. HST20 107 v Kent, High Wycombe, 2015 (1st). BBT20 2/19 v Notts, Merchant Taylors' S, Northwood, 2017 (2nd).

Oliver William SMITHSON (Bradfield C) b Lisbon, Portugal 6.1.96. RHB LMF. Debut Glos 2014; MCC YC 2015; Durham & Northants 2017. HS 12* (Glos) v Hants, WE Nursery 2014. BB 3/24 v Glos, Shenley, 2016. HSSET 27 (Glos) v Northants, Thornbury CC 2014. BBSET 3/41 v Leics, Merchant Taylors' S, Northwood, 2017. HST20 15 v Worcs, Merchant Taylors' S, Northwood, 2017 (2nd). BBT20 3/15 v Notts, Merchant Taylors' S, Northwood, 2017 (1st).

Ishwarjot Singh SOHI (Isleworth & Syon S; Brunel U) b Punjab, India, 7.8.94. RHB RFM. Debut Northants & Surrey 2014; MCCYC 2016. HS 49 (Essex) v Sussex, Halstead, 2017. BB 3/83 (Northants) v Glos, Thornbury, 2014. HSSET 1* (Northants) v Somerset, Milton Keynes, 2014. BBSET 1/25 (Northants) v Sussex, Desborough, 2014. HST20 21* (Surrey) v Glam, 2017 (1st). BBT20 2/29 (Surrey) v Kent, Polo Farm SG, Canterbury, 2017 (1st).

Benjamin Steven TWINE (Eastbourne Coll) b Eastbourne, Sussex, 25.11.98. RHB RFM. Debut Sussex 2015; MCC YC 2017. BB 2/13 v Sussex, Eastbourne, 2017. HSSET 4 (Sussex) v Essex, Southend-on-Sea, 2015. BBSET 1/58 in the same match.

Kiel van VOLLENHOVEN (Pretoria Boys HS, S Africa) b 6.6.98. RHB LB. Debut MCC YC & Sussex 2017. HS 6 v Sussex, Eastbourne, 2017 & (Sussex) v Essex, Star Stile, 2017. BB 3/95 (Sussex) v Essex, Star Stile, 2017. BBT20 5/12 v Durham, Merchant Taylors' S, Northwood, 2017 (1st).

Matthew Brian WAREING (Manningtree HS; Colchester SFC) b Colchester, 17.1.94. LHB LMF. Debut Essex & Leics 2015; Unc 2016; Worcs & MCC YC 2017. HS 8 (Essex) v Kent, Maidstone, 2015 & (Unc) v MCC YC, Saffron Walden, 2017. BB 3/48 (Worcs) v Lancs, Great Crosby, 2017. HSSET 7* (Unc) v Glam, Newbury, 2017. BBSET 3/55 (Unc) v Hants, Ageas Bowl Nursery, 2017. HST20 2* (Leics) v Unc, Long Marston, 2016 (1st). BBT20 2/35 (Leics) v Unc, Long Marston, 2016 (2nd).

MIDDLESEX

PLAYING RECORDS 2017
Championship – P9 W3 D5 Ab1 – second in the southern group
2nd XI Trophy – P8 W5 L2 NR1 - second in the southern group
2nd XI T20 Competition – P12 W7 L5 – third in the southern group

2nd XI SUCCESSES
Championship –Winners – 1974, 1989, 1993, 1999, 2000, 2013 (joint
with Lancashire)
2nd XI Trophy – Winners – 1989, 2007.
2nd XI T20 Competition – Winners – 2015, 2016

SECOND ELEVEN CHAMPIONSHIP AVERAGES

BATTING	M	I	NO	Runs	HS	Avge	100s	C/S
N A Sowter	3	3	2	240	1228	240.00	1	1
G F B Scott	4	4	1	288	212*	96.00	1	-
R G White	5	6	2	330	160*	82.50	2	9/1
M K Andersson	4	5	1	284	192	71.00	1	1
J A R Harris	3	5	1	243	146	60.75	1	-
R F Higgins	2	3	1	109	54	54.50	-	1
T C Lace	7	9	0	363	106	40.33	1	9
M D E Holden	3	5	0	170	84	34.00	-	1
S Perera	4	7	2	150	64	30.00	-	1
J Davies	3	3	0	67	56	22.33	-	5/1
L B K Hollman	2	3	0	66	31	22.00	-	1
R H Patel	4	4	1	64	28*	21.33	-	1
S D Robson	3	4	0	80	40	20.00	-	7
T N Walallawita	5	6	2	77	27	19.25	-	1
O P Rayner	2	3	0	45	37	15.00	-	1
C F B Scott	2	3	0	35	35	11.66	-	1
H W Podmore	4	3	0	20	14	6.66	-	2

BOWLING	O	M	Runs	Wkt	Avge	BB
R F Higgins	28	9	66	5	13.20	3/22
O P Rayner	57.3	21	108	8	13.50	4/33
R H Patel	110.4	26	285	17	16.76	3/23
J A R Harris	87.2	18	254	14	18.14	3/41
T E Barber	89.1	15	348	19	18.31	5/27
E R Bamber	74.3	15	212	10	21.20	3/65
H W Podmore	105	29	270	12	22.50	3/35
G F B Scott	30	4	104	3	34.66	3/11
T J Murtagh	42.2	7	140	4	35.00	2/47
T N Walallawita	163.1	21	521	13	40.07	3/55

Also bowled – M K Andersson 19-1-72-0; F Baharami 16-1-48-1;
B Cullen 10-1-36-1; A D Duke 22-1-132-1; J K Fuller 15-3-59-2;
A Godsal 26-4-115-1; T G Helm 23-7-61-2; M D E Holden 10-0-
57-2; L B K Hollman 21.4-0-106-2; M John 7-0-47-2; S Reingold
25.4-7-81-2; N A Sowter 29.2-2-112-1; R S Wijeratne 11.5-1-53-0.

Also batted – 5 matches – A Godsal 3, 15* (2ct). 4 matches – T
E Barber 1. 3 matches – E R Bamber 0 (1ct). 2 matches – N R D
Compton 107, 3 (1ct); A D Duke 1* (1ct); D S Manuwelege 2, 11
(1ct); T J Murtagh 2. 1 match – F Baharami 0, 2*; A J Coleman
DNB (1ct); J Cracknell 27; B Cullen 4, 0; J M de Caires 14; S S
Eskinazi 97 (ct); J K Fuller 47; N R T Gubbins 6, 27 (1ct); T G
Helm 6 (1ct); M John 5 (1ct); A Rath 34 (2ct); S Reingold 38 (2ct);
A Thomas 4 (2ct & 1st); R S Wijeratne 6 (1ct).

SECOND ELEVEN TROPHY AVERAGES

BATTING	M	I	NO	Runs	HS	Avge	100s	C/S
G F B Scott	8	7	1	504	153*	92.98	3	4
R G White	3	3	2	73	54*	73.00	-	4
N R D Compton	5	4	0	139	57	34.75	-	3
D S Manuwelege	5	4	2	63	40	31.50	-	1
T C Lace	6	5	1	122	93	30.50	-	1
R F Higgins	5	4	0	106	83	26.50	-	-
H W Podmore	6	3	1	36	36*	18.00	-	2
J Davies	5	5	0	83	30	16.60	-	4/3
S Perera	5	3	1	25	11	12.50	-	1

BOWLING	O	M	Runs	Wkt	Avge	BB
N A Sowter	19.4	1	111	7	15.85	4/31
R H Patel	24	0	112	6	18.66	4/50
A Godsal	28	0	179	8	22.37	4/46
G F B Scott	18	0	102	4	25.20	2/17
J K Fuller	14.2	0	77	3	25.66	2/28
T G Helm	16	0	87	3	29.00	3/54
H W Podmore	44	5	232	7	33.14	3/50
T E Barber	44.5	2	321	6	53.50	2/29

Also bowled – E R Bamber 6.1-0-38-1; R F Higgins 18-2-80-2; L B
K Hollman 4-0-45-0; T J Murtagh 5-0-28-1; O P Rayner 20-0-116-
1; P R Stirling 1-0-11-0; T N Walallawita 27-0-138-2.

Also batted – 8 matches – T E Barber 9, 0 (1ct). 7 matches – A
Godsal 5*, 2 (3ct). 4 matches – N A Sowter 0, 2* (3ct); T N Walallawita 1*. 3 matches – R H Patel 10* (2ct); O P Rayner 49*, 62
(1ct). 2 matches – E R Bamber DNB (1ct); S S Eskinazi 149; J K
Fuller 19, 27 (3ct); T G Helm 6, 13* (1ct). 1 match – L B K Hollman 18; T J Murtagh 3; A Rath 123; C F B Scott 3; P R Stirling 64.

SECOND ELEVEN T20 AVERAGES

BATTING	M	I	NO	Runs	HS	Avge	100s	C/S
G F B Scott	10	9	3	268	75*	44.66	-	6
N R T Gubbins	3	3	0	116	71	38.66	-	1
R G White	11	9	3	213	65*	35.50	-	3/1
S S Eskinazi	5	5	1	131	50	32.75	-	4
T C Lace	9	9	2	226	80*	32.28	-	6
M K Andersson	8	8	0	212	54	26.50	-	2
R F Higgins	3	3	0	57	46	19.00	-	2
M D E Holden	3	3	0	48	32	16.00	-	1
H W Podmore	9	7	1	93	31*	15.50	-	2
J A R Harris	6	4	1	45	27	15.00	-	4
R S Wijeratne	4	3	0	45	24	15.00	-	2
S Perera	6	4	0	54	46	13.50	-	-
A Godsal	6	4	0	14	7	3.50	-	6
N A Sowter	5	4	1	9	4*	3.00	-	2
R H Patel	7	5	2	6	3	2.00	-	3

BOWLING	O	M	Runs	Wkt	Avge	BB
A D Duke	7	0	41	4	10.25	2/14
L B K Hollman	8	0	58	5	11.60	5/26
T N Walallawita	22	1	150	9	16.66	3/26
N A Sowter	19	0	121	7	17.28	2/16
R H Patel	28	0	167	9	18.55	3/24
G F B Scott	9	0	85	4	21.25	3/10
J A R Harris	23	0	194	8	24.25	2/23
T E Barber	24	0	215	6	35.83	3/30
H W Podmore	31.2	0	281	7	40.14	2/25
A Godsal	13.5	0	145	3	48.33	1/19

Also bowled – M K Andersson 4-0-33-1; E R Bamber 8-0-58-1; J E C Franklin 4-0-39-2; T G Helm 3-0-9-0; R F Higgins 7-0-66-2; M D E Holden 3-0-21-1; M John 3-0-29-1; O P Rayner 8-0-62-2; S Reingold 6-0-67-2; P R Stirling 1-0-5-1; R S Wijeratne 8-0-48-2.

Also batted – 7 matches – T E Barber 2*, 4*, 5* 1* (2ct). 6 matches – T N Walallawita 9, 20 (2ct). 3 matches – M John 6* (1ct). 2 matches – E R Bamber DNB; J Cracknell 5; A D Duke DNB; J E C Franklin 1*, 68 (1ct); L B K Hollman DNB (1ct); O P Rayner 0 (1ct); S Reingold 1* (3ct); C F B Scott 4, 16*. 1 match – N R D Compton 0 (1ct); J Davies 20 (1ct & 1st); J M de Caires 26 (1ct); T G Helm 19; P R Stirling 16.

HOME MATCHES: SECOND ELEVEN CHAMPIONSHIP

v Kent (Radlett) – 18-20 April – Kent 151 (C J Haggett 72*; T E Barber 4/41) & 234 (A J Ball 86, K C Appleby 54; R F Higgins 3/22) lost to Middx 492/9d (N R D Compton 107, T C Lace 94, N A Sowter 81, R F Higgins 54; Imran Qayyum 3/66, I A A Thomas 3/100) by an inns & 107 runs.

v Somerset (Radlett) – 5-7 June - Middx 161 (P A van Meekeren 5/44, B G F Green 3/27) & 52/0d drew with Somerset 197 (T E Barber 4/47, H W Podmore 3/35)

v Sussex (Richmond) – 19-21 June – Middx 356 (N A Sowter 122*, M D E Holden 84; G S Whittingham 3/57, N S Oxley 3/66) beat Sussex 152 (T E Barber 5/27, R H Patel 3/23) & 136 (A J Robson 66; G F B Scott 3/11, R H Patel 3/27) by an inns & 68 runs.

v Glamorgan (Merchant Taylors' S) – 11-13 July – Glam 213 (T N Cullen 69; O P Rayner 3/28, E R Bamber 3/65) & 165 (O P Rayner 4/33, T N Walallawita 3/55) lost to Middx 195 (L J Carey 3/12, K Szymanski 3/25) & 185/7 (C R Brown 3/45) by three wkts.

HOME MATCHES: FRIENDLIES

v Leicestershire (Uxbridge CC) – 28 June – Match 1 – Middx 138/9 (G F B Scott 51; R A Jones 4/18, T J Wells 3/35) lost to Leics 142/1 (C S Delport 99*) by nine wkts.

v Leicestershire (Uxbridge CC) – 28 June – Match 2 – Leics 88 (T N Walallawita 3/14) lost to Middx 89/1 by nine wkts.

v Essex (Radlett) – 11-13 Sept – Middx 177 (M K Andersson 62; M W Dixon 5/29) & 334 (T C Lace 81, N R T Gubbins 54, G F B Scott 50) lost to Essex 280 (R K Patel 67, K S Velani 53; E R Bamber 4/58, M K Andersson 3/50, R H Patel 3/73) & 232/5 (R K Patel 50) by five wkts.

v Warwickshire (Merchant Taylors' S) – 18-21 Sept – Warwicks 505 (A R I Umeed 162, S R Hain 101, E J Pollock 78, A J Mellor 60*; R F Higgins 4/67, R H Patel 3/89) & 24/0 beat Middx 246 (M K Andersson 66; T R G Hampton 4/60, O J Hannon-Dalby 4/61) & 278 (M K Andersson 73*, R G White 58; Sukhjit Singh 6/74) by 10 wkts.

HOME MATCHES: SECOND ELEVEN TROPHY

v Kent (Radlett) – 17 Apr – Middx 364/7 (G F B Scott 153*, A Rath 123; C F Hartley (3/63) beat Kent 182 (N A Sowter 4/31, R H patel 4/50) by 182 runs.

v Essex (Radlett) – 26 Apr – Middx 229/9 (G F B Scott 100; M W Dixon 3/51) lost to Essex238/2 (V Chopra 109*, J S Foster 67*, C J Taylor 50) by eight wkts (DLS).

v Sussex (Southgate) – 2 May – Sussex 254/6 (P D Salt 102, A J Robson 74) lost to Middx 258/3 (T C Lace 93, G F B Scott 81; S G Whittingham 3/60) by seven wkts.

v Lancashire (Blackpool) – 2 June – Lancs 128/9 lost to Middx 131/5 (R G White 54*; M W Parkinson 3/14) by five wkts. *This was the Semi-Final of the One-Day Trophy.*

v Yorkshire (Headingley) – 8 June – Yorks 265/5 (H C Brook 112, R Gibson 78, W M H Rhodes 50*) beat Middx 179 (N R D Compton 57; J W Shutt 4/19) by 99 runs (DLS) *This was the Final of the One-Day Trophy.*

HOME MATCHES : SECOND ELEVEN T20 COMPETITION

v Surrey (Sunbury-on-Thames) – 14 June – Match 1 – Surrey 150/7 (N R Welch 71; T E Barber 3/30) beat Middx 101(G S Virdi 3/15) by 49 runs.

v Surrey (Sunbury-on-Thames) – 14 June – Match 2 – Middx 147/7 (M W Pillans 3/25) beat Surrey 125 (R H Patel 3/28) by 19 runs.

v Somerset (Uxbridge) – 30 June – Match 1 – Middx 168/9 (G F B Scott 75*; M T C Waller 3/18) beat Somerset 153/9 (R H Patel 3/28) by 15 runs.

v Somerset (Uxbridge) – 30 June – Match 2 – Somerset 195/4 (J Allenby 91*, P D Trego 78) beat Middx 169/9 (S S Eskinazi 50; O R T Sale 3/36, B G F Green 3/38) by 26 runs.

v Glamorgan (Richmond) – 10 July – Match 1 – Glam 146/6 lost to Middx 148/2(N R T Gubbins 71) by eight wkts.

v Glamorgan (Richmond) – 10 July – Match 2 – Middx 209/6 (J E C Franklin 68; R A J Smith 3/51) beat Glam 178/5 (N Brand 56) by 31 runs.

PLAYERS WHO HAVE REPRESENTED MIDDLESEX 2nd XI IN SEASON 2017 (43)

M K Andersson	A D Duke	M John	S Reingold
F Baharami	S S Eskinazi	*O M D Kolk	S D Robson
E R Bamber	J E C Franklin	T C Lace	C F B Scott
T E Barber	J K Fuller	D S Manuwelege	G F B Scott
*D Bartlett	A Godsal	T J Murtagh	N A Sowter
A J Coleman	N R T Gubbins	* T M Nugent	P R Stirling
N R D Compton	J A R Harris	R H Patel	A Thomas
J Cracknell	T G Helm	S Perera	T N Walallawita
B Cullen	R F Higgins	H W Podmore	R G White
J Davies	M D E Holden	A Rath	R S Wijeratne
J M de Caires	L B K Hollman	O P Rayner	

MIDDLESEX CRICKETERS

Martin Kristoffer ANDERSSON (Reading Blue Coat S; Leeds U) b Reading, Berks, 6.9.96. RHB RM. Debut 2013, aged 16 yrs & 242 days. F/C debut (Leeds/Bradford MCCU) v Kent, Canterbury, 2017. HS 192 v Essex, Coggeshall, 2017. BB 3/21 v Sussex, Blackstone, 2017. HSSET 47* v Sussex, Fulking, 2016. BBSET 2/52 v Unc, Saffron Walden, 2014. HST20 54 v Hants, Ageas Bowl Nursery, 2017 (2nd). BBT20 2/21 v Essex, Radlett, 2016 (1st).

Fahim BAHARAMI (Dormers Wells HS, Ealing; West Thames Coll) b Maidan Waldak, Afghanistan, 8.3.97. RHB RMF.Debut 2017. HS 2* v Surrey, New Malden, 2017. BB 1/37 in the same match.

Ethan Read BAMBER (Mill Hill S) b Westminster, Middx, 17.12.98. RHB RA. Debut 2015, aged 16 yrs & 180 days. Eng U19 to SA 2017/18. HS 16* v Somerset, Merchant Taylors' S, 2015. BB 5/37 v Kent, Beckenham, 2016. BBSET 1/38 v Sussex, Southgate, 2017. BBT20 2/23 v Somerset, Merchant Taylors' S, 2015 (2nd).

Thomas "Tom" Edward BARBER (Bournemouth GS) b Poole, Dorset, 31.8.95. RHB LFM. Debut Hants 2012. List A Debut (Hants) v Sri Lanka A, the Ageas Bowl, 2014. Debut Somerset 2016; Middx & MCC YC 2017. Eng U19 to S Africa, 2012/13; v Pak & Bang 2013. HS 27* (Hants) v Somerset, Taunton Vale, 2015. BB 5/27 v Sussex, Richmond, 2017. HSSET 17 (MCC YC) v Warwicks, Merchant Taylors' S, Northwood, 2017. BBSET 2/29 v Lancs, Blackpool, 2017. HST20 5* v Somerset, Uxbridge, 2017 (2nd). 3/12 (Hants) v Surrey, Purley, 2015 (1st).

*D BARTLETT Debut 2017. Debut v Somerset, Taunton Vale, but did not bat or bowl.

Alan James COLEMAN (Longford Community S, Feltham) b Ashford, 13.12.83. RHB RFM. Debut 2000. List A debut v Sussex, Richmond, 2001. HS 51* v Essex, Chelmsford, 2002. BB 4/41 v Durham, Chester-le-Street, 2002.HSSET 14 v Northants, Ealing, 2001. BBSET 3/12 v Leics, Finchley, 2003. Played one T20 match in 2015 v Hants, Ageas Bowl Nursery, but did not bat or bowl.

Nicholas Richard Denis COMPTON (Harrow S; Durham U) b Durban, Natal, SA, 26.6.83. Tests (Eng) 12 (2012/13-2016). Debut Middx 2001 aged 16 years and 60 days; F/C debut v Cambridge UCCE, Fenner's, 2004; Middx Cap 2006; debut Somerset 2010. Cap 2011. RHB OB. Son of R. (Natal, 1978-79 – 1980/81), Grandson of D.C.S (Middlesex, England 1936-64), Great Nephew of L.H. (Middx 1938-56). HS 120 v MCC YC, Radlett, 2008. BB 2/0 v Essex, Chelmsford, 2002. HSSET 86 v Essex, Shenley, 2006. BBSET 3/28 v Notts, Uxbridge, 2005. HST20 118 (Somerset) v Glam, Diamond Ground, Cardiff, 2012 (1st). HSKO 72 (Somerset) v Derbys, Derby, 2010.

Joseph Benjamin CRACKNELL (London Oratory S) b Enfield, 16.3.00. RHB WK. Debut 2017. HS 27 v Sussex, Richmond, 2017. HST20 5 v Hants, Ageas Bowl Nursery, 2017 (2nd).

Blake C CULLEN Debut 2017.HS 4 v Glam, Merchant Taylors' S, Northwood, 2017. BB 1/18 in the same match.

Jack DAVIES (Wellington Coll) b Reading, Berks, 30.3.00. LHB WK. Debut 2017. Son of A G (Cambridge 192/89; Glam & Glos 2nd XIs 1979/81). Great nephew of H G (Glam 1935-1958). Eng U19 to SA, 2017/18. HS 56 v Surrey, New Malden, 2017. HSSET 30 v Lancs, Blackpool, 2017. HST20 20 v Essex, Coggeshall, 2017 (1st).

Joshua Michael de CAIRES b Paddington, 25.4.02. RHB RM. Debut 2017. Son of M A Atherton (Lancs 1984-2001) Tests (Eng) 115; 1989 to 2001 & 54 ODIs. HS 14 v Essex, Coggeshall, 2017. HST20 26 v Essex, Coggeshall, 2017 (2nd).

Alfie D DUKE (Oaklands Coll, Herts) b London, 15.2.98. LHB LM. Debut 2016. HS 5 v Somerset, Taunton Vale, 2017. BB 1/46 v Essex, Coggeshall, 2017. HSSET 0* v Surrey, Sunbury-on-Thames, 2016. BBSET 1/56 in the same match. HST20 6* v Glam, Port Talbot, 2016 (2nd). BBT20 2/14 v Essex, Coggeshall, 2017 (2nd).

Stephen Sean ESKINAZI (Christ Church GS, Claremont, W Aus; U of W Australia) b Johannesburg, South Africa, 28.3.94. RHB WK. Debut 2013. F/C debut v Yorks, Lords, 2015. HS 126 v Notts, Radlett, 2015. HSSET 149 v Unc, Newbury, 2017. HST20 67 v Essex, Billericay, 2015 (2nd). Middx staff.

James Edward Charles FRANKLIN b Wellington, New Zealand, 7.11.80. LHB LFM. Tests (NZ) 31 & 110 ODIs, 2000/01 to 2013. F/C debut (Wellington) v the Indians, Basin Reserve, 1998/99. Debut Glos 2004; Glam & Cap 2006; Glos 2010; Essex 2012; Notts 2014; Middx 2015. HS 13* (Notts) v Warwicks, Edgbaston, 2014. BB 1/28 in the same match. HSSET 159 (Notts) v Warwicks, Edgbaston, 2014. BBSET 0/26 in the same match. HST20 68 v Glam, Richmond, 2017 (2nd). BBT20 2/39 v Glam, Richmond, 2017 (1st).

James Kerr FULLER (Otago U, NZ) b Cape Town, S.Africa 24.1.90. RHB RFM. F/C debut (Otago) v N.Districts, Whangarei 2009/10; debut Glos 2011; Middx 2016. HS 75* (Glos) v Middx, Bristol 2011. BB 4/27 (Glos) v Kent, Lansdown CC, 2015. HSSET 40 v MCCYC, Radlett, 2016. BBSET 2/28 v Kent, Radlett, 2017. HST20 47* v Somerset, Taunton Vale, 2016 (2nd). BBT20 3/18 (Glos) v Glam , Bristol 2013 (1st).

Arthur GODSAL (Chiswick S) b Chiswick, 23.9.97. RHB RMF. Debut 2013. Eng U19 to Ind 2016/17; v Ind 2017. HS 24 v Somerset, Taunton Vale, 2017. BB 4/15 v Hants, Radlett, 2015. HSSET 12 v Kent, Beckenham, 2016. BBSET 5/56 v Surrey, Sunbury-on-Thames, 2016. HST20 7 v Kent, Polo Farm SG, Canterbury, 2017 (2nd). BBT20 1/6 v Glam, Port Talbot, 2016 (2nd).

Nicholas Richard Trail GUBBINS (Radley Coll; Leeds Un) b Richmond, Surrey, 31.12.93. LHB LB. Debut 2012. F/C debut (Leeds/Bradford MCCU) v Yorks, Headingley, 2013. HS 134 v MCCYC, Radlett, 2012. BB 6/23 v Essex, Coggeshall, 2013 (and match figs of 10/62). HSSET 71 v Hants, Radlett, 2014. HST20 110 v Essex, Radlett, 2016 (1st). Middx staff.

James Alexander Russell HARRIS (Pontarddulais S, Swansea; Gorseinon SFC, Swansea) b Morriston, Swansea, 16.5.90. RHB RFM. Debut Glam 2005; F/C debut (Glam) v Notts, Trent Bridge, 2007. Glam Cap 2010. Debut Middx 2013; Cap 2015. HS 146 v Surrey, New Malden, 2017. BB 3/41 v Surrey, New Malden, 2017. HSSET 32 v Surrey, Radlett, 2014. BBSET 5/56 v Sussex, Richmond, Surrey, 2015. HST20 27 v Somerset, Uxbridge, 2017 (1st). BBT20 2/23 v Hants, Ageas Bowl Nursery, 2017 (2nd). Middx Staff.

Thomas George HELM (Misbourne S, Great Missenden) b Stoke Mandeville, Bucks 7.5.94. RHB RFM. Debut 2011. F/C debut v Yorks, Headingley, 2013. HS 52* v Glos, Thornbury CC, 2013. BB 4/22 v Sussex, Hove, 2013. HSSET 22 v Surrey, Radlett, 2014. BBSET 3/40 v Glam, St Helen's, Swansea, 2012. HST20 24* (Eng

U19) v Worcs, Arundel, 2012. BBT20 5/37 v Surrey, Arundel, 2013. Middx Staff.

Ryan Francis HIGGINS (Bradfield Coll, Berks) b Harare, Zimbabwe, 6.1.95. RHB OB. Debut 2012. List A debut v Glam, the SWALEC, 2014. Eng U19 v Bang, Pak, 2013; to UAE 2013/14 (Tri-Series). HS 303* v Worcs, Kidderminster, 2016. BB 5/11 v MCCYC, Radlett, 2016. HSSET 93 v Glos, Richmond, 2014. BBSET 3/14 v Surrey, Sunbury-on-Thames, 2013. HST20 94 v Durham, 2016 (SF). BBT20 3/20 v Kent, Uxbridge, 2016 (1st). Joins Gloucestershire for the 2018 season.

Max David Edward HOLDEN (Sawston Village Coll, Cambridge) b Cambridge, 18.12.97. LHB OB. Debut Middx 2013, debut Northants (on loan) 2017. Eng U19 v Aus 2014/15; v Aus 2015; v Sri Lanka (Capt) 2016. HS 140 v Lancs, Liverpool, 2015. BB 1/2 v Essex, Billericay, 2015. HSSET 127 v Surrey, Sunbury-on-Thames, 2016. BBSET 1/17 v Sussex, Fulking, 2016. HST20 54 v Glam, Port Talbot, 2016 (1st). BBT20 1/13 v Durham., Arundel, 2016 (SF) & v Surrey, Sunbury, 2017 (2nd). Middx Staff.

Luke Barnaby Kurt HOLLMAN (Acland Burghley S, Camden) b Islington, 16.9.00. LHB LB. Debut 2017. Eng U19 v SA 2017/18. HS 31 v Sussex, Richmond, 2017. BB 1/0 in the same match. HSSET 18 v Essex, Radlett, 2017. BBSET 0/45 in the same match. BBT20 5/26 v Essex, Coggeshall, 2017 (1st).

Max JOHN (Merchant Taylors' S, Northwood) b London, 10.11.00. RHB RM. Debut 2016. HS 5 v Hants, Ageas Bowl Nursery, 2017. BB 2/47 in the same match. HST20 6* v Hants, Ageas Bowl Nursery, 2017 (2nd). BBT20 1/19 v Essex, Coggeshall, 2017 (2nd).

*Oskar Magnus David KOLK (Reed's S, Cobham, Surrey) b Guildford, Surrey, 9.1.97. RHB RMF OB. Debut Leics 2016; Notts & Surrey 2017. HS 59 (Notts) v MCC YC, High Wycombe, 2017. BB 0/6 (Leics) v Yorks, York, 2016.

Thomas Creswell LACE (Millfield S) b Hammersmith, 27.5.98. RHB WK. HS 112 v Worcs, Kidderminster, 2016. HSSET 93 v Sussex, Southgate, 2017. HST20 80* v Hants, Ageas Bowl Nursery, 2017 (1st).

Don Sithira MANUWELGE (Heathlands S) b Colombo, Sri Lanka, 25.9.96. RHB. Debut Middx 2014; MCC YC 2017. HS 92 v Essex, Billericay, 2016. BB 2/65 (MCC YC) v Yorks, High Wycombe, 2017. HSSET 89 v Sussex, Fulking, 2016. BBSET 2/6 v MCC YC, Radlett, 2015. HST20 35 v Glam, Port Talbot, 2016 (2nd). BBT20 2/8 v Surrey, Purley, 2016 (1st).

Timothy James MURTAGH (John Fisher S, Purley; St Mary's Coll, Twickenham) b Lambeth, 2.8.81. LHB RFM. Debut Surrey 2001, aged 16 years & 303 days; debut Middx 2007; Cap 2008. F/C debut (B Univs) v Zimbabweans, Fenner's, 2000. ODIs (Ireland) 36 (2012 to date). Brother of C P (Surrey 2008 to 2009); nephew of A J (Hants & E Province 1973/77). HS 74 (Surrey) v Essex, Colchester, 2002. BB 5/23 v Somerset, Merchant Taylors' S, 2015. HSSET 19 (Surrey) v Kent, Banstead, 2003. BBSET 5/30 (Surrey) v Sussex, Stirlands, 2006. Middx Staff.

Thomas Michael NUGENT (Loughborough U) b Bath, Somerset, 11.7.94. Debut Hants 2012; Middx 2017. F/C debut (Loughborough MCCU) v Notts, Trent Bridge, 2015. HS 35 (Hants) v Somerset, the Ageas Bowl, 2013. BB 3/32 (Hants) v Glos, Lansdown CC, 2013. HSSET 23* (Hants) v Sussex, Horsham, 2012. BBSET 2/19 in the same match. HST20 7* (Hants) v MCCYC, the Ageas Bowl, 2013 (2nd). BBT20 1/30 (Hants) v MCCYC, the Ageas Bowl, 2013 (1st).

Ravi Hasmukh PATEL (Merchant Taylors' S, Northwood) b Harrow 4.8.91. RHB SLA. Debut 2008. F/C debut v Oxford MCCU. The Parks, 2010. HS 36 v Sussex, Blackstone, 2017. BB 8/115 v Lancs. Radlett, 2016 (and match figs of 14/161). HSSET 10* v Lancs, Radlett, 2010 & v Kent, Radlett, 2017. BBSET 5/43 v Gloucs, Radlett, 2010. HST20 3 v Surrey, Sunbury, 2017 (1st). BBT20 4/16 v Northants, Uxbridge CC, 2012 (2nd). HSKO 21 v Surrey, Wimbledon, 2010. BBKO 1/37 in the same match. Middx Staff.

Savin PERERA (Kingston Coll, Kingston-u-Thames) b Colombo, Sri Lanka, 3.5.99. LHB OB. Debut 2016. Eng U19 v SA 2017/18. HS 64 v Surrey, New Malden, 2017. HSSET 11 v Essex, Radlett, 2017. HST20 46 v Kent, Polo Farm SG, Canterbury, 2017 (1st).

Harry William PODMORE (Twyford HS, Acton) b Hammersmith,, 23.7.94. RHB RM. Debut Middx 2011; Glam (on loan) 2016. F/C debut (Glam) v Kent, Canterbury, 2016. Debut Durham (on loan) 2017. HS 116* v Essex, Billericay, 2015. BB 6/52 v Somerset, Merchant Taylors' S, 2015. HSSET 36* v Surrey, Purley, 2017. BBSET 4/41 v Kent, Radlett, 2015. HST20 31* v Hants, Ageas Bowl Nursery, 2017 (2nd). BBT20 3/4 v Somerset, Merchant Taylors' S, 2015 (2nd). Middx staff.

Anshuman RATH (Harrow S) b Hong Kong, 5.11.197. LHB SLA. Debut 2015. ODIs (Hong Kong) 12 (2014/15 to date). F/C debut (HK) v United Arab Emirates, Dubai, 2015/16. HS 140 v Warwicks, EFCSG, 2016. BB 3/70 in the same match. HSSET 123 v Kent, Radlett, 2017. BBSET 2/42 v Sussex, Fulking, 2016. HST20 35 v Somerset, Arundel, 2016 (Final). BBT20 1/16 in the same match.

Oliver Philip RAYNER (St Bede's S, Upper Dicker, Hailsham) b Fallingbostel, Lower Saxony, Germany, 1.11.85. RHB OB. Debut Sussex 2002; F/C debut (Sussex) v Sri Lankans, Hove, 2006; debut MidWest Rhinos, Zim, 2009/10; Middx 2012. HS 127 (Sussex) v Glam, Usk, 2007. BB 8/65 (Sussex) v Middx, Horsham, 2006. HSSET 78* (Sussex) v Northants, Hove, 2009. BBSET 4/48 (Sussex) v Middx, Uxbridge, 2009. HST20 59 (Sussex) v Durham, Fenner's, 2011. BBT20 3/10 (Sussex) v Surrey, Fulking, 2011. HSKO 34 (Sussex) v Essex, Chelmsford, 2010. BBKO 2/40 (Sussex) v Derbys, Horsham, 2010. Middx Staff.

Steven Jack REINGOLD (Jewish Free S, London) b Cape Town, SA, 7.8.98. RHB OB. Debut 2017. HS 38 v Essex, Coggeshall, 2017. BB 2/74 in the same match. HST20 1* v Essex, Coggeshall, 2017 (2nd). BBT20 2/39 in the same match.

Samuel David ROBSON (Marcellin Coll, Randwick, Sydney, Aus) b Paddington, Sydney, 1.7.89. RHB LB. Brother of A J (Leics & Sussex to date). Debut 2008; F/C debut v Essex, Chelmsford, 2009. Cap 2013. Tests (England) 7 (2014). HS 206 v Lancs, Great Crosby, 2011. BB 2/35 v Surrey, Charterhouse S, 2009. HSSET 127* v Essex, Winchmore Hill 2008. BBSET 1/31 v Northants, Vine Lane 2008. HST20 44* v Northants, Bedford S, 2013 (1st). Middx staff.

Charles Fergus Buchan SCOTT (St Albans School) b Hemel Hempstead, Herts, 13.10.99. RHB RFM. Debut 2015, aged 15 yrs & 217 days. Brother of G F B (as below). HS 37 v Hants, Ageas Bowl Nursery, 2015. HSSET 3 v Kent, Radlett, 2017. HST20 16* v Essex, Coggeshall, 2017 (2nd).

George Frederick Buchan SCOTT (St Albans S; Leeds U) b Hemel Hempstead, Herts, 6.11.95. RHB RM. Debut 2013. Brother of C F B (as above). F/C debut (Leeds-Bradford MCCU) v Sussex, Hove, 2015. HS 212* v MCCU, Radlett, 2017. BB 4/24 v Surrey, Radlett, 2014. HSSET 153* v Kent, Radlett, 2017. BBSET 3/22 v Essex, Billericay, 2016. HST20 75* v Somerset, Uxbridge, 2017 (1st). BBT20 3/10 v Kent, Polo Farm SG, Canterbury, 2017 (1st). Middx Staff

Nathan Adam SOWTER (Hills Sport HS, Seven Hills, NSW, Australia) b Penrith, NSW, Australia, 12.10.92. RHB LB. Debut 2014. F/C debut v Warwicks, Lords, 2017. HS 122* v Sussex, Richmond, 2017. BB 6/70 v Sussex, Richmond, Surrey, 2015. HSSET 41 v Unc, Saffron Walden, 2014. BBSET 4/31 v Kent, Radlett, 2017. HST20 24 v Unc, Saffron Walden, 2014 (1st). BBT20 6/19 v Glam, Radlett, 2015 (1st).

Patrick Robert STIRLING (Belfast HS) b Belfast, NI, 3.9.90. RHB OB. Brother of R.B (Ireland U19 2006) Debut Ireland 2008; F/C debut (Ireland) v U.A.E., Abu Dhabi 2008. ODI 71 (Ireland), 2008 to date. Debut Middx 2008. Cap 2016. HS 254 v Glam Radlett, 2015. BB 4/92 v Sussex, Radlett, 2013. HSSET 110 v Northants, Dunstable, 2014. BBSET 2/23 Northants, Radlett, 2013. HST20 116 v Hants, Ageas Bowl Nursery, 2015 (2nd). BBT20 1/2 v Northants, Dunstable, 2011 (1st). HSKO 30 v Surrey, Wimbledon, 2010. BBKO 0/31 in the same match. Middx Staff.

Andrew THOMAS RHB WK. Debut 2017. HS 4 v Sussex, Richmond, 2017.

Thilan Nipuna WALALLAWITA (Oaklands S, Cheshire) b Colombo, Sri Lanka, 23.6.98. LHB SLA. Debut 2015. HS 44 v Sussex, Blackstone, 2017. BB 3/52 v Warwicks, EFCSG, 2016. HSSET 6 v Kent, Beckenham, 2016. BBSET 4/45 v Glos, Radlett, 2016. HST20 20 v Kent, Polo Farm SG, Canterbury, 2017 (2nd). BBT20 3/26 v Kent, Polo Farm SG, Canterbury, 2017 (1st).

66

Robert George WHITE (Harrow S; Loughborough U) b Ealing, Middx 15.9.95, RHB RFM. WK. Debut Middx 2013. F/C debut (Loughborough MCCU) v Hants, Ageas Bowl Nursery, 2015. HS 160* v MCCU, Radlett, 2017. HSSET 54* v Lancs, Blackpool, 2017. HST20 65* v Essex, Coggeshall, 2017 (1st). Middx Staff.

Rahul S WIJERATNE RHB OB Debut 2017. HS 6 v Essex, Coggeshall, 2017. BB 0/26 in the same match. HST20 24 v Kent, Polo Farm SG, Canterbury, 2017 (2nd). BBT20 1/17 v Hants, Ageas Bowl Nursery, 2017 (2nd).

NORTHAMPTONSHIRE

PLAYING RECORDS 2017
Championship – P9 L4 D5 – tenth in the northern group
2nd XI Trophy – P6 W3 L3 – sixth in the northern group
2nd XI T20 Competition – P12 W5 L7 – sixth in the northern group

2nd XI SUCCESSES
2nd XI Champions – 1960, 1998
2nd XI Trophy – Winners 1986, 1998
2nd XI T20 – Best - 3rd in the group in 2011

SECOND ELEVEN CHAMPIONSHIP AVERAGES

BATTING	M	I	NO	Runs	HS	Avge	100s	C/S
D Murphy	3	4	3	163	92*	163.00	-	4
J M Kettleborough	5	8	1	376	150*	53.71	2	7
D Davies	6	9	1	246	60	30.75	-	2
C O Thurston	4	7	1	179	48	29.83	-	1
E A J Cox	5	10	1	268	62	29.77	-	1
S M Sharif	3	4	0	93	33	23.25	-	1
H R D Adair	9	15	0	340	98	22.66	-	2/1
T B Sole	9	12	3	198	37*	22.00	-	4
M A Richardson	3	3	0	52	28	17.33	-	2
A Kapil	6	7	0	107	66	15.28	-	4
S A Zaib	8	12	1	135	36	12.27	-	3
Z H Khawaja	3	3	0	19	11	6.33	-	8/1
C A Barrett	2	3	0	11	4	3.66	-	-
A Sheikh	6	6	1	16	7	3.20	-	-

BOWLING	O	M	Runs	Wkt	Avge	BB
P A Sivirajah	20	6	40	4	10.00	4/40
C A Barrett	47	10	122	8	15.25	5/18
R J Gleeson	18	3	56	3	18.66	3/56
S C Kerrigan	40.3	5	128	5	25.60	5/128
R N Sidebottom	41.4	10	115	4	28.75	2/28
D Davies	39	3	191	6	31.83	3/57
S M Sharif	40	10	129	3	43.00	2/54
C P H Haddow	34	4	136	3	45.33	2/38
A Sheikh	91	11	362	7	51.71	2/36
A Kapil	59	8	272	5	54.40	3/33
M Bilal	44	5	219	4	54.75	2/79
S A Zaib	110.4	16	424	5	84.80	4/92
T B Sole	127.2	18	465	3	155.00	2/60

Also batted – 3 matches – M Bilal 1* (1ct). 2 matches – C P W Haddow 1, 0; C E Home 1, 0, 1* (1ct); A E King 0, 2, 2 (2ct); M S Pepper 4, 51 (1ct); R N Sidebottom 0*, 1*; H J H Stow 5, 0; G Wade DNB (1ct). 1 match – M Y Ahmadzai DNB (1ct); S F G Bullen 15, 0; S P Crook DNB (1ct); M H Cross 7, 23 (2ct & 1st); H R C Ellison 6; R J Gleeson DNB; T D Heathfield DNB (1ct); W J Heathfield 0*; J B R Holling DNB (1ct); C F Hughes 24*, 22; S C Kerrigan 29*; F Niyazi 0*, 0 (1ct); S E Rippington 10*, 0; A Shahzad 0; B J Shoare 21, 4; P A Sivirajah DNB; O W Smithson 1*, 0; M J G Taylor 3, 0; K O Walters DNB; N R Welch 1, 15.

Also bowled – M Y Ahmadzai 14-5-33-2; E A J Cox 3-0-17-0; S P Crook 11-3-32-1; T D Heathfield 14-2-39-1; W J Heathfield 5-0-30-0; J B R Holling 14-1-62-1; C F Hughes 1.1-0-4-0; J M Kettleborough 9.3-0-39-3; F Niyazi 8-0-38-0; M A Richardson 40-4-168-2; S E Rippington 16-1-91-0; A Shahzad 10-1-37-2; O W Smithson 18-4-41-2; H J H Stow 38-5-147-2; M J G Taylor 7-0-31-0; C O Thurston 1-0-4-0; G Wade 29-3-121-2; K O Walters 4-1-14-0.

SECOND ELEVEN TROPHY AVERAGES

BATTING	M	I	NO	Runs	HS	Avge	100s	C/S
T B Sole	4	3	2	99	53*	99.00	-	3
M A Richardson	4	4	3	58	46*	58.00	-	2
S A Zaib	5	5	0	102	30	20.40	-	2
A Bramley	3	3	0	44	28	14.66	-	1
C E Home	4	4	0	45	23	11.25	-	-
B Claydon	3	3	0	25	14	8.33	-	1
H R D Adair	5	5	1	28	23*	7.00	-	-

BOWLING	O	M	Runs	Wkt	Avge	BB
B M R Akram	6.5	0	20	4	5.00	4/20
A Sheikh	21	1	87	6	14.50	3/35
R J Gleeson	15	0	65	4	16.25	3/19
S A Zaib	28.1	2	144	7	20.57	3/2
G G White	20	0	103	3	34.33	2/63
M A Richardson	31	0	193	5	38.60	3/41
A Kapil	20	0	143	3	47.66	3/68

Also batted – 3 matches – C A Barrett, 45 (3ct); A Sheikh 4, 9*. 2 matches – J J Cobb 52, 32 (2ct); E A J Cox 3, 15; R J Gleeson 2 (1ct); A Kapil 14, 34 (1ct); R I Newton 3, 14 (1ct); G G White 74, 19. 1 match – B M R Akram DNB; M Azarullah DNB (1ct); A W R Barrow 18 (1ct & 1st); N L Buck DNB; S P Crook 115* (1ct); M H Cross 26 (1ct); D Davies 47 (3ct); B M Duckett 83 (1ct); C P W Haddow DNB; J S Kendall 14* (2ct); R I Keogh 63 (1ct); J M Kettleborough 1; Z H Khamaja 15 (1ct); D Murphy 34; H M Nicholls 14; A M Rossington 34 (1ct); M J G Taylor 0; A G Wakely 39.

Also bowled – M Azarullah 6-0-61-1; C A Barrett 22-1-123-2; A Bramley 7-0-48-2; N L Buck 5-0-33-0; B Claydon 10-0-67-0; J J Cobb 10-0-64-2; S P Crook 7-0-45-2; D Davies 10-0-39-1; C P W Haddow 5-1-9-1; C E Home 7-0-15-1; R I Keogh 6-0-18-1; T B Sole 35-1-157-2; M J G Taylor 9-0-54-1.

SECOND ELEVEN T20 AVERAGES

BATTING	M	I	NO	Runs	HS	Avge	100s	C/S
S A Zaib	10	10	0	411	76	41.10	-	9
R E Levi	3	3	1	68	35	34.00	-	1
M Bilal	6	6	5	31	16*	31.00	-	1
R I Newton	4	3	0	76	56	25.33	-	1
C O Thurston	10	10	0	214	54	21.40	-	-
A Kapil	10	10	1	178	47	19.77	-	-
E A J Cox	3	3	0	55	33	18.33	-	-
C F Hughes	4	4	0	55	29	13.75	-	-
M S Pepper	6	6	1	67	38	13.40	-	3/2
H P Kingston	4	4	1	38	17*	12.66	-	2
J S Kendall	4	4	0	50	1	12.50	-	2
T B Sole	10	10	1	73	22	8.11	-	4
A E King	5	3	0	23	14	7.66	-	3/1
C E Home	3	3	0	16	10	5.33	-	1
A Sheikh	8	3	1	7	4	3.50	-	-

BOWLING	O	M	Runs	Wkt	Avge	BB
B W Sanderson	4	0	31	4	7.75	4/31
H P Kingston	11	0	76	4	19.00	2/9
A Kapil	18	0	122	6	20.33	2/12
L S Perry	9	0	63	3	21.00	2/18
T B Sole	29	1	194	9	21.55	4/17
S A Zaib	21	0	137	5	27.40	2/21`
R J Gleeson	12	0	84	3	28.00	2/15
A Sheikh	23.5	1	201	5	40.20	2/17
M Bilal	16.5	0	147	3	49.00	2/22

Also bowled – M Azarullah 8-0-71-1; A D F Brewster 11-0-118-1; N L Buck 7-0-46-0; J J Cobb 4-0-21-1; S P Crook 3-0-29-1; C P W Haddow 14-0-98-2; C F Hughes 1-0-3-0; R I Keogh 2-0-13-1; R K Kleinveldt 3-0-20-1; A Shahzad 5.4-0-46-1; S M Sharif 5.5-0-82-1; G G White 8-0-73-1.

Also batted – 5 matches – C P W Haddow 2* (2ct). 4 matches – R J Gleeson 1*. 3 matches – L S Perry 0*, 2. 2 matches – H R D Adair 1*, 41*(1ct); M Azarullah DNB (1ct); A D F Brewster 4, 5*; N L Buck 19*; J J Cobb 52, 16; S P Crook 4*, 15* (1ct); B M Duckett 34, 40 (2ct); R I Keogh 7, 15; D Murphy 4, 11; S M Sharif 1, 24 (1ct); A Shahzad 17*, 13; A G Wakely 23, 41 (1ct); G G White 4*. 1 match – R K Kleinveldt 13* (1ct); B W Sanderson DNB.

HOME MATCHES: SECOND ELEVEN CHAMPIONSHIP

v Durham (Milton Keynes) – 2-4 May – Durham 434/3d (G J Harte 183, M A Jones 172) beat Northants 124 (J Coughlin 3/15, S Reeves 3/21) & 250 (J M Kettleborough 150*; S Reeves 6/79) by an inns & 60 runs.
v Nottinghamshire (Milton Keynes) – 23-25 May – Notts 387/8d (G P Smith 146, A K Dal 125) & 154/8d (C A Barrett 5/18) drew with Northants 264 (J M Kettleborough 117; C R Marshall 3/32) & 92/3.

v Worcestershire (Holcot Oval) – 20-22 June – Worcs 380/9d (B J Twohig 83, A N Kervezee 74, J D Shantry 61*; A Hepburn 54; S A Zaib 4/92) beat Northants 167 (D Davies 60; A Hepburn 3/27) & 142 (D Davies 54; P R Brown 4/34, A Hepburn 3/40) by an inns & 71 runs.
v MCC Young Cricketers (Milton Keynes) – 7-9 Aug – MCC YC 300/9d (S M Imtiaz 78, M D Lezar 58, B L Brookes 53; P A Sivirajah 4/40) drew with Northants 3/2.

HOME MATCHES: FRIENDLIES

v Glamorgan (Northampton) – 12-14 Apr – Glam 180 (A Carter 5/53) & 200 (S J Pearce 58; C A Barrett 3/44) lost to Northants 390/7d (D Murphy 96, C A Barrett 77, H R D Adair 62; L Dixon 3/67) by an inns & 10 runs.

COMBINED FRIENDLY MATCHES INVOLVING NORTHAMPTONSHIRE

Kent & Northamptonshire v Warwickshire (Canterbury) – 13-16 June – Kent & Northants 241 (C J Basey 57; O J Hannon-Dalby 3/41, M R Adair 3/55) & 425 (S A Zaib 114, J M Kettleborough 84, H R D Adair 69; Sukhjit Singh 5/87, G D Panayi 3/74) lost to Warwicks 255 (S R Hain 115, A J Mellor 60; R J Gleeson 6/78, M D Hunn 3/61) & 415/3 (A R I Umeed 174, S R Hain 149*) by seven wkts.

Kent & Northamptonshire v Scotland A (Northampton) – 12-14 Sept – Kent & Northants 329 (A P Rouse 108, S A Zaib 61; A C Evans 4/84, S M Sharif 3/67) & 151/9d (A C Evans 5/66, S M Sharif 3/29) lost to Scotland A 99 (N L Buck 4/35, G Wade 3/22) & 382/7 (C S MacLeod 145, S M Sharif 75*, M H Cross 63) by three wkts.

HOME MATCHES: SECOND ELEVEN TROPHY

v MCC Young Cricketers (Lancot Park, Totternhoe) – 18 Apr – MCC YC 246/9 (F H Allen 64; M A Richardson 3/41) lost to Northants 248/8 (R I Keogh 63, J J Cobb 52; O W Smithson 3/43, B L Brookes 3/45) by two wkts.

v Leicestershire (Northampton) – 19 Apr – Nortants 431/7 (S P Crook 115*, B M Duckett 83, G G White 74) beat Leics 332 (C S Delport 157, A M Ali 57) by 99 runs.

v Durham (Milton Keynes) – 1 May – Durham 93 (B M R Akram 4/20, S A Zaib 3/2) lost to Northants 94/4 (G T Main 3/21) by six wkts.

v Nottinghamshire (Bedford S) – 22 May – Notts 217/9 (G P Smith 103*; A Sheikh 3/35) beat Northants 194 (L Wood 4/15, W T Root 4/32) by 23 runs.

HOME MATCHES: SECOND ELEVEN T20 COMPETITION

v Worcestershire (Wantage Road) – 19 June – Match 1 - Worcs 138/9 lost to Northants 139/4 (J J Cobb 52; P R Brown 3/10) by six wkts.

v Worcestershire (Wantage Road) – 19 June – Match 2 – Northants 195/5 (R I Newton 56) beat Worcs 180/6 (A O Wiffen 99; B W Sanderson 4/31) by 15 runs.

v Lancashire (Wantage Road) –3 July – Match 1 – Northants 120/6 lost to Lancs 122/3 by seven wkts.

v Lancashire (Wantage Road) –3 July – Match 2 – Lancs 161/3 (K R Brown 101) lost to Northants 165/8 (M W Parkinson 4/18) by two wkts.

PLAYERS WHO HAVE REPRESENTED NORTHAMPTONSHIRE 2nd XI IN 2017 (66

H R D Adair	D Davies	A E King	B J Shoare
M Y Ahmadzai	B M Duckett	H P Kingston	R N Sidebottom
B M R Akram	H R C Ellison	R K Kleinveldt	P A Sivirajah
M Azarullah	R J Gleeson	R E Levi	O W Smithson
C A Barrett	C P W Haddow	D Murphy	T B Sole
A W R Barrow	T D Heathfield	R I Newton	H J H Stow
M Bilal	W J Heathfield	H M Nicholls	M J G Taylor
A Bramley	M D E Holden	F Niyazi	C O Thurston
A D F Brewster	J B R Holling	M S Pepper	G Wade
N L Buck	C E Home	L S Perry	A G Wakely
S F G Bullen	C F Hughes	M A Richardson	K O Walters
*A Carter	A Kapil	S E Rippington	N R Welch
B Claydon	J S Kendall	A M Rossington	G G White
J J Cobb	R I Keogh	B W Sanderson	S A Zaib
E A J Cox	S C Kerrigan	A Shahzad	
S P Crook	J M Kettleborough	S M Sharif	
M H Cross	Z H Khawja	A Sheikh	

NORTHAMPTONSHIRE CRICKETERS

Harry Robert David ADAIR (Shrewsbury S) b Chesterfield, Derbys, 14.12.97. RHB LB. Debut 2016. HS 98 v Lancs, Liverpool., 2017. BB 0/1 v Durham, Riverside, 2016 & v Glam, Northampton, 2017. HSSET 80 v Notts, Finedon Dolben, 2016. HST20 41* v Warwicks, Scorers, 2017 (2nd).

Basil Mohammad Ramzan AKRAM (Brentwood S; Loughborough U), b Leytonstone, Essex, 23.2.93. RHB RFM. Debut Essex 2010; Northants 2011; Notts 2013; Hants, Leics & MCC Univs 2014. F/C debut (Loughborough MCCU) v Sussex, Hove, 2014. Debut Sussex 2016. HS 77 (MCCU) v Durham, Gosforth, 2016. BB 2/49 (MCCU) v Somerset, Taunton Vale, 2014. HSSET 23 (Hants) v Kent, Canterbury, 2014 & v Surrey, Horsham, 2016. BBSET 4/20 v Durham, Milton Keynes, 2017. HST20 1* (Hants) v Somerset, Taunton Vale, 2015 (2nd). BBT20 1/13 (Sussex) v MCCYC, Eastbourne, 2016 (2nd).

Chad Anthony BARRETT (King Edward VII S, Johannesburg) b Johannesburg, Transvaal (Gauteng), S.Africa, 22.5.89. RHB RFM. Debut Somerset 2009. MCC YC 2011; Derbys 2012; Glos 2013 & Middx 2013. Northants 2014. F/C debut v S Lankans,

Northampton, 2014. HS 77 v Glam, Northampton, 2017. BB 5/18 v Notts, Milton Keynes, 2017. HSSET 65* v Unc, Long Marston, Herts, 2014. BBSET 4/32 in the same match. HST20 26 (MCC YC) v Kent, Canterbury, 2012 (1st). BBT20 2/27 (MCC YC) v Sussex, Radlett, 2011 (1st). Northants Staff.

Alexander William Rodgerson BARROW (Selwood S, Frome; King's C, Taunton) b Bath 6.5.92. RHB OB WK. Debut Somerset 2009, Eng U19 v SL 2010, F/C debut (Somerset) v Hants, Rose Bowl, 2011; debut Glos & Northants 2017. HS 150* (Somerset) v Kent, Maidstone 2011. HSSET 93 (Somerset) v MCCYC, North Perrott 2011. HST20 56* (Somerset) v Glos, Taunton Vale 2015 (2nd).

Andrew BRAMLEY (The Leys S, Cambridge) b Cambridge, 21.2.00. RHB OB. Debut 2017. HSSET 28 v Notts, Bedford S, 2017. BBSET 2/37 v Lancs, Northop Hall, 2017.

Andrew David Francis BREWSTER (Tadcaster GS & SFC) b York, 1.2.97. RHB RFM. Debut Glam 2016; Durham, Northants & MCCU 2017. F/C debut (Cardiff MCCU) v Glam, SWALEC, 2017. BB 4/33 (Durham) v Essex, Richmond, N Yorks, 2017. HST20 5*

v Notts, Grantham, 2017 (2nd). BBT20 1/6 (Durham) v Worcs, Burnopfield CC, 2017 (2nd).

Nathan Liam BUCK (Ashby S) b Leicester 26.4.91. RHB RMF. Debut Leics 2008, F/C debut (Leics) v Loughborough MCCU, Grace Road, 2009. Eng U19 to S.Africa 2008/09; v Bangladesh 2009; to NZ 2009/10 (World Cup). Leics Cap 2011. Debut Lancs 2015; debut Northants 2017. HS 50 (Lancs) v Notts, Aigburth, 2016. BB 5/55 (Leics) v Lancs, Grace Road, 2013. HSSET 15 (Leics) v Yorks, Grace Road, 2013. BBSET 2/31 (Leics) v Notts, Notts SG, 2013. HST20 19* v Leics, Lutterworth, 2017 (1st). BBT20 3/22 (Leics) v Northants, Hinckley, 2013 (2nd).

Steven Frank Gregory BULLEN (Sheldon S, Chippenham, Wilts; Filton Coll, Bristol; Leeds Beckett U) b Watford, Herts, 12.7.92. RHB WK. Debut Hants & Glos 2009; Surrey 2010; Somerset 2011; Derbys 2012; Leics 2013; MCCU 2015. F/C debut (Leeds-Bradford MCCU) v Yorks, Headingley, 2015. Debuts Durham, 2016; Northants 2017. HS 113 (MCCU) v Worcs, Worcester RGS, 2015. HSSET 12 (Leics) v Yorks, Grace Road, 2013. HST20 11 (Leics) v Essex, Hinckley, 2013 (1st).

***Andrew CARTER** (Lincoln C) b Lincoln 27.8.88. RHB RM. Brother of M (Notts 2014 to date) Debut Notts 2006, F/C debut (Notts) v Oxford MCCU, the Parks, 2009. Debut Essex 2010. Ret to Notts 2011. Debut Derbys & Hants 2016; Northants 2017. HS 16* (Notts) v Surrey, Sutton 2006. BB 7/56 (Notts) v Warwicks, Welbeck Colliery 2009. HSSET 16* (Notts) v Leics, Notts HS, 2011. BBSET 5/38 (Notts) v Minor Counties, Welbeck Colliery 2008. HST20 3 (Derbys) v Lancs, Glossop, 2016 (2nd). BBT20 2/13 (Derbys) v Yorks, Harrogate, 2016 (1st).

Benjamin CLAYDON (Bottisham Village Coll, Cambridge) b Cambridge, 31.3.00. RHB RMF. Debut 2015, aged 15 yrs & 41 days. HS 22 v MCCU, Desborough, 2016. BB 2/13 v Glam , Northampton, 2017. HSSET 14 v Derbys, Denby, 2016. BBSET 1/38 v Notts, Finedon Dolben, 2016.. HST20 2* v Worcs, Milton Keynes, 2015 (2nd). BBT20 0/2 in the same match.

Joshua James COBB (Bosworth C; Oakham S) b Leicester 17.8.90. Son of R.A. (Leics, N.Transvaal B 1980/1989). RHB LB. Debut Leics 2006 aged 16 years and 3 days; F/C debut (Leics) v Northants, Grace Road, 2007. Debut Northants 2015. Eng U19 to S.Africa 2008/09 and v Bangladesh 2009. HS 208* (Leics) v Lancs, Leicester Ivanhoe, 2011. BB 3/28 (Leics) v Worcs, Kidderminster, 2011. HSSET 79* (Leics) v Derbys, Hinckley 2008. BBSET 2/12 (Leics) v Derbys, Hinckley 2008. HST20 71* v Worcs, Worcester, 2016 (2d). BBT20 3/23 (Leics) v Middx, Uxbridge. 2013 (2nd), HSKO 77* (Leics) v Northants, Dunstable, 2010. BBKO 1/19 in the same match. Northants Staff.

Ewan Andrew Jake COX (Bedford S; Moulton Coll) b Holland, 25.6.99. RHB RM. Debut 2017.   HS 62 v Lancs, Liverpool, 2017. HSSET 15 v Notts, Bedford S, 2017. HST20 33 v Lancs, Northampton, 2017 (2nd).

Steven Paul CROOK (Rostrevor Coll, Woodforde; U of S Australia, Maghill) b Modbury, S.Australia 28.5.83. Brother of A.R (S.Aus, Lancs, Northants 1999/2008). RHB RFM. Debut Lancs 2002; F/C debut (Lancs) v Durham MCCU, the Racecourse, 2003; debut Middx 2011. HS 142 (Lancs) v Notts, Notts Unity, 2003. BB 8/37 (Kent/Northants) v Warwicks, Beckenham, 2015. HSSET 115* v Lancs, Northampton, 2017. BBSET 3/61 (Lancs) v Derbts, Glossop, 2005. HST20 47 (Middx) v Northants, Dunstable, 2011. BBT20 2/16 (Middx) v Leics, Grace Road, 2012 (1ˢᵗ). Northants Staff.

Matthew Henry CROSS (Robert Gordon Coll; Loughborough U) b Aberdeen, Scotland, 15.10.92. RHB WK. Debut Scotland A 2009; 32 ODIs & 23 T20s (Scotland), 2013 to date. Debut Notts 2011. F/C debut (Loughborough MCCU) v Sussex, Hove, 2013. Debuts Leics 2015; Essex 2016; MCC YC, Kent & Northants 2017. HS 105* (Notts) v MCCU, Notts Sports Ground, 2012. HSSET 80 (Notts) v Derbys, Notts SG, 2014. HST20 69 (MCC YC) v Merchant Taylors' S, Northwood, 2017 (1st).

Daniel DAVIES (Prestatyn HS) b Bodelwyddan, Denbighshire, N Wales, 28.6.95. RHB OB Debut Glam 2015; Northants 2017. HS 60 v Worcs, Holcot, 2017. BB 3/57 v Lancs, Liverpool, 2017. HSSET 47 v Notts, Bedford S, 2017. BBSET 1/39 in the same match.

Ben Matthew DUCKETT (Stowe S, Bucks) b Farnborough, Kent, 17.10.94. LHB WK. Debut 2011. F/C debut v Leics, Northampton, 2013. Northants Cap 2016. Tests (Eng) 4 & 3 ODIs (2016/17). HS 95 v Derbys, Milton Keynes, 2012. HSSET 83 v Leics, Northampton, 2017. HST20 99 v Leics, Grace Road, 2015 (2nd). Northants Staff.

Harry Richard Clive ELLISON (Millfield S; Anglia Ruskin U) b Canterbury, Kent, 22.2.93. RHB OB. F/C debut (Cambridge MCCU) v Essex, Fenner's, 2014. Debut MCCU 2015; Kent & Northants 2017. HS 68 v Yorks, Weetwood, 2015.

Richard James GLEESON b Blackpool, Lancs, 2.12.87. RHB RM. Debut Warwicks 2012; Northants 2015. F/C debut v Australians, Northampton, 2015. HS 30 v MCCU, Desborough, 2015. BB 6/22 v Derbys, Swarkestone, 2015. HSSET 6 v Unc, Great Tew, 2016. BBSET 3/19 v Derbys, Denby, 2017. HST20 1* v Notts, Grantham, 2017 (1st). BBT20 2/19 v Worcs, Northampton, 2017 (1st).

Conner Paul William HADDOW (John Hampden GS, High Wycombe; Henley Coll) b High Wycombe, Bucks, 6.6.00. RHB SLA. Debut 2017. HS 1 v Notts, Milton Keynes, 2017. BB 2/38 in the same match. BBSET 1/9 v Durham, Milton Keynes, 2017. HST20 2* v Lancs, Northampton, 2017 (2nd). BBT20 1/13 v Worcs, Northampton, 2017 (1st).

Thomas David "Tom" HEATHFIELD (Northampton S for Boys) b Northampton, 10.5.97. RHB RMF. Debut 2016. Brother to W J (below) HS 19* v MCCU, Desborough, 2016. BB 2/48 in the same match. HSSET 0 v Notts, Finedon Dolben, 2016. BBSET 0/50 in the same match.

William James "Will" HEATHFIELD (Northampton S for Boys) b Northampton, 19.9.98. RHB RM. Debut 2017. Brother to T (above). HS 0* v Notts, Milton Keynes, 2017. BB 0/30 in the same match.

Max David Edward HOLDEN (Sawston Village Coll, Cambridge) b Cambridge, 18.12.97. LHB OB. Debut Middx 2013; Northants (on loan). Eng U19 to Aus 2014/15; v Aus 2015; v Sri Lanka (Capt) 2016; v Ind 2017. HS 140 (Middx) v Lancs, Liverpool, 2015. BB 1/2 (Middx) v Essex, Billericay, 2015. HSSET 127 (Middx) v Surrey, Sunbury-on-Thames, 2016. BBSET 1/17 (Middx) v Sussex, Fulking, 2016. HST20 54 (Middx) v Glam, Port Talbot, 2016 (1st). BBT20 1/13 (Middx) v Durham., Arundel, 2016 (SF).

Joshua Brynmor Rusby HOLLING (Silcoates S, Wakefield & SFC; Leeds Beckett U) b Barnsley, S Yorks, LHB LM. Debut 2017. HS 26 (Kent/Northants) v Warwicks, Canterbury, 2017. BB 1/40 in the same match.

Charles Edward HOME (Shrewsbury S) b Shrewsbury, Salop, 10.2.99. RHB OB. Debut 2014. HS 122 v MCCU, Desborough, 2016. BB 0/16 in the same match. HSSET 23 v Notts, Bedford S, 2017. BBSET 1/15 in the same match. HST20 10 v Notts, Grantham, 2017 (1st).

Chesney Francis HUGHES (Albana Lake Hodge CS) b Anguilla, W Indies, 20.1.91. LHB SLA. Debut Derbys 2009. F/C debut (Derbys) v Middx, Leeds, 2010. HS 178 (Derbys) v Notts, Denby. 2014. BB 4/33 (Derbys) v Leics, Leicester, 2009. HSSET 117 (Derbys) v Worcs, Worcester RGS, 2015. BBSET 5/35 (Drbys) v Leics, Denby, 2014. HST20 82 (Derbys) v Durham, Repton S, 2012. BBT20 2/9 (Derbys) v Lancs, Glossop, 2012 & (Derbys) v Leics, Grace Road, 2015 (1st).

Aneesh KAPIL b Wolverhampton, Staffs. b 3.8.93. RHB RFM Debut Worcs 2008; F/C debut (Worcs) v Sussex, Horsham, 2011. Debuts Surrey 2014; Northants & Unc 2017. Eng U19 v S.Africa, 2011; to Bangladesh 2011/12; to Australia (World Cup) 2012. HS 161 (Surrey) v Kent, New Malden, 2016. BB 4/12 (Worcs) v Derbys, Belper Meadows, 2010. HSSET 106 (Worcs) v Derbys, Kidderminster, 2013. BBSET 4/40 (Surrey) v Sussex, Horsham, 2016. HST20 82 (Surrey) v MCC YC, Purley, 2015 (1st). BBT20 3/26 (Unc) v Hants, Great Tew, 2017 (1ˢᵗ).

Joseph Samuel KENDALL (Oakham S) b Leicester, 2.12.96. RHB LB. Debut 2014. HS 12 v Worcs, Kidderminster, 2016. HSSET 14* v Durham, Milton Keynes, 2017. HST20 23 v Yorks, Stowe S, 2016 (1st).

Robert Ian KEOGH (Queensbury S; Dunstable Coll) b Dunstable, Beds 21.10.91. RHB OB. Debut 2009. F/C debut v Glam,

SWALEC, 2012 . HS 128 v Leics, Stowe S, 2012. BB 4/23 v MCC Univs, Weetwood, 2010. HSSET 63 v MCC YC, Totternhoe, 2017. BBSET 3/22 v Minor Counties, Long Marston, 2010. HST20 39* v Warwicks, Finedon Dolben, 2016 (2nd). BBT20 2/18 v Leics, Grace Road, 2011 (2nd). HSKO 5 v Leics, Dunstable, 2010. BBKO 3/34 in the same match. Northants Staff.

Simon Christopher KERRIGAN (Preston Coll) b Preston 10.5.89. RHB SLA. Debut Lancs 2007. F/C debut v Warwicks, Old Trafford, 2010. Lancs Cap 2013. Tests (Eng) 1, 2013. Debut Northants (on loan) 2017. HS 52 (Lancs) v Notts, Liverpool 2009. BB 6/26 (Lancs) v Leics, Desborough, 2017. HSSET 42 (Lancs) v Leics, Hinckley, 2017 BBSET 4/8 (Lancs) v Yorks, Pudsey Congs, 2015. HST20 14 (Lancs) v Durham, Gosforth, 2012 (2nd). BBT20 2/14 (Lancs) v MCC YC, Westhoughton, 2017 (2nd). BBKO 0/5 (Lancs) v Derbys, Glossop, 2010.

James Michael KETTLEBOROUGH (Bedford S) b Huntingdon, Cambs, 22.10.92. RHB OB Debut Middx 2011; Northants 2012. F/C debut (Northants) v Sri Lankans, 2014. Debut Glam 2015; Derbys, Unc & ret to Northants 2017. HS 209* (Glam) v Essex, Bishop's Stortford, 2016. BB 2/24 v Notts, Milton Keynes, 2017. HSSET 143* (Unc) v Somerset, Taunton Vale, 2017. BBSET 1/28 (Middx) v MCCYC, Radlett, 2011. HST20 52* (Glam) v Essex, Chelmsford, 2016 (1st). BBT20 2/13 (Unc) v Kent, Saffron Walden, 2017 (2nd).

Zaakir Husnain KHAWAJA (Northampton S for Boys, Moulton SFC, Northampton) b Northampton, 3.12.94. RHB WK. Debut 2012. HS 78* v MCCU, Desborough, 2014. HSSET 31 v Unc, Desborough, 2015. HST20 49* v Leics, Grace Road 2015 (1st).

Adam E KING (Stowe S) b Aylesbury, Bucks, 14.9.99. LHB WK. Debut 2016. HS 38 v Yorks, Market Harborough, 2016. HSSET 12 v Durham, Riverside 2016. HST20 14 v Lancs, Northampton, 2017 (1st).

Hamish Philip KINGSTON (St Virgil`s Coll, Hobart, Tasmania) b Hobart, Tasmania, 17.12.90. RHB RFM. Debut 2017. HST20 17* v Leics, Lutterworth, 2017 (2nd). BBT20 2/9 in the same match.

Rory Keith KLEINVELDT (Plumstead HS, Cape Town, Cape Province, S Africa) b Cape Town, 15.3.83.RHB RMF. F/C debut (W Province) v Border, Belleville, Cape Town, 2002/03. Tests 4 (S Africa) 2012/13 & 10 ODIs. Debut W Province 2002/03; W Province Boland 2004/05; Cape Cobras 2005/06; Hants 2008; Northants 2015. HSSET 47 (Hants) v Surrey, West End Nursery, 2008. BBSET 1/33 in the same match. HST20 13* v Worcs, Northampton, 2017 (1st), BBT20 1/20 in the same match. Northants Staff.

Richard Ernst LEVI b Johannesburg, Transvaal (Gauteng), S Africa, 14.1.88. RHB RM. Int T20 (SA) 4 (2011/12). Debut Western Province 2004/05; Cape Cobras 2005/06; F/C debut (WP) v Border, East London, 2006/07; debut Glam 2009; Somerset 2012; Northants 2014. HS 103* (Glam) v MCCYC, Radlett, 2009. HSSET 52 (Glam) v MCC YC, Radlett, 2009. HST20 51 v Unc, Great Tew, Oxon, 2014 (1st). Northants Staff.

MOHAMMED YOUNAS AHMADZAI (Barnfield West Academy, Luton; Barnfield Coll) b Kabul, Afghanistan, 28.8.97. RHB SLA. Debut 2017. BB 2/33 v Durham, Milton Keynes, 2017.

MOHAMMAD AZARULLAH (M C Model, Burewala, Punjab, Pakistan; G C Coll, Burewala; Bahauddin Zakariya University, Multan) b Burewala, Punjab, Pakistan, 25.12.83. RHB RMF. Debut Multan (2004/05 to 2006/07); Water & Power Dev Auth (2004/05 to 2013/13); Quetta (2005/06); Baluchistan (2007/08 to 2008/09).F/C debut (Multan) v Karachi Whites, Karachi, 2004/05. Debut Northants 2013. HS16* v Hants, the Ageas Bowl, 2013 BB 6/67 v Leics (11/117 in the match), Finedon Dolben, 2013. HSSET 2* v Middx, Radlett, 2013. BBSET 4/19 v Somerset, Taunton Vale, 2013. HST20 1* v Leics, Hinckley, 2013 (1st). BBT20 4/32 v Essex, Northampton, 2014 (1st). Released at the end of the 2017 season.

MOHAMMED BILAL (Admy Public S; Bradford Coll) b Sialkot, Pakistan, 8.2.94. LHB LM. Debut 2017. HS 1* v Yorks, York, 2017. BB 2/79 in the same match. HST20 16* v Lancs, Northampton, 2017 (2nd). BBT20 2/22 v Yorks, Pudsey Congs, 2017 (2nd).

David MURPHY (Richard Hale S, Hertford; Loughborough U) b Welwyn Garden City, Herts 24.6.89. RHB WK. Debut 2007, F/C debut (Loughborough UCCE) v Leics, Grace Road, 2009. Debut Scotland 2013. HS 147 v MCCU, Desborough, 2015. BB 1/27 v Durham, Northampton, 2015. HSSET 100* v Glos, Thornbury, 2014. HST20 71* v Yorks, Barnsley (2nd). BBT20 1/18 v Worcs, Finedon Dolben, 2016 (2nd). Retired at the end of the 2017 season. .

Robert Irving NEWTON (Framlingham Coll) b Taunton, Somerset, 18.1.90. RHB LB. Debut 2006 aged 16 years and 181 days. F/C debut v Worcs, New Road, 2010. HS 134 v Surrey, Whitgift S, 2010. HSSET 113 v Warwicks, Stowe S, 2011. HST20 88 v Essex, Chelmsford, 2011 (1st). Northants Staff.

Henry Michael NICHOLLS (St Andrew's Coll, Christchurch, N Zealand) b Christchurch, N Zealand, 15.11.91. LHB OB. 2017. HSSET 14 v Notts, Bedford S, 2017.

Fazel NIYAZI (Moulton S & SFC) b Kabul, Afghanistan, 14.3.96. LHB LFM. Debut 2017. HS 0* v Durham, Milton Keynes, 2017. BB 0/38 in the same match.

Michael-Kyle Steven PEPPER (The Perse S) b Harlow, 25.6.98. Brother of C A (Essex 2013 to 2016). RHB WK. Debut Unc 2016; Essex & Northants 2017. HS 136 (Essex) v Middx, Coggeshall, 2017. HSSET 103 (Unc) v Middx, Radlett, 2017. HST20 38 v Lancs, Northampton, 2017 (2nd).

Laurence Samuel PERRY (Bushloe HS, Wigston; Guthlaxton Coll, Wigston; U of Leicester) b Leicester Jan 1992 LHB SLA. Debut 2012. HS 4* v MCCU, Finedon Dolben, 2012. BB 1/9 v MCCU, Finedon Dolben, 2012, BBSET 0/48 v Notts, the John Fretwell Sporting Centre, Nettleworth, 2012. HST20 2 v Leics, Lutterworth, 2017 (1st). BBT20 2/18 in the same match.

Miles Andrew RICHARDSON (Sackville S, E Grinstead, Sussex) b Maidstone, 26.8.91. RHB RMF. Debut Surrey & Kent 2014; Northants 2016. F/C debut v Loughborough MCCU, Northampton, 2017. Ret to Surrey 2017. HS 84* v Worcs, Kidderminster, 2016. BB 3/74 v Derbys, Northampton, 2016. HSSET 46* v Lancs, Northop Haaal, 2017. BBSET 3/41 v MCC YC, Totternhoe, 2017. HST20 10 v Lancs, Westhoughton, 2016 (1st). BBT20 4/25 v Lancs, Westhoughton , 2016 (2nd).

Samuel Edward RIPPINGTON (Abbey Coll, Ramsey) b Waltham Forest, Essex, 8.1.94. LHB LFM. Debut Northants & MCCU 2017. F/C debut (Cambridge MCCU) v Notts, Fenner`s, 2017. HS 10* v Warwicks, EFCSG, 2017. BB 3/96 (MCCU) v Hants, Horsham, 2017

Adam Matthew ROSSINGTON (Belmont Prep S; Mill Hill S) b Edgware, 5.5.93. RHB WK. Debut Middx 2009. F/C Debut (Middx) v Oxford MCCU, the Parks, 2010. Eng U19 v Sri Lanka 2010; to S Lanka, 2010/11; v S Africa 2011. Debut Northants (on loan) 2014. HS 161 (Middx) v Northants, Northampton, 2010. BB 0/1 (Middx) v Gloucs, Radlett, 2010. HSSET 130 (Middx) v Essex, Chelmsford, 2011. HST20 107 (Middx) v Unicorns A, Uxbridge, 2013 (2nd).

Ben William SANDERSON (Ecclesfield S; Sheffield Coll) b Sheffield, Yorks 3.1.89. RHB RMF. Debut Yorks 2006; Eng U19 v NZ, 2008; debut Durham 2011; Unc & Worcs 2014; Northants 2015. F/C debut (Yorks) v Durham, Chester-le-Street, 2008. HS 44 (Yorks) v Kent/ Northants, Beckenham, 2011. BB 6/30 (Yorks) v Notts, Stamford Bridge, 2008. HSSET30 (Yorks) v Notts, Headingley, 2009. BBSET 4/25 (Yorks) v Derbys, York, 2009. HST20 12* (Yorks) v Derbys, Headingley, 2011 (1st). BBT20 4/31 v Worcs, Northampton, 2017 (1st).

Ajmal SHAHZAD (Woodhouse Grove S, Bradford) b Huddersfield, Yorks, 27.7.85. RHB RMF. Debut Yorks 2003;F/C debut (Yorks) v Middx, Scarborough, 2006. Cap 2010. Debut Lancs 2012 (on loan); Debut Notts 2013; Sussex 2015; Leics & Northants 2017. Tests (Eng) 1 & 11 ODIs (2010-2010/11). HS 57 (Yorks) v Derbys, Barnsley, 2008. BB 6/42 in the same match. HSSET 91 (Yorks) v Leics, Bingley, 2008. BBSET 3/55 (Yorks) v Durham, Seaton Carew, 2006. HST20 27 (Sussex) v Surrey, Purley, 2016 (1st). BBT20 3/29 (Sussex) v Surrey, New Malden, 2017 (1st).

Safyaan Mohammed SHARIF (Buckhaven HS, Fife) b Huddersfield, Yorks 24.5.91. RHB RFM. Debut (Scotland) 2010; Glos 2014; Northants 2016. 26 ODIs (Scot) 2011 to date. F/C debut (Scot) v Namibia, Windhoek 2011/12. Debut Glos 2014. HS 48* (Scot) v Lancs, Blackpool, 2015. BB 4/78 (Scot) v Yorks, Scarborough, 2014. HSSET 27 v Durham, Riverside, 2016. BBSET

2/28 v Unc, Bath CC 2014. HST20 24 v Yorks, Pudsey Congs, 2017 (2nd). BBT20 1/47 v Yorks, Pudsey Congs, 2017 (1st).

Atif SHEIKH (Bluecoat S, Nottingham) b Nottingham, 18.2.91. RHB LMF. Debut Derbys 2008, F/C debut (Derbys) v Glos, Derby, 2010. Eng U19 to S Africa 2009/10; v Sri Lanks, 2010. Debut Leics & Worcs 2012. Northants 2017. HS 37 (Derbys) v Worcs (Worcester RGS) 2010. BB 6/49 (Leics) v Worcs, Lutterworth, 2014. HSSET 28* (Derbys) v Leics, Leicester 2009. BBSET 4/35 (Leics) v Lancs, Grace Road, 2015. HST20 15 (Leics) v Warwicks, Edgbaston, 2015 (2nd). BBT20 2/17 v Leics, Lutterworth, 2017 (2nd). HSKO 1 (Derbys) v Sussex, Horsham, 2010. BBKO 1/23 (Derbys) v Lancs, Glossop, 2010.

Benjamin John SHOARE (Reigate GS; Collyer`s SFC, Horsham) b Crawley, 21.9.95. RHB OB. Debut Sussex 2013; MCC YC 2016; Northants 2017. . HS 63 (Sussex) v Essex, Hove, 2013. BB 1/5 in the same match. HSSET 40 (Sussex) v Essex, Fulking, 2013. HST20 16* (Sussex) v Kent, Birdham, 2013 (2nd).

Ryan Nathan SIDEBOTTOM (Wanganui Park Sec Coll, Shepparton, Victoria, Aus) b Shepparton, Victoria. Aus, 14.8.89. RHB RFM. Debut Victoria 2012/13; F/C debut (Victoria) v Tasmania, Hobart, 2012/13; debuts Notts, Northants & Warwicks 2017. HS 1* v Lancs, Liverpool, 2017. BB 8/33 (Warwicks) v Northants, EFCSG, 2017. HST20 2* (Warwicks) v Durham, S Northumberland, 2017 (2nd). BBT20 5/11 (Warwicks) v Durham, S Northumberland, 2017 (1st).

Praven Ashley SIVIRAJAH (Haberdashers`Aske`s S, Elstree, Herts; U of Southampton Solent) b Islington, 3.4.94. RHB SLA. Debut MCC YC 2016; Northants 2017. HS 21* (MCC YC) v Sussex, Eastbourne, 2016. BB 5/78 (MCCYC) v Leics, High Wycombe, 2017. HSSET 20* (MCC YC) v Worcs, Kidderminster, 2017. BBSET 2/40 (MCC YC) v Warwicks, Merchant Taylors`s S, Northwood, 2017. HST20 5 (MCC YC) v Worcs, Merchant Taylors' S, Northwood, 2017 (2nd). BBT20 2/1 (MCC YC) v Essex, Southend-on-Sea, 2016 (1st).

Oliver William SMITHSON (Bradfield C) b Lisbon, Portugal 6.1.96. RHB LMF. Debut Glos 2014; MCC YC 2015; Durham & Northants 2017. HS 12* (Glos) v Hants, WE Nursery 2014. BB 3/24 (MCC YC) v Glos, Shenley, 2016. HSSET 27 (Glos) v Northants, Thornbury CC 2014. BBSET 3/41 (MCC YC) v Leics, Merchant Taylors`s S, Northwood, 2017. HST20 15 (MCC YC) v Worcs, Merchant Taylors`s S, Northwood, 2017 (2nd). BBT20 3/15 (MCC YC) v Notts, Merchant Taylors' S, Northwood, 2017 (1st).

Tom Barclay SOLE (Merchiston Castle S, Edinburgh; Cardiff Met) b Edinburgh, 12.6.96. RHB OB. Son of D Sole (Scotland RU & British Lions). Debut 2015. List A debut v S Africans, Northampton, 2017. HS 40* v Glam, Northampton. 2017. BB 3/42 v Warwicks, Shirley, 2015. HSSET 53* v Derbys, Denby, 2017. BBSET 4/24 v Leics, Lancot Park Totternhoe, 2015. HST20 22 v Warwicks, Shirley, 2017 (1st). BBT20 4/17 v Leics, Lutterworth, 2017 (2nd).

Harry Jonathan Hugh STOW (Dumeriah Eng speaking S , Dubai; Ellesmere Coll, Cheshire; Leeds Beckett U) b Lincoln, 21.9.97. RHB RMF. Debut 2017. HS 5 v Durham, Milton Keynes, 2017. BB 2/78 v Leics, Desborough, 2017.

Matthew John George TAYLOR (Wymondham Coll, Norfolk; Rugby S) b Norwich, Norfolk, 1.10.96. RHB LB. Debut 2014. HS 46 v Surrey, Guildford, 2014. BB 4/120 v Durham Riverside, 2016. HSSET 19 v Derbys, Belper, 2015. BBSET 2/49 in the same match. HST20 1* v Warwicks, Finedon Dolben, 2016 (1st). BBT20 2/36 v Leics, Bedford S, 2016 (2nd)

Charles Oliver THURSTON (Bedford S) b Cambridge, 17.8.96. RHB RM. Debut Middx 2013; Northants 2015. F/C debut (Loughborough MCCU) v Surrey, the Oval, 2016. HS 203* v Durham, Northampton, 2015. BB 1/14 v Durham, Riverside, 2016. HSSET 34 v Durham, Riverside, 2016. HST20 54 v Yorks, Pudsey Congs, 2017 (2nd).

Gareth WADE (Prudhoe Comm HS, Northumberland; U of Sunderland) b Hexham, Northumberland., 11.1.91. RHB RF. Debut Unc & Worcs 2015.; Northants 2017. F/C debut v Loughborough MCCU, Northampton, 2017. HS 5* (Worcs) v Leics, Kidderminster, 2015. BB 1/37 v MCC YC, Milton Keynes, 2017. BBT20 2/36 (Unc) v Durham, Burnopfield, 2015 (1st).

Alexander George WAKELY (Bedford S) b Hammersmith, Middx, 3.11.88. RHB OB. Debut 2004 aged 15 yrs & 294 days. F/C debut v Somerset, Taunton, 2007. Cap 2012. Eng U19 to Malaysia (World Cup), 2006/07; v Pakistan, 2007; to Sri Lanka 2007/08; v New Zealand 2008. HS 115 v Sussex, Hove, 2009. BB 1/3 v Lancs, Southport, 2008. HSSET 74 v Middx, Milton Keynes, 2008. BBSET 3/51 v Hants, Rose Bowl Nursery, 2009. HST20 50 v Unicorns A, Northampton, 2013 (2nd). Northants Staff.

Kelbert Orlando WALTERS b Anguilla, W Indies, 4.12.90. RHB RFM. Debut Derbys 2009.Hants 2010. F/C debut (Anguilla) v Barbados, North Sound, 2010/11. Debut Northants 2017. HS 13* v Ireland A, Rose Bowl, 2010. BB 1/56 in the same match.

Nicholas Roy WELCH (St John`s Coll, Harare, Zim) b Harare, Zim, 5.2.98. RHB LB. F/C debut (Mashonaland Eagles, Zim) v Mountaineers, Harare, 2013/14. Debuts Surrey 2015, Sussex 2016, Essex & Northants 2017. HS 88 (Surrey) v Middx, New Malden, 2017. HSSET 72* (Sussex) v Kent, Canterbury, 2017. HST20 75* (Surrey) v Unc, New Malden, 2017 (2nd).

Graeme Geoffrey WHITE (Royal Latin S, Buckingham; Stowe S) b Milton Keynes, Bucks 18.4.87. RHB SLA. Debut Northants 2003, F/C debut v Derbys, Northampton, 2006; Debut Notts 2010. On loan to Northants 2013. Eng U19 v India 2006. HS 111 v Glos, Thornbury, 2014. BB 6/36 (Notts) v Worcs, Ombersley, 2010. HSSET 104* (Notts) v MCCYC, Caythorpe CC, 2010. HSSET 4/32 (Notts) v Durham, Notts Sports Ground, 2011. HST20 35* (Notts) v Lancs, Long Eaton, 2011 (2nd). BBT20 4/20 (Notts) v Eng U19, Trent Coll, Long Eaton, 2012. (2nd) Northants Staff.

Saif Ali ZAIB (Royal GS, High Wycombe, Bucks) b High Wycombe, 22.5.98. LHB SLA. Debut 2013. F/C debut v Kent, Canterbury, 2015. HS 114 (Kent/Northants) v Warwicks, Canterbury, 2017. BB 4/92 v Worcs, Holcot, 2017. HSSET 121 v Notts, Notts SG, 2015. BBSET 4/35 v Durham, Finedon Dolben, 2015. HST20 76 v Leics, Lutterworth, 2016 (2nd). BBT20 2/12 v Worcs, Worcester, 2016 (1st).

NOTTINGHAMSHIRE

PLAYING RECORDS 2017
Championship – P9 W3 L2 D3 Ab1– sixth in the northern group
2nd XI Trophy – P6 W3 L3 – fifth in the northern group
2nd XI T20 Competition – P12 W5 L7 – seventh in the northern group

2nd XI SUCCESSES
Championship – Winners – 1972, 1985, 2015
2nd XI Trophy – Winners – 1991, 2011
2nd XI T20 Competition – Best finish – 4th in the group in 2011, 2015

SECOND ELEVEN CHAMPIONSHIP AVERAGES

BATTING	M	I	NO	Runs	HS	Avge	100s	C/S
J D Libby	4	6	1	357	170*	71.40	2	-
B R M Taylor	2	3	1	140	104*	70.00	1	1
L W James	2	3	1	105	54*	52.50	-	2
A K Dal	8	11	2	449	125	49.88	2	1
G P Smith	3	5	0	209	146	41.80	1	3
C R Marshall	8	10	5	188	64*	37.60	-	3
T J Moores	4	6	1	162	101*	32.40	1	13
C F Gibson	3	6	0	181	58	30.16	-	-
M E Milnes	7	5	2	90	47*	30.00	-	4
W T Root	3	5	0	113	66	22.60	-	1
L Wood	3	6	1	106	57	21.20	-	-
W A R Fraine	2	4	1	58	55	19.33	-	-
M Carter	8	10	1	140	52	15.55	-	12
B M Kitt	6	4	0	57	27	14.25	-	4
T G Keast	8	10	0	123	35	12.30	-	8/1
B A Hutton	4	7	0	40	18	5.71	-	5

BOWLING	O	M	Runs	Wkt	Avge	BB
R N Sidebottom	26	7	108	8	13.50	4/53
M E Milnes	140	34	425	20	21.25	4/41
D D A Brown	27	5	69	3	23.00	2/28
B A Hutton	126.5	18	436	17	25.64	7/44
L Wood	58	18	161	6	26.83	3/60
C R Marshall	94.4	20	290	10	29.00	3/32
M Carter	211.5	59	524	18	29.11	4/47
B M Kitt	123	31	386	11	35.09	3/87

Also bowled – J T Ball 10-3-38-1; J M Blatherwick 11-2-42-2; J D Cook 2-0-29-0; A K Dal 41-12-103-2; M H A Footitt 27-7-73-2; l James 4-0-14-0; J D Libby 11-1-34-0; R A Parker-Cole 26-4-127-2; L A Patterson-White 1-0-3-0; M A Raza 7-0-24-1; W T Root 17-6-42-1; G P Smith 4.2-0-57-1; B R M Taylor 5-0-32-0.

Also batted – 3 matches – R A Parker-Cole 19* (2ct). 2 matches – D D A Brown 18, 6 (1ct); M H A Footitt 7; L P J Kimber 14 (2ct). 1 match – J T Ball DNB; J M Blatherwick 17; J D Cook DNB; J D M Evison 9, 54; J E P Hebron 54 (12ct); O M D Kolk 59; Z McKaskie 9, 24* (1ct); L A Patterson-White 3, 13 (2ct); M A Raza DNB; S D P Reeves 4, 12* (1ct); R N Sidebottom DNB.

SECOND ELEVEN TROPHY AVERAGES

BATTING	M	I	NO	Runs	HS	Avge	100s	C/S
G P Smith	4	4	1	209	103*	69.66	1	-
W T Root	3	3	0	175	123	58.33	1	1
J D Libby	3	3	1	112	57*	56.00	-	-
B A Hutton	4	4	0	147	119	36.75	1	-
T G Keast	6	6	2	114	66*	28.50	-	-
A K Dal	4	4	0	106	83	26.50	-	-
M Carter	6	5	1	98	57	24.50	-	2
B R M Taylor	3	3	0	62	44	20.66	-	2
B M Kitt	5	4	2	37	11	18.50	-	4
M E Milnes	6	4	3	14	8	14.00	-	1
T J Moores	6	6	0	83	26	13.83	-	5/1
L A Patterson-White	3	3	0	38	28	12.66	-	4
D D A Brown	4	4	0	21	11	5.25	-	1

BOWLING	O	M	Runs	Wkt	Avge	BB
L Wood	8.2	2	15	4	3.75	4/15
L A Patterson-White	25	0	127	6	21.16	3/44
W T Root	29	0	116	5	23.20	4/32
B M Kitt	45	2	246	8	30.75	4/37
B A Hutton	45	2	163	5	32.60	2/35
M Carter	51	56	227	6	37.83	3/28
M E Milnes	38	2	197	4	49.25	2/18

Also bowled – L R Bhabra 5-0-18-1; D D A Brown 11-0-81-0; A K Dal 11-2-57-1; H F Gurney 10-0-52-1; J D Libby 6-0-15-2; C R Marshall 12-0-55-1; S J Mullaney 6-0-24-0.

Also batted – 2 matches – C R Marshall 16, 0; L Wood 121, 28 (1ct). 1 match - L R Bhabra DNB; C F Gibson 1; H F Gurney DNB; L P J Kimber 20; S J Mullaney 0.

SECOND ELEVEN T20 AVERAGES

BATTING	M	I	NO	Runs	HS	Avge	100s	C/S
T J Moores	4	3	1	134	88	67.00	-	-
G P Smith	10	10	2	286	70	35.75	-	3
A K Dal	6	6	1	142	56*	28.40	-	1
C R Marshall	10	7	2	107	42*	21.40	-	2
W T Root	9	8	0	150	65	18.75	-	4
T G Keast	10	7	3	68	22	17.00	-	4/4
B A Hutton	9	8	2	97	30*	16.16	-	2
M Carter	9	5	1	45	17	11.25	-	4
L Wood	12	10	0	107	23	10.70	-	5
L W James	3	3	1	15	6	7.50	-	-
M E Milnes	11	5	2	15	5*	4.00	-	2

BOWLING	O	M	Runs	Wkt	Avge	BB
L J Fletcher	4	0	31	4	7.75	4/31
S R Patel	4	0	34	3	11.33	3/34
D T Christian	6	0	48	3	16.00	3/37
M Carter	32	1	204	11	18.54	4/11
M E Milnes	24	0	159	8	19.87	2/20
B M Kitt	13.2	0	117	5	23.40	2/21
B A Hutton	21	0	146	5	29.20	2/14
L Wood	26.5	0	206	7	29.42	2/12
J M Blatherwick	15	0	167	5	33.40	1/19
C R Marshall	25	0	176	5	35.20	2/17
W T Root	26.1	0	211	5	42.20	1/10

Also batted – 11 matches – J M Blatherwick 0* (2ct). 8 matches – B M Kitt 1*, 0. 2 Matches – D T Christian 1, 90* (2ct); M H A Footitt DNB (2ct); L P J Kimber 20, 8; M D Lezar 5, 0; J D Libby 22*, 42. 1 match – L J Fletcher DNB; C F Gibson DNB; A D Hales 2; M J Lumb 95; Z McCaskie 12; S J Mullaney 44*; S R Patel 5; L A Patterson-White DNB; S D P Reeves 1; R N Sidebottom 0*; I S Sodhi DNB (1ct); B R M Taylor 49* (1ct); M H Wessels 23 (1ct).

Also bowled – A K Dal 8.1-0-57-1; M H A Footitt 5-0-40-12; J D Libby 2-0-16-0; S J Mullaney 3-0-18-2; L A Patterson-White 2-0-17-0; S D P Reeves 4-0-32-1; R N Sidebottom 3-0-28-1; I S Sodhi 3-0-27-0.

HOME MATCHES: SECOND ELEVEN CHAMPIONSHIP

v Leicestershire (Notts SG) – 10-12 Apr – Leics 328 (L J Hill 87, H E Dearden 83; M E Milnes 3/55, B M Kitt 3/87) & 250/7d (A M Ali 60, M L Pettini 50; M E Milnes 3/67) beat Notts 165 (W T Root 66; C F Parkinson 4/8, R A Jones 3/36) & 257 (C F Gibson 58) by 156 runs.

v Warwickshire (Notts SG) – 15-17 May – Warwicks 244/4 (R M Yates 102, M J Lamb 95) drew with Notts DNB.

v Lancashire (Notts SG) – 5-7 June – Lancs 280/8d (B D Guest 96*, R P Jones 75) & inns forfeited lost to Notts inns forfeited & 284/5 (B R M Taylor 104*, C R Marshall 64*) by five wkts.

v Worcestershire (Notts SG) – 31 July to 2 Aug – Notts 198 (W A R Fraine 55; B J Twohig 3/45) & 328/5d (J D Libby 170*, J Evison 54) drew with Worcs 395 (T C Fell 128, A G Milton 63, Z A Malik 57, B J Twohig 50*; M Carter 4/107, B A Hutton 4/112)

HOME MATCHES: FRIENDLIES

v Yorkshire (Notts SG) – 3 Apr – Yorks 300/5d (M J Waite 101*, W M H Rhodes 63, D J Willey 53) drew with Notts 69/8 (J C Wainman 4/9)

v Yorkshire (Notts SG) – 4 Apr – Notts 177/4d (A D Hales 52, C F Gibson 50) drew with Yorks 166/3 (R Gibson 78)

v Leicestershire (Notts SG) – 29-31 Aug – Leics 335/7d (R J Sayer 89, A J Ball 82, T J Wells 59; J D Cook 3/74) & 163/3d (S T Evans 65*) beat Notts 220/4d (C F Gibson 92; Z J Chappell 3/23) & 159 by 119 runs.

HOME MATCHES: SECOND ELEVEN TROPHY

v Leicestershire (Notts SG) – 13 Apr – Leics 257/8 (T J Wells 78) lost to Notts 258/8 (W T Root 123; D Klein 3/48) by two wkts.

v Worcestershire (Oakham S) – 1 May – Worcs 244/6 (G H Rhodes 134*, A Hepburn 56) beat Notts 229/9 (A K Dal 83, M Carter 57) by 15 runs.

HOME MATCHES : SECOND ELEVEN T20 COMPETITION

v Warwickshire (Worksop C) – 19 June – Match 1 – Notts 132/5 (A K Dal 56*) lost to Warwicks 134/3 (E J Pollock 93*) by seven wkts.

v Warwickshire (Worksop C) – 19 June – Match 2 – Warwicks 119/7 lost to Notts 120/5 (G P Smith 50*) by five wkts.

v Lancashire (Trent C) – 22 June – Match 1 – Notts 143/6 lost to Lancs 145/6 (C K Turner 55) by four wkts.

v Lancashire (Trent C) – 22 June – Match 2 – Notts 140/7 (W T Root 65; T J Lester 3/8) lost Lancs 143/3 by seven wkts.

v Northamptonshire (Grantham) – 5 July – Match 1 – Northants 166 (L J Fletcher 4/31, S R Patel 3/34) lost to Notts 170/5 (M J Lumb 95*) by five wkts.

v Northamptonshire (Grantham) – 5 July – Match 2 – Northants 131/6 (S A Zaib 58) lost to Notts 135/1 (G P Smith 60*) by nine wkts.

v Derbyshire (Worksop C) – 17 July – Match 1 – Notts 173/4 (T J Moores 88) beat Derbys 143/8 by 30 runs.

v Derbyshire (Worksop C) – 17 July – Match 2 – Derbys 194/7 (T A Wood 60, C A J Brodrick 60; D T Christian 3/37) lost to Notts 195/4 (D T Christian 90*) by six wkts.

J T Ball	C F Gibson	M D Lezar	S D P Reeves
L R Bhabra	H F Gurney	J D Libby	W T Root
J M Blatherwick	A D Hales	M J Lumb	R N Sidebottom
D D A Brown	*R Hassan	Z McCaskie	G P Smith
M Carter	J E P Hebron	C R Marshall	I S Sodhi
D T Christian	B A Hutton	M E Milnes	B R M Taylor
J D Cook	L W James	T J Moores	M H Wessels
A K Dal	T G Keast	S J Mullaney	*A O Wiffen
J D M Evison	L P J Kimber	R A Parker-Cole	L Wood
L J Fletcher	*N J H Kimber	S R Patel	
M H A Footitt	B M Kitt	L A Patterson-White	
W A R Fraine	O M D Kolk	M A Raza	

NOTTINGHAMSHIRE CRICKETERS

Jacob Timothy BALL (Meden CS,Warsop) b Mansfield 14.3.91. RHB RFM. Notts Cap 2016. Brother of J.J. (Notts 2007). Tests 4 (Eng) & 16 ODIs, 2016/17. Nephew of B N French (Notts & England, 16 Tests, 13 ODIs). Eng U19 v Sri Lanka, 2010. Debut 2008. F/C debut v MCC, Abu Dhabi, 2011. HS 75 v Durham, Notts Sports Ground, 2011. BB 6/56 v Northants, Notts SC, 2010. HSSET 56 v Durham, Gosforth, 2014. BBSET 5/18 v Worcs, Notts Sports Ground, 2011. HST20 11 v Yorks, Headingley, 2011 (1st). BBT20 4/29 v Lancs, Parkgate Neston, 2012 (1st). HSKO 5 v Derbys, Alvaston & Boulton, 2010. BBKO 0/68 in the same match. Notts Staff.

Louis Robert BHABRA (Becket S, West Bridgford) b Huddersfield, Yorks, 12.3.01. RHB RFM. Debut 2017. HS 7* v Leics, Notts SG, 2017. BB 1/19 in the same match. BBSET 1/18 v Leics, Notts SG, 2017.

Jack Morgan BLATHERWICK (The Holgate Acad, Hucknall, Notts; Central Coll, Nottingham) b Nottingham, 4.6.98. RHB RFM. Debut 2016. Eng U19 to India 2016/17; v India 2017. HS 17 v Derbys, Denby, 2016 & v MCC YC, High Wycombe, 2017. BB 3/29 v Derbys, Denby, 2016. HSSET 0* v Worcs, Worcester, 2016. BBSET 1/33 v Derbys, Worksop, 2016. HST20 1* v Unc, Notts SG, 2016 (2nd). BBT20 2/24 in the same match.

Dominic David Anthony BROWN (Trinity S, Nottingham & Trinity SFC) b Nottingham, 18.12.94. RHB RM. Debut 2015. HS 65 v MCCU, Notts SG, 2016. BB 3/17 v Yorks, Trent Coll, 2016. HSSET 49 v Worcs, New Road, 2016. BBSET 3/22 v Northants, Finedon Dolben, 2016. HST20 45* v Yorks, Trent Coll, 2016 (2nd). BBT20 3/12 v Yorks, Trent Coll, 2016 (1st).

Matthew CARTER (Branston S, Lincs) b Lincoln, 26.5.96. RHB OB. Brother of A (Notts, Essex, Glam, Derbys & Hants; 2006 to 2016). Debut 2014. F/C debut v Somerset, Taunton, 2015. HS 52 v Derbys, Swarkestone, 2017. HS 43 v Durham, Notts SG, 2016. HSSET 57 v Worcs, Oakham S, 2017. BBSET 4/25 v Worcs, Worcester, 2016. HST20 24* v Derbys, Derby, 2016 (1st). BBT20 4/11 v MCC YC, Merchant Taylors' S, 2017 (2nd).

Daniel Trevor CHRISTIAN b Camperdown, NSW, Australia 4.5.83. RHB RFM. T20s (Aus) 19 (2011/12 to 2013/14). F/C debut (S.Australia) v Victoria, Melbourne 2007/08. Debut Hants 2010; Glos & Cap 2013; Middx 2014; Notts & Cap 2015. HS 60 (Hants) v Surrey, West End 2010. BB 2/18 v Glos, Bristol, 2015. HSSET 115 v Derbys, Derby, 2015. BBSET 3/23 in the same match. HST20 90* v Derbys, Worksop Coll, 2017 (2nd). BBT20 3/37 in the same match.

Jordan David COOK (Tollbar Acad, Grimsby; Franklin Coll, Grimsby) b Grimsby, Lincs, 7.1.00. RHB OB. Debut 2017. HS 27 v Leics, Notts SG, 2017. BB 3/74 in the same match.

Anuj Kailash DAL (Durban HS, S Africa; Nottingham HS) b Newcastle-upon-Tyne, Northumberland 8.7.96. RHB RM. Debut 2013. Eng U19 v Pak & Bang, 2013. HS 125 v Northants, Milton Keynes, 2017. BB 2/2 v Middx, Radlett, 2015. HSSET 83 v Worcs, Oakham S, 2017. BBSET 2/56 v Worcs, Trent Coll, 2015. HST20 80 v Northants, Northampton, 2015 (1st). BB 1/17 v Lancs, Trent Coll, 2017 (1st).

Joey David Michael EVISON (Stamford S) b Peterborough, Hunts, 14.11.01. RHB RM. Debut 2017. HS 54 v Worcs, Notts SG, 2017.

Luke Jack FLETCHER (Henry Mellish S, Nottingham) b Nottingham 18.9.88. RHB RMF. Debut 2006, F/C debut v Oxford UCCE, The Parks, 2008. Eng U19 v N.Zealand 2008. HS 106 v Derbys, Notts SC, 2010. BB 6/40 v Leics, Kibworth, 2012. HSSET 40 v Northants, Rugby S, 2008. BBSET 4/52 v Middx, Radlett, 2013. HST20 38* v Lancs, Ormskirk, 2014 (1st). BBT20 4/31 v Northants, Grantham, 2017 (1st). Notts staff.

Mark Harold Alan FOOTITT (Carlton le Willows S, Gedling; West Notts C, Mansfield) b Nottingham 25.11.85. RHB LF. Debut Notts 2001 aged 15 years and 270 days, F/C debut v Glam, Trent Bridge, 2005; debut Northants 2009; Derbys 2010; Cap 2014; debut Surrey 2016. HS 66* v MCCYC, Radlett 2009. BB 6/61 v Somerset, Notts SC 2006. HSSET 21* (Derbys) v Glam, SWALEC, 2010. BBSET 4/23 v Yorks, Headingley 2009. BBT20 2/20 (Derbys) v Lancs, Glossop, 2014 (2nd). BBKO 0/26 (Derbys) v Notts, Alvaston & Boulton, 2010. Joins Notts for the 2018 season.

William Alan Richard FRAINE (Silcoates S, Wakefield; Bromsgrove SFC; Durham U) b Huddersfield, Yorks, 13.6.96. RHB RM. Debut Worcs 2015; MCCU & Notts 2017. F/C debut (Durham MCCU) v Glos, Bristol, 2016. HS 87* (Worcs) v Yorks, Scarborough, 2016. HSSET 75 (Worcs) v Lancs, Worcester RGS, 2016. HST20 27* (Worcs) v Leics, Kidderminster, 2015 (1st).

Christopher Francis GIBSON (Helston Comm Coll, Cornwall; Trent Coll) b Truro, Cornwall, 24.5.99. RHB LB. Debut 2016. HS 92 v Leics, Notts SG, 2017. BB 0/21 v Leics, Coalville, 2016. HSSET 1 v Leics, Notts SG, 2017.

Harry Frederick GURNEY (Garendon HS, Loughborough; Loughborough GS; Leeds U) b Nottingham, 25.10.86. RHB LMF. Brother of J.H. (Leics 2008 & 2011). ODIs (Eng) 10 (2014 to 2014/15). Debut Leics 2006; F/C debut (Leics) v Grace Road, 2007. Debut Notts & Cap 2014. HS 14* (Leics) v Durham, Hinckley, 2008. BB 5/43 v Derbys, Denby, 2009. HSSET 33 (Leics) v Glam, SWALEC, 2010. BBSET 4/40 (Leics) v Lancs, Old Trafford, 2008. HST20 0 v Yorks, Trent Coll, 2014 (1st). BBT20 3/24 v Unc, Notts SG, 2016 (1st). Notts staff.

Alexander Daniel HALES (Chesham HS) b Hillingdon, Middx, 3.1.89. RHB RM. Debut MCCYC 2006; Glos & Notts 2007. F/Cdebut v Somerset, Trent Bridge, 2008. Notts Cap 2011. Tests 11 (Eng) & 53 ODIs, 2014 to date. HS 246 v Derbys, Derby, 2009. BB 1/26 v Yorks, Notts SC. HSSET 63 v Essex, Bishop's Stortford, 2008. HST20 39 v Lancs, Long Eaton, 2011 (2nd). Notts Staff.

* Rehan HASSAN (Brentwood S, Essex; Felsted S, Essex) b King George Hospital, Ilford, Essex 24.1.95. LHB LB. Debut Essex 2011; Derbys 2014; Notts 2017. HS 150* (Essex) v MCC Un, Bishop's Stortford, 2013. BB 1/19 (Derbys) v Durham, Belper, 2014. HSSET 42 (Essex) v Sussex, Fulking, 2013. BBSET 0/16 (Derbys) v Yorks, Swarkestone, 2014. HST20 19 (Derbys) v Middx, Southend-on-Sea, 2013 (1st) & (Derbys) v Yorks, Derby, 2014 (1st). BBT20 2/22 (Derbys) v Durham, Brandon, 2014 (2nd).

Jack Edward Percy HEBRON (Felsted S) b Haroldwood, Essex, 13.6.96. RHB RM. Debut 2017. HS 54 v MCC YC, High Wycombe, 2017.

Brett Alan HUTTON (Worksop Coll) b Doncaster, Yorks 6.2.93. RHB RM. Debut 2009 aged 16 years and 207 days. F/C debut v MCC, Abu Dhabi, 2011. Eng U19 v South Africa, 2011; to

Bangladesh & to Australia 2011/12; to Australia, World Cup, 2012. HS 123* v Leics, Notts SG, 2013. BB 7/44 v Durham, Riverside, 2017. HSSET 119 v Derbys, Denby, 2017. BBSET 4/40 v Warwicks, Notts Sports Ground, 2011. HST20 42 v Durham, Trent Coll, 2013 (1st). BBT20 3/21 v Yorks, Harrogate, 2015 (1st). Joins Northants for the 2018 season.

Lyndon Wallace JAMES (Oakham S) b Worksop, 27.12.98. RHB RMF. Debut 2016. HS 93 v Derbys, Chesterfield, 2017. BB 0/14 v Worcs, Notts SG, 2017. HSSET 27 v Northants, Finedon Dolben, 2016. HST20 6 v Yorks, Barnsley, 2017 (2nd).

Thomas George KEAST (De Aston S, Market Rasen, Lincs; Worksop Coll) b Barnet, Herts, 25.6.98. RHB WK. Debut 2014 aged 15 years and 301 days. HS 48* v Durham, Gosforth, 2014. HSSET 70 v Worcs, Trent Coll, 2015. HST20 22 v Lancs, Trent Coll, 2017 (2nd).

Louis Philip James KIMBER (William Farr C of E S, Lincoln) b Lincoln, 26.2.97. RHB OB. Brother to N J H (below). Debut Kent, 2016; Notts 2017. HS 15 (Kent) v Sussex, Blackstone, 2016. HSSET 20 v Derbys, Denby, 2017. HST20 20 v Yorks, Barnsley, 2017 (1st).

*Nicholas John Henry KIMBER (William Farr C of E S, Lincoln) b Lincoln, 16.1.01. RHB RMF. Brother to L P J (above). Debut 2017. HS 6 v Yorks, Notts G, 2017 (Match 1). BB 1/19 v Yorks, Notts G, 2017 (Match 2).

Benjamin Michael KITT b Plymouth, Devon, 18.1.95. RHB RMF. Debut 2012. HS 36* v Derbys, Denby, 2016. BB 6/38 v Essex, Southend-on-Sea, 2014. HSSET 15* v Durham, Gosforth, 2014. BBSET 4/37 v Warwicks, Scorers, 2017. HST20 17* v Yorks, Trent Coll, 2016 (1st). BBT20 3/18 v Lancs, Worksop Coll, 2015 (2nd).

Oskar Magnus David KOLK (Reed`s S, Cobham, Surrey) b Guildford, Surrey, 9.1.97. RHB RMF OB. Debut Leics 2016; Notts 2017. HS 59 v MCC YC, High Wycombe, 2017. BB 0/6 v Yorks, York, 2016.

Marc Daniel LEZAR (Filton C, Bristol) b Johannesburg, S.Africa 14.11.95. RHB RM. Brother of D.R. (Glos 2013). Debut Glos 2013; MCC YC 2015; Notts 2017. HS 87 (MCC YC) v Hants, Ageas Bowl Nursery, 2016. BB 3/17 (MCC YC) v Glos, Shenley, 2016. HSSET 54 (Glos) v Sussex, Hove 2014. BBSET 0/12 (MCC YC) v Somerset, High Wycombe, 2016. HST20 59 (Glos) v Somerset, Taunton Vale 2014 (1st). BBT20 0/10 (Glos) v Kent, Cheltenham Coll, 2015 (1st) & (MCC YC) v Hants, Shenley, 2016 (2nd).

Jacob Daniel "Jake" LIBBY (Plymouth Coll; Truro Coll; Cardiff Met) b Plymouth, Devon, 3.1.93. RHB OB. Debut Somerset & Cardiff MCCU 2013; Notts 2014. F/C debut (Cardiff MCCU) v Glam, SWALEC, 2014. Debut (on loan) Northants 2016. HS 225* v Warwicks, Edgbaston, 2014. BB 2/56 v Leics, Hinckley, 2016. HSSET 109 v Leics, Loughborough CC, 2016. BBSET 2/15 v Warwicks, Scorers, 2017. HST20 42 v Derbys, Worksop Coll, 2017 (2nd). BBT20 0/16 in the same match.

Michael John LUMB (St Stithians Coll, Johannesburg) b Johannesburg, Transvaal ,S Africa, 12.2.80. LHB RM. Son of R G (Yorks 1970/84). Debut (Yorks) 2000; F/C debut (Yorks) v Zimbabweans, Headingley, 2000. Cap 2003. Debut Hants 2007; Cap 2008. Debut & Cap Notts 2012. ODIs (Eng) 3 (2013/14) & 27 T20s. HS 191 (Yorks) v Notts, Middlesbrough, 2000. BB 3/12 (Yorks) v Durham, Middlesbrough, 2001. HSSET 50 v Northants, Notts SG, 2015. HST20 95 v Northants, Grantham, 2017 (1st). Retired at the end of the 2017 season.

Zachary McCASKIE (Christ Church Foundation; Barbados Community Coll; U of WI) b Barbados, WI, 18.11.96. RHB OB. Debut Hants 2016; Notts 2017. HS 69 (Hants) v Glam, Newport, 2016. HST20 12 v Yorks, Barnsley, 2017 (2nd).

Connor Robert MARSHALL (Trent Coll) LHB LB. Debut 2014 v Leics, Notts SG. HS 64* v Lancs, Notts SG, 2017. BB 5/29 v MCCU, Notts SG, 2016. HSSET 54* v Worcs, Trent Coll, 2015. BBSET 1/38 v Worcs, Trent Coll, 2015. HST20 42* v Yorks, Barnsley, 2017 (2nd). BBT20 2/9 v Warwicks, Edgbaston, 2016 (1st).

Matthew Edward MILNES (West Bridgford CS & SFC; Durham U) b Nottingham 29.7.94. RHB RMF. Debut Durham 2013; Durham MCCU 2014; F/C Debut (Durham MCCU) v Derbys. Derby, 2014; debut MCC Un 2015; debut Notts 2016. HS 59 v Derbys, Denby, 2016. BB 4/41 v Durham, Riverside, 2017.

HSSET 49 (Durham) v Yorks, Marske-by-the-Sea, 2014. BBSET 5/39 (Durham) v Derbys, Ticknall, 2014. HST20 5* v MCC YC, Merchant Taylors` S, Northwood, 2017 (2nd). BBT20 2/20 v Lancs, Trent Coll, 2017 (1st).

Thomas James MOORES (Loughborough GS; Millfield S, Somerset) b Brighton, Sussex, 4.9.96. LHB WK. Son of Peter (Worcs & Sussex 1982-98 & later Coach of Lancs and Eng) Debut Leics 2013, Notts 2014; Lancs (on loan) 2016. F/C debut (Lancs) v Durham, Southport, 2016. Eng U19 v Aus, 2015; v Sri Lanka, 2016. HS 139 v Durham, Notts SG, 2016. BB 0/9 v Derbys, Notts SG, 2015. HSSET 155 v Durham, Notts SG, 2016. HST20 88 v Derbys, Worksop Coll, 2017 (1st).

Steven John MULLANEY (St Mary's RCS, Astley) b Warrington, Lancs, 19.11.86. RHB RM. Debut Lancs 2004, F/C debut (Lancs) v Durham MCCU, the Racecourse, 2006; debut Notts 2010. Cap 2013. Eng U19 to India 2004/05, v India 2006. HS (Lancs) 207 v Worcs, Southport 2009. BB 6/39 v Yorks, Notts SC, 2010. HSSET 75 v Unicorns A, Trent Coll, Long Eaton, 2012. BBSET 2/8 v Warwicks, Bulls Head Ground, Coventry, 2012. HST20 103* v Yorks, Trent Coll, 2014 (2nd). BBT20 2/18 v Northants, Grantham, 2017 (1st). Notts Staff.

Riecko Antonio PARKER-COLE (Worksop Coll) b Nottingham, 30.10.99. RHB LMF. Debut 2016. HS 19* v Worcs, Notts SG, 2017. BB 1/28 v Leics, Notts SG, 2017 (1st).

Samit Rohit PATEL (Worksop Coll) b Leicester 30.11.84. RHB SLA. Tests 6 (Eng) & 36 ODIs (2008-2015/16). Brother of Akhil (Derbys, Notts, Kent, Northants & Surrey 2007 to date). Debut 1999 aged 14 yrs & 274 days. F/C debut v W Indies A, Trent Bridge, 2002. Notts Cap 2008. HS 144 v Leics, Hinckley, 2005. BB 6/55 v Durham, Gosforth, 2005. HSSET 163 v Essex, Worksop Coll, 2008. BBSET 3/26 v Essex, Billericay, 2008. HST20 5 v Northants, Grantham, 2017 (1st). BBT20 3/34 in the same match. Notts Staff.

Liam Anthony PATTERSON-WHITE (Worksop Coll) b Sunderland, Durham, 8.11.98. LHB SLA. Debut 2016. Eng U19 to India 2016/17; v India 2017. HS 58 v Yorks, Scarborough, 2016. BB 4/86 v Leics, Hinckley, 2016. HSSET 28 v Worcs, Oakham S, 2017. BBSET 3/44 v Warwicks, Scorers, 2017. BBT20 0/17 v Northants, Grantham, 2017 (2nd).

Mohammed Anis RAZA (St Peter's Acad, Stoke-on-Trent; Central Coll, Notts) b Stoke-on- Trent, 21.5.99. LHB SLA. Debut 2017. BB 1/24 v Lancs, Notts SG, 2017.

Stephen Dean Puttenham REEVES (Hilton Coll, Johannesburg, KwaZulu-Natal, SA; Teesside U) b Johannesburg, 1.10.95. RHB SLA. Debut Durham 2016; Notts 2017. HS 24* (Durham) v Northants, Riverside, 2016. BB 1/4 (Durham) v Warwicks, ECFSG, 2016. HST20 1 v MCC YC, Merchant Taylors` S, Northwood, 2017 (2nd). BBT20 1/32 in the same match.

William Thomas ROOT (Worksop Coll; Leeds Beckett U) b Sheffield, Yorks 5.8.92. LHB OB. Brother of J.E. (Yorks & Eng 2007 to date). Debut Yorks 2009. Notts & Worcs 2011. Leics, Surrey & MCCYC 2012; Middx 2014. F/C debut (Leeds/Bradford MCCU) v Sussex, Hove, 2015. HS 200 v Derbys, Notts SG, 2014. BB 4/57 (MCCYC) v Hants, Rose Bowl, 2012. HSSET 139* v Northants, Finedon Dolben, 2016. BBSET 4/32 v Northants, Bedford S, 2017. HST20 85* (Leics) v Essex, Hinckley, 2013(1st), BBT20 2/14 (MCCYC) v Hants, the Ageas Bowl, 2013 (1st).

Ryan Nathan SIDEBOTTOM (Wanganui Park Sec Coll, Shepparton, Victoria, Aus) b Shepparton, Victoria. Aus, 14.8.89. RHB RFM. Debut Victoria 2012/13; F/C debut (Victoria) v Tasmania, Hobart, 2012/13; debuts Notts, Northants & Warwicks 2017. HS 1* (Northants) v Lancs, Liverpool, 2017. BB 8/33 (Warwicks) v Northants, EFCSG, 2017. HST20 2* (Warwicks) v Durham, S Northumberland, 2017 (2nd). BBT20 5/11 (Warwicks) v Durham, S Northumberland, 2017 (1st).

Gregory Philip SMITH (Oundle S; Durham U) b Leicester 16.11.88. RHB LB. Debut Leics 2007; F/C debut (Leics) v Bangladesh A, Grace Road, 2008; debut Notts 2015. Eng U19 v N.Zealand 2008. HS 146 (Leics) v Northants, Hinckley 2008 & v Northants, Milton Keynes, 2017. BB 1/57 v Lancs, Notts SG, 2017. HSSET 138 v Derbys, Derby, 2015. HST20 101 (Leics) v Northants, Northampton, 2012 (1st). HSKO 17 (Leics) v Surrey, Purley CC, 2010. Retired at the end of the 2017 season.

Inderbir Singh SODHI b Ludhiana, Punjab, India, 31.10.92. RHB LB. Debut (& F/C debut) N Districts, NZ v Otago, Hamilton, 2012/13. Debut Notts 2017. Tests 14 (NZ) & 18 ODIs (2013/14 to 2016/17). BB 1/46 v Leics, Notts SG, 2017. BBT20 v Northants, Grantham, 2017 (1st).

Brendan Ross Murray TAYLOR (St John's Coll, Harare, Zim) b Harare, Zimbabwe, 6.2.86. RHB OB WK. Notts Cap 2015. Tests 23 (Zim) 2004/05 to 2014/15 & 167 ODIs. F/C debut (Mashonaland A) v CFX Academy, Harare Country Club, 2001/02. Debut Notts 2016. HS 104* v Lancs, Notts SG, 2017. BB 0/32 in the same match. HSSET 44 v Leics, Notts SG, 2017. HST20 68 v Warwicks, Edgbaston, 2016 (2nd).

Mattheus Hendrik "Ricky" WESSELS (Woodbridge Coll, Port Elizabeth, S.Africa; Northampton U) b Maroochydore, Queensland, Australia. 12.11.85. RHB WK. Son of KC (Aus & S.Africa, 1982/83-1994/95; Free State, Sussex, Western Province,

Northern Transvaal, Queensland, Eastern Province, Griqualaland West 1973/74-1999/00). Debut Northants & MCC 2004; F/C debut (MCC) v West Indians, Arundel, 2004; debut Notts 2011. HS 170 v Yorks, Barnsley, 2011. HSSET 77 v Derbys, Trent Coll, 2013. HST20 29 v Eng U19s, Loughborough, 2013 (1st). Notts Staff.

*__Adam Oldsworth WIFFEN__ (Maritzburg Coll, Pietermaritzburg, SA; Pershore HS) b Johannesburg, 12.3.98. LHB. Debut Notts & Worcs 2017. HS 77 (Worcs) v Leics, Worcester RGS, 2017. HST20 99 (Worcs) v Northants, Northampton, 2017 (2nd).

Luke WOOD (Portland CS, Worksop; Worksop Post 16 Centre) b Sheffield, Yorks, 2.8.95. LHB LMF. Debut 2012. F/C debut v Sussex, Trent Bridge, 2014. Eng U19 to UAE 2013/14 (Tri/ Series). HS 61* v Warwicks, EFCSG, 2016. BB 6/75 v Warwicks, Edgbaston, 2014. HSSET 121 v Durham, Riverside, 2017. BBSET 4/15 v Northants, Bedford S, 2017. HST20 23 v Yorks, Barnsley, 2017 (1st). BBT20 4/31 v Eng U19s, Loughborough, 2013 (1st).

SCOTLAND A

Friendlies – P5 W3 L2 (1 Abandoned)

All were played away from home.

SCOTLAND A CRICKETERS

Ryan G BROWN (St Leonards Senior S, St Andrews) b Redhill, Surrey, 2.1.97. RHB OB. Debut Scotland A 2017. HS 4* v Durham, Burnopfield, 2017 (2nd). BB 1/27 in the same match.

Dylan Evers BUDGE (Woodhouse Grove S, Bradford) b Leeds, 11.9.95. RHB RM. Debut Durham 2014; Scotland A 2017. HS 86 (Durham) v Northants, Northampton, 2014. BB 3/36 (Durham) v Sussex, Fulking, 2014. HSSET 67 v Durham, Riverside, 2017. BBSET 1/27 (Durham) v Unc, Burnopfield, 2015. HS T20 38* (Durham) v Warwicks, Benwell Hill, 2015 (2nd). BBT20 3/20 in the same match.

Scott James CAMERON (Craigie High School, Dundee) b Dundee, Scotland 24.9.96. RHB RMF. Debut MCC YC & Scotland A 2017.HS 10* (MCC YC) v Glos, Rockhampton, 2017. BB 2/19 v Glos, Bath, 2017.

Harris Gordon CARNEGIE (Arbroath HS) b Arbroath, 4.2.98. RHB WK. Debut 2016. HS 5 v Durham, Riverside, 2016.

Kyle James COETZER (Aberdeen GS) b Aberdeen, Scotland, 14.4.84. RHB RMF. ODIs (Scot) 10 (2008 to date) Debut Scotland 2003; Durham 2003; F/C debut (Durham) v Glam, Sophia Gardens, 2004; debut Northants 2011. Cap 2013. HS 250* v Derbys, Northampton, 2015. BB 3/62 v Notts, Stowe S, 2015. HSSET 149* (Durham) v Notts, Worksop College 2009. BBSET 5/30 (Durham) v Northants., Bedford S, 2011. HST20 49 v Unc, Great Tew, Oxon, 2014 (1st). BBT20 3/13 (Durham) v Notts, Brandon, 2011 (1st). HSKO 36 (Durham) v Lancs, Parkgate, Neston, 2010.

Matthew Henry CROSS (Robert Gordon Coll; Loughborough U) b Aberdeen, Scotland, 15.10.92. RHB WK. Debut Scotland A 2009; 32 ODIs & 23 T20s (Scotland), 2013 to date. Debut Notts 2011. F/C debut (Loughborough MCCU) v Sussex, Hove, 2013. Debut Leics 2015; Essex 2016; MCC YC & Northants 2017. HS 105* (Notts) v MCCU, Notts Sports Ground, 2012. HSSET 80 (Notts) v Derbys, Notts SG, 2014. HST20 69 (MCC YC) v Merchant Taylors' S, Northwood, 2017 (1st).

James William DICKINSON (Loretto S, Musselburgh) b Edinburgh, 14.9.98. RHB LB. Debut 2017. HS 2* v Kent & Northants, Northampton, 2017. BB 2/41 in the same match.

Michael Miller ENGLISH b Paisley, Renfrewshire, Scotland, 2.5.95. RHB MF. Debut 2016. HS 76 v Durham, Burnopfield, 2017.

Alasdair Campbell EVANS (George Watson's Coll, Edinburgh; Loughborough U) b Tunbridge Wells, Kent, 12.1.89. RHB RMF. ODIs (Scot) 19 (2009 to date). Debut Scotland 2009; F/C debut (Loughborough U) v Leics, Grace Road, 2009; debut Derbys 2011; Durham 2014. HS 24 (Durham) v Yorks, Scarborough, 2014. BB 7/133 (Derbys) v Lancs, Derby, 2012. HSSET 0* (Derbys) v Notts, Trent Coll, 2013 & (Derbys) v MCC YC, Denby, 2013. BBSET 2/38 (Derbys) v Warwicks, Dunstall, 2012. HST20 4* (Derbys) v Eng U19, Loughborough, 2012 (1st). BBT20 1/9 (Derbys) v Eng U19, Loughborough, 2012 (2nd).

Christopher Nicholas GREAVES b 12.10.90. RHB LB. Debut 2016. HS 54* v Glos, Alveston, 2016.

Riyaad HENRY (Paul Roos Gymnasium, Stellenbosch, W Cape, S Africa; Stellenbosch U) b Falkirk, Scotland, 4.7.92. RHB RM. Debut Scotland 2016; Scotland A 2017. Son of Omar 3 Tests (SA) 1992/93. HS 32 v Durham, Burnopfield, 2017.

Michael Alexander JONES (Ormskirk GS; Myerscough Coll) b Ormskirk, Lancs, 5.1.98. RHB OB. Debut Derbys, Durham, Leics & Scotland A 2017. HS 173* v Durham, Riverside, 2017. HSSET 34 (Durham) v Lancs, Bowden, 2017. HST20 35 (Leics) v Durham, Riverside, 2017 (1st).

Ihtisham MALIK (Renfrew HS) b Glasgow, 1.3.99. RHB RFM. Debut Scotland A 2017. BB 3/20 v Durham, Burnopfield, 2017.

Calum Scott MacLEOD (Hillpark S, Glasgow) b Glasgow, 15.11.88. RHB RM. ODIs (Scot) 46 (2008 to date) F/C debut (Scotland) v UAE, Cambusdoon, Ayrshire, Scotland, 2007. Debut Warwicks 2006; Kent 2011; Northants 2012; Durham 2014. HS 145 v Kent & Northants, Northampton, 2017. BB 6/37 (Warwicks) v Worcs, Moseley, 2008. HSSET 116* (Northants) v Notts, Nettleworth, 2012. BBSET 2/6 (Durham) v Yorks, Chester-le-Street, 2015. HST20 103* (Durham) v Yorks, York, 2014 (1st). BBT20 2/25 (Kent) v Surrey, Folkestone, 2011. (2nd). HSKO 5* (Warwicks) v Somerset, Taunton, 2010. BBKO 1/34 (Warwicks) v Worcs, New Road, 2010.

Henry George **MUNSEY** (Loretto S, Musselburgh, Scotland) b Oxford, 22.2.93. LHB RMF. Debut Northants & Notts 2015. F/C debut (Northants) v Australians, Northampton, 2015; debut Lancs 2016. T20s (Scotland) 8 (2015 to date). HS 68 v Glos, Bath, 2017. BB 1/30 (Northants) v Derbys, Northampton, 2016. HSSET 77 (Northants) v Leics, Kibworth, 2016. HST20 48* (Northants) v Worcs, Milton Keynes 2015 (1st). BBT20 0/4 (Northants) v Warwicks, Finedon Dolben, 2016 (2nd).

Adrian **NEILL** (Nairn Academy, Inverness) b Western Cape, S Africa, 22.3.94. RHB RFM. Debut 2016. HS 8 v Lancs, Blackpool, 2016. BB 2/25 v Durham, Riverside, 2017.

Mitchell David **RAO** (Prestwick Acad, S Ayrshire; U of Glasgow) b Glasgow, 3.4.97. RHB OB. Debut 2016. HS 34* v Lancs, Blackpool, 2016. BB 1/54 v Glos, Bath, 2017.

Elliot Euan **RUTHVEN** b Melrose, 2.2.96. RHB RMF. Debut 2016. HS 1 v Glos, Bath, 2017. BB 4/93 v Glos, Alveston, 2016.

Syed Mohammed **Owais SHAH** (Bellahouston Acad, Glasgow) b Glasgow, 1.10.98. LHB LB Debut 2016. HS 61 v Durham, Burnopfield, 2017.

Safyaan Mohammed **SHARIF** (Buckhaven HS, Fife) b Huddersfield, Yorks 24.5.91. RHB RFM. Debut 2010. 11 ODIs (Scot) 2011 to date. F/C debut (Scot) v Namibia, Windhoek 2011/12.

Debut Glos 2014. HS 75* v Kent & Northants, Northampton, 2017.. BB 4/78 v Yorks, Scarborough, 2014. HSSET. (Glos) 2 v Unc, Bath CC 2014. BBSET 2/28 in the same match.

Tom Barclay **SOLE** (Merchiston Castle S, Edinburgh; Cardiff Met) b Edinburgh, 12.6.96. RHB OB. Son of D Sole (Scotland RU & British Lions). Debut Northants 2015. List A debut (Northants) v S Africans, Northampton, 2017. Debut Scotland A 2017. HS 40* (Northants) v Glam, Northampton. 2017. BB 5/51 v Durham, Burnopfield, 2017. HSSET 53* (Northants) v Derbys, Denby, 2017. BBSET 4/24 (Northants) v Leics, Lancot Park Totternhoe, 2015. HST20 22 (Northants) v Warwicks, Shirley, 2017 (1st). BBT20 4/17 (Northants) v Leics, Lutterworth, 2017 (2nd).

Craig Donald **WALLACE** (Dundee HS) b Dundee, Angus, 27.6.90. RHB WK. ODIs (Scot) 3, 2012. Debut Scotland 2012. F/C debut (Scot) v Kenya, Aberdeen, 2013. Debut Durham 2013. HS 94 v Northants, Desborough, 2012. HSSET 36 (Durham) v Lancs, The Tyldesleys, Westhoughton, 2013. HST20 10 (Durham) v Lancs, Parkgate, Neston, 2013 (2nd).

Mark Robert James **WATT** (Heriot's) b Edinburgh 29.7.96. LHB SLA. Debut 2013. HS 57* v Durham, Riverside, 2016. BB 4/45 v Durham, Seaton Carew, 2015.

SOMERSET

PLAYING RECORDS 2017

Championship – P9 2W D6 L1 – seventh in the southern group
2nd XI Trophy – P7 W5 L2 – winners of the southern group & beaten semi-finalists
2nd XI T20 Competition – P12 W4 L8 – ninth in the southern group

2nd XI SUCCESSES

2nd XI Champions – 1994, 2004.
2nd XI Trophy – Beaten Finalists in 1990, 2001, 2007, 2016
2nd XI T20 Competition – Beaten Finalists 2014, 2016.

SECOND ELEVEN CHAMPIONSHIP AVERAGES

BATTING	M	I	NO	Runs	HS	Avge	100s	C/S
M E Trescothick	3	4	0	293	162	73.25	1	4
T B Abell	4	5	0	261	151	52.20	1	2
M A Leask	4	3	0	135	79	45.00	-	4
M J Leach	4	5	2	120	82	40.00	-	1
E J Byrom	7	9	0	337	141	37.44	2	7
T D Rouse	7	9	0	302	84	33.55	-	7
R C Davies	9	10	1	297	124	33.00	1	11
T A Lammonby	3	4	1	81	29	27.00	-	1
P A van Meekeren	7	4	1	72	27	24.00	-	4
G A Bartlett	8	1		147	56	21.00	-	4
B G F Green	5	5	2	56	26	18.66	-	4
F Hand	3	3	1	35	24*	17.50	-	-
R Bridgens	2	3	1	34	28	17.00	-	-
T Banton	6	7	1	101	64	16.83	-	3
W C F Smeed	3	3	0	43	21	14.33	-	1
L J P Shaw	2	3	0	38	33	12.66	-	1
D M Bess	5	5	1	34	17	8.50	-	2

BOWLING	O	M	Runs	Wkt	Avge	BB
J H Davey	43	12	108	9	12.00	3/22
P D Trego	59	20	153	9	17.00	5/36
N Dunning	00	0	57	3	19.00	3/32
M J Leach	71.2	20	205	10	20.50	3/46
P A van Meekeren	130.1	33	404	17	23.76	5/44
O R T Sale	73.4	18	195	8	24.37	4/33
B G F Green	97	32	263	10	26.30	3/27
R Bridgens	26	7	125	4	31.25	3/40
D M Bess	89	26	314	9	34.88	4/90
W J N Pereira	42	6	141	4	35.25	3/42
T D Rouse	60.2	9	217	3	72.33	2/75

Also bowled – T B Abell 7.3-0-31-1; J Allenby 9-4-18-0; G A Bartlett 3.4-1-17-0; E J Byrom 1-0-2-0; L P Goldsworthy 15-4-48-2; J C Gore 28-23-135-1; F Hand 20.5-4-89-2; C G Harrison 14-0-77-0; T A Lammonby 24-3-83-2; M A Leask 9-1-37-2; L J P Shaw 1.1-1-0-2; M T C Waller 21-5-68-2; W S A Williams 19-5-57-0.

Also batted – 4 matches – J C Gore 0*; W J N Pereira 2*, 7, 0*. 3 matches – J H Davey 8, 24; O R T Sale 7* (3ct); P D Trego 36, 30 (2ct). 2 matches – L P Goldsworthy 3 (1ct); F R Trenouth 31 (3ct). 1 match – J Allenby 38; N Dunning DNB (1ct); C G Harrison DNB (1ct); A J Hose DNB (1ct); J G Myburgh 16; J Overton 14; M T C Waller 1; W S A Williams 28*.

SECOND ELEVEN TROPHY AVERAGES

BATTING	M	I	NO	Runs	HS	Avge	100s	C/S
R C Davies	7	7	1	396	135	66.00	1	4/6
J Allenby	3	3	0	188	101	62.66	1	3
G A Bartlett	7	7	1	375	142*	62.50	1	1
E J Byrom	6	5	1	224	75	56.00	-	-
M J Leach	4	3	2	51	38	51.00	-	-
J G Myburgh	5	5	1	177	101	44.25	1	-
M A Leask	7	6	0	148	82	24.66	-	2
B G F Green	7	6	2	87	24	21.75	-	2
D M Bess	6	4	2	21	9*	10.50	-	1

BOWLING	O	M	Runs	Wkt	Avge	BB
M T C Waller	20	0	73	4	18.25	3/39
D M Bess	56	2	269	14	19.21	5/63
M J Leach	34	0	175	6	29.16	4/41
P A van Meekeren	48	3	234	5	46.80	4/42
B G F Green	46.5	1	324	6	54.00	2/40

Also bowled – J Allenby 13-1-74-1; J H Davey 8-2-38-0; N N Gilchrist 8-0-49-0; T D Groenewald 10-0-57-2; T A Lammonby 0.2-0-4-0; M A Leask 20-0-141-2; J G Myburgh 12.1-0-65-1; J Overton 16-3-57-0; T D Rouse 6-0-36-0.

Also batted – 6 matches – P A van Meekeren 5*, 2 (1ct). 3 matches – A J Hose 76, 19 (1ct). 2 matches – T B Abell 7, 9 (1ct); T Banton 4, 1; J Overton 0 (1ct); T D Rouse 41, 64 (2ct); M T C Waller 2. 1 match – J H Davey 17 (2ct); N N Gilchrist 0*; J C Gore 0*; T D Groenewald DNB; T A Lammonby 31; M E Trescothick 19.

SECOND ELEVEN T20 AVERAGES

BATTING	M	I	NO	Runs	HS	Avge	100s	C/S
P D Trego	5	5	1	176	78	44.00	-	-
T Banton	12	12	3	376	94	41.77	-	9/2
B G F Green	6	3	2	39	26*	39.00	-	2
D M Bess	8	7	2	139	72	27.80	-	4
T B Abell	8	8	0	171	62	21.37	-	7
T D Rouse	6	5	0	102	68	20.40	-	3
M A Leask	10	8	1	125	40*	17.85	-	1
R C Davies	10	10	1	129	31	14.33	-	4/1
J G Myburgh	7	7	0	90	41	12.85	-	5
T A Lammonby	4	3	0	37	25	12.33	-	1
G A Bartlett	6	5	0	58	39	11.60	-	1
E J Byrom	6	6	0	62	33	10.33	-	-
P A van Meekeren	6	3	1	13	9*	6.50	-	1
L J P Shaw	3	3	0	16	12	5.33	-	-
W J N Pereira	6	3	2	5	4*	5.00	-	1

BOWLING	O	M	Runs	Wkt	Avge	BB
B G F Green	20.1	0	169	13	13.00	4/22
M T C Waller	20	0	115	8	14.37	3/18
O R T Sale	20	0	176	10	17.60	3/23
J H Davey	7	0	59	3	19.66	3/37
W J N Pereira	16.5	0	139	5	27.80	2/24
D M Bess	30	0	239	7	34.14	2/18
P A van Meekeren	20.3	0	164	4	41.00	2/24
M A Leask	13	0	138	3	46.00	1/15

Also bowled – T B Abell 5-0-43-1; J Allenby 3-0-23-0; Z G G Bess 2-0-25-0; N N Gilchrist 1-0-6-0; L P Goldsworthy 5-0-39-0; J C Gore 6-0-75-2; F Hand 3-0-41-2; T A Lammonby 10-0-111-1; M J Leach 4-0-35-0; J G Myburgh 9-0-65-2; T D Rouse 2-0-18-1; L J P Shaw 8-0-67-1; P D Trego 7-0-59-1; R E van der Merwe 8-0-52-2; W S A Williams 6-0-41-2.

Also batted – 6 matches – O R T Sale 0*, 1 (1ct). 5 matches – M T C Waller 1, 15 (3ct). 2 matches – J Allenby 0, 91* (1ct); J H Davey 9*, 5 (1ct); L P Goldsworthy 1, 12; J C Gore 1; F Hand 0*, 5* (1ct); F R Trenouth 9, 1; R E van der Merwe 7, 3* (1ct); M S A Williams 6*, 4*. 1 match – Z G G Bess 16*; N N Gilchrist DNB; M J Leach 1.

HOME MATCHES: SECOND ELEVEN CHAMPIONSHIP

v Kent (Taunton Vale) – 16-18 May – Kent 206/5d (C J Basey 85) drew with Somerset 89/5d.

v Glamorgan (Taunton Vale) – 13-15 June – Glam 366/9d (D L Lloyd 100; J R Murphy 70; B G F Green 3/54) & 196/6d (C A J Meschede 61, A O Morgan 52; N Dunning 3/32) drew with Somerset 278/5d (T D Rouse 84, T Banton 64, R C Davies 50*) & 201/5 (T D Rouse 60, G A Bartlett 56)

v MCC Universities (Taunton Vale) – 12-14 July – MCCU 242 (W A R Fraine 65; D M Bess 4/90) & 308/5 (J D Marshall 93*, J M

Cooke 59) drew with Somerset 403 (T B Abell 151, M A Leask 56; A D Tilcock 6/162, J A Clifford 3/68)

v Hampshire (Taunton Vale) – 7-9 Aug - Somerset 280 (M A Leask 79; C B Sole 4/69) beat Hants 92 (A H J A Hart 51*; P D Trego 5/36, J H Davey 3/22) & 138 (P A van Meekeren 4/30) by an inns & 50 runs.

v Essex (Taunton Vale) – 21-23 Aug - Essex 282/8d (C J Taylor 64, N L J Browne 61; M J Leach 3/46, J H Davey 3/47) & 50/1d lost to Somerset inns forfeited & 335/9 (E J Byrom 100, M J Leach 82) by one wicket.

HOME MATCHES: FRIENDLIES

v Worcestershire (Taunton Vale) – 11-13 Apr – Worcs 131 (J H Davey 4/23, O R T Sale 3/40) & 213 (T Kohler-Cadmore 55; P A van Meekeren 7/48) lost to Somerset 471 (A J Hose 137, M A Leask 86, G A Bartlett 50; C A J Morris 3/75, P R Brown 3/83) by an inns & 127 runs.

v Middlesex (Taunton Vale) – 10-12 May – Middx 179 (H W Podmore 52; T B Abell 4/23, J C Gore 3/23, P A van Meekeren 3/62) & 329 (G F B Scott 92, H W Podmore 77; B G F Green 5/66) lost to Somerset 545/8d (B G F Green 107*, E J Byrom 96, T D

Rouse 71, M A Leask 67, D M Bess 65*; H W Podmore 3/107) by an inns & 37 runs.

v Hampshire (Bath CC) – 12 June – Hants 194 (M T C Waller 4/33) lost to Somerset 197/6 (E J Byrom 71; B J Taylor 3/54) by four wkts.

v Gloucestershire (Taunton Vale) – 12-14 Sept – Glos 189 (B A C Howell 101; P A van Meekeren 5/50) drew with Somerset 191/6 (C J W Gregory 3/22)

HOME MATCHES: SECOND ELEVEN TROPHY

v Unicorns (Taunton Vale) – 26 Apr – Unc 265/2 (J M Kettleborough 143*, S S Arthurton 78) lost to Somerset 268/2 (G A Bartlett 142*) by eight wkts.
v Essex (Taunton Vale) – 1 May – Somerset 253/9 (M A Leask 82) lost to Essex 256/6 (P I Walter 145*; D M Bess 4/33) by four wkts.
v Kent (Taunton Vale) – 15 May – Somerset 323/8 (R C Davies 93, E J Byrom 75; M D Hunn 4/48) beat Kent 285 (A J Ball 62, J J Weatherley 50; D M Bess 5/63) by 38 runs.

v Yorkshire (The County Ground, Taunton) – 2 June - Somerset 328 (J Allenby 101, T D Rouse 64, E J Byrom 51; M D Fisher 4/67) lost to Yorks 76/1. No result. Yorks won by virtue of a better record in the qualifying groups.
This was the Semi-Final of the One-Day Trophy.

HOME MATCHES : SECOND ELEVEN T20 COMPETITION

v Gloucestershire (Taunton Vale) – 3 July – Match 1 – Glos 154/8 (M D Taylor 51*) lost to Somerset 155/4 (P D Trego 72*) by six wkts.
v Gloucestershire (Taunton Vale) – 3 July – Match 2 – Somerset 184/5 (T Banton 54*) beat Glos 156/9 (O R T Sale 3/23) by 28 runs.
v Hampshire (Taunton Vale) – 5 July – Match 1 – Hants 145/9 (B G F Green 4/22) beat Somerset 119 (R J W Topley 3/15, B J Taylor 3/23) by 26 runs.

v Hampshire (Taunton Vale) – 5 July – Match 2 – Somerset 122/5 (T Banton 68*; C B Sole 3/10) lost to Hants 128/3 (C M Dickinson 57) by seven wkts.
v Glamorgan (Taunton Vale) – 27 July – Match 1 – Somerset 170/8 (T Banton 94; R A J Smith 3/32) lost to Glam 172/5 (N J Selman 63*) by five wkts.
v Glamorgan (Taunton Vale) – 27 July – Match 2 – Somerset 171/9 (D M Bess 72) lost to Glam 172/2 (N J Selman 58*, R A J Smith 53) by eight wkts.

PLAYERS WHO HAVE REPRESENTED SOMERSET 2nd XI IN THE 2017 SEASON (40)

T B Abell	R C Davies	T M Lammonby	W C F Smeed
J Allenby	N Dunning	M J Leach	P D Trego
T Banton	N N Gilchrist	M A Leask	F R Trenouth
G A Bartlett	L P Goldsworthy	J G Myburgh	M E Trescothick
D M Bess	J C Gore	J Overton	*P Tweddle
Z G G Bess	B G F Green	W J N Pereira	*R E van der Merwe
R Bridgens	T D Groenewald	*C Reed	P A van Meekeren
E J Byrom	F Hand	T D Rouse	M T C Waller
*D Caddy	C G Harrison	O R T Sale	*B Wells
J H Davey	A J Hose	L J P Shaw	W S A Williams

SOMERSET CRICKETERS

Thomas Benjamin ABELL (Taunton S, Exeter U) b Taunton, 5.3.94. RHB RM. Debut 2010. F/C debut v Warwicks, Taunton, 2014. HS 205* v MCCU, Taunton Vale, 2014. BB 4/23 v Middx, Taunton Vale, 2017. HSSET 112* v Essex, Taunton Vale, 2013. BBSET 1/15 v Middx, Radlett, 2013 HST20 76 v Glos, Bristol, 2013 (2nd). BBT20 2/24 v Glos, Taunton Vale, 2015 (2nd). Somerset Staff.
James "Jim" ALLENBY (Christ Church GS, Perth, W Aus) b Perth, WA, 12.9.82. RHB RM. Debut Leics 2002; F/C debut (Leics) v West Indies A, Grace Road, 2006; debut & Cap Glam 2010; Somerset 2015. HS 161 (Leics) v Warwicks, Kenilworth Wardens, 2005. BB 3/28 (Leics) v Worcs, Grace Road, 2005. HSSET 104* (Leics) v Derbys, Derby, 2006. BBSET 2/20 (Leics) v Derbys, Belper Meadows, 2005. HST20 93* v Essex, Taunton Vale, 2016 (2nd). BBT20 v Middx, Uxbridge, 2017 (2nd). Released at the end of the 2017 season.
Thomas "Tom" BANTON (Bromsgrove S) b Chiltern, Bucks, 11.11.98. RHB WK. Debut Warwicks 2015; Somerset 2016. List A (T20) debut v Middx, Uxbridge CC, 2017. Eng U19 to India, 2016/17; v India 2017; to S Africa 2017/18. HS 117 v Glam, Newport, 2017. HSSET 14 v Surrey, Bath, 2016. HST20 94 v Glam, Taunton Vale, 2017 (1st).
George Anthony BARTLETT (Millfield S) b Frimley, Surrey, 14.3.98. RHB OB. Debut 2015. F/C debut v Warwicks, Edgbaston, 2017. Eng U19 v Sri Lanka, 2016; to India 2016/17; v India 2017. HS 106 v Yorks, Headingley, 2016. BB 0/2 v Kent, Taunton Vale, 2017. HSSET 142* v Unc, Taunton Vale, 2017. BBSET 1/29 v Surrey, Taunton Vale, 2015. HST20 58 v Middx, Arundel, 2016(F). BBT20 4/25 v 2016 (2nd).
Dominic Mark BESS (Blundell's S, Tiverton) b Exeter, Devon 22.7.97. RHB OB. Cousin of JJ (Unicorns A, Worcs & Surrey 2010/13) & ZGG (Surrey & Somerset, 2011/12. See below). F/C debut v Pakistanis, Taunton, 2016. Eng U19 v Sri Lanka, 2016.

Debut 2013. F/C debut v Pakistasnis, Taunton, 2016. HS 126 v Glos, Longwood, Bristol, 2016. BB 3/50 in the same match. HSSET 32* v Lancs, Old Trafford, 2016. BBSET 5/63 v Kent, Taunton Vale, 2017. HST20 72 v Glam, Taunton Vale, 2017 (2nd). BBT20 4/25 v Glam, Newport, 2016 (2nd).
Zachary George Gerald BESS (Blundell's S, Tiverton, Devon; Exeter U) b Exeter, Devon, 26.2.93. LHB RFM. Brother of J J (above). Debut Surrey 2011, Somerset 2012. HS 7 v MCC YC, Radlett, 2012. HSSET 11 v MCC YC, Radlett, 2012. HST20 16* v Essex, Chelmsford, 2017 (1st). BBT20 0/25 in the same match.
Rhett BRIDGENS (Uplands Coll, Mpumalanga, S Africa) b S Africa, 23.2.93. RHB RMF Debut 2017. HS 28 v Middx, Radlett, 2017. BB 3/40 v Sussex, Horsham, 2017.
Edward James BYROM (St John's Coll, Harare, Zim; Kings Coll) b Harare, Zim, 17.6.97. LHB OB. Debut 2015. F/C debut v Hants, Ageas Bowl, 2017. HS 179 v Kent, Taunton Vale, 2015. BB 0/2 v MCCU, Taunton Vale, 2017. HSSET 89 v Essex, Taunton Vale, 2015. HST20 33 v Essex, Chelmsford, 2017 (1st).
***Dylan CADDY** (Camborne Sec S, Cornwall) b Trelisk, Cornwall, 22.6.99. RHB RMF. Debut 2017. BB 1/29 v Glos, Taunton Vale, 2017.
Joshua Henry DAVEY (Culford S, Bury St Edmunds) b Aberdeen, Scotland 3.8.90. RHB RM. ODIs 26 (Scotland) 2010 to date. Debut Middx 2008. F/C debut (Middx) v Oxford MCCU, the Parks, 2010; debut 1.3.80. LHB SLA. Debut 2015. (on loan) 2013. HS 149 (Middx) v Lancs, Radlett, 2012. BB 5/42 v Glos, Taunton Vale, 2014. HSSET 83* (Middx) v Minor Counties, Radlett 2009. BBSET 5/63 v Glos, Taunton Vale, 2016. HST20 60 v Hants, Taunton Vale, 2015 (2nd). BBT20 4/28 v Sussex, Horsham, 2015 (2nd). HSKO 8 (Middx) v Surrey, Wimbledon, 2010. Somerset Staff.
Ryan Christopher DAVIES (Sandwich Tech S) b Margate, Kent, 5.11.96. RHB WK Debut Kent 2013 aged 16 years & 212 days. F/C

debut (Kent) v Derbys, Canterbury, 2015. Debut Somerset 2016. Eng U19 to Aus, 2014/15; v Aus 2015. HS 124 v Glos, Longwood, Bristol, 2017. HSSET135 v Glos, Bristol U, 2017. HST20 64* (Kent) v Surrey, Maidstone, 2015 (1st). Released at the end of the 2017 season.

Ned DUNNING (Millfield S) b Guildford, Surrey, 31/3/00. LHB OB. Debut 2017. BB 3/32 v Glam, Taunton S, 2017.

Richard Daniel EDWARDS (Isgol Gyfun Ystalyfera; Canulfan Gwenullt; Cardiff Met) b Neath, Wales, 30.12.94. LHB RMF. Debut 2017. F/C debut (Cardiff MCCU) v Glam, SWALEC, 2017. HS 2 v Glam, Newport, 2017. BB 4/54 in the same match.

Nathan Nicholas GILCHRIST (St Stithians S, Johannesburg, S Africa; King`s Coll, Taunton) b Harare, Zimbabwe, 11.6.00. RHB RM. Debut 2016. HS 3* v Sussex, Taunton Vale, 2016. BB 1/36 in the same match. HSSET 0* v Glos, Bristol U, 2017. BBSET 0/6 v Hants, Taunton Vale, 2017 (2nd).

Lewis Peter GOLDSWORTHY (Camborne Science & International Acad) b Cornwall, 8.1.01. RHB SLA.Debut 2017. HS 3 v Hants, Taunton Vale, 2017. BB 2/39 v Surrey, New Malden, 2017. HST20 12 v Glam, Taunton Vale, 2017 (2nd). BBT20 0/12 v Glam, Taunton Vale, 2017 (1st).

Joseph "Joe" Christopher GORE (Exmouth Comm Coll) b Exeter, Devon, 8.8.99. RHB RFM. Debut 2015, aged 15 yrs & 362 days. HS 1* v Glam, Taunton Vale, 2016. BB 3/23 v Middx, Taunton Vale, 2017. HSSET 0* v Yorks, Taunton, 2017. HST20 1 v Sussex, Horsham, 2017 (2nd). BBT20 2/45 in the same match.

Benjamin "Ben" George Frederick GREEN (Exeter S) b Exeter, Devon, 28.9.97. RHB RM. Debut 2014. Eng U19 v India 2017. List A (T20) debut v Hants, Ageas Bowl, 2016. Eng U19 to Aus 2014/15; v Aus 2015; v Sri Lanka 2016. HS 107* v Middx, Taunton Vale, 2017. BB 5/66 in the same match. HSSET 24 v Kent, Taunton Vale, 2017. BBSET 5/45 v Leics, Taunton, 2016. HST20 26* v Middx, Arundel, 2016 (F) & v Hants, Taunton Vale, 2017 (2nd). BBT20 4/22 v Hants, Taunton Vale, 2016 (1st).

Timothy Duncan GROENEWALD (Maritzburg Coll) b Pietermaritzburg, Natal, S Africa, 10.1.84. RHB RFM. Debut Warwicks 2004; F/C debut (Warwicks) v Cambridge UCCE, Fenner`s, 2006; debut Derbys 2009. Derbys Cap 2011. Debut Somerset 2014. HS 125* (Warwicks) v Leics, Kenilworth Wardens, 2006. BB 7/47 (Warwicks) v Northants, Stratford-u-Avon, 2006. HSSET 80* (Warwicks) v Glos, Bristol West Indians, 2006. BBSET 4/32 v MCC YC, Taunton Vale, 2015. HST20 2* v Essex, Taunton Vale, 2016 (1st). BBT20 3/6 in the same match. Somerset Staff.

Fionn HAND (Ardgillon Comm Coll, Balbriggan R of Ireland; Queens Coll, Taunton) b Dublin, 1.7.98. RHB RMF. Debut 2017. HS 24* v Hants, Taunton Vale, 2017. BB 1/2 in the same match. HST20 5* v Sussex, Horsham, 2017 (2nd). BBT20 2/28 in the same match.

Calvin Grant HARRISON (King's Coll, Taunton) b Durban, Kwa-Zulu Natal, S Africa, 29.4.98. RHB LB. Debut Somerset 2015; Worcs 2017. HS 26 v Derbys, Taunton S, 2016. BB 3/24 in the same match. HSSET 12* v Essex, Taunton Vale, 2015. BBSET 0/28 in the same match. BBT20 0/23 v Sussex, Taunton Vale, 2016 (1st).

Adam John HOSE (Carisbrooke S, Newport) b Newport, Isle of Wight, 25.10.92. RHB RM. Debut MCCYC 2011; Glam 2012; Northants 2013; Hants & Kent 2014; Somerset 2015. F/C debut v Pakistanis, Taunton, 2016. HS 222 v Glos, Taunton Vale, 2015. BB 2/23 (MCC YC) v Worcs, High Wycombe, 2013. HSSET 141 v Surrey, Taunton Vale, 2015. BBSET 3/36 (MCC YC) v Durham, Shenley, 2014. HST20 82* (Hants) v Kent, The Ageas Bowl, 2014 (1st). BBT20 2/28 (MCC YC) v Kent, Radlett, 2013 (2nd).

Thomas (Tom) Alexander LAMMONBY (Exeter S) b Exeter, Devon, 2.6.00. LHB LM. Debut 2015, aged 15 yrs & 35 days. Eng U19 v India 2017; to S Africa 2017/18. HS 48 v Kent, Polo Farm SG, Canterbury, 2016. BB 2/17 v Glos, Taunton Vale, 2016. HSSET 31 v Essex, Taunton Vale, 2017. BBSET 0/4 in the same match. HST20 25 v Glam, Taunton Vale, 2017 (2nd). BBT20 1/29 v Glam, Taunton Vale, 2017 (1st).

Matthew Jack LEACH (Bishop Fox's Community S; Richard Huish S; UWIC) b Taunton 22.6.91. LHB SLA. Debut 2009. F/C debut v Cardiff MCCU, Taunton Vale, 2012. HS 123* v Notts,

Taunton, 2015. BB 6/62 v Middx, Merchant Taylors' S, 2015. HSSET 44 v Essex, Bishop's Stortford, 2014. BBSET 4/41 v Glos, Bristol U, 2017. HST20 38* v Glam, Newport, 2014 (2nd). BBT20 5/18 in the same match. BBKO 1/17 v Hants, Rose Bowl Nursery, 2011. Somerset staff.

Michael Alexander LEASK b Aberdeen, 29.10.90. RHB OB. Debut (Scotland) 2011. List A debut (Scotland) v Essex, Edinburgh, 2013. ODIs (Scot) 15 (2013/14 to date). Debut Northants 2014; Somerset 2015. HS 173* (Scotland) v Yorks, Scarborough. 2014. BB 3/90 (Scotland) v Glos, Bristol, 2013. HSSET 82 v Essex, Taunton Vale, 2017. BBSET 2/24 v Glos, Taunton Vale, 2016. HST20 83 v Glam, Newport, 2016 (2nd). BBT20 3/44 v Hants, Ageas Bowl Nursery, 2016 (1st). Released at the end of the 2017 season.

Johannes Gerhardus MYBURGH (Pretoria BHS; U. of SA) b Pretoria, Transvaal, South Africa 22.10.80.RHB OB. Brother of SJ (Northerns 2005/06-2009/10) F/C debut Northerns v Western Province, Centurion, 1997/98. Debut Hants 2010; Durham 2012; Somerset 2014. HS 129 (Hants) v Kent, Rose Bowl Nursery, 2011. BB 1/18 (Hants) v Surrey, Wimbledon, 2011 & v Warwicks, EFCSG, 2017. HSSET 101 v Glam, Newport, 2017. BBSET 2/20 v Lancs, Middlesbrough, 2012. HST20 77* v Hants, Ageas Bowl Nursery, 2016. BBT20 2/16 in the same match. Somerset staff.

Jamie OVERTON (West Buckland S) b Barnstaple, Devon, 10.4.94. RHB RM. Twin brother of C (Somerset 2011 to date & 2 Tests for Eng, 2017/18). Debut 2011. F/C debut v Surrey, the Oval, 2012. Eng U19 v S.Africa, 2011; to Bangladesh & to Australia 2011/12; to Australia, World Cup, 2012; to S Africa, 2012/13. HS 54 v Sussex, Blackstone, 2015. BB 6/38 v MCCU. Taunton Vale, 2014. HSSET 50* v Unc, Sidmouth, 2014. BBSET 4/63 v MCCYC, North Perrott, 2011. HST20 21* v Sussex, Horsham, 2015 (2nd). BBT20 2/15 v Sussex, Horsham, 2015 (2nd). Somerset staff.

William James Nirananda PEREIRA (Boxhill S, Dorking, Surrey; Loughborough U) b Wandsworth, London, 11.10.96. RHB LFM. Debut Surrey 2014; Somerset 2017. HS 9* (Surrey) v Glam, Guildford, 2016. BB 4/46 (Surrey) v Glos, Cheam, 2015. HSSET 8* (Surrey) v Somerset, Taunton Vale, 2014. BBSET 4/50 (Surrey) v Hants, Ageas Bowl Nursery, 2015. HST20 7* (Surrey) v Glam, Purley, 2016 (1st). BBT20 2/24 v Essex, Chelmsford, 2017 (2nd).

Charley James REED (King Edward's S, Bath) b Bath, 21.4.01. RHB WK. Debut 2017 v Hants, Bath, but did not bat.

Timothy David ROUSE (Kingswood S, Bath; Cardiff U) b Sheffield, Yorks, 9.4.96. Brother of HP (Somerset & Leeds/ Bradford MCCU, 2012 to date). RHB OB. Debut 2012. F/C debut (Cardiff MCCU) v Glam, SWALEC, 2015. HS 175 v Glos, Taunton Vale, 2016. BB 5/86 v Glos, Taunton Vale, 2015. HSSET 71 v Essex, Bishop`s Stortford, 2014. BBSET 2/47 v Essex, Taunton Vale, 2015. HST20 81 v Glam, Taunton Vale, 2015 (1st). BBT20 1/5 v Worcs, Taunton Vale, 2013 (1st).

Oliver Richard Trethowan SALE (Sherborne S, Dorset) b Newcastle-under-Lyme, Staffs, 30.9.95. RHB RFM. Debut 2014. List A (T20) debut v Hants, Ageas Bowl, 2016. HS 33 v Middx, Merchant Taylors' S, 2015. BB 5/64 v Surrey, Bath, 2016. HSSET 4 v Surrey, Taunton Vale, 2015. BBSET 3/22 in the same match. HST20 7* v Hants, Taunton Vale, 2015 (1st). BBT20 3/23 v Glos, Taunton Vale, 2017 (2nd).

Louie Joseph Patrick SHAW (Clifton Coll) b Bristol, 4.1.99. RHB OB. Debut 2016. Eng U19 to India 2016/17. HS 34* v. Glos, Taunton Vale, 2017. BB 2/0 v Hants, Taunton Vale, 2017. HST20 16 v Glam, Newport, 2016 (1st). BBT20 1/15 v Glam, Taunton Vale, 2017 (2nd).

William "Will" Conrad Francis SMEED (King's Coll, Taunton) b Cambridge, 26.10.01. RHB OB. Debut 2017. HS 21 v Glos, Longwood, Bristol, 2017.

Peter David TREGO (Wyvern Comp, Weston-super-Mare) b Weston-super-Mare, 12.6.81. RHB RFM. Debut Somerset 1997 aged 16 yrs & 20 days; F/C debut v Oxford U, Taunton, 2000. Eng U19 v Sri Lanka, 2000. Debut Kent 2003; Worcs & Northants 2004; Middx & Minor C, 2005; Ret to Somerset 2006; Cap 2007. Debut Central Districts, NZ, 2012/13. HS 188 v Warwicks, Knowle & Dorridge, 2000. BB 7/42 v Glam, Taunton, 2002. HSSET 112* v

Glam, Tondu, 2006. BBSET 5/25 (Kent) v Sussex, Tonbridge S, 2003. HST20 78 v Middx, Uxbridge, 2017 (2nd). BBT20 1/5 v Warwicks, Taunton, 2014 (1st). Somerset staff .

Finlay Robert TRENOUTH (Clifton Coll; Millfield S) b London, 22.9.98. RHB WK (occ). Debut 2016. Eng U19 to S Africa, 2017/18. HS 54 v Glam, Newport, 2017. BB 0/30 in the same match.

Marcus Edward TRESCOTHICK (Sir Bernard Lovell S) b Keynsham, 25.12.75. LHB RM. Debut 1992. F/C debut v Lancs, Taunton, 1993. Cap 1999. Tests (Eng) 76 & 123 ODIs (2000 to 2006). HS 322 v Warwicks, Taunton, 1997. BB 4/41 in the same match. HSSET 79 v Hants, Southampton, 1992. BBSET 4/56 v Glos, Taunton, 1997. HST20 67 v Warwicks, Taunton, 2014 (2nd). Somerset staff. Awarded MBE in 2006 for services to cricket.

Paul Michael TWEDDLE b Devizes, Wiltshire 20.4.1988. RHB WK. Debut 2017 v Glam, Newport, but did not bat or bowl.

Roelof Erasmus van der MERWE (Pretoria HS) b Johannesburg, Gauteng, S Africa, 31.12.84. RHB SLA. ODIs 13 (S Africa) 2008/09 to 2010). Debut & F/C debut (Northerns) v Limpopo, Duiwelskloof, 2006/07; debut Titans 2007/08; Netherlands 2015; Somerset 2016. HS 111 v Yorks, Headingley, 2016. BB 3/4 in the same match. HST20 56* v Middx, Taunton Vale, 2016 (1st). BBT20 4/12 v Sussex, 2016 (1st).

Paul Adriaan van MEEKEREN b Amsterdam 15.1.93. RHB, RFM. Debut Glam & Somerset 2016. F/C debut (Holland) v Canada, King City, 2013. 2 ODIs (Holland) 2013 to date. HS 41 v Glos, Longwood, Bristol, 2016. BB 5/20 v Kent, Polo Farm SG, Canterbury, 2016. HSSET 23* v MCCYC, High Wycombe, 2016. BBSET 4/42 v Glam, Newport, 2017. HST20 9* v Glam, Taunton Vale, 2017 (1st). BBT20 2/24 in the same match.

Max Thomas Charles WALLER (Millfield S, Street) b Salisbury, Wilts 3.3.88. RHB LB. Debut 2006. F/C debut v Sussex, Hove, 2009. HS 211 v Glos, Taunton Vale, 2013. BB 6/83 v Sussex, Taunton Vale, 2011. HSSET 67 v Glos, Taunton Vale, 2014. BBSET 4/40 v MCCYC, High Wycombe, 2016. HST20 47 v Middx, Merchant Taylors' S, 2015 (1st). BBT20 4/25 v Worcs, Taunton Vale, 2011 (2nd). HSKO 2 v Derbys, Derby, 2010. BBKO 2/3 v Warwicks, Taunton, 2010. Somerset staff.

*Ben WELLS (Monkton Combe S, Bath) b Bath, 30/7/00. RHB WK. Debut 2017. HS 18 v Glam, Newport, 2017.

William Salter Austen WILLIAMS (Christchurch Boys HS, N Zealand; Canterbury Aero Club) b Christchurch, 6.10.92. RHB RFM. Debut 2017. F/C debut (Canterbury, NZ) v Otago, University Oval, Dunedin, 2012/13. HS 28* v Essex, Taunton Vale, 2017. BB 0/26 in the same match. HST20 6* v Glam, Taunton Vale, 2017 (1st). BBT20 1/15 v Glam, Taunton Vale, 2017 (2nd).

SURREY

PLAYING RECORDS 2017
Championship – P9 W3 L2 D4 – third in the southern group
2nd XI Trophy – P6 W2 L3 Ab1 – seventh in the southern group
2nd XI T20 Competition – P12 W4 L5 NR1 Ab2 – sixth in the southern group

2nd XI SUCCESSES
2nd XI Champions – 1966, 1968, 1975, 1988, 1992, 2009, 2010.
2nd XI Trophy – Winners – 1992, 1997, 2001.
2nd XI T20 – Winners - 2013.

SECOND ELEVEN CHAMPIONSHIP AVERAGES

BATTING	M	I	NO	Runs	HS	Ave	100	C/S	BOWLING	O	M	Runs	Wkt	Avge	BB
O J D Pope	4	6	0	349	92	58.16	-	6	M W Pillans	85.3	21	221	13	17.00	5/42
A Harinath	7	9	1	399	127	49.87	1	1	R R Jafri	15.4	3	57	3	19.00	2/22
R Patel	8	12	0	598	226	49.83	1	3	B J Currie	88.1	16	287	14	20.50	3/35
M W Pillans	4	5	2	137	43*	45.66	-	-	G S Virdi	202.3	60	533	26	20.50	6/77
R Ratnasabapathy	4	4	0	171	90	42.75	-	3	M P Dunn	31	11	90	4	22.50	2/30
F O E van den Bergh									F O E van den Bergh						
	9	13	3	404	135	40.40	1	2		171.2	18	525	23	22.82	5/57
N R Welch	4	7	0	220	88	31.42	-	2	C McKerr	123	39	325	14	23.21	5/25
E D Woods	6	10	1	259	67	28.77	-	7	A A P Atkinson	84.1	21	252	10	25.20	3/68
C McKerr	5	5	2	83	28*	27.66	-	1	R Patel	39.4	8	129	4	32.25	3/15
W G Jacks	3	6	1	103	45	20.60	-	2	G C H Barlow	55	6	217	6	36.16	2/31
A A P Atkinson	5	6	1	86	31*	17.20	-	-	M A Richardson	31.4	2	159	4	39.75	2/32
A A Shafique	3	4	0	62	21	15.50	-	15/1							
G S Virdi	6	6	4	28	23	14.00	-	3							
S J W Hall	3	4	0	41	16	10.25	-	4							
G C H Barlow	4	4	0	18	14	4.50	-	-							

Also bowled – A Bhuyian 3-0-13-0; S G Borthwick 22-0-109-1; M H A Footitt 31-10-83-2; A Harinath 7-1-13-0; T M Homes 27.5-5-94-2; W G Jacks 8-1-15-0; S C Meaker 18-8-46-2; R J Montgomery 9-2-23-2; R Rampaul 29-6-67-1; I S Sohi 8-1-31-0; T G Sturgess 15-2-76-0; M D Teale 7-0-33-0; E D Woods 31-4-103-1.

Also batted – 7 matches – T M Homes 3, 1 (1ct). 4 matches – B J Currie 1* (2ct). 2 matches – M P Dunn 14(1ct); M A Richardson 18; I S Sohi 16, 16 (1ct); N J Tilley 13, 15 (1ct). 1 match – FH Allen 30 (1ct); O R Batchelor 1; L Bedford 0; A Bhuyian DNB; S G Borthwick 42 (2ct); J E Culff 6*; A E C Dahl 45, 56 (2ct); M H A Footitt DNB; S M Imtiaz 18 (6ct); R R Jafri 27*, 13; S C Meaker 18, 0; R J Montgomery 8*; R Rampaul 4, 16 (1ct); T G Sturgess 0; M D Teale 1 (1ct); C J Whittock 47, 9 (1ct).

SECOND ELEVEN TROPHY AVERAGES

BATTING	M	I	NO	Runs	HS	Avge	100s	C/S	BOWLING	O	M	Runs	Wkt	Avge	BB
F O E van den Bergh									R J Montgomery	7	0	31	3	10.33	2/12
	5	4	1	180	96*	60.00	-	-	M W Pillans	8	0	37	3	12.33	3/37
A Harinath	6	5	0	237	115	47.70	1	2	R Patel	23	3	121	9	13.44	3/22
O J D Pope	4	3	0	140	83	46.66	-	2	G S Virdi	30.4	2	177	9	19.66	7/33
S C Meaker	3	3	0	112	58	37.33	-	1	F O E van den Bergh						
M W Pillans	4	3	0	78	49	26.00	-	1		26	2	149	7	21.28	2/13
R Patel	6	5	0	100	57	20.00	-	-	R Rampaul	19	0	96	3	32.00	2/55
A A P Atkinson	5	4	1	54	32	18.00	-	-							
C McKerr	6	5	1	61	29*	15.25	-	2							
R J Montgomery	3	3	0	44	27	14.66	-	-							
E D Woods	4	3	0	38	20	12.66	-	2							
G S Virdi	6	4	2	22	12	11.00	-	3							

Also bowled – A A P Atkinson 4-0-37-0; T M Homes 11-1-46-1; C McKerr 23-0-140-1; S C Meaker 19.5-0-145-1; T G Sturgess 1-0-13-0; E D Woods 10-0-69-0.

Also batted – 3 matches – T M Homes 8*. 2 matches – S J W Hall 6, 30 (6ct); R Rampaul 54, 8 (1ct); R Ratnasabapathy 10, 3*; J D Smith 5, 7 (1ct). 1 match - G C H Barlow DNB; W G Jacks DNB; T G Sturgess 6.

BATTING	M	I	NO	Runs	HS	Avge	100s	C/S
O J D Pope	4	4	2	182	81*	91.00	-	1/1
N R Welch	4	4	1	213	75*	71.00	-	2
W G Jacks	8	8	1	290	65*	41.42	-	2
F O E van den Bergh	10	8	1	173	45	24.71	-	1
S J W Hall	6	3	0	56	28	18.66	-	2
R Patel	8	8	1	119	40	17.00	-	1
A Harinath	6	6	1	75	20	15.00	-	-
M W Pillans	4	4	0	38	23	9.50	-	-
O R Batchelor	7	5	1	37	13	9.25	-	1
G S Virdi	5	3	1	14	8	7.00	-	1
A A P Atkinson	10	6	2	27	13*	6.75	-	2

BOWLING	O	M	Runs	Wkt	Avge	BB
M W Pillans	12.2	0	88	6	14.66	3/25
G S Virdi	18.4	0	89	5	17.80	3/15
T M Homes	30.3	1	199	11	18.09	3/14
W G Jacks	11	0	61	3	20.33	2/13
S C Meaker	15.3	1	116	5	23.20	2/27
F O E van den Bergh	33.4	1	204	8	25.50	4/15
A A P Atkinson	26.2	1	238	9	26.44	3/24

Also batted – 10 matches – T M Homes 8*, 0. 6 matches – I S Sohi 21*, 1* (3ct). 4 matches – S C Meaker, 13* (4ct); A S Sambi DNB (1ct); A A Shafique 1*, 4, 2 (5ct & 3st); E D Woods 3, 6. 2 matches – 1 (1ct); M D Teale 1*, 17 (1ct); N J Tilley 0. 1 match – S S Mann DNB; N Reifer 1 (1ct).

Also bowled – A Harinath 1.2-0-15-0; A S Sambi 6-0-42-1; I S Sohi 6-0-53-2; T G Sturgess 2-0-28-0; E D Woods 7-0-54-0.

HOME MATCHES: SECOND ELEVEN CHAMPIONSHIP

v Gloucestershire (Purley) – 9-11 May – Surrey 446/5d (R Patel 226, A Harinath 86, R Ratnasabapathy 65) beat Glos 147 (C McKerr 5/25) & 271 (G H Roderick 105; M W Pillans 5/42) by an inns & 28 runs.
v Somerset (LSE SG, New Malden) – 27-29 June – Surrey 186 (R Patel 54; O R T Sale 4/33) & 203/3 (O J D Pope 86, R Patel 70) drew with Somerset 212 (T D Rouse 81; F O E van den Bergh 3/32, A A P Atkinson 3/68).

v Middlesex (LSE SG, New Malden) – 14-16 Aug - Middx 339 (S Perera 64, M K Andersson 61, J Davies 56, M D E Holden 51; F O E van den Bergh 3/66 & 254/9d (J A R Harris 146; B J Currie 3/41) drew with Surrey 276/4d (A Harinath 127, E D Woods 55; J A R Harris 3/41) & 314/7 (N R Welch 88, F O E van den Bergh 65*, A Harinath 64, R Patel 61; J A R Harris 3/71, T N Wallalawita 3/92)
v MCC Universities (LSE SG, New Malden) – 23-25 Aug - Surrey 356/8d (F O E van den Bergh 135; X G Owen 3/41) & 179 (A E C Dahl 56) beat MCCU 287 (J W Tetley 94, M Lake 58) & 141 (B J Currie 3/35, G S Virdi 3/43) by 107 runs.

HOME MATCHES: SECOND ELEVEN FRIENDLIES

v Middlesex (Richmond) – 30-31 May – Middx 179 (A A P Atkinson 7/67) & 190/2 (P R Stirling 80, R F Higgins 62) drew with Surrey 361/8d (A Harinath 90, F O E van den Bergh 68, O J D Pope 50)

v Yorkshire (Wimbledon CC) – 13-15 Sept – Surrey 288 (S G Borthwick 159; J C Wainman 3/70) & 58 (K Carver 3/14, M D Fisher 3/24) lost to Yorks 164/7d (J A Tattersall 76*; B J Currie 3/25) & 184/4 (M J Waite 69*, J A Tattersall 66) by six wkts.

HOME MATCHES: SECOND ELEVEN TROPHY

v Somerset (Purley) – 24 Apr – Somerset 349/7 (A J Hose 76, G A Bartlett 65, R C Davies 62, E J Byrom 60*; R Patel 3/50) beat Surrey 235 (R Rampaul 54, S C Meaker 53; M T C Waller 3/39) by 114 runs.
v Middlesex (Purley) – 25 Apr – Middx 332/7 (R F Higgins 83, P R Stirling 64, N R D Compton 51) beat Surrey 267 (O J D Pope 83, S C Meaker 58; H W Podmore 3/52, T G Helm 3/54) by 65 runs.

v Hampshire (Whitgift S) – 1 May – Match abandoned without a ball bowled.
v Gloucestershire (Purley) – 8 May – Surrey 288/7 (R Patel 57, A Harinath 54; G S Drissell 3/44) beat Glos 182 (D J Lincoln 78; R Patel 3/22, M W Pillans 3/37) by 106 runs.

HOME MATCHES: SECOND ELEVEN T20 COMPETITION

v Sussex (New Malden) – 4 July – Match 1 – Surrey 111/8 (A Shahzad 3/29) lost to Sussex 115/6 (A J Robson 59*) by eight wkts.
v Sussex (New Malden) – 4 July – Match 2 – Sussex 136 (F O E van den Bergh 4/15) lost to Surrey 137/2 (O J D Pope 80*) by eight wkts.

v Unicorns (New Malden) – 11 July – Match 1 – Surrey 165/9 (W G Jacks 62; Waqas Hussain 3/37) lost to Unc 166/2 (Waqas Hussain 69) by eight wkts.
v Unicorns (New Malden) – 11 July – Match 2 – Surrey 118/3 (N R Welch 75*) v Unc DNB. No result.

PLAYERS WHO HAVE REPRESENTED SURREY 2ND XI IN 2017 (43)

F H Allen	A E C Dahl	S C Meaker	J D Smith
A A P Atkinson	M P Dunn	R J Montgomery	I S Sohui
G C H Barlow	M H A Footitt	R Patel	T G Sturgess
O R Batchelor	S J W Hall	M W Pillans	M D Teale
L Bedford	A Harinath	O J D Pope	N J Tilley
A Bhuiyan	T M Homes	R Rampaul	F O E van den Bergh
O D W Birts	S M Imtiaz	R Ratnasabapathy	G S Virdi
S G Borthwick	W G Jacks	N Reifer	N R Welch
*B L Brookes	R R Jafri	M A Richardson	C J Whittock
J E Culfe	C McKerr	A S Sambhi	E D Woods
B J Currie	S S Mann	A A Shafique	

SURREY CRICKETERS

Finnley Hugh ALLEN (St Kentigern Coll, Auckland, NZ) b Auckland, NZ, 22.4.99. RHB WK. Debut MCC YC & Surrey 2017. List A debut (T20) (Auckland) v Central Districts, Auckland, 2016/17. HS 95 (MCC YC) v Yorks, High Wycombe, 2017. BB 1/28 (MCC YC) v Leics, High Wycombe, 2017. HSSET 64 (MCC YC) v Northants, Totternhoe, 2017. HST20 21 (MCC YC) v Leics, Kibworth, 2017 (2nd). BBT20 1/23 (MCC YC) v Durham, Merchant Taylors' S, Northwood, 2017 (1st).

Angus "Gus" Alexander Patrick ATKINSON (Bradfield Coll, Berks) b Chelsea, 19.1.98. RHB RMF. Debut 2016. HS 51* v Hants/Sussex, Ageas Bowl Nursery, 2016. BB 7/67 v Middx, Richmond, 2017. HSSET 32 v Middx, Purley, 2017. BBSET 2/27 v Somerset, Bath, 2016. HST20 13* v Kent, Polo Farm SG, Canterbury, 2017 (2nd). BBT20 3/24 v Kent, Polo Farm, Canterbury, 2017 (1st).

George Charles Herbert BARLOW (Charterhouse S) b Windsor, Berks, 21.3.00. RHB RFM. Debut 2017. HS 14 v Sussex, Hove, 2017. BB 2/31 v MCCU, New Malden, 2017.

Oliver Richard BATCHELOR (Charterhouse S, Godalming) b Chelsea, 2.10.96. RHB. Debut 2013. HS 79 v Glam, Guildford, 2016. HSSET 132 v Glos, Guildford, 2015. HST20 63* v Sussex, 2016 (2nd).

Lewis BEDFORD (Cranleigh S) b Guildford, 10.3.99. RHB. Debut 2017. HS 0 v Middx, New Malden, 2017.

Arafat BHULYAN (Rokeby S, Kingston-upon-Thames; Newham SFC; London City U) b Dhaka, Bangladesh, 11.10.96. RHB RFM. Debut 2017. HS 2 v Kent, Beckenham, 2017. BB 0/13 in the same match.

Oliver Donald W BIRTS (Bradfield Coll, Berks) b Basingstoke, Hants, 21.8.97. RHB SLA. Debut Surrey & Sussex 2016. HS 0* v Somerset, Bath, 2016. BB 1/5 in the same match.

Scott George BORTHWICK (Farrington Com. Sports C, Sunderland) b Sunderland 19.4.90. LHB LB. Debut Durham 2006 aged 16 years and 133 days, F/C Debut (Durham) v Hants, Rose Bowl, 2009. Debut Surrey 2017. Tests 1 (Eng) 2013/14 & 2 ODIs. HS 159 v Yorks, Wimbledon, 2017. BB 6/83 (Durham) v Glam, Cardiff CC 2009. HSSET 133 (Durham) v Hants, Riverside, 2010. BBSET 4/42 (Durham) Leics, Gosforth 2009 HST20 31* (Durham) v Lancs, Gosforth, 2012 (2nd) . BBT20 1/8 (Durham) v Lancs, Gosforth, 2012 (1st). Surrey Staff.

***Benjamin Louis BROOKES** (Tudor Grange S, Solihull; Alden SFC) b Solihull, 29.6.97. RHB LM. Brother of H J H (Warwicks). Debut Warwicks 2015; MCC YC & Surrey 2017. HS 84 (MCC YC) v Warwicks, High Wycombe, 2017. BB 4/44 (Warwicks) v Kent/Northants, Beckenham, 2015. HSSET 25 (Warwicks) v Yorks, Knowle & Dorridge, 2016. BBSET 3/45 (MCC YC) v Northants, Totternhoe, 2017. HST20 14 (MCC YC) v Notts, Merchant Taylors' S, Northwood, 2017 (1st). BBT20 2/12 (Warwicks) v Leics, Edgbaston, 2015 (2nd).

James Edward CULFF (Whitgift S) b Epsom, 18.9.98. RHB RM. Debut 2017. HS 6* v Kent, Beckenham, 2017.

Bradley James CURRIE (Poole GS; Millfield S) b Poole, Dorset, 8.11.98. RHB LFM. Debut 2016. HS 3 v Yorks, Wimbledon, 2017. BB 3/25 in the same match.

Angus Edward C DAHL (Cranleigh S) b Islington, Middx, 15.7.99. LHB SLA. Debut 2017. HS 56 v MCCU, New Malden, 2017.

Matthew Peter DUNN (Bearwood C, Wokingham) b Egham 5.5.92. LHB RFM. Debut 2009. Eng U19s v Bangladesh, 2009; to NZ, U19 World Cup, 2009/10; v SL, 2010. F/C Debut v the Bangladeshis, the Oval, 2010. HS 51 v Northants, Milton Keynes, 2013. BB 6/34 v Hants, Ageas Bowl Nursery, 2016. HSSET 32 v Glam, Charterhouse S, Godalming, 2012. BBSET 3/19 v Essex, New Malden, 2016. HST20 10* v Sussex, Fulking, 2011 (2nd). BB 3/24 v Kent, Folkestone, 2011 (2nd). Surrey Staff.

Mark Harold Alan FOOTITT (Carlton le Willows S, Gedling; West Notts C, Mansfield) b Nottingham 25.11.85. RHB LFM. Debut Notts 2001 aged 15 years and 270 days, F/C debut (Notts) v Glam, Trent Bridge, 2005; debut Northants 2009; Derbys 2010; Surrey 2016. HS (Notts) 66* v MCCYC, Radlett 2009. BB (Notts) 6/61 v Somerset, Notts SC 2006. HSSET 21* (Derbys) v Glam, SWALEC, 2010. BBSET (Notts) 4/23 v Yorks, Headingley 2009. BBT20 2/20 (Derbys) v Lancs, Glossop, 2014 (2nd). BBKO 0/26 (Derbys) v Notts, Alvaston & Boulton, 2010. Re-joins Notts for the 2018 season.

Samuel John Wade HALL (Whitgift S; Reigate GS) b Croydon, 6.12.99.RHB WK.Debut 2017. HS 38 v Worcs, Kidderminster, 2017. HSSET 30 v Glos, Purley, 2017. HST20 28 v Kent, Polo Farm SG, Cantewrbury, 2017 (2nd).

Arun HARINATH (Tiffin S, Kingston upon Thames; Loughborough U) b Sutton 26.3.87. LHB OB. Brother of M. (Surrey 2010). Debut 2003 aged 16 years and 146 days. Debut Loughborough MCCU 2007. F/C debut (Loughborough) v Somerset, Taunton, 2007. Debut MCC 2008; Surrey 2009. HS 166 v Hants, The Rose Bowl, 2010. BB 2/12 v MCC Un, Fenner's, 2013. HSSET 127* v Northants, Charterhouse, 2014. BBSET 2/35 v Somerset, Bath, 2016. HST20 56 v Hants, Rose Bowl, 2012 (2nd). BBT20 1/21 v Sussex, The Oval, 2012 (2nd). HSKO 19* v Leics, Purley, 2010. Surrey staff.

Thomas Matthew HOMES (Glyns S & SFC, Epsom, Surrey) b Epsom, 25.1.98. RHB SLA. Debut MCCYC 2015; Surrey 2016. HS 12* v Yorks, Wimbledon, 2017. BB 1/4 in the same match. HSSET 8* v Somerset, Purley, 2017. BBSET 1/33 in the same match. HST20 8* v Middx, Sunbury, 2017 (2nd). BBT20 3/14 v Glam, Neath, 2017 (2nd).

Safwaan M "Saf" IMTIAZ (Chigwell S) b London 16.3.96. RHB WK. Debut Essex 2013; Durham, MCCYC & Northants 2016; Kent & Surrey 2017. HS 175 (MCC YC) v Essex, High Wycombe, 2016. BB 0/129 (MCC YC) v Lancs, Urmston, 2017. HSSET 100 (MCC YC) v Somerset, Taunton Vale, 2015. HST20 67 (MCC YC) v Surrey, High Wycombe, 2016 (1st).

William George JACKS (St George's S, Weybridge) b Chertsey, 21.11.98. RHB RM. Debut 2015. Eng U19 to India 2016/17; v India 2017; to S Africa 2017/18. HS 45 v Glam, Neath, 2017. BB 1/21 v Middx, Richmond, 2017. HSSET 33 v Essex, New Malden, 2016. HST20 65* v Glam, Neath, 2017 (2nd). BBT20 2/13 v Glam, Neath, 2017 (1st).

Rafeh Raheem JAFRI (Southborough HS, Surbiton) b Sutton, Surrey, 10.11.98. RHB RFM. Debut 2015. HS 54 v Worcs, Kidderminster, 2017. BB 2/20 v Essex, Coggeshall, 2015. HST20 2* v Hants, Purley, 2015 (1st). BBT20 1/16 v Hants, Purley, 2015 (2nd).

Conor McKERR (St John's Coll, Johannesburg, S Africa) b Johannesburg, S Africa, 19.1.98. RHB RFM. Debut 2016; Derbys 2017. F/C debut (Derbys) v Notts, Trent Bridge, 2017. HS 124 v Worcs, Kidderminster, 2017. BB 5/25 v Glos, Purley, 2017. HSSET 41 v Somerset, Bath , 2016. BBSET 2/60 v Glos, Victoria Gd, Cheltenham, 2016. Surrey Staff.

Satbir Singh MANN (City of London S; Reading U) b Croydon, 15.5.97. RHB RFM. Debut 2017. Made T20 debut v Unc, New Malden, 2017 (2nd match) but did not bat or bowl.

Stuart Christopher MEAKER (Cranleigh S) b Pietermaritzburg, KwaZulu-Natal, S Africa, 21.1.89. RHB RMF. ODIs 2 (Eng) 2011/12. Debut 2007. F/C debut v Loughborough MCCU. The Oval, 2008. Cap 2012. HS 150* v Somerset, the Oval, 2010. BB 7/99 v Middx, Radlett, 2010. HSSET 58 v Middx, Purley, 2017. BBSET 4/43 v Somerset, Taunton Vale, 2014. HST20 38 v Hants, Rose Bowl Nursery, 2014 (2nd). BBT20 3/38 v MCCYC, High Wycombe, 2016 (2nd). Surrey Staff.

Robbie Jay MONTGOMERY (Mindarie Senior C, Perth, WA, Australia) b Taunton 22.9.94. RHB RMF. Debut Somerset 2011, Glos 2014. List A (T20) debut (Glos) v Glam, SWALEC, 2014. Debut Sussex 2016; Surrey 2017. HS 106 (Glos) v Northants, Thornbury CC 2014. BB 4/30 (Glos) v Somerset, Taunton Vale, 2015. HSSET 69 (Glos) v Middx, Downend CC, 2015. BBSET 3/46 (Glos) v MCC YC, Bath, 2015. HS T20 15* (Glos) v Somerset, Taunton Vale, 2015 (2nd). BBT20 5/15 (Somerset) v Glam, Taunton, 2013 (2nd).

Ryan PATEL (Whitgift S, Croydon) b Sutton, Surrey, 26.10.97. LHB RM. Debut 2016. Eng U19 v Ind 2017. HS 226 v Glos, Purley, 2017. BB 6/60 v Sussex, New Malden, 2016. HSSET 65 v Hants, Ageas Bowl Nursery, 2016. BBSET 3/22 v Glos, Purley, 2017. HST20 40 v Hants, Purley, 2016 (1st) & v Unc, New Malden, 2017 (1st). BBT20 v Hants, Purley, 2016 (1st)..

Mathew William PILLANS (Pretoria Boys HS, Gauteng, S Africa; U of Pretoria) b Westville, KwaZulu-Natal, S Africa, 4.7.91. RHB RFM. F/C debut (Northerns) v N West, Pretoria, 2012/13; debut KZN & Dolphins 2013/14; Somerset 2014; Glam 2015; Surrey 2016; Leics 2017. HS 73 v Hants, Ageas Bowl Nursery, 2016. BB 5/42 v Glos, Purley, 2017. HSSET 49 v Essex, Billericay, 2017. BBSET 3/37 v Glos, Purley, 2017. HST20 23 v Middx, Sunbury, 2017 (1st). BBT20 3/23 v MCCYC, High Wycombe, 2016 (1st). Surrey Staff.

Oliver John Douglas POPE (Cranleigh S) b Chelsea, Middx, 2.1.98. RHB WK. Debut 2015. F/C debut v Oxford MCCU, 2017. Eng U19 v Sri Lanka, 2016; to India 2016/17. HS 92 v Hants, Ageas Bowl Nursery, 2017. HSSET 83 v Middx, Purley, 2017. HST20 81* v Kent, Polo Farm SG, Canterbury, 2017 (1st). Surrey Staff.

Ravindranath "Ravi" RAMPAUL b Preysal, Trinidad, W Indies, 15.10.84. LHB RFM. Tests 18 (WI) 2009/10 to 2012/13 & 92 ODIs. Debut & F/C debut (Trinidad & Tobago) v Barbados, Port of Spain, 2001/02; debut Surrey 2016. HS 21* v Hants/Sussex, Ageas Bowl Nursery, 2016. BB 1/13 v Glos, Bath, 2016. HSSET 54 v Somerset, Purley, 2017. BBSET 2/55 in the same match. Surrey Staff. Joins Derbys for the 2018 season.

Rehan RATNASABAPATHY (Blenheim HS, Epsom; Kingston Coll) b Kingston-upon-Thames, 16.7.00. LHB RFM. Debut 2017, aged 16 yrs & 292 days. HS 90 v Essex, Billericay. 2017. HSSET 10 v Sussex, Horsham, 2017.

Nico REIFER (Queen's Coll, Bridgetown, W Indies; Whitgift S) b Bridgetown, 11.11.00. RHB RM. Debut 2017, aged 16 yrs & 184 days. HST20 1 v Middx, Sunbury, 2017 (2nd).

Miles Andrew RICHARDSON (Sackville S, E Grinstead, Sussex) b Maidstone, 26.8.91. RHB RMF. Debut Surrey & Kent 2014; Northants 2016. F/C debut (Northants) v Loughborough MCCU, Northampton, 2017. Ret to Surrey 2017. HS 84* (Northants) v Worcs, Kidderminster, 2016. BB 3/74 (Northants) v Derbys, Northampton, 2016. HSSET 46* (Northants) v Lancs, Northop Hall, 2017. BBSET 3/41 (Northants) v MCC YC, Totternhoe, 2017. HST20 10 (Northants) v Lancs, Westhoughton, 2016 (1st). BBT20 4/25 (Northants) v Lancs, Westhoughton , 2016 (2nd).

Ajit Singh SAMBHI (Delhi Pub S, Nolda; Institute of Tech & Science, Delhi, India) b Isleworth, Middx. 21.9.85. RHB LB. Debut 2017. BBT20 1/18 v Sussex, New Malden, 2017 (2nd).

Adeel Ahmad SHAFIQUE (Fernwood Comp S; Bilborough Coll) b Nottingham, 7.6.94. RHB WK. Debut Notts 2011; Derbys 2013; Durham & MCCYC 2014; Sussex & Worcs 2016. Debut Surrey 2017. HS 83 (MCCYC) v Essex, Halstead, 2015. HSSET 43 (MCCYC) v Durham, Shenley, 2014. HST20 39 (MCCYC) v Glam, Shenley, 2015 (2nd).

Jamie Daniel SMITH (Whitgift S, Croydon) b Epsom, 12.7.00. RHB WK. Debut 2016. HS 35 v Hants/Sussex, Ageas Bowl Nursery, 2016. HSSET 7 v Middx, Purley, 2017.

Ishwarjot Singh SOHI (Isleworth & Syon S; Brunel U) b Punjab, India, 7.8.94. RHB RFM. Debut Northants & Surrey 2014; MCCYC 2016. HS 49 (Essex) v Sussex, Halstead, 2017. BB 3/83 (Northants) v Glos, Thornbury, 2014. HSSET 1* (Northants) v Somerset, Milton Keynes, 2014. BBSET 1/25 (Northants) v Sussex, Desborough, 2014. HST20 21* v Glam, 2017 (1st). BBT20 2/29 v Kent, Polo Farm SG, Canterbury, 2017 (1st).

Tommy Graham STURGESS (Wellington S, Taunton) b Truro, Cornwall, 18.1.98. RHB RFM. Debut 2016. HS 34 v Glos, Bath, 2016. BB 0/17 in the same match. HSSET 6 v Essex, Billericay, 2017. BBSET 0/13 in the same match. HST20 1 v Unc, New Malden, 2017 (1st). BBT20 0/28 in the same match.

Matthew David TEALE (St Bede`s Coll, Christchurch, NZ) b Christchurch, 10.6.89. RHB RFM. Debut 2015. HS 30 v Kent, Maidstone, 2015. BB 3/45 in the same match. BBSET 4/18 v Sussex, Guildford, 2015. HST20 17 v Middx, Sunbury, 2017 (2nd). BBT20 1/22 v Kent, Maidstone, 2015 (1st).

Nathan John TILLEY (Reed`s S, Cobham) b Guildford, 6.1.00. RHB OB. Debut 2017. HS 15 v Sussex, Hove, 2017. HST20 0 v Sussex, New Malden, 2017 (1st).

Frederick Oliver Edward van den BERGH (Whitgift S, Croydon; U of Durham) b Bickley, Kent 14.6.92. RHB SLA. Debut 2009 aged 16 years and 326 days. F/C debut v Cambridge MCCU, Fenner`s, 2011. HS 135 v MCCU, New Malden, 2017. BB 6/29 (Surrey/Hants) v Sussex, Horsham, 2014. HSSET 96* v Sussex, Horsham, 2017. BBSET 3/12 v Sussex, Guildford, 2015. HST20 45 v Sussex, New Malden, 2017 (2nd). BBT20 4/15 in the same match. Surrey Staff.

Guramar Singh VIRDI (Guru Nayak Sikh Academy, Hayes, Middx) b Chiswick, Middx, 19.7.98. RHB OB. Debut 2013. F/C debut v Essex, Chelmsford, 2017. Eng U19 v Sri Lanka, 2016; v India 2017. HS 23 v Hants, Ageas Bowl Nursery, 2017. BB 6/77 v Glam, Neath, 2017. HSSET 12 v Somerset, Purley, 2017. BBSET 7/33 v Sussex, Horsham, 2017. HST20 8 v Middx, Sunbury, 2017 (2nd). BBT20 3/15 Middx, Sunbury, 2017 (1st). Surrey Staff.

Nicholas Roy WELCH (St John's Coll, Harare, Zim) b Harare, Zim, 5.2.98. RHB LB. F/C debut (Mashonaland Eagles, Zim) v Mountaineers, Harare, 2013/14. Debuts Surrey 2015, Sussex 2016, Essex & Northants 2017. HS 88 v Middx, New Malden, 2017. HSSET 72* (Sussex) v Kent, Canterbury, 2017. HST20 75* v Unc, New Malden, 2017 (2nd).

Christopher Jonathan WHITTOCK (Aldridge S, Walsall) b Walsall, W Midlands, 8.5.93. RHB RM. Debut Leics 2012; MCC YC 2013; Unc 2015; Surrey 2017. HS 47 v MCCU, New Malden, 2017. BB 1/7 (Leics) v Glam, Ratcliffe Coll, 2012. HSSET 88 * (Unc) v Durham, Burnopfield CC, 2016. BBSET 3/15 (MCC YC) v Derbys, Denby. 2013. HST20 70* (Unc) v Notts, Notts SG, 2016 (1st).

Euan David WOODS (Piggott S, Wargrave, Berks) b Reading, Berks, 30.9.98. LHB OB. Debut 2016. Eng U19 to India 2016/17. HS 67 v Sussex, Hove, 2017. BB 1/39 v Glam, Neath, 2017. HSSET 20 v Glos, Purley, 2017. BBSET 0/34 v Somerset, Purley, 2017. HST20 6 v Kent, Polo Farm SG, 2017 (2nd). BBT20 0/16 v Glam, Neath, 2017 (1st).

SUSSEX

2nd XI T20 WINNERS 2017

PLAYING RECORDS 2017
Championship – P9 W2 L3 D4 – fifth in the southern group
2nd XI Trophy – P6 W4 L2 – fourth in the southern group
2nd XI T20 Competition – P14 W10 Tie 1 L3 – southern group &
competition winners

2nd XI SUCCESSES
Championship – Winners – 1978, 1990, 2007
2nd XI Trophy – Winners – 2005
2nd XI T20 Competition – Winners – 2011, 2017

SECOND ELEVEN CHAMPIONSHIP AVERAGES

BATTING	M	I	NO	Runs	HS	Avge	100s	C/S
H Z Finch	3	6	1	284	82	56.80	-	4
A J Robson	9	17	2	775	137	51.66	2	-
M G K Burgess	5	7	2	258	84*	51.60	-	11/1
N S Oxley	4	6	2	202	57*	50.50	-	1
P D Salt	6	10	1	323	84	35.88	-	3
L P Smith	5	7	1	180	82*	30.00	-	2
O E Robinson	7	11	1	285	74*	28.50	-	4
A Shahzad	3	3	1	49	34	24.50	-	3
T J Haines	5	9	2	160	42	22.85	-	1
D M W Rawlins	7	13	0	297	55	22.84	-	7
E O Hooper	4	5	2	68	67*	22.66	-	2
J W Jenner	6	10	1	153	48	17.00	-	9
S G Whittingham	9	9	4	78	38*	15.60	-	4
A J Woodland	4	7	1	89	40	14.83	-	1
S G Budinger	2	4	0	46	29	11.50	-	-
T G R Clark	2	3	1	22	13*	11.00	-	2
A P Barton	7	3	0	26	24	8.66	-	1
A Sakande	7	8	2	32	19	5.33	-	-
W A T Beer	3	3	0	15	11	5.00	-	-

BOWLING	O	M	Runs	Wkt	Avge	BB
G H S Garton	28	8	79	5	15.80	3/36
E O Hooper	74	8	300	16	18.75	6/110
A J Woodland	16	2	64	3	21.33	1/14
S G Whittingham	177.3	34	668	30	22.26	6/66
O E Robinson	147.5	27	430	17	25.29	5/37
A Sakande	148.1	21	577	22	26.22	6/96
W A T Beer	48	7	139	5	27.80	5/61
K van Vollenhoven	31	1	126	4	31.50	3/95
N S Oxley	32.1	1	182	4	45.50	3/66
A Shahzad	53	12	173	3	57.66	1/17
A P Barton	75	14	235	4	58.75	2/15
D M W Rawlins	61	9	241	3	80.33	1/7

Also bowled – W C H Collard 4-1-24-1; T J Haines 1-0-7-0; T R G Hampton 16-1-69-0; J W Jenner 10-0-57-0; S C Johnson 3-0-20-0; S J Magoffin 24.2-8-45-2.

Also batted – 1 match – J Billings 42* (1ct & 1st); L G Cammish 16, 1 (5ct); W C H Collard DNB; G H S Garton DNB (1ct); T R G Hampton DNB (1ct); J W Hutson DNB (4ct); S C Johnson 7, 3; S J Magoffin DNB; J C Martin DNB (7ct); K van Vollenhoven 6; N R Welch 12, 16* (2ct); L W P Wells 208.

SECOND ELEVEN TROPHY AVERAGES

BATTING	M	I	NO	Runs	HS	Avge	100s	C/S
P D Salt	6	6	0	280	123	76.92	2	2
M G K Burgess	4	4	1	98	62	32.66	-	5
A J Woodland	4	4	1	79	33*	26.33	-	-
A J Robson	6	6	0	154	74	25.66	-	1
A Shahzad	3	3	1	40	29*	20.00	-	-
D M W Rawlins	6	6	0	114	43	19.00	-	1
J W Jenner	4	4	1	39	17*	13.00	-	1
S G Whittingham	4	3	2	9	5*	9.00	-	-

BOWLING	O	M	Runs	Wkt	Avge	BB
T R G Hampton	10	1	51	3	17.00	3/51
N S Oxley	15	0	92	5	18.40	4/40
A Shahzad	27	2	90	4	22.50	2/24
W A T Beer	18	1	80	3	26.66	2/33
S G Whittingham	37	0	213	7	30.42	3/44
A Sakande	53.1	6	244	7	34.85	3/43
A P Barton	21	0	105	3	35.00	2/40
D M W Rawlins	43.1	3	193	4	48.25	2/24

Also batted – 6 matches – A Sakande 2* (2ct). 3 matches – A P Barton 0; N S Oxley 6, 13 (2ct). 2 matches – W A T Beer 0, 99* (2ct); G H S Garton 13* (1ct); N R Welch 24, 72*. 1 match – D R Briggs 70; L G Cammish 47* (2ct); W C H Collard DNB; B N Evans DNB; L J Evans 3; H Z Finch 16; T R G Hampton DNB; S C Johnson 11; J C Martin DNB; L P Smith 65 (1ct).

Also bowled – D R Briggs 10-2-25-1; W C H Collard 6-0-38-0; B N Evans 8-1-43-0; G H S Garton 18.1-1-107-2; J W Jenner 3-0-9-0; S C Johnson 4-0-16-1; A J Robson 2-0-13-0; A J Woodland 11-0-46-2.

SECOND ELEVEN T20 AVERAGES

BATTING	M	I	NO	Runs	HS	Avge	100s	C/S
A J Robson	12	12	5	471	90*	67.28	-	8
M G K Burgess	8	7	2	155	40	31.00	-	4/2
J W Jenner	12	9	4	150	42*	30.00	-	6
D M W Rawlins	10	10	1	239	59	26.55	-	4
P D Salt	8	8	0	174	74	21.75	-	3
L W P Wells	8	8	0	167	80	20.87	-	3
H Z Finch	8	8	0	157	54	19.62	-	2
N S Oxley	7	5	3	29	15	14.50	-	1
O E Robinson	12	6	0	66	29	11.00	-	3
S G Whittingham	12	4	1	29	16*	9.66	-	1
T J Haines	8	5	0	29	14	5.80	-	-
E O Hooper	7	5	2	12	5*	4.00	-	1

BOWLING	O	M	Runs	Wkt	Avge	BB
A J Woodland	12	0	58	6	9.66	2/14
W A T Beer	16	0	78	8	9.75	3/20
J W Jenner	3.4	0	33	3	11.00	2/23
A Shahzad	18.1	1	110	10	11.00	3/29
A P Barton	22.3	0	137	10	13.70	3/9
O E Robinson	46.5	1	299	20	14.95	5/33
D M W Rawlins	35	0	242	11	22.00	4/15
S G Whittingham	42.3	0	283	12	23.58	3/19
A Sakande	29.4	0	233	9	25.88	3/26
E O Hooper	27	0	176	4	44.00	2/28

Also bowled – G H S Garton 4-0-14-1; T S Mills 4-0-38-0; N S Oxley 11-0-80-1; S van Zyl 2-0-22-0.

Also batted – 10 matches – A Sakande 1*, 1 (2ct). 6 matches – A P Barton DNB (3ct). 5 matches – A Shahzad 1 (2ct). 4 matches – W A T Beer 30* (2ct); J Billings 0, 1, 2* (4ct/3st) L P Smith 31*, 5 (3ct); A J Woodland DNB (2ct). 2 matches – B J Gayler DNB 1ct). 1 match – T G R Clark DNB; L J Evans 20*; G H S Garton 2* (2ct); T S Mills DNB (1ct); S van Zyl 79* (1ct).

HOME MATCHES: SECOND ELEVEN CHAMPIONSHIP

v Glamorgan (Fulking) – 23-25 May – Glam 323 (C A J Meschede 91; T N Cullen 85; A Sakande 4/46, G H S Garton 3/36) & 224/9d (N Brand 57; S G Whittingham 4/22) drew with Sussex 290/7d (A J Robson 97, L P Smith 64, N S Oxley 57*; R A J Smith 3/61) & 22/0.

v Gloucestershire (Blackstone CC) – 27-29 June – Sussex 302/6d (A J Robson 110*; M A H Hammond 3/50) & inns forfeited lost to Glos inns forfeited & 306/5 (M A H Hammond 70, B A C Howell 66, P J Grieshaber 57, I A Cockbain 53; E O Hooper 3/42) by five wkts.

v Somerset (Horsham) – 19-21 July - Somerset 173 (M E Trescothick 89; S G Whittingham 6/66) & 294/8d (M E Trescothick 162, T B Abell 76; E O Hooper 5/102) lost to Sussex 181 (H Z Finch 82; R Bridgens 3/40, W J N Pereira 3/42) & 289/4 (M G K Burgess 84*, O E Robinson 74*) by six wkts.

v Surrey (County Ground, Hove) – 24-26 July – Sussex 400/9d (L W P Wells 208, H Z Finch 57; F O E van den Bergh 5/57) & 188/4 (P D Salt 84, D M W Rawlins 55) drew with Surrey 272 (F O E van den Bergh 72, E D Woods 67; W A T Beer 5/61)

HOME MATCHES: FRIENDLIES

v Surrey (Blackstone CC) – 10-12 Apr – Surrey 380/3d (R Patel 119, A Harinath 107, O J D Pope 60, F O E van den Bergh 56*)& 193/4d (O J D Pope 89*) beat Sussex 356/3d (W A T Beer 155*, P D Salt 76) & 68 (G S Virdi 5/6) by 149 runs.

v MCC Young Cricketers (Eastbourne) – 21-23 Aug – MCC YC 163 (O E Robinson 5/48) & 173 (S M Imtiaz 50; O E Robinson 4/50) lost to Sussex 323 (P D Salt 70, O E Robinson 67, H Z Finch 50; A Karvelas 4/74) & 14/0 by 10 wkts.

v Hampshire (Horsham) – 29-31 Aug – Sussex 426/7d (L J Evans 118, P D Salt 55) & inns forfeited drew with Hants 31/1d & 83/0.

v Middlesex (Blackstone) – 4-7 Sept – Sussex 188 (J Goodwin 71*; E R Bamber 4/80, M K Andersson 3/21, T E Barber 3/46) & 295/7d (T Hains 105; R H Patel 3/48) beat Middx 177 (G H S Garton 5/50) & 282 (M D E Holden 76, T C Lace 58; A Sakande 4/55, W A T Beer 3/54) by 24 runs.

HOME MATCHES: SECOND ELEVEN TROPHY

v Hampshire (Fulking) – 27 Apr – Hants 288/7 (J H Barrett 109, F S Hay 75; T R G Hampton 3/51) lost to Sussex 289/3 (P D Salt 123) by seven wkts.

v Surrey (Horsham) – 4 May – Surrey 209/9 (F O E van den Bergh 96*; N S Oxley 4/40) beat Sussex 91 (G S Virdi 7/33) by 118 runs.

v Glamorgan (Blackstone) – 22 May – Glam 298/7 (N Brand 102, J L Lawlor 90; A Sakande 3/43) lost to Sussex 300/6 (W A T Beer 99*, L P Smith 65) by four wkts.

HOME MATCHES: SECOND ELEVEN T20 COMPETITION

v Kent (East Grinstead) – 9 June – Match 1 – Kent 85 (O E Robinson 3/15) lost to Sussex 87/1 by nine wkts.

v Kent (East Grinstead) – 9 June – Match 2 – Kent 114/8 (W A T Beer 3/20) lost to Sussex 118/3 by seven wkts.

v Gloucestershire (Fulking) – 26 June – Match 1 – Glos 127/9 (S G Whittingham 3/19) lost to Sussex 128/2 (A J Robson 63*) by eight wkts.

v Gloucestershire (Fulking) – 26 June – Match 2 – Glos 137/8 lost to Sussex 139/2 (A J Robson 70*) by eight wkts.

v Somerset (Horsham) – 18 July – Match 1 – Somerset 193/7 (T D Rouse 68; O E Robinson 4/38) lost to Sussex 194/3 (S van Zyl 79*, P D Salt 74) by seven wkts.

v Somerset (Horsham) – 18 July – Match 2 – Sussex 207/7 (L W P Wells 80) beat Somerset 148 (T B Abell 62) by 59 runs.

v Lancashire (Arundel) – 10 Aug – Lancs 149/5 lost to Sussex 150/6 (A J Robson 90*) by four wkts.
This was the second Semi-Final of the 2017 competition

v Hampshire (Arundel) – 10 Aug – Sussex 171/6 (H Z Finch 54) beat Hants 147 (A P Barton 3/9, A Sakande 3/26) by 24 runs. *This was the Final of the 2017 competition*

PLAYERS WHO HAVE REPRESENTED SUSSEX 2nd XI IN 2017 (43)

A P Barton	L J Evans	S J Magoffin	L P Smith
W A T Beer	H Z Finch	J C Martin	* J J Swift
J Billings	G H S Garton	T S Mills	*B S Twine
D R Briggs	B J Gayler	N S Oxley	K van Vollenhoven
*B C Brown	*J Goodwin	D M W Rawlins	S van Zyl
S G Budinger	T J Haines	O E Robinson	N R Welch
M G K Burgess	T R G Hampton	A J Robson	L W P Wells
L G Cammish	E O Hooper	A Sakande	S G Whittingham
T G R Clark	J W Hutson	P D Salt	A J Woodland
W C H Collard	J W Jenner	A Shahzad	*L J Wright
B N Evans	S C Johnson	* W Sheffield	

SUSSEX CRICKETERS

Adam Paul BARTON (Anglia Ruskin U); b Surrey, May 1995. RHB LMF. Debut 2016. F/C debut (Cambridge MCCU) v Essex, Fenner's, 2014. HS 24 v Kent, Polo Farm SG, Canterbury, 2017. BB 2/15 v Essex, Star Stile, 2017. HSSET 0 v Surrey, Horsham, 2017. BBSET 2/40 in the same match. BBT20 3/9 v Hants, Arundel, 2017 (F).

William Andrew Thomas BEER (Reigate GS; Collyer's SFC, Horsham) b Crawley 8.10.88. RHB LB. Debut 2006, F/C debut v MCC, Lords, 2008. Eng U19 v N.Zealand 2008. HS 155* v Surrey, Blackstone, 2017. BB 7/48 v Gloucs, Horsham, 2010. HSSET 99* v Glam, Blackstone, 2017. BBSET 4/24 v Somerset, Hove, 2012. HST20 36* v Surrey, Purley, 2016 (1st). BBT20 5/24 v MCCYC, Horsham, 2012 (1st). HSKO 1 v Essex, Chelmsford, 2010. BBKO 0/36 in the same match. Sussex staff.

Joe BILLINGS (St Bede's S, Hailsham) b Haywards Heath, 15.12.98. RHB WK. Debut 2015. HS 42* v MCCU, Hastings, 2017. HST20 2* v Hants, Newclose CC, I of Wight, 2017 (2nd).

Danny Richard BRIGGS (Carisbrooke HS, Newport) b Newport, IOW 30.4.91. RHB SLA. Eng U19 v Bangladesh 2009 and to New Zealand (U19 World Cup) 2009/10. Debut Hants 2007 aged 16 years and 120 days; F/C debut (Hants) v Somerset, the Ageas Bowl, 2009. Hants Cap 2012. HS 49 (Hants) v Somerset, Ageas Bowl Nursery, 2011. BB 6/73 (Hants) v Middx, Ageas Bowl, 2015. HSSET 70 v Essex, Star Stile, 2017. BBSET 3/26 (Hants) v MCCYC, I of Wight, 2015. HST20 40 v Surrey, Purley, 2016 (2nd). BBT20 1/16 (Hants) v MCCYC, Shenley, 2012. HSKO 2 (Hants) v Sussex, Stirlands CC, 2010. BBKO 1/34 in the same match.

Ben Christopher BROWN (Ardingly C) b Crawley 23.11.88. RHB WK. Debut 2004, F/C debut v S.Lanka A, Hove, 2007. Eng U19 to Malaysia, 2006/07; v Pakistan 2007; to Sri Lanka 2007/08; to Malaysia 2007/08 (WC); v New Zealand 2008. HS 117 v Essex, Coggeshall, 2010. HST20 135 v Hants, Horsham, 2010. HST20 89 v Hants, Rose Bowl Nursery, 2011(1st). HSKO 93 v Derbys, Horsham, 2010. Sussex staff.

Soloman G BUDINGER b Harare, Zimbabwe, 21.8.99. RHB RA Bowler. Debut 2016. HS 29 v Middx, Richmond, 2017. HSSET 10* v Kent, Blackstone, 2016.

Michael Gregory Kerran BURGESS (Cranleigh S; Loughborough U) b Epsom. 8.7.94. RHB RM. Occ WK. Debut Surrey 2011; MCCU 2014; F/C debut (Loughborough U) v Sussex, Hove, 2014. Leics 2015; Sussex 2017. HS 84* v Somerset, Horsham, 2017. HSSET 62 v Essex, Billericay, 2017. HST20 64* v Unc, Loughborough CC, 2015 (1st).

Leo George CAMMISH (Hurstpierpoint Coll; Brighton & Hove Albion SFC) b Pembury, Kent, 22.11.96. RHB WK. Debut 2013. HS 69 v Yorks, Hove, 2015. HSSET 55* v Middx, Hove. 2014. HST20 21* Kent, Birdham, v 2013 (1st). HST20 8* v MCCYC, Arundel, 2014 (2nd).

Thomas Geoffrey Reeves CLARK (Ardingly Coll, Haywards Heath) b Haywards Heath, 2.7.01. LHB RM. Debut 2017. HS 13* v Glos, Blackstone, 2017.

William Charles Henry COLLARD (Hurstpierpoint Coll) b Haywards Heath, 13.10.99. RHB LB. Debut 2017. BB 1/24 v MCCU, Hastings, 2017. BBSET 0/38 v Middx, Southgate, 2017.

Bradley Neil "Brad" EVANS (St John's Coll, Harare ; Eastbourne Coll) b Harare, Zimbabwe, 24.3.97. RHB RMF. Debut 2015. HS 12 v Essex, Blackstone, 2016. BB 3/40 v Surrey, New Malden, 2016. BBSET 1/40 v Glam, St Fagans, 2016.

Laurie John EVANS (Whitgift S, Croydon; John Fisher S, Purley; Durham U) b Lambeth, Surrey, 12.10.87. RHB RFM. Debut Surrey 2005; F/C debut (Durham UCCE) v Notts, the Racecourse, Durham, 2007; debut Warwicks 2010; Sussex 2017. HS 239 (Warwicks) v MCC Un, Edgbaston, 2011. BB (Surrey) 3/73 v Durham, Seaton Carew, 2010. HSSET (Surrey) 119 v Minor Counties, Cheam, 2010. BBSET (Surrey) 1/20 v Gloucs, Bristol, 2010. HS T20 111 (Warwicks) v Glos, Olton & W Warwicks, 2013 (2nd). BB T20 1/12 (Warwicks)v Glos, Cheltenham, 2014 (2nd). HSKO (Surrey) 35 v Leics, Purley, 2010. BBKO 1/30 in the same match.

Harry Zachariah FINCH (St Richard's Cath Coll, Bexhill; Eastbourne Coll) b Hastings 10.2.95. RHB RMF. Debut 2011. F/C debut v Durham, Chester-le-Street, 2013. Eng U19 to S Africa, 2012/13; v Pak & Bang, 2013; to UAE 2013/14 (Tri/Series). HS 165 v Hants/Surrey, Blackstone, 2015. BB 3/24 v Essex, Southend-on-Sea, 2013. HSSET 120 v Kent, Fulking, 2014. BBSET 2/28 v Hants, the Ageas Bowl, 2013. HST20 68 v MCC YC, High Wycombe, 2015 (1st). BBT20 2/20 v Somerset, Taunton Vale, 2016 (1st). Sussex staff.

George Henry Simmons GARTON (Hurstpierpoint Coll & SFC) b Brighton, 15.4.97. LHB LM. Eng U19 v Aus, 2015. Debut 2013. F/C debut v Leeds/Bradford MCCU, 2016. HS 34 v Hants, Horsham, 2017. BB 5/50 v Middx, Blackstone, 2017. HSSET 16 v Middx, Hove, 2014. BBSET 1/26 v Hants, Eastbourne, 2014. HST20 11* v Surrey, Purley, 2016 (1st). BBT20 2/14 v Somerset, Horsham, 2017 (2nd).

Bradley James GAYLER (Hurstpierpoint Coll; Loughborough U) b Redhill, Surrey, 5.9.94. RHB WK. Debut 2017. T20 debut v Kent, E Grinstead, 2017, but did not bat in either match.

*Jake GOODWIN (Kingsdown S, Swindon) b Swindon, Wilts, 19.1.98. RHB RM. Debut 2015. List A (T20) debut (Hants) v Somerset, Ageas Bowl, 2016. Debut Sussex 2017. HS 131 (Hants) v Surrey, Ageas Bowl Nursery, 2016. BB 1/47 (Hants) v Kent, Newclose, I of Wight, 2016. HSSET 44 (Hants) v Essex, Coggeshall, 2016. BBSET 2/20 (Hants) v MCCYC, Ageas Bowl Nursery, 2016. HST20 29 (Hants) v Somerset, Ageas Bowl Nursery, 2016 (1st). BBT20 1/7 (Hants) v MCCYC, Shenley, 2016 (1st).

Thomas Jacob HAINES (Tanbridge House S; Hurstpierpoint C) b Crawley, West Sussex 28.10.1998. LHB RM. Debut 2014 aged 15 years and 190 days. F/C debut v Kent, Hove, 2016. HS 86 v Surrey, New Malden, 2016. BB 1/22 Hants, Horsham, 2016. HSSET 120* v Glam, St Fagans, 2016. BBSET 1/9 in the same match. HST20 45 v MCCYC, Eastbourne, 2016 (2nd). BBT20 0/12 v Kent, Horsham, 2015 (2nd).

Thomas Robert Garth HAMPTON (John Hampden GS, High Wycombe) b Kingston upon Thames, Surrey 5.10.90. RHB RFM. Brother of DOD (MCCYC 2012 to date). Debut Middx 2008; MCCYC 2011; Lancs 2012; Hants, Kent, Somerset 2013; Glos 2014; Sussex, Warwicks & Worcs 2017. F/C debut (Middx) v Oxford MCCU, Oxford 2010. HS 37 (Kent) v Glos, Bristol 2013. BB 5/19 (Glos) v Glam, Bristol 2014. HSSET 27 (MCCYC) v Kent, Shenley 2012. BBSET 4/38 (Kent), Richmond 2009. HST20 20* (MCCYC) v Hants, Shenley 2012 (1st). BBT20 3/15 (MCCYC) v Surrey, Purley 2011 (2nd).

Elliot Owen HOOPER (St Bede's S, Upper Dicker, Hailsham) b Eastbourne, 22.3.96. LHB SLA. Debut 2012. HS 67* v MCCU, Hastings, 2017. BB 6/110 v MCCU, Hastings, 2017. HSSET 41 v Hants, Eastbourne, 2014. BBSET 2/28 v Glos, Hove, 2014. HST20 5* v Lancs, Arundel, 2017 (SF). BBT20 2/28 v Lancs, Arundel, 2017 (SF).

Jacob "Jake" William HUTSON (Kemnal Tech Coll, Bromley; NW Kent Coll; U of Brighton) b Sidcup, Kent, 22.6.94. RHB WK. Debut Kent & Sussex 2016. HS 8 (Kent) v Glam, Canterbury, 2016. HSSET 38 (Kent) v Glam, Canterbury, 2016. HST20 17* (Kent) v Glam, Polo Farm SG, Canterbury, 2016 (2nd).

Jonty William JENNER (Hurstpierpoint Coll) b Jersey, 2.12.97. RHB WK. Debut Sussex 2015; Jersey 2015 (T20s). F/C debut v S Africa A, Arundel, 2017. HS 116 v Surrey, New Malden, 2016. BB 0/4 v Somerset, Horsham, 2016. HSSET 48 v Hants, Horsham, 2016. BBSET 0/9 v Surrey, Horsham, 2017. HST20 42* v Kent, E Grinstead, 2017 (2nd). BBT20 2/23 v Somerset, Horsham, 2017 (2nd).

Shawn Craig JOHNSON (Bexhill HS; Bexhill Coll) b Harare, Zim, 31.1.95. RHB RM. Debut 2013. HS 34 v Glos, Frocester, 2013. BB 0/15 in the same match. HSSET 11 v Kent, Canterbury, 2017. BBSET 1/16 in the same match.

Steven James MAGOFIN (Indooroopilly HS, W Aus; Curtin U, W Aus) b Corinda, Queensland, 17.12.79. LHB RFM. Debuts W Aus 2004; F/C debut (W Aus) v Tasmania, WACA, 2004/05; debuts Leics & Surrey 2006; Worcs 2008; Queensland 2011/12; Sussex 2012. HS 5* (Surrey) v Essex, the Oval, 2006. BB 3/22 in the same match. Re-joins Worcestershire for the 2018 season.

Jason Charles MARTIN RHBWK. b 18.3.95. Debut 2017 v Glam, Fulking, but did not bat.

Tymal Solomon MILLS (Mildenhall CT) b Dewsbury, Yorks 12.8.92. RHB LMF. Debut 2009. T20s (Eng) 4, 2016 to 2016/17. F/C debut (Essex) v the Sri Lankans, Chelmsford, 2011. Debut Sussex 2015. HS 27* (Essex) v Hants, Southend-on-Sea, 2011. BB 4/26 (Essex) v Somerset, Bishop's Stortford, 2014. HSSET 15 v Surrey, Guildford, 2013. BBSET 4/19 (Essex) v Surrey, Bishop`s Stortford, 2013. HST20 4 v Kent, Horsham, 2015 (1st). BBT20 5/27 (Essex) v Unicorns A, Chelmsford , 2012 (2nd).

Nicholas S OXLEY (Worthing Coll) b Worthing. RHB SLA (Chinaman). Debut 2016. HS 57* v Glam, Fulking, 2017. BB 3/66 v Middx, Richmond, 2017. HSSET 41 v Surrey, Horsham, 2016. BBSET 4/40 v Surrey, Horsham, 2017. HST20 15 v Lancs, Arundel, 2017 (SF). BBT20 1/3 v Surrey, New Malden, 2017 (2nd).

Delray Millard Wendell RAWLINS (St Bede`s S, Hailsham) b Bermuda, 14.9.97. LHB SLA. Debut 2015. F/C debut v Kent, Hove, 2017. Eng U19 to Ind, 2016/17. HS 117* v Durham, Blackstone, 2016. BB 6/79 v MCCYC, Eastbourne, 2016. HSSET 43 v Hants, Fulking, 2017. BBSET 2/24 v Surrey, Horsham, 2017. HST20 59 v Hants, Newclose CC, I of Wight, 2017 (2nd). BBT20 4/15 in the same match.

Oliver Edward ROBINSON (King's S, Canterbury) b Margate, Kent 1.12.93. RHB RM & OB. Debut Kent 2011; debut Yorks & Leics 2013; Hants 2014; Sussex 2015. F/C debut v Durham, Chester-le-Street, 2015. HS 119 (Yorks) v Glos, Bristol, 2014. BB 5/37 v Essex, Star Stile, 2017. HSSET 79 v Essex, Blackstone, 2016. BBSET 3/50 v Glam, St Fagans, 2016. HST20 40 (Yorks) v Durham, York (1st) 2013. BBT20 5/33 v Unc, Long Marston, 2017 (2nd).

Angus James ROBSON (Marcellin Coll, Randwick, NSW; Australian Coll of PE) b Sydney, NSW, Aus, 19.2.92. RHB LB. Debut Glos, Leics & Worcs 2012. F/C debut (Leics) v Glos, Bristol, 2013. Debut Sussex 2017. Brother of S D (Middx & Eng) 7 Tests (Eng) 2014. HS 145 (Leics) v Glos, Bristol, 2012. BB 3/16 (Leics) v Northants, Finedon Dolben, 2013. HSSET 122 (Leics) v Notts, Loughborough CC, 2016. BBSET 2/34 (Leics) v Lancs, Lutterworth, 2013. HST20 90* v Lancs, Arundel, 2017 (SF). BBT20 1/17 (Leics) v Essex, Hinckley, 2013 (1st).

Abidine SAKANDE (Ardingly Coll. Ardingly; St John's Coll, Oxford U) b Chester, Cheshire, 22.9.94. RHB RMF. Debut 2011. F/C debut (Oxford U) v Cantab U, the Parks, 2014. Eng U19 v Bang & Pak, 2013. HS 32* v Durham, Blackstone, 2016 . BB 6/96 v Kent, Polo Farm SG, Canterbury, 2017. HSSET 4* v Glos,

Frocester, 2013. BBSET 5/45 v Middx, Hove, 2014. HST20 1* v Hants, Newclose, I of Wight, 2017 (1st). BBT20 3/26 (Eng U19s) v Derbys, Alvaston & Boulton, 2013 (1st) & v Hants, Arundel, 2017 (F).

Philip Dean SALT (Reed's S, Surrey) b Bodelwyddan, North Wales, 28.6.96. RHB OB. Debut 2013. F/C debut v Pakistanis, Hove, 2016. HS 94 v Worcs, Kidderminster, 2016. BB 0/0 v MCCYC, Eastbourne, 2016. HSSET 123 v Hants, Fulking, 2017. BBSET 0/25 v Kent, Fulking, 2014. HST20 74 v Somerset, Horsham, 2017 (1st).

Ajmal SHAHZAD (Woodhouse Grove S, Bradford) b Huddersfield, Yorks, 27.7.85. RHB RMF. Debut Yorks 2003; F/C debut (Yorks) v Middx, Scarborough, 2006. Cap 2010. Debut Lancs 2012 (on loan); Debut Notts 2013; Sussex 2015; Leics & Northants 2017. Tests (Eng) 1 & 11 ODIs (2010-2010/11). HS 57 (Yorks) v Derbys, Barnsley, 2008. BB 6/42 in the same match. HSSET 91 (Yorks) v Leics, Bingley, 2008. BBSET 3/55 (Yorks) v Durham, Seaton Carew, 2006. HST20 27 v Surrey, Purley, 2016 (1st). BB 3/29 v Surrey, New Malden, 2017 (1st). Sussex Staff.

***William SHEFFIELD** (Hurstpierpoint Coll) b Haywards Heath, 13.10.99. RHB RM. Debut MCC YC & Sussex 2017. BB 0/10 (MCC YC) v Sussex, Eastbourne, 2017.

Liam P SMITH b Johannesburg, S Africa, 11.5.97. RHB. Debut Sussex 2017. F/C debut v S Africa A, Arundel, 2017. HS 82* v MCCU, Hastings, 2017. HSSET 65 v Glam, Blackstone, 2017. HST20 31* v Kent, E Grinstead, 2017 (1st).

***Jason James SWIFT** b Muswellbrook, NSW, Aus, 30.10.70. LHB RM. Debut Sussex 2017. List A debut (Australian Capital Territory) v Queensland, Manuka Oval, Canberra, 1997/98. Debut v Hants, Horsham, but did not bat or bowl.

***Benjamin Steven TWINE** (Eastbourne Coll) b Eastbourne, Sussex, 25.11.98. RHB RFM. Debut Sussex 2015; MCC YC 2017. HS 12 v Surrey, Blackstone, 2017. BB 2/13 (MCC YC) v Sussex, Eastbourne, 2017. HSSET 4* (Sussex) v Essex, Southend-on-Sea, 2015. BBSET 1/58 in the same match.

Kiel van VOLLENHOVEN (Pretoria Boys HS, S Africa) b 6.6.98. RHB LB. Debut MCC YC & Sussex 2017. HS 6 (MCC YC) v Sussex, Eastbourne, 2017 & v Essex, Star Stile, 2017. BB 3/95 v Essex, Star Stile, 2017. BBT20 5/12 (MCC YC) v Durham, Merchant Taylors' S, Northwood, 2017 (1st).

Stiaan van ZYL b Cape Town, S Africa, 19.9.87. Tests (SA) 12, 2014/15 to 2016/17. Debut & F/C debut (Boland, SA) v Kei, Stellenbosch, 2006/07; Cape Cobras 2007/08; W Province 2014/15; Sussex 2017. HST20 79* v Somerset, Horsham 2017 (1st). BBT20 0/22 in the same match.

Nicholas Roy WELCH (St John`s Coll, Harare, Zim) b Harare, Zim, 5.2.98. RHB LB. F/C debut (Mashonaland Eagles, Zim) v Mountaineers, Harare, 2013/14. Debuts Surrey 2015, Sussex 2016, Essex & Northants 2017. HS 88 (Surrey) v Middx, New Malden, 2017. HSSET 72* v Kent, Canterbury, 2017. HST20 75* (Surrey) v Unc, New Malden, 2017 (2nd).

Luke William Peter WELLS (St Bede's S, Upper Dicker, Hailsham) b Eastbourne 29.12.90. Son of A.P. (Sussex, Kent & England 1978-2001). Nephew of CM (Sussex & England ODIs 1979-93) LHB OB. Debut 2008; F/C debut v Worcs, New Road, 2010. Sussex Cap 2016. Eng U19 v Bangladesh 2009. HS 208 v Surrey, Hove, 2017. BB 3/6 v Somerset, Blackstone, 2014. HSSET 94 v Essex, Southend-on-Sea, 2014. BBSET 6/21 v Glam, Fulking, 2015. HST20 80 v Somerset, Horsham, 2017 (2nd). BBT20 3/9 v Surrey, the Oval, 2012 (1ˢᵗ). HSKO 17 v Hants, Stirlands CC, 2010. BBKO 2/14 in the same match. Sussex staff.

Stuart Gordon WHITTINGHAM (Christ`s Hospital, Horsham; Loughborough U) b Derby, 10.2.94. RHB RFM. Debut MCC Un & Sussex, 2015. F/C debut (Loughborough U) v Hants, Ageas Bowl Nursery, 2015. HS 44* v Northants, Finedon Dolben,2014. BB 6/66 v Somerset, Horsham, 2017. HSSET 30* v Surrey, Horsham, 2016. BBSET 3/44 v Essex, Billericay, 2017. HST20 16* v Unc, Long Marston, 2017 (2nd). BBT20 3/19 v Glos, Fulking, 2017 (1st).

Alexander James WOODLAND (St Edward's S, Oxford) b Windsor, Berks 16.1.98. LHB RM. Debut Hants 2015, Glos 2016. Unc & Sussex 2017. HS 40 v Kent, Polo Farm SG, Canterbury, 2017. BB 3/39 v Somerset, Taunton Vale, 2015. HSSET 55*

(Unc) v Hants, Ageas Bowl Nursery, 2017. BBSET 2/20 v Kent, Canterbury, 2017. HST20 1 (Unc) v Somerset, Bristol U, 2016 (1st). BBT20 2/14 v Kent, East Grinstead, 2017 (1st)
Luke James WRIGHT (Belvoir HS, Bottesford, Leics; Ratcliffe Coll, Leicester; Loughborough U) b Grantham, Lincs, 7.3.85. RHB RM. ODIs (Eng) 50 (2007 to 2013/14). Debut Leics 2001 aged 16 yrs & 69 days; F/C debut (Leics) v Sussex, Hove, 2003; debut Sussex 2004; cap 2007; debut Wellington, NZ, 2010/11. HS 184 (Leics) v Derbys, Derby, 2003. BB 6/58 v Essex, Halstead, 2006. HSSET 54 v MCC YC, Horsham, 2005. BBSET 4/20 (Leics) v Warwicks, Hinckley, 2003. HST20 109 v Hants, Hove, 2015 (1st). Sussex staff.

UNICORNS

(Formerly the Minor Counties)

PLAYING RECORDS 2017
2nd XI Trophy – P6 L6 – tenth in the southern group
2nd XI T20 Competition – P12 W2 T1 L6 NR1 Ab2 – tenth in the southern group

2nd XI SUCCESSES
2nd XI Trophy – Best finish – Beaten Semi-Finalists in 2013
2nd XI T20 Competition – Best finish – 2nd in the group in 2013.

SECOND ELEVEN CHAMPIONSHIP AVERAGES

BATTING	M	I	NO	Runs	HS	Avge	100s	C/S
M S Pepper	6	5	0	235	103	47.00	1	5/3
E R Kilbee	6	6	1	146	77	29.20	-	-
L J Thomason	4	4	0	109	45	27.25	-	1
T Bulcock	4	3	1	44	25	22.00	-	1
J P Harrison	4	4	0	45	18	11.25	-	1
R O Gordon	6	5	0	45	17	9.00	-	2
A S T West	3	3	0	17	14	5.66	-	-
C J Whittock	6	5	0	12	6	2.40	-	1

BOWLING	O	M	Runs	Wkt	Avge	BB
M B Wareing	23	0	152	5	30.40	3/55
B S Phagura	15	0	100	3	33.33	3/36
T Bulcock	37	1	145	3	48.33	1/19
R O Gordon	53.4	5	304	5	60.80	2/65

Also bowled – A S Brown 5-0-35-0; P I Burgoyne 10-0-47-1; L J Chapman 10-1-61-0; D O Conway 8-0-35-2; C J Guest 10-0-73-1; S Kelsall 10-0-69-0; J M Kettleborough 9-0-59-1; M H McKiernan 20-1-105-2; J Parmar 2-0-20-0; S A Sweeney 17.2-0-133-2; L J Thomason 7-0-44-2; A S T West 7-0-29-0; H M Whitlock 10-0-47-2; A J Woodland 3-0-19-0.

Also batted – 4 matches - M B Wareing 0, 7* (1ct). 2 matches - S S Arthurton 78, 30; R C J Aucott 11; S Kelsall 47, 2; J M Kettleborough 143*, 7 (1ct); M H McKiernan 31, 35; B S Phagura 21 (1ct); S A Sweeney 2*, 4 (1ct). 1 match - A S Brown 7*; P I Burgoyne 18 (2ct); L J Chapman 9; D O Conway 11; C J Guest 12; H J Palmer 22; J Parmar 17*; H M Whitlock 0; A J Woodland 55*.

SECOND ELEVEN T20 AVERAGES

BATTING	M	I	NO	Runs	HS	Avge	100s	C/S
S Kelsall	4	4	2	121	84*	60.50	-	1
L J Thomason	10	8	3	152	47*	30.40	-	3/3
C J Whittock	10	9	2	206	58*	29.42	-	4
E R Kilbee	9	8	0	208	62	26.00	-	5
J M Kettleborough	4	4	0	89	51	22.25	-	3
A Kapil	4	4	1	62	27	20.66	-	1
M H McKiernan	4	2	2	35	18*	17.50	-	-
P I Burgoyne	10	7	0	99	30	14.14	-	3
M S Pepper	4	3	0	36	19	12.00	-	1/1
J P Harrison	4	3	1	11	6*	5.50	-	1

BOWLING	O	M	Runs	Wkt	Avge	BB
B A Waring	8	0	33	5	6.60	3/15
T Bulcock	6.5	0	39	5	7.80	4/13
A Kapil	14.2	0	99	6	16.50	3/26
Waqas Hussain	6	0	62	3	20.66	3/37
P I Burgoyne	32	0	238	11	21.63	4/33
L J Chapman	24	0	216	8	27.00	2/10
L J Thomason	8	0	81	3	27.00	2/11
R O Gordon	13	0	105	3	35.00	2/22
B S Phagura	13.1	0	107	3	35.66	2/25

Also bowled – U Amjaid 7.4-0-83-1; D O Conway 4-0-25-1; C J Guest 9-0-75-2; S Kelsall 3-0-42-0; J M Kettleborough 2-0-13-2; M H McKiernan 30-0-226-2.

Also batted – 10 matches – L J Chapman 11 (3ct). 5 matches – C J Guest 8 (2ct). 4 matches – U Amjaid DNB; R O Gordon 9*; S S E Gumbs 0, 0 (2ct); I A Karim 13, 1(1ct/1st) ; B S Phagura 18*, 5* (2ct). 2 matches – T Bulcock 11 (2ct); D O Conway 1*; Waqas Hussain 69 (2ct); B A Waring DNB (1ct).

HOME MATCHES: FRIENDLIES

v MCC Young Cricketers (Saffron Walden) – 5-6 April – Unc 244
(A D Todd 89; T E Barber 3/37) & 115/3 (M S Pepper 73*) drew
with MCC YC 333 (T F Smith 82, J H Barrett 75, M H Cross 75;
M B Wareing 4/31)

HOME MATCHES: SECOND ELEVEN TROPHY

v Middlesex (Enborne Lodge, Newbury) – 9 May – Middx 338/4
(S S Eskinazi 149, G F B Scott 106, O P Rayner 62) beat Unc 325
(M S Pepper 103, E R Kilbee 77; A Godsal 4/46, H W Podmore
3/50) by 13 runs.

v Glamorgan (Enborne Lodge, Newbury) – 10 May – Unc 185
(O M R Pringle 3/30) lost to Glam 190/6 (A O Morgan 56) by four
wkts.

HOME MATCHES: SECOND ELEVEN T20 COMPETITION

v Essex (Great Tew) – 13 June – Match 1 – Unc 171/3 (S Kelsall
84*, E R Kilbee 55) lost to Essex 173/1 (A J A Wheater 83, V
Chopra 73*) by nine wkts.
v Essex (Great Tew) – 13 June – Match 2 – Essex 145/5 beat Unc
124/8 by 21 runs.
v Hampshire (Great Tew) – 14 June – Match 1 – Hants 124 (A
Kapil 3/26) beat Unc 111/7 (B J Taylor 4/23) by three wkts.
v Hampshire (Great Tew) – 14 June – Match 2 – Unc 146/6 (I G
Holland 3/14) lost to Hants 148/3 by seven wkts.

v Kent (Saffron Walden) – 10 July – Match 1 – Unc 134/7 (A J
Ball 3/14) lost to Kent 135/2 (S R Dickson 68, Z Crawley 52*)
by eight wkts.
v Kent (Saffron Walden) – 10 July – Match 2 – Kent 212/7 (S W
Billings 84, A P Rouse 53; P I Burgoyne 4/43) beat Unc 190/6 (E R
Kilbee 62, J M Kettleborough 51) 22 runs.
v Sussex (Long Marston) – 3 Aug – Match 1 – Sussex 125 (T
Bulcock 4/13) lost to Unc 126/2 (C J Whittock 58*) by eight wkts.
v Sussex (Long Marston) – 3 Aug – Match 2 – Sussex 120/7 (B A
Waring 3/15) tied with Unc 120/9 (O E Robinson 5/33)

PLAYERS WHO HAVE REPRESENTED THE UNICORNS IN 2017 (29)

S S Arthurton	C J Guest	H J Palmer	M B Wareing
R C J Aucott	J P Harrison	J Parmar	A S T West
A S Brown	A Kapil	M S Pepper	H M Whitlock
T Bulcock	S Kelsall	B S Phagura	C J Whittock
P I Burgoyne	J M Kettleborough	S A Sweeney	A J Woodland
L J Chapman	E R Kilbee	L J Thomason	
D O Conway	*A D Maskell	Uzair Amjaid	
R O Gordon	M H McKiernan	Waqas Hussain	

UNICORNS CRICKETERS

Uzair AMJAID b High Wycombe, Bucks, 29.11.98. RHB
OB.Debut 2017. HS 5 v MCC YC, Saffron Walden, 2017. BB 2/77
in the same match. BBT20 1/16 v Kent, Saffron Walden, 2017 (1st)
* Joshua Benjamin Thomas ARKSEY (Bottisham S, Cambridge;
Long Road SFC, Cambridge; Anglia Ruskin Univ) b Cambridge,
20.12.94. RHB SLA. Debut Surrey 2015. F/C debut (Cambridge
MCCU) v Northants, Fenner's, 2015. Debut Unc 2017. HS 10 v MCC
YC, Saffron Walden, 2017. BB 5/53 (Surrey) v Sussex, Horsham,
2015. BBT20 1/21 (Surrey) v Glam, Cardiff CC, 2015 (1st).
Samuel Shaun ARTHURTON (Reepham HS; Easton SFC) b
Norwich, Norfolk 22.7.92. RHB LB. Debut 2017. MCCYC
2013; Kent 2014; Northants & Unc 2016. HS 150 (Essex) v Glam,
Halstead 2009. BB 1/17 (Essex) v MCCYC, Radlett, 2011. HSSET
89* (MCCYC) v Notts, Notts SG, 2014. BBSET 2/13 (Essex) v
Middx, Radlett, 2010. HST20 53* (MCCYC) v Middx, Southend-
on-Sea, 2013 (2nd). BBT20 1/4 v Leics, Long Marston, 2016 (1st).
Ross Charles John AUCOTT (Idsall S, Shifnal, Salop; Wrekin
Coll, Wellington, Salop) b Shrewsbury, 7.3.96. RHB RFM.
Debut Northants 2013; Worcs 2015; Unc 2017. HS 3* v MCC YC,
Saffron Walden, 2017. BB 1/28 in the same match. HSSET 11 v
Hants, Ageas Bowl Nursery, 2017. HST20 22 (Northants) v Leics,
Hinckley, 2013 (1st).
Ayden Sean BROWN (Melbourne Central HS, Australia) b
Melbourne, 10.3.96. RHB RFM. Debut 2017. HSSET 7* v Essex,
Billericay. BBSET 0/35 in the same match.
Tobias (Toby) BULCOCK b Blackburn Lancs, 5.9.90. LHB
SLA. Debut Unicorns A & Worcs 2013. HS 1 (Worcs) v Derbys,
Kidderminster, 2013. BB 1/51 in the same match. HSSET 36 v
Durham, Burnopfield, 2015. BBSET 2/15 v Warwicks, Great Tew,

2015. HST20 13* v Leics, Loughborough Town CC, 2015 (2nd).
BBT20 4/13 v Sussex, Long Marston, 2017 (1st).
Peter Ian BURGOYNE (St John Houghton S, Ilkeston; Derby
SFC) b Nottingham 11.11.93. RHB OB. Debut Derbys 2011.
F/C debut Southern Rocks (Zim) v Mashonaland Eagles, Harare,
2012/13; debut Sussex 2015; Unc 2017. Eng U19 v S.Africa 2011.
HS 150 (Derbys) v Northants, Derby, 2013. BB 7/171 (Sussex) v
Hants, Ageas Bowl Nursery, 2015. HSSET 80 (Sussex) v Essex,
Southend-on-Sea, 2015. BBSET 3/14 (Derbys) v Unicorns A, Long
Marston , 2012. HST20 30 v Essex, Great Tew, 2017 (2nd). BBT20
4/18 (Derbys) v Notts, Trent Coll, Long Eaton, 2011 (2nd).
Luke James CHAPMAN (Cambridge U) b Stevenage, Herts.,
21.8.98, RHB OB. Debut 2017. F/C debut (Cambridge MCCU) v
Notts, Fenner's, 2017. HSSET 9 v Essex, Billericay, 2017. BBSET
0/61 in the same match. HST20 11 v Sussex, Long Marston, 2017
(2nd). BBT20 2/10 v Hants, Great Tew, 2017 (1st).
Danny Oliver CONWAY (Nunthorpe CS; Middlesbrough Coll;
Oxford Brookes U) b Stockton-on-Tees, Co Durham, 1.5.85. RHB
RM. Debut Yorks 2004; Derbys 2007; Kent, MCCU & Northants
2010; Unc 2017. F/C debut (Oxford MCCU) v Northants, the Parks,
2010. HS 34* v (MCCU) v Surrey, Cranleigh S, 2010. BB 3/43
(Yorks) v Lancs, Blackpool, 2004. HSSET 20* (Yorks) v Durham,
Sunderland, 2004. BBSET 2/30 (Kent) v Glos, Beckenham,
2010. HST20 1* v Sussex, Long Marston , 2017 (2nd). HSKO
57 (Northants) v Leics, Dunstable, 2010. BBKO 0/26 in the same
match.
* Alexander Joseph M CHRISTIE b 3.10.95, Nottingham. RHB
LM. Debut Leics 2014; Unc 2017. BB 1/40 (Leics) v Kent, Market
Harborough, 2014.

Recordo Olton GORDON (Aston Manor S, Birmingham; Hamstead Hall SFC. Halesowen) b St Elizabeth, Jamaica, 12.10.91. RHB RM. Debut Warwicks 2011. F/C debut (Warwicks) v Oxford MCCU, the Parks, 2013. Debut Unc 2017. HS 35* (Warwicks) v Durham, Chester-le-Street, 2015. BB 6/27 (Warwicks) v Lancs, Southport, 2014. HSSET 18 (Warwicks) v Worcs, Worcester RGS, 2016. BBSET 3/24 (Warwicks) v MCCYC, Olton, 2013. HST20 42 (Warwicks) v Durham, Edgbaston, 2016 (2nd). BBT20 5/13 (Warwicks) v Notts, Edgbaston, 2016 (2nd).

Callum Jake GUEST (St Bede's S, Upper Dicker, Hailsham, Sussex; Cambridge U) b May 1995, Hastings. RHB OB. Debut 2017. F/C debut (Cambridge MCCU) v Notts, Fenner's, 2017. HSSET 12 v Essex, Billericay, 2017. BBSET 1/73 in the same match. HST20 8 v Sussex, Long Marston , 2017 (2nd). BBT20 2/7 v Hants, Great Tew, 2017 (1st)

Shelvin Sameer Emanuel GUMBS (Loughborough U) b Slough, Bucks, 29.8.91. RHB OB. Debut Hants 2010; Unc 2011. HS 1 (Hants) v Northants, Stowe S, 2010. HSSET 10 v Northants, Great Tew, 2016. HST20 0 v Kent, Saffron Walden 2017 (1st). BBT20 1/22 v Middx, Ealing, 2011.

Jamie Paul HARRISON (Arthur Terry S, Sutton Coldfield) b Alberton, Johannesburg, Gauteng, S Africa, 13.5.98. LHB SLA. Debut 2017. HSSET 18 v Glam, Newbury, 2017. HST20 6* v Hants, Great Tew, 2017 (2nd).

Aneesh KAPIL b Wolverhampton, Staffs. b 3.8.93. RHB RFM Debut Worcs 2008; F/C debut (Worcs) v Sussex, Horsham, 2011. Debuts Surrey 2014; Northants & Unc 2017. Eng U19 v S.Africa, 2011; to Bangladesh 2011/12; to Australia (World Cup) 2012. HS 161 (Surrey) v Kent, New Malden, 2016. BB 4/12 (Worcs) v Derbys, Belper Meadows, 2010. HSSET 106 (Worcs) v Derbys, Kidderminster, 2013. BBSET 4/40 (Surrey) v Sussex, Horsham, 2016. HST20 82 (Surrey) v MCC YC, Purley, 2015 (1st). BBT20 3/26 v Hants, Great Tew, 2017 (1st).

Irfan Ali KARIM (Braeburn HS, Nairobi, Kenya; Braeburn SFC; Loughborough U) b Hendon, Middx, 25.9.92. LHB OB. ODIs (Kenya) 9 (2011 to 2013/14) & 7 T20s. Debut MCCU 2014; Leics 2016; Durham & Unc 2017. F/C debut (Kenya) v Ireland, Mombassa SC, 2011/12. HS 68 (Leics) v Notts, Hinckley, 2016. HSSET 50* (Leics) v Notts, Loughborough CC, 2016. HST20 13 v Kent, Saffron Walden, 2017 (1st).

Samuel "Sam" KELSALL (Trentham HS) b Stoke-on-Trent, Staffs 14.3.93. RHB RM. Debut Notts 2008 aged 15 years and 158 days. F/C debut (Notts) v Durham, Chester-le-Street, 2014. Eng U19 v S.Africa, 2011; to Bangladesh & to Australia 2011/12, HS 154 (Notts) v Warwicks, Edgbaston, 2014. BB 0/38 (Notts) v Leics, Market Harborough, 2010. HSSET 113 (Notts) v Middx, Radlett, 2013. BBSET 0/14 v Warwicks, Bulls Head Gd, 2016. HST20 84* v Essex, Great Tew, 2017 (1st). BBT20 1/20 v Lancs, Knypersley, 2016 (1st). HSKO 19 (Notts) v Derbys, Alvaston & Boulton, 2010.

James Michael KETTLEBOROUGH (Bedford S) b Huntingdon, Cambs, 22.10.92. RHB OB Debut Middx 2011; Northants 2012. F/C debut (Northants) v Sri Lankans, 2014. Debut Glam 2015; Derbys, Unc & ret to Northants 2017. HS 209* (Glam) v Essex, Bishop`s Stortford, 2016. BB 2/24 (Northants) v Notts, Milton Keynes, 2017. HSSET 143* v Somerset, Taunton Vale, 2017. BBSET 1/28 (Middx) v MCCYC, Radlett, 2011. HST20 52* (Glam) v Essex, Chelmsford, 2016 (1st). BBT20 2/13 v Kent, Saffron Walden, 2017 (2nd).

Edward Richard KILBEE (Marlborough Coll, Wilts; U of Cape Town, S Africa) b Lambeth, Surrey, 20.1.88. LHB SLA. Debut Worcs & Surrey 2011; Somerset 2014; Unc 2017. HS 56 (Worcs) v Lancs, Nantwich, 2011. HSSET 77 v Middx, Newbury, 2017. HST20 62 v Kent, Saffron Walden, 2017 (2nd).

*Alexander David MASKELL (Cambridge U) b Harlow, Essex, March 1994. RHB. Debut 2017 . HS 0 v MCC YC, Saffron Waldon, 2017.

Matthew Harry "Mattie" McKIERNAN (Lowton HS, Leigh; St John Rigby Coll, Wigan) b Billinge, Merseyside, 14.6.94. RHB LB. Debut Lancs 2011; Northants 2012 (on loan). Ret to Lancs 2013; Leics & Unc 2016; Durham 2017. HS 49 (Lancs) v Lancs, Liverpool, 2014. BB 4/64 (Leics) v Northants, Desborough, 2017. HSSET 42 (Lancs) v Leics, Grace Road, 2014. BBSET 5/45

(Durham) v Worcs, New Road, 2017. HST20 18* v Hants, Great Tew, 2017 (2nd). BBT20 3/11 v Leics, Long Marston, 2016 (2nd).

Harrison John PALMER b Enfield, Middx, 13.10.96. RHB WK. F/C debut (Cambridge MCCU) v Essex, Fenner`s, 2016. Debut Unc 2017. HSSET 22 v Essex, Billericay, 2017.

Jay Jitesh PARMAR b Waltham Forest, Essex, 11.5.94. Debut 2016. HSSET 2 v Worcs, East Challow, 2016. HSSET 17* v Glos, Bristol U, 2017. BBSET 0/20 in the same match.

Michael-Kyle Steven PEPPER (The Perse S) b Harlow, 25.6.98. Brother of C A (Essex 2013 to 2016). RHB WK. Debut Essex 2016; Essex & Northants 2017. HS 136 (Essex) v Middx, Coggeshall, 2017. HSSET 103 v Middx, Radlett, 2017. HST20 38 (Northants) v Lancs, Northampton, 2017 (2nd).

Brinder Singh PHAGURA (Q3 Academy, Birmingham; Bishop Vesey GS, Sutton Coldfield) b West Bromwich, W Midlands, 23.2.96. RHB RM. Debut Warwicks 2013; Northants & Unc 2016. HS 45 v MCC YC, Saffron Walden, 2017. BB 4/17 (Warwicks) v MCCYC, High Wycombe, 2014. HSSET 36* (Warwicks) v Unc, Great Tew, 2015. BBSET 4/26 (Warwicks) v Notts, Bulls Head, Coventry, 2015. HST20 18* v Essex, Great Tew, 2017 (2nd). BBT20 3/23 v Leics, Long Marston, 2016 (1st).

Samuel Alan SWEENEY (Parklands HS, Chorley; Myerscough C, Manchester) b Preston, Lancs 15.3.90. RHB RM. List A debut (Northants) v Warwicks, Edgbaston 2011. Debut Northants & Worcs 2011, Glos 2015; Unc 2017. HS 63 (Northants) v Worcs, Northampton, 2011. BB 7/72 (Worcs) v MCC Univs, Fenner's, 2011. HSSET 4 v Glam, Newbury, 2017. BBSET 4/50 (Northants) v Leics, Stowe S, 2012. HST20 4* (Northants) v Leics, Leicester, 2011 (1st). BBT20 3/22 (Northants) v Middx (2nd), Uxbridge 2012.

Adam James SYDDALL (Bolton S; U of St. Andrews) b Bolton, Lancs 10.6.80. RHB LFM. Debut Lancs 1999, Glam, Hants and Worcs 2000, Minor Counties 2007; Unc 2011. HS 15 (Worcs) v Durham, Riverside 2000. BB 3/37 (Glam) v Lancs, Southport 2000. HSSET 8 v Warwicks, Marlins, Long Marston, 2012. BBSET 5/5 v Lancs, Chester Boughton Hall, 2011.

Lee James THOMASON (Barr Beacon S, Walsall; U of Wolverhampton) b Sutton Coldfield, 22.1.95. RHB WK. Brother of A D (Warwicks 2013 to date). Debut Warwicks & Unc 2014; Derbys 2017. HS 31 v MCC YC, Saffron Walden, 2017. HSSET 58 v Durham, Burnopfield, 2015. BBSET 2/32 v Glos, Bristol U, 2017. HST20 47* v Sussex, Long Marston, 2017 (1st). BBT20 2/11 v Hants, Great Tew, 2017 (1st)

*Adam David TODD (Bungay HS, Suffolk) b Norwich, Norfolk, 29.2.92. RHB RFM. Debut Essex 2015. HS 89 v MCC YC, Saffron Walden, 2017. BB 2/54 v MCC YC, Halsted, 2015.

WAQAS HUSSAIN (West London Acad.; Harrow S; Uxbridge C) b Brent, Middx 11.5.92. RHB RM. Debut Glos, Unicorns 2014. HSSET 66 v Sussex, East Challow 2014. BBSET 5/53 v Durham, Burnopfield, CC, 2016. HST20 89 v Lancs, Knypersley, 2016 (2nd). BBT20 6/33 v Durham, Burnopfield CC, 2016 (2nd).

Matthew Brian WAREING (Manningtree HS; Colchester SFC) b Colchester, 17.1.94. LHB LMF. Debut Essex & Leics 2015; Unc 2016; Worcs & MCC YC 2017. HS 8 (Essex) v Kent, Maidstone, 2015 & v MCC YC, Saffron Walden, 2017. BB 3/48 (Worcs) v Lancs, Great Crosby, 2017. HSSET 7* v Glam, Newbury, 2017. BBSET 3/55 v Hants, Ageas Bowl Nursery, 2017. HST20 2* (Leics) v Unc, Long Marston, 2016 (1st). BBT20 2/35 (Leics) v Unc, Long Marston, 2016 (2nd).

Ben Alexander WARING b Harlow, 12.4.98. RHB SLA. Debut Essex 2015; Unc 2017. HS 14 v Hants, Ageas Bowl Nursery, 2017. BB 2/36 v Somerset, Halstead, 2016. HSSET 0 v Hants, Ageas Bowl Nursery, 2017. BBSET 3/55 v Somerset, Taunton Vale, 2015. BBT20 3/15 (Unc) v Sussex, Long Marston, 2017 (2nd).

Aaron Spencer Thomas WEST (Brentwood S) b Romford, Essex 30.1.91. RHB RM WK. Debut Essex 2007 aged 16 years and 197 days. Debut Leics 2010. Debut Unicorns A 2012. Kent 2013; debut Derbys, Hants, Surrey, 2014. HS 121 (Essex) v Hants, West End Nursery, 2010. BB (Essex) 0/4 v MCCU, Billericay,2010. HSSET (Essex) 113 v Kent, Southend, 2010. BBSET BBSET 2/32 (Hants) v Sussex, Horsham, 2016112* v Middx, Saffron Walden, 2014 (2nd). HSKO (Essex) 67 v Sussex, Chelmsford, 2010.

Hugo M WHITLOCK (S Devon Steiner S; Richard Huish Coll, Taunton) b Torquay, Devon, 25.12.96. RHB RM. Debut 2017. HSSET 0 v Glos, Bristol U 2017. BBSET 2/47 in the same match.
Christopher Jonathan WHITTOCK (Aldridge S, Walsall) b Walsall, W Midlands, 8.5.93. RHB RM. Debut Leics 2012; MCC YC 2013; Unc 2015. HS 11 (Leics) v Warwicks, Hinckley, 2012 & v MCC YC, Saffron Walden, 2017. BB 1/7 (Leics) v Glam, Ratcliffe Coll, 2012. HSSET 88 * v Durham, Burnopfield CC, 2016. BBSET 3/15 (MCC YC) v Derbys, Denby. 2013. HST20 70* v Notts, Notts SG, 2016 (1st).

Alexander James WOODLAND (St Edward's S, Oxford) b Windsor, Berks 16.1.98. LHB RM. Debut Hants 2015, Glos 2016. Unc & Sussex 2017. HS 40 (Sussex) v Kent, Polo Farm SG, Canterbury, 2017. BB 3/39 (Sussex) v Somerset, Taunton Vale, 2015. HSSET 55* v Hants, Ageas Bowl Nursery, 2017. BBSET 2/20 (Sussex) v Kent, Canterbury, 2017. HST20 1 v Somerset, Bristol U, 2016 (1st). BBT20 2/14 (Sussex) v Kent, East Grinstead, 2017 (1st).

WARWICKSHIRE

PLAYING RECORDS 2017
Championship – P9 W3 L1 D5 - second in the Northern group
2nd XI Trophy – P6 W3 L2 Ab1 – fourth in the Northern group
2nd XI T20 Competition – P12 W7 L5 - fourth in the Northern group

2nd XI SUCCESSES
Championship – Winners – 1979, 1996, 2011
2nd XI Trophy – Winners - 2006
2nd XI T20 Competition – second in the northern group and beaten semi-finalists in 2016

SECOND ELEVEN CHAMPIONSHIP AVERAGES

BATTING	M	I	NO	Runs	HS	Avge	100s	C/S
J E Poysden	5	5	4	82	42	82.00	-	4
I J Westwood	3	5	0	358	142	71.60	1	1
M J Lamb	8	9	1	542	164	67.75	2	2
L Banks	7	11	1	570	181	57.00	1	3
A Javid	2	4	0	211	105	52.75	1	-
A R I Umeed	7	11	0	535	203	48.63	1	5
M R Adair	4	6	2	180	66	45.00	-	2
A D Thomason	5	7	3	163	91*	40.75	-	2
G T Thornton	4	4	1	111	71*	37.00	-	1
R M Yates	4	5	0	178	102	35.60	1	1
A J Mellor	6	8	1	219	94	31.28	-	13
S R Hain	2	3	0	93	45	31.00	-	1
H J H Brookes	4	5	3	38	20	19.00	-	-
G D Panayi	6	7	1	90	29	15.00	-	1
C G Harrison	4	3	0	42	25	14.00	-	1
Sukhjit Singh	7	7	0	20	10	2.85	-	7

BOWLING	O	M	Runs	Wkt	Avge	BB
R N Sidebottom	42.5	8	133	15	8.86	8/33
B S Phagura	18	4	58	4	14.50	3/2
M J Lamb	52.2	11	134	9	14.88	4/30
W B Rankin	19.4	3	60	3	20.00	2/22
M R Adair	38.4	7	139	5	27.80	3/55
C J C Wright	42	7	142	5	28.40	2/26
A D Thomason	46	2	201	7	28.71	3/31
Sukhjit Singh	148.1	34	510	16	31.87	4/93
C G Harrison	20	0	98	3	32.66	3/73
O J Hannon-Dalby	35	5	116	3	38.66	2/49
G T Thornton	63	14	198	5	39.60	3/66
G D Panayi	71	6	297	7	42.42	3/31
J E Poysden	77.2	18	263	6	43.83	2/34
M T Spencer	109	18	436	8	54.50	2/31
H J H Brookes	56.4	8	219	3	73.00	3/69

Also batted – 6 matches – M T Spencer 0*, 0* (3ct). 3 matches - C J C Wright 4, 12. 2 matches – O J Hannon-Dalby DNB; B S Phagura 17, 29; E J Pollock 13, 31; R N Sidebottom DNB; A T Thomson 95, 43* (1ct); C R Woakes 19, 14 (1ct). 1 match – T R Ambrose 118* (7ct); B J Curran 45 & 21*; S E Grant 76 (1ct); B J Griffin 2* (2ct); N A Hammond 0; H D Johnson 11 & 1; Khayam Khan DNB; W B Rankin DNB; D P Richardson 10 & 14 (1ct); J H Sookias DNB (1ct); O P Stone DNB; I J L Trott 29.

Also bowled – L Banks 15-1-68-0; S E Grant 8.3-2-43-0; S R Hain 1.1-0-22-0; A Javid 5-0-30-1; Khayam Khan 10-1-54-0; D P Richardson 1-0-18-0; J H Sookias 6.5-0-47-0; O P Stone 16-3-47-1; A T Thomson 1.2-1-1-0; A R I Umeed 10.4-0-60-2; C R Woakes 15-4-53-2.

SECOND ELEVEN TROPHY AVERAGES

BATTING	M	I	NO	Runs	HS	Avge	100s	C/S
A Javid	3	3	2	128	87*	128.00	-	-
M R Adair	4	3	2	88	49	88.00	-	4
M J Lamb	3	3	1	169	103*	84.50	1	-
A R I Umeed	4	4	0	214	87	53.50	-	3
L Banks	5	5	0	148	78	29.60	-	1
A D Thomason	3	3	0	62	33	20.66	-	-
Sukhjit Singh	4	3	0	19	12	6.33	-	-
G D Panayi	4	3	0	13	10	4.33	-	-
A J Mellor	4	4	0	15	7	3.75	-	2/2
J E Poysden	5	3	1	6	3*	3.00	-	4

BOWLING	O	M	Runs	Wkt	Avge	BB
K H D Barker	8	0	29	3	9.66	3/29
A D Thomason	22	0	118	7	16.85	16.85
G D Panayi	18.4	0	139	6	23.16	4/76
J E Poysden	48.3	0	262	10	26.20	5/47
Sukhjit Singh	38	2	164	5	32.80	3/21
M T Spencer	32.2	0	187	5	37.40	2/31

Also bowled – M R Adair 11-0-91-1; H J H Brookes 2-0-14-0; O J Hannon-Dalby 7-1-36-0; A Javid 22-0-75-2; M J Lamb 6-0-26-1; G T Thornton 14-12-90-2; A R I Umeed 12-0-53-2.

Also batted – 5 matches – M T Spencer 0, 0* (3ct). 2 matches – E J Pollock 13, 40; G T Thornton 0, 31 (1ct). 1 match – K H D Barker 13; H J H Brookes 12 (ct); B J Griffin DNB (1ct); S R Hain 62; O J Hannon-Dalby DNB (2ct); K Harrison 0 (1ct); H D Johnson 48.

SECOND ELEVEN T20 AVERAGES

BATTING	M	I	NO	Runs	HS	Avge	100s	C/S
N A Hammond	4	4	1	122	56*	40.66	-	1
M J Lamb	11	11	3	210	54	26.25	-	4
E J Pollock	9	9	1	208	93*	26.00	-	5
Sukhjit Singh	7	3	1	43	29	21.50	-	2
A J Mellor	9	9	0	170	47	18.88	-	9/4
A Javid	10	5	1	70	36	17.50	-	4
A R I Umeed	4	4	0	70	28	17.50	-	3
W T S Porterfield	3	3	0	50	23	16.66	-	1
A T Thomson	8	6	2	60	39*	15.00	-	2
L Banks	4	4	0	57	28	14.25	-	-
J E Poysden	12	5	1	50	21	12.50	-	1
A D Thomason	6	5	1	38	17	9.50	-	2

BOWLING	O	M	Runs	Wkt	Avge	BB
O J Hannon-Dalby	20.2	0	138	11	12.54	4/14
R N Sidebottom	10.5	0	81	6	13.50	5/11
M T Spencer	10	0	71	5	14.20	2/30
Sukhjit Singh	23	0	159	9	17.66	3/23
A Javid	32	0	173	8	21.62	3/22
J E Poysden	46	0	303	14	21.64	2/15
H J H Brookes	17	1	136	4	34.00	1/3
K H D Barker	11	1	108	3	36.00	2/35

Also bowled – R Clarke 4-0-28-0; C de Grandhomme 4-0-33-2; G D Elliott 3-0-23-0; K S Leverock 3-0-26-1; Mohammed Ahmed 1-0-15-0; B S Phagura 7-0-48-0; W B Rankin 4-0-30-2; D P Richardson 1-0-9-0; O P Stone 4-0-21-2; A D Thomason 12-0-78-2; A T Thomson 10.1-0-80-2; G T Thornton 8-0-76-2.

Also batted – 6 matches – O J Hannon-Dalby 2* (4ct). 5 matches - H J H Brookes 11, 2* (1ct). 4 matches – M T Spencer DNB (1ct); G T Thornton 11, 8 (4ct). 3 matches – K H D Barker 4*, 12; R N Sidebottom 2* (1ct). 2 matches – B Chapman-Lilley 4; S R Hain 50, 59; K S Leverock DNB (1ct); B S Phagura 0 (2ct); D P Richardson 8, 33. 1 match – T R Ambrose 33 (1ct); R Clarke 21; C de Grandhomme 26*; G D Elliott 68*; B J Griffin DNB; H D Johnson 1* (2ct); Mohammed Ahmed 25*; W B Rankin 0; O P Stone 1; R M Yates 41*.

HOME MATCHES: SECOND ELEVEN CHAMPIONSHIP

v Leicestershire (Edgbaston Foundation Community Sports Ground) – 3-5 May – Warwicks 234 (I J Westwood 77; C E Shreck 4/77) & 455/9d (A R I Umeed 203, I J Westwood 84, L Banks 82; J E Bailey 4/57, D Manthorpe 3/89) drew with Leics 495/9d (P J Horton 277*)

v Derbyshire (EFCSG) – 22-24 May - Derbys 222 (T A Wood 68; G D Panayi 3/31) & 376 (M J J Critchley 135; M R Adair 3/55) lost to Warwicks 573/5d (L Banks 181, M J Lamb 113, A J Mellor 94, A

D Thomason 91*) & 27/0 by 10 wkts.

v Lancashire (EFCSG) - 10-12 July - Warwicks 279 (A R I Umeed 91, L Banks 55; L A Procter 3/64, L J Hurt 3/66) drew with Lancs 301/5d (L A Procter 97, J J Bohannon 75, H Hameed 71).

v Northamptonshire (EFCSG) – 25-27 July – Northants 154 (B S Phagura 3/2; R N Sidebottom 8/33) lost to Warwicks 356/5d (T R Ambrose 118*, A R I Umeed 62, M J Lamb 55) by an inns & 71 runs.

HOME MATCHES: FRIENDLIES

v Somerset (EFCSG) – 29-31 May v Somerset 513/7d (A J Hose 194, T D Rouse 123, E J Byrom 74; M R Adair 5/108) & 196/8d (J Allenby 56*; J E Poysden 5/42) drew with Warwicks 287 (A J Mellor 57; J H Davey 4/62, P A van Meekeren 4/80) & 172/5 (E J Pollock 72)

v Worcestershire (Bulls Head Gd, Coventry) – 22-25 Aug – Worcs 59 (G T Thornton 4/13, H J H Brookes 3/24) & 169 (K H D Barker

v Lancashire (EFCSG) – 3/15, G T Thornton 3/37) lost to Warwicks 391 (A T Thomson 101*, L Banks 85; J D Shantry 3/47) by an inns & 163 runs.

v Gloucestershire (Bulls Head Gd, Coventry) – 5-7 Sept – Warwicks 391/6d (A J Hose 181, A J Mellor 118*) drew with Glos 192 (J E Poysden 5/26) & 105/4.

HOME MATCHES: SECOND ELEVEN TROPHY

v Worcestershire (Scorers, Shirley) – 25 Apr – Worcs 307 (R A Whiteley 90, O E Westbury 82, A N Kervezee 76; A D Thomason 4/57) beat Warwicks 207/8 (A R I Umeed 87, S R Hain 62) by 13 runs (DLS)
v Nottinghamshire (Scorers, Shirley) – 28 Apr – Warwicks 187 (B M Kitt 4/37, L A Patterson-White 3/44) beat Notts 181 (J D Libby 57*, K H D Barker 3/29) by six runs.
v Derbyshire (Bulls Head Gd, Coventry) – 25 May – Derbys 239 (H R Hosein 66; J E Poysden 5/47) lost to Warwicks 240/3 (M J Lamb 103*, A Javid 87*) by seven wkts.

HOME MATCHES: SECOND ELEVEN T20 COMPETITION

v Leicestershire (Scorers, Shirley) – 26 June – Match 1 – Leics 159/7 (C S Delport 60; A Javid 3/22) lost to Warwicks 163/3 (G D Elliott 68*) by seven wkts.
v Leicestershire (Scorers, Shirley) – 26 June – Match 2 – Warwicks 133/8 (C F Parkinson 4/13) beat Leics 106/7 by 27 runs.
v Lancashire (Bulls Head Gd, Coventry) – 13 July – Match 1 – Lancs 161/8 beat Warwicks 157 (S R Hain 50; D J Lamb 3/48) by four runs.
v Lancashire (Bulls Head Gd, Coventry) – 13 July – Match 2 – Lancs 154/8 lost to Warwicks 157/4 (S R Hain 59) by 6 wkts.
v Northamptonshire (Scorers, Shirley) – 24 July – Match 1 – Northants 139/8 lost to Warwicks 140/2 (N A Hammond 56*) by eight wkts.
v Northamptonshire (Scorers, Shirley) – 24 July – Match 2 – Northants 103/9 (O J Hannon-Dalby 4/14) lost to Warwicks 107/3 by seven wkts.

PLAYERS WHO HAVE REPRESENTED WARWICKSHIRE 2ndXI IN 2017 (47)

M R Adair	S R Hain	A J Mellor	O P Stone
T R Ambrose	N A Hammond	Mohammed Ahmed	Sukhjit Singh
L Banks	*T R G Hampton	G D Panayi	A D Thomason
K H D Barker	O J Hannon-Dalby	B S Phagura	A T Thomson
H J H Brookes	C G Harrison	E J Pollock	G T Thornton
B Chapman-Lilley	K Harrison	W T S Porterfield	I J L Trott
R Clarke	*A J Hose	J E Poysden	A R I Umeed
B J Curran	A Javid	W B Rankin	I J Westwood
C de Grandhomme	H D Johnson	D P Richardson	C R Woakes
G D Elliott	Khayam Khan	R N Sidebottom	C J C Wright
S E Grant	M J Lamb	J H Sookias	R M Yates
B J Griffin	K S Leverock	M T Spencer	

WARWICKSHIRE CRICKETERS

Mark Richard ADAIR (Sullivan Upper S, Holywood, Co Down, N Ireland) b Belfast, 27.3.96. RHB RFM. Debut 2013. F/C debut v Somerset, Taunton, 2017. HS 66 v MCC YC, High Wycombe, 2017. BB 45/108 v Somerset, EFCSG, 2017. HSSET 49 v Yorks, Harrogate, 2017. BBSET 4/19 v Unc, Great Tew, 2015. HST20 6* v Durham, Benwell Hill, 2015 (2nd). BBT20 3/15 v Notts, Trent Coll, 2015 (1st). Released at the end of the 2017 season..
Timothy Raymond AMBROSE (Merewether HS, NSW, Aus; Training and Further Education Coll, NSW, Aus) b Newcastle, NSW, 1.12.82. RHB WK. Tests (Eng) 11 (2007/08 to 2008/09) & 5 ODIs. Debut Sussex 2001; F/C Debut (Sussex) v Warwicks, Edgbaston, 2001; Cap 2003; debut Warwicks 2006; Cap 2007. HS 121* v Worcs, Ombersley, 2006. HSSET 104 v Somerset, North Perrott, 2006. HST20 33 v Lancs, Bulls Head Gd, Coventry, 2017 (2nd). Warwicks Staff.
Liam BANKS (Newcastle-u-Lyme S & SFC) b Newcastle-u-Lyme, Staffs, 3.6.99. RHB OB. Debut 2015, aged 16 yrs & 44 Days. F/C debut v Yorks, Headingley, 2017. Eng U19 v Ind 2017; to SA 2017/18. HS 181 v Derbys, EFCSG, 2017. BB 0/8 v Worcs, Worcester RGS, 2015. HSSET 78 v MCC YC, Merchant Taylors' , Northwood, 2017. BBSET 1/20 v Worcs, Worcester RGS, 2016. HST20 40 v Worcs, Shirley, 2016 (2nd).
Keith Hubert Douglas BARKER (Moorhead HS, Accrington; Preston Coll) b Manchester, 21.10.86. LHB LM. Debut 2008. F/C debut v Notts, Edgbaston, 2009. Cap 2013. HS 170 v Yorks, York, 2010. BB 7/52 v MCCYC, High Wycombe, 2010. HSSET 52* v Yorks, Edgbaston, 2009. BBSET 5/9 v Derbys, Dunstall, 2010. HST20 12 v Durham, S Northumberland, 2017 (2nd). BBT20 2/35 v Lancs, Bulls Head Gd, Coventry, 2017 (2nd). HSKO 56 v Worcs, Worcester, 2010. BBKO 2/43 in the same match. Warwicks Staff.
Henry James Hamilton BROOKES (Tudor Grange Acad, Solihull, Warwicks) b Solihull, 21.8.99. RHB RMF. Brother of B L (Warwicks 2015/16). Eng U19 v Ind, 2016/17; v India 2017. Debut 2016. F/C debut v Essex, Edgbaston, 2017. HS 20 v Leics, EFCSG, 2017. BB 3/24 v Worcs, Bulls Head Gd, Coventry, 2017.

HSSET 12 v Notts, Scorers, Shirley, 2017. BBSET 0/14 in the same match. HST20 11 v Leics, Scorers, Shirley, 2017 (2nd). BBT20 1/3 in the same match.
Benjamin Joseph CHAPMAN-LILLEY (St Benedict Catholic Voluntary Academy, Derby; Repton S) b Derby, 13.1.00. RHB RM. Debut 2017. HST20 v Notts, Worksop Coll, 2017 (2nd).
Rikki CLARKE (Broadwater S, Godalming, Surrey; Godalming Coll) b Orsett, Essex, 29.9.81. RHB RFM. Tests 2 (Eng) 2003/04 & 20 ODIs. Debut MCCYC & Surrey 2000; F/C debut (Surrey) v Cambridge MCCU, Fenner`s, 2002; debut Derbys 2008; Warwicks 2009. HS 89 (Surrey) v Glam, Whitgift S, 2001. BB 4/25 (Surrey) v Somerset, Taunton, 2001. HSSET 84 Surrey) v Essex, Colchester, 2002. BBSET 4/36 (MCCYC) v Surrey, the Oval, 2000. HST20 21 v Worcs, Worcester RGS, 2017 (2nd). BBT20 3/23 v Worcs, Shirley, 2017 (1st).
Benjamin Jack CURRAN (Wellington Coll) b Northampton, 7.6.96. LHB OB. Brother of T K Tests 1 (Eng) 2017/18 & 1 ODI (2017) & S M (both Surrey) and son of K M (Northants, Glos, Boland, SA & Natal, SA, 1980/81 to 1999. ODIs 11 (Zim) 1983 to 1987/88). Debut MCC YC 2015; Notts & Surrey 2016; Warwicks & Leics 2017. HS 192 (MCC YC) v Yorks, High Wycombe, 2017. HSSET 141* (MCC YC) v Middx, Radlett, 2016. HST20 87* (MCC YC) v Notts, Merchant Taylors' S, Northwood, 2017 (2nd).
Colin de GRANDHOMME b Harare, Zim, 22.7.86. RHB RFM. Tests 6 (NZ), 2016/17 & 12 ODIs. Debut Manicaland, Zim, 2004/05, Midlands , Zim, 2005/06. F/C debut (Zimbabwe A) v Kenya, Harare, 2005/06; debut Auckland 2006/07;Warwicks 2017. HST20 26* v Lancs, Bulls Head Gd, Coventry, 2017. BBT20 2/33 in the same match.
Grant David ELLIOTT (St Stithians S, Johannesburg; U of Orange Free State) b Johannesburg, SA, 21.3.79. RHB RFM Tests 5 (NZ) & 83 ODIs, 2007/08 to 2015/16. Debut & F/C debut Transvaal B v Natal B, Durban, 1996/97. Debuts Griqualand West 1999/00; Gauteng 2001/02; Wellington, NZ, 2005/06; Sussex 2008; Surrey 2009; Leics 2015; Warwicks 2017. HS 25 (Sussex) v Warwicks,

Birdham, 2008. BB 0/0 in the same match. HST20 68* v Leics, Shirley, 2017. BBT20 0/23 in the same match.

Samuel Edward GRANT (Brighton Coll; Loughborough U) b Shoreham-by-Sea, Sussex, 30.8.95. LHB LMF. Debut Sussex 2013; F/C debut (Loughborough MCCU) v Kent, Canterbury, 2014. Debuts Durham & Somerset 2016; Warwicks & Worcs 2017. HS 76 v MCC YC, High Wycombe, 2017. BB 4/19 (Sussex) v Surrey, Blackstone, 2013. HSSET 15* (Sussex) v Unc, East Challow, Oxon. 2014. BBSET 2/18 (Sussex) v Somerset, Arundel, 2014. HST20 29* (Somerset) v Hants, Ageas Bowl Nursery, 2016 (1st). BBT20 3/4 (Somerset) v Warwicks, Arundel, 2016 (SF).

Ben Jai GRIFFIN (King Edward VI GS, Aston) b Solihull, 13.11.00. RHB WK. Debut 2016. Made debut v Worcs, Worcester RGS, 2016. HS 2* v MCC YC, High Wycombe, 2017.

Samuel Robert HAIN (The Southport S, Gold Coast, Queensland) b Hong Kong 16.7.95. RHB RM. Debut 2011; F/C debut v Middx, Edgbaston, 2014. HS 176* v Worcs, Worcester RGS. 2015. BB 1/56 v Worcs, Bull`s Head, Ground, 2014. HSSET 147 v Leics, Grace Road, 2014. HST20 74* v Worcs, Shirley, 2016 (2nd). Warwicks Staff.

Nicholas Alexander HAMMOND (King's S, Worcester) b Worcester, 3.2.98. RHB RM. Debut Worcs 2015, Warwicks 2017. HS 67 (Worcs) v Lancs, Southport, 2015. HSSET 21 (Worcs) v Notts, New Road, 2016. HST20 56* v Northants, Scorers, Shirley, 2017 (1st).

***Thomas Robert Garth HAMPTON** (John Hampden GS, High Wycombe) b Kingston upon Thames, Surrey 5.10.90. RHB RFM. Brother of DOD (MCCYC 2012 to date). Debut Middx 2008; MCCYC 2011; Lancs 2012; Hants, Kent, Somerset 2013; Glos 2014; Worcs 2017. F/C debut (Middx) v Oxford MCCU, Oxford 2010. HS 37 (Kent) v Glos, Bristol 2014. BB 5/19 (Glos) v Glam, Bristol 2014. HSSET 27 (MCCYC) v Kent, Shenley 2012. BBSET 4/38 (Middx) v Kent, Richmond 2009. HST20 20* (MCCYC) v Hants, Shenley 2012 (1ˢᵗ). BBT20 3/15 (MCCYC) v Surrey, Purley 2011 (2ⁿᵈ).

Oliver James HANNON-DALBY (Brooksbank S, Elland) b Halifax 20.6.89. LHB RMF. Debut Yorks 2006. F/C debut (Yorks) v Surrey, the Oval, 2008. Debut Warwicks 2013. HS 30 v Durham, EFCSG, 2016. & v Middx, Merchant Taylors' S, Northwood, 2017. BB 6/32 (Yorks) v Scotland, Stamford Bridge 2007. HSSET 15* (Yorks) v Warwicks, Weetwood, 2012. BBSET 5/29 (Yorks) v Worcs, New Road, 2011. HST20 13* v Lancs, Walmley, 2015 (2nd). BBT20 4/14 v Northants, Scorers, Shirley, 2017 (2nd). Warwicks Staff.

Calvin Grant HARRISON (King's Coll, Taunton) b Durban, KwaZulu-Natal, S Africa, 29.4.98. RHB LB. Debut Somerset 2015; Worcs 2017. HS 26 (Somerset) v Derbys, Taunton S, 2016. BB 3/24 in the same match. HSSET 12* (Somerset) v Essex, Taunton Vale, 2015. BBSET 0/28 in the same match. BBT20 0/23 (Somerset) v Sussex, Taunton Vale, 2016 (1st).

K HARRISON Debut 2017. HSSET 0 v Yorks, Harrogate, 2017.

***Adam John HOSE** (Carisbrooke S, Newport) b Newport, Isle of Wight, 25.10.92. RHB RM. Debut MCCYC 2011; Glam 2012; Northants 2013; Hants & Kent 2014; Somerset 2015. F/C debut (Somerset) v Pakistanis, Taunton, 2016. Debut Warwicks 2017. HS 222 (Somerset) v Glos, Taunton Vale, 2015. BB 2/23 (MCC YC) v Worcs, High Wycombe, 2013. HSSET 141 (Somerset) v Surrey, Taunton Vale, 2015. BBSET 3/36 (MCC YC) v Durham, Shenley, 2014. HST20 82* (Hants) v Kent, The Ageas Bowl, 2014 (1st). BBT20 2/28 (MCC YC) v Kent, Radlett, 2013 (2nd).

Ateeq JAVID (Aston Manor Acad, Birmingham) b Birmingham 15.10.91. RHB OB. Debut 2008 aged 16 years and 316 days, F/C debut v Durham UCCE, the Racecourse, Durham, 2009. Eng U19 v Bangladesh 2010; to New Zealand (U19 World Cup) 2009/10 and v Sri Lanka 2010. HS 141 v Leics, Barnt Green 2009. BB 5/83 v MCCU, New Close Cricket Ground, Newport, Isle of Wight, 2012. HSSET 118* v Leics, Stratford-upon-Avon 2009. BBSET 3/21 v Yorks, York, 2015. HST20 64* v Glos, Olton v W Warwicks, 2013 (2nd). BBT20 3/22 v Leics, Edgbaston, 2015 (1st) & v Leics, Scorers, Shirley, 2017 (1st). HSKO 28* v Worcester, Worcester, 2010. Joins Leicestershire for the 2018 season.

Harry David JOHNSON (Kenilworth S) b Warwick, 14.12.98. RHB WK. Debut 2016. HS 12* v Somerset, EFCSG, 2017. HSSET 48 v Yorks, York, 2017. HST20 1* v Nortnants, Scorers, Shirley, 2017 (2nd).

KHAYAM KHAN (George Salter Acad, W Bromwich) b West Bromwich, 26.11.98. RHB RFM. Debut 2017. BB 0/54 v Leics, EFCSG, 2017.

Matthew James LAMB (N Bromsgrove HS) b Wolverhampton, Staffs 19.7.96. RHB RFM. Debut 2013. F/C debut v Somerset, Taunton, 2016. HS 205 v Middx, EFCSG, 2016. BB 4/30 v MCC YC, High Wycombe, 2017. HSSET 103* v Derbys, Bulls Head Gd, Coventry, 2017. BBSET 1/26 v MCC YC, Merchant Taylors', Northwood, 2017. HST20 54 v Durham, S Northumberland, 2017 (1st).

Kamau Sadiki LEVEROCK (Bermuda Institute of Higher Education; Priory SFC, Dorking, Surrey; Cardiff Met U) b Hamilton, Bermuda, 19.10.94. LHB RFM. Nephew of D, 32 ODIs (Bermuda) 2006/09. T20s (Bermuda) 16 (2011/12 to 2013/14). Debut Surrey & Sussex 2011; MCC YC 2014; Glam & MCCU 2015. F/C debut (Cardiff MCCU) v Glos, Bristol, 2015. Debut Somerset 2016; Warwicks 2017. HS 34 (Sussex) v Middx, Radlett, 2011. BB 2/32 Middx, Merchant Taylors' S, Northwood, 2017. HSSET 13 (Glam) v Glos, Diamond Ground, Cardiff, 2015. BBSET 3/45 (Somerset) v Essex, Halstead, 2016. BBT20 1/26 v Northants, Scorers, Shirley, 2017 (1st).

Alexander James MELLOR (Westwood Coll, Leek, Staffs; U of Staffs) b. Stoke-on-Trent, Staffs 22.7.91. LHB, WK. Debut Northants 2011; Somerset 2012; Notts 2013; Glam & Unc 2014; Warwicks 2015; Derbys 2016. F/C debut (Derbys) v Leics, Grace Road, 2016. HS 118* v Glos, Bulls Head Gd, Coventry, 2017. HSSET 47 (Glam) v Yorks, SWALEC Stadium, 2014. HST20 54* (Notts) v Durham, Trent Coll, 2013 (2nd).

MOHAMMED AHMED b Birmingham, 18.3.99. LHB SLA. Debut 2017. HST20 25* v Worcs, Worcester RGS, 2017 (2nd). BBT20 0/15 in the same match.

George David PANAYI (Shrewsbury S) b Enfield, Middx, 23.9.97. RHB RFM. Debut Worcs 2011; Warwicks 2013. Eng U19 v India, 2017. F/C debut (Oxford MCCU) v Notts, The Parks, 2014. Eng U19 v Sri Lanka, 2016. HS 37 v Glos, Bristol, 2016. BB 3/31 v Yorks, Harrogate, 2015 & v Derbys, EFCSG, 2017. HSSET 31* v Worcs, Olton, 2015. BBSET 4/76 v Yorks, York, 2017. HST20 14 v Somerset, Arundel, 2016 (SF). BBT20 1/28 v Worcs, Shirley, 2016 (2nd).

Brinder Singh PHAGURA (Q3 Academy, Birmingham; Bishop Vasey GS, Sutton Coldfield) b West Bromwich, W Midlands, 23.2.96. RHB RM. Debut Warwicks 2013; Northants & Unc 2016. HS 45 (Unc) v MCC YC, Saffron Walden, 2017. BB 4/17 v MCCYC, High Wycombe, 2014. HSSET 36* v Unc, Great Tew, 2015. BBSET 4/26 v Notts, Bulls Head, Coventry, 2015. HST20 18* (Unc) v Essex, Great Tew, 2017 (2nd). BBT20 3/23 (Unc) v Leics, Long Marston, 2016 (1st).

Edward John POLLOCK (Worcester RGS) b High Wycombe, Bucks, 10.7.95. LHB OB. Debut Unc 2014; Durham & Warwicks 2015. F/C debut (Durham MCCU) v Somerset, Taunton Vale, 2015. HS 107 (Durham) v Northants, Northampton, 2015. HSSET 106 (Durham) v Sussex, East Challow, Oxon, 2014. HST20 93* v Notts, Worksop Coll, 2017 (1st).

William Thomas Stuart PORTERFIELD (Strabane GS, Co Tyrone, N Ireland; Leeds Met U) b Londonderry, N Ireland, 6.9.84. LHB OB. Debut MCCYC & Durham, 2004; Derbys, Kent & Northants 2006; Glos 2007; Warwicks 2011. Cap 2014. F/C debut (Ireland) v Namibia, Dublin, 2006. HS 163* (MCCYC) v Northants, Radlett, 2006. HSSET 92 (MCCYC) v Kent, Beckenham, 2006. HST20 81 v Notts, Edgbaston, 2016 (1st). HSKO 0 (Glos) v Somerset, Taunton Vale, 2010. Released at the end of the 2017 season.

Joshua Edward POYSDEN (Cardinal Newman CS, Hove; Anglia Ruskin Met U) b Shoreham-by-Sea, Sussex, 8.8.91. LHB LB. Debut Sussex & Hants 2010; F/C debut (Cambridge MCCU) v Essex, Fenner's, 2011. Debut MCC Un 2012. Debut Unc A & Warwicks 2013. HS 42 v MCC YC, High Wycombe, 2017. BB 5/42 v Somerset, EFCSG, 2107. HSSET 14* v Worcs, Worcester

RGS, 2016. BBSET 6/47 v Unc, Bulls Head Ground, 2016. HST20 21 v Lancs, Bulls Head Gd, Coventry, 2017 (1st). BBT20 3/8 v Lancs, Rookwood, Sale, 2016 (1st). Warwicks Staff.

William Boyd RANKIN (Strabane GS; Harper Adams Un Coll, Newport, Salop) b Londondery, N Ireland, 5.7.84. LHB RFM. Test 1 (Eng) & 7 ODIs (& 37 ODIs for Ireland) 2006/07 to 2013/14. Debut Midddx 2004; Derbys 2007; Warwicks 2008 (& Cap 2013). F/C debut (Ireland) v UAE, Abu Dhabi, 2006/07. HS 68* v. Surrey, Walmley, 2012. BB 5/38 (Middx) v Essex, Billericay, 2004. HSSET 38* v Derbys, Repton S, 2016. BBSET 4/48 (Derbys) v Lancs, Middleton, 2006. HST20 0 v Lancs, Bulls Head Gd, Coventry, 2017 (1st). BBT20 3/9 v Leics, Edgbaston, 2015 (1st). Warwicks Staff.

Daniel Philip RICHARDSON (King Edward VI S, Stratford-upon-Avon; Stafford Coll; U of Staffs) b Stafford, 19.1.95. RHB RM. Debut (Northants) 2015; Warwicks 2017. HS 14 v Yorks, Harrogate, 2017. BB1/16 v Glos, Bulls Head, Gd, Coventry, 2017 & v Middx, Merchant Taylors' S, Northwood, 2017. HST20 33 v Worcs, Worcester RGS, 2017 (2nd). BBT20 v Worcs, Worcester RGS, 2017 (1st).

Ryan Nathan SIDEBOTTOM (Wanganui Park Sec Coll, Shepparton, Victoria, Aus) b Shepparton, Victoria. Aus, 14.8.89. RHB RFM. Debut Victoria 2012/13; F/C debut (Victoria) v Tasmania, Hobart, 2012/13; debuts Notts, Northants & Warwicks 2017. HS 1* (Northants) v Lancs, Liverpool, 2017. BB 8/33 v Northants, EFCSG, 2017. HST20 2* v Durham, S Northumberland, 2017 (2nd). BBT20 5/11 v Durham, S Northumberland, 2017 (1st).

James Hovannes SOOKIAS (Repton S) b Solihull, Warwicks, 7.5.99. RHB WK.Debut (Derbys) 2016; Warwicks 2017. HS 16* (Derbys) v MCC Un, Weetwood, 2016. BB 0/47 v Worcs, Worcester RGS, 2017. HSSET 21 (Derbys) v Yorks, Alvaston & Boulton, 2016.

Mitchell Thomas SPENCER (Maryhill HS & SFC, Stoke-on-Trent) b Stoke-on-Trent, 8.3.93. RHB RMF. Debut Northants 2015; Unc & Warwicks 2016. HS 21 v Northants, Rugby S, 2016. BB 6/27 (Northants) v Derbys, Swarkestone, 2015. HSSET 3 (Northants) v Lancs, Westhoughton, 2015. BBSET 4/65 v Leics, Bull`s Head Ground, 2016. HST20 7 (Northants) v Leics, Grace Road, 2015 (1st). BBT20 2/30 v Leics, Scorers, Shirley, 2017 (1st).

SUKHJIT "Sonny" SINGH (George Dixon International S; South & City Coll, Birmingham) b India, 3.5.96. LHB SLA. Debut 2014. F/C debut v Oxford MCCU, The Parks, 2017. HS 57 v Middx, EFCSG, 2016. BB6/87 v Middx, Merchant Taylors' S, Northwood, 2017. HSSET 21 v Unc, Great Tew, 2015. BBSET 3/21 v Notts, Scorers, Shirley, 2017. HST20 29 v v Durham, S Northumberland, 2017 (2nd). BBT20 3/5 v Worcs, Shirley, 2016 (1st).

Oliver Peter STONE (Thorpe St Andrew S, Norwich) b Norwich, Norfolk, 9.10.93. RHB RM. Debut Northants 2010; Warwicks 2017. Eng U19 v S Africa, 2012/13. F/C debut (Northants) v Yorks, Headingley, 2012. HS 117 (Northants) v Essex, Stowe S, 2013. BB 4/15 (Kent & Northants) v Warwicks, Canterbury, 2013. HSSET 43 (Northants) v Kent, Beckenham, 2013. BBSET 2/33 (Northants) v Kent, Beckenham, 2013. HST20 22 (Northants) v Warwicks, Finedon Dolben, 2016 (2nd). BBT20 4/10 (Northants) v Worcs, Milton Keynes, 2015 (1st).

Aaron Dean THOMASON (Barr Beacon S, Walsall, Staffs) b Birmingham, 26.6.97. RHB RFM. Brother of L J (Unc) to date. Debut 2013. List A debut v Middx, Lords, 2014. Eng U19 to Aus, 2014/15; v Aus 2015. HS 145 v Surrey, Guildford, 2015. BB 3/24 v Hants/Surrey, Coventry & N Warwicks, 2013. HSSET 57 v Derbys, Repton S, 2016. BBSET 5/62 v Notts, Edgbaston, 2014. HST20 53* v Notts, Trent Coll, 2015 (2nd). BBT20 2/19 v Lancs, Bulls Head Gd, Coventry, 2017 (1st). Warwicks Staff.

Alexander Thomas THOMSON (The King's S, Macclesfield, Cheshire; Denstone Coll, Uttoxeter; Cardiff Met) b Macclesfield, Cheshire, 30.10.93. RHB OB. Debut Leics 2013; Unc 2015. F/C debut (Cardiff MCCU) v Glam SWALEC, 2015. Debut MCCU 2016; Warwicks 2017. HS 101* v Worcs, Bulls Head Gd, 2017. BB 7/148 (MCCU) v Sussex, Hastings, 2017. HST20 39* v Notts, Worksop Coll, 2017 (2nd). BBT20 2/20 in the same match.

Grant Thomas THORNTON (The Woodlands S & Sports Acad, Coventry; Coventry U) b Coventry, Warwicks, 29.8.92. LHB RMF. Debut Leics 2015; Warwicks 2016. F/C debut v Somerset, Taunton, 2017. HS 71* v MCC YC, High Wycombe, 2017. BB 3/37 v Yorks, EFCSG, 2016. HSSET 31 v Yorks, York, 2017. BBSET 2/60 v Worcs, Scorers, Shirley, 2017. HST20 11 v. Lancs, Bulls Head Gd, Coventry (2017) (1st) BBT20 2/42 v Somerset, Arundel, 2016 (SF).

Ian Jonathan Leonard TROTT (Rondebosch Boys HS; Stellenbosch U) b Cape Town, Cape Province, S Africa, 22.4.81. RHB RM. Tests 49 (Eng) & 68 ODIs, 2009 to 2013/14. F/C debut (Boland) v Free State, Paarl, 2000/01; debut W Province 2001/02; Warwicks 2003 & Cap 2005; Otago 2005/06. HS 248 v Worcs Barnt Green 2003 (the only example of a double hundred on 2nd XI Championship debut); BB 3/39 v Yorks, Stamford Bridge, 2014. HSSET 70 v Yorks, Pudsey Congs, 2014. BBSET 1/32 v Sussex, Knowle & Dorridge, 2005. Warwicks Staff.

Andrew Robert Isaac UMEED (The HS of Glasgow) b Glasgow, 19.4.96. RHB LB. Debut 2013. F/C debut (Scotland) v Afghanistan, Stirling, 2015. HS 203 v Leics, EFCSG, 2017. BB 2/51 in the same match. HSSET 98 v Yorks, Knowle & Dorridge, 2016. BBSET 1/25 v Notts, Scorers, Shirley, 2017. HST20 38 v Northants, Finedon, Dolben, 2016 (2nd). Warwicks Staff.

Ian James WESTWOOD (Wheelers Lane Coll, Kings Heath; Solihull SFC) b Birmingham 13.2.82. LHB OB. Debut Warwicks 2003. F/C Debut v India A, Edgbaston, 2003; Cap 2008. HS 250* v Worcs, Barnt Green, 2003. BB 6/50 v Leics, Leicester, 2004. HSSET 82 v Worcs, Kenilworth Wardens, 2005. BBSET 5/44 Glam, Usk, 2006. HS T20 23 v Somerset, Taunton Vale, 2012 (1st). BB T20 2/19 v Glam, SWALEC, 2011 (1st). Retired at the end of the 2017 season.

Christopher Roger WOAKES (Barr Beacon Lang Coll) b Birmingham, 2.3.89. RHB RMF. Debut Warwicks 2005. F/C debut v West Indies A, Edgbaston, 2006; Warwicks Cap 2009. Temporary debut Notts 2015 (at the special request of ECB, to allow the player some meaningful practice before returning to England duty). Tests 19 (Eng) 2013 to date & 67 ODIs. HS 93* (Notts) v Worcs, Notts SG, 2015. BB 3/14 (Warwicks) v Surrey, Cheam, 2008. HSSET 58 (Warwicks) v Worcs, Hinckley, 2008. BBSET 3/36 (Warwicks) v MCCYC, High Wycombe, 2010. HST20 20 v Notts, Edgbaston, 2016 (1st). BBT20 0/18 in the same match. Warwicks Staff.

Christopher Julian Clement WRIGHT (Eggar's S, Alton, Hants; Anglia Poly U, Cambridge) b Chipping Norton, Oxon, 14.7.85. RHB RFM. Debut Hants, 2003; Middx 2004; Tamil Union 2005/06; MCCYC 2007; Essex 2008; Warwicks 2011 & Cap 2013. F/C debut (Cambridge MCCU) v Essex, Fenner's, 2004. HS 104* (Middx) v Glos, Radlett, 2007. BB 6/72 (Essex) v Lancs, Chelmsford, 2008. HSSET 41 (Middx) v Notts (Worksop Coll) 2005 & (Middx) v M Counties, Ealing, 2006. BBSET 3/24 (Middx) v M Counties, Ealing, 2004. BBT20 4/12 v Glos, Cheltenham, 2014 (1st). Warwicks Staff.

Robert Michael YATES (Warwick S) b Solihull, 19.9.99. LHB OB. Debut 2017. HS 102 v Notts, Notts SG, 2017. HST20 41* v Worcs, Worcester RGS, 2017 (1st).

PLEASE NOTE – EFCSG stands for Edgbaston Foundation Community Sports Ground and is the former Mitchell & Butler Sports Ground in Edgbaston. It is now the regular base for Warwickshire CCC 2nd XI home games.

WORCESTERSHIRE

PLAYING RECORDS 2017
Championship – P9 W3 L2 D3 Ab1 – third in the Northern group
2nd XI Trophy – P6 W4 L2 - third in the Northern group
2nd XI T20 Competition – P12 W4 L8 – ninth in the Northern group

2nd XI SUCCESSES
Championship – Winners – 1962, 1963, 1982
Trophy – Winners - 2004
2nd XI T20 Competition – Beaten Semi-Finalists in 2012

SECOND ELEVEN CHAMPIONSHIP AVERAGES

BATTING	M	I	NO	Runs	HS	Avge	100s	C/S
T C Fell	6	9	0	626	223	69.55	3	6
A Hepburn	8	13	2	556	98	50.54	-	4
A N Kervezee	5	8	0	395	140	49.37	1	2
G H Rhodes	4	7	1	296	77	49.33	-	5
B J Twohig	8	11	3	317	83	39.62	-	8
R A Whiteley	2	3	0	114	65	38.00	-	3
J J Dell	6	8	0	303	60	37.87	-	4
A G Milton	5	8	1	209	91	29.85	-	14/1
A O Wiffen	2	3	0	88	77	29.33	-	1
Z A Malik	6	9	1	216	63*	27.00	-	4
C A J Morris	4	4	1	80	37*	26.66	-	2
J M H Dodd	3	4	2	47	20*	23.50	-	6/1
D Y Pennington	2	3	0	57	49	19.00	-	-
P R Brown	6	6	2	60	30*	15.00	-	1
G L S Scrimshaw	3	4	3	14	10*	14.00	-	1
J A Haynes	3	4	0	52	21	13.00	-	2
O E Westbury	8	13	0	160	44	12.30	-	4

BOWLING	O	M	Runs	Wkt	Avge	BB
M B Wareing	15	1	57	3	19.00	3/48
A R Wilkinson	31	2	140	7	20.00	4/53
A Hepburn	170.4	30	595	28	21.25	5/43
C A J Morris	74	11	262	10	26.20	2/19
A W Finch	108.3	14	358	12	29.83	5/19
G H Rhodes	76	9	279	9	31.00	3/66
B J Twohig	196.3	18	698	22	31.72	5/87
Z A Malik	51	3	194	6	32.33	2/11
P R Brown	123	28	453	12	37.75	4/34
G L S Scrimshaw	50	8	245	6	40.83	4/63

Also bowled – A N Kervezee 20-3-92-1; D Y Pennington 16-3-61-2; J D Shantry 30-1-61-1; Z Ul-Hassan 23-4-72-2; O E Westbury 10-0-52-1; R A Whiteley 19-2-58-0.

Also batted – 6 matches – A W Finch 0* (1ct). 2 matches – Z Ul-Hassan 16 (1ct); A R Wilkinson 7* (1ct). 1 match – C M Dudley 35, 15*; N A Hammond 8; J D Shantry 61* (2ct); M B Wareing DNB.

SECOND ELEVEN TROPHY AVERAGES

BATTING	M	I	NO	Runs	HS	Avge	100s	C/S
O E Westbury	6	6	0	383	143	63.83	2	2
G H Rhodes	6	6	1	262	134*	52.40	1	-
A Hepburn	6	6	1	172	56	34.40	-	4
T C Fell	3	3	0	103	62	34.33	-	2
A N Kervezee	6	6	0	204	76	34.00	-	2
J J Dell	5	5	1	66	34*	16.50	-	2
Z A Malik	5	5	0	77	44	15.40	-	2
B J Twohig	6	6	3	46	15*	15.33	-	2

BOWLING	O	M	Runs	Wkt	Avge	BB
A Hepburn	47	3	233	11	21.18	4/56
Z A Malik	29.1	0	191	5	38.20	3/43
B J Twohig	44	0	242	6	40.33	2/56
P R Brown	39	2	218	5	43.60	2/28
G H Rhodes	42	0	264	5	52.80	3/54

Also bowled – M C Davis 4-0-23-0; B L D`Oliveira 9-0-563-1; A N Kervezee 19-0-87-2; D K H Mitchell 8-0-49-1; C A J Morris 16-0-85-2; J D Shantry 8-0-35-0; J C Tongue 9-1-24-2; Z Ul-Hassan 7-0-39-1.

Also batted – 5 matches - P R Brown 9, 0* (3ct). 4 matches - J M H Dodd 20* (4ct/2st). 2 matches – C A J Morris 0 (1ct); Z Ul-Hassan 6; R A Whiteley 90, 65. 1 match - M C Davis DNB; B L D`Oliveira 2; C M Dudley 2; T Kohler-Cadmore 121 (2ct); A G Milton 16 (1ct); D K H Mitchell 12 (1ct); J D Shantry7; J C Tongue 11*.

SECOND ELEVEN T20 AVERAGES

BATTING	M	I	NO	Runs	HS	Avge	100s	C/S
A O Wiffen	5	5	0	167	99	33.40	-	1
R A Whiteley	3	3	0	89	56	29.66	-	-
A Hepburn	10	10	1	261	53	29.00	-	4
Z A Malik	5	4	1	85	52*	28.33	-	1
G H Rhodes	4	3	1	53	46*	26.50	-	4
E G Barnard	3	3	1	47	32*	23.50	-	2
T C Fell	8	8	0	122	28	15.25	-	3
O E Westbury	9	8	1	94	22	13.42	-	1
B J Twohig	11	9	3	74	17	12.33	-	5
A N Kervezee	6	5	0	55	26	11.00	-	-
A G Milton	8	7	0	74	21	10.57	-	2/1
P R Brown	9	4	2	19	9	9.50	-	3
J D Shantry	6	5	2	26	10	8.66	-	2
C A J Morris	9	5	3	16	9	8.00	-	-

BOWLING	O	M	Runs	Wkt	Avge	BB
G L S Scrimshaw	14	1	68	10	6.80	5/12
M J Santner	8	0	29	4	7.25	2/11
G H Rhodes	10	0	64	5	12.80	3/38
A N Kervezee	15	0	92	5	18.40	2/19
P R Brown	26.1	0	184	9	20.44	3/30
E G Barnard	8	0	83	3	27.66	2/30
B J Twohig	37.1	0	277	10	27.70	3/20
C A J Morris	18	0	171	5	34.20	3/27
J D Shantry	17	0	138	4	34.50	1/8

Also bowled – B L D'Oliveira 6-0-41-1; A W Finch 10-0-78-1; S E Grant 2-0-12-0; A Hepburn 25-0-213-2; J Leach 3-0-32-0; Z A Malik 7-0-48-2; D K H Mitchell 5-0-29-1; D Y Pennington 3-0-16-2; J C Tongue 3-0-20-0; O E Westbury 2-0-13-0.

Also batted – 5 matches – J J Dell 5, 14 (2ct). 4 Matches - A W Finch DNB (1ct); G L S Scrimshaw 0*, 1*.
2 matches – J M Clarke 20, 13; O B Cox 0, 15 (4ct/2st); J M H Dodd 10 (1st); B L D'Oliveira 13, 49*; C M Dudley 3; S E Grant 3*; J Leach 22, 0* (1ct); D K H Mitchell 51, 23 (3ct); M J Santner 28, 32 (1ct). 1 match – J W Hastings 10; J A Haynes 1; D Y Pennington 6; J C Tongue 3; Z Ul-Hassan 13.

HOME MATCHES: SECOND ELEVEN CHAMPIONSHIP

v **Warwickshire** (Worcester RGS, Flagge Meadow) – 18-20 Apr – Worcs 347/8d (G H Rhodes 77, J J Dell 60; G T Thornton 3/66) & 196/2d (G H Rhodes 76*, A Hepburn 74*) lost to Warwicks 353/4d (A Javid 68, I J Westwood 52) & 291/7 (A R I Umeed 72, L Banks 66; G H Rhodes 3/66) by three wkts.
v **MCC Young Cricketers** (Barnt Green) – 10-12 May – MCC YC 235 (T F Smith 79, F J Hudson-Prentice 68; A Hepburn 5/77, A R Wilkinson 4/53) & 153 (A Hepburn 5/43 {and match figs of 10/120]) lost to Worcs 521/9d (T C Fell 223, A N Kervezee 94; S E Grant 3/64) by an inns & 133 runs.
v **Derbyshire** (War Memorial Gd, Amblecote) – 13-15 June – Worcs 223 (J J Dell 57, T C Fell 51; T P Milnes 4/38, M J J

Critchley 3/48) & 326/6 (A N Kervezee 140) drew with Derbys 390 (H R Hosein 105*, C A J Brodrick 76; B J Twohig 5/87).
v **Leicesterhire** (Worcester RGS, Flagge Meadow) – 4-6 July – Leics 318 (A M Ali 99, H J Swindells 60; B J Twohig 3/95) & 302/8d (A M Ali 80) lost to Worcs 295/8d (A Hepburn 98, B J Twohig 52; D Manthorpe 3/36) & 326/3 (T C Fell 101, A O Wiffen 77, A Hepburn 76*) by seven wkts.
v **Yorkshire** (Worcester RGS, Flagge Meadow) – 25-27 July - Worcs 283 (A G Milton 91; J A Brooks 3/47) & 177/9d (A Hepburn 56) drew with Yorks 197 (A Z Lees 50; A W Finch 5/19, A Hepburn 3/35) & 260/7 (A Z Lees 135; G L S Scrimshaw 4/63, B J Twohig 3/100).

HOME MATCHES: FRIENDLIES

v **Surrey** (Kidderminster) – 5-8 Sept – Surrey 385 (C McKerr 124, R R Jafri 54; A Hepburn 4/76) drew with Worcs 270/5 (R Tongue 70)

HOME MATCHES: SECOND ELEVEN TROPHY

v **Derbyshire** (Kidderminster) – 4 May – Worcs 383/6 (O E Westbury 143, T Kohler-Cadmore 121; H Qadri 3/73) beat Derbys 355/9 (H R Hosein 87, T A I Taylor 66; A Hepburn 4/63) by 28 runs.
v **MCC Young Cricketers** (Kidderminster) – 9 May – Worcs 327/6 (O E Westbury 100, T C Fell 62) beat MCC YC 284/9 (B J Curran 83, L A Jones 53*; Z A Malik 3/43, G H Rhodes 3/54) by 43 runs.

v **Durham** (New Road) – 15 May – Durham 227/4 (G J Harte 124*) beat Worcs 219 (A N Kervezee 60, O E Westbury 50; M H McKiernan 5/45) by eight runs.

HOME MATCHES : SECOND ELEVEN T20 COMPETITION

v **Leicesterhire** (New Road) – 3 July – Match 1 - Worcs 168/9 (D K H Mitchell 51) lost to Leics 169/4 (M L Pettini 81*) by six wkts.
v **Leicesterhire** (New Road) – 3 July – Match 2 – Leics 144/9 (E J H Eckersley 61; G H Rhodes 3/38) beat Worcs 106 (C F Parkinson 3/23) by 38 runs.
v **Yorkshire** (Worcester RGS, Flagge Meadow) – 24 July – Match 1 – Yorks 137/9 (G L S Grimshaw 5/12) beat Worcs 129/9 (J A Thompson 3/18) by eight runs.

v **Yorkshire** (Worcester RGS, Flagge Meadow) – 24 July – Match 2 – Yorks 145/7 lost to Worcs 146/6 by four wkts.
v **Warwickshire** (Worcester RGS, Flagge Meadow) – 3 Aug – Match 1 – Warwicks 116/8 (C A J Morris 3/27) lost to Worcs 122/3 by seven wkts.
v **Warwickshire** (Worcester RGS, Flagge Meadow) – 3 Aug – Match 2 – Warwicks 146/8 (G L S Grimshaw 3/28) lost to Worcs 150/5 (R A Whiteley 56; Sukhjit Singh 3/23) by five wkts.

E G Barnard	A W Finch	A G Milton	*R Tongue
P R Brown	S E Grant	D K H Mitchell	B J Twohig
J M Clarke	N A Hammond	C A J Morris	Z Ul-Hassan
O B Cox	J W Hastings	D Y Pennington	M B Wareing
M C Davis	J A Haynes	G H Rhodes	O W Westbury
J J Dell	A Hepburn	M J Santner	*R J Wheldon
J M H Dodd	A N Kervezee	G L S Scrimshaw	R A Whiteley
B L D'Oliveira	T Kohler-Cadmore	J D Shantry	A O Wiffen
C M Dudley	J Leach	*A C Simpson	A R Wilkinson
T C Fell	Z A Malik	J C Tongue	*A J Woods

WORCESTERSHIRE CRICKETERS

Edward George BARNARD (Meole Brace S, Shrewsbury; Shrewsbury S) b Shrewsbury, Salop, 20.11.95. RHB RM. Debut 2013. F/C debut v Hants, The Ageas Bowl, 2015. Eng U19 to S Africa, 2012/13; to UAE 2013/14 (Tri/Series); v S Africa 2014. HS 133 v Warwicks, Barnt Green, 2015. BB 6/31 v Notts, Notts SG, 2015. HSSET 58 v Lancs, Ombersley, 2014. BBSET 2/60 v Warwicks, Olton, 2015. HST20 32* v Warwicks, Worcester RGS, 2017 (2nd). BBT20 3/17 v Northants, Milton Keynes, 2015 (2nd). Worcs staff.

Patrick Rhys BROWN (Bourne GS, Lincs) b Peterborough, Cambs, 23.8.98. RHB RM. Debut 2015. F/C debut v Sussex, New Road, 2017. HS 34 v Warwicks, Bulls Head Gd, Coventry, 2017. BB 4/34 v Northants, Holcot, 2017. HSSET 9 v Durham, New Road, 2017. BBSET 2/28 v Notts, Oakham S, 2017. HST20 9 v MCC YC, Merchant Taylors' S, Northwood, 2017 (1st). BBT20 3/30 v Northants, Northampton, 2017 (1st).

Joseph Michael CLARKE (Llanfyllin HS, Powys, Wales) b Shrewsbury, Salop, 26.5.96. RHB WK. Debut 2013. F/C debut v Hants, The Ageas Bowl, 2015. Eng U19 to UAE 2013/14 (Tri/Series); v S Africa, 2014. HS 222 v MCC YC, Kidderminster, 2014. HSSET 44v Lancs, Ombersley, 2014. HST20 56 v Yorks, Barnt Green 2015 (2nd). Worcs staff.

Oliver Benjamin COX (Bromsgrove S) b Wordsley, Staffs, 2.2.92. RHB WK. Debut 2009, F/C debut v Somerset, New Road, 2009. HS 83 v Northants, Kidderminster, 2011. HSSET 41 v Yorks, Pudsey Congs, 2012. HST20 65* v Warwicks, Balsall Common, 2012 (2nd). HSKO 21 v Warwicks, Worcester, 2010. Worcs Staff.

Matthew Cullis DAVIS (Blessed Edward Old Corne CC, Worcester; Worcester SFC) b Worcester, 19.4.01. RHB RM. Debut 2017, aged 16 yrs & 15 days. BB 1/42 v Hants, Ageas Bowl Nursery, 2017. BBSET 0/23 v Derbys, Kidderminster, 2017.

Joshua Jamie DELL (Cheltenham Coll) b Tenbury Wells, 26.9.97. RHB RMF. Debut 2015. Eng U19 v Sri Lanka, 2016. HS 95* v Glam, Abergavenny, 2017. HSSET 34* v Derbys, Kidderminster, 2017. HST20 41 v Leics, Kibworth, 2016 (2nd).

Joseph Michael Harry DODD (Studley HS, Warwicks; NE Worcs Coll, Redditch) b Redditch, 4.10.92. RHB WK. Debut 2012. HS 39 v Derbys, Kidderminster, 2013. HSSET 20* v Durham, New Road, 2017. HST20 10 v MCC YC, Merchant Taylors' S, Northwood, 2017 (1st).

Brett Louis D'OLIVEIRA (Worcester SFC) b Worcester 28.2.92. RHB LB. Brother of M.D (MCCYC 2006); Son of D.B (Worcs 1982/1995); Grandson of B.L (Worcs 1964/1980 and 44 Tests and 4 ODIs for England). Debut 2010. Cap 2012. F/C debut v Warwicks, Edgbaston, 2012. HS 135 v Warwicks, Barnt Green, 2015. BB 7/54 v Derbys, Derby, 2012. HSSET 122 v Unc, Kidderminster, 2015. BBSET 3/32 v Northants, Northampton, 2011. HST20 100* v Warwicks, Kidderminster, 2015 (1st). BBT20 2/24 v Glam, Kidderminster, 2012 (2nd). Worcs Staff.

Connor M DUDLEY (Pulteney GS, Adelaide, S Australia) b Sydney NSW, Aus, 1.12.98. RHB RM. Debuts Worcs 2016; Lancs 2017. HS 35 v Lancs, Great Crosby, 2017. HSSET 2 v Lancs, Parkgate, Neston, 2017. HST20 18 (Lancs) v Warwicks, Bulls Head Gd, 2017 (1st).

Thomas 'Tom' Charles FELL (Oakham S; Oxford Brookes U) b Hillingdon, Middx, 17.10.93. RHB OB WK. Debut 2010. F/C debut v Oxford MCCU, the Parks, 2013. Cap 2013. HS 223 v MCC YC,

Barnt Green, 2017. BB 0/3 v Lancs, Aigburth, 2013. HSSET 77 v Yorks, New Road, 2011.HST20 46 v Warwicks, West Bromwich, 2014 (1st). BBT20 1/9 v Northants, New Road, 2016 (1st). Worcs Staff.

Adam William FINCH (Kingswinford S, Dudley, W Midlands; Oldswinford Hospital SFC, Stourbridge, W Midlands) b Wordsley, Stourbridge, 28.5.00. RHB RMF. Debut 2016. Eng U19 v Ind 2017; to SA 2017/18. HS 4 v Somerset, Taunton Vale, 2017. BB 5/19 v Yorks, Worcester RGS, 2017. HSSET 1 v Warwicks, Worcester RGS, 2016. HST20 0* v Warwicks, Shirley, 2016 (1st). BBT20 1/35 v Warwicks, Worcester RGS, 2017 (1st).

Samuel Edward GRANT (Brighton Coll; Loughborough U) b Shoreham-by-Sea, Sussex, 30.8.95. LHB LMF. Debut Sussex 2013; F/C debut (Loughborough MCCU) v Kent, Canterbury, 2014. Debuts Durham & Somerset 2016; Warwicks & Worcs 2017. HS 76 (Warwicks) v MCC YC, High Wycombe, 2017. HSSET 15* (Sussex) v Surrey, Blackstone, 2013. BBSET 2/18 (Sussex) v Somerset, Arundel, 2014. HST20 29* (Somerset) v Lancs, Ageas Bowl Nursery, 2016 (1st). BBT20 3/4 (Somerset) v Warwicks, Arundel, 2016 (SF).

Nicholas Alexander HAMMOND (King's S, Worcester) b Worcester, 3.2.98. RHB RM. Debut 2015. Warwicks 2017. HS 67 v Lancs, Southport, 2015. HSSET 21 v Notts, New Road, 2016. HST20 56* (Warwicks) v Northants, Scorers, Shirley, 2017 (1st).

John Wayne HASTINGS (St Dominic's Cath Coll, Penrith, Sydney, Aus; Aus Coll of PE, Sydney) b Penrith, Sydney, 4.11.85. RHB RFM. Debut & F/C debut v Indians, St Kilda CC, Melbourne, Aus, 2007/08; debut Durham 2014; Worcs 2017. Tests (Aus) 1 & 29 ODIs (2010/11 to 2017). HST20 10 v Warwicks, Worcester RGS, 2017 (2nd). Worcs Staff.

Jack Alexander HAYNES (Malvern Coll) b Worcester, 30.1.01. RHB OB. Brother of J L (Worcs 2015/16) and son of Gavin (Worcs 1991/99). Debut 2016, aged 15 yrs & 183 days. HS 21 v Yorks, Worcester RGS, 2017. HSSET 2* v Notts, New Road, 2016. HST20 1 v Yorks, Worcester RGS, 2017 (1st).

Alex HEPBURN (Aquinas Coll, Perth, W Aus) b Subiaco, W Australia, 21.12.95. RHB RM. Debut 2013. List A debut v Leics, New Road, 2015. HS 149 v Northants, Kidderminster, 2016. BB 5/43 (& match figs of 10/120) v MCC YC, Barnt Green, 2017. HSSET 119* v Unc, Kidderminster, 2015. BBSET 4/56 v Lancs, Parkgate, Neston, 2017. HST20 53 v Durham, Burnopfield CC, 2017 (1st). BBT20 4/14 v Durham, Chester-le-Street CC, (2nd). Worcs Staff.

Alexei Nicolaas KERVEZEE (Duneside HS, Namibia; Grenoobi HS, SA; Segbroek C, Holland) b Walvis Bay, Namibia, 11.9.89. RHB OB. ODIs (Netherlands) 39 (2006 to 2011/12). Debut Netherlands 2005; F/C debut (Netherlands) v Scotland, Utrecht, 2005; debut Worcs 2007; debut Dhaka Gladiators 2011/12. HS 156 v Derbys, Derby, 2012. BB 7/61 v Notts, Worcester RGS, 2016. HSSET 102 v Warwicks, Olton, 2015. BBSET 4/57 v Durham, Kidderminster, 2015. HST20 65 v Warwicks, Kidderminster, 2015 (2nd). BBT20 2/19 v MCC YC, Merchant Taylors' S, Northwood, 2017 (2nd). Worcs Staff.

Tom KOHLER-CADMORE (Malvern C) b Chatham, Kent, 19.8.94. RHB OB. Debut 2010. Brother of B (Worcs 2016). F/C debut v Hants, the Ageas Bowl, 2014. HS 153 v Yorks, Barnt Green, 2015. BB 1/12 v MCCU, Kidderminster, 2012. HSSET 121 v

Derbys, Kidderminster, 2017. HST20 110* v Glam, Kidderminster, 2014 (2nd). Worcs staff.

Joseph LEACH (Shrewsbury S; U of Leeds) b Stafford 30.10.90. RHB RM. Debut 2008. F/C debut (Leeds/Bradford MCCU) v Surrey, the Oval, 2012. Worcs Cap 2012. HS 162 v Warwick, Ombersley, 2013 BB 4/46 v MCCYC. High Wycombe, 2013. HSSET 66 v Glam, Kidderminster, 2010. BBSET 4/19 v Warwicks, Worcester RGS, 2011. HST20 58* v Warwicks, West Bromwich, 2014 (1st). BBT20 3/23 v Somerset, Ombersley, 2012 (1st). HSKO 31 v Warwicks, Worcester, 2010. BBKO 0/18 in the same match. Worcs Staff.

Zen-Ul-Abideen MALIK (Malvern Coll) b Stoke-on-Trent, Staffs, 9.4.98. RHB LB. Debut 2015. Eng U19 v Sri Lanka, 2016 HS 112 v Warwicks, Barnt Green, 2016. BB 4/55 v Glam, Abergavenny, 2017. HSSET 44 v Lancs, Parkgate, Neston, 2017. BBSET 3/43 v MCC YC, Kidderminster, 2017. HST20 52* v MCC YC, Merchant Taylors' S, Northwood, 2017 (2nd). BBT20 2/18 v Warwicks, Worcester RGS, 2017 (1st).

Alexander Geoffrey MILTON (Malvern C; Cardiff U) b Redhill, Surrey, 19.5.96. RHB WK. Debut Worcs 2012; MCCYC 2014; Glam 2015. F/C debut (Cardiff MCCU) v Hants, Ageas Bowl, 2016. HS 103* (MCCYC) v Middx, Radlett, 2014. HSSET 50* v Warwicks, Worcester RGS, 2016. HST20 71 (Glam) v MCCYC, Shenley, 2015 (2nd).

Darryl Keith Henry MITCHELL (Prince Henry's HS, Evesham, University Coll, Worcester) b Badsey, Nr Evesham, 25.11. 83. RHB RM. Debut 2002. F/C debut v Loughborough MCCU, Kidderminster, 2005. HS181 v Warwicks, Ombersley, 2005. BB 3/42 v Glam, Panteg, 2005. HSSET 141 v Glam, Old Hill, 2006. BBSET 5/21 v Glam, Neath, 2007. HST20 68 v Glam, 2014 (1st). BBT20 1/18 v Warwicks, Worcester RGS, 2017 (2nd). Worcs Staff.

Charles Andrew John MORRIS (King's Coll, Taunton; Oxford Brookes U) b Hereford, 6.7.92. RHB RMF. Debut Kent, MCC Un & Worcs 2012. F/C debut (Oxford MCCU) v Glam, The Parks, 2012. HS 44* v Warwicks, Bulls Head Gd, Coventry, 2017. BB 5/27 (Kent) v MCCYC, Shenley, 2012. HSSET 30* v Lancs, Middlewich, 2013. BBSET 5/38 v Unc, East Challow, 2016. HST20 10 v Durham, Amblecote, 2016 (1st). BBT20 3/27 v Warwicks, Worcester RGS, 2017 (1st). Worcs staff.

Dillon Young PENNINGTON (Wrekin Coll) b Shrewsbury, Salop, 26.2.99. RHB RMF. Debut 2017. Eng U19 to SA 2017/18. HS 49 v Yorks, Worcester RGS, 2017. BB 1/8 v Notts, Notts SG, 2017. HST20 6 v Yorks, Worcester RGS, 2017 (1st). BBT20 2/16 in the same match.

George Harry RHODES (The Chase HS & SFC, Malvern) b Birmingham, 26.10.93. RHB OB. Son of S J (Yorks, Worcs & Eng, 1984 to 2004) and grandson of W E (Notts 1961 to 1964). Debut 2012. F/C debut v Northants, Northampton, 2016. HS 137 v Glos, Cheltenham Coll, 2016. BB 4/55 v Glos, Cheltenham Coll, 2017. HSSET 134* v Notts, Oakham S, 2017. BBSET 3/54 v MCC YC, Kidderminster, 2017. HST20 61* v Warwicks, Shirley, 2016 (2nd). BBT20 4/19 v Yorks, Marske, 2016 (1st). Worcs staff.

Mitchell Josef SANTNER b Hamilton, Waikato, N Zealand, 5.2.92. LHB SLA. Debut & F/C debut N Districts v Otago, Dunedin, 2011/12; debut Worcs 2016. Tests (NZ) 15 & 42 ODIs, 2015/16 to date. HST20 32 v Warwicks, Worcester RGS, 2017 (1st). BBT20 2/11 v Leics, New Road, 2017 (2nd). Worcs Staff.

George Louis Sheridan SCRIMSHAW (John Taylor HS, Burton-on-Trent) b Burton-on-Trent, Staffs, 10.2.98. RHB RMF. Debut 2015. List A (T20) debut v Northants, New Road, 2017. HS 13 v Lancs, Worcester RGS, 2016. BB 4/46 v Hants, Ageas Bowl (Nursery), 2016. HSSET 24 v Lancs, Worcester RGS, 2016. BBSET 1/27 v Notts, New Road, 2016. HST20 15 v Warwicks, Shirley, 2016 (1st). BBT20 5/12 v Yorks, Worcester RGS, 2017 (1st). Worcs Staff.

Jack David SHANTRY (Priory S; Shrewsbury SFC; Manchester U) b Shrewsbury, Salop, 29.1.88. LHB LM. Brother of A.J. (Minor Counties, Northants, Warwicks, Glam 2001 to 2102), son of B.K. (Gloucs 1978/79). Debut 2008, F/C debut v Notts, New Road, 2009. HS 61* v Northants, Holcot, 2017. BB 7/34 v Leics, Himley 2008.

HSSET 56* (Minor Counties) v Notts, Welbeck Colliery 2008. BBSET 4/39 v Glos, Malvern College 2008. HST20 10 v Durham, Burnopfield, 2017 (2nd). BBT20 2/18 v Warwicks, Ombersley, 2011 (1st). Worcs staff.

* Alexander Charles SIMPSON (Sedbergh S) b Darlington Co Durham, 6.2.98. RHB RM. Debut Durham 2014; Worcs 2017. HS 39 (Durham) v Sussex, Fulking, 2014. BB 1/69 v Surrey, Kidderminster, 2017.

Joshua Charles TONGUE (The King's S,Worcester; Worcester SFC) b Redditch, 15.11.97. RHB RM. (Brother of R B below) Debut 2015. Eng U19 v Sri Lanka, 2016; v Ind 2017. F/C debut v Oxford MCCU, The Parks, 2016. HS 50* v Sussex, Kidderminster, 2016. BB 6/27 v Hants, Kidderminster, 2015. HSSET 11* v Notts, Oakham S, 2017. BBSET 2/24 v Notts, Oakham S, 2017. HST20 10* v Yorks , Marske, 2016. (1st). BBT20 1/13 v Northants, Milton Keynes, 2015 (2nd). Worcs Staff.

*Ryan Benjamin TONGUE (Nunnery Wood HS, Worcester; Worcester SFC) b Redditch, 22.7.97. Brother of J C (above). LHB OB. Debut 2017. HS 70 v Surrey, Kidderminster, 2017.

Benjamin Jake TWOHIG (Malvern Coll) b Dewsbury, Yorks, 13.4.,98. RHB SLA. Debut 2014. Eng U19 v Sri Lanka, 2016. HS 99 v Leics, Oakham S, 2016 .BB 6/74 v Lancs, Southport, 2015. HSSET 20 v Lancs, Old Trafford, 2015. BBSET 2/56 v Lancs, Parkgate, Neston, 2017. HST20 28 v Warwicks, Shirley, 2016 (2nd). BBT20 3/12 v Yorks, Marske, 2016 (2nd). Worcs Staff.

Zain UL-HASSAN (Pedmore Tech Coll, Stourbridge) b Islamabad, Pakistan, 28.10.00. LHB RM. Debut 2017. HS 28 v Hants, Ageas Bowl Nursery, 2017. BB 3/78 in the same match. HSSET 6 v Durham, New Road, 2017. BBSET 1/26 v MCC YC, Kidderminster, 2017. HST20 13 v Durham, Burnopfield, 2017 (2nd).

Matthew Brian WAREING (Manningtree HS; Colchester SFC) b Colchester, 17.1.94. LHB LMF. Debut Essex & Leics 2015; Unc 2016; Worcs & MCC YC 2017. HS 8 (Essex) v Kent, Maidstone, 2015 & (Unc) v MCC YC, Saffron Walden, 2017. BB 3/48 v Lancs, Great Crosby, 2017. HSSET 7* (Unc) v Glam, Newbury, 2017. BBSET 3/55 (Unc) v Hants, Ageas Bowl Nursery, 2017. HST20 2* (Leics) v Unc, Long Marston, 2016 (1st). BBT20 2/35 (Leics) v Unc, Long Marston, 2016 (2nd).

Oliver Edward WESTBURY (Ellowes Hall Sports Coll, Dudley; Shrewsbury S) b Dudley, W Midlands, 2.7.97. RHB OB. Debut 2015. Eng U19 v Sri Lanka, 2016. HS 151 v Glos, Cheltenham Coll, 2016. BB 1/24 v Leics, Worcester RGS, 2017. HSSET 143 v Derbys, Kidderminster, 2017. HST20 22 v Northants, Northampton, 2017 (2nd). BBT20 0/13 v Yorks, Worcester RGS, 2017 (1st). Worcs staff.

*Ryan James WHELDON (Kidderminster Coll) b Shrewsbury, Salop, 10.5.00. RHB RMF. Debut 2017. BB 0/12 v Glam, Abergavenny, 2017.

Ross Andrew WHITELEY (Repton S) b Sheffield, Yorks 13.9.88. LHB LM. Brother of A.J. (Derbys 2003-05). Debut Derbys 2006, F/C debut, (Derbys) v Leics, Grace Road, 2008. Debut Worcs & Cap 2013. HS 82 (Derbys) v Lancs, Belper, 2013. BB 5/23 (Derbys) v Leics, Ashby-de-la-Zouch, 2011. HSSET 135 v Notts, Trent Coll, 2015. BBSET 6/74 (Derbys) v Yorks, Denby 2008. HST20 65* (Derbys) v Lancs, Derby, 2011 (1st). BBT20 1/19 (Derbys) v Notts, Long Eaton, 2011 (1st). HSKO 0 (Derbys) v Sussex, Horsham, 2010. BBKO 0/15 (Derbys) v Lancs, Glossop, 2010. Worcs Staff.

Adam Oldsworth WIFFEN (Maritzburg Coll, Pietermaritzburg, S Africa; Pershore HS) b Johannesburg, Gauteng, S Africa, 12.3.98. Debut Notts & Worcs 2017. HS 77 v Lancs, Worcester RGS, 2017. HST20 99 v Northants, Northampton, 2017 (2nd).

Alex Ross WILKINSON (Bromsgrove S) b Birmingham, 4.9.96. LHB LMF. Debut 2016. HS 21 v Durham, Amblecote, 2016. BB 4/53 v MCC YC, Barnt Green, 2017. HSSET 3* v Unc, East Challow, 2016. HST20 5 v Warwicks, Shirley, 2016 (1st). BBT20 1/32 v Durham, Amblecote, 2016 (2nd).

* Alexander James WOODS (The Piggott S, Wargrave, Berks) b Reading, Berks, 22.1.92. RHB RM. Debut 2017. F/C debut (Oxford MCCU) v Surrey, The Parks, 2017.

YORKSHIRE

2nd XI TROPHY WINNERS 2017

PLAYING RECORDS 2017
Championship – P9 W2 L0 D6 Ab1 – fourth in the Northern group
2nd XI Trophy – P8 W5 L0 NR1 Ab2 - second in the Northern group & competition winners
2nd XI T20 Competition – P13 W7 L3 Ab3 - Winners of the Northern group & beaten semi-finalists

2nd XI SUCCESSES
2nd XI Champions – 1977, 1984, 1991, 2003.
(And one Championship shared with Kent in 1987)
2nd XI Trophy – Winners – 1988, 1994, 2009, 2017.
2nd XI T20 – best – northern group winners & beaten semi-finalists 2017.

SECOND ELEVEN CHAMPIONSHIP AVERAGES

BATTING	M	I	NO	Runs	HS	Avge	100s	C/S
J A Leaning	2	3	2	192	112*	192.00	1	-
A Z Lees	4	6	0	610	202	101.66	3	4
T Kohler-Cadmore	2	3	0	252	230	84.00	1	1
H C Brook	3	4	0	332	161	83.00	2	3
J Shaw	4	5	1	219	100*	54.75	1	-
W M H Rhodes	7	11	0	551	147	50.09	1	2
J A Tattersall	8	14	2	501	117	41.75	2	5
M J Waite	4	6	1	201	85	40.20	-	1
E Callis	3	5	2	120	39*	40.00	-	2
A J Hodd	5	7	1	237	93	39.50	-	12/3
J A Thompson	6	7	0	226	127	32.28	1	4
J C Wainman	7	7	1	162	56*	27.00	-	6
R Gibson	5	6	1	114	71	22.80	-	1
J A Brooks	5	5	2	53	38	17.66	-	4

BOWLING	O	M	Runs	Wkt	Avge	BB
B O Coad	26	5	51	4	12.75	2/21
J A Thompson	32	11	92	6	15.33	2/9
R J Sidebottom	61	24	119	7	17.00	2/17
W M H Rhodes	63.1	12	212	10	21.20	4/23
M D Fisher	67	23	158	7	22.57	4/43
K Carver	150	43	432	16	27.00	6/53
J D Warner	53	10	192	7	27.42	2/25
J E G Logan	75.4	12	292	10	29.20	4/107
J C Wainman	146.5	30	596	18	33.11	5/79
J A Brooks	114	19	391	11	35.54	4/52
A Drury	29	6	147	4	36.75	3/74
J Shaw	89.2	18	335	9	37.22	3/37
J W Shutt	67	14	193	4	48.25	2/67

Also batted – 5 matches – K Carver 2*, 1*, 0, 2 (2ct). 3 matches – E Barnes 9, 27*; M D Fisher 1, 38 (2ct); J E G Logan DNB (3ct); J Read 15, 14 (13ct/1st); J W Shutt DNB; R J Sidebottom 0*; J D Warner 6*, 4 (2ct). 2 matches – B D Birkhead 8, 9* (9ct/1st). 1 match – B L Ainsley 9, 0; Azeem Rafiq 59 (1ct); G S Ballance 69 (1ct); B O Coad 6; A Drury 0; S A Patterson 13, 45*; L E Plunkett 24, 7 (1ct).

Also bowled – Azeem Rafiq 25-6-78-1; E Barnes 40-4-204-2; H C Brook 2-1-11-0; R Gibson 4.5-1-15-1; A J Hodd 1-0-4-0; T Kohler-Cadmore 1-0-1-0; J A Leaning 10-2-33-1; A Z Lees 1-0-1-0; S A Patterson 27-5-86-1; L E Plunkett 20-5-58-2; J A Tattersall 20-6-59-1; M J Waite 52-8-176-2.

SECOND ELEVEN TROPHY AVERAGES

BATTING	M	I	NO	Runs	HS	Avge	100s	C/S
H C Brook	3	3	1	217	112	108.50	1	1
R Gibson	5	5	2	237	76*	79.00	-	1
J A Leaning	3	3	1	115	77*	57.50	-	2
J A Tattersall	5	5	0	195	98	39.00	-	2
W M H Rhodes	6	4	1	54	50*	18.00	-	2

BOWLING	O	M	Runs	Wkt	Avge	BB
J W Shutt	3.3	0	19	4	4.75	4/19
D J Willey	6.3	1	34	3	11.33	3/34
R Gibson	15	0	80	5	16.00	3/35
J Shaw	18	2	91	5	18.20	3/24
M D Fisher	19	2	107	5	21.40	4/67
J E G Logan	12	1	68	3	22.66	3/53
K Carver	35	2	211	9	23.44	3/17
J C Wainman	25.1	1	143	5	28.60	2/45

Also batted – 5 matches – K Carver 2* (1ct); J C Wainman 16*, 14* (3ct). 4 matches – J Shaw 1*, 14*, 2* (1ct). 3 matches – M D Fisher 22, 2; A J Hodd 22, 8 (4ct). 2 matches – Azeem Rafiq 20, 42; J A Brooks DNB (1ct); E Callis 55, 17 (2ct); A Z Lees 27, 21; J E G Logan DNB; J Read DNB (2ct/2st); J A Thompson 11, 0 (4ct); M J Waite 70, 51 (1ct). 1 match – J M Bairstow 60; B D Birkhead 24; A Lyth 4 (2ct); L E Plunkett 11; J W Shutt DNB; J D Warner DNB; D J Willey 54 (1ct).ain 48; A Z Lees 119*; A MacQueen 0; J Shaw 18; J W Shutt DNB.

Also bowled – Azeem Rafiq 7-1-36-1; J A Brooks 13-0-68-1; J A Leaning 4-0-14-0; L E Plunkett 8-0-38-2; W M H Rhodes 15-0-95-2; J A Thompson 12-0-71-2; M J Waite 11-0-75-0; J D Warner 4-0-12-0.

BATTING	M	I	NO	Runs	HS	Avge	100s	C/S
J A Leaning	3	3	2	167	85*	167.00	-	1
K Carver	10	3	2	53	41*	53.00	-	-
A Z Lees	5	5	1	208	116*	52.00	-	4
R Gibson	3	3	0	147	103	49.00	1	-
W M H Rhodes	8	7	2	130	54*	26.00	-	3
Bilal Anjum	4	4	0	90	41	22.50	-	1
J A Tattersall	8	8	2	123	38*	20.50	-	4
B D Birkhead	8	6	2	67	37*	16.75	-	-
M J Waite	8	7	0	112	32	16.00	-	3
J A Thompson	10	7	1	88	36	14.66	-	4
J C Wainman	9	5	1	58	45	14.50	-	3
J W Shutt	6	3	2	10	9*	10.00	-	-

BOWLING	O	M	Runs	Wkt	Avge	BB
Azeem Rafiq	6.1	0	28	5	5.60	4/5
J W Shutt	15	0	85	6	14.16	4/12
E Barnes	15	0	107	7	15.28	2/3
M D Fisher	24	0	199	11	18.09	3/46
J C Wainman	22.3	0	208	11	18.90	4/21
J A Thompson	13	0	122	4	30.50	3/18
K Carver	33	0	233	7	33.28	2/26
W M H Rhodes	18	0	168	4	42.00	1/17

Also bowled – J A Brooks 6-0-36-1; R Gibson 2-0-19-0; S A Patterson 3-0-24-0; M J Waite 5-0-41-2; J D Warner 5-0-43-1.

Also batted – 7 matches – M D Fisher 7*, 1 (4ct). 6 matches – E Barnes 3, 2* 0 (2ct). 3 matches – J D Warner 6 (3ct). 2 matches – Azeem Rafiq 7 (1ct); J A Brooks 0; A J Hodd 13*, 11; T Kohler-Cadmore 94, 28 (1ct). 1 match – E Callis 3; G C H Hill DNB (1ct); S A Patterson DNB; J Read DNB (1ct).

HOME MATCHES: SECOND ELEVEN CHAMPIONSHIP

v Warwickshire (Harrogate) – 9-11 May - Warwicks 294 (I J Westwood 142; J A Brooks 4/52) & 232 (L Banks 72; J Shaw 3/37) lost to Yorks 388 (A Z Lees 125, W M H Rhodes 76; S Singh 4/93, H J H Brookes 3/69, C G Harrison 3/73) & 141/3 by seven wkts.
v Lancashire (Scarborough) – 13-15 June - Lancs 350 (R P Jones 93, B D Guest 67, L A Procter 62; J C Wainman 5/79) & 212/6 (L A Procter 65*, D J Lamb 58) drew with Yorks 585/8d (H C Brook 161, J A Thompson 127, J Shaw 89, J C Wainman 56*; A M Lilley 3/105)

v Derbyshire (York) – 20-22 June - Yorks 302 (J A Leaning 76*, Azeem Rafiq 59; S Connors 3/59) & 426/3d (T Kohler-Cadmore 230, J A Leaning 112*) drew with Derbys 383 (M A Jones 100, G T G Cork 75; K Carver 4/76)
v Nottinghamshire (Stamford Bridge CC) – 27-29 June - Match abandoned without a ball bowled
v Northamptonshire (York) – 11-13 July - Yorks 402/5d (J A Tattersall 109, A Z Lees 97, A J Hodd 51*) & 30/0d drew with Northants 71/2 d & 321/9 (H R D Adair 80, A Kapil 66; M D Fisher 4/43)

HOME MATCHES: FRIENDLIES

v Gloucestershire (Headingley) – 18-20 Apr – Yorks 332 (J A Tattersall 72, W M H Rhodes 71, J A Leaning 64; M D Taylor 3/32) & 225/6d (R Gibson 62*, E Callis 54) lost to Glos 275/5d (G T Hankins 124, I A Cockbain 75) & 286/6 (G T Hankins 88, B S Gilmour 80, J R Bracey 77) by four wkts.

v Derbyshire (Harrogate) – 29-31 Aug – Yorks 390/6d (A Z Lees 145*, T Kohler-Cadmore 68, L E Plunkett 58; W S Davis 3/75) & 85/2 drew with Derbys 360 (J M Kettleborough 180)
v Durham (Scarborough) – 19-21 Sept – Durham 364/7d (S W Poynter 159*, J Coughlin 61) & 95/4 drew with Yorks 310/5d (T Kohler-Cadmore 88, M J Waite 64)

HOME MATCHES: SECOND ELEVEN TROPHY

v Lancashire (Scarborough) – 25 Apr – Yorks 259/8 (M J Waite 70; S C Kerrigan 3/22) v Lancs 7/0. No result.
v Derbyshire (York) – 27 Apr – Yorks 295 (J M Bairstow 60, D J Willey 54, M J Waite 51; M J J Critchley 4/26, T A I Taylor 3/75) beat Derbys 184 (K Carver 3/17, D J Willey 3/34) by 111 runs.
v Warwickshire (Harrogate) – 8 May – Yorks 362/7 (J A Tattersall 98, R Gibson 64, H C Brook 58, E Callis 55; G D Panayi 4/76) beat Warwicks 270 (A R I Umeed 51; K Carver 3/86) by 92 runs.

v Somerset (The County Ground, Taunton) – 2 June - Somerset 328 (J Allenby 101, T D Rouse 64, E J Byrom 51; M D Fisher 4/67) lost to Yorks 76/1. No result. Yorks won by virtue of a better record in the qualifying groups.
This was the Semi-Final of the One-Day Trophy.
v Middlesex (Headingley) – 8 June – Yorks 265/5 (H C Brook 112, R Gibson 58, W M H Rhodes 50*) beat Middx 179 (N R D Compton 57; J W Shutt 4/19) by 99 runs (DLS) *This was the Final of the One-Day Trophy.*

HOME MATCHES: SECOND ELEVEN T20 COMPETITION

v Nottinghamshire (Barnsley) – 26 June – Match 1 – Yorks 207/7 (T Kohler-Cadmore 94) beat Notts 98 (Azeem Rafiq 4/5) by 109 runs.
v Nottinghamshire (Barnsley) – 26 June – Match 2 – Notts 130/7 lost to Yorks 135/3 by seven wkts.
v Durham (Marske-by-the-Sea) – 6 July – Match 1 – Match abandoned without a ball bowled.
v Durham (Marske-by-the-Sea) – 6 July – Match 2 – Yorks 210/3 (R Gibson 103, J A Leaning 85*; U Arshad 3/54) lost to Durham 168/3 (U Arshad 70) by seven wkts (DLS)

v Northamptonshire (Pudsey Congs CC) – 10 July – Match 1 – Northants 173/3 (S A Zaib 50; J C Wainman 3/33 [inc hat-trick]) lost to Yorks 174/2 (W M H Rhodes 54*) by eight wkts.
v Northamptonshire (Pudsey Congs CC) – 10 July – Match 2 – Yorks 201/4 (A Z Lees 116*) beat Northants 200/6 (S A Zaib 65, C O Thurston 54; M D Fisher 3/46) by one run.
v Hampshire (Arundel) – 10 Aug – Yorks 100 lost to Hants 101/1 (J H K Adams 57*) by nine wkts.
This was the first Semi-Final of the 2017 competition.

PLAYERS WHO HAVE REPRESENTED YORKSHIRE 2ND XI IN 2017 (38)

B L Ainsley	E Callis	A Z Lees	R J Sidebottom
Azeem Rafiq	K Carver	J E G Logan	J A Tattersall
J M Bairstow	B O Coad	*T W Loten	* M D Taylor
G S Ballance	A Drury	A Lyth	J A Thompson
E Barnes	M D Fisher	S A Patterson	JC Wainman
Bilal Anjum	R Gibson	L E Plunkett	M J Waite
B D Birkhead	G C H Hill	J Read	J D Warner
*T T Bresnan	A J Hodd	W M H Rhodes	D J Willey
H C Brook	T Kohler-Cadmore	J Shaw	
J A Brooks	J A Leaning	J W Shutt	

YORKSHIRE CRICKETERS

Benjamin Lewis AINSLEY (Prior Purseglove College, Guisborough, Yorks) b Middlesbrough 19.11.97. Debut 2014. HS 61 v Glos, Bristol, 2016. BB 0/3 v Durham, York, 2016. HSSET 26 v Derbys, Alvaston & Boulton, 2016. Released midway through the 2107 season.

AZEEM RAFIQ (Holgate S; Barnsley Coll) b Karachi, Pakistan 27.2.91. RHB OB. Debut Yorks 2008, F/C debut (Yorks) v Sussex, Headingley, 2009. Debut (Derbys) 2011 (on Loan). Eng U19 to S.Africa 2008/09; v Bangladesh 2009; to Bangladesh, 2009, to New Zealand (U19 World Cup) 2009/10 and v Sri Lanka 2010. Cap 2016. HS 87* v Notts, Notts Sports Ground, 2014. BB 5/51 v Lancs, Headingley 2008. HSSET 80 v Glam, Pudsey Congs, 2013. BBSET 5/33 v Hants, Headingley 2009. HST20 49 v Notts, Headingley, 2013 (1st). BBT20 4/5 v Notts, Barnsley, 2017 (1st). HSKO 3 v Durham, Weetwood, 2010. BBKO 2/39 in the same match.

Jonathan Marc BAIRSTOW (St Peter`s S, York) b Bradford, 26.9.89. RHB WK. Tests 45 (Eng) & 32 ODIs (2011 to date). Son of D L (Yorks, Griqualandland W; Tests 4 (Eng) & 21 ODIs (1978/79 to 1984). Brother of A D (Warwicks, Lancs, Derbys, Somerset & Sussex, 1993-2000). Debut 2007. F/C debut v Somerset, Headingley, 2009. HS 202* v Leics, Oakham, 2009. HSSET 81* v Leics, Grace Road, 2009. Yorks Staff.

Gary Simon BALLANCE (Peterhouse Boys S, Marondera, Zim; Harrow S) b Harare, Zim, 22.11.89. LHB LB. Nephew of D L Houghton (Rhodesia / Zim 1978/79 to 1997/98). Tests (Eng) 23 (2013/14 to 2017) & 16 ODIs. Debut Derbys 2006, aged 16 yrs & 162 days. Debut Yorks 2008. F/C debut v Kent, Canterbury, 2008. HS 212 v MCC YC, Stamford Bridge, 2009. BB 2/20 v Notts, Barnsley, 2011. HSSET 129 v Notts, Headingley, 2011. HST20 2 v Durham, Chester-le-Street, 2011 (2nd). HSKO 12 v Durham, Weetwood, 2010. BBKO 2/11 in the same match.

Edward "Ed" BARNES (King James's S, Knaresborough, Yorks) b York, 26.11.97. RHB RFM. Debut 2016. Eng U19 v Sri Lanka, 2016. HS 65 v Scot Dev XI, Harrogate, 2016. BB 3/23 v Notts, Scarborough, 2016. HSSET 58 v Warwicks, Knowle & Dorridge, 2016. BBSET 1/42 in the same match. HST20 3 v Derbys, Harrogate, 2016 (1st) & v Worcs, Worcester RGS, 2017 (1st). BBT20 2/3 v Notts, Barnsley, 2017 (1st).

BILAL ANJUM (Oakwood HS, Rotherham; Queen Ethleburga's SFC) b Rotherham, S Yorks, 30.1.99. RHB OB. Debut 2017. HS 40 v Durham, Riverside, 2017. HST20 41 v Northants, Pudsey Congs, 2017 (1st).

Benjamin "Ben" David BIRKHEAD (Huddersfield New Coll) b Halifax, 28.10.98. RHB WK. Debut 2016. HS 36 v Durham, Scarborough, 2017. HSSET 24 v Warwicks, York, 2017. HST20 37* v Derbys, Alvaston & Boulton, 2017 (2nd).

Timothy "Tim" Thomas BRESNAN (Castleford HS; Pontefract New Coll) b Pontefract, 28.2.85. RHB RMF. Debut 2003, aged 16 yrs & 118 days. F/C debut v Northants, Northampton, 2003. Tests (Eng) 23 & 85 ODIs (2006 to 2015). HS 102 v Lancs, Stamford Bridge, 2003. BB 4/26 v Durham, Stockton-on-Tees, 2003. HSSET 42* v Derbys, Glossop, 2001. BBSET 4/42 v Notts, York, 2002. Yorks Staff.

Harry Cherrington BROOK (Sedbergh S) b Keighley, 22.2.99. RHB RM. Debut 2015. F/C debut v Pak A, Headingley, 2016. Eng U19 to India, 2016/17; v Ind 2017 (as Capt); to SA 2017/18 (as Capt). HS 161 v Lancs, Scarborough, 2017. BB 0/3 v MCCU,

Stamford Bridge, 2016. HSSET 112 v Middx, Headingley, 2017. HST20 29 v Notts, Trent Coll, 2016 (2nd).

Jack Alexander BROOKS (Wheatley Park S, Holton, Oxon) b Oxford, 4.6.84. RHB RFM. Debuts Northants & Surrey 2008. F/C debut (Northants) v the Australians, Northampton, 2009. Northants Cap 2012. Debut Yorks & Cap 2013. HS 43 (Northants) v Warwicks, Northampton, 2009. BB 6/9 in the same match. HSSET 17* (Northants) v Surrey, Wellingborough S, 2009. BBSET 3/34 (Northants) v Kent, King's S, Canterbury, 2009. HST20 0 v Worcs, Worcester RGS, 2017 (1st). BBT20 1/15 v Worcs, Worcester RGS, 2017 (1st). Yorks Staff.

Eliot CALLIS (Worksop Coll) b Sheffield, 8.11.94. RHB LB. Debut 2013. F/C debut v Pakistan A, Headingley, 2016. HS 125 v Warwicks, EFCSG, 2016. BB 0/3 v Lancs, Todmorden, 2014. HSSET 78 v Notts, Notts SG, 2014. HST20 66* v Notts, Trent Coll, 2016 (2nd). Yorks Staff.

Karl CARVER (Thirsk S & SFC) b Northallerton, Yorks , 26.3.96. LHB SLA Debut 2012. F/C debut v Warwicks, Edgbaston, 2014. Eng U19 v Pak & Bang, 2013; v S Africa, 2014. HS 53* v Derbys, Scarborough, 2015. BB 6/43 v Middx, Merchant Taylors' S, Northwood, 2013. HSSET 66* v Warwicks, Knowle & Dorridge, 2016. BBSET 3/17 v Derbys, York, 2017. HST20 41* v Worcs, Worcester RGS, 2017 (1st). BBT20 5/20 v Worcs, Barnt Green, 2015 (2nd). Yorkshire Staff .

Benjamin "Ben" Oliver COAD (Thirsk HS & SFC) b Harrogate, 10.1.94. RHB RMF. Debut 2012. F/C debut v Durham, Riverside, 2016. HS 27 v Lancs, Todmorden, 2014. BB 6/57 v Northants, Market Harborough, 2016. HSSET 17* Glam, SWALEC, 2014. BBSET 4/27 v Derbys, Alvaston & Boulton, 2016. HST20 7 v Derbys, Derby, 2014 (1st). BBT20 3/17 v Northants, Stowe S, 2016 (1st). Yorkshire Staff .

Alec DRURY (Driffield Sec S, E Yorks) b Hull, 25.7.00. RHB OB. Debut 2017. HS 0 v MCC YC, High Wycombe, 2017. BB 3/74 in the same match.

Matthew David FISHER (Easingwold S, N Yorks) b York 9.1.97. Debut 2013 aged 15 yrs & 199 days. RHB RMF. F/C debut v Notts, Trent Bridge, 2015. Debut Eng U19 v Pak & Bang, 2013, aged 15 yrs and 269 days, the youngest-ever England U19 International Cricketer; to UAE 2013/14 (Tri/Series); v S Africa, 2014; to Ind 2016/17. HS 96* v Scot Dev XI, Harrogate, 2016. BB 5/31 v Worcs, York, 2014. HSSET 22 v Lancs, Headingley, 2017. BBSET 6/25 v Leics, Market Harborough, 2013. HST20 29 v Durham, York, (1st) 2013. BBT20 3/46 v Northants, Pudsey Congs, 2017 (2nd). Yorks Staff .

Ryan GIBSON (Fylinghall S & SFC) b Middlesbrough, 22.1.96. RHB RM. Debut 2012. F/C debut v Pak A, Headingley, 2016. Eng U19 to S.Africa, 2012/13. HS 162* v Leics, York, 2016. BB 3/1 v Northants, York, 2015. HSSET 87 v Durham, York, 2016. BBSET 3/35 v MCC YC, Merchant Taylors' S, Northwood, 2017. HST20 103 v Durham, Marske CC, 2017 (2nd). BBT20 2/37 v Derbys, Harrogate, 2016 (2nd). Released midway through the 2017 season.

George Christopher Hindley HILL (Sedbergh S) b Keighely, W Yorks, 24.1.01. RHB RMF. Debut 2017 v Derbys (T20 at Alvaston & Boulton) but did not bat or bowl (2nd).

Andrew John HODD (Bexhill HS; Bexhill Coll; Loughborough U) b Chichester, Sussex, 12.1.84. RHB WK. Debut Sussex 2002; Surrey 2005; ret to Sussex 2006; debut Yorks 2012. F /C Debut

105

(Sussex) v Zimbabweans, Hove 2003. Yorks Cap 2016. Eng U19 to Australia 2002/03, and v S.Africa 2003. HS 179 v Kent, Polo Farm, Canterbury, 2015. BB 0/20 (Sussex) v Surrey, Horsham, 2011. HSSET 112 v Warwicks, Pudsey Congs, 2014. HST20 36 v Derbys, Derby, 2014 (1st). HSKO 74 (Sussex) v Essex, Chelmsford, 2010. HST20 41 v Durham, York, 2015 (2nd). Yorks Staff.

Tom KOHLER-CADMORE (Malvern C) b Chatham, Kent, 19.8.94. RHB OB. Debut 2010. F/C debut (Worcs) v Hants, the Ageas Bowl, 2014. HS 230 v Derbys, York, 2017. BB 1/12 (Worcs) v MCCU, Kidderminster, 2012. HSSET 46 (Worcs) v Lancs, Old Trafford, 2015. HST20 110* (Worcs) v Glam, Kidderminster, 2014 (2nd).

Jack Andrew LEANING (Archbishops Holgate S; York; York Coll) b Bristol 18.10.93; RHB OB. Eng U19 to Bang & Aus 2011/12. Debut 2011. F/C debut v Surrey, Headingley, 2013. Cap 2016. HS 150* v Worcs, New Road, 2011. BB 3/28 v Notts, York, 2013. HSSET 77* v MCC YC, Merchant Taylors' S, Northwood, 2017. BBSET 2/25 v Glam, Pudsey Congs, 2013. HST20 102 v Notts, Trent Coll, 2014 (2nd) BBT20 1/22v Durham, York, 2013 (1st). Yorks Staff.

Alexander Zak LEES (Holy Trinity S) b Halifax, 14.4.93. LHB LB. Debut 2010; F/C Debut v India "A", Headingley, 2010. Cap 2014. HS 202 v Durham, Riverside, 2017. BB 0/1 in the same match. HSSET 119* v Durham, York, 2016. HST20 116* v Northants, Pudsey Congs, 2017 (2nd). Yorks Staff.

James Edwin Graham LOGAN (Normanton Freeston HS; Pontefract New Coll) b Wakefield 12.10.97. LHB SLA. Debut 2014. HS 12* v MCCYC, Shenley, 2014. BB 8/76 v Lancs, Scarborough, 2015. HSSET 28 v Leics, Barnsley, 2014. BBSET 3/53 v MCC YC, Merchant Taylors' S, Northwood, 2017. HST20 1* v Derbys, Harrogate, 2016 (1st). BBT20 2/20 v Notts, Trent Coll, 2016 (2nd).

***Thomas William LOTEN** (Pocklington S) b York, 8.1.99. RHB RMF. Debut 2017. HS 6 v Lancs, Old Trafford, 2016. BB 0/8 in the same match.

Adam LYTH (Caedmon S, Whitby; Whitby Community Coll) b Whitby, Yorks 25.9.87. LHB RM. Debut 2004; F/C debut v Loughborough UCCE, Headingley, 2007. Cap 2010. Tests 7 (Eng) 2015. HS 165* v Durham, Stamford Bridge 2006. BB 1/59 v Leics, Hinckley, 2011. HSSET 152* v Worcs, Kidderminster 2009. BBSET 2/30 v MCC YC, Weetwood, 2013. Yorks Staff.

Steven Andrew PATTERSON (Malet Lambert S, Hull; St Marys SFC, Hull; Leeds U) b Beverley, 3.10.83. RHB RM. Debut 2002. F/C debut v Bangladesh "A", Headingley, 2005. Cap 2012. HS 62* v Warwicks, Edgbaston, 2007. BB 5/24, Durham, S Northumberland, 2013. HSSET 37 v Leics, Bingley, 2008. BBSET 4/18 v Leics, Hinckley, 2007. HST20 18* v Notts, Harrogate, 2015 (1st). BBT20 1/11 in the same match. Yorks Staff.

Liam Edward PLUNKETT (Nunthorpe CS, Middlesbrough; Teesside Coll, Middlesbrough) b Middlesbrough, Yorks, 6.4.85. RHB RFM. Debut 2001, aged 16 yrs and 139 days. F/C Debut (Durham) v Durham UCCE, the Racecourse, 2003. Debut Durham 2003. Ret to Yorks 2013. Tests (Eng) 13 (2005/06-2007) & 34 ODIs. HS 101 v Kent, Polo Farm, Canterbury, 2015. BB 3/40 (Durham) v Notts, Darlington, 2003. HSSET 42 (Durham) v Lancs, Seaton Carew, 2004. BBSET 2/38 v Derbys, York, 2017. HST20 33* (Durham) v Notts, Brandon, 2011 BBT20 2/27 (Durham) v Lancs, Gosforth, 2012 (1ˢᵗ). Yorks Staff.

Jonathan READ (Lady Lumley`s S & SFC) b Scarborough, 2.2.98. RHB WK. Debut 2015. F/C debut v Pak A, Headingley, 2016. HS 42 v MCCU, Stamford Bridge, 2016. HSSET 0 v Derbys, Alvaston & Boulton, 2016. HST20 5* v Derbys, Harrogate, 2016 (1st).

William Michael Harry RHODES (Cottingham HS & SFC) b Nottingham 2.3.95. LHB RM. Debut 2012. . Eng U19 v Pak & Bang, 2013; to UAE 2013/14 (Tri/Series); v S Africa, 2014. F/C debut v MCC, Abu Dhabi, 2014/15. HS 176 v Lancs, Old Trafford, 2017. BB 5/43 v Scot Dev XI, Harrogate, 2016. HSSET 124 v Worcs, Stamford Bridge, 2014. BBSET 3/34 v Unc, Barnsley, 2016. HST20 85 v Durham, York, 2014 (1st). BBT20 3/21 (inc hat/trick) v Durham, York, 2014 (2nd). Joins Warwickshire for the 2018 season.

Joshua SHAW (Crofton HS, Wakefield; Skills Exchange Coll, Wakefield) b Wakefield 3.1.96. RHB RMF. Debut Yorks 2012; Glos (on loan) 2016. F/C debut (Glos) v Durham MCCU, Bristol, 2016. Eng U19 to S Africa, 2012/13 v Pak & Bang, 2013; to UAE 2013/14 (Tri/Series); v S Africa, 2014. HS100* v MCC YC, High Wycombe, 2017. BB 5/28 v Durham, Harrogate, 2014 (and match figs of 10/71). HSSET 19 v Glam, SWALEC, 2014. BBSET 2/24 v Warwicks, York, 2017. HST20 25 (Eng U19) v Yorks, Loughborough, 2013 (1st). BBT20 3/25 v Derbys, Derby, 2014 (1st). Yorkshire Staff .

Jack William SHUTT (Kirk Balk S, Barnsley; Thomas Rotherham Coll, Rotherham) b Barnsley 24.6.97. RHB OB. Debut 2015. HS 8 v Sussex, Hove, 2015. BB 3/17 v Durham, York, 2016 & v Scot Dev XI, Harrogate, 2016. BBSET 4/19 v Middx, Headingley, 2017. HST20 9* v Worcs, Worcester RGS, 2017 (1st). BBT20 4/12 v Derbys, Alvaston & Boulton, 2017 (1st).

Ryan Jay SIDEBOTTOM (King James's GS, Almondbury) b Huddersfield 15.1.78. LHB LFM. Tests (Eng) 22 & 25 ODIs (2001 to 2009/10). Son of A (Yorks & Eng, 1971 to 1991 and 1 Test). Debut Yorks 1995; F/C debut v Leics, Grace Road, 1997; Cap 2000. Debut & Cap Notts 2004. HS 55* v MCCU, York, 2012. BB 5/19 v Notts, Trent Coll, 2016. HSSET 21* v Notts, Farnsfield, 1997. BBSET 3/10 v Durham, Stockton/on/Tees, 1998. Yorks Staff.

***Matthew Adam TAYLOR** (St Thomas a Becket S, Wakefield; Pontefract New Coll) b Wakefield, 18.12.97. RHB RFM. Debut 2015. BB 3/48 v MCCU, Weetwood, 2015.

Jonathan Andrew TATTERSALL (King James's S, Knaresborough) b Harrogate 15.12.94. Brother of J H (Yorks 2011). RHB LB. Debut 2011. List A debut v Glam, Headingley, 2013. Eng U19 to S Africa, 2012/1 v Pak & Bang, 2013; to UAE 2013/14 (Tri/Series); v S Africa, 2014. HS 137 v Glos, Bristol, 2014. BB 1/26 v Lancs, Scarborough, 2017. HSSET 98 v Warwicks, York, 2017. BBSET 0/8 Leics, Grace Road, 2013. HST20 38* v Northants, Pudsey Congs, 2017 (1st). BBT20 1/16 v Derbys, Derby, 2014 (1st).

Jordan Aaron THOMPSON (Benton Park S, Leeds) b Leeds 9.10.96. LHB RM. Debut 2013. HS 146* v Worcs, Scarborough, 2016. BB 5/60 v Derbys, Belper Meadows, 2016. HSSET 43* v Leics, Leics Ivanhoe CC, 2015. BBSET 2/29 v Middx, Headingley, 2017. HST20 36 v Notts, Barnsley, 2017 (1st). BBT20 3/18 v Worcs, Worcester RGS, 2017 (1st).

James Charles WAINMAN (Leeds GS) b Harrogate 25.1.93. RHB LM. Debut 2010. Missed the whole of the 2012 season through injury. List A debut v Sri Lanka, Headingley, 2014. HS 56* v Lancs, Scarborough, 2017. BB 5/24 v Warwicks, EFCSG, 2016. HSSET 38 v Unc, Long Marston, 2015. BBSET 3/2 v Warwicks, Pudsey Congs, 2014. HST20 45 v Worcs, Worcester RGS, 2017 (1st). BBT20 4/21 v Derbys, Alvaston & Boulton, 2017 (1st). Yorks Staff.

Matthew James WAITE (Brigshaw HS) b Leeds 24.12.95. RHB RMF. Debut 2014. F/C debut v Somerset, Taunton, 2017. HS 143 v Lancs, Scarborough, 2015. BB 4/33 v Lancs, Old Trafford. 2017. HSSET 70 v Lancs, Headingley, 2016. BBSET 1/16 v Derbys, Alvaston & Boulton, 2016. HST20 49 v Derbys, Harrogate, 2016 (2nd). BBT20 3/16 v Northants, Stowe S, 2015 (1st). Yorks Staff.

Jared David WARNER (Kettleborough Park HS, Wakefield; Silcoates SFC, Wakefield) b Wakefield 14.11.96. RHB RFM. Debut 2014. Eng U19 to Aus 2014/15; v Aus 2015. HS 20 v Lancs, Headingley, 2014. BB 2/25 v Lancs, Scarborough, 2017. HSSET 19 v Warwicks, Knowle & Doridge, 2016. BBSET 2/53 in the same match. HST20 6 v Hants, Arundel, 2017 (SF). BBT20 2/14 v Notts, Trent Coll, 2016 (1st). Yorks Staff.

David Jonathan WILLEY (Northampton S) b Northampton, 28.2.90. Son of P. (Northants, Leics & England 1965/91). LHB LM. Debut Northants 2007. F/C debut (Northants) v Leics, Grace Road, 2009. Northants Cap 2013. Yorks Cap 2016. ODIs (Eng) 22 (2015 to date). HS 80 (Northants) v Notts, Finedon Dolben, 2011. BB 4/25 (Northants) v Derbys, Denby, 2011. HSSET 101* (Northants) v Unicorns A, Chester Boughton Hall, 2011. BBSET 3/34 v Derbys, York, 2017. HST20 108 v Durham, Brandon, 2016 (2nd). BBT20 4/21 (Northants) v Leics, Grace Road, 2011(1ˢᵗ). Yorks Staff.

TABLE OF CHAMPIONSHIP RESULTS 1959-2017

	P	W	L	D	T	A
DERBYS	679	132	173	374	0	19
DURHAM	301	92	74	135	0	10
ESSEX	677	143	234	299	1	13
GLAM	741	152	215	371	3	30
GLOUCS	638	140	180	317	1	22
HANTS	705	189	169	346	1	15
KENT	742	216	158	367	1	13
LANCS	749	219	129	405	1	21
LEICS	774	176	195	402	1	28
MIDD	748	213	169	366	0	28
NORTHANTS	860	204	188	467	1	35
NOTTS	801	190	193	417	1	21
SOMERSET	599	131	190	277	1	10
SURREY	792	241	174	376	1	20
SUSSEX	687	183	189	315	0	17
WARWICKS	933	253	218	460	2	31
WORCS	802	178	230	392	2	31
YORKS	601	193	111	296	1	18
GL/SOM	24	5	8	11	0	0
MCCYC	121	16	42	63	0	10
SCOT A	12	1	7	4	0	0
MCCUNIVS	80	6	27	47	0	1
TOTALS	**13066**	**3273**	**3273**	**6507**	**18**	**393**

Abandoned matches do not count in the total played.

2ND XI T20 RESULTS 2011 TO 2017

	P	W	L	D	T	A
DERBYS	48	25	20	3	0	8
DURHAM	55	37	16	1	1	5
ESSEX	47	19	25	3	0	10
GLAM	47	21	26	0	0	9
GLOUCS	41	22	19	0	0	17
HANTS	50	25	23	1	1	7
KENT	47	28	18	1	0	11
LANCS	50	33	13	3	1	8
LEICS	49	20	26	2	1	10
MIDD	46	30	12	3	1	14
NORTHANTS	53	19	31	3	0	3
NOTTS	52	19	28	4	1	4
SOMERSET	58	32	23	2	1	0
SURREY	49	21	23	3	2	9
SUSSEX	47	25	19	2	1	13
WARWICKS	48	19	26	2	1	8
WORCS	46	19	26	1	0	11
YORKS	45	13	29	3	0	11
UNICORNS	46	15	27	3	1	10
MCCYC	50	16	30	4	0	6
ENGLAND U19	18	10	8	0	0	0
TOTALS	**992**	**468**	**468**	**44**	**12**	**174**

Abandoned matches do not count in the total played.

2ND XI TROPHY RESULTS 1986 TO 2017

	P	W	L	D	T	A
DERBYS	243	88	144	0	11	30
DURHAM	198	102	83	1	12	21
ESSEX	262	106	138	0	18	12
GLAM	224	90	115	2	17	34
GLOUCS	232	101	112	1	18	30
HANTS	261	143	105	0	13	21
KENT	259	132	104	1	22	18
LANCS	251	136	104	1	10	30
LEICS	258	133	105	1	19	20
MIDD	253	135	102	0	16	22
NORTHANTS	256	136	106	1	13	23
NOTTS	256	133	109	0	14	22
SOMERSET	231	102	117	3	9	34
SURREY	254	140	102	2	10	22
SUSSEX	258	131	113	1	13	17
WARWICKS	241	116	113	0	12	26
WORCS	240	95	132	0	13	23
YORKS	246	126	106	1	13	31
MCC YC	199	57	131	1	10	21
MINOR COUNTIES	17	5	11	0	1	1
MINOR COUNTIES U25	104	24	71	0	9	8
UNICORNS	21	9	11	0	1	0
UNICORNS A	26	10	16	0	0	2
TOTALS	**4790**	**2250**	**2250**	**16**	**274**	**468**

Abandoned matches do not count in the total played.

SECOND ELEVEN CHAMPIONSHIP RECORDS 1959-2017

CHAMPIONS

1959	Gloucestershire	1989	Middlesex
1960	Northamptonshire	1990	Sussex
1961	Kent	1991	Yorkshire
1962	Worcestershire	1992	Surrey
1963	Worcestershire	1993	Middlesex
1964	Lancashire	1994	Somerset
1965	Glamorgan	1995	Hampshire
1966	Surrey	1996	Warwickshire
1967	Hampshire	1997	Lancashire
1968	Surrey	1998	Northamptonshire
1969	Kent	1999	Middlesex
1970	Kent	2000	Middlesex
1971	Hampshire	2001	Hampshire
1972	Nottinghamshire	2002	Kent
1973	Essex	2003	Yorkshire
1974	Middlesex	2004	Somerset
1975	Surrey	2005	Kent
1976	Kent	2006	Kent
1977	Yorkshire	2007	Sussex
1978	Sussex	2008	Durham
1979	Warwickshire	2009	Surrey
1980	Glamorgan	2010	Surrey
1981	Hampshire	2011	Warwickshire
1982	Worcestershire	2012	Kent
1983	Leicestershire	2013	Lancashire & Middlesex
1984	Yorkshire	2014	Leicestershire
1985	Nottinghamshire	2015	Nottinghamshire
1986	Lancashire	2016	Durham
1987	Kent & Yorkshire	2017	Lancashire
1988	Surrey		

Wins

9 – Kent (including one joint victory)

7 – Surrey

6 - Middlesex (including one joint victory)

5 - Hampshire, Lancashire (including one joint victory), Yorkshire (including one joint victory)

3 – Nottinghamshire. Sussex, Warwickshire, Worcestershire

2 - Durham , Glamorgan, Leicestershire, Northamptonshire, Somerset.

1 –Essex, Gloucestershire.

Derbyshire, MCC Universities & MCC Young Cricketers have yet to become 2nd XI Champions.

New records for 2017 are shown thus

HIGHEST INNINGS TOTALS

697/8d	Middx v Glam (Radlett)	2015
686	Worcs v Warwicks (Barnt Green)	2003
682	Surrey v Derbys (The Oval)	2003
680/9d	Warwicks v Somerset (Knowle & Dorridge)	2002
678/7d	Surrey v Sussex (Hove)	1997
676	Leics v Essex (Chelmsford)	2014
674/9d	Lancs v Warwicks (Stratford-upon-Avon)	2003
652/9d	Derbys v Essex (Coggeshall)	1999
646/4	Warwicks v Worcs (Barnt Green)	2003
643/4d	Glos v Somerset (Taunton)	1999
632/9d	Middx v Derbys (RAF Vine Lane)	2000
628/7d	Essex v MCCYC (Billericay)	2005
621/7d	Notts v MCC Young Cricketers (Notts Sports Ground)	2010
613/6d	Notts v Durham (South Northumberland)	2005
612/4d	*Middx v MCCU (Radlett)*	*2017*
605/9d	Surrey v Essex (Guildford)	2001
605	Somerset v Warwicks (Taunton) (Fourth Innings chasing 612 to win)	1997
603/8d	Glos v Somerset (Taunton)	2001
600/8d	Sussex v Hants (Hove)	2002
600/8d	Surrey v Somerset (Taunton)	2003

600/8d	Somerset v Glam (Taunton)	2004
600	Notts v Derbys (Denby)	2005
594/9d	Durham v Leics (Riverside)	2001
592/7d	Somerset v Worcs (Taunton Vale)	2007
590	Somerset v MCC Young Cricketers (North Perrott)	2011
590	Durham v Northants (Northampton)	2015
589/7d	Worcs v Warwicks (Ombersley)	2002
588/8d	MCCYC v Somerset (High Wycombe)	2016
587/9d	Leics v Derbys (Leicester)	2007
585/8d	*Yorks v Lancs (Scarborough)*	*2017*
581/7d	Warwicks v Glam (Studley)	1997
580/5d	Kent v Essex (Chelmsford)	1992
580/7d	Derbys v Surrey (The Oval)	2003
579/8d	Notts v Derbys (Denby)	2005
578/6d	Somerset v Leics (Hinckley)	2001
577/8d	Warwicks v Worcs (Kidderminster)	1984
575/5d	Surrey v Glam (Diamond Ground, Cardiff)	2015
575	Surrey v Sussex (Hove)	2003
573/5d	*Warwicks v Derbys (EFCSG)*	*2017*
573/7d	Glos v MCC Universities (Victoria Ground, Cheltenham)	2013
572/6d	Kent v Leics (Oakham School)	1999
572/7d	Somerset v Sussex (Hastings)	2001
572/8d	Surrey v Durham (Oxted)	1994
570/8d	Kent v Glam (Ammanford)	1999
570/8d	Lancs v Leics (Middleton)	2005
568/5d	Warwicks v Worcs (Barnt Green)	2001
568	Northants v Glos (Bristol)	2003
567/7d	Middx v Yorks (RAF Vine Lane)	2000
563/9 d	Middx v Glos (Radlett)	2010
561/7	Sussex v Middx (Harefield)	1976
557	Somerset v Worcs (Kidderminster)	1997
556	Northants v Essex (Northampton)	1997
556	Somerset v Glam (Taunton)	2000
555/7d	Surrey v Notts (The Oval)	1999
555/7d	Derbys v Yorks (Stamford Bridge)	2002
554/3d	Lancs v Glos (Bristol)	1998
553/7d	Glos v Worcs (Kidderminster)	1998
553/8d	*Hants v Kent (Polo Farm SG, Canterbury)*	*2017*

HIGHEST FOR OTHER TEAMS

549	MCC Universities v Surrey (Whitgift School)	2009
523/8d	Glam v Somerset (Taunton Vale)	2011
400/6d	Scotland A v Yorks (Scarborough)	2014

LOWEST INNINGS TOTALS

24	Kent v Lancs (Folkestone)	1986
26	Kent v Surrey (Purley)	1984
29	Middx v Essex (Ealing)	1979
31*	Leics v Warwicks (Nuneaton)	1959
32	Lancs v Worcs (Urmston)	1974
33	Worcs v Somerset (Halesowen)	1961
35	Sussex v Surrey (Guildford)	1989
36	Lancs v Yorks (Elland)	1979
36*	Essex v Kent (Sittingbourne)	1969
36	Warwicks v Lancs (Knowle & Dorridge)	1985
37	Northants v Essex (Witham)	1966
39	Derbys v Warwicks (Leamington Spa)	1962
* one batsman absent		

LOWEST FOR OTHER COUNTIES

42	Notts v Northants (Peterborough)	1966
43	Somerset v Northants (Corby)	1964
45	Glos v Worcs (Cheltenham)	2011
48	Hants v Kent (Beckenham)	1962
53	Durham v Hants (Boldon)	1993
53	Surrey v Middx (Teddington)	1979
56	Glam v Leics (Lutterworth)	1975
62	MCCYC v Yorks (High Wycombe)	2005

62   Scotland A v Derbys (Denby)   2007
66   Yorks v Notts (Trent College)   2016
79   MCC Universities v Worcs (Kidderminster)   2012

HIGHEST INDIVIDUAL SCORES

322	M.E.Trescothick (Somerset) v Warwicks (Taunton)	1997
306*	P.C.McKeown (Lancs) v Gloucs (Bristol)	1998
303*	W.I.Jefferson (Essex) v MCCYC (Billericay)	2005
300	C.G.Taylor (Gloucs) v Somerset (Taunton)	1999
294	R.A.Kettleborough (Middx) v Warwicks (Walmley)	1999
293	W.R.Smith (Notts) v Durham	
	(South Northumberland)	2005
284	S.A.Newman (Surrey) v Derbys (The Oval)	2003
277*	P.R.Pollard (Notts) v Gloucs (Nottingham HS)	1994
*277**	*P J Horton (Leics) v Warwicks (EFCSG)*	*2017*
273*	R.J.Blakey (Yorks) v Northants (Northampton)	1986
272	N.Shahid (Surrey) v Sussex (Hove)	2003
267	I.J.Thomas (Glam) v Somerset (North Perrott)	2003
266	N.Shahid (Surrey) v Derbys (The Oval)	2003
264*	J.W.Lloyds (Somerset) v Glam (Ebbw Vale)	1981
261	K.P.Dutch (Middx) v Somerset (RAF Vine Lane)	1986
258*	P.J.Prichard (Essex) v Sussex (Eastbourne)	1988
258*	C A L Davis (Sussex) v Glam (Abergavenny)	2016
258	G.J.Kennis (Surrey) v Leics (Kibworth)	1995
255*	T.L.Penney (Warwicks) v Somerset	
	(Knowle & Dorridge)	2002
255	G.R.Cowdrey (Kent) v Glam (Sittingbourne)	1985
255	T.A.Tweats (Derbys) v Essex (Coggeshall)	1999
254	P R Stirling (Middx) v Glam (Radlett)	2015
253*	M.Asif Din (Warwicks) v Middx (Studley)	1995
252	D.L.Maddy (Warwicks) v MCCYC	
	(High Wycombe)	2010
251	M.Keech (Hants) v Glam (Usk)	1995
250*	I.J.Westwood (Warwicks) v Worcs (Barnt Green)	2003
250	N.J.Llong (Kent) v Worcs (Kidderminster)	1994
250	M E Trescothick (Somerset) v MCC Un	
	(Taunton Vale)	2013
249*	B A Godleman (Derbys) v Notts (Derby)	2015
248*	T.A.Tweats (Derbys) v Sussex	
	(Abbotsholme School)	1997
248	I.J.L.Trott (Warwicks) v Worcs (Barnt Green)	2003
246	A.D.Hales (Notts) v Derbys (Derby)	2009
245	I.J.L.Trott (Warwicks) v Somerset	
	(Knowle & Dorridge)	
	First double century on debut in the competition	2002
244*	D.W.Varey (Lancs) v Derbys (Blackpool)	1984
244	D.J.Bicknell (Surrey) v Gloucs (Bristol)	1997
243	D L Lloyd (Glam) v Warwicks	
	(Bulls Head Ground, Coventry)	2014
241	J.S.Laney (Hants) v Essex (Wickford)	1998
241	*T W M Latham (Durham) v MCC YC*	
	(Highb Wycombe)	*2017*

HIGHEST FOR OTHER COUNTIES

236	A.Fordham (Northants) v Worcs (Kidderminster)	1989
223	*T C Fell (Worcs) v MCC YC (Barnt Green)*	*2017*
192	*B J Curran (MCC YC) v Yorks (High Wycombe)*	*2017*
185	C M Dickinson (MCC Universities) v Warwicks	
	(EFCSG)	2016
173*	M A Leask (Scotland A) v Yorks (Scarborough)	2014

MOST RUNS IN A SEASON

	Avge		
1498	55.48	D.L.Maddy (Leics)	1994
1485	57.11	S.Jayasinghe (Leics)	1961
1481	67.31	B.Parker (Yorks)	1996
1436	49.55	P.C.McKeown (Lancs)	1996
1432	57.28	G.P.Burnett (Sussex)	1990
1432	46.19	P.Johnson (Notts)	1982
1393	63.31	R.J.Bartlett (Somerset)	1991
1367	68.35	R.I.H.B.Dyer (Warwicks)	1983
1362	61.90	D.D.J.Robinson (Essex)	1992
1357	41.12	M.Diwan (Derbys & Kent)	1995
1300	54.16	G.R.Cowdrey (Kent)	1985
1287	55.95	N.J.Speak (Lancs)	1989
1283	55.78	R.I.Alikhan (Surrey)	1989
1279	45.67	M.J.Wood (Yorks)	1997
1274	43.93	N.J.Speak (Lancs)	1990
1274	47.19	A.Gordon (Warwicks)	1971
1273	38.57	A.M.R.Sim (Northants)	1964
1271	70.61	G.D.Hodgson (Worcs & Gloucs)	1989
1269	52.87	M.J.Walker (Kent)	1994
1269	66.78	N.Shahid (Surrey)	2003
1261	54.82	R.A.Kettleborough (Yorks)	1997
1250	54.34	J.W.Cook (Northants)	1999
1228	58.47	S.A.Newman (Surrey)	2003
1223	49.92	R.M.F.Cox (Hants)	1991
1221	43.60	V.J.Wells (Kent)	1989
1212	93.23	S.P.Titchard (Lancs)	1991
1209	60.45	S.A.Newman (Surrey)	2002
1203	63.31	B.Leadbeater (Yorks)	1977

MOST FOR OTHER COUNTIES

1195	44.25	C.D.Fearnley (Worcs)	1961
1183	73.94	G.D.Hodgson (Glos)	1989
1155	50.21	T.J.G.O'Gorman (Derbys)	1995
1107	50.31	J.C.Pooley (Middx)	1989
1066	48.45	A.W.Evans (Glam)	1996
941	47.05	C D Piesley	
		(Kent, MCC YC & Sussex)	2014
930	66.42	G.J.Muchall (Durham)	2008
820	45.55	R.J.Woodman (MCC YC)	2008
545	41.92	H L Thompson (MCC Universities)	2014
366	40.66	M A Leask (Scotland A)	2014

HIGHEST WICKET PARTNERSHIPS

552	1st	S.A.Newman (284) & N.Shahid (266) Surrey	
		v Derbys (The Oval)	2003
402	2nd	M.A.G.Boyce (201) and J.J.Cobb (208*)	
		Leics v Lancs (Leicester Ivanhoe)	2011
399	3rd	I A Cockbain (224) & C L Herring (203*) (Glos)	
		v MCC Universities	
		(Victoria Ground, Cheltenham)	2013
397	4th	I.J.L.Trott (245) & T.L.Penney (255*)	
		Warwicks v Somerset, (Knowle & Dorridge)	2002
*389**	*5th*	*G F B Scott (212*) & R G White (160*)*	
		Middx v MCCU (Radlett)	*2017*
325	6th	N.A.James (234) & I.Hassan (139)	
		Glam v Hants (Rose Bowl Nursery)	2011
423	7th	D.W.Varey (244*) & H.Pilling (181)	
		Lancs v Derbys (Blackpool)	1989
251	8th	P.E.Robinson (233) & C.Johnson (102)	
		Yorks v Kent (Canterbury)	1983
240	9th	B A Godleman & T A I Taylor (Derbys) v	
		Notts (Derby)	2015
166	10th	O.J.Newby (133) & G.Yates (52*)	
		Lancs v Derbys (Derby)	2004

TWO HUNDREDS IN A MATCH

109* & 100*	R.J.Turner (Somerset) v Notts (Clevedon)	1994
122* & 178*	I.D.Austin (Lancs) v Glam (Usk)	1994
109 & 136*	A.A.Metcalfe (Yorks) v Somerset	
	(North Perrott)	1994
123* & 126	J.C.Pooley (Middx) v Hants (Southampton)	1994
200* & 110	W.P.C.Weston (Worcs) v Hants	
	(Kidderminster)	1994
134 & 108	D.A.Leatherdale (Worcs) v Leics	
	(Worcester)	1995
157 & 179	W.G.Khan (Warwicks) v Leics (Leicester)	1996
123 & 192*	R.A.Kettleborough (Yorks) v Notts	
	(Todmorden)	1996
114 & 119*	C.M.Tolley (Notts) v Middx (Trent Bridge)	1996
130* & 144*	M.J.Powell (Glam) v Kent (Pontardulais)	1997

115 & 102*	T.Frost (Warwicks) v Worcs (Studley)	1998
132 & 123*	M.T.E.Peirce (Sussex) v Derbys (Eastbourne)	1998
131 & 100	A.J.Swann (Northants) v Yorks (York)	1998
114 7 114	G.J.Kennis (Somerset) v Yorks (York)	1999
104 7 115	S.J.Adshead (Leics) v Glam (Hinckley)	1999
158 & 112	A.W.Evans (Glam) v Somerset (Taunton)	2000
101 & 128*	Hassan Adnan (Derbys) v Notts (Notts Unity)	2002
205* & 125	J.S.Laney (Hants) v Sussex (Hove)	2002
130 & 201*	W.J.House (Sussex) v Northants (Hastings)	2002
100* & 113	C.D.Hopkinson (Sussex) v Northants (Hastings)	2002
141 & 100	R.A.White (Northants) v Sussex (Hastings)	2002
137 & 143	A.N.Cook (Essex) v Surrey (The Oval)	2003
123 & 124	J.R.C.Hamblin (Hants) v Sussex (Hove)	2003
126 & 141	S.C.Moore (Worcs) v Northants (Kidderminster)	2003
120 & 103*	A.Dale (Glam) v Hants (Cardiff)	2004
181 & 120	D.K.H.Mitchell (Worcs) v Warwicks (Ombersley)	2005
108 & 110	C.P.Murtagh (Surrey) v Yorks (Whitgift School)	2005
201* & 129	C.R.Taylor (Yorks) v Sussex (Hove)	2005
129 & 118	M.J.Brown (Hants) v Surrey (WE Nursery)	2006
131 & 123	A.W.Gale (Yorks) v Somerset (Taunton)	2006
118 & 124	J.A.Lowe (Durham) v Northants (Stowe School)	2006
22** & 103*	J.K.Maunders (Leics) v Essex (Billericay)	2006
157 & 105	J.J.Sayers (Yorks) v Lancs (Headingley)	2007
125 & 105	S.J.Walters (Surrey) v Warwicks (Cheam)	2008
186 & 152*	L.J.Evans (Surrey) v Northants (Whitgift School)	2010
103 & 116	S.J.Walters (Surrey) v Warwicks (Wormsley – 2nd XI Championship Final)	2010
163 & 138*	I.J.Westwood (Warwicks) v Notts (Notts Sports Ground)	2011
100 & 104	M.D.Birrell (Kent) v MCC Young Cricketers (Beckenham)	2011
146 & 113	J.C.Mickleburgh (Essex) v Kent (The King`s School, Canterbury)	2011
162 & 101*	J C Mickleburgh (Essex) v Glam (Southend-on-Sea)	2012
119 & 111	M A Comber (Essex) v MCC Young Cricketers (Southend-on-Sea)	2012
120 & 102	S A Northeast (Kent) v Sussex (Fulking)	2014
118 & 123	B T Slater (Derbys) v Worcs (Worcester RGS)	2015
118* & 120*	A J Hose (Somerset) v Essex (Halstead)	2016
113 & 117	N J Selman (Glam) v Surrey (Guildford)	2016

Note: Instances of two hundreds in a match between 1959 and 1992 can be found in Annuals 1992/94.

CARRYING BAT THROUGH COMPLETED INNINGS

	Out of		
74*	128	J.B.Sedgley (Worcs) v Warwicks (M&B, Birmingham)	1959
83*	188	A.Gill (Notts) v Derbys (Derby)	1962
128*	250	B.Ward (Essex) v Surrey (Chelmsford)	1967
68*	151	B.Hedges (Glam) v Warwicks (Cardiff)	1967
87*	213	D.A.Laycock (Kent) v Hants (Sittingbourne)	1968
107*	311	B.Leadbeater (Yorks) v Worcs (Worcester)	1978
122*	272	D.A.Francis (Glam) v Warwicks (Coventry & N.War)	1979
40*	188	R.I.H.B.Dyer (Warwicks) v Middx (Griff & Coton, Nuneaton)	1982
86*	217	A.C.Storie (Warwicks) v Sussex (Edgbaston)	1978
133*	213	A.M.Brown (Derbys) v Glam (Ilkeston)	1989
93*	198	R.I.Alikhan (Surrey) v Yorks (The Oval)	1989

90* (*)187		J.J.B.Lewis (Essex) v Sussex (Hove)	1990
109*	207	D.D.J.Robinson (Essex) v Hants (Bournemouth)	1991
90*	184	D.D.J.Robinson (Essex) v Hants (Southampton)	1992
123*	out of 275	W.G.Khan (Warwicks) v Essex (Griff & Coton)	1992
102*	188	G.K.Brown (Durham) v Warwicks (Shildon)	1992
91*	189	M.Diwan (Essex) v Gloucs (Bristol)	1993
80*	200	M.R.Fletcher (Kent) v Lancs (Old Trafford)	1995
53*	132	T.A.Radford (Middx) v Worcs (Worcester)	1995
147*	369	M.R.May (Derbys) v Glam (Swansea)	1996
126*	315	R.M.S.Weston (Durham) v Yorks (Shildon)	1996
132*	262	P.Whitticase (Leics) v Sussex (Oakham School)	1996
88*	204	A.J.E.Hibbert (Essex) v Gloucs (Bristol)	1997
134*	252	G.E.Welton (Notts) v Lancs (Trent Bridge)	1997
133*	251	R.C.Driver (Worcs) v Hants (Bournemouth SC)	1999
53*	135	W.A.Kirby (Notts) v Surrey (Notts Unity)	1999
90*	191	M.D.R.Sutliff (Gloucs) v Hants (West End)	2000
93*	201	W.M.Noon (Notts) v Yorks (Stamford Bridge)	2002
54*	110	C.R.Taylor (Yorks) v Durham (Stockton)	2003
128*	243	D.C.Shirazi (Hants) v Sussex (WE Nursery)	2004
79*	164	R.T.Timms (Somerset) v Gloucs (Hatherley & Reddings)	2005
132*	213	I.A.Cockbain (MCCYC) v Glam (Radlett)	2007
152*	288	L.J.Evans (Surrey) v Northants (Whitgift School)	2010
56*	91	J.J.Sayers (Yorks) v Durham (Darlington)	2011
24*	62	C.R.G.Vernon (Kent) v Sussex (Canterbury)	2011
66*	125	N.L.J.,Browne (Essex) v Somerset (Taunton Vale)	2011
156*	260	G Pardoe (Worcs) v Yorks (Barnsley)	2012
103*	210	A Harinath (Surrey) v Hants (Rose Bowl)	2012
135*	299	S P Terry (Hants) v MCC Universities (The Ageas Bowl)	2013
56*	121	A Patel (Surrey) v Sussex (Arundel)	2013
249*	445	B A Godleman (Derbys) v Notts (Derby)	2015
150	*250*	*J M Kettleborough (Northants) v Durham (M Keynes)*	*2017*

(*) One batsman absent

BEST BOWLING IN AN INNINGS

10/13	D.Gibson (Surrey) v Sussex (Guildford)	1969
9/20	J A Tomlinson (Hants) v Kent (Maidstone)	2012
9/26	A.J.Dibble (Somerset) v Hants (Rose Bowl Nursery)	2011
9/27	G.A.Cope (Yorks) v Northants (Northampton)	1979
9/35	R.M.Ratcliffe (Lancs) v Warwicks (Old Trafford)	1974
9/35	J.A.North (Sussex) v Derbys (Heanor)	1991
9/36	R.L.Pratt (Leics) v Notts (Wollaton)	1959
9/37	A.Wright (Warwicks) v Derbys (Burton-on-Trent)	1960
9/41	A.Richardson (Warwicks) v Notts (Knowle & Dorridge)	2003
9/43	D.G.Moir (Derbys) v Northants (Peterborough)	1983
9/44	G.Monkhouse (Surrey) v Sussex (Cranleigh)	1980
9/46	G.E.Sainsbury (Essex) v Kent (Dartford)	1982
9/47	S.J.Marshall (Lancs) v Notts (Worksop College)	2004
9/48	C.P.Wood (Hants) v Kent (Canterbury)	2010
9/50	I.L.Pont (Essex) v Notts (Southend)	1988
9/51	M.J.Boyes (Essex) v Northants (Hadleigh)	1969
9/59	E.E.Hemmings (Warwicks) v Notts (Coventry & Nth War)	1978
9/60	J.J.Bates (Sussex) v Surrey (The Oval)	1998
9/62	M.K.Bore (Yorks) v Warwicks (Scarborough)	1976
9/69	W.Jones (Gloucs) v Hants (Southampton)	1972
9/70	R.D.O.Earl (Warwicks) v Gloucs (Cheltenham)	1988

9/72   M.J.Vernon (Gloucs) v Warwicks (Bristol)   1977
9/78   P.C.R.Tufnell (Middx) v Hants (Southampton)   1986
9/78   D.J.P.Boden (Gloucs) v Notts (Bristol)   1995
9/79   A.A.Barnett (Lancs) v Gloucs (Crosby)   1995
9/90   C.E.Sketchley (Glam) v Somerset (Pontypridd)   1996
9/94   J.E.Melville (Kent) v Sussex (Hove)   1960
9/94   N.V.Radford (Worcs) v Northants (Halesowen)   1990

BEST FOR OTHER COUNTIES
7/32   C.L.Campbell (Durham) v Kent (Riverside)   1995
8/17   B.Lobb (Gloucs & Somerset) v Northants (Ashton)   1967
8/95   N.Chowdhury (MCC YC) v Essex (Radlett)   2005
8/24   A.B.Palfreman (Notts) v Leics (Ashby-de-la-Zouch)   1965
8/25   P.G.Lee (Northants) v Essex (Chelmsford)   1967
8/45   B.P.Kruger (MCC Univs) v Middx (Radlett)   2009
5/61   G.Goudie (Scotland A) v Lancs (Blackpool)   2008

BEST BOWLING IN A MATCH
16/111   D.G.Moir (Derbys) v Northants (Peterborough)   1983
15/54   B.Lobb (Gloucs & Somerset) v Northants (Ashton)   1967
15/142   B.T.P.Donelan (Sussex) v Middx (Hove)   1990
15/147   M.C.Ilott (Essex) v Lancs (Lytham)   1990
15/157   K.P.Dutch (Middx) v Leics (Hinckley)   1996
14/74   R.D.Jackman (Surrey) v Essex (Walthamstow)   1969
14/84   K.Higgs (Leics) v Northants (Bletchley)   1981
14/88   D.J.Balcombe (Hants) v Gloucs (WE Nursery)   2007
14/92   K.Stevenson (Hants) v Middx (Southgate)   1983
14/103   C.C.Clifford (Warwicks) v Essex (Leamington Spa)   1978
13/36   S.C.G.MacGill (Somerset) v Hants (Clevedon)   1997
13/42   A.R.Windows (Gloucs) v Essex (Bristol)   1963
13/54   R.M.Ratcliffe (Lancs) v Worcs (Urmston)   1974
13/64   P.D.Watts (Northants) v Derbys (Derby)   1960
13/65   B.D.Wells (Gloucs) v Leics (Cheltenham)   1959
13/65   I.J.Jones (Glam) v Surrey (Margam)   1964
13/65   J.H.Shackleton (Gloucs) v Warwicks (Gloucester)   1971
13/67   Mushtaq Mohammad (Northants) v Warwicks   1965
13/75   D.G.A'Court (Gloucs) v Glam (Bristol)   1960
13/77   T.J.Mason (Leics) v Durham (Hinckley)   1994
13/79   A.J.M.Hooper (Kent) v Sussex (Redhill)   1967
13/80   G.Yates (Lancs) v Durham (Southport)   1997
13/81*   K.J.Wheatley (Hants) v Gloucs & Som (Bournemouth)   1967
13/88   G.Yates (Lancs) v Durham (Southport)   1993
13/89   M.J.Hilton (Lancs) v Northants (Corby)   1959
13/91   M.Ashenden (Gloucs) v Warwicks (Bristol)   1976
13/92   E.E.Hemmings (Warwicks) v Notts (Coventry & Nth War)   1978
13/92   M.K.Bore (Yorks) v Lancs (Harrogate)   1976
13/95   G.H.Hall (Somerset) v Worcs (Halesowen)   1961
13/99   A.Carter (Notts) v Warwicks (Welbeck Colliery)   2009
13/100   N.J.Perry (Glam) v Yorks (Cardiff)   1978
13/108   J.J.Bates (Sussex) v Surrey (The Oval)   1998
13/110   J.D.Batty (Yorks) v Leics (Bradford)   1992
13/111   M.K.Bore (Yorks) v Warwicks (Scarborough)   1976
13/111   R.Mayhew (Leics) v Notts (Lutterworth)   1959
13/114   V.C.Drakes (Sussex) v Surrey (Banstead)   1994
13/114*   K.J.Wheatley (Hants) v Middx (Bournemouth)   1967
13/120   P.Aldred (Derbys) v Notts (Trent Bridge)   1997
13/122   G.J.Parsons (Leics) v Northants (Market Harborough)   1983
13/123   R.T.Bates (Notts) v Hants (Worksop College)   1996
13/127   G.J.Batty (Surrey) v Northants (Sutton)   2001
* In consecutive matches

BEST FOR OTHER COUNTIES
12/48   S.Chapman (Durham) v Worcs (Worcester)   1999
12/144   C.P.Roberts (Worcs) v Lancs (Urmston)   1974
1/154   A MacQueen (MCCU) v Durham (Maiden Castle)   2012
9/93   R G Querl (MCCYC) v Worcs (Kidderminster)   2010
8/70   R M Haq (Scotland A) v Warwicks (Rugby Sch)   2010

MOST WICKETS IN A SEASON
96	12.84	A.R.Caddick (Somerset)	1991
95	15.24	P.N.Broughton (Leics)	1961
91	16.65	P.J.Martin (Lancs)	1989
87	9.28	B.D.Wells (Glos)	1959
83	19.12	S.Greensword (Leics)	1966
81	15.54	B.M.Brain (Worcs)	1964
74	17.94	H.Sully (Northants)	1964
73	24.53	A.R.Roberts (Northants)	1995
72	16.13	C.C.Clifford (Warwicks)	1980
71	19.77	A.A.Barnett (Middx)	1990
71	22.02	R.Palmer (Somerset)	1965
71	14.29	B.L.D'Oliveira (Worcs)	1994
69	15.71	M.K.Bore (Yorks)	1976
69	18.11	P.J.Lewington (Warwicks)	1974
68	18.50	J.D.Fitton (Lancs)	1987
68	16.38	B.Stead (Notts)	1968
68	13.88	P.J.Robinson (Worcs)	1963
65	18.47	R.C.Smith (Leics)	1960
65	17.69	V.C.Drakes (Sussex)	1994

MOST FOR OTHER COUNTIES
61	16.73	P.J.Lindsey (Essex)	1964
61	21.73	N.M.Kendrick (Surrey)	1991
59	18.71	D.W.Baker (Kent)	1963
59	17.40	D.G.Moir (Derbys)	1981
53	20.11	D.W.White (Hants)	1959
53	23.83	D.J.P.Flint (Hants)	1991
52	17.11	H.D.S.Miller (Glam)	1966
52	15.09	C.Hughes (Glam)	1963
51	22.70	D.M.Cox (Durham)	1995
38	27.18	A MacQueen (MCCU)	2012
33	20.12	P Joshi (MCC YC, Northants, Surrey)	2014
15	31.13	G.Goudie (Scotland A)	2008

HAT-TRICKS
D.J.Spencer (Kent) v Leics (Oakham C.C.)   1993
J.M.de la Pena (Gloucs) v Somerset (Bath)   1993
T.C.Walton (Northants) v Leics (Kibworth)   1993
G.Welch (Warwicks) v Durham (Edgbaston)   1993
I.R.J.McLaren (Worcs) v Gloucs (Worcester)   1994
J.D.Lewry (Sussex) v Somerset (King's Col, Taunton)   1995
U.Afzaal (Notts) v Somerset (Trent Bridge)   1995
P.Aldred (Derbys) v Warwicks (Knowle & Dorridge)   1996
D.A.Altree (Warwicks) v Hants (Southampton)   1996
D.A.Altree (Warwicks) v Kent (Coventry & Nth War)   1996
J.J.Bates (Sussex) v Somerset (Horsham)   1996
N.Killeen (Durham) v Glam (Cardiff)   1996
G.Welch (Warwicks) v Worcs (Moseley)   1996
R.J.Kirtley (Sussex) v Hants (Hove)   1997
M.P.L.Bulbeck (Somerset) v Northants (Taunton)   1998
J.Ormond (Leics) v Northants (Northampton)   1998
G.Prince (Worcs) v Northants (Barnt Green)   2000
J.M.Anderson (Lancs) v Warwicks (Stratford-upon-Avon)   2001
A.D.Mascarenhas (Hants) v Middx (Harrow)   2001
I.Pattison (Durham) v Notts (Trent Bridge)   2002
M.S.Mason (Worcs) v Glam (Worcester)   2002
T.J.Murtagh (Surrey) v Lancs (Crosby)   2003
Z.K.Sharif (Essex) v Sussex (Hove)   2004
S.I.Mahmood (Lancs) v Leics (Middleton)   2005
B.W.Harmison (Durham) v Notts (Notts SC)   2007
K.D.Hodnett (MCCYC) v Northants (Radlett)   2008
T.W.Parsons (Hants) v Somerset (Taunton Vale)   2008
M.A.G.Nelson (Northants) v Essex (Milton Keynes)   2009
J A Glover (Sussex) v Somerset (Stirlands)   2010
J A Porter (MCC YC) v Hants (Rose Bowl)   2012
N R T Gubbins (Middx) v Essex (Coggeshall)   2013
L J Fletcher (Notts) v Worcs (Worcs RGS)   2014
Note: Instances of hat-tricks between 1959 and 1992 can be found in the Annuals 1992-2000.

FOUR WICKETS IN FOUR BALLS

A.J.Shantry (Northants) v Warwicks (Kenilworth Wardens) 2004

MATCHES ENDING IN A TIE

Essex v Northants	1960
Warwicks v Glam	1960
Glam v Notts	1961
Hants v Somerset	1963
Warwicks v Glos	1970
Lancs v Kent	1987
Worcs v Surrey	1990
Worcs v Glam (one innings match)	1998
Leics v Yorks	2011

MATCH DOUBLE

B.L.D'Oliveira 64,92 & 5-66,6-25
        Worcestershire v Leicestershire (Worcester) 1964
K.J.Wheatley 112 & 7-53,6-61
        Hampshire v Middlesex (Bournemouth) 1967
R.M.Ratcliffe 90*,18 & 6-41,4-94
        Lancashire v Nottinghamshire (Worksop) 1977
D.N.Patel 23,103* & 5-39,6-81
        Worcestershire v Glamorgan (Worcester) 1978
M.C.Dolman 82,23* & 4-92,7-38
        Warwickshire v Leicestershire (Edgbaston) 1982
P.N.Kasiwal 132* & 6-23,4-57
        Middlesex v Surrey (Enfield) 1986
S.R.Lampitt 38,80 & 6-104,6-63
        Worcestershire v Gloucestershire (Old Hill) 1986
R.J.Scott 147,26* & 4-94,6-68
        Hampshire v Sussex (Southampton) 1988
K.P.Dutch 261 & 5-26,5-137
        Middlesex v Somerset (RAF Vine Lane) 1996
M.J.Rawnsley 133 & 6-39,4-99
        Worcestershire v Gloucestershire (Bristol) 1997
M.A.Wagh 156 & 4-35,6-82
        Warwickshire v Derbyshire (Kenilworth Wardens) 1999

MOST DISMISSALS IN AN INNINGS

8 (all ct)	A.D.Shaw (Glam) v Gloucs (Usk)	1998
8 (7 ct; 1 st)	D.J.Malan (MCCYC) v Essex (Halstead)	2007
7 (all ct)	J.W.Elliott (Worcs) v Notts (Worcester)	1963
7 (5ct ; 2st)	G.R.Cass (Essex) v Warwicks (Harlow)	1964
7 (6ct ; 1st)	S.A.Westley (Gloucs) v Northants (Northampton)	1971
7 (all ct)	R.J.Parks (Hants) v Kent (Canterbury)	1979
7 (all ct)	C.H.Pegg (Essex) v Sussex (Horsham)	1989
7 (all ct)	R.J.Blakey (Yorks) v Notts (Middlesbrough)	2000
7 (all ct)	S.D.Snell (Gloucs) v Hants (WE Nursery)	2005
7 (all ct)	T.G.Burrows (Hants) v Middx (WE Nursery)	2005
7 (all ct)	A A Shafique (MCC YC) v Leics (High Wycombe)	2014

MOST DISMISSALS IN A MATCH

12 (all ct)	A.D.Shaw (Glam) v Gloucs (Usk)	1998
11 (all ct)	N.F.Sargeant (Surrey) v Hants (Basingstoke)	1993
11 (all ct)	R.J.Rollins (Essex) v Hants (Colchester)	1994
11 (all ct)	D.Murphy (Northants) v Derbys (Denby)	2011
10 (8ct ;2 st)	G.R.Cass (Essex) v Warwicks (Harlow)	1964
10 (all ct)	J.N.Batty (Derbys) v Somerset (Taunton)	1994
10 (all ct)	S.D.Snell (Gloucs) v Hants (WE Nursery)	2005
10 (all ct)	S.D.Snell (Gloucs) v Hants (WE Nursery)	2006
10 (all ct)	N.J.O'Brien (Northants) v Warwicks (M.Keynes)	2007
10 (all ct)	A M Gowers (Lancs) v Warwicks (Coventry)	2015
9 (8ct ; 1st)	L.A.Johnson (Northants) v Surrey (Northampton)	1964
9 (8ct ; 1st)	M.Khan (Northants) v Worcs (Kidderminster)	1989

9 (all ct)	T.Frost (Warwicks) v Kent (Coventry & N.War)	1996
9 (all ct)	T.Frost (Warwicks) v Essex (Walmley)	1996
9 (all ct)	R.C.J.Williams (Gloucs) v Somerset (Taunton)	1997
9 (all ct)	R.J.Blakey (Yorks) v Notts (Middlesbrough)	2000
9 (all ct)	J.N.Batty (Surrey) v Somerset (North Perrott)	2000
9 (all ct)	T.G.Burrows (Hants) v Middx (WE Nursery)	2005
9 (all ct)	L.J.Goddard (Derbys) v Lancs (Derby)	2005
9 (all ct)	J.A.Simpson (Notts) v Derbys (Notts SC)	2007
9 (all ct)	R L Jenkins (Somerset) v Middx (Taunton Vale)	2010
9 (8 ct; 1 st)	S A Stanworth (Notts) v Lancs (Cleethorpes)	2010
9 (8 ct; 1 st)	L K Parkinson (Lancs) v Derbys (Southport)	2012
9 (all ct)	G Knight (Warwicks) v Glam (Dianond Ground, Cardiff)	2013
9 (8 ct; 1st)	A M Rossington (Northants) v Somerset (Milton Keynes)	2014

MOST DISMISSALS IN A SEASON

58 (39ct ; 19st)	J.W.Elliott (Worcs)	1963
57 (47ct ; 10st)	L.A.Johnson (Northants)	1959
54 (50ct ; 4st)	G.J.Kersey (Kent)	1992
53 (52ct ; 1st)	T.Frost (Warwicks)	1996
53 (44ct ; 9st)	L.A.Johnson (Northants)	1961
52 (40ct ; 12st)	G.R.Cass (Essex)	1964
51 (43ct ; 8st)	L.A.Johnson (Northants)	1962
51 (30ct ; 21st)	N.D.Burns (Essex)	1984
51 (40ct ; 11st)	B.J.M.Maher (Derbys)	1992
51 (46ct ; 5st)	R.C.J.Williams (Glos)	1992
51 (45ct ; 6st)	S.C.Willis (Kent)	1995

MOST OUTFIELD CATCHES IN AN INNINGS

6	S.B.Hassan (Notts) v Lancs (Old Trafford)	1973
6	A.D.Brown (Surrey) v Kent (The Oval)	1989
5	A.J.W.McIntyre (Surrey) v Essex (The Oval)	1959
5	C.D.Fearnley (Worcs) v Notts (Halesowen)	1962
5	M.K.Kettle (Northants) v Essex (Duston)	1963
5	N.Hussain (Essex) v Notts (Southend)	1988
5	R.S.M.Morris (Hants) v Gloucs (Southampton)	1995
5	C A L Davis (Sussex) v Glam (Abergavenny)	2016

MOST OUTFIELD CATCHES IN A MATCH

7	R.S.M.Morris (Hants) v Gloucs (Southampton)	1995
7	H G Munsey (Northants) v MCCU (Desborough)	2016
6	M.K.Kettle (Northants) v Essex (Duston)	1963
6	G.S.Warner (Warwicks) v Northants (Ashton)	1972
6	S.B.Hassan (Notts) v Lancs (Old Trafford)	1973
6	A.D.Brown (Surrey) v Kent (The Oval)	1989
6	R.T.Bates (Notts) v Surrey (Worksop College)	1995
6	W.R.Smith (Notts) v Derbys (Denby)	2005
6	N.L.J.Browne (Essex) v Kent (The King`s School, Canterbury)	2011
6	S L Elstone (Derbys) v Worcs (Derby)	2016
6	Craig Cachopa (Sussex) v Surrey (New Malden)	2016
6	*S D Robson (Middx) v Glam (Merchant Taylors` S, Northwood)*	*2017*

MOST OUTFIELD CATCHES IN A SEASON

33	M D Bates (Hants)	2013
32	R.J.Blakey (Yorks)	1984
32	S S Eskinazi (Middx)	2013
30	M G K Burgess (Surrey)	2013
28	W.A.Bourne (Warwicks)	1973
28	J A Regan (Somerset)	2013
27	C.Johnson (Yorks)	1984
26	R.J.Maru (Hants)	1993
25	P.J.Robinson (Worcs)	1963
25	P.J.Robinson (Worcs)	1964

BAIN-DAWES / BAIN-CLARKSON / BAIN-HOGG /AON RISKS/ SECOND ELEVEN TROPHY WINNERS AND RUNNERS-UP

1986	Northamptonshire beat Essex by 14 runs	2002	Kent beat Hampshire by 5 wickets
1987	Derbyshire beat Hampshire by 7 wickets	2003	Hampshire beat Warwickshire by 8 wickets
1988	Yorkshire beat Kent by 7 wickets	2004	Worcestershire beat Essex by 8 wickets
1989	Middlesex beat Kent by 6 wickets	2005	Sussex beat Nottinghamshire by 6 wickets
1990	Lancashire beat Somerset by 8 wickets	2006	Warwickshire beat Yorkshire by 93 runs
1991	Nottinghamshire beat Surrey by 8 wickets	2007	Middlesex beat Somerset by 1 run
1992	Surrey beat Northamptonshire by 8 wickets	2008	Hampshire beat Essex by 7 runs
1993	Leicestershire beat Sussex by 142 runs	2009	Yorkshire beat Lancashire by 2 wickets
1994	Yorkshire beat Leicestershire by 6 wickets	2010	Essex beat Lancashire by 14 runs
1995	Leicestershire beat Gloucestershire by 5 wickets	2011	Nottinghamshire beat Lancashire by 4 wickets
1996	Leicestershire beat Durham by 46 runs	2012	Lancashire beat Durham by 76 runs
1997	Surrey beat Gloucestershire by 3 wickets	2013	Lancashire beat Nottinghamshire by 76 runs
1998	Northamptonshire beat Derbyshire by 5 wickets	2014	Leicestershire beat Lancashire by 168 runs
1999	Kent beat Hampshire by 106 runs	2015	Derbyshire beat Durham by 10 runs
2000	Leicestershire beat Hampshire by 25 runs	2016	Lancashire beat Somerset by 10 wickets (DLS)
2001	Surrey beat Somerset by 6 wickets	2017	Yorkshire beat Middlesex by 99 runs (DLS)

APPEARANCES IN THE SEMI-FINALS
11	Lancashire
9	Hampshire, Middlesex, Nottinghamshire
8	Leicestershire, Somerset, Sussex
7	Kent, Surrey, Warwickshire, Yorkshire
6	Durham
5	Northamptonshire
4	Gloucestershire
3	Derbyshire, Essex
2	Glamorgan, Worcestershire
1	Unicorns A

There were no Semi-Finals in 1986 and 1987 (Bain Dawes) and in 1988 (Bain Clarkson)

APPEARANCES IN THE FINAL
8	Lancashire
6	Hampshire, Leicestershire
5	Yorkshire
4	Essex, Kent, Nottinghamshire, Somerset, Surrey,
3	Derbyshire, Durham, Middlesex, Northamptonshire
2	Gloucestershire, Sussex, Warwickshire
1	Worcestershire

Only Glamorgan have yet to appear in the Final.

WINS
5	Leicestershire
4	Lancashire, Yorkshire
3	Surrey
2	Derbyshire, Hampshire, Kent, Middlesex, Northamptonshire, Nottinghamshire
1	Essex, Sussex, Warwickshire, Worcestershire

SECOND ELEVEN TROPHY RECORDS 1986-2017
(Incorporating Bain Dawes, Bain Clarkson, Bain Hogg and AON Risk matches)
The One-Day Trophy comprised 55 overs from 1986 to 1996, and then 50 from 1997 to 2010.
It became a 40-Over competition for the first time in 2011.
It reverted to 50 overs for the 2014 season.

New records for 2017 are shown thus.

HIGHEST INNINGS TOTALS (350 or better)

				368/4	Somerset v Gloucestershire (Taunton Vale)	2016
				367/5	Yorkshire v Northamptonshire (Bingley)	1991
				367/9	Kent v Hampshire (Polo Farm SC, Canterbury)	2015
437/5	Essex v Surrey (The Oval)	2010		366/4	Sussex v Middlesex (Uxbridge)	2009
431/7	*Northants v Leics (Northampton)*	*2017*		364/1	Surrey v Kent (The Oval)	1992
407/3	Northants v Glos (Thornbury)	2014		*364/7*	*Middx v Kent (Radlett)*	*2017*
404/5	Hants v MCC YC (Ageas Bowl Nursery)	2016		363	Lancs v Worcs (Old Trafford)	2015
400/9	Surrey v MCC YC (Banstead)	2001		362	Somerset v Glam (Cardiff)	2002
395/7	Worcestershire v Warwickshire (Olton)	2015		362/7	Somerset v MCCYC (High Wycombe)	2016
391/5	Glamorgan v Somerset (Cardiff)	2002		*362/7*	*Yorks v Warwicks (York)*	*2017*
388/1	Surrey v MCCYC (The Oval)	1993		360/4	Somerset v Gloucestershire (Lansdown, Bath)	1990
386/6	Durham v Nottinghamshire (Philadelphia)	1995		360/4	Worcestershire v Warwickshire (Barnt Green)	2008
385/8	Leicestershire v Middlesex (Leicester)	1996		360/6	Kent v Middlesex (Canterbury)	1988
383/5	Yorkshire v Durham (Harrogate)	2014		359/2	Somerset v Worcestershire (Taunton)	1993
383/6	*Worcs v Derbys (Kidderminster)*	*2017*		359/5	Leicestershire v Derbyshire (Hinckley)	2008
382/8	Gloucestershire v Worcestershire (Old Hill)	2004		356/5	Hampshire v Kent (Canterbury)	2006
381/5	Middlesex v Gloucestershire (Downend CC)	2015		*355/9*	*Derbys v Worcs (Kidderminster)*	*2017*
379/6	Nottinghamshire v Derbyshire (Derby)	2015		355	Durham v Derbyshire (Duffield)	1996
378/6	Worcestershire v MCC YC (Bromsgrove)	2014		352/4	Worcestershire v Glamorgan (Swansea)	1988
371/5	Gloucestershire v Worcestershire (Ombersley)	2003		352/4	Nottinghamshire v Leicestershire (Notts SC)	2015

352/5 Warwickshire v Worcestershire (Harborne) 2006
352/7 Kent v Hampshire (Canterbury) 2006
352/9 Surrey v Gloucestershire (Guildford) 2015
351/7 MCC YC v Kent (Radlett) 2006
351/9 Worcestershire v Warwickshire (Harborne) 2006

HIGHEST FOR OTHER COUNTIES
290/8 Unicorns v Yorks (Todmorden) 011
275/3 Minor Counties v Northants (Milton Keynes) 2006

LOWEST INNINGS TOTALS (90 or lower)
35 Derbys v Warwicks (Dunstall) 2010
41 Unicorns A v Notts (Trent College) 2012
46 Leics v Middx (Finchley) 2003
50 Warwicks v Hants (Edgbaston) 1991
50 Leics v Northants (Milton Keynes) 1999
50 Northants v Kent (Northampton) 2000
51 Middx v Surrey (The Oval) 1990
52 Unicorns A v Yorks (Abbeydale Park, Sheffield) 2012
55 Warwicks v Glam (Leamington) 2007
62 Notts v Lancs (Neston) 2009
64 Essex v Kent (Folkestone) 2000
65 Notts v Yorks (Hull) 1987
66 Worcestershire v Unicorns (East Challow) 2016
69 Notts v Northants (Thoresby Park, Nottm) 1986
72 Somerset v Northants (Taunton Vale) 2013
73 Sussex v Surrey (Guildford) 2015
74 Worcs v Glam (Worcester) 1999
76 Surrey v Kent (Cheam) 2011
77 Sussex v Essex (Chelmsford) 1986
77 Northants v Warwicks (West Bromwich) 2003
77 Warwicks v Somerset (Coventry & Nth Warwicks) 2008
78 Durham v Lancs (Lytham St Anne's) 2011
80 Leics v Minor Counties (Leicester) 1998
82 Essex v Surrey (Saffron Walden) 1996
82 Glos v Surrey (Whitgift School) 2009
82 Lancs v MCC YC (Radlett) 2013
83 Kent v Hants (Basingstoke) 2007
84 Kent v Hants (Bournemouth SC) 2005
84 Essex v Middx (Merchant Taylors' School, Northwood) 2012
84 Unicorns A v Glos (Bradfield College) 2013
85 Glos v Warwicks (Cheltenham C.C.) 2006
86 Leics v Lancs (Ramsbottom) 1988
86 Worcs v Hants (Barnt Green) 1999
86 Glam v Hants (Newport, Mon) 2002
86 Glamorgan v Gloucestershire (Diamond Ground, Cardiff) 2015
86 Kent v Sussex (Stirlands) 2007
88 Minor Counties v Warwicks (Solihull) 1999
88 Durham v Glam (Panteg) 2013
89 Lancs v Yorks (Old Trafford) 1998
89 Kent v Leics (Canterbury) 2000
90 Derbys v Notts (Derby) 1989
90 Essex v Kent (Wickford) 1993

LOWEST FOR OTHER COUNTIES
91 MCCYC v Surrey (Uxbridge) and v Surrey (Radlett) 2000 & 2011
92 Yorks v Notts (Headingley) 2009
95 Hants v Glam (Ebbw Vale) 1999

HIGHEST INDIVIDUAL SCORES (150 or better)
216* B.A.Godleman (Essex) v Surrey (The Oval) 2010
210 A.D.Brown (Surrey) v Kent (The Oval) 1992
203* F.du Plessis (Notts) v Minor Counties (Notts Unity) 2006
202* S.C.Goldsmith (Derbys) v Lancs (Checkley) 1992
196* S.A.Marsh (Kent) v Essex (Chelmsford) 2000
193* D.J.Pipe (Worcs) v Glam (Neath) 2004
193 J.M.Dakin (Leics) v Middx (Leicester) 1996
190* M A H Hammond (Gloucestershire)v MCC YC (Bath) 2015

188 P.Bainbridge (Durham) v Notts (Philadelphia) 1995
182 S.M.Davies (Worcs) v Warwicks (Harborne) 2006
180* D.M.Ward (Surrey) v MCCYC (The Oval) 1993
180* S W Billings (Kent) v Glos (Beckenham) 2012
176* F K Cowdrey (Kent) v Gloucestershire (Canterbury) 2015
172* A.J.E.Hibbert (Essex) v Sussex (Chelmsford) 1996
172* S.L.Elstone (Derbyshire) v Northamptonshire (Belper) 2015
172 J.C.Pooley (Middx) v MCCYC (Southgate) 1994
171 A.Fordham (Northants) v Yorks (Todmorden) 1990
170* W.P.C.Weston (Worcs) v Hants (Old Hill) 2002
170 J.H.K.Adams (Hants) v Glam (Cardiff) 2008
170 J.E.R.Gallian (Lancs) v Yorks (Bradford) 1994
169 P.D.Atkins (Surrey) v MCCYC (The Oval) 1993
169 A.Fordham (Northants) v Leics (Bedford School) 1997
167* K.A.Parsons (Somerset) v Worcs (Taunton) 1993
166 B.Parker (Yorks) v Northants (Bingley) 1991
163* N.Shahid (Essex) v MCCYC (Wickford) 1993
163 S.R.Patel (Notts) v Essex (Worksop College) 2008
162 V.S.Solanki (Worcs) v Somerset (Bromsgrove) 1997
162 T.L.Maynard (Glam) v MCCYC (Usk CC) 2010
162 L S Livingstone (Lancashire) v Worcestershire (Old Trafford) 2015
161* T.C.Walton (Northants) v Middx (Milton Keynes) 1998
161* D.D.Cherry (Glam) v Worcs (Usk) 2002
161 J.R.Wileman (Notts) v Lancs (Trent Bridge) 1996
160 M.A.Thornely (Sussex) v Middx (Canterbury) 2009
159 J E C Franklin (Notts) v Warwicks (Edgbaston) 2014
157 C S Delport (Leics) v Northants (Northampton) 2017
156* M J diVenuto (Durham) v Northants (Brandon) 2012
155 S.C.Moore (Worcs) v Somerset (Ombersley) 2004
155 M A Comber (Essex) v Middx (Chelmsford) 2011
155 T J Moores (Notts) v Durham (Notts SG) 2016
154* R.S.M.Morris (Hants) v Warwicks (Finchampstead)1993
154* W.A.Dessaur (Notts) v Yorks (Scarborough) 1994
154 R.J.Bartlett (Somerset) v Gloucs (Lansdown, Bath)1990
153 G F B Scott (Middx) v Kent (Radlett) 2017*
152* A.Lyth (Yorks) v Worcs (Kidderminster) 2009
152* S.A.Northeast (Kent) v Surrey (Canterbury) 2010
152 A J Ball (Kent) v Glos (Beckenham) 2017*
151* K K Jennings (Durham) v Yorkshire (Chester-le-Street) 2015
151 N.J.Llong (Kent) v Surrey (Canterbury) 1992
151 A J Blake (Kent) v Hampshire (Polo Farm SG, Canterbury) 2015
151 T P Alsop (Hants) v MCCYC (Ageas Bowl Nursery) 2016
150 N.Pratt (MCC YC) v Essex (Ilford) 1992
150 A.J.E.Hibbert (Essex) v Kent (Maidstone) 1996

HIGHEST FOR OTHER COUNTIES
146* M.A.Fell (Minor Counties) v Middx (Marlow) 1995
143 J M Kettleborough (Unicorns) v Somerset (Taunton Vale) 2017*
129 D.J.Lovell (Warwicks) v Leics (Leicester) 1996

THREE CENTURIES IN ONE INNINGS
P Mustard (104), N R Hobson (125*) & C S MacLeod (105*) for Durham v Northants at the Riverside 2016

BEST BOWLING (6 wickets or better)
9/27 K.Adams (Kent) v Northants (Northampton) 2000
8/19 C.J.Jordan (Surrey) v MCC YC (Radlett) 2011
8/28 J.W.Dike (Hants) v Gloucs (Bristol) 1994
7/12 M J Rippon (Sussex) v Kent (Hove) 2012
7/19 R.M.Amin (Surrey) v MCCYC (Wormsley) 2002
7/33 G S Virdi (Surrey) v Sussex (Horsham) 2017
7/36 G Burrows (Lancs) v Leics (Hinckley) 2017
7/44 T.M.Smith (Leics) v Warwicks (Harborne) 2002
6/8 H W Powell (Glam) v MCC YC (Newclose, Isle of Wight) 2013

6/9	D A Payne (Gloucestershire) v Glam	
	(Diamond Ground, Cardiff)	2015
6/12	A.K.Golding (Essex) v Sussex (Leigh-on-Sea)	1987
6/14	S.P.D.Smith (Surrey) v Kent (Tonbridge School)	2007
6/14	A.J.Dibble (Somerset) v Essex (Taunton Vale)	2011
6/18	J.A.North (Sussex) v Middx (Ealing)	1991
6/20	I.D.Austin (Lancs) v Leics (Old Trafford)	1991
6/21	P.A.Booth (Yorks) v Notts (Thoresby Park, Nottm)	1986
6/21	O.J.Newby (Lancs) v Durham (Liverpool)	2006
6/21	L W P Wells (Sussex) v Glamorgan (Fulking)	2015
6/22	L E Beaven (Hants) v Middx (Radlett)	2012
6/24	M.J.Thursfield (Hants) v Warwicks (Edgbaston)	1991
6/25	A.M.Smith (Gloucs) v Somerset (Bristol)	1993
6/25	M.A.Sharp (Minor Counties) v Middx (Uxbridge)	1997
6/25	M D Fisher (Yorks) v Leics (Grace Road)	2013
6/26	A M Lilley (Lancs) v Unicorns A (Old Trafford)	2013
6/27	M.Beardshall (Derbys) v Notts (Derby)	1988
6/27	L.Savident (Hants) v Worcs (Kidderminster)	1997
6/27	C J Haggett (Kent) v Glos (Maidstone)	2014
6/27	G T Griffiths (Hants) v Kent (Ageas Bowl Nursery)	2016
6/28	J.M.M.Averis (Gloucs) v Worcs	
	(Hatherley & Reddings)	2006
6/28	M W Parkinson (Lancs) v Glam (SWALEC)	2014
6/29	D.A.Leatherdale (Worcs) v Hants (Southampton)	1996
6/29	S.Lugsden (Hants) v Worcs (Barnt Green)	1999
6/29	S.M.J.Cusden (Kent) v Surrey	
	(Charterhouse School)	2006
6/30	A.R.Lilley (Lancs) v Yorks (Great Crosby)	2010
6/31	I.L.Pont (Essex) v Surrey (Southend-on-Sea)	1987
6/31	O.T.Parkin (Glam) v Warwicks	
	(Coventry & N.War.)	1993
6/32	R.J.Doughty (Surrey) v Middx (The Oval)	1986
6/32	T.M.Smith (Derbys) v Lancs (Belper Meadows)	1996
6/33	M.A.Feltham (Surrey) v Sussex (Horsham)	1987
6/33	J.M.Dakin (Leics) v Minor Counties (Barwell)	1995
6/33	C.J.Yates (Hants) v Somerset (West End)	2001
6/33	Adnan Ghaus (Lancs) v Notts (Great Crosby)	2013
6/34	J.M.Dakin (Leics) v Northants (Oakham School)	2001
6/34	G.W.Mike (Notts) v Yorks (Hull)	1987
6/35	L.A.Dawson (Hants) v MCC YC (Vine Lane)	2008
6/37	D S Lucas (Worcs) v Lancs (Middlewich)	2013
6/38	J.C.Hallett (Somerset) v Glam (Bridgend)	1993
6/39	D.R.Law (Durham) v Derbys (South Shields)	2002
6/39	N.J.Clewley (Warwicks) v Leics (Harborne)	2003
6/39	T.S.Roland-Jones (Middx) v Surrey (Radlett CC)	2010
6/47	J E Poysden (Warwicks) v Unicorns	
	(Bulls Head Ground)	2016
6/53	A M Reynoldson (Unicorns) v Somerset	
	(Sidmouth)	2014
6/53	*T J Wells (Leics) v Lancs (Hinckley)*	*2017*
6/58	D P Sibley (Surrey) v Middlesex	
	(Sunbury-on-Thames)	2015

BEST FOR OTHER COUNTIES

| 5/22 | S.J.E.Brown (Northants) v Notts (Peterborough) | 1988 |
| 5/14 | J.D.Harvey (MCCYC) v Kent (Norbury) | 1992 |

HIGHEST STAND FOR EACH WICKET

1st	333 by P D Atkins & A D Brown (Surrey) v Kent	
	(The Oval)	1992
2nd	374* by P D Atkins & D M Ward (Surrey) v	
	MCC Young Cricketers (The Oval)	1993
3rd	324* by A Lyth & C R Taylor (Yorkshire) v	
	Worcestershire (Kidderminster)	2009
4th	213 by M E Cassar & T A Tweats (Derbyshire) v	

	Nottinghamshire (Belper)	1998
5th	194 by V S Solanki & I Dawood (Worcestershire) v	
	Somerset (Bromsgrove)	1997
6th	187 by J M Dakin & V P Clarke (Leicestershire) v	
	Middlesex (Leicester)	1996
7th	170* by A A Metcalfe & G M Hamilton (Yorkshire) v	
	Lancashire (Bradford)	1995
8th	134* by A Javid & N S Tahir (Warwickshire) v	
	Leics (Stratford-upon-Avon)	2009
9th	*106 by T B Sole & C A Barrett (Northants) v*	
	Derbys (Denby)	*2017*
10th	90 by R A G Cummins & C J Liddle (Leicestershire) v	
	Yorkshire (Grace Road)	2006

The above records have been compiled by Philip Bailey of Cricket Archive and the Editor is very grateful for his help in filling this previous gap in the Annual. The records of the One-Day Trophy are not complete, particularly in the early years, so if any County Archivist or 2nd XI Scorer has confirmation of a higher stand for any wicket, please get in touch with the Editor.

HAT-TRICKS

S.J.Dennis (Glam) v Hants (Panteg)	1991
D.B.Pennett (Yorks) v Notts (Bawtry Rd, Sheffield)	1991
K.J.Shine (Middx) v Sussex (Harrow)	1994
K.P.Dutch (Middx) v Leics (Leicester)	1995
J.F.Brown (Northants) v Leics (Leicester)	1996
M.V.Steele (Northants) v Middx (Southgate)	1997
D.R.Law (Essex) v Surrey (The Oval)	1999
W.G.Khan (Sussex) v Surrey (Sutton)	2000
J.E.Bishop (Essex) v Northants (Milton Keynes)	2000
J.P.Hewitt (Middx) v Warwicks (Ealing)	2001
I.J.Westwood (Warwicks) v Northants (West Bromwich)	2003
R.H.Joseph (Kent) v Sussex (Maidstone)	2005
A.J.Blake (Kent) v Hants (Bournemouth SC)	2008
C.J.Jordan (Surrey) v Kent (Beckenham)	2008
A.P.Palladino (Essex) v Kent (Southend-on-Sea)	2010
G.R.Breese (Durham) v Warwicks (Longhirst Hall, Morpeth)	2011
C.J.Jordan (Surrey) v MCC YC (Radlett)	2011
I.A.A.Thomas (Kent) v Surrey (Cheam)	2011
D J Redfern (Derbys) v Yorks (Stamford Bridge)	2013
R J Gleeson (Northants) v Derbys (Denby)	*2017*

FOUR WICKETS IN FOUR BALLS

| B.E.A.Preece (Worcs) v Glamorgan (Panteg) | 1996 |

MOST DISMISSALS BY A WICKET-KEEPER IN AN INNINGS

5	*W E L Buttleman (Essex) v Somerset*	
	(Taunton Vale)	*2017*
5	*S J W Hall (Surrey) v Glos (Purley)*	*2017*

MATCH DOUBLE

| 122 | 5/22 | M.J.Weston (Worcs) v Glamorgan (Swansea) | 1988 |
| 126* | 6/33 | J.M.Dakin (Leics) v Minor Counties (Barwell) | 1995 |

TIED MATCHES

Somerset v Glam (Taunton Vale)	2008
Leics v Lancs (Grace Road)	2009
Durham v Glam (Darlington)	2010
Northants v Kent (Bedford School)	2010
Surrey v Sussex (Purley CC)	2010
Somerset v Surrey (Taunton Vale)	2011
Glos v Somerset (Bristol)	2011
Yorks v MCC YC (Weetwood)	2013

SECOND ELEVEN T20 COMPETITION RECORDS
2011 ONWARDS

WINNERS

2017   Sussex (beat Hampshire in the Final at Arundel)
    (Semi-Finals – Hampshire beat Yorkshire and
    Sussex beat Lancashire)

2016   Middlesex (beat Somerset in the Final at Arundel)
    (Semi-Finals – Middlesex beat Durham and
    Somerset beat Warwickshire)

2015   Middlesex (beat Kent in the Final at Arundel)
    (Semi-Finals – Kent beat Durham and
    Middlesex beat Lancashire)

2014   Leicestershire (beat Somerset in the Final at Arundel)
    (Semi-Finals – Leicestershire beat Lancashire and
    Somerset beat Hampshire)

2013   Surrey (beat Middlesex in the Final at Arundel)
    (Semi-Finals – Middlesex beat Durham and
    Surrey beat Gloucestershire)

2012   England U19 (beat Sussex in the Final at Arundel)
    (Semi-Finals – England U19 beat Worcestershire and
    Sussex beat Essex)

2011   Sussex (beat Durham in the Final at Fenner's)
    (Semi-Finals – Durham beat Gloucestershire and
    Sussex beat Leicestershire)

WINNERS & APPEARANCES

Winners

2	Middlesex, Sussex
1	England U19; Leicestershire; Surrey

Finalists

3	Middlesex, Sussex
2	Somerset
1	Durham; England U19; Hampshire; Kent; Leicestershire; Surrey.

Semi-Finalists

4	Durham
3	Lancashire, Middlesex; Sussex.
2	Gloucestershire; Hampshire; Leicestershire; Somerset.
1	England U19; Essex; Kent; Surrey; Warwickshire; Worcestershire; Yorkshire

Derbyshire, Glamorgan, MCC YC, Northamptonshire, Nottinghamshire and the Unicorns have yet to appear at Finals Day.

New records for 2017 are shown thus.

HIGHEST INNINGS TOTALS (Top 10)

232/4	Middlesex v Hampshire (Ageas Bowl Nursery)	2015
225/4	Worcestershire v Warwickshire (Kidderminster)	2015
225/4	Somerset v Warwickshire (Walmley)	2013
224/4	Lancashire v Yorkshire (Marske-by-the-Sea)	2013
224/5	Worcestershire v Glamorgan (Kidderminster)	2014
223/4	Kent v MCC YC (High Wycombe)	2015
222/5	Worcestershire v Warwickshire (Ombersley)	2011
221/5	Notts v Unc (Notts SG)	2016
221/7	Kent v MCC YC (High Wycombe)	2015
219/1	*Kent v Middx (Polo Farm SG, Canterbury)*	*2017*

HIGHEST FOR OTHER TEAMS

214/5	Warwickshire v Worcestershire (Kidderminster)	2015
211/3	Gloucestershire v Glamorgan (SWALEC)	2014
210/3	*Yorks v Durham (Marske CC)*	*2017*
207/3	Derbyshire v Durham (Brandon)	2014
207/7	*Sussex v Somerset (Horsham)*	*2017*
206/5	Essex v Unicorns A (Chelmsford)	2012
205/5	Hampshire v Surrey (Purley)	2011
205/3	Durham v Yorks (Brandon CC)	2016
204/3	Glamorgan v Somerset (Taunton Vale)	2012
200/1	Surrey v Sussex (Fulking)	2013

200/4	MCC YC v Surrey (Purley)	2015
200/6	*Northants v Yorks (Pudsey Congs)*	*2017*
199/6	Unicorns A v Notts (Notts SG)	2016
190/6	Leicestershire v Northamptonshire (Grace Road)	2015
181/6	England U19 v Durham (Loughborough)	2012

LOWEST INNINGS TOTALS (Lowest 10)

59	Somerset v Gloucestershire (Bristol)	2011
62	Worcs v Warwicks (Scorers, Shirley)	2016
71	Kent v MCC Young Cricketers (Canterbury)	2014
72	Nottinghamshire v Lancashire (Ormskirk CC)	2014
73	Lancashire v Durham (Parkgate, Neston)	2013
73	*Leics v Northants (Lutterworth CC)*	*2017*
79	Essex v Kent (Billericay)	2016
80	Surrey v Hampshire (Purley)	2015
81	Northamptonshire v Essex (Chelmsford)	2013
81	Yorkshire v Derbyshire (Denby)	2013
82/8	England U19 v Durham (Brandon)	2013

LOWEST FOR OTHER TEAMS

83	Glamorgan v Middlesex (Radlett)	2015
83	Gloucestershire v Surrey (Arundel)	2013
90	Warwickshire v Lancashire (Walmley)	2015
94	*Derbys v Lancs (Westhoughton)*	*2017*
96	*MCC YC v Lancs (Westhoughton)*	*2017*
105/7	Sussex v Surrey (Fulking)	2011
109	Durham v Derbys (Repton School)	2012
114/3	Middx v Northants (Dunstable)	2011
115	Hants v Sussex	
	(Spen Cama Memorial Ground, Fulking)	2012
117/7	Unicorns A v Northants (Bishop's Stortford)	2012

HIGHEST INDIVIDUAL SCORES (Top10)

127*	J J Roy (Surrey) v Sussex (Fulking)	2013
118	N R D Compton (Somerset) v Glamorgan (Diamond Ground, Cardiff)	2012
*116**	*A Z Lees (Yorks) v Northants (Pudsey Congs)*	*2017*
116	P R Stirling (Middlesex) v Hampshire (Ageas Bowl Nursery)	2015
115	G J Maxwell (Hampshire) v MCC Young Cricketers (Shenley)	2012
113*	J P Webb (Warwicks) v Somerset (Taunton)	2014
112*	A S T West (Unicorns) v Middlesex (Saffron Walden)	2014
111	B M Shafayat (Hampshire) v Kent (The Ageas Bowl)	2012
110*	T Kohler-Cadmore (Worcestershire) v Glamorgan (Kidderminster)	2014
110*	A J Hose (MCC YC) v Surrey (Purley)	2015

HIGHEST FOR OTHER COUNTIES

110	K Ali (Leics) v Unicorns A (Grace Road)	2012
109*	D L Lloyd (Glamorgan) v Surrey (Diamond Ground, Cardiff)	2015
*109**	*C T Steel (Durham) v Warwicks (S Northumberland)*	*2017*
*109**	*Z Crawley (Kent) v Middx (Polo Farm SG, Canterbury)*	*2017*
109	L J Wright (Sussex) v Hampshire (Hove)	2015
109	B T Foakes (Essex) v Northamptonshire (Northampton)	2014
103*	S J Mullaney (Nottinghamshire) v Yorkshire (Trent Coll)	2014
103*	L S Livingstone (Lancashire) v Warwickshire (Liverpool)	2015
99*	T C Knight (Derbyshire) v Durham (Brandon)	2014
99	R.I.Newton (Northamptonshire) v Essex (Chelmsford)	2011

97*	J M R Taylor (Gloucestershire) v Glamorgan	
	(Diamond Ground, Cardiff)	2012
74	R F Higgins (England U19) v Durham (Brandon)	2013

MOST RUNS IN A SEASON (Top 10)

471	*A J Robson (Sussex)*	*2017*
469	T F Smith (Glamorgan & MCC YC)	2015
439	N J Selman (Glam)	2016
415	L S Livingstone (Lancashire)	2015
411	*S A Zaib (Northants)*	*2017*
404	*Z Crawley(Kent)*	*2017*
390	A J Hose (MCC YC & Somerset)	2015
380	A S T West (Hampshire & Unicorns)	2014
376	*T Banton (Somerset)*	*2017*

MOST FOR OTHER TEAMS

353	A M Rossington (Middlesex)	2013
343	A J Mellor (Lancs, Somerset, Unc & Warwicks)	2015
339	J J Roy (Surrey)	2013
338	T P Lewis (Warwickshire)	2015
329	A J Hose (Hants, MCC YC)	2014
326	R F Higgins (Middx / England U19)	2013
319	C J Whittock (Unc)	2016
316	B M Shafayat (Hampshire)	2012
297	A L Hughes (Derbys)	2016
290	A N Kervezee (Worcestershire)	2015
289	M.D.Stoneman (Durham)	2011
281	S Hicks (MCC YC)	2015
270	S R Dickson (Kent)	2015
254	N D Pinner (Leicestershire)	2015
252	S K W Wood (Nottinghamshire)	2015
249	D M Hodgson (Yorkshire)	2015
240	H.J.H.Marshall (Gloucestershire)	2011
236	J C Mickleburgh (Essex)	2015
232	A L Davies (England U19)	2012

HIGHEST WICKET PARTNERSHIPS

First Wicket (Top 10)

177	P R Stirling & D J Malan (Middlesex) v Hampshire	
	(Ageas Bowl Nursery)	2015
160	C D Nash & L J Wright (Sussex) v Hampshire	
	(Hove)	2015
148	A M Rossington & D J Malan (Middx) v Unicorns A	
	(Uxbridge CC)	2013
137	K Ali & M J Wiley (Leics) v Unicorns A	
	(Grace Road)	2012
137	*V Chopra & A J A Wheater (Essex) v Unc*	
	(Great Tew)	*2017*
135	*A P Rouse & S W Billings (Kent) v Unc*	
	(Saffron Walden) (2nd match)	*2017*
132	M E Trescothick & C Kieswetter (Somerset) v	
	Warwicks (Taunton)	2014
132	*S Kelsall & E R Kilbee (Unc) v Essex (Great Tew)*	*2017*
131	M D T Roberts & S P Terry (Hants) v Sussex	
	(Ageas Bowl)	2013
130	*S R Dickson & Z Crawley (Kent) v Unc*	
	(Saffron Walden) (1st match)	*2017*

Second Wicket

*195**	*Z Crawley & J D S Neesham (Kent) v Middx*	
	(Polo Farm SG, Canterbury)	*2017*
162*	J J Roy & A Patel (Surrey) v Sussex (Fulking)	2013
156*	M W Machan & J S Gatting (Sussex) v Hants	
	(Ageas Bowl)	2013
153	D L Lloyd & M P O'Shea (Glam) v Worcs	
	(Kidderminster)	2012
150	L S Livingstone & L A Procter (Lancs) v Unicorns	
	(Liverpool)	2015
150	*R Gibson & J A Leaning (Yorks) v Durham*	
	(Marske CC)	*2017*
146	*J Allenby & P D Trego (Somerset) v Middx*	
	(Uxbridge)	*2017*

144*	T C Lac e & R G White (Middx) v Hants	
	(Ageas Bowl Nursery)	2017
138	M D E Holden & R F Higgins (Middx) v Durham	
	(Arundel)	2016
134	S C Moore & S J Croft (Lancs) v Notts	
	(Worksop College)	2013

Third Wicket

143	K R Brown & J Clark (Lancs) v Yorks	
	(Marske-by-the-Sea)	2013
137	L D McManus & J J Weatherley (Hants) v Sussex	
	(Ageas Bowl Nursery)	2016
128	T C Knight & P Drysdale (Derbys) v Durham	
	(Brandon)	2014
126	J Clark & R P Jones (Lancs) v Northants	
	(Westhoughton)	2016
124*	L A Procter & R P Jones (Lancashire) v Derbyshire	
	(Parkgate, Neston)	2015
124	B M Shafayat & S P Terry (Hants) v Kent	
	(The Rose Bowl)	2012
117	T A Wood & C J Whittock (Unc) v Notts	
	(Notts SG)	2016
114*	W J Durston & S L Elstone (Derbyshire) v Unicorns	
	(Derby)	2015
114	M L Pettini & B T Foakes (Essex) v Northants	
	Chelmsford)	2013
*113**	*C J Whittock & L J Thomason (Unc) v Sussex*	
	(Long Marston)	*2017*

Fourth Wicket

158	G J Maxwell & H Riazuddin (Hants) v	
	MCC Young Cricketers (Shenley)	2012
125	*F I N Khushi & A P Beard (Essex) v Somerset*	
	(Chelmsford)	*2017*
114*	C S MacLeod & G J Muchall (Durham) v Yorks	
	(York)	2014
113	J J Weatherley & A S T West (Hants) v Surrey	
	(Purley)	2016
110	J A Leaning & W M H Rhodes (Yorks) v Durham	
	(York)2014	
108*	G J Muchall & S G Borthwick (Durham) v Lancs	
	(Gosforth)	2012
107*	A W R Barrow & J H Davey (Somerset) v	
	Gloucestershire (Taunton Vale)	2015
107	L C Paternott & S Prasanna (Northants) v Leics	
	(Bedford S)	2016
104	A J Hose & S S McKechnie (MCC YC) v Sussex	
	(Shenley)	2013
103	M N W Spriegel & A Harinath (Surrey) v Hants	
	(The Rose Bowl)	2012

Fifth Wicket

128*	J R Levitt & Zain Abbas (MCC Young Cricketers) v	
	Leics (Grace Road)	2012
115	*M J Lumb & S J Mullaney (Notts) v Northants*	
	(Grantham)	*2017*
106	N.A.James and D.S.Roberts (Glam) v Warwicks	
	(SWALEC)	2011

Sixth Wicket

102	T Banton & M T C Waller (Somerset) v Warwicks	
	(Arundel)	2016
*93**	*T Banton & R C Davies (Somerset) v Glos*	
	(Taunton Vale)	*2017*
84	C R Hemphrey & S J Cook (Kent) v Hants	
	(The Rose Bowl)	2012
78	R G White & A Rath (Middx) v Somerset	
	(Arundel)	2016
77*	G J Muchall & P Coughlin (Durham) v Warwicks	
	(Edgbaston)	2016
76	C.P.Wood and B.A.C.Howell (Hants) v Sussex	
	(Rose Bowl Nursery)	2011

Seventh Wicket

98*	A Javid & T W Allin (Warwicks) v Glos (Olton)	2013
98	B T Foakes & M E T Salisbury (Essex) v Northants (Northampton)	2014
72*	T Kohler-Cadmore & M A Johnson (Worcs) v Warwicks (Kidderminster)	2013
66*	J.P.Thompson and C.Macleod (Kent) v MCC YC (Radlett)	2011

Eighth Wicket

74*	R S Buckley & I S Sohi (MCCYC) v Hants (Shenley)	2016
59*	S M Park & J P Kettle (Unicorns A) v Northants (Bishop's Stortford)	2012
55	T.B.Abell and M.T.C.Waller (Somerset) v Glam (Taunton Vale)	2011

Ninth Wicket

*72**	*D M Bess & S E Grant (Somerset) v Hants (Ageas Bowl Nursery)*	*2016*
71*	G P W Bacon & L Wood (Notts) v Lancs (Worksop College)	2013
69*	A DTillcock & L J Fletcher (Notts) v Lancs (Ormskirk)	2014
63*	L J Hill & D T Reed (Unicorns A) v Northants (Northampton)	2013
62	*J C Wainman & K Carver (Yorks) v Worcs (Worcester RGS)*	*2017*

Tenth Wicket

*48**	*K Carver & J W Shutt (Yorks) v Worcs (Worcester RGS)*	*2017*
47*	P J Mackay & J O Grundy (Warwicks) v Glos (Bristol)	2012

TWO HUNDREDS IN A MATCH

103*	S J Mullaney (Notts) & 102 by J A Leaning (Yorks) (Trent College)	2014
100	B L D'Oliveira (Worcs) & 101 by T P Lewis (Warwicks) (Kidderminster)	2015
108	D J Willey (Yorks) & 104 by P Mustard (Durham) (Brandon CC)	2016

BEST BOWLING IN AN INNINGS (TOP 10 RETURNS)

6/19	N A Sowter (Middlesex) v Glamorgan (Radlett)	2015
6/33	Waqas Hussain (Unc) v Durham (Burnopfield CC)	2016
5/10	U Arshad (Durham) v Lancs (Parkgate, Neston)	2013
5/11	*R N Sidebottom (Warwicks) v Durham (S Northumberland)*	*2017*
5/12	*G L S Scrimshaw (Worcs) v Yorks (Worcester RGS)*	*2017*
5/12	*K van Vollenhoven (MCC YC) v Durham (Merchant Taylors' S, Northwood)*	*2017*
5/13	R O Gordon (Warwicks) v Notts (Edgbaston)	2016
5/14	L C Norwell (Glos) v Kent (Polo Farm SG, Canterbury)	2016
5/15	R J Montgomery (Somerset) v Glam (Taunton)	2013
5/16	M E Hobden (Sussex) v Surrey (Purley)	2014

OTHER 5 WICKET PERFORMANCES

5/17	M W Parkinson (Lancs) v Unc (Knypersley)	2016
5/18	M J Leach (Somerset) v Glam (Newport)	2014
5/20	G T Park (Unicorns A) v Leics (Bishop's Stortford)	2013
5/20	K Carver (Yorkshire) v Worcestershire (Barnt Green)	2015
5/22	*A M Ali (Leics) v Northants (Lutterworth)*	*2017*
5/25	D J Lamb (Lancashire) v Nottinghamshire (Worksop Coll)	2015
5/24	J N J Rollings (MCC Young Cricketers) v Sussex (Horsham)	2012
5/27	T S Mills (Essex) v Unicorns A (Chelmsford)	2012

BEST FOR OTHER COUNTIES

4/10	O P Stone (Northants) v Worcs (Milton Keynes)	2015
4/11	*M Carter (Notts) v MCC YC (Merchant Taylors' S, Northwood)*	*2017*
4/13	J W Dernbach (Surrey) v Kent (Polo Farm Sports Club, Canterbury)	2013
4/14	A Hepburn (Worcs) v Durham (Chester-le-Street CC)	2015
4/15	A M Davies (Kent) v MCC YC (Radlett)	2013
4/18	P.D Burgoyne (Derbys) v Notts (Long Eaton)	2011
4/18	*J B Lintott (Hants) v Middx (Ageas Bowl Nursery)*	*2017*
4/28	S W Griffiths (Glam) v Warwicks (Cardiff CC)	2013
3/18	B F Collins (England U19) v Durham (Loughborough)	2012

MOST WICKETS IN A SEASON

20	G S Randhawa (Durham)	2016
20	*O E Robinson (Sussex)*	*2017*
19	A D Tillcock (Nottinghamshire)	2015
19	Zain Shahzad (Essex & MCC YC)	2015
17	G T Park (Unicorns A)	2013
17	C J Russell (Worcestershire)	2015
17	Imran Qayyum (Kent)	2015
17	O J Hannon-Dalby (Warwicks)	2016
16	B J McCarthy (Durham)	2015
16	M H McKiernan (Unc)	2016
16	*B J Taylor (Hants)*	*2017*
15	N.A.James (Glamorgan)	2011
15	P.B.Muchall (Durham & MCC YC)	2011
15	T M J Smith (Glos / Middx)	2013

MOST FOR OTHER COUNTIES

14	N A Sowter (Middlesex)	2015
14	H W Podmore (Middlesex)	2015
14	S Mahmood (Lancashire)	2015
14	T J Lancefield (Glam / Glos / Northants / Unicorns A)	2013
14	M T C Waller (Somerset)	2016
13	B F Collins (England U19)	2012
12	A MacQueen (MCC YC)	2015
12	T.S.Mills (Essex)	2013
12	C J Jordan (Surrey)	2012
11	J.Needham (Derbyshire)	2011
10	M D Taylor (Gloucestershire)	2013
10	D.J.Willey (Northamptonshire)	2011
10	G G White (Northamptonshire)	2016
10	Azeem Rafiq (Yorkshire)	2013
9	M.N.Malik (Leicesershire)	2011

HAT-TRICKS

W A White (Lancs) v Notts (Worksop College)		2013
W M H Rhodes (Yorks) v Durham (York CC)		2014
G R Napier (Essex) v Leics (Chelmsford) *		2014
O H Freckingham (Leics) v Essex (Chelmsford) *		2014
J C Wainman (Yorks) v Northants (Pudsey Congs)		*2017*
T Bulcock (Unc) v Sussex (Long Marston)		*2017*

* Two hat-tricks in the same match.

FOUR WICKETS IN FOUR BALLS

No instances have, as yet, occurred.

CARRYING BAT THROUGH COMPLETED INNINGS

No instances have, as yet, occurred.

MATCHES ENDING IN A TIE

Middx v Leics (Uxbridge CC) (D/L)	2011
Lancs v Notts (Parkgate, Neston) (D/L)	2012
Somerset v Warwicks (Taunton)	2014
Hampshire v Surrey (The Ageas Bowl Nursery)	2014
Durham v Unicorns (Burnopfield)	2015
Surrey v Sussex (Purley)	2016

Unc v Durham (Long Marston)   **2017**
Derbys v Durham (Belper Meadows)   **2017**

MOST DISMISSALS IN A SEASON

15	S S Eskinazi (Middx) (7 ct & 8 st)	2016
14	A J Mellor (Lancs, Somerset, Unicorns	
	& Warwicks) (12 ct & 2 st)	2015
13	*A J Mellor (Warwicks) (9 ct & 4 st)*	*2017*
12	A M Gowers (Lancashire) (11 ct & 1 st)	2015
12	T.J.Poynton (Derbys) (3 ct & 9st)	2011
12	S W Poynter (Durham) (5 ct & 7 st)	2016
12	B J Yates (Lancs) (11 ct & 1 st)	2016
11	G Knight (Glam / Northants) (7 ct & 4 st)	2013
11	S W Poynter (Durham) (6 ct & 5st)	2014
11	*G H Roderick (Glos) (10 ct & 1 st)*	*2017*
11	*T Banton (Somerset) (9 ct & 2 st)*	*2017*

MOST OUTFIELD CATCHES IN A SEASON

10	M T C Waller (Somerset)	2013

MOST DISMISSALS IN AN INNINGS

5	H J Swindells (Leics) v Worcs (Kibworth CC)	
	(4 ct & 1 st)	2016
5	S S Eskinazi (Middx) v Kent (Uxbridge CC)	
	(2ct & 3st)	2016
5	A J Mellor (Lancs, Somerset, Unicorns	
	& Warwicks)	2015
5	C B Cooke (Glam) v Glos (3 ct & 2 st)	2012
5	*G H Roderick (Glos) v Essex (Chelmsford)*	
	(4ct & 1st)	*2017*
5	*A J A Wheater (Essex) v Glam (St Fagans) (5ct)*	*2017*

MOST OUTFIELD CATCHES IN AN INNINGS

4	J D S Neesham (Derbys) v Unc (Long Marston)	2016
4	T M J Smith (Gloucestershire) v Glamorgan	
	(Bristol U)	2015
4	D W Lawrence (Essex) v Kent (Maidstone)	
4	L J Kinch (Leics) v Middx	2011
4	*N O Priestley (Derbys) v Yorks*	
	(Alvaston & Boulton)	*2017*

Other T20 records may be found in the 2015 Annual, pp 115 to 118

2018 FIXTURES

Abbreviations:

SEC	Second Xl Championship
SET	Second Xl Trophy
SET20	Second Xl T20
SEF 1	1-day friendly
SEF 2	2-day friendly
SEF 3	3-day friendly
SEF 4	4-day friendly

Date	Match	Venue
April		
9 SEF 3	Derbyshire v Warwickshire	3aaa County Ground
10 SEF 4	Gloucestershire v Yorkshire	Brightside Ground
10 SEF 3	Essex v MCC YC	Billericay CC
10 SEF 3	Northamptonshire v Kent	County Ground
16 SEC	Leicestershire v MCC YCs	Kibworth CC
16 SEC	Nottinghamshire v Derbyshire	Notts Sports Club (Lady Bay)
16 SET	Sussex v Essex	Hove
16 SEF 4	Middlesex v Durham	
17 SEC	Sussex v Essex	Hove
17 SEF 1	Gloucestershire v Ireland	Rockhampton CC
17 SEF 4	Kent/Northamptonshire v Warwickshire	Beckenham
17 SEF 3	Lancashire v Yorkshire	Emirates Old Trafford
18 SEF 3	Glamorgan v Gloucestershire	SSE SWALEC
18 SEF 3	Somerset v Worcestershire	Taunton Vale
19 SET	Leicestershire v MCC YCs	
23 SEC	Lancashire v Derbyshire	Liverpool CC
23 SEC	MCC YCs v Northamptonshire	High Wycombe CC
23 SET	Kent v Somerset	Polo Farm
23 SEF 3	Yorkshire v Nottinghamshire	Scarborough
23 SEF 4	Hampshire/Surrey v Essex/Sussex	Ageas Bowl
23 SEF 1	Gloucestershire v Scotland	Bristol CC
24 SEC	Kent v Somerset	Polo Farm
24 SEC	Warwickshire v Worcestershire	EFSG Portland Road
24 SEF 1	Durham v Leicestershire	Brandon CC
25 SEF 3	Durham v Leicestershire	Emirates Riverside
26 SET	MCC YCs v Northamptonshire	
26 SEF 1	Yorkshire v Nottinghamshire	Scarborough
30 SET	Hampshire v Unicorns	Saffron Walden CC
30 SET	Northamptonshire v Derbyshire	
May		
1 SEC	Middlesex v Gloucestershire	Uxbridge Sports Club
1 SEC	Somerset v Surrey	Taunton Vale
1 SET	Unicorns v Essex	
1 SET	Worcestershire v Warwickshire	
2 SET	Leicestershire v Northamptonshire	
2 SEF 3	Hampshire v Glamorgan	Ageas Bowl
3 SET	Derbyshire v Worcestershire	Alvaston & Boulton
3 SET	Nottinghamshire v Warwickshire	Notts Sports Club (Lady Bay)
4 SET	Yorkshire v Leicestershire	Stamford Bridge CC
7 SEC	Derbyshire v Warwickshire	Hem Heath
7 SET	Gloucestershire v Surrey	Rockhampton CC
8 SET	Hampshire v Sussex	Ageas Bowl
8 SET	Kent v Middlesex	Beckenham
8 SET	MCC YCs v Worcestershire	
8 SET	Northamptonshire v Lancashire	
8 SET	Somerset v Surrey	Taunton Vale
8 SET	Yorkshire v Durham	Emerald, Headingley
9 SEC	Kent v Middlesex	Beckenham
9 SEC	MCC YCs v Worcestershire	High Wycombe CC
9 SEC	Northamptonshire v Lancashire	
9 SEC	Yorkshire v Durham	Emerald, Headingley
9 SET	Gloucestershire v Glamorgan	Rockhampton CC
10 SET	Derbyshire v Warwickshire	Hem Heath

10	SET	Somerset v Glamorgan	Taunton Vale
13	SET	Middlesex v Unicorns	Uxbridge Sports Club
14	SET	Glamorgan v Sussex	Newport CC
14	SET	Hampshire v Kent	Ageas Bowl
14	SET	Northamptonshire v Nottinghamshire	
14	SET	Surrey v Essex	LSE, New Malden
14	SET	Unicorns v Somerset	
14	SET20	Warwickshire v Durham	
15	SEC	Glamorgan v Sussex	Newport CC
15	SEC	Hampshire v Kent	Ageas Bowl
15	SET	Lancashire v Yorkshire	Liverpool CC
15	SET	MCC YCs v Durham	
15	SET	Middlesex v Gloucestershire	Southgate CC
15	SET	Warwickshire v Leicestershire	
15	SET	Worcestershire v Nottinghamshire	
16	SET	Derbyshire v Yorkshire	Repton School
16	SET	Somerset v Gloucestershire	Taunton Vale
17	SET	Durham v Worcestershire	
17	SET	Essex v Middlesex	Garon Park, Southend
17	SET	Lancashire v Derbyshire	Northern CC
21	SET	Durham v Northamptonshire	Emirates Riverside
21	SET	Essex v Hampshire	Billericay CC
21	SET	Gloucestershire v Kent	Bristol CC
21	SET	Leicestershire v Nottinghamshire	
21	SET	Warwickshire v Yorkshire	
21	SET	Worcestershire v Lancashire	
22	SEC	Durham v Northamptonshire	
22	SEC	Essex v Hampshire	Billericay CC
22	SEC	Glamorgan v Somerset	Newport CC
22	SEC	Leicestershire v Nottinghamshire	Kibworth CC
22	SEC	Warwickshire v Yorkshire	EFSG Portland Road
22	SEC	Worcestershire v Lancashire	
22	SET	Middlesex v Surrey	TBC
24	SET	Surrey v Sussex	LSE, New Malden
24	SET	Unicorns v Gloucestershire	
25	SET	Glamorgan v Unicorns	SSE SWALEC
28	SET	Middlesex v Surrey	Southgate CC
28	SEC	Nottinghamshire v Durham	Notts Sports Club (Lady Bay)
28	SEF 4	Gloucestershire v Worcestershire	Cheltenham College
29	SEC	Northamptonshire v Derbyshire	
29	SET	Glamorgan v Hampshire	Neath CC
29	SET	Lancashire v Leicestershire	Northern CC
29	SET	Sussex v Kent	Hove
30	SEC	Glamorgan v Hampshire	Neath CC
30	SEC	Sussex v Kent	Hove
31	SET	Nottinghamshire v Durham	Grantham CC
31	SET	Warwickshire v MCC YCs	TBC

June

4	SET	Durham v Lancashire	Emirates Riverside
4	SET	Essex v Somerset	Bishop Stortford
4	SET	Kent v Glamorgan	Bromley CC
4	SET	Nottinghamshire v Derbyshire	Notts Sports Club (Lady Bay)
4	SEF 3	Warwickshire v Surrey	EFSG Portland Road
5	SEC	Durham v Lancashire	Emirates Riverside
5	SEC	Essex v Somerset	Bishop Stortford
5	SEC	Kent v Glamorgan	Beckenham
5	SEC	Worcestershire v Nottinghamshire	
5	SET	Sussex v Middlesex	Blackstone
5	SET	Yorkshire v MCC YCs	York CC

6	SEC	Sussex v Middlesex	Blackstone
6	SEC	Yorkshire v MCC YCs	York CC
8	SET	Surrey v Hampshire	LSE, New Malden
11	SEC	Gloucestershire v Surrey	Rockhampton CC
11	SEC	Warwickshire v MCC YCs	
11	SET20	Derbyshire v Nottinghamshire	3aaa County Ground
11	SET20	Essex v Glamorgan	Chelmsford
11	SET20	Worcestershire v Durham	
11	SEF 4	Leicestershire v Kent	
12	SEC	Essex v Glamorgan	Billericay CC
12	SEC	Lancashire v Yorkshire	Southport CC
12	SEC	Worcestershire v Durham	
13	SEC	Sussex v Unicorns	Eastbourne
14	SET20	Unicorns v Hampshire	Newclose, IOW
15	SET SF	TBC v TBC	TBC
15	SET SF	TBC v TBC	TBC
18	SEC	Kent v Gloucestershire	Polo Farm
18	SEC	Middlesex v Hampshire	Radlett CC
18	SEC	Surrey v Sussex	LSE, New Malden
18	SET20	MCC YCs v Leicestershire	
19	SET20	Derbyshire v Lancashire	3aaa County Ground
19	SET20	Durham v Yorkshire	Brandon CC
20	SEF 3	Derbyshire v Glamorgan	Belper Meadows
21	SET Final	TBC v TBC	TBC
21	SET20	Kent v Gloucestershire	Polo Farm
25	SEC	Nottinghamshire v MCC YCs	Notts Sports Club (Lady Bay)
25	SET20	Durham v Derbyshire	
25	SET20	Lancashire v Warwickshire	Westhoughton
25	SET20	Surrey v Middlesex	LSE, New Malden
25	SET20	Worcestershire v Northamptonshire	
26	SEC	Durham v Derbyshire	
26	SEC	Lancashire v Warwickshire	Chester Boughton Hall CC
26	SEC	Worcestershire v Northamptonshire	
26	SEC	Yorkshire v Leicestershire	York CC
26	SET20	Gloucestershire v Somerset	Bristol CC
26	SET20	Middlesex v Kent	Uxbridge Sports Club
26	SET20	Sussex v Hampshire	Horsham
27	SET20	Surrey v Kent	LSE, New Malden
28	SET20	Glamorgan v Somerset	Port Talbot CC
28	SET20	Kent v Sussex	Beckenham
28	SET20	Middlesex v Hampshire	Richmond CC
28	SET20	Nottinghamshire v MCC YCs	Oakham School

July

2	SET20	Glamorgan v Middlesex	Newport CC
2	SET20	Leicestershire v Worcestershire	
2	SET20	MCC YCs v Derbyshire	
2	SET20	Northamptonshire v Warwickshire	
2	SEF 1	Somerset v Hampshire	Taunton Vale
2	SEF 1	Nottinghamshire v Essex	
3	SEC	Glamorgan v Middlesex	Neath CC
3	SEC	Leicestershire v Worcestershire	
3	SEC	MCC YCs v Derbyshire	High Wycombe CC
3	SEC	Warwickshire v Durham	EFSG Portland Road
3	SET20	Sussex v Surrey	East Grinstead
4	SET20	Somerset v Essex	Taunton Vale
4	SET20	Yorkshire v Lancashire	Harrogate CC
5	SET20	Essex v Unicorns	Billericay CC
5	SET20	Hampshire v Surrey	Ageas Bowl

Date	Comp	Match	Venue
5	SET20	Nottinghamshire v Northamptonshire	Worksop College TBC
6	SET20	Kent v Unicorns	Folkestone
9	SEC	Derbyshire v Yorkshire	Glossop
9	SET20	Durham v MCC YCs	South Northumberland CC
9	SET20	Glamorgan v Gloucestershire	Newport CC
9	SET20	Lancashire v Northamptonshire	Emirates Old Trafford
9	SET20	Leicestershire v Warwickshire	
9	SET20	Middlesex v Essex	Radlett CC
10	SEC	Durham v MCC YCs	South Northumberland
10	SEC	Hampshire v Surrey	LSE, New Malden
10	SEC	Leicestershire v Warwickshire	
10	SEC	Middlesex v Essex	Uxbridge Sports Club
10	SET20	Somerset v Sussex	Taunton Vale
11	SEC	Somerset v Sussex	Taunton Vale
11	SEF 3	Gloucestershire v Lancashire	Rockhampton CC
11	SEF 3	Northamptonshire v Glamorgan	
12	SET20	Yorkshire v Derbyshire	Barnsley CC
16	SET20	Gloucestershire v Essex	Bedminster CC
16	SET20	Hampshire v Somerset	Ageas Bowl
16	SET20	Warwickshire v Worcestershire	
16	SEF 4	Middlesex v Kent	
17	SEC	Gloucestershire v Essex	Bristol CC
17	SEC	Hampshire v Somerset	Ageas Bowl
17	SEF 1	Lancashire v Leicestershire	
18	SET20	Nottinghamshire v Yorkshire	Worksop College TBC
18	SET20	Worcestershire v MCC YCs	
19	SET20	Derbyshire v Leicestershire	Denby
23	SET20	Gloucestershire v Sussex	Bath CC
23	SET20	MCC YCs v Lancashire	
23	SET20	Northamptonshire v Yorkshire	
23	SET20	Somerset v Middlesex	Taunton Vale
23	SET20	Surrey v Glamorgan	LSE, New Malden
23	SET20	Warwickshire v Nottinghamshire	
23	SEF 4	Derbyshire v Kent	Denby
24	SEC	Gloucestershire v Sussex	Bath CC
24	SEC	MCC YCs v Lancashire	High Wycombe CC
24	SEC	Northamptonshire v Yorkshire	
24	SEC	Somerset v Middlesex	Taunton Vale
24	SEC	Surrey v Glamorgan	LSE, New Malden
24	SEC	Warwickshire v Nottinghamshire	EFSG Portland Road
24	SET20	Leicestershire v Durham	
25	SEC	Leicestershire v Durham	Kibworth CC
30	SET20	Hampshire v Gloucestershire	Ageas Bowl
30	SET20	Lancashire v Nottinghamshire	Liverpool CC
30	SET20	Northamptonshire v Leicestershire	
30	SET20	Yorkshire v Worcestershire	Marske CC
31	SEC	Essex v Kent	Coggeshall CC
31	SEC	Hampshire v Gloucestershire	Ageas Bowl
31	SEC	Lancashire v Nottinghamshire	Liverpool CC
31	SEC	Northamptonshire v Leicestershire	
31	SEC	Yorkshire v Worcestershire	Harrogate CC

August

Date	Comp	Match	Venue
1	SET20	Unicorns v Surrey	
2	SET20	Unicorns v Glamorgan	
3	SET20	Essex v Kent	Coggeshall CC
6	SEC	Derbyshire v Worcestershire	Belper Meadows
6	SEC	Nottinghamshire v Northamptonshire	Notts Sports Club (Lady Bay)
6	SEC	Surrey v Kent	LSE, New Malden
6	SEF 3	Somerset v Hampshire	Taunton Vale
6	SEF 3	Sussex v Middlesex	Horsham
9	SET20	Finals Day TBC v TBC	Arundel
13	SEC	Nottinghamshire v Yorkshire	Notts Sports Club (Lady Bay)
13	SEC	Surrey v Essex	LSE, New Malden
13	SEF 4	Hampshire v Middlesex	Ageas Bowl
13	SEF 1	Glamorgan v Gloucestershire	SSE SWALEC
13	SEF 4	Worcestershire v Warwickshire	
14	SEC	Somerset v Gloucestershire	Taunton Vale
15	SEC	Lancashire v Leicestershire	Blackpool CC
20	SEC	Derbyshire v Leicestershire	Chesterfield
20	SEC	Sussex v Hampshire	Preston Nomads
20	SEF 1	Durham v Essex	Burnopfield CC
20	SEF 4	Kent v MCC YC	Canterbury
21	SEC	Gloucestershire v Glamorgan	Bristol CC
21	SEF 3	Durham v Essex	Burnopfield CC
22	SEC	Northamptonshire v Warwickshire	
27	SEF 4	Kent v Essex	Canterbury
27	SEF 3	Nottinghamshire v Surrey	
27	SEF 4	Middlesex v Lancashire	
28	SEF 4	Gloucestershire v Warwickshire	Rockhampton CC
28	SEF 3	MCC YC v Sussex	
28	SEF 3	Somerset v Yorkshire	Cooper Associates County Ground
28	SEF 3	Worcestershire v Glamorgan	

September

Date	Comp	Match	Venue
3	SEF 4	Worcestershire v Surrey	
4	SEC	Final TBC v TBC	TBC
4	SEF 3	Glamorgan v Nottinghamshire	SSE SWALEC
4	SEF 4	Leicestershire v Yorkshire	
4	SEF 3	Northamptonshire v Scotland	County Ground
4	SEF 3	Sussex v Durham	Blackstone
10	SEF 4	Lancashire v Hampshire	Southport CC
10	SEF 4	Essex v Middlesex	Billericay CC
10	SEF 4	Somerset v Warwickshire	Taunton Vale
12	SEF 3	Surrey v Yorkshire	Guildford
17	SEF 3	Hampshire v Worcestershire	Ageas Bowl
18	SEF 3	Warwickshire v Nottinghamshire	
18	SEF 3	Yorkshire v Durham	Scarborough
18	SEF 3	Sussex v Derbyshire	Blackstone

INDEX OF VENUES

2nd XI SCORERS FOR SEASON 2018

Where there are no personal details for a named scorer, please get in touch with the appropriate County Cricket Club or MCC

DERBYSHIRE – John Wallis via john.wallis5@btinternet.com & 07718 645426 and
Jane Hough via SecondTeam.Scorer@derbyshireccc.co.uk

DURHAM – Grahame Maddison via dcccscorer@gmail.com or 07742097107 and
Peter Connolly via dcccscorer@gmail.com or 07782399608

ESSEX – Paul Parkinson via parkinson-jp@supanet.com or use 07985 382744

GLAMORGAN – Byron Jones / Gareth Watkins

GLOUCESTERSHIRE – S Cashmore or Gloucestershire ACO appointed.

HAMPSHIRE – Alan Mills via a.c.mills@hotmail.co.uk and
Peter Danks via pandedanks@btinternet.com or phone 01243 371947

KENT – Andy Bateup via andybateup@icloud.com

LANCASHIRE – Mike Dixon – please use 07939-738163 or mikedixon21954@gmail.com

LEICESTERSHIRE – Peter Johnson via pete.johnson@hotmail.co.uk

MCC YOUNG CRICKETERS – Neil Smith via neilsmith38@hotmail.com or 07802-155734.

MIDDLESEX – Martyn Fryer via martyn.fryer@middlesexccc.com

NORTHAMPTONSHIRE – Mick Woolley via mick_woolley@hotmail.co.uk or 07746 640318

NOTTINGHAMSHIRE – Anne Cusworth via 07891-243744

SOMERSET – Polly Rhodes via pollyrhodes@aol.com or C Crees

SURREY – Debbie Beesley via 07766-103082 or dbeesley11@gmail.com

SUSSEX – Graham Irwin via sussexcricket@hotmail.com or via 07826-947888

UNICORNS - Kevin O'Connell

WARWICKSHIRE – Steve Smith

WORCESTERSHIRE – Phil Mellish & Sue Drinkwater

YORKSHIRE – J R Virr via johnvirr@yahoo..co.uk or 07808778609